GREEK POETRY FOR EVERYMAN

The Works of John Webster (*Chatto & Windus*)

Criticism:

Authors Dead and Living (*Chatto & Windus*)
Tragedy (*Hogarth Press*)
Ten Victorian Poets (*Cambridge University Press*)
The Decline and Fall of the Romantic Ideal (*Cambridge University Press*)
Studies French and English (*Cassell*)
Literature and Psychology (*Cassell*)

Anthologies:

Beddoes *(Cambridge University Press)*
Crabbe *(Cambridge University Press)*
D. G. Rossetti *(Cambridge University Press)*
Tennyson *(Cambridge University Press, Clarendon Press)*

Travel:

From Olympus to the Styx (*Cassell*)

Politics:

Journal under the Terror, 1938 (*Cassell*)

Fiction:

Dr. Dido (*Cassell*)
The Woman Clothed with the Sun (*Cassell*)

Drama:

The Bear Dances (*Cassell*)
Four Plays (*Cambridge University Press*)

Poetry:

Poems 1935 (*Cambridge University Press*)
Ariadne (*Cambridge University Press*)
Gilgamesh (*Golden Cockerel Press*)
Aphrodite (*Cambridge University Press*)

(See also page xvii)

GREEK POETRY
FOR
EVERYMAN

F. L. LUCAS

Fellow of King's College, Cambridge
University Reader in English

LONDON

J. M. DENT & SONS LTD

Copyright, 1951,
by
J. M. DENT & SONS LTD.
Aldine House · Bedford St. · London

Made in Great Britain
by
The Temple Press · Letchworth · Herts
First published 1951

TO

GEORGE BOAS

Where lowlands stretch for ever,
Rank pasture, mud-banked river,
And bullocks flick and browse,
    And flies carouse;
Or the city's smoke-pall thickens
And the sullied sunlight sickens—
There the heart cries 'How far
    The mountains are!'

Till, on some windless even,
Vast cloud-peaks rampart Heaven,
And sunset hues with rose
    Their timeless snows;
Above this age's shuffle,
Its buzz, and rush, and scuffle,
So towers, far off, at peace,
    The world of Greece.

CONTENTS

PART THREE
ALEXANDRIAN PERIOD

PART FOUR

ROMAN AND EARLY BYZANTINE PERIOD

xi

PREFACE

It must be faced that the 'dead languages' are in some danger of dying a second death. It becomes harder and harder to find time for Greek or Latin in a world where knowledge grows ever more multitudinous, life more hustled—and more herded.

The Renaissance gave rebirth both to Classics and, thereby, to Science: to-day Science, like a giant cuckoo, pushes Classics more and more from the nest. To decry Science is senseless and thankless; we have misused its benefits; but without it we should starve. (Indeed mankind will need all its help to avoid starving in the next hundred years.) Yet intelligent scientists themselves deplore the narrowness produced by the study of Science alone. And it is curious that as the world grows more scientific, it now grows less scientific also. The twentieth century has shown, not less, but more besotted fanaticism than the eighteenth or nineteenth.

Yet Life itself still remains more an art than a science. And art, though it ceaselessly changes, has in the last three thousand years found it often hard to progress. The two greatest poems of western man are still, in many eyes, the two oldest. And the grace and sanity of Greece are not so common in our modern world that we can afford to forget them. Once already the West has forgotten Greek. That period we call 'the Dark Ages.'

Since, then, the place of Greek in higher education has declined, and seems likely to decline still more, what possible remedy is there but more translation and selection of the best Greek literature? Excellent books *about* it are produced every year; but books about books are no substitute for books—though many moderns seem to think so. All translations, indeed, remain inadequate. 'Everything,' as Chesterfield said, 'suffers by translation except a Bishop.' Yet on translations Alfred the Great thought it worth while to spend some of his hard-won leisure a thousand years ago, to bring his England in touch again with the classic past; in our very different English-speaking world the need remains. Who, again, would burn our Bibles and demand that we read Hebrew literature in Hebrew or not at all? The Renaissance itself translated enthusiastically. The pity is that our Tudor and Jacobean translators did not render the great writers of the Hellenes, as of the Hebrews, into a collected volume of their admirable prose (for their verse-renderings are largely debased, like Chapman's overrated *Homer*, by tawdry efforts to be witty and ornate).

But that is a vain regret. There are now plenty of modern versions of Greek poetry; but not, to my knowledge, any attempt to combine all the best of that poetry in a single homogeneous book, with the introductions and notes needed by the non-classical.[1] If this work sends some back to the originals, so much the better.[2] It has been done at intervals over the last twenty-five years. I do not know if I have wasted my time. At least I have enjoyed it.

I have used verse, because modern prose translations, though often useful, remain for me unsatisfying. They seem like songs robbed of their music, or birds whose wings are clipped. Take, for example, the appeal of Elpēnor's ghost to Odysseus (*Od.* xi, 69–78):

> 'For well I know that, returning from Hades' house, awhile
> Thou wilt stay thy stout-built galley again at Aeaea's isle.
> There, O my lord, I charge thee, once more remember me,
> Nor leave me unwept, unburied, as thou sailest out to sea;
> Lest haply the wrath of Heaven upon thy head I bring.
> But burn me there and, with me, the arms of my warfaring,
> And heap a mound above me, beside the grey sea-flow,
> The grave of a man unhappy, for men unborn to know;
> Do this for me, I beg thee; and on my barrow raise
> The oar I pulled with my comrades, living, in other days.'

[1] *The Oxford Book of Greek Verse in Translation* contains versions by a hundred and twenty-four different translators and is, I feel, more suited to the classical than the non-classical reader. And, to be quite frank—though this is only personal taste, or lack of it—I find in some of its versions neither truth nor beauty.

[2] Those attracted by Greek need not be frightened off by the supposed difficulty of the language. Nineteenth-century educators took seven or eight years of boys' lives for Greek and Latin; after which most of their pupils never opened a classic author again, nor could have read him if they had. This was partly because many of these pedagogues planted the road to Helicon with grammatical prickly pears; partly because they chose to inflict on their victims classic authors who are either bores (there are plenty) or too difficult for novices to enjoy. To-day, no doubt, teaching of the humanities has become more human; but the harm is done. In fact, the death of classical education, though partly from natural causes, was partly suicide. I have always cherished, for example, the memory of the pundit who at some conference objected to his boys reading Herodotus, because it spoilt their 'Attic style.' ('Quelle perte irréparable!' as Comte is said to have modestly observed on his own deathbed.)

Schliemann, on the other hand, being a practical business-man with no 'Attic style' round his neck, learnt Greek in four months. And in middle age. True Schliemann was unusually gifted; but still . . .! I believe that, equipped with the minimum of grammar, one should plunge straight into Homer and Herodotus, the two Greek writers who are still most vividly alive. Then perhaps the best of the *Anthology*, Hēsiod's *Works and Days*, and Theócritus. After that anyone should be able to pursue his own bent. (Plutarch's *Lives*, which I follow Montaigne—despite the purists—in thinking one of our most precious pictures of the ancient world, should certainly be also read; but in translation.) Admirably vital introductions to the life of Hellas will be found in books like Gilbert Murray's *Ancient Greek Literature* (though I cannot accept his Homeric theories), Livingstone's *Greek Genius*, and Zimmern's *Greek Commonwealth*.

Put the same passage into prose: 'For I know that departing hence from the House of Hades you will bring your stout ship to land at the isle of Aeaea; there, my king, I charge you to remember me. Do not sail away again leaving me unwept and unburied, for fear I bring upon you the anger of the Gods; but burn me with the arms that were mine, and heap a mound above me on the shore of the grey sea, the memorial of a man ill-fated, for men to know hereafter. Do all this for me and set above my barrow the oar I pulled among my comrades while I lived.' Tastes may differ; but without metre it seems to me still harder to recapture some of that desolate sadness which catches at the heart in Homer's Greek. By the measure of verse this measureless sorrow is heightened and yet controlled. I know that some prefer prose versions; but the *Odyssey* is not *Robinson Crusoe*. To say that is not to undervalue Defoe. But the rhythm of verse can be like the movement of a horse that gathers its great limbs under one and devours the plain. If some find my horse lame, I am sorry. But here I prefer to ride.

Diction presents another problem. Too archaized, it becomes 'Wardour Street' English, a style to some so emetic that to avoid it they lurch into Cheapside, or beyond. That seems going farther only to fare worse. Better King Lear in woad, even, than King Lear in a lounge suit. For two reasons at least. First, the society of Agamemnon or Lear was a primitive society; too modernized a setting inflicts constant jars of incongruity on anyone with a historic sense. This historic sense may itself be a modern thing. But it is there. To ignore it is not 'modern'; it is merely insensitive. When in some film-script a spacious Elizabethan courtier replies to his sovereign 'O.K., Queen!', we smile; but there are modern translations on lines not very different.

These seem to me not only crude, but false. For, secondly, the Ancients believed that the higher kinds of literature demanded dignity. Much modern writing appears to have forgotten that such a thing even exists. But it did. And what the originals valued, it is not for translators to neglect. Accordingly I have tried to shun both aggressively ancient and aggressively modern words.[1] After all, the English language is rich enough.

Then comes the vexed question of literalness. The first business of a translator is to be readable; if a translation reads like a translation, it must be bad. The literal jargon into which Browning turned the *Agamemnon*— as if in later life he had developed a sort of spite against beauty—seems to me worse than the wildest licences sometimes practised by FitzGerald. At least FitzGerald remains a pleasure to read. All the same I believe it is possible to be a good deal more literal than most verse translators.[2] It merely means a lot of trouble. On the other hand there is a tendency for

---

[1] For two extreme examples, see p. 186.
[2] One simple point is of importance: in Greek the emphasis tends to lie on the words at the beginning of the sentence; in English, on the words at the end. In translation this often entails changes of order.

those who pore over ancient texts with microscopes, forgetting that they were composed mainly to be heard—not read—and sometimes heard only through music, to insist on subtleties that no ancient audience could have noticed. (The same fallacy underlies much niggling modern analysis of what Shakespeare wrote for the noisy bustle of the stage.)   There is a wise passage in a letter from Lawrence of Arabia: 'The worst of being a habitual translator is that one gets in the way of trying to squeeze every sponge dry—and so few authors really intend *all* the contents of their sponges.'

In short, as Pope says in that preface to his *Homer* which seems to me finer than his translation, 'a mere modern wit can like nothing that is not modern, and a pedant nothing that is not Greek.'

Lastly there is the question of selection.   Some snort at all anthologies. But here, for a large and important public, it is a case of anthologies or nothing.   Much cant gets talked about 'artistic wholes,' particularly by critics of that special psychological type which cares more for the form and organization of a work than for its spirit, its content, its supreme moments. Yet in practice we make automatic selections of our own from every book we read (if we remember them at all).   Even before we turn the last page of *Iliad* or *Divina Commedia* or *Paradise Lost*, we have forgotten the greater part; all that we can hope to carry with us through life is an imperfect outline of the whole and an involuntary selection by our memories of the lines and phrases that moved us most.   All ink is mixed with water of Lethe.   And was it not the great Johnson who asked tartly, 'Sir, do *you* read books *through*?'

It may be recalled how one day a Sibyl came to King Tarquin in Rome and asked three hundred pieces of gold for nine volumes that she brought. Refused, she went away, burnt three, and came back to ask the same price for the rest.   Again refused, she burnt three more; and the astonished king gave her for the remaining three the price of all the nine.   Rome, we are told, did not regret the bargain.   It seems to me that our own and future ages must more and more imitate King Tarquin.

Besides—why not face it?—much even of Greek poetry was, inevitably, minor; much has been superannuated by time.   Some of Homer himself has lost savour—who wants *all* his battles?   Sometimes, as Hēsiod already knew, 'the half is more than the whole.'

> Greece with calm eyes I see,
> Her pure white marbles have not blinded me,
>   But breathe on me the love
> Of earthly things as bright as things above:
>   There is (where is there not?)
> In her fair regions many a desart spot;
>   Neither is Dirce clear,
> Nor is Ilissus full throughout the year.[1]

[1] Landor.

'Of the Greeks,' wrote that master-critic, Sainte-Beuve, 'a page, an idyll from time to time suffices me. It is not deep knowledge of them that I require: it is their flavour.' Let those who love and believe in Hellas not make too extravagant claims on this hurried modern world. They will be refused. Let us ask less—only so can we hope for more.

Each author here is preceded by a brief notice and followed by a brief commentary. Both must ask the indulgence of the classical reader.[1] They are not meant for him, but for others less informed. *Ecce convertimur ad gentes.*

Note

Most of the renderings of the *Odyssey* given here were first issued as a separate volume by the Folio Society in 1948; most of those of the *Iliad* in a companion volume in 1950. The *Hymn to Aphrodite* was published by the Golden Cockerel Press in 1949 and in a cheaper edition, along with the *Pervigilium Veneris*, by the Cambridge University Press in the same year under the title *Aphrodite*. The Golden Cockerel likewise produced *Hero and Leander* in 1950; and most of the epigrams in 1937, as *The Golden Cockerel Greek Anthology* (reprinted in enlarged and cheaper form, as *A Greek Garland*, by the Oxford University Press, 1939; second edition, Cohen & West, 1949). My thanks are also due to the Hogarth Press for permission to reprint several of the pieces of Theognis, which first appeared in *Time and Memory* (1929). Finally, I am deeply indebted to Mr. A. S. F. Gow for allowing me to see in proof the notes to his new edition of Theocritus.

[1] On the same principle of consideration for the non-classical reader, I have marked the length of syllables in proper names, or their accentuation, wherever there seemed any possibility of mispronunciation. An accent on a syllable means that it is short, but *stressed* in English. (This has, of course, nothing to do with Greek accents, which marked *pitch*.) It need hardly be added that in Greek names a final *e* is pronounced, and pronounced long. Similarly with the spelling of Greek names I have been more concerned to be helpful than consistent.

CHRONOLOGICAL TABLE

B.C.	Greek Literature and Art	Greek History	Events elsewhere
1500			Sixth city of Troy
		Destruction of Cnossus (1450–1400)	
1400			Religious reform of Iknaton (c. 1375) Tutankhamen (c.1360)
1300		Beginning of Heroic Age	Ramses II (1292–1225) Israelite Exodus? (c. 1240)
1200		Fall of Troy First Greek settlements in Asia Minor	Ramses III repels sea-raids on Egypt (c. 1190)
1100		Dorian invasion	Judges in Israel Samuel Saul (c. 1025) David (c. 1000)
1000			Solomon (c. 974)
900	Homer?		Ahab (c. 876) Carthage founded (c. 820)
800	Hēsiod		
		Olympic Games founded (776)	
	Cyclic Epics and most Homeric Hymns (800–600)	Greek colonization in Black Sea, Sicily, and Italy	Amos (c. 760) Traditional founding of Rome (753)
		Sparta conquers Messenia (c. 736–716)	Assyrians take Samaria (722)
700	Archílochus (c. 700–650)		Midas, king of Phrygia (d. c. 693)

xix

B.C.	Greek Literature and Art	Greek History	Events elsewhere
700			Assyria conquers Egypt (681)
		Byzantium founded (660)	Gyges, king of Lydia (680–660)
	Tyrtaeus (c. 650–600)	Second war of Sparta with Messenia (c. 630)	
	Alcman (c. 650–600)		
	Mimnermus (c. 620)		Assurbanipal (Sardanapalus) (d. 626)
			Fall of Nineveh (606)
600	Semōnides		Nebuchadnezzar (605–562)
	Solon (c. 640–560)		
	Thales the philosopher (c. 624–546)		Nebuchadnezzar takes Jerusalem (597)
	Stesíchorus (c. 610–550)	Laws of Solon at Athens (594)	
	Alcaeus (b. c. 620)		
	Sappho (c. 610–565)		
		Peisístratus tyrant of Athens (561; d. 527)	Croesus, king of Lydia (560–546)
			Cyrus the Persian conquers the Medes (550)
	Ibycus (c. 535)		
			Cyrus conquers Lydia (546)
		Persia conquers the Greeks of Asia Minor (545)	
	Pythágoras (c. 530)		Takes Babylon (538)
	Thespis founds drama at Athens (c. 534)		
	Anácreon (c. 570–485)		
	Xenóphanes (c. 565–470)		
	Theognis (c. 540)		Cyrus slain by the Massagetae (529)
	Simōnides (556–467)		Cambyses conquers Egypt (525)
			Zerubbabel rebuilds the Temple (520–516)
		Hippias dethroned at Athens (510)	Tarquins dethroned at Rome (510)

B.C.	Greek Literature and Art	Greek History	Events elsewhere
		New constitution at Athens (507)	
500	Heraclītus (c. 500)		Confucius (551–479)
		Ionia revolts from Persia (499–494)	
		Persian defeat at Marathon (490)	
	Parménides (c. 520–455)		
	Aeschylus (525–456)	Thermópylae and Salamis (480)	
	Pindar (c. 518–438)		
	Bacchýlides (c. 510–430)		
	Anaxágoras (c. 500–428)		
	Temple of Zeus at Olympia finished (c. 456)		
	Sophocles (495–406)		
	Empédocles (c. 494–434)		
	Euripides (c. 485–406)		
	Heródotus (c. 484–430)		
	Parthenon finished (433)	Peloponnesian War between Athens and Spartan League (432–404)	
	Socrates (c. 469–399)		
	Demócritus (c. 460–351)		
	Thucydides (c. 455–400)		
	Aristophanes (c. 450–385)		
	Timótheüs (c. 450–360)	Fall of Athens (404)	
		Thrasybūlus restores Athenian democracy (403)	
400			
		Socrates executed (399)	Ezra returns to Jeru salem (397)

B.C.	Greek Literature and Art	Greek History	Events elsewhere
400	Plato (c. 427–347) Aristotle (384–322) Demosthenes (384–322)		
		Philip defeats the Greeks at Chaerōnēa (338) Alexander invades Asia (334) Alexander dies at Babylon (323)	
	Epicurus (c. 341–270)		
300	Philētas (c. 300) Arātus (c. 315–240) Theócritus (b. c. 312) Callímachus (c. 310–240) Archimēdes (c. 287–212) Apollonius of Rhodes (c. 280–200)	Sicily a Roman province (241) First War of Rome with Macedon (214–205)	Pyrrhus invades Italy (280) First War of Rome with Carthage (264–241) Second (Hannibalic) War (218–202)
200		Second War (200–197) Third War (172–168). End of Macedonian kingdom	Rising of Maccabees (166)
	Bion Antípater of Sidon	Rome destroys Corinth (146)	Rome destroys Carthage (146)
100	Meleāger (c. 135–65) Philodēmus (c. 110–40) Zōnas Crinágoras	Greece overrun by Mithridates and reconquered by Sulla (88–85)	

Greek Literature and Art	Greek History	Events elsewhere
		Death of Caesar (44)
Antípater of Thessalonica		Octavian defeats Antony at Actium (31 B.C.)
A.D.		
1		
Lucílius		Nero (54–68 A.D.)
Plutarch (c. 46–126)		Titus takes Jerusalem (70)
100		
Ptolemy the astronomer (c. 100–78)		
Lucian (c. 115–85)		Marcus Aurelius (121–180)
200		
Oppian (c. 200)		
300		
Quintus of Smyrna	Constantinople founded (330)	
400		St. Augustine of Hippo (354–430)
Pallãdas		
Nonnus		Romans leave Britain (c. 410)
		Alaric sacks Rome (410)
		Attila defeated near Châlons (451)
Musaeus (*Hero and Leander*)		End of Western Empire (476)
500	Reign of Justinian (527–65)	Clovis makes Paris his capital (510)
Julianus		
Macedonius	Closes schools of Athens (529)	
Paulus Silentiarius		
Agáthias	St Sophia dedicated (537)	
		St. Columba brings Christianity to Scotland (563)
		St. Augustine lands in Kent (596)
800–1000		
		Alfred the Great (871–901)
Anthology of Cephalas under Constantine VII (912–59)		

A.D.	*Greek Literature and Art*	*Greek History*	*Events elsewhere*
1300	Anthology of Pla- nūdes (1301)		
	Manuel Chrysoloras begins teaching Greek at Florence (1396)		Dante d. (1321)
1400		Fall of Constanti- nople (1453)	End of Hundred Years War (1453)

INTRODUCTION

THE happy traveller who approaches Greece may enter, like most of her barbarian invaders, from the mountains of the north or, like the Roman, from the western sea. The sea-gate is perhaps even finer. And more sudden. Here at first sight stands revealed the character of Hellas, in full contrast to her richer sister, Italy. Yesterday the eye rested on the green hills of Samnium, the sun-baked flats of Apulia: but now, beyond the Straits of Otranto, dawn reddens on gaunt mountains towering like a rampart sheer from the Ionian Sea. No European coast I know, but Norway, stands up in such grim splendour. All day one's ship steams southward—past fertile Corcӯra (Corfu), perhaps the ancient Phaeacia that sent the sea-worn Odysseus home; past the death-grey ranges of Epīrus, where Ácheron and Cōcȳtus, the infernal rivers of Woe and Wailing, wind through dark gorges down to the shore that rang with unseen lamentations one night two thousand years ago, at the news that Pan was dead; past the gulf of Actium, ringed with the mountains that watched Antony lose a world for Cleopatra; past the sheer white Leucadian headland of Sappho's legendary leap; past the rugged little Ithaca of Odysseus, nestling beneath Mount Nēritus, bare now of the 'tossing leaves' that Homer knew; past the low coasts of Cálydon and Missolonghi, where Meleāger died for Atalanta and Byron for Greece—to anchor under Mount Panachaïcus in the harbour of Patras.

The northern land-gate through Jugoslavia brings contrasts of a different kind. In March the snowflakes may still be drifting down on that dreary Siberian plain south of the Drave, a muddy infinitude beneath a muddy sky, broken at last by the great mud-brown swirl of Save and Danube as they meet before Belgrade. South from Belgrade, gaunt and black on its height amid the snow, the train pants up the gorges of featureless hills towards Nish and the watershed of the Aegean; till beyond it, on a moorland desolate as Rannoch, watched from eastward by the blue peaks of Thrace, winter vanishes and there comes a sudden sense of the approaching south, of the magic of the Mediterranean world. The same night at the frontier station of Ghevghelí (in those happier years before the states of eastern Europe had become a block of prisons) the traveller would suddenly see shining out of the darkness a word in Greek characters—ΑΙΘΟΥΣΑ. It was a word he had last encountered in Homer; but three thousand years had not killed it; it had merely changed its meaning from the 'vestibule' of an Achaean king to the 'waiting-room' of a modern railway. And one felt, suddenly, as if at last one had come home.

Next morning, standing where Xerxes and St. Paul stood long ago, on the shore of Salonīka, one would vaguely glimpse, across fifty miles of blue Aegean, a far-off mist-capped whiteness—and cry, all at once, 'Olympus!' Beyond it, to southward along the sea, loomed the peak of Ossa; and then, dimmer still, the seaward ridge of Pēlion, the mountain of the Centaurs, where the little Jason and the little Achilles were once reared in Chiron's cave.

Thus, whether one comes from the land of the Latin or the Slav, Greece reveals itself at once (though one must see it to realize) as a country of endless mountains jostling mountains, till they fall at last into the sea. From Salonīka turn your back on the wind that shrieks down the Vardar valley, as blustering still as when men prayed to him as 'Bóreas,' and take the southward road—past Pydna where Macedon went down before the legions (168 B.C.); through Piéria, the Muses' ancient home between the roots of Olympus and the sea; to where 'Pēneus rolls his fountains Against the morning star.' There the seaward crags of Ossa bar all progress, and the track turns west inland, between the precipices of Ossa and Olympus, through the forest-gorge of Tempe.[1] At its western end, where green grasses wave on the ruined mosque of Babá, for the only time in Greece proper a great plain opens—Thessaly. Like Lombardy beneath the Alps, it lies magnificently walled with mountains—Olympus to the north, Ossa to north-east, to westward the long white rampart of Pindus through which Caesar marched from the Adriatic in 48 B.C., to win the world at Pharsālus on the plain's southern edge. To southward, too, you must breast more mountain-bastions—Othrys; then Oeta above the deathless gate of Thermópylae; then Parnassus towering above the fatal field of Chaerōnēa—before you can look from the narrow ledge of Apollo's Delphi, across the blue Gulf of Corinth two thousand feet below, to the further peaks of Arcadia and Argŏlis. All this land of tossing stone recalls Odysseus' words of his own Ithaca:

> Rugged, and yet a brave mother of men. In all wide earth
> No sight I know so lovely as the land of a man's own birth.

Such, then, is Greece: a labyrinth of sharp grey-white mountains, green valleys, all-embracing seas—mountains that hardened, valleys that gladdened, seas that widened the spirit of her race. Only one-fifth of the country is level: and, with an area one-sixth of Spain and Portugal, it has three hundred miles more coast. For first the land was crumpled upwards into ranges; then it sank downwards again, turning glens to fiords and peaks to islands.[2] Its mountain barriers bred individuality, but disunity; yet they made its sea more navigable by giving countless landmarks and harbours; and this sea, beautiful enough to have given birth to Beauty's Goddess, brought

---

[1] When Alexander turned the pass of Tempe in 336 B.C. by scaling the side of Ossa, he had to cut steps in its crags.

[2] See M. Cary, *The Geographic Background of Greek and Roman History*.

home to Hellas wealth and experience from other shores. It was the sea alone that prevented the mountain chains of Greece from becoming chains indeed.

A land in itself poor and barren. Yet, if crops were scanty save for vine and olive, its earth gave limestone and marble for builder and sculptor, clay for the potter's kiln. Its air is clear and brilliant as the Greek spirit at its best. The climate, with its summer drouth and glare, keeps the nerves tense, even over-tense; but its winds are bracing and its winters far from soft.[1]

Such a country was a fit cradle for its race: but men are not made only by their cradles. Greek greatness was brief. Through most of the two thousand years that followed, this remained an obscure and downtrodden land. Partly, perhaps, because in Europe the loveliness of the South seems to need ever and again to be reinvigorated by the energy of the North. That stands out from the history not only of Greece, but of Italy, France, and Spain. What these owed to Lombard, Frank, and Goth, early Greece received from Achaean and Dorian, as they swept down from the northern mountains on a decaying Minoan world. First the avalanche, then the flowers; and afterwards the autumn dust. A heroic age of splendid and passionate kings; then a dark period, after the Dorian invasion, of oppressive landowners and grumbling peasantry; then a growth of cities, where the nobles slowly gave place to moneyed oligarchy, or popular dictatorship, or democracy, as the new bourgeoisie gained wealth by trade, colonization, and industry, with a perilously increasing exploitation of the slave. In the great conflict with Persia Hellas reached her height; in mad conflict with herself—Athens against Sparta, Sparta against Thebes—she fell. Partly through loss of wisdom and the simpler virtues, the city-states with all their brilliance went down before the rise of nations, of Macedon and Roman Italy. Yet even in this final phase, like an aloe in its supreme flowering before death, Hellenism could still conquer Asia with the sword of Alexander, and Rome by the force of her inspiration and her intellect. So was prepared the way for the spread of Roman Empire and Christian faith and for that thousand-year reign of Byzantium (330–1453 A.D.) which, with all its decadence and bigotry, yet preserved the seeds of Greek civilization for Europe's Renaissance.

Within seven centuries (c. 900–200 B.C.—and most of it was done in the last four) this race invented for itself epic, elegy, lyric, tragedy, comedy, opera, pastoral, epigram, novel, democratic government, political and economic science, history, geography, philosophy, physics, and biology; and made revolutionary advances in architecture, sculpture, painting, music,

---

[1] C. 1000–300 B.C. Greece may have been cooler in summer and wetter (and so less malarial), owing to a southward shift of the belt of cyclonic storms, which are believed to foster maximum human energy. (Ellsworth Huntington, *Civilization and Climate*, 3rd ed., 22 ff.)

oratory, mathematics, astronomy, medicine, anatomy, engineering, law, and war. One need not be a frenzied philhellene to find this a stupendous feat for a race whose home was only half the area of England and Wales (with a third of it barren) and whose most brilliant state, Attica, was the size of Hertfordshire, with a free population (including children) of perhaps 160,000 —less than Southampton.

But all this, however extraordinary, might be of merely antiquarian interest. It is not because they were ancient that the Greeks still matter, but because they are in many ways so modern. In science, indeed, they were children to us; one armed trawler could annihilate all their navies, one aircraft their armies. Even in art we can challenge them with Michelangelo and Mozart and Shakespeare. They were not more heroic; England in 1940 had a finer hour even than Greece at Salamis. They were more superstitious, more cruel than nineteenth-century Europe (we had better not speak of the twentieth); they took for granted a slavery which our modern age, outside Russia, has left behind.. Their deepest fascination rests, I think, rather on our sense of the balance, completeness, and lucidity of their miniature world, our feeling that they had found a way of life where human beings could realize themselves with a grace, sanity, and freedom since attained only by a few favoured exceptions like Goethe. They had no anaesthetics, no medical or dental experts like ours, no aids for failing sight and hearing, not a hundredth part of our luxuries, toys, and pleasures in this world, no consoling faith in a world beyond. Their view of life was often tragic; their poets have cried again and again that it was better never to be born. And yet what vitality, what versatility, what vivid minds in vivid bodies! Their consolation lay not in divine, but human grace. The transience and sadness of existence were made bearable by their splendour and their poetry. Tolstoy protested that it was bad Russian to use the same word (like our 'fine') for 'beautiful' and 'good': but it was very good Greek. From Homer onward their καλός means both. Many of them, I feel (like a few people one has known), carried into the art of living, consciously or not, a certain fineness, a certain sense of style, which redeemed them from the sterile futility of most human struggling. Such characters can suffer, grow old, be forgotten; but they were never ugly, nor squalid, nor ridiculous. If anything could justify the world, it would be its beauty; and they were a part of that. Much Greek history, I know, is very different. Much medieval history is very different from the knightly ideal of Malory. If ideals were easy to realize they would not be ideals. But in Homer and the best Greek writing, in the marbles of Olympia and the Parthenon, in the grave-reliefs of the Cerameicus, in many of the characters of Plutarch, this ideal seems to me to live.

It is curious to contrast their writers with those of the last two hundred and fifty years, since literature tended to become professionalized and specialized. Undeniable though modern genius has often been, what processions of eccentrics and neurotics, decadents and suicides!—figures like Swift, Rousseau, Gray, Collins, Chatterton, Blake, Coleridge, Byron, Shelley, Hölderlin, Hoffmann, Lenau, Musset, Baudelaire, Dostoevsky, Carlyle, Poe, Rossetti, Swinburne, Nietzsche, Flaubert, Verlaine, Zola, Huysmans, Proust, D. H. Lawrence, Joyce (not to mention Surrealists and Existentialists). Our 'intellectuals' in their jaded restlessness, like haunted hypochondriacs scurrying from quack to quack, have genuflected before Negro mumbo-jumbos, or day-dreamed of Aztec atrocities, or adored the sombre decadence of Etruria, or sighed for the picturesque superstition of the Middle Ages once again. Until this playing at barbarians helped to bring the grim earnest of two world wars.

There is a curious passage in the memoirs of Ethel Smyth: 'I even remember a few years later, when for the first time I saw Paestum, standing in the centre of the Neptune temple and suddenly being possessed with such an overwhelming horror of Wagner's art as compared to this, that it seemed as though one were physically seized and shaken by one of the ancient gods.' Much even of Greek art may be bad, much may be boring; but they did not crave blue wine—red was enough; they did not cultivate green carnations—enough the wild iris that Sappho saw trodden beneath the shepherds' feet upon the hills. There are human beings so anaemic that they need drink or drugs to feel alive; there are others so alive that, like Wordsworth, they can find intoxication in a mountain burn. There is no need to romanticize the Greeks in the style of Lord Leighton: the truth is remarkable enough. These men were much poorer than we; but they would have thought that most of us, rich and poor alike, lived the lives of slaves. They were much nearer to the primitive than we; but they were much farther from the madhouse.

'First,' says an old Greek poem on life's aims, 'is health'; in that—in uninhibited, clear-headed health of mind—lies perhaps no small part of their peculiar and enduring appeal.

This book contains extracts from the poetry of nearly fifteen hundred years (tenth century B.C.? to sixth A.D.)—as long a span as separates us from Roman Britain, or Hitler from Attila. Naturally this is only a fragment of what survives; what survives is only a fragment of what existed once. But one need not too much regret what time has lost. Those who never revisit the past may become crude barbarians: those who stay too long there may become senile ghosts. It was the Greeks themselves who invented the maxim 'Nothing too much.'

There are books that give a couple of hours' pleasure, like fellow-travellers on a journey or fellow-guests at a party, then pass out of our lives forgotten; there are books that satisfy mere curiosity—and die with it; and there are books that influence all our years. We may never reopen them; we may even forget them; but something in them has left its mark somewhere in our brains. Such, for me, are Horace, Chaucer, Shakespeare, Montaigne,

Johnson, Flaubert, Ibsen. These are the books that matter. Their authors have become our friends. I am not trying to introduce a few more modern readers to a few dead writings: I am trying to introduce them to certain living people who happen to have left their bodies, some time since, to mingle with the dust of Greece. Often it may be only a glimpse, through the haze of translation; and yet how much one reads sometimes even in a face that passes in the street! Whitman said that his readers would touch, not a book, but a man: here are many men—and women; and children even. They rise like the wraiths before Odysseus, by his pit of blood on the desolate shore of the Ocean-stream:

> Young brides, and youths unwedded, and old men's weary years,
> And maids in their tender girlhood, with young hearts new to tears,
> And, from the grapple of Ares, many a mighty man
> Slain with the bronze of battle—still red their armour ran.

It is not only a question of great poets; the minor writers are not always the least vivid—Hēsiod with his peasant grumblings (you can meet him on Greek hillsides still); the laughing yet savage Archílochus; the embittered aristocrat Theognis, who could see no good in democrat or merchant, yet could turn his bitterness into such passionate beauty that even merchant and democrat must listen; Simōnides, that quieter, more reticent man of the world who could undertake undismayed, where other voices might have trembled, the task of saying for all Hellas the last laconic words above the dead who had saved her from the Orient; Theócritus, the returner to nature, hearing in the glare of Alexandrian streets the sough of the sea-wind through the pines of Etna; Callímachus, the Parnassian, irritable, pen-proud, pedantic, yet suddenly full of overmastering pity for child or friend laid in the tomb; his hated rival Apollonius, the bookworm who yet gave Europe its first clear picture of love's blind stirrings in a young girl's heart; Musaeus who, when the Greek world was dying, yet lent a new and lasting life to Hero and Leander; and many another half-seen face of dimmer writers whom Meleāger and later anthologists saved from the thickening dusk of time— Asclēpiades, so passionately gathering his rosebuds; Leōnidas, singing of the rustic and the poor; Ányte, the poetess of Tégea, whose lines on a Hermes by the wayside seem to me a perfect symbol of what Greek poetry has peculiarly to offer—not raptures, not rhapsodies, not even the Water of Life—only the limpid purity of bright spring-water leaping beside a hot and stony track.

> Beside the grey sea-shingle, here at the cross-roads' meeting,
> I, Hermes, stand and wait, where the wind-swept orchard grows.
> I give, to wanderers weary, rest from the road and greeting:
> *Cool and unpolluted from my spring the water flows.*

(Only for those interested in prosody)

The greater part of the Greek poetry here translated is either in hexameters

$$(-\,\smile\smile\,|\,-\,\smile\smile\,|\,-\,\|\,-\,|\,-\,\smile\smile\,|\,-\,\smile\smile\,|\,-\,\smile)$$ or in that kindred metre, which also

flourished for over a thousand years, the elegiac, where hexameters alternate

with pentameters $(-\,\smile\smile\,|\,-\,\smile\smile\,|\,-\,\|\,\smile\smile\,|\,\smile\smile\,|\,\smile)$.[1] What, then, is the best
equivalent for Greek hexameters? Matthew Arnold thought, English ones.
But I cannot believe in English hexameters, except for semi-burlesque, as
used by Arnold's friend Clough:

> But for the|funeral|train||which the|bridegroom|sees in the|distance
> Would he so|joyfully,|think you,||fall|in with the|marriage pro|cession?

The Elizabethan Nash has already summed the matter: 'The Hexamiter
verse I graunt to be a Gentleman of an auncient house (so is many an english
begger), yet this Clyme of ours hee cannot thrive in; our speech is too
craggy for him to set his plough in: hee goes twitching and hopping in our
language like a man running upon quagmiers, up the hill in one Syllable,
and down the dale in another, retaining no part of that stately smooth gate
which he vaunts himselfe with amongst the Greeks and Latins.' And surely
Nash was justified by grotesqueries like—

> All travell|ers do|gladly||re|port great|praise of U|lysses
> For that he|knew many|men's||mann|ers and|saw many|cities.

Yet the last two centuries have seen persistent attempts to acclimatize this
alien growth, despite the scepticism of Swinburne and the protest of
Tennyson:

> These lame|hexamet|ers||the|strong-wing'd|music of|Homer!
> No—but a|most burl|esque||barbarous|experi|ment.
> When was a|harsher|sound||ever|heard, ye|Muses, in|England?
> When did a|frog coars|er||croak upon|our Helic|on?

Perhaps the most successful example is Cotterill's *Odyssey*; here is his
version of the prayer of Elpēnor quoted above (p. xiv):

> Well do I|know that de|parting||from|here, from the|mansion of|Hades,
> Back thou 'lt|hold for the|isle||Ae|aea thy|well-built|vessel—
> Here when thou|com'st, O|bear me||in|memory,|prince, I im|plore thee,
> Neither un|wept and un|buried||ab|andon me|homeward re|turning,

[1] The Greek fondness for these two metres involves a certain lack of variety
in this book. I had hoped to diversify it by including also a selection of the
dramatists (iambic and lyric); but for reasons of length these must wait for a
later volume.

Parting in|haste—lest|aye||as a|curse from the|gods I shall|haunt thee.
Burn me, I|pray, on a|pyre||with my|armour and|all my e|quipment;
Also e|rect me a|tomb||on the|strand of the|grey-green|ocean,
Haply for|ages to|come||of a|luckless|man a re|membrance!
These my en|treaties ful|fil,||and my|oar set a|loft on the|barrow,
Rowing with|which when a|live||so|often I|toiled with my|comrades.

The objections to this seem to me, first, that the whole movement is too like a rocking-horse; secondly, that many of its spondees ($- -$) are really trochees ($- \smile$)—we do not say 'lūck*lēss*' but 'lūcklĕss'[1]; thirdly, that whereas

Greek can vary the final rhythm of its lines between $- \smile \smile | - -$ and $- \smile \smile | - \smile$, in English the monotonous 'jiggledy-jiggle' of the verse-endings soon grows maddening. As for partly quantitative hexameters like George Ernle's

Queen Helen|a ex|cepted||a|lone, as|being an|Argive,

this does not seem verse at all. Despite Matthew Arnold, I find myself still of Campion's mind: '*Carmen Exametrum* doth rather trot and hobble than run smoothly in our English tongue.'

What alternatives? Chapman's fourteener seems too lumbering; Pope's ten-syllable couplet too short, too epigrammatic, too intolerant of extra syllables to match the variety of a Greek verse that ranges, in practice, from thirteen syllables to seventeen. Cowper, Lord Derby, Sir William Marris, Maurice Hewlett, and others have used blank verse. But, without sharing William Morris's view that blank verse should be banned by Act of Parliament for at least two generations, I do feel with Goldsmith that it tends to a 'disgusting solemnity' (as seen in bad Wordsworth); and that it lacks that rapidity which Arnold stressed as one of the four key-qualities of Homer.[2] It can march superbly; but it gallops ill.

We are driven back, then, to rhyme. And why not? As Johnson said of Adam Smith, whom he did not much like: 'Sir, had I known that he loved rhyme as much as you tell me he does, I should have HUGGED him.' But what form of rhyme? Maginn's ballad-metre and Gladstone's imitations of Scott are open to Arnold's charge of lacking Homer's dignity. Worsley and Mackail tried the stanzas of Spenser and *Omar Khayyám*; but stanzas break the rush of Homer's narrative and still more of his speeches. What was a torrent becomes a river with locks. And translating Greek epic is hard enough without shackling oneself to triple and quadruple rhymes.

[1] 'The translator,' says Arnold, 'must learn to use spondees freely.' He should. But how, when most such English 'spondees' are really trochaic?

[2] This quality specially struck Pope: 'His fancy . . . becomes on fire, like a chariot-wheel, by its own rapidity'—'a tide of verse, the most rapid, and yet the most smooth imaginable'—'Homer hurries and transports us with a commanding impetuosity.'

The obvious equivalent for a Greek verse of six feet might seem an English verse of that number. But the pure iambic Alexandrine in English (unlike French) develops a sort of gouty stiffness when used continuously. Drayton ruined his *Polyolbion* with it; and it does its full share in making Browning's *Fifine* intolerable. But suppose we try a freer six-foot line based on ballad-metre—just as the Greek hexameter may have grown from a shorter line (possibly four-foot) used in shorter lays now lost?

> They hae slain the Earl of Murray
> And hae laid him on the green.

Print both lines as one and you have the metre sometimes appearing in Tennyson's *Maud*, *Revenge*, and *Maeldune*, and employed by Morris for his *Sigurd* and his *Odyssey*. It is, roughly, as if the last syllable of a hexameter were simply shifted from the end of the line to the beginning. This slight change turns a falling rhythm of dactyl (– ‿ ‿) and spondee (– –) into a rising rhythm of anapaest (‿ ‿ –) and iamb (‿ –), to which the natural run of English speech takes far more kindly.

Hexameter: – ‿ ‾ – ‿ ‾ ‿ ‿ ‖ ‿ – ‿ ‾ – ‿ ‾ ‿ ‿ (13–17 syllables)

This metre: ‿ ‿ ‾ ‿ ‿ ‿ ‿ ‿ ‿ ‖ ‿ ‿ ‿ ‿ ‿ ‿ ‿ ‿ – (13–18 syllables) [1]

All the same, while my admiration for *Sigurd* is immense (an admiration I was delighted to find shared by T. E. Lawrence), I cannot feel Morris's *Odyssey* a success. The language seems too archaic, the metre too rough and too monotonous. To avoid that monotony I have tried to introduce more variety of both stress and pause; partly by occasional twelve-syllable Alexandrines, or by fourteeners (on the analogy of the Alexandrines that Dryden and Pope mingle with their decasyllables), or by triple rhymes (with similar precedent), or by shifting the main pause from the middle of the fourth foot to its end. And in rendering elegiacs I have alternated feminine and masculine rhymes to match the different endings of hexameter (– ‿) and pentameter (–).

One point, however, remains vital if this metre is to work. *As in the Greek, a just perceptible pause must be made at the central break or caesura in each verse.* If this is ignored, a line of this length just runs breathlessly off its feet.

But the only test is practice. Here are four strangely modern lines from the *Iliad* (xix, 221–4) on the grim waste of war:

Aīpsă tē | phūlŏpĭ|dōs ‖ pĕlĕ|tāi kŏrŏs | ānthrō|pŏīsĭn,
Hēs tē | pleîstēn | mēn ‖ kălă|mēn chthŏnĭ | chālkŏs ĕ|cheūĕn,
Āmē|tōs d'ŏlĭ|gīstŏs, ‖ ĕ|pēn klĭ|nēsĭ tă|lāntă
Zēus, hōs t'|ānthrō|pōn ‖ tămĭ|ēs pŏlĕ|mŏīŏ tĕ|tūktāī.

[1] For, in practice, Greek lines *all* spondees (*i.e.* twelve syllables) or English *all* anapaests (*i.e.* nineteen syllables, with the extra syllable before the caesura) are too rare to need considering.

In Chapman this becomes:

> We quickly shall have store
> And all satiety of fight, whose steel heaps store of straw
> And little corn upon a floor, when Jove, that doth withdraw
> And join all battles, once begins t' incline his balances,
> In which he weighs the lives of men.

(Curious that Chapman, whose ear for blank verse was sometimes splendid, could perpetrate this jingle of 'store . . . store . . . straw . . . floor . . . withdraw.') In Pope it runs (far better, though still very free as a translation):

> The bravest soon are satiate of the field;
> Though vast the heaps that strow the crimson plain,
> The bloody harvest brings but little gain:
> The scale of conquest ever wavering lies,
> Great Jove but turns it, and the victor dies!

In Cowper (who does not seem quite to grasp the meaning):

> Men, satiate soon with battle, loath the field
> On which the most abundant harvest falls,
> Reap'd by the sword; and when the hand of Jove,
> Dispenser of the great events of war,
> Turns once the scale, then farewell ev'ry hope
> Of more than scanty gleanings.

And in the metre that I have, rightly or wrongly, preferred:

> Soon of the shock of battle men surfeit and grow sick.
> There are no swathes so heavy as the sword reaps, nor so thick;
> But never a thinner harvest than men receive therefor,
> Weighed in the scales of God, that casts the account of war.

Of other Greek metres there is little to add. One can ask no better equivalent for Greek iambics than English blank verse (even though it is a foot or half a foot shorter); to turn them into rhymed couplets seems perverse. But in lyrics I feel the need for rhyme. No doubt the choruses of Swinburne's *Atalanta* and Murray's Euripides, despite their beauty, are too romantic for Greek. But far better that than the creaking boredom of Arnold's *Merope*, so inferior to Arnold's own rhymed verse. In any case their rhyme cannot be blamed for their romanticism. I have tried throughout not to romanticize the Greek. But I have *not* tried, except with Sapphics, to reproduce Greek lyric metres exactly; only to match their general structure as closely as I could without torturing English rhythm. Attempts to do more, though they seem always to give immense satisfaction to the writers, keep the reader in constant uncertainty which syllables to stress. It is like walking on cobbles. One cannot lose oneself in the poetry. And in poetry, unless one can lose oneself, one is losing one's time.

PART ONE

===

EPIC PERIOD
10TH(?)–7TH CENTURIES B.C.

===

HOMER

ILIAD

For not to have been dipt in Lethe lake,
Could save the son of Thetis from to die;
But that blind bard did him immortal make
With verses, dipt in dew of Castaly.

Spenser, *Ruins of Time.*

IN 1870 (a year when his countrymen were less well employed) a German business-man began digging the hill of Hissarlik to find Homeric Troy. For even as a poor grocer's lad in Mecklenburg Heinrich Schliemann had loved Homer. German scholars smiled pityingly at the credulous amateur. They knew that Troy and Homer were alike fables. Yet the faith which, year after year, moved mountains of soil from Hissarlik, was astoundingly rewarded. Schliemann and his young Greek wife found, not one, but seven Troys. With equal success he next unearthed the treasures of Homer's 'golden Mycenae' and the palace of 'Tiryns of the mighty walls.' Only obstructive landowners prevented him from excavating Cnossus also. Most of his finds we now know to be pre-Homeric. But Schliemann's dream had come true—Homer's world was not a dream.

So with Homer himself. Following Wolf (1795), nineteenth-century scholars busied themselves reducing the *Iliad* to a scrapbook and multiplying Homer into a team of bards (just as Shakespeare has been divided into seven Shakespeares). But these men were better at splitting hairs than poems. Poets like Goethe, Schiller, Tennyson, Arnold, knowing better how poetry is written, were less easily convinced; though Coleridge (in my heretical belief a much overrated critic) accepted the idea. But much modern scholarship, while admitting possible later interpolations in certain places, has gradually swung back from this paradoxical notion that the two best-constructed epics in the world were somehow constructed like patchwork quilts. A masterpiece involves a master. Critics have talked about re-handling by a series of poets as if it were an easy process. The rehandling of good poetry is a good deal more likely to spoil it than to improve. Chaucer could remould Boccaccio; Shakespeare, Kyd; but only because they were still better writers—even Dryden only degraded Chaucer and Shakespeare when he tried revising them in turn. Shakespeare, indeed, may be our best analogy for Homer—a final genius taking the rude brick-structures of older days and rebuilding them in marble.

3

Many now would further agree (though this is more open to question) that if there lived a genius great enough to compose the *Iliad*, it seems rather unlikely, in the teeth of all ancient tradition, that there appeared almost simultaneously a second equal genius to compose the world's other greatest epic—the *Odyssey*. From being chopped up like old Aeson, Homer has risen only the stronger. We can again believe that there *was* a siege of Troy; and a great poet who immortalized it.[1]

In the second millennium B.C. there pressed down into the Aegean world invaders from the North—men who in weapons and habits and a proud independence towards God and man strangely resembled the great Scandinavians of Edda and Saga two thousand years afterwards. Cnossus they gave to the flames. They shook even Egypt. About 1200 B.C. they plundered Troy. Then from the northern darkness followed the Dorians. Achaean Mycenae shared the fate it had inflicted on Dardan Ilios; and a stream of settlers was driven east to the coasts of Asia Minor. There, perhaps in the tenth or ninth century B.C. and in the area of Smyrna or Chios, were created from earlier poetry and legend the two masterpieces we know. (A similar gap of some three centuries separates the *Chanson de Roland* from the events of which it tells.) Ancient lives of Homer are apocryphal; but he may well have been blind, as tradition says, since in a primitive society blind men have obvious reasons for becoming bards. Yet it seems clear also that he cannot have been born so—that this poet had eyes, and used them, as few men ever have. Beyond this, conjecture fails: Homer remains more self-effacing even than Shakespeare, who at least wrote his Sonnets. Yet some may find this superb aloofness, though tantalizing, yet impressive in an age like ours, when the personal lyric has almost killed other forms of verse and we hear little but the chirping of introverted poets over the straws of their private emotions.

The strange thing is that Homer should preserve, so long after, glimpses of that lost Mycenaean world which, like his Troy, only the modern spade has revealed; and on the other hand should avoid anachronisms, on the whole, so carefully that we should never guess from his story that the ruder Dorians had since overrun the Sparta, Argos, and 'golden Mycenae' where his sons of Atreus or of Tydeus ruled.

[1] See J. A. Scott, *The Unity of Homer*; C. M. Bowra, *Tradition and Design in the Iliad*; T. W. Allen, *Homer, the Origins and Transmission*; M. P. Nilsson, *Homer and Mycenae*; G. Thomson, *The Prehistoric Aegean*. The last, with great learning, argues that *Iliad* and *Odyssey* 'could not have been produced either by a single artist or by a succession of artists working separately for their own ends. They were the work of a school in which generations of disciplined and devoted masters and pupils had given their lives to perfecting their inheritance.' But I remain unconvinced of the ability of any 'school' to produce poetry like this. Ballads, indeed, may be moulded in transmission through anonymous generations, with some gifted poets among them; but the Homeric epics show a very different order of unity, complexity, and (I feel) *personality*.

4

He must have had a strong tradition behind him. 'There lived before Agamemnon,' says Horace, 'heroes now forgot': so, doubtless, there lived before Homer forgotten bards who sang of Troy. His language and metre, more perfect even than Virgil's or Milton's, imply a long development. Lost geniuses before him must have begun the creation of that most magnificent of all mythologies, which we owe to Greece. The great Pantheon of the Olympian Gods did not spring full-grown from Homer's brain, like Athene from the head of Zeus. The poet takes for granted legends like those of Hēracles and Meleāger and indeed of Troy itself. His heroes are introduced as figures already known; and it was only because his hearers were familiar with the story that he could make a whole epic out of an episode—the Anger of Achilles. Thereby he gave that epic a unity that no relation of the entire siege, no complete life of Achilles, could ever have possessed. In short, he built on other men's foundations; just as his Troy rose on the ruins of six earlier Troys. Genius is often the art of taking pains; but often, also, the art of economizing them. Really original minds do not fuss about 'originality.' Homer's work took its place so surely that, from the eighth century to the sixth, other poets were content to write introductions or sequels to it—the so-called 'Epic Cycle.' But these were smaller men; after many centuries their poems vanished, while manuscripts of Homer are still counted by the hundred. Greek poetry—European poetry—was not to see his like again.

'An epic poem,' writes Horace Walpole, 'is a mixture of history without truth and of romance without imagination. We are well off when from that *mésalliance* there spring some bastards called episodes, that are lucky enough to resemble their romantic mother, more than their solemn father.' Only too many epics have deserved this gay disparagement; indeed no literary form has a more paradoxical history. It is the oldest surviving species of European literature; it has existed nearly three thousand years; it has been produced in hundreds (Sir Richard Blackmore alone wrote four); and yet nearly all its births have proved degenerate. While its descendant, the Novel, remains so vigorous and prolific, hardly a dozen specimens of Epic are still really alive and perhaps only two—the two earliest—are completely successful. Most modern poets would as soon breed elephants. Hardly an instance of 'Progress.'

Yet though the Epic has become ever more difficult as men lose the patience for long poems, even when readers were ravenous it was never easy—as is shown by the inferiority to Homer of his immediate successors; of Apollonius, Lucan, and Statius; even of Virgil and Milton. Not a little of Homer's unique success is due to his masterly sense of structure. The *Iliad* stands like a great bridge with five massive piers—the quarrel of Achilles with his overlord (Book I); his refusal to forgive (IX); the resulting death of his friend Patroclus, which turns his glory to gall (XVI); his vengeance on that friend's slayer, Hector (XXII); and the final scene

(XXIV) where Achilles learns at last the quality of mercy and gives back that hated body to the prayers of Priam. So, as Dr. J. T. Sheppard has pointed out, the tragedy that began with the old father of Chrȳsēïs hounded from the Greek camp ends with the old father of Hector sent from that camp with honour and compassion home. Homer does not preach; but the moral is plain; all literature can show few as fine.

The other nineteen books are filled with episodes that postpone, but cannot avert, the inevitable end—the conflicts of Gods, the victories and defeats of men. Some of these have faded now; we can no longer throw ourselves without reserve into this ancient 'joy of battle.' The wonder is that Homer's power of character and style can still grip us through catalogues of carnage. And some of these episodes, like the parting of Hector and Andrómache, even Homer never surpassed.

It is amazing how much of later European literature—not only epic, but elegy and tragedy and comedy, oratory and character-portrait, novel and short story and description of nature—already takes shape in this sudden and splendid dawn. Classic, Romantic, Realist—Homer is already all three.

But when all has been said of technical excellences and influences, the greatest thing in Homer remains, I believe—Homer. If he is finer than other epic poets, as Shakespeare than other Elizabethan dramatists, that is partly, I feel, because he was a finer person—more vigorous and vital than Virgil, more merciful than Dante, more generous than Milton. It is not just a matter of a style like cloth of gold, nor of a metre never equalled for narrative again. For these hardly survive translation; yet Homer survives it. The greatest poetry *is* translatable; for it does not live by form alone. And Homer lives, above all, by the essential poetry of his men and women and his vision of the world. Like Chaucer and Shakespeare, he is supremely tolerant (without tolerance, how understand men's ways?); and yet he is never indifferent (with indifference, what values has life left?). People stare if you talk of 'the philosophy of Homer'; but I know few thinkers in these three thousand years who seem to me as true. Plato (who, unlike the great Ionian philosophers before him, cared more for what he thought to be morality than for truth) denounced Homer's Gods as immoral. Yet how else should they incarnate the forces of a beautiful, yet ruthless world? Homer's Poseidon can be cruel—but what sense in a God of the Sea who could not? Homer's Aphrodite can be wanton and heartless—but what truth in an embodiment of human passion that were otherwise? Homer saw (as we too have lived to see) that men of violence and blood may come, blinded by Ate, to violent and bloody ends. He saw the beauty of compassion—that Prayers are the daughters of Zeus Himself. But he saw as clearly another daughter of Zeus, Artemis, 'rejoicing in her arrows' and with them dealing death not only to the wild things of the waste, but also to the daughters of men. Life is often unjust; Death also. Often the guilty

6

suffer; but, with them, the innocent.   One should make the best of it: not
pretend the best of it.

It is for men, Homer seems to have felt, to be finer than the Gods.
Often, indeed, they fail.   Man's passions are strong: and who knows how
far his will is really free?   Helen has ruined both Greece and Troy; but
Hector never reproaches her who, he knows, will cost him his life and more
than life; and the old King Priam is too generous to rail at her, as they sit
together on the ramparts of the city she has doomed.

> I blame not *thee*.   Nay rather, it is the Gods I blame,
> Through whom this war and its sorrows upon my country came.

Yet no reader of Homer doubts an instant, though Helen is divine, that
Andrómache was better.   Helen herself knows it.   Achilles, too, is half-
divine; yet he causes almost as much misery by his pride as Helen by her
falsity; none the less he becomes tragic because Patroclus was more to him
even than the splendour of that pride.   The astounding thing about Homer
is that his sympathies are so strong and yet so fair—that he sees with equal
eyes the magnificence of Achilles and his folly, the glories of Achaea and
the hopeless gallantry of Troy.   Roman and medieval poets blackened and
belittled the Greeks in favour of Ilios; but Homer is unalterably just.   If
his Achilles is superb, above all in that passionate eloquence with which he
denounces the eternal insolence of the rulers of the world; yet his Hector is
more moving still, in his farewell to the wife and child he will not see again
or that agonizing conflict, as he faces his last fight, between honour and fear
in a heart without reproach.

'No creature,' says Zeus, 'is unhappier than Man, of all that go or creep
upon the earth'; and yet Homer still calls his heroes 'godlike.'   All life is
a tragedy; and yet it still remains enthralling, not only in its vitality and
its courage, but also in the quiet beauty of the moonlight that gladdens
the shepherd on the hills, the peace of the forest where the woodman takes
his lonely meal far from the thunders and the shrieks of war.

Later writers of epic were less happy.   Lucretius is a great poet, but not
a great epic poet.   As *dramatis personae,* atoms are inadequate.   Virgil
remains a master stylist; but he lacked Homer's individual freedom—behind
him loom the State, the Dictator, the propaganda machine.   In the quiet of
his own Italian countryside he is at his best; but in the councils or conflicts
of men or Gods that sensitive voice grows often strained.   Virgil's Aeneas
is an admirable public servant—but he is not Achilles.   Dante forged from
the new metal of Italian a style like steel; but Heaven and Hell seem better
in the background, where Homer kept them, than as an epic's central theme;
and through the magnificence of Dante's painting there runs, like a red
streak, the cruelty of medieval theology—as if at times he had dipped his
brush in human blood.   This seems not to trouble Dante's idolaters.   But
inhumanity is no mere foible; it is the human quality that may in a few

years end by destroying mankind itself. Spenser, again, lives by his gifts as painter and musician; but neither he nor his stanza can tell a story. Milton labours under some of the same difficulties as Dante; he too shackled himself to a theology that, once it ceased to be devoutly believed, became grotesque—a celestial sultan with a magic apple-tree. Milton's poor devils attacking Omnipotence are as gnats against a mammoth. Perhaps the most Homeric poem in English is Morris's *Sigurd*; but Morris, with all his generous greatness, lacked Homer's gifts of construction and character, of metre and style. Hardy's *Dynasts* remains one of the few epics that can be not only read but reread; yet its tragic Universe somewhat dwarfs its individuals; and its rugged fabric seems built of iron and granite, not of gold and ivory like Homer's utterance.

Homer was not merely a genius. In our modern world genius has too often become a sort of disease, of mania, so that none knows if it be more blessing or curse. But Homer is unfalteringly sane—passionate without losing balance, realist without growing ugly, infinitely pitiful without becoming soft. He does not try to justify the ways of God to man: he justifies, despite all human follies, miseries, and crimes, the ways of men and women at their finest and their best.

ILIAD

The Wrath of Achilles

Of the wrath of the son of Pēleus—of Achilles—Goddess, sing—
That ruinous wrath, that brought sorrows past numbering
Upon the host of Achaea, and to Hades cast away
The valiant souls of heroes, and flung their flesh for prey
To hounds, and all the fowls of air—yet the will of Zeus was done.
Sing it from that first moment when fierce disunion
Sundered the noble Achilles and Atrīdes, king of men.
    What God was it first caused them to clash in conflict then?
The Son of Zeus and Lēto. For wroth with the high king's pride,
With an evil plague he smote the host, that fast the people died,
Because the son of Atreus had put his priest to shame.
To the swift Achaean galleys that old man, Chrȳses, came,
Bringing a priceless ransom for his daughter's liberty,
While high on a golden sceptre he bore for all to see
The wreath of the Archer Apollo, and prayed the Achaean lords—
All, but most the Atrīdae, the marshallers of swords:
'O Atreus' sons, O Achaeans glittering-greaved, I pray
That the Gods who hold Olympus' halls grant ye one day
The sack of King Priam's city, and a happy homecoming.
Yet ransom me my dear daughter, receive these gifts I bring,
Revering the Son of Zeus, Apollo, the Archer-king.'

Then the other lords of Achaea in the old man's cause spoke fair—
'Twere well to honour his priesthood and take the gifts he bare.
But the heart of Agamemnon, son of Atreus, brooked it ill
And he spurned old Chrȳses from him, with words of evil will:
'Never again let me find thee loitering in the way
Here by our hollow ships, old man—now nor another day—
Lest the God's own wreath and sceptre protect thee not at all!
I will *not* set free thy daughter—nay, in my palace-hall
In Argos, far from her homeland, old age shall bow her head,
Plying her loom and serving to cheer her master's bed.
Begone!—and beware my anger, if home thou wouldst come whole!'
   The old man heard, and obeyed him, with terror in his soul;
Where the surges broke in thunder, silent he went and there
In loneliness he lifted his voice with many a prayer
Unto the Lord Apollo, whom fair-tressed Lēto bore:
'Hear me, Lord of the Silver Bow, that evermore,
O Smintheus, standest master of Chrȳse in Thy might,
Of Ténedos, of fair Killa!—if ever in Thy sight
Shrine that I built found favour, if ever I burnt the thighs
Of goats and fatted oxen to Thee in sacrifice,
Bitterly let Thine arrows repay the Greeks my tears!'
   So he prayed; and his prayer rose up to Apollo's ears.
Then from the brow of Olympus in anger Phoebus swept,
And his bow and his close-shut quiver about his shoulders leapt;
Yea, on his shoulders the arrows, in the fierceness of his flight,
Rattled; and his coming was like the coming night.
Aside from the ships he sat him down, and let an arrow go—
Terrible, as he loosed it, the clang of his silver bow,
First the mules he slaughtered, and the lightfoot hounds; and then
A shaft of bitter bale he turned to aim at men,
And shot; then, thick and ceaseless, the fires smoked for the dead.
   Nine days Apollo's arrows against the host were sped;
Then on the tenth Achilles bade summon all the folk
(By the will of white-armed Hēra that thought in his heart awoke,
For she pitied the Achaeans, as she saw her people die).
So, when they all had gathered to his summons and stood nigh,
Thus spoke the swift Achilles, rising amid the host:
'It seems to me, son of Atreus, that soon, with purpose lost,
To shun our own destruction we shall turn us homeward hence,
If alike the Greeks must perish by sword and pestilence.
Come then, let us ask a priest, or a prophet, who can tell—
Ay, or a reader of dreams (from God come dreams as well)—
Why is Apollo's anger so fierce against us now?—
Is it sacrifice forgotten?   Or some neglected vow?

9

The fat of lambs, it may be, or spotless goats has power
To change his heart, and save us, in this our evil hour?'
    With that he ceased and sat him down; then from the rest
Up rose the son of Thestor, of prophets far the best,
Calchas, that knew things present, things past, and things at hand,
And guided the keels of Achaea unto the Trojan land
By the grace of Phoebus Apollo, that gave him the prophet's art.
Now he arose among them, and spoke with loyal heart:
'Thou bidst me, Achilles dear to Zeus, reveal what thing
It is that has roused to anger Apollo the Archer-king.
Speak then I will.   But thou—mark me and swear, at need
With thy best will to aid me, alike in word and deed.
For it well may be I shall rouse to wrath, by what I say,
One that is mighty in Argos, one whom the Greeks obey.
And weak is a meaner man to meet the ire of a king—
To-day he may swallow his anger and seem long-suffering,
But none the less thenceforward it rankles in his soul,
Till his vengeance falls.   Weigh well, then, if thou wilt keep me whole.'
    And then the swift Achilles made answer—'Have no fear!
Whatever thou knowest, by God revealed, speak out!—and speak it clear!
For, by Apollo dear to Zeus, who suffers thee,
His servant, to reveal us God's will in prophecy,
Long as I live and look on earth, so long, I swear,
To wrong thee here by the hollow ships no man shall dare—
Not one among the Achaeans!—though Atrīdes' self it be,
Who claims over all Achaea to hold the sovranty.'
    So then the prophet without reproach took heart and spoke:
'It was neither for vow nor offering that Apollo's wrath awoke;
It was for his priest's dear sake, whom Atrīdes set at nought,
And would not ransom his daughter, nor take the gifts he brought.
For *that* Apollo smites us—ay, and will smite us more.
He will not lift from the Argives this shame and ruin before
We yield again to her father that maid with glancing eyes,
*Un*redeemed, *un*ransomed; and send for sacrifice
A hecatomb to Chrȳse.   *Thus* might we gain us grace.'
    So saying he sat him down again; but in his place
The hero Agamemnon, Atrīdes, mighty king,
Rose up in wrath—his great, black chest all quivering
With passion—his eyes aglitter, fierce as a gleaming fire.
First of all upon Calchas he turned with looks of ire:
'Prophet of evil, *never* according to my will
Came word of thine—'tis thy pleasure to prophesy me ill.
No good hast thou ever promised, nor brought to happy end;
And now among the Achaeans thy soothsay must pretend

That the Archer-king for *my* fault sends them calamity,
Because for no wealth of ransom brought would I set free
The maid Chrȳsēïs—rather, I wish to keep her here,
Under my roof.   I own it—to me she is grown more dear
Than my own queen Clytemnestra, to whom she yields not place
In handicraft, nor wisdom, nor beauty of form and face.
None the less, if need be, I will let the maiden go—
Safe I would see my people, not watch their overthrow.
But find me forthwith some other gift, lest I, the king,
Alone of the Greeks go giftless.   For *that* were a shameful thing.
And well ye may see that, *now*, the prize that I had is fled.'

 Then Achilles, the swift of foot, the noble, rose and said:
'Most glorious son of Atreus, greediest of men,
How should the gallant Argives find *thee* a new gift, then?
Nothing we know of treasures laid up in common store,
For all the spoil is divided, from the towns we took in war.
'Twere an insult to our peoples to have it gathered back.
Nay, let the girl in God's name go!   And if we sack,
By the grace of Zeus, the mighty walls of Ilios,
We, the Greeks, will repay thee threefold, fourfold, thy loss.'

 Thereto the son of Atreus, the mighty king, replied:
'Seek not, godlike Achilles, for all thy valiant pride,
To cozen *me*.   Thou canst not; by soft words, nor by guile.
Must *I* sit stripped of all I won, and thou the while,
To keep thine own share safely, bid *me* yield up *my* part!
Enough!—if the gallant Argives will satisfy my heart
With a gift as good as this I lose—then be it so.
But if they grudge to give it, then I myself will go
And seize *thy* share, or the share that Odysseus or Ajax won—
Though bitter be his anger on whom my will is done.
Of this we will determine, hereafter, what shall be;
But a black ship, at once, let us launch on the sacred sea,
And gather the rowers needful, and there within her lade
The victims; then aboard her we will bring the fair-cheeked maid,
Chrȳsēïs; and as captain shall one of our wise depart,
Idómeneus, or Ajax, or Odysseus, noble heart—
Ay, or thyself, Pēlīdes, most terrible of men!—
To sacrifice to the Archer-king and win his grace again.'

 To that the swift Achilles made answer, with a scowl:
'Out on thee, lapt in shamelessness, in craft most foul!
How should any Achaean be eager, any more,
To go upon thine errands or fight for thee in war?
It was for no fault of the spears of Troy that here I came
To battle.   Never Trojan to *me* gave cause for blame,

11

Never in fertile Phthīa, dear mother of men, did they
Lift *my* herds of cattle, nor drive *my* steeds away,
Nor waste *my* fruitful acres.   For indeed, 'twixt them and me
Stretch mountains mighty-shadowed and wastes of thundering sea.
To pleasure *thee*, O shameless—for *thy* sake—we drew sword,
To win for Menelaus and for thee, thou hound-faced lord,
Vengeance upon the Trojans.   Yet thou heedest not our toil,
For *that* thou carest never.   And now wilt thou seize the spoil,
For which so hard I laboured—the gift the Greeks made mine!
Yet always in our plunder my share is less than thine,
When we sack some teeming city within the realm of Troy.
Bigger, indeed, is the portion that these my hands enjoy
In the buffetings of battle; but when its fruits we share,
Thy part is far the greater—back to my ships I bear
A small prize, yet a dear one, all wearied out with war.
But now I will turn me homeward, to Phthīa.   Better far
In my curved ships to get me hence.   I am not made
To gather thee gold and riches, and with insult be repaid.'

   Then cried King Agamemnon in answer: 'Hence, away!
Flee, if thy heart so wishes.   *I* shall not beg thee stay,
To do *me* any pleasure.   There are others hear my call
And render me due honour—and the wise Zeus most of all.
But thee I hold most hateful of all God-cherished kings,
For strife is all thou lovest, and wars, and slaughterings.
What though thy strength be mighty?   God gave that strength to thee.
Sail then, with ships and comrades!   Exert thy sovranty
Over thy Myrmidons!   I count thee not at all,
And scorn thy spleen.   Yet listen!   I warn thee what shall fall.
Seeing that Phoebus Apollo takes from me Chrȳsēïs,
My ship and my companions shall bring her home; for this
To *thy* tent I will come myself, and take *thy* prize,
The lovely-cheeked Brīsēïs.   So shalt thou too grow wise,
And learn how much I am master; and others, too, shall fear
To bandy words and outface me, as if I were their peer.'

   He ceased; and the heart of Achilles within his shaggy breast
Groaned, and was torn with division, wondering were it best
To snatch the keen blade from his side, and thrust apart
The other chiefs, and plunge it in Agamemnon's heart;
Or should he curb his spirit and his rage control?
But, as he stood debating thus within his soul,
Great sword half heaved from the scabbard, down from the firmament
To his side sped Pallas Athene, by the white-armed Hēra sent
(For both of the kings she loved, both were alike her care).
Behind him came the Goddess and grasped his golden hair,

Revealing herself to him alone, else hid from view:
But at her touch, in wonder, Achilles turned and knew
The face of Pallas Athene, with dreadful eyes aflame.
Then from his lips to greet her the words swift-winging came:
'Daughter of Aegis-bearing Zeus, why comest Thou?
Is it to see the presumption of this son of Atreus?   Now
I tell Thee—ay, and truly, I trust to prove it so—
His insolence in a moment may make his heart's blood flow.'
    Then the flashing-eyed Athene made answer in his ear:
'Nay, but from Heaven to check thy heat, if thou wilt hear,
I come—the white-armed Hēra has sent me from above,
(For both of you alike she cares, both share her love).
Hold then, have done with conflict, and set not hand on sword;
Threaten him only with ills to come, in many a bitter word.
For this I say (and truly, as I say, so shall it be)
Gifts of a threefold value he shall one day bring to thee,
To expiate this insult.   But now—take heed, refrain.'
    Then the fleet-footed Achilles answered her again:
'What ye both bid, O Goddess, needs must a man obey,
However hot his anger.   I know 'tis the wiser way—
Who heeds the Gods' commandment, the Gods too hear his call.'
So on his silver swordhilt he let his strong hand fall
And thrust the great blade homeward, obeying her behest.
Then straightway vanished Athene—back to Olympus' crest,
To the hall of the Aegis-wielder and the gathered Gods, she came.
But anew the son of Pēleus with biting words of blame
Taunted King Agamemnon; for his rage still kept its smart:
'Besotted bibber of wine, dog's face and deer's faint heart,
Never hadst *thou* the courage to arm with the host for the fray,
Nor to march with us out to the ambush, though there the noblest lay
Of the Argive land—as dreadful as death to thee are these!
Far better in our wide leaguer, sitting at thine ease,
To rob any man of his portion that answers thee one word,
Our common wealth's devourer, lord of a craven herd!
For had they hearts, Atrīdes, thine insolence this day
Had been thy last.   But listen.   I will seal this word I say
With a great oath—I swear it, by this staff whose leaves of green
And boughs shall never spring again, now it hath been
Hewn from its root on the mountain and the blade of bronze hath shorn
Both leaf and bark, to smooth it, and high in hand 'tis borne
By the sons of the Achaeans, the justicers that keep
The laws by Zeus delivered—sure be this oath and deep!
I say the sons of Achaea, one and all, shall bewail
The day that they lost Achilles; and thou—thy soul shall fail,

Yet find no help, as they perish in multitudes of slain
Before the murderous Hector's spear.   Then, then, in vain
Thou shalt gnaw thy heart, that the bravest of the Greeks thou didst disdain.'
    So spoke the son of Pēleus, and hurled down in his heat
That sceptre set with golden nails, and took his seat
While, facing him, Atrīdes raged.   But Nestor rose,
The clear-voiced lord of Pylos—no sweeter honey flows
Than from his lips the winning words; and in his day
He had seen two generations of mortals pass away.
They that had shared his infancy, his boyhood, lived no more,
But still he ruled their grandsons, on Pylos' goodly shore.
With loyal heart towards either, now in his turn he spoke:
'Alas, what a day of sorrow is come on Achaea's folk!—
A thing to fill King Priam, and Priam's sons, with joy
And thrill with exultation all the hearts of Troy!
If they knew that thus you quarrelled, how deep were their delight!—
You, Achaea's noblest in counsel and in fight!
Nay, hark to me—you are younger, both of you, than I.
With better men, even than *ye* are, I dealt in days gone by,
Yet *they* heeded what I told them.   For I have not looked on—nay,
Never again shall I look on such mighty men as they—
Dryas, his people's shepherd, Polyphemus' godlike worth,
Exádius, and Caeneus, and Peiríthoüs. . . .   On earth
The mightiest of *all* men those heroes were, and best—
The mightiest they were, and warred with the mightiest,
With the Centaurs of the mountains, and slew them terribly.
With these did *I* too play my part (they sent for me
Out of my home in Pylos, far off although it lay);
As a champion at their side I fought—though none to-day,
As men are *now*, could venture to face them in the fight.
And yet to my words they hearkened and deemed my counsels right.
Then hearken *ye*!—far better to heed my words in this.
Great as thou art, Agamemnon, take not the maid that's his;
Leave her—the sons of Achaea gave her to be his prize.
And thou too, son of Pēleus, let not thy passion rise
Against the King.   For greater is the honour must reside
In a king who wields the sceptre, whom Zeus hath glorified.
Maybe, thou art the stronger, and a Goddess gave thee birth;
Yet he has more that obey him, and his the higher worth.
But thou, Atrīdes, check thy wrath.   Myself I call
On thee to forgive Achilles, that stands a mighty wall
To guard the sons of Achaea against the ills of war.'
    But then King Agamemnon answered him once more:
'Indeed, old sir, there is wisdom in all that thou hast said.

14

But all of us under his heel this fellow seeks to tread.
We *all* must own him master, *all* own his royal sway,
All heed his beck: yet *one*, methinks, will not obey.
If the deathless Gods have made him mighty with the sword,
Is *that* a cause for his tongue to bandy taunts abroad?'
   Then upon Agamemnon the noble Achilles broke—
'Nay, let me be called a thing of nought, a coward among the folk,
If *I* must stoop in all things to *thy* authority!
Issue to others such commands, lay not on *me*
Orders of thine: for *I*, methinks, will not obey.
Nay, mark well what I tell thee—this too I have to say.
Neither with thee nor another will I battle for the sake
Of a girl—it was ye that gave her, and yours she is to take.
But, from my other possessions, think not in thy pride
To plunder aught that is lying at my swift black galley's side.
Nay come, do thou but try it!—that the Greeks too may know;
Quickly about my spearpoint thy own dark blood shall flow.'
   So, with a clash of insults, from their places rose the twain
And the host by the ships assembled dispersed to their camp again.
With Patroclus and his comrades Achilles went his way
To where his own stout ships and his own leaguer lay;
But Atrīdes ordered the launching of a swift ship into the foam
With twenty chosen rowers and beasts for a hecatomb
In sacrifice to Apollo. Fair Chrȳsēïs he led
Aboard, and the guileful Odysseus he gave to be their head.

                          (I, 1–311.)

After the assembly had broken up, Agamemnon sent two reluctant heralds to
fetch the maiden Brīsēïs from Achilles' hut. Achilles let her go, but himself
went weeping with anger down to the sea-shore and called to his mother Thĕtis,
who rose from the deep to console her son. He begged her to persuade Zeus to
vindicate his honour by making the Trojans victorious, now that he had quit the
field. Meanwhile Odysseus escorted the maiden Chrȳsēïs home to her old father
at Chrȳse and the anger of Apollo was appeased with sacrifice.

   On the twelfth day, when the Gods had returned from feasting with the
blameless Ethiopians, Thĕtis sought out Zeus, where he sat alone on the topmost
peak of Olympus, and prayed on her son's behalf.

'O father Zeus, if ever among the Gods I gave
Service to Thee, in word or deed, grant me this boon I crave.
To him that is doomed untimely, beyond all men—my son—
Do honour. Since dishonour to *him* hath now been done
By the King of Men, Agamemnon, that has snatched away his prize
And keeps her. Yet honour him Thou, Olympus' Lord all-wise!

Give victory to the Trojans, till honour due is paid
My son by the Achaeans, and retribution made.'
    So Thĕtis spoke; but never a word storm-gathering Zeus replied.
Long time He sat in silence.   Yet Thĕtis on her side
Clasped still His knees.   Then again she asked: 'Grant this to me
And with Thy nod confirm it, or else deny!   For Thee,
Denial hath no danger. *So* let me learn aright
How much, of all the Immortals, I am meanest in Thy sight.'
    Then Zeus, the Lord of Tempests, answered with troubled glance:
'Nay, this is an evil doing—to set me at variance
With Hēra and her bitter tongue.   Now, as it is,
Among the deathless Gods she rails at me for this,
Saying that I help the Trojans.   Begone then, lest she know
Thy coming!   And *I* will bethink me how all shall happen so.
See now, my nod shall seal it, to show that this shall be.
For in the house of Heaven there is no pledge from me
Solemn as this—the promise that once my nod hath willed,
Never shall it be voided, or false, or unfulfilled.'
    Then Zeus with His dark brows nodded, to seal the words He said,
And the ambrosial locks were shaken about the deathless head
Of the great Lord of Heaven; and Olympus quaked for dread.

                    (I, 503–30.)

*As soon as Zeus re-entered the assembly of the Gods, Hēra guessed what
had happened and upbraided him bitterly, until his threats silenced her; then
good humour was restored in Heaven by the jests of the lame Hephaestus.*

*That night Zeus sent Agamemnon a deceiving dream, promising victory.
Next morning, filled with confidence, the King called together his host and
rashly made trial of their spirit after nine years of war by suggesting that they
return home.   This proved wellnigh disastrous, so homesick grew the army's
mood; but Odysseus rallied them and silenced with blows the scurrilous Thersītes.
Then, after other speeches by Nestor and Agamemnon, the Achaeans mustered
once again for war.*

    As when, high up the mountains, through the endless woodland ways
A fire leaps on, devouring, with far-off glittering blaze;
So from their glorious armour, marching to the fight,
Dazzling, the brazen splendour to Heaven flashed its light.
And as in the Asian meadow, where Caÿster's current winds,
Gather the wingéd birds in all their divers kinds—
Cranes, or wild geese, or long-necked swans—with joyous wings
Hither and thither wheeling, or with loud chatterings
Settling to earth, till around them all the meadow rings;
So did those divers nations from their leaguer and their fleet
Come pouring o'er Scamander's plain.   Beneath the feet

Of warriors and horses the earth drummed terribly,
Till there they stood in their thousands on Scamander's flowery lea,
Numberless as in springtime the leaves and flowers arise.
Yea, like the clouds, uncounted, of densely swarming flies,
That all about the steading of the herdsman dart and hum,
When the milk pours into the milkpail and the days of May are come;
So thick in the plain there mustered, burning to destroy,
The long-haired sons of Achaea against the ranks of Troy.
And easily as the goatherds divide their goats that stand
Huddled in confusion across the pastureland,
So hither and thither hurried the chieftains marshalling
Their ranks to charge; and, foremost, Agamemnon the King,
With head and glance like Zeus, that thunders over earth—
With great breast like Poseidon—like Ares in his girth.
As o'er the herds around him some great bull in his pride
Towers up, amid the heifers that crowd on every side,
So Zeus that day made Atrīdes mighty among the rest,
In all that host of heroes the first, the lordliest.

(II, 455–83.)

*The poet now enumerates the leaders and contingents of the Achaean host.
As they marched towards Troy, Zeus sent Iris, in the shape of Polītes son of
Priam, to warn the Trojans assembled at the king's palace. So with a mighty
uproar Hector led forth the hosts of Ilios from her gates, to muster at a mound
before the walls. Then follows a similar catalogue of Trojans and allies.*

But when the bands were mustered round their leaders on each side,
On marched the Trojans shouting, like flocks of birds, and cried
Loudly as rings from Heaven the calling of the cranes,
When, fleeing the storms of winter and the intolerable rains,
Towards the stream of Ocean they fly and cry afar,
And bringing upon the Pygmies the cruel clash of war,
With slaughter and destruction through the mists of morn they come.
But the Achaeans moved to meet them, resolute and dumb,
Steadfast in heart together to conquer or to fall.
As when on a mountain-summit the south wind spreads a pall
Of mist, no friend to the shepherd, more dear to the thief than night
(For beyond the cast of a stone the world lies hid from sight);
So thick beneath their marching feet up rose the dust,
Whirling; but swiftly onward, across the plain, they thrust.

(III, 1–14.)

*As the armies closed, Menelaus saw the hated Paris strutting before the
Trojan line and challenging the Achaean chiefs to combat; he rushed upon him
and the seducer fled. Then, bitterly reproached by Hector, Paris proposed a duel*

17

*between Menelaus and himself, which should decide the whole issue of the war
and the fate of Helen. The Achaeans agreed and King Priam was summoned
from Troy to seal the solemn covenant.*

Priam and Helen on the Wall

But to tell the white-armed Helen came Iris—shaped was she
In the likeness of Priam's fairest child, Laódice,
Sister-in-law to Helen (the same that Antēnor's heir,
Lord Helicāon wedded). And now she found Helen there
Within her hall embroidering, on a web of purple grain—
A great web double-woofed, the tale of all that pain
The Trojans, tamers of horses, and Achaea's brazen bands
Bore for her sake in battle beneath the War-god's hands.
Then close to her drew Iris, the swift of foot, and cried;
'Come hither and see, dear sister, what strange things now betide
Betwixt the bronze-clad Achaeans and the Trojans, tamers of steeds.
Erewhile in the plain they struggled, with all the bitter deeds
Of Ares, mad with passion for the rage and ruin of war;
But now they sit in silence—hushed is the battle's roar:
On their shields they lean, and beside them their long spears planted stand.
But warlike Menelaus and Paris, spear in hand,
For thee shall fight; and whoever shall win the victory,
By the common voice, henceforward, his dear wife thou shalt be.'
    So saying, the Goddess wakened sweet longing in her mind
For her homeland, and her parents, and her husband left behind.
At once, with a mantle round her of snow-white linen thrown
And all in tears, she hurried from her chamber—not alone,
For fast in her footsteps followed two handmaidens beside,
Aethra, daughter of Pittheus, and Clýmene lustrous-eyed.
Swiftly they came to where, about King Priam, sate
Thymoetes, Clýtius, Lampus, above the Scaean Gate,
Panthöüs, Hiketāon, that ancient scion of war,
Ucálegon and Antēnor, wise both and full of lore—
Grey elders of the people, too old for battle now,
Yet noble still in counsel. As on a woodland bough
Cicadas chirp, with voices thin and frail as a flower,
So those old chiefs of the Trojans sat waiting on their tower.
But when they saw how Helen towards the rampart came,
Softly among them the winged words passed: 'What man can blame
Trojans and well-greaved Achaeans so long and terribly
To war for such a woman? Fearful, how fair is she!—
Like to some deathless Goddess! And yet let her sail back home,
However fair; lest she ruin us, and all our race to come!'

But Priam called: 'Dear child, come sit at my feet, and behold
Him that was once thy husband, thy kin and friends of old.
I blame not *thee*.   Nay, rather, it is the Gods I blame,
Through whom this war and its sorrows upon my country came.
Tell me, then, who is yon mighty man?   How do they call
That great and towering Achaean?   There are some there still more tall,
But never so noble a figure these eyes of mine descried,
Never a man so stately—with the look of a king in his pride.'

Then the noble Helen answered: 'Dear father of my lord,
I honour and I fear thee.   Would God some death abhorred
I had chosen, ere to Troyland with Paris thy son I fled,
Leaving my little daughter, my kin, my marriage-bed,
And the loved friends of my girlhood!   But it might not be.   And so
My sorrows now must waste me.   But the warrior thou wouldst know
Is Agamemnon, Atreus' son, the lord of a mighty realm—
Great he is on the throne, and valiant under helm,
And brother-in-law to me, poor bitch, in other days—
If such days were.'   Then cried King Priam, with wondering gaze:
'Ah happy, happy Atrīdes, blest child of destiny,
How many sons of Achaea are subject unto thee!
To Phrygia I have ridden, land where the vines grow fair,
And seen the people of Otreus and godlike Mygdon there,
The countless Phrygian armies, the lords of lightfoot steeds,
All moving up to battle beside Sangárius' reeds.
(For there in alliance with them I too was mustered, when
The Amazons came against us, that matched in war with men.)
And yet the quick-eyed Achaeans are a mightier host than they.'

Then the old king saw Odysseus, and again he asked her—'Say,
What is the name, dear daughter, of yonder other lord,
Less in stature than Atreus' son, and yet more broad
In chest and shoulders?   See, his weapons in a pile
Rest on the kindly earth, and through their ranks meanwhile
Like a bell-wether he ranges—ay, like a thick-fleeced ram
That moves through a mighty flock, amid white ewe and lamb.

Then Zeus-born Helen answered: 'Yon is that man of guile,
Odysseus, son of Laertes, from Ithaca's rugged isle,
Whose heart is keen with cunning, and many a stratagem.'

Then in his turn Antēnor, the prudent, answered them:
'Lady, indeed thou hast spoken truth.   Here once before
The noble Odysseus came, long since, as ambassador
Concerning thee; and, with him, Menelaus great in war.
Within my house I lodged them, as guests to entertain,
And so I learnt their looks, and the mind of each grew plain.
When they stood amid the Trojans, gathered to meet them there,

19

Menelaus' mighty shoulders showed taller of the pair;
But when they sat, Odysseus seemed kinglier to behold.
Then, as their web of cunning speech they both unrolled,
King Menelaus uttered his words right fluently—
Few, yet exceeding clear—no wordy man was he,
Although in years the younger—to the mark his sayings went;
But whenever Odysseus rose, with eyes on the earth down-bent
There he would stand, in silence; his staff he never shook
Forward nor back, but held it stiff; and by his look
You would think him only some sullen clown, that nothing knew.
Yet when from that deep chest his mighty voice he threw
And out the words came whirling, as winter snowflakes drive,
Then to match Odysseus there breathed no man alive;
And then the less we wondered to mark his outward mien.'

　　But a third time now the old king asked—for he had seen
Ajax: 'What other Achaean is yonder, fine and tall,
Whose head and stalwart shoulders rise towering over all?'
And then the queenly Helen in her long robe answered him:
'Yon is Achaea's bulwark, Ajax the huge and grim.
And there on the other side, fair as a God, there stands
Idómeneus, and about him the chiefs of the Cretan bands.
Oft Menelaus gave him hospitality
At home, when he came sailing from Crete across the sea.
And the other quick-eyed Achaeans—I see them all as well,
Easy it is to know them, easy their names to tell.
Only two of the chieftains—two only I have missed,
Castor, the tamer of horses, Polydeuces strong of fist,
My brothers, whom aforetime the selfsame mother bore.
Maybe they have never quitted fair Lacedaemon's shore;
Or though indeed they followed across the sea to war,
Yet to the clash of battle they will not come, in shame,
Dreading the taunts and insults that shower upon my name.'
So she said; but, already, in the arms of life-giving earth
Both lay, in Lacedaemon, the dear land of their birth.

(III, 121–244.)

*Priam was now brought from the city and a solemn covenant sworn between
the armies that, if Menelaus lost the duel, the Achaeans should sail home; if he
won, Helen and her wealth should be restored. Paris drew the lot to hurl his
spear first, but only struck Menelaus' shield.*

Then Menelaus, shaking his own long-shadowed spear,
Hurled—on the orbéd shield of Paris it struck clear
And through that shining circle the mighty spearhead clove
And through his inlaid corslet and through his tunic drove,
Skimming the flank of Paris.   From that black doom of death
He shrank aside; then Atreus' son tore from its sheath
His sword with silver studded, and whirled it high in air,
And struck his foe on the helmet-crest.   But, shivered there
In threefold, fourfold fragments, from his fingers burst the blade.
Then lifting his eyes to Heaven's height, cried Atreus' son, dismayed:
'There is no God so grievous, O Father Zeus, as Thou!
I thought to have had my vengeance on this traitor here.   But now
My sword in my hand is shattered.   Just as fruitlessly
My spear was flung against him.   And scatheless still is he.'
    Then, hurling himself on Paris, by the crested helm he caught
His enemy and, turning, towards Achaea's ranks he sought
To drag the Trojan, choking.   For the broidered strap, that passed
Under his chin from the helmet, round his soft throat clung fast.
And now would Menelaus have hauled him clear, and won
Undying fame—but swiftly, beholding what was done,
The Zeus-born Aphrodite dissevered suddenly
That thong of a slaughtered bullock's hide.   The helm flew free
In the stalwart hand of the victor—he slung its empty shell
In the Greek midst, and his comrades upcaught it where it fell.
Then spear in hand Menelaus leapt back into the fray,
Raging to kill; but lightly, as an Immortal may,
Aphrodite lifted Paris, close-wrapped in cloudy gloom,
And set him safe in his chamber, fragrant with sweet perfume.
    Then to summon Helen the Goddess passed, and found
Her still on that lofty tower, while the women of Troy thronged round:
The scented robe of Helen she plucked with her hand, and shook,
While in their eyes the semblance of an ancient dame she took—
One that dressed wool for Helen, in days when she used to dwell
At home in Lacedaemon; and Helen loved her well.
Wearing that old dame's likeness, fair Aphrodite said:
'Come!   For now Paris calls thee home.   On his carved bed
He waits there in your chamber, clad gloriously—his face
Radiant in its beauty—thou couldst not dream such grace
In one new-come from battle.   He looks as he were dressed
To dance; or else from dancing this moment turned to rest.'
    But at the Goddess' whisper sore troubled grew the queen;
The neck of Aphrodite she saw in its beauty's sheen,

And the loveliness of her bosom, and the splendour in her eyes;
And then she cried in answer, with wonder and surprise:
'Lady, with what strange purpose art come to cheat me so?
Is there some city farther yet, where I must go—
Some teeming town of Phrygia, or the fair Maeonian land,
Where haply some other mortal in thy good grace may stand?
Is it because Menelaus has worsted now in war
Fair Paris, and so must lead me—poor wretch!—back home once more,
That thus again thou comest with treachery at heart!
Go!—sit *thyself* by Paris' side—from Heaven depart,
And never again set foot within Olympus' door—
Ay, vex *thyself* to watch and tend him evermore,
Till for his wife he take thee—or for his slave, maybe!
But I—to him I go not—it were shame and blame for me
To seek his bed! No woman, in all Troy, but would hold
My name accurst. And already my heart bears griefs untold.'

    Then, angered, Aphrodite made answer: 'Tempt me not,
Stubborn one, lest I leave thee—lest in my heart grown hot,
Deep as the love I gave thee, so fierce a hate arise,
And I make thee a thing of loathing in either nation's eyes—
To Trojan alike and Achaean—and thou die a death of shame.'

    Then Zeus-born Helen trembled; without a word she came,
Close around her wrapping her robe of radiant white,
Unseen by the Trojan women, as the Goddess led her flight.
But when they came, together, to Paris' fair-built hall,
Each to her tasks appointed her handmaids hurried all,
While into her high bedchamber passed on that lady fair
And the Queen of Smiles, Aphrodite, before her set a chair,
Face to face with Paris. Then with averted eyes
Down sat Zeus-born Helen, and stung him with mockeries:
'So, thou art back from battle! Would God, there thou hadst died,
Slain by that strong fighter who won me once for bride!
It was thy boast, aforetime, that in arms and valiancy
The warlike Menelaus could never match with thee—
Well then, go back and challenge to fight with thee once more
The warlike Menelaus! Nay, mark my word—in war
Wiser thou wert to shun him. Face not that golden head
In the bitter clash of battle, lest, by thy folly led,
One day thou come to perish by Menelaus' spear.'

    But Paris answered: 'Lady, have done with taunt and sneer.
To-day by Menelaus—whom Pallas helped—I fell:
But *I* may triumph hereafter. There are Gods love me as well.
But come, to bed—let us turn again to the joys of love.
For never yet in my heart did I feel such passion move!

Not even when first I stole thee in my ships across the sea
From lovely Lacedaemon, and in sea-girt Cránaë
First in bed together we mingled our desire,
Did such love stir within me, nor such sweet longing fire.'
    So saying he passed to bedward; whither he led, she came,
And the two lay down together in that bed of fair-wrought frame.
But through the press Menelaus raged like a beast of the wood,
Peering to see where Paris in his godlike beauty stood;
But never a man of the Trojans, or their famed allies, that day
Could tell the son of Atreus where Paris hidden lay;
Not out of love—had they seen him, not one had sought to save—
For with one heart they loathed him, as the black pit of the grave.

(III, 355–454.)

*By the terms of the truce Helen should now have been handed back to her
husband and the war concluded. But the Gods held council on Olympus and
Hēra insisted that the Ilios she hated must not thus escape unsacked. Zeus
gave way to her and Athene was sent to instigate some Trojan to violate the
truce. Disguising herself as a Trojan, the Goddess suborned the Lýcian archer
Pandarus to shoot a treacherous shaft at Menelaus, which, however, only slightly
wounded him. In fury for his beloved brother, Agamemnon renewed the
conflict, encouraging each of his chiefs in turn.*

The Achaeans Renew the Battle

    As when from his mountain-outlook a goatherd spies a cloud,
Far out at sea, swept landward by west winds piping loud—
Far out across the surges, as it comes, he sees it loom,
Blacker—like pitch—and blacker, with a whirlwind mid its gloom,
And with fear his heart grows troubled, and he hurries his flock to its cave;
So now around the Aiantes the ranks of the young and brave,
Beloved of Zeus, drove onward towards the battlefield,
In masses darkly bristling with serried spear and shield. . . .
As off some echoing shore a wind from out the west,
Ridge upon ridge, lifts a roller—and far away its crest
Rears up at first to seaward, then breaks in towards the land,
Roaring, and round the jutting crags on either hand
It surges arching onward and spits its salt sea-spray;
So there, rank after rank, on swept the Greek array,
With never a check, to battle. To his own band each chief
Shouted commands; else hushed were all—nay, past belief
It seemed that all those thousands had voices in their breasts,
So quiet, in awe of their captains, onward still they pressed;
Only their inlaid armour flashed as they marched along.
But as in a rich man's farmstead an innumerable throng

23

Of sheep that wait for milking, stand and bleat ceaselessly
(For all the while the mothers can hear their young lambs cry),
So clamoured all the Trojans through their leaguer's wide extent.
For no one tongue was among them—no single speech—but blent
Their language was, in that army mustered from many a land.
One host was urged by Ares, but on the opposing hand
Moved flashing-eyed Athene, and Panic, and Affright,
And Strife with rage unsated, companion in the fight
Of her murdering brother Ares—when first men see her rise,
Little and low she is; but soon to the very skies
She towers from the earth she tramples. And now through the hosts amain
She strode, inflaming hatred, multiplying pain.

But when in one place together the meeting armies clashed,
Then spears and bucklers and raging men, one on the other, crashed
With a clatter of brazen corslets. Shield against bossy shield
Battered, until their thunder filled all the foughten field.
Loud the lamentations, loud the prayers and screams
Of the slayers and the dying, while the red blood ran in streams.
As when two rushing torrents, sprung from great fountain-heads
High in the hills, and swirling adown their torrent-beds,
At a waters'-meet together come clashing, tide on tide,
And the shepherd hears their thunder, high up the mountainside;
Such were the shock and the shouting, as those two armies met.

(IV, 275–82, 422–56.)

*Inspired by Athene, Diomed now carried all before him, killing the treacherous
Pandarus, and wounding not only Aeneas but even the divine Aphrodite and
Ares, who were helping the ranks of Troy. By the advice of his brother Hélenus,
Hector hastened back to the city and bade Queen Hecuba offer a sacred robe in
Athene's temple, in the hope that she might stay the fury of Diomed. Then he
again reproached Paris for dallying in his chamber while his countrymen died
for him; and Paris, once more ashamed, promised to return to the fight. On
his own way back to the battle Hector turned aside to his home, to take farewell
of his wife Andrómache; but found she had gone to the ramparts.*

Hector and Andrómache

But when through Troy's wide city Hector had turned again
To the Scaean Gate, where he purposed to pass to the Trojan Plain,
There came to meet him, running, the wife his gifts had won,
Andrómache, the daughter of noble Eëtion—
Eëtion of Thēbe, the Cilicians' king,
Who dwelt beneath Mount Plăcos, where high the woodlands cling.
His daughter bronze-helmed Hector had chosen for his bride,
And now by the Gate she met him, with a handmaid at her side

That bore a babe on her bosom in its first innocency,
By his sire he was named 'Scamandrius'; but all men called the boy
'Astýanax,' for his father—none else—was the stay of Troy.
There Hector stood and watched him, in silence, with a smile,
And by his side Andrómache, that wept the while.
Clasping her hand in her husband's, 'Dear one, thy dauntless heart,'
She said, 'will surely slay thee—ah, pitiless thou art
Both to thy little son and my unhappiness.
For soon I shall be thy widow—I know the Greeks will press,
Massed as one man, to kill thee.   And once I sit bereft
Of thee, the grave were better—there is no comfort left
In the whole world for me, the day that thou shalt die—
Nothing but grief.   No father, no mother's love have I;
For the noble son of Pēleus struck my father down
When the Cicilians' city, the fair tall-gated town
Of Thēbe, fell before him—my father's blood he shed,
Yet spared to strip his armour, honouring him dead.
High on a pyre he burnt him, with his weapons fashioned fair,
And heaped a barrow above his bones.   And elm-trees there
The Aegis-bearer's daughters, the nymphs of the mountain, set.
Once, too, I had seven brothers, in my father's house—and yet
In a single day they too passed down to Hades' hall;
For the noble Achilles, the swift of foot, he slew them all,
As they herded their shambling oxen, their snowy flocks of sheep.
But my mother, once a queen beneath the wooded steep
Of Plăcos, he brought hither, with all the booty his,
And freed for a countless ransom; yet after, Artemis,
The Archer-queen, in the palace of her father pierced her heart.
Ah, Hector, *thou* art my father, my mother too thou art,
My brother thou, and my life's dear lord!   Then in this hour
Have some pity upon me, stay here upon the tower,
Lest thou leave thy wife a widow, and fatherless thy boy.
There by the fig-tree range our host, where the wall of Troy
Is easiest for the stormer and our battlements most weak.
For thrice the Achaean bravest have gathered there to seek
An entry—both the Aiantes, the great and the lesser one,
Idómeneus, and the Atrīdae, and Tydeus' valiant son.
Maybe some prophet told them, who reads what the high gods hide,
Maybe 'twas their native wit, needing no other guide.'
    Then to her in answer the bright-helmed Hector said:
'Dear wife, I share thy sorrows.   Yet my honour stands in dread
Of the men of Troy, and their long-robed wives—what will they think
If, from the clash of battle, back like a coward I shrink?

That my heart cannot suffer.   Ever it was my way
To fight as a brave man should, far in the foremost fray,
That the honour of my father and my name may still endure.
For well in my heart I know it, my soul foresees for sure,
One day for sacred Troy shall doom at last draw near,
For Priam, and for all the people of Priam of the ashen spear.
Yet never so much I sorrow for the Trojans' suffering,
Nor for Hecuba, even, nor for Priam the king,
Nor for my many brothers, those noble hearts that must
Before the spears of battle lie stricken to the dust,
As for *thee*, whom some Achaean in bronze shall drag away,
Weeping, bereft for ever of thy freedom's day.
Then, as a slave in Argos, thou shalt weave another's wool,
Or to the spring Messeïs, or Hypereia's pool
Go, sick at heart, for water, a drudge beneath the yoke.
There as they watch thee weeping, they will say among the folk:
"Yon was the wife of Hector, who fought the best of all
The Trojans, tamers of horses, when they warred round Ilios' wall."
So they will say; and within thee thy grief shall spring again,
That thou hast no such husband, now, to save thee from thy chain.
Ah, deep be the earth of my grave-mound above me, ere the day
I hear the sound of thy crying, thy carrying away!'
   So saying, the glorious Hector stretched out his hands to his son;
But into the maid's deep bosom, with a wail, the little one
Shrank back, crying out in terror on his father's head to see
Bronze casque and crest of horsehair, nodding so fearsomely
High on top of his helmet.   At that there laughed aloud
Fond father and loving mother; and the hero glittering-browed
Lifted the helm from his forehead and laid its flashing pride
Low on the earth; then kissed the babe, and dandled it, and cried:
'O Zeus, O Gods of Heaven, grant to me that my son
May win among the Trojans such fame as I have won.
Mighty as mine be his arm, and valiant be his reign
In Ilios; let men say, as they see him ride again
From battle with spoils all bloody, that once a foeman clad,
"He is better far than his father"—till his mother's heart grows glad.'
   So saying, in his dear wife's arms once more he laid the child;
To her fragrant breast she clasped it, while through her tears she smiled,
And, struck by pity, her husband, with hand that caressed her, said:
'Dear heart, let not thy spirit be too oppressed with dread.
There liveth none that shall hurl me down to Hades' gate
Before mine hour appointed.   But no man flees his fate,
Neither the brave nor the craven, when his life has once begun.
But come now, turn thee homeward, to the toil that must be done!

Back to thy loom and distaff; and bid thy maids once more
Bow to their tasks.   On men must fall the weight of war,
And on me beyond all others that the Trojan land has bred.'
   So spoke the glorious Hector and helmed once more his head.

(VI, 392–494.)

*With the return of Hector and Paris to the field, the battle regained its fury.
Hector in his turn now challenged the Achaean chiefs to single combat.   Nine
accepted and from these Ajax was drawn by lot to fight.   After the duel had
lasted till evening, with some advantage to Ajax, the pair parted with mutual
gifts.   Both armies burned their dead; and by Nestor's counsel the Achaeans
built a wall to defend their ships.*

   *Next day, remembering his promise to glorify Achilles, Zeus forbade the
Gods to help either side; and himself sat down on the summit of Mount Gargărus
to assure the triumph of Troy.*

The Scales of War

   In haste the sons of Achaea, where the huts of their leaguer lay,
Took their first meal and, after, made ready for the fray;
And within Troy the Trojans upon the other part,
A smaller host, yet armed them with no less eager heart
To fight for wives' and children's sake, since so they must.
Then all Troy's gates flew open and out her people thrust,
Both horse and foot; and loudly their onset's thunder pealed.
But when the hosts encountered, then hard clashed shield on shield,
And the spears, and the brazen corslets, of mighty men of war,
And shield-boss rang on shield-boss, and terrible the roar,
As rose above that tumult the shouts of triumph, the screams,
Voices of slain and slayer, while earth ran blood in streams.
   Now while it yet was morning and day's divine light grew,
On both sides bit the weapons; on both, men fell and slew:
But when the sun at length bestrode the middle sky,
Then hung the Father of Heaven His scales of gold on high.
Twin dooms He laid within them, of death and overthrow,
For the Trojans, tamers of horses, and the bronze-clad Greeks—and lo!
As He poised the scales by the middle, the doom of Achaea's might
Towards the kindly earth sank downward; and towards the Heaven's
      height
Troy's fate rose up.   From Ida Zeus thundered loud—the light
Of His levin-bolt fell blinding where the ranks of Argos stood.
Sorely they wondered, seeing; and pale fear chilled their blood.

(VIII, 53–77.)

In the ensuing panic the Achaean bravest fled. Nestor, with one of his horses killed by an arrow from the bow of Paris, was saved from Hector by the courage of Diomed alone. And Diomed's horses in their turn, as he drove again into the Trojan ranks, were frightened by the thunderbolt of Zeus. The Achaean host was hurled back behind their new-built ditch and wall. There, however, Agamemnon rallied them and for a moment Zeus relented at his prayer. Again the Achaeans charged, while the arrows of Teucer slew Trojan after Trojan, until Hector smote him with a stone. Then again the tide of battle turned towards the ships. In vain Hēra and Athene set forth to aid the Greeks; they were stayed by the angry threats of Zeus. Only night saved the vanquished; and Hector ordered his army to camp in the open plain, that they might burn the Achaean ships at dawn.

The Trojans Encamp Before the Achaean Wall

So Hector; and loud the Trojans acclaimed the words he spoke,
And loosed their horses, steaming, from underneath the yoke,
And haltered them by their chariots, and brought in haste
Kine and fat sheep and wine, honey-sweet to the taste,
And corn from their homes in the city, and piled the faggots high;
Then fat the smoke of their feasting blew rolling up the sky.
On the bridges of the battle, with spirits high upraised,
All night they sat; and thickly their leaguer's campfires blazed.
As when, high up in Heaven, the stars shine sharp and bright
All round the moon in her splendour, while windless lies the night;
Each glen, each hill, each mountain-peak shows clear its face,
And far above bursts open the Heaven's infinite space
With all its stars; and the heart of the shepherd fills with joy;
So thick flamed through the darkness the fires of the hosts of Troy
Between the ships and Xanthus, before the Trojan wall.
There in the plain a thousand burned; and fifty men by all
Sat in the blaze, with their horses by the chariots champing rye
And barley white, as they waited for Morning throned on high.
So waited and watched the Trojans. But on the Achaean part
Lay deadly Fear, the comrade of Flight that chills the heart.
Even their bravest spirits were numbed with utter woe.
As when o'er the teeming surges, all of a sudden, blow
From Thrace two winds together, Zephyr and Boreas—
Dark swell the crested rollers and high on shore they mass
The wild sea-wrack. So troubled the hearts of Achaea grew.

(VIII, 542–IX, 8.)

The discouraged Agamemnon now assembled his host and proposed that they sail home; but was hotly rebuked for his faint heart by Diomed. Nestor

*supported him and advised Agamemnon to call his chiefs to a feast and council;
here Nestor urged that the time was come to placate Achilles. Agamemnon
owned his fault and promised generous redress. By Nestor's advice, Odysseus,
Ajax, and old Phoenix were sent as envoys. They found Achilles, with
Patroclus beside him, chanting the glories of heroes; though surprised at their
coming, he gave his guests warm welcome.*

Achilles Rejects the Embassy

So spoke the noble Achilles; they followed where he led,
And he seated them on settles with purple covers spread,
Then quickly called to Patroclus, waiting near at hand:
'Bring a mightier mixing-bowl, Menoetius' son, to stand
Before us. And set cups for each. And mix us stronger wine,
Since the comrades I love dearest are come to this hearth of mine.'
And then Patroclus, hearkening to his loved friend's desire,
Set down a mighty fleshing-block, full in the light of the fire;
The backs of a full-fed goat, and a sheep, he laid on that,
And the chine of a sleek hog's carcass, with all its weight of fat.
There, while Autómedon held them, Achilles stood to hew,
And the flesh he had cut in slices, upon the spits he drew;
But the godlike hero Patroclus sent the fire leaping high,
And when its blaze was over and the flame had come to die,
He scattered the glowing embers and above them laid each spit
Upon its rest, and sprinkled sacred salt on it.
But when the flesh was roasted and all in platters spread,
To their guests about the table Patroclus served the bread,
Heaped in shapely baskets, and Achilles dealt the meat;
Then, facing the godlike Odysseus, himself he took his seat
By the other wall. To the Gods he bade Patroclus bring
Their portion; and his comrade scattered the offering
Into the flame. Then together they set their hands to the fare.
But when they had eaten and drunk their fill, then Ajax there
Signed with a nod to Phoenix. But Odysseus saw his sign
And, filling his cup, to Achilles he pledged the brimming wine,
And said: 'Hail now, Achilles! No lack have we of cheer
Either beside the hearth of Atreus' son, or here
This night with thee. Most nobly thou hast feasted us. And yet
Not on the joys of feasting this night our thoughts are set.
For, O beloved of Zeus, there looms before our eyes
Too grim a dread—in the balance 'twixt ruin and safety lies
The stout fleet of Achaea, if thou rise not in thy might.
Close to our ships and leaguer there lie encamped to-night

The hosts of haughty Trojans and allies called from afar.
Thick through the lines their campfires flame—resolved they are
There by our own black galleys to end our overthrow.
Now Zeus the son of Crŏnus lightens from Heaven to show
Sure omens of His favour; and Hector, trusting Him,
Exultant in his valour, storms through the battle, grim
With a madness that has seized him, till he heeds nor Gods nor men.
He prays but for the coming of Dawn divine again,
Quickly; for from our galleys he has sworn to hew away
Their sternposts, and burn their timbers with roaring flame, and slay
Beside them the Achaeans, all blinded 'mid the smoke.
Sorely my heart misgives me lest now upon our folk
The Gods fulfil his menace; and it be doomed for us,
Far from horse-rearing Argos, in Troy to perish thus.
Up, then, if thou hast any pity for the Argives; if, though late,
As they faint mid the Trojan onset, thou wilt avert their fate!
Thou too wilt grieve one day for this; yet lack the power,
When the ill is done, to mend it.   Bethink thee ere that hour,
How thou wilt save the Achaeans from calamity.
Ah friend, recall how thy father, old Pēleus, counselled thee,
When he sent thee forth from Phthīa to Agamemnon's side:
"Strength, O my son, Athene and Hēra will provide,
If so they will.   But thou—curb well within thy breast
Thy own proud soul.   In all things, a wise heart still is best.
Beware of strife, that counsels ill—so shalt thou hold
Honour among the Argives, alike with young and old."
Thus thy old father charged thee.   Thou hast forgot.   But still
Cease, even now, thine anger.   'Tis Agamemnon's will,
If thou wilt put it from thee, most fully to atone.
Ah come, Achilles, hear me yet, while I make known
What gifts, that he hath promised, the huts of Atrīdes hold—
Seven unfired tripods, and talents ten of gold,
Twenty gleaming cauldrons, twelve horses stout of breed—
Racers all, that have won him prizes by their speed.
No lack of golden treasure, no dearth of wealth were his
That made himself the master of riches such as this,
That Agamemnon's horses have gained him in the race.
And seven women, skilful in handicrafts of grace,
Lesbians, he will give thee, that he himself kept back—
Earth's fairest—when rich Lesbos by thee was put to sack.
These he will give; and, with them, shall she that he took be there,
The maid begot of Brīseus; and a great oath will he swear
That never he hath taken, O king, her maidenhead
In the way of man and woman, nor lain within her bed.

These presents shall be thine forthwith; and if one day
The Gods grant that great city of Priam to be our prey,
Thine it shall be to enter and fill thy galley's hold,
When we share out the plunder, with store of bronze and gold.
And twenty Trojan women thou shalt choose from all the rest,
That, after Argive Helen's self, shall be the loveliest.
And if to Achaean Argos we come, earth's richest shore,
For son-in-law he will take thee—nor prize Orestes more,
His cherished son that grows there in all prosperity.
There in his fair-built palace the King hath daughters three,
Laódice, Iphianassa, and Chrysóthemis;
Take her that thy heart desireth, whichever one it is,
Gift-free, to the house of Pēleus.   And a dowry he will add
Richer than ever bridegroom from his bride's father had.
And seven well-peopled cities he offers to thy will—
Cardámyle, holy Phĕrae, and Hĭre's grassy hill,
Énope, fair Aipeia, Antheia with her kine
In deepest pastures grazing, and Pēdasus of the vine.
Bordering on sandy Pylos, close beside the deep
They lie, and blest are their peoples with cattle and with sheep;
Honour to thee all these, as to a God, will pay,
Yielding rich dues and bounties beneath thy sceptre's sway.
Faithfully will he perform this, if thine anger but abate;
But if towards the son of Atreus too deep has grown thy hate,
Towards him and all he offers thee—yet pity now
The rest of Achaea's stricken host; and they shall bow,
As to some God, before thee.   How great thy glory were!
For haply thou mayst kill Hector, too.   To face thee he will dare
Now—since he deems him greater, in his grim savagery,
Than all whom the ships of Achaea have borne across the sea.'
   Then the swift Achilles answered: 'Odysseus subtly-wise,
Son of Laertes Heaven-sprung, without disguise
'Tis well that I should utter the things that I feel indeed,
Even as I shall do them—and then ye may cease to plead,
Crowding here about me, with tongues that moan and crave.
For I hold that man as hateful as the very gates of the grave
Who says one thing, while another lies hidden in his breast.
Therefore I tell ye clearly what seems to me the best.
In vain, methinks, will Atrīdes labour to persuade
Me; and in vain the Achaeans.   Too little thanks were paid
For all my toil in battling with the Trojans evermore;
The same was his share that sat at home, and his that was first to war—
Honoured alike were the coward and the noblest of the brave.
Yet alike for the man of deeds and the deedless waits the grave.

C   31

What gained I then from the travail whereto my soul was steeled?—
From hazarding my life upon the battlefield?
As a bird that brings each morsel that ever she finds, to fill
The beaks of her unfledged nestlings, and fares herself but ill,
So have I too watched sleepless, many and many a night,
And filled my days with bloodshed, matching myself in fight
With desperate men defending the wives they left at home.
Twelve cities have I sacked now, with my ships, beyond the foam,
And in the fertile marches of Troy eleven more;
Many a costly treasure I plundered there, and bore
To Atrīdes, lying easy by the swift ships of our host—
He took them, and gave some few away, and kept the most.
Yet the gifts he gave to honour the other chiefs and kings,
At least are not snatched from them. But her whom I loved he wrings
From me alone of Achaeans. So be it! Let him take
His pleasure, lying by her! Yet why do the Argives make
War, then, on Troy? What made the son of Atreus bring
Our people hither, if not fair Helen's ravishing?
Is it only the Atrīdae, of all men born on earth,
That love their wives? Ah no! Any man with heart of worth
Loves the woman he makes his own—as *I* held dear,
With all my heart, Brīsēïs, though I won her with my spear.
But now that he has deceived me and grasped his gift again,
Let him not tempt me further. I know him. His words are vain.
'Twere best that with thee, Odysseus, and the other kings, he planned
How to defend his galleys from the foeman's flaming brand.
Many things he has done already, great things, without my aid—
He has built a wall and, before it, a great moat he has made,
Spacious, and deep, and guarded with sharpened stakes in rows;
And yet, for all that, too feeble to-day his power grows
To hold back murderous Hector—who durst not fight at all,
In the days when I warred in Achaea's ranks, save near the Trojan wall;
Past the Scaean Gate and the oak-tree he never dared to go.
There, once, he gave me battle—and hardly, even so,
Escaped before my onset. But now—since I will not fight
Henceforth with noble Hector—to-morrow in the sight
Of Zeus and the other Immortals I will make offering,
And launch my ships, and lade them; and then, if anything
It may concern thee, watch—in the first grey light of morn
Down teeming Hellespont thou shalt see swiftly borne
My galleys, with my comrades all eager at the oar.
So the third day may find me on fertile Phthīa's shore,
If haply the great Earth-shaker shall send a helping gale.
There wait my great possessions, that once I left, to sail

On this fool's quest; from here, too, my ships shall bring away
More gold, fair-girdled women, red bronze and iron gray,
My share of our common plunder.   But the gift he once gave me
Himself, the son of Atreus hath now despitefully
Taken again.   So tell him, as I bid thee—speak it forth
In all the Achaeans' presence, and rouse them too to wrath,
In case he still is hoping for still more Greeks to cheat;
Clothed as he is in insolence—yet dares not meet
Me face to face, though shameless as a hound he is at heart.
I will not share his counsels; still less, in his deeds have part.
He has wronged me, he has tricked me, he shall not fool me still
With words—let once suffice him!   Let him run now, at his will,
To ruin!   Since Zeus in His wisdom has surely crazed his wit.
I loathe his gifts; and his greatness—I care not a straw for it!
Ten times his wealth he can offer, or twenty times—in vain!—
Ay, twenty times the treasure that he has, or hopes to gain—
Nay, all the wealth that enters Orchómenus' treasury,
Or comes to Thebes in Egypt, of all the towns there be
The richest (for a hundred are its gates, and from each one
With chariots and horses two hundred warriors run).
Not even with gifts like the dust, like the sand in multitude,
Shall King Agamemnon have power to melt my mood,
Until he has paid to the utmost for the wound he dealt my pride.
Nor yet will I take the daughter of Atreus' son for bride;
Not though she vied in beauty with the golden Queen of Love,
And with flashing-eyed Athene in handicraft she strove—
Not even so would I wed her.   For her husband let him try
Some Argive that better suits him, one kinglier than I.
For if the Gods shall bring me safely across the sea,
Pēleus himself shall find some maid to match with me.
Many daughters of Achaea in Hellas and Phthīa dwell,
Children of princely fathers that ward their cities well;
And the bride that I wish among them, I will take for love and life.
Often my own high heart has longed to wed a wife,
Some helpmate meet and fitting, with whom, forgetting care,
At home to enjoy the riches my sire has gathered there.
More worth than all is life to me—than all the gold
Men say the fair-set city of Ilios used to hold
Ere came the sons of Achaea, when peace lay on the land;
Or all the hoards that, guarded by his stone-built threshold, stand
In the hall of the Archer Apollo, by Pytho's craggy steep.
For a man may plunder cattle and drive fat flocks of sheep,
And chestnut steeds, and tripods, with gold a man may gain;
But life!—no sword can gain it, to buy it is in vain

For ever, once the spirit between man's lips is fled.
The silver-footed Thĕtis, my goddess-mother, said
I have two fates before me, whereby my death may fall:
If here I stay to battle about the Trojan wall,
My hope of home I forfeit, yet ever my fame shall stand;
But if I turn me homeward to my dear fatherland,
Then forfeit is my glory, but long shall my years be yet,
Ere Death, that endeth all things, on me his hand shall set.
You others, too, I counsel back homeward to depart;
For now that goal escapes you, whereon ye set your heart—
High-builded Troy.   Too clearly far-thundering Zeus doth hold
His hand out to defend her; and her hosts again grow bold.
But now—to the ships of Achaea go back and tell them clear
My answer—for, as elders, it is their right to hear;
So that they may take counsel and plan some happier stroke
To save their ships and, with them, the whole Achaean folk,
Since *this* attempt has failed them, and my anger shall not cease.
But here let Phoenix stay with *me*, to sleep in peace;
Then with my ships to-morrow to our dear land again
He too can sail, if he chooses—his choice I will not constrain.'
    He ceased.   And on all a silence fell, that no sound broke,
So deep they wondered hearing how vehemently he spoke;
Until the old knight Phoenix opened at last his lips,
While from his eyes fast streamed the tears, in dread for Achaea's ships:
'If, most noble Achilles, thy heart is set to sail,
If nothing can persuade thee to ward these fires of bale
From the swift ships of Achaea, because thy soul is wild
With wrath—then here without thee how should *I* stay, dear child,
Alone?   For the old knight Pēleus first set me by thy side
When to King Agamemnon from Phthïa he bade thee ride,
An innocent lad, not knowing aught of the shock of swords
Or of speech before the people, where men win fame with words.
Therefore he set me by thee, to guide thee and to teach,
And make thee a doer of deeds and a master, too, of speech.
So now I could not, ever, forsake thy fellowship,
Dear child!—though God Himself should promise me to strip
My years away, and make me as when in my prime of age
From Hellas, land of fair women, I fled, and my father's rage—
Amyntor, the son of Ormĕnus; with whom I came to strife
For the sake of the fair-tressed mistress that he loved—and scorned his
        wife,
My mother.   For still my mother begged me with tears and prayers
To win the girl, and bring her to hate my sire's grey hairs.
I hearkened, and I did it.   But guessing himself forestalled

34

Unto the grim Erīnyes my father called,
Cursing me—never thereafter might I set upon his knee
A dear son sprung of my body. (And thus the Gods bade it be—
The Zeus that reigns in Hades, and the dread Persephone.)
Then in my rage I was tempted to slay him with my sword;
Yet some God stayed my anger, remembering how abhorred
In men's mouths it would make me—how my name should be decried
And cursed through all Achaea for the guilt of parricide.
And yet my soul no longer could bear to sit and wait
There at the hearth of my father, beneath my father's hate.
Vainly my friends, my kinsmen, gathered to press and pray
That I should not flee my father's roof. They turned to slay
Many a fatted wether and shambling curl-horned kine,
And there in the flame of Hephaestus many a fatted swine
Hung singeing; and in plenty ever they drank the wine,
Drawn from the old man's jars, to keep the feast alight.
Nine days they watched all round me there, night after night,
Taking their turn to guard me—never there ceased the glow
Of fires kept burning brightly—one in the portico
Of our stout-builded courtyard, one in the porch before
My room. But when there darkened the tenth night, through the door,
Fast-bolted, of my room I broke, and forth I crept,
And over the wall of the courtyard I lightly climbed and leapt,
Unseen by the serving-women and the guards on every side.
So then through the land of Hellas, stretching far and wide,
To the fertile fields of Phthīa, mother of flocks, I fled,
And the royal court of Pēleus. Shelter for my head
His kindness gave—he loved me, with all a father's care
For a son late-born, an only son, to great possessions heir.
Riches as well he gave me, and a mighty folk with these,
And I dwelt in the ends of Phthīa, ruling the Dólopes.
So was it, godlike Achilles, that I bred thee what thou art.
With none wouldst thou go but me, who loved thee from my heart,
Into the hall to banquet; ne'er wouldst thou taste of meat,
Till first upon my knee I had made for thee a seat,
And cut thy food, and fed thee, and held to thy lips the wine.
Oft hast thou drenched my tunic, here on this breast of mine,
Spilling thy drink upon me, in childish heedlessness;
Many a toil have I suffered, many a sharp distress,
For the sake of thee, recalling that to me the Gods forbade
Child of my own. Ah, Achilles, fair as the Gods, I made
Thee my dear son, to keep me from shame and misery.
Yet curb thy proud spirit, Achilles. It suits not well with thee
To have a heart without pity. The Gods themselves can bend,

Though theirs is a loftier might than ours, and glory without end;
And yet with sacrifices and the gentleness of prayer,
With incense and libation, men move their hearts to spare,
When those that have sinned and offended, once more for mercy cry.
For Prayers, indeed, are the daughters born of Zeus most high—
Timid of glance they are, and wrinkled, and lame from birth,
But 'tis their task to follow on Sin through all the earth.
Now Sin is strong, and swift of foot, and far before
Rushing she goes upon her way, the wide world o'er,
Blinding men's hearts.   But Prayers with healing come behind;
And he that honours God's daughters, when they come to him, shall find
Their blessing—*they* shall hear him, when he too comes to pray;
But, if a man denies them and harshly turns away,
They quit him, and then their voices on the Son of Crŏnus call
To let Sin blind him also, that he may pay for all.
So hear God's daughters, Achilles!   From thee too let them find
Reverence such as, always, restrains a noble mind.
Had not Atrīdes brought thee gifts—and sworn to bring
Others beside—were he still as blunt and blustering,
Then I would never urge thee to soften or abate
Thy anger, and aid the Achaeans—however sore their strait.
But now—rich gifts he proffers, and more he promises,
And the noblest of his princes he sends to offer these,
Choosing from out the Achaean host those in thine eyes
Dearest of all.   Then, Achilles, do not thou despise
Their words, nor insult their errand.   Thy past wrath none could blame;
But *this* we can learn from the stories of men of ancient fame,
The heroes—though in their spirits wild fury could break forth,
Yet gifts they took in atonement, and words could calm their wrath.
A thing long-past I remember, that happened years ago,
Just as it was.   Friends all, I tell you what I *know*.
It chanced that the Cūrētes, once fought round Cálydon
With the stout spears of Aetōlia, and the slaying had begun—
The Aetōlians defending Cálydon the fair,
And the Cūrētes eager to sack and not to spare.
For Artemis gold-enthronéd had caused this curse to fall,
Because in his fruitful orchard, at harvest-festival,
King Oeneus brought her nothing—hecatombs of their own
To all the Gods he offered, save the Child of Zeus alone,
Forgetting, or not thinking, in folly infatuate.
Then the Child of Zeus, the Archer-queen, in wrath and hate
Roused up to raven against him a great white-tusked wild boar,
That brake into his orchards, and wasted more and more.
Many a tall tree headlong he hurtled to the ground,

36

With their very roots uptwisted, and their blossom scattered round.
Him the son of Oeneus, Meleāger, slew
Helped by hounds and huntsman that from many a land he drew
(For no small band it needed to make that great beast quail,
And dead he laid many a hunter on the bitter fire of bale):
Yet even then for the wild boar's head, and his shaggy skin,
Queen Artemis stirred new tumult and furious battle-din,
Setting at odds Cūrētes and Aetōlians high of heart.
Now while brave Meleāger in the battle bore his part,
Ill went it with the Cūrētes and, though their host was great,
They durst not offer battle outside their city-gate;
But then on Meleāger came anger (that can rise
To madness, even in hearts of men that are most wise),
And furious with his mother, Althaea, by the side
Of fairest Cleopatra he lay—his wedded bride,
Whose mother had been Euēnus' lovely-ankled child,
Marpessa, and her father that Idas who was styled
Strongest of all men living—the same that dared to take
His bow against Apollo's self, for fair Marpessa's sake.
(But unto Cleopatra the name 'Halcyone'
Her father and her mother gave—so ceaselessly,
Like some sad halcyon, Marpessa weeping lay,
When the Archer Phoebus Apollo had carried her away.)
So now by Cleopatra lay Meleāger, grim
And furious for the curses his mother called on him,
When she cried to the Gods in her anguish for the sake of her brother slain.
(Ay, on all-nurturing earth, again and yet again,
She beat her hands, as she kneeled, with tears on her bosom shed,
Calling loud on Hades and Persephone the dread,
To slay her son; till the Fury that stalks in the Nether Gloom
From the deep of Erebus heard her, with pitiless heart of doom.)
But now round the gates there thundered loud tumult and the roar
Of battered towers; and the elders of Cálydon begged him sore
To rise up and defend them.   They sent to him to plead
The holiest priests of Heaven; they promised in their need
A princely gift—where lies fair Cálydon's fattest soil,
They bade him take at pleasure, to recompense his toil,
Rich lands of fifty acres—half, cleared for growing grain,
And half laid out in vineyards.   Again and yet again
The old knight Oeneus begged him—without the doors he stood
Of that high-vaulted chamber, beating the panelled wood,
Praying to his son; and loudly the queen his mother cried,
Beseeching, and his sisters.   But he the more denied.
His comrades came, the dearest of all he loved, the best—

37

Not even they could soften that fury in his breast;
Till now the room was shaking, now the Cūrētes came
Scaling the towers and setting the great town all in flame.
Then to Meleāger his own wife girdled-fair
Cried out, in tears, repeating what sorrows men must bear
Whose city falls—burnt lie its streets, its men in graves,
Their children, their wives deep-girdled, are led away as slaves.
So she awoke his pity, to think such griefs must be.
To his feet he leapt and seized his glittering panoply
And, yielding to compassion, at last he turned to save
Aetōlia from destruction. Yet his people never gave
Those great and gracious gifts to him—he saved them unrepaid.
Dear son, be not *thou* so stubborn! Let no spirit of ill persuade
Thee to do thus! For truly, when the ships already burn,
Late it will be for rescue. Up, while thou yet canst earn
Their gifts—and *then* the Argives shall hold thee as divine.
But if, having scorned their offer, to the murderous battle-line
Thou comest, the less thine honour, though then thou turn the tide.'
   Then to his words Achilles, the fleet of foot, replied:
'Phoenix, old father, of race divine, I love but ill
Such "honour"—better the honour assigned me by God's will.
That I shall keep, remaining beside my ships, so long
As the breath abides in my body and my knees beneath are strong.
Ay, and another thing!—keep it in memory!
Do not with tears and wailings trouble the heart in me,
For the sake of the son of Atreus—no cause hast thou to choose
Him for thy love!—lest haply my own love thou shouldst lose.
The man that does not spare me, thou likewise shouldst not spare;
And in return my kingship, my honour, *thou* shalt share.
Let these now take their tidings back; and rest thee here
In the soft bed that waits thee. As soon as day breaks clear,
We will resolve if homeward 'tis best to sail, or stay.'
   Silently to Patroclus he nodded then, to lay
Thick rugs for the bed of Phoenix, that quickly the rest might take
Thought for their returning. Then godlike Ajax spake,
Of Télamon begotten: 'Odysseus, subtle heart,
Son of Laertes Heaven-sprung, let us depart.
I see that no words we utter can gain the end we sought;
At least upon this journey. We must bring swift report,
However ill our tidings, for the Danaan lords to learn,
Where now they sit and wait us. To a cruel mood, and stern,
Achilles now has hardened that great heart in his breast.
Implacable, he cares not for the friends that loved him best,
Nor the honour that we gave him—and gave to none beside.

Ruthless he is.   Yet even a man whose son has died,
Or brother hath been murdered, a blood-price will receive
And curb at last his passion, sore though his proud heart grieve;
So that the murderer pays his gold, and thenceforth lives
Safe in the land.   But *thee*, with an anger that forgives
Nothing, the Gods have maddened—all for a woman's sake,
A single girl!   Now seven such we bid thee take,
Our fairest; and many a gift beside!   Have done, relent!
Respect this hearth we sit by, as guests of thine own, now sent
By the whole host of Achaea—how gladly would we stand
Nearest to thee, and dearest, of all the Argive land!'
    Then the swift Achilles answered: 'Royal son of Télamon,
Sprung from the Gods; with thy reasons I am, indeed, at one—
And yet the heart in my bosom boils up too bitterly,
When I think how the son of Atreus hath put such shame on me,
Like some dishonoured outcast, before the Danaï.
Nay, get you back and tell them that *this* is my reply:
"To the bloody work of battle I will not give a thought
Until the noble Hector, wise Priam's son, has brought
His sword to the very vessels and camp of the Myrmidons,
Slaying as he goes, and the flame among these galleys runs.
Methinks, by my own black hull and hut, this arm shall stay
Hector at last!—whatever his stomach for the fray."'
    He ceased; from a cup two-handled each of them poured a last
Libation.   Then, by Odysseus led, back by the ships they passed.

                                            (IX, 199–657.)

*When the envoys reported to Agamemnon that Achilles remained implacable,
the Achaean leaders were plunged in despair, but Diomed again encouraged
them and they went to rest.   But Agamemnon could not sleep, nor Menelaus.
A new council was called and Nestor advised a night-raid on the Trojan lines.
Diomed and Odysseus set forth; intercepted and killed the Trojan Dŏlon, bent
on a like errand in the Achaean camp; and slaughtered the sleeping Rhēsus,
King of Thrace (who had just arrived to succour Troy) together with twelve of
his men.*

At daybreak the battle was renewed.

    But as some star of bale amid night's misty skies
Shines out, then hidden again in the darkening cloudrack lies,
So Hector now to vanward glittered in all men's eyes,
Now, hidden, urged the rearmost.   Fierce blazed his brazen form
As the flash the Aegis-wielder hurls across the storm.
But the battling hosts—as reapers in row opposed to row
Cut swathes of wheat or barley, what time their sickles mow
* C

Some rich man's field, and thickly fall the severed ears,
So Trojans and Achaeans leapt in the press of spears
And struck, alike unheeding the fatal thought of flight.
Line against line stood balanced, and they raged like wolves in fight,
And Strife rejoiced to see them—that bringer of bane to men—
For alone she watched the battle.   But the other Gods by then
Had turned away and were sitting, each in his hall, at rest,
Where stand their noble mansions in the folds of Olympus' crest.
Towards Zeus that gathers the stormrack, hot grew their hearts with blame,
Because His will shed glory upon the Trojan name;
But them the All-father heeded not.   For in that hour
Alone He sat, rejoicing in His glory and His power.
Before Him the keels of Achaea, the walls of Troy stood plain,
The flashing of brazen armour, the slayers and the slain.
Now while it yet was morning, and day's divine light grew,
On both sides bit the weapons; on both, men fell and slew;
But at the hour when the woodman turns to break his fast,
High in the glens of the mountains, as his arms grow tired at last
And his heart has had its fill of felling the towering trees
And longing comes upon him to take his meal at ease,
Then the Danaï in their valour, loud cheering man to man,
Broke through the line, with Atrīdes charging in the van.
There he smote down Biēnor, that shepherd of his folk,
There fell his driver, Oïleus, before the king's spearstroke.

(XI, 62–93.)

*At first Agamemnon performed prodigies and forced the Trojans right back
to the Scaean Gate.   But when he finally withdrew wounded, Hector rallied
his men and the tide of war turned anew.   One Achaean chief after another was
disabled—Diomed, Odysseus, Machāon; and despite the efforts of Ajax the
Trojans again advanced.*

But now Zeus throned in the highest made Ajax' heart turn cold
With terror—he stood bewildered, and thrust his seven-fold
Shield of bull's hide behind him and with anxious glances paced
Back towards the ranks of Achaea, like some beast of the waste,
With short, slow steps, oft turning—as a tawny lion gives ground,
Chased from a cattle-steading by herdsman and by hound.
All night they have repelled him, unsleeping, hour by hour,
From the fattest of their oxen, that he hungers to devour.
Ever anew he charges—in vain; too thick and fast
Rain javelins upon him, that fearless hands have cast,
And flaming faggots with them, that even his valour fears.
So, rage in heart, he turns away as morning nears.

With just such rage did Ajax from the hosts of Troy that day
(For sore he feared for Achaea's ships) reluctant turn away.
As when some dullard ass has strayed aside from the track,
Despite the boys that lead him and the sticks broke on his back,
To browse some waving cornfield—with blows their cudgels rain
Hard on his ribs, yet childish is all their strength and vain,
And hardly at last they drive him forth, when his feast is done;
So, by the Trojans driven, Télamon's mighty son—
By them and Troy's far-sought allies—passed from the field,
With spearpoints thrust unceasing against his midmost shield.

(XI, 544–65.)

*Meanwhile Achilles saw the wounded Machāon returning and sent for news
his own comrade Patroclus; who was begged by Nestor to ask Achilles, even
if he would not fight himself, at least to send Patroclus with the Myrmidons to
help.   Already the Achaeans were driven back within their wall; now the
Trojans forced the ditch and assaulted the rampart, headed by Sarpēdon,
king of Lÿcia.*

The Storming of the Achaean Wall

But as on a day in winter thickly the flakes of snow
Fall, when wise Zeus is minded before men's eyes to show
These arrows of His armoury—first fast asleep
He lays His winds; then He snoweth, with never a pause, till deep
The towering crags are hidden and the mighty mountain's brow,
And the meadows of the clover, and the fat fields of the plough;
Snow drives on the beaches, even, and the bays of the grey sea-tide.
There the wash of the breakers beats it back; but all beside
Lies thickly mantled over by that blizzard from on high;
So dense, betwixt the armies, stones hurtled through the sky. . . .
But now the godlike Sarpēdon felt in his heart the call
To leap high up the rampart and breach the Achaean wall;
And he cried to Glaucus his comrade, son of Hippólochus:
'Come, Glaucus, wherefore is it that we are honoured thus
With the highest seat, and the choicest flesh, and brimming cups of wine
In Lÿcia?   Why do our people look to us as divine?
Why by the banks of Xanthus do we hold a fair domain
Rich with many an orchard and fertile fields of grain?
'Tis *our* part now to repay it by standing to the fore
In the Lÿcian ranks, and leading in the fiery clash of war,
So that the bands embattled of Lÿcia may say:
"The Kings of our Lÿcian land—no deedless kings are they!
Our fat beasts fill their table, of our honeyed wine they drink
The best—but valour to match it is theirs, that does not shrink

41

To lead the Lўcian vanguard in the thickest of the fight."
Dear heart, if once escaping this battle's shock we might
Live deathless still, and ageless, henceforward evermore,
Ah *then* I would not thrust me to the forefront of the war,
Nor urge thee too to the combat that yieldeth men renown;
But—since so many shapes of doom about us frown,
Past numbering, past man's power to avoid or escape at all—
Now let us on!—whether glory to us or the foe shall fall.'

    .   .   .   .

    Then on in mass the Trojans broke, and Hector led,
Thrusting forward in fury, as from a mountain-head
Some boulder, that a torrent from the crown of a crag has thrown,
Sapping with weight of waters the roots of the ruthless stone.
High through mid-air it bounds and flies; the forest-trees
Crash; and yet nought can hold it, as onward still it flees
Down to the plain—but *there* its rage can roll no more.
So awhile Hector threatened, unchecked, to reach the shore,
Clean through the camp of Achaea, and their galleys, striking dead
All in his way; but when he met the serried tread
Of those dense ranks, he halted and onward stormed in vain.
And now the sons of Achaea hurled him back again
With swords and double-pointed spears.   Rearward he reeled,
Yet loud he cried to the Trojans far down the foughten field:
'Now, Trojans, Lўcians, Dardans, ye grapplers hand to hand,
Hold fast!   Not long the Achaeans shall bring me to a stand,
Although they have massed their columns like towers of a city-wall.
Soon my spear shall break them, if aright I heard the call
Of the thunderous lord of Hēra, the mightiest God of all.'
                       (XII, 278–87, 307–28, XIII, 136–54.)

Meanwhile Poseidon, watching the battle from the wooded heights of Samo-
thrace, had pitied the hard-pressed Achaeans and hurried in his chariot across the
sea to their aid.   Taking the shape now of Calchas, now of Thoas, he heartened
their bravest; especially Idómeneus the Cretan who, though his hair was touched
with grey, struck down hero after hero, among them Othrýoneus, the betrothed
of Priam's daughter Cassandra.   None the less to such straits were the Achaeans
driven that the wounded Agamemnon again proposed to launch their ships and
flee; but was restrained by Odysseus and encouraged by the disguised Poseidon.
To distract Zeus from Poseidon's succour of the Greeks, Hēra made herself
irresistibly lovely with the girdle of Aphrodite and lured her lord to her arms
upon Mount Ida.   While he slept among the mountain flowers, Ajax struck
Hector with a huge stone so that he was carried from the battle; and the Trojans
were again flung back beyond the wall.

    But now Zeus woke.   Bitterly rebuking Hēra, he sent Iris to warn Poseidon

from the field.   Revived by Apollo, Hector repassed the Achaean rampart and   Homer
this time reached the outermost line of Achaean ships, where Ajax made a last   Iliad
desperate stand.

The Last Stand at the Ships

Easily as a child that plays in his innocency,
When high he has built a castle in the sand beside the sea,
Tumbles it back to nothing with hands and feet in his play;
So easily, Lord Apollo, in ruin thou didst lay
The wall of the Achaeans, that cost such toil and pain
To build, and hurl their army in headlong flight again. . . .
But the high-hearted Ajax still held it scorn to yield
And join the sons of Achaea fallen back from the field;
From poop to poop of the galleys ever with giant stride
He leapt, and in his hand a boarding-pike he plied,
Of two and twenty cubits, with vast and jointed shaft.
And as some man that is cunning in all the horseman's craft,
From a herd of steeds will harness four, and across the plain
Towards some populous city go galloping amain
Along the crowded highway, while men and women stare
To see how sure and safely, while fast his horses tear,
He leaps from one to other—so now did Ajax bound
From one swift ship to another, with vast strides, and the sound
Of his great voice pealed to Heaven—terrible from his lips
Rang his call to the Greeks to rally, for their leaguer and their ships.
Nor yet did Hector linger amid Troy's serried troops,
But as some dark-red eagle on the birds of Heaven swoops—
A flock of cranes, it may be, or slim-necked swans, or geese—
When they feed, in their multitudes, along a river's leas,
So towards a black-prowed galley charged Hector down the shore.
With mighty hand on his shoulders, Zeus thrust him on before
And roused the Trojan spearmen to follow him amain.
Then a grim and bitter battle raged by the ships again:
It seemed no stress of conflict could tame them or could tire
On either side, so fiercely they grappled in their ire.
And yet far different were their thoughts.   For in despair
Of safety, the Achaeans looked but to perish there;
But high in the hearts of the Trojans one hope, for all, rose plain—
To see the Achaean ships ablaze, and Achaea's heroes slain.

(xv, 362–6, 674–702.)

Patroclus now returned to Achilles, weeping for the peril of his countrymen.

Then seeing him the noble Achilles, the swift of foot, was moved;
And the words came winging from him, and he said to the friend he loved:
'Why all in tears, Patroclus?—as a little maid will cry,
Plucking her mother's dress, to be lifted up on high—
Running beside and clinging, as her mother hurries past,
And looking up all tearful, till she wins her way at last.
Like such a child, Patroclus, thou weepest piteously.
Hast thou some news for the Myrmidons? Some tale for me?
Come tidings out of Phthīa, that are unknown to us?
And yet they say that Actor's son, Menoetius,
Is living—and Pēleus lives, among the Myrmidons—
Whose death were bitter hearing for us that are their sons.
Or are thy tears for the Argives, as they perish in their need
There by the hollow galleys, for their own evil deed?
Speak out. Hide not thy feeling. Best that we both should know.'
    Then saidst thou, knightly Patroclus, with voice of utter woe:
'O Achilles, son of Pēleus, Achaea's goodliest,
Do not be vexed—so sorely the Argives now are pressed.
For all the chiefs that aforetime they counted first in might,
Now by the ships are lying, wounded or maimed in fight—
For Diomed, Tydeus' gallant son, is wounded sore,
Wounded are Agamemnon and Odysseus famed in war;
Eurýpylus is smitten—in his thigh a shaft;
And round them, with all their simples, the leeches ply their craft,
Healing their hurts. O Achilles, what man may deal with thee!
Never may *I* nurse anger so implacably,
Thou dreadful heart of valour! Wilt thou serve some race unborn,
When in shame and ruin the Argives have perished by thy scorn?
Ah pitiless!—never Thĕtis bare *thee* within her womb,
No knightly Pēleus sired thee—nay, of the grey sea's gloom
And the mountain-crags wast *thou* begot, inexorable one!
Yet, if there is some soothsay thy heart warns thee to shun,
Or thy noble mother has told thee some word that Zeus hath spoke,
Still, in thy place, oh send me!—and let me lead thy folk
Of the Myrmidons, if haply, through me, some light may shine
For the Danaan host. And lend me the armour that is thine,
That the Trojans may think me Achilles and fall back from the war,
Till the martial sons of Achaea have time to breathe once more,
Pressed as they are. In battle soon tells a breathing-space.
Unwearied against men weary, easily we shall chase
Their lines from our ships and leaguer, back to the Trojan wall.'
    So, blind of heart, Patroclus prayed; nor guessed at all

44

That for himself he was praying a deadly doom and grim.
But the swift-footed Achilles, sore troubled, answered him:
'Ay me, Patroclus Heaven-sprung, what hast thou said!
It is no prophet's soothsay that I have heard and dread,
Nor hath my noble mother brought word from Zeus to me:
Nay, but my heart and soul are wrung intolerably
That a man, because he is greater in sovereignty, should dare
Thus to rob his equal of the prize that was his share!
Bitter to me past bearing the wrongs that my heart has known—
That she whom the sons of Achaea chose out as mine alone—
She whom my own spear won me, the day I put to sack
Her towered town—by Atrīdes should thus be ravished back,
As if I were some poor vagrant, devoid of name or worth.
Still, bygones must be bygones now.   No heart on earth
Can nurse its rage for ever.   Indeed I had meant, before,
Never to stay my anger till to the very shore
Where my own ships are lying, the clamour of battle came.
But now—upon thy shoulders buckle my arms of fame,
Lead forth my Myrmidons, all thirsting for the fight,
If true it is that the Trojans, in a cloud as dense as night,
Press on the ships and pen there, against the wave-washed strand,
The Argives, masters only of one poor strip of land,
While, with high-mounting courage, comes thrusting forward now
All Ilios, since no longer men see my helmet's brow
Glitter at hand.   They should turn them, fast enough, to flee
And choked with their slaughtered bodies the riverbeds should be,
Had but Atrīdes used me well!   But now they fight
Here in our camp.   No longer, in the Danaans' evil plight,
Rages the spear of Tydeus' son, the spear of Diomed;
Nowhere across the tumult I hear the warcry sped
From Agamemnon's hateful lips.   Nought echoes in my ears
But Hector crying slaughter and the roar of Trojan cheers,
As they beat down our Achaeans and master all the plain.
Nevertheless, Patroclus, do thou fall on amain
To clear them from our galleys, lest with devouring fire
They cut us off for ever from the homes of our desire.
Yet listen!   Let this last word be fixed in thy memory,
That so thou mayst gather glory and high renown for me
And the Argives may restore me that girl in her beauty's pride
And satisfy my honour with splendid gifts beside.
When from our ships thou hast swept them, then turn thee back.   For
      though
Glory on thee Queen Hēra's loud-thundering lord bestow,
Strive not alone, Patroclus—without me—still to press

Against Troy's valiant spearmen.   Thou wilt leave my honour less.
Nor let thy own heart lure thee, drunk with the battle's joy
As the Trojans fall before thy spear, to thrust as far as Troy;
Lest one of the Gods that die not, from Olympus, meet with thee
In wrath.   For the Archer Apollo loves Troy exceedingly.
Nay, turn again as I tell thee, once thou hast shed thy light
Over the ships.   Across the plain, let others press the fight.
Ah would to Apollo and Pallas and Zeus the sire of all,
That every man of the Trojan race were doomed to fall,
And every man of the Argives, and no arms left but ours
To loose, alone together, Troy's sacred crown of towers!'
　　But while the two held converse with one another there,
Ajax could stand no longer.   Too fierce for him to bear
That storm of spears the Trojans hurled, and the manifested will
Of Zeus; too grim the rattle about his temples still,
As darts on each stout cheekpiece, darts on his bright helm pealed,
And faint grew his left shoulder with the load of his gleaming shield.

(XVI, 5–107.)

*Hector now struck off the point of the great boarding-spear wielded by Ajax
and the Trojans were able to lay a firebrand to the first Achaean ship; but
quickly Patroclus, in the arms and the chariot of Achilles, led out the Myrmidons.*

Patroclus goes to Battle

　　But now—as ravening wolves, with hearts to flinch at nought,
That rend high up the hills some tall stag they have caught,
Till all their jowls run crimson with the blood of their banqueting,
Then gallop off together to some dark-shadowed spring,
Where the whole pack, with long thin tongues, will slake their thirst,
Lapping the dark wave's surface, their bellies gorged to burst,
Reckless in their fury, belching their quarry's gore—
So mustered the chiefs and leaders of the Myrmidons to war,
About the gallant comrade of swift Aeácides;
And Achilles, loved of Ares, stood in the midst of these,
Urging on the spearmen and their horses to the fray. . . .
Then back to his hut turned Achilles and opened a chest fair-wrought
That the silver-footed Thĕtis in other days had brought
Aboard his galley, filled with many a mantle proof
Against the winds, and tunics, and rugs of fleecy woof.
There lay a finely fashioned cup, whence none but he
Tasted the wine that glitters red and fierily—
No God he honoured with it save Zeus the Heavenly Sire.
Taking it forth he cleansed it, first of all with fire

And brimstone; then with water, drawn from a stainless spring;
And washed his hands, and filled it with wine red-glittering.
Then in the court he poured it forth, and made his prayer
With eyes upraised to Heaven (and the Thunderer marked him there):
'Pelasgian Zeus, Dōdōna's lord, that hast Thy seat
Far off in bleak Dōdōna; where with unwashen feet,
Couching on earth, Thy Selloi dwell round Thee evermore
To speak Thy will! Thou hast granted what I asked of Thee before
And brought on the Achaeans, for my honour, grievous ill;
Once more I call upon Thee, this prayer no less fulfil.
For here by our gathered galleys I stay yet, but my friend
With all my mighty host of the Myrmidons I send
To battle. O Lord of Thunder, with glory let him go!
Strengthen the heart within him, that Hector too may know
Whether my squire can show his mettle in the fight
Alone—or whether his hands are matchless in their might
Only when *I* march *with* him into the moil of war.
But when from our swift galleys he hath turned the battle's roar,
Back to me, waiting beside them, oh send him safe and sound—
Back let him come, with all his arms, and his gallant comrades round.'
    Then Zeus, the all-devising, heard him as there he cried,
And part the All-father granted, part of his prayer denied.
That Patroclus should thrust the battle from the ships back to the plain,
He granted; but denied him to come safe home again.
But when to Zeus Achilles had poured the wine and prayed,
Back to his hut he turned once more, and the cup in its coffer laid;
Yet by the doorway still he stood, keen to discern
'Twixt Trojan and Achaean how the tides of war would turn.
Meanwhile around Patroclus his warriors kept their way
Unfaltering—till on the Trojans they burst in proud array.
Swiftly they streamed as hornets, that in their wayside nest
A band of boys makes angry and teases without rest
(As boys will in their mischief)—a plague for wayfarers.
For whenever some passer-by, all unsuspecting, stirs
Their fury, all together out pours that fearless swarm,
Full in his face, defending their little ones from harm.
Like these the Myrmidons—in courage and in will—
Poured from the ships, arousing a tumult nought could still.

(XVI, 156–67, 220–67.)

*At first Patroclus was brilliantly successful. He hurled back the Trojans
from the ships, slaying Sarpēdon of Lўcia, and pursued them to the very wall
of Ilios.*

Then indeed had the sons of Achaea, led by Patroclus' might,
Burst through the high-built gates of Troy—so fierce he raged in fight.
But there, to succour the Trojans, on a great tower's battlement,
Apollo stood—towards Patroclus grim now grew his intent.
Thrice on the high wall's angle Patroclus set amain
His foot, and thrice Apollo forced him back again,
Thrusting with hands immortal his glittering shield away;
But when with more than a mortal's might a fourth time through the fray
He rushed, from the lips of Apollo a dreadful cry rang clear:
'Give back, God-sprung Patroclus! 'Tis not before thy spear
That the gallant Trojans' city is doomed at last to bow—
Nor even before Achilles, that is mightier far than thou.'
Then at his shout far backward Patroclus, shuddering,
Shrank before the anger of Phoebus the Archer-king.
But Hector now by the Scaean Gate had drawn his rein,
Doubtful if into the tumult to lash his steeds again
Or bid his host fall backward to the wall of Ilios;
Yet Apollo stood beside him, as he paused there at a loss,
Transformed into the likeness of a warrior stout and young—
Āsius, Hecuba's brother, from the loins of Dÿmas sprung,
Who dwelt in Phrygia's marches, by the banks of Sangárius,
Own uncle unto Hector. Then cried Apollo thus:
'Why shrink from battle, Hector? No time for shrinking now!
Were I as much thy better, as I am worse than thou,
Thy hanging back from combat should cost thee bitterly.
Come, lash against Patroclus thy strong-hoofed team, and see
If to thy spear Apollo will vouchsafe victory.'
The God passed on through the battle, where warriors smote and died,
And straight to wise Kebríones the glorious Hector cried
To lash his steeds to battle. Deep through the thickest fray
Apollo plunged—mid the Argives terror and dismay
He spread, and gave the Trojans and Hector new renown.
But Hector stayed for no man, his spear struck no Greek down—
Only against Patroclus his gallant coursers swept.
Then from his car, to meet him, earthward Patroclus leapt,
Spear in left hand—in the other, with firmly taken stand,
He grasped a jagged and gleaming stone, that more than filled his hand,
And hurled—on no idle errand was that great missile sped,
Nor long upon its passage—for full against the head
It struck, with its sharp edges, of Hector's charioteer,
Kebríones, the bastard of glorious Priam. Sheer
It broke through the bone of his forehead, while yet to the reins he clung,

And crushed both brows together, and both his eyes were flung
Down in the dust before his feet.   Headlong he fell
From his chariot, as a diver plunges amid the swell,
And life was fled.   Then, Patroclus, loud didst thou mock at him:
'Gods, how he tumbles nimbly, this fellow light of limb!
Could he but make his business to dive for oysters, then
From the teeming main he might gather a feast for many men,
Diving over a vessel's side, though stormy raged the deep,
Since upon land so lightly from chariots he can leap.
Who would have thought in Troyland such tumbling men were kept!'
So crying, above the body of Kebríones he leapt
With the spring of a lion that is wounded, as he rushes to surprise
Some cattlefold, clean through the breast, and by his daring dies.
So furiously, Patroclus, didst thou spring upon the slain,
And Hector, too, sprang down to earth.   And then the twain
Battled above the body as two great lions fight
Above a slain deer's carcass on some far mountain-height,
When both are grim with hunger, both fearless in their pride.
So there above Kebríones, on either side
Menoetius' son, Patroclus, and glorious Hector fought,
Those champions of the war-cry, as each other's blood they sought.
For Hector seized the dead man's head, and gave not ground,
Patroclus haled him by the foot; and all around
The Trojans and Achaeans clashed in the battle's rage.
As when, in the glens of the mountains, South Wind and East Wind wage
Wild war, and vie in tossing the forest-depths, and dash
Together the smooth-barked cornel, and the oak tree, and the ash,
Till one and all together in deafening tumult shake
The long sweep of their branches, that thunder as they break;
So Trojans and Achaeans leapt headlong to the fight
And hacked and slew, while neither took thought of fatal flight.
Thickly the wingéd arrows came whizzing from the string,
Thickly about Kebríones the spears stuck quivering,
Thickly the mighty boulders, in the madness of the fray,
Rang on the shields; but quiet in the whirling dust-cloud lay
That mighty one mightily fallen, the steeds that he loved forgot.
   Now while in the highest heaven the noontide sun stood hot,
On both sides bit the weapons, on both sides died the folk;
But when the sun sank westward, when oxen quit the yoke,
The Achaeans grew the stronger, in the very teeth of fate,
And dragged from the storm of missiles Kebríones the great,
Despite the Trojan war-cries, and stripped his arms from him.
But Patroclus charged the Trojans with murderous heart and grim.
Thrice with a leap like Ares into the thick he thrust—

Fearful his shout, as thrice he smote nine heroes in the dust.
But when, like a God in his valour, a fourth time on swept he,
Then Death at last, Patroclus, rose up revealed for thee.
For Apollo stood to meet him across the battle's storm,
Terrible. Yet Patroclus saw not that deathless form
Coming—so thick a mantle of mist veiled him from all,
As he passed behind Patroclus and let his flat hand fall
On back and mighty shoulders. The hero's eyes spun round
Beneath the blow of Apollo, and his helmet hit the ground—
Under the hoofs of the horses that great casque rolled and rung,
And the plumes that waved above it, defiled in the dust were flung,
Besmirched with the blood of battle—that horsehair crest of war
That never had been fated for dust to foul before,
Through all the days while it warded the head and noble brow
Of the godlike son of Pēleus. Indeed Zeus gave it now
To Hector for his wearing: yet *his* doom too was near.
But now, in the hand of Patroclus, snapped his long-shafted spear,
Bronze-barbed and heavy and huge and strong; and on the field
There fell from Patroclus' shoulders his fringed and belted shield.
And then the lord Apollo unbraced his habergeon,
And his glorious limbs were loosened—dazed now and all undone
His wit; and he stood bewildered. Then a Trojan drove the keen
Point of a lance, from close behind, his shoulder-blades between—
Panthöüs' son, Euphorbus, surpassing all his peers
In speed of foot, and horsemanship, and hurling spears;
From their chariots twenty heroes that day to the earth he bore,
Driving through his first battle, a novice yet in war.
He first, O knightly Patroclus, planted his spear in thee,
Yet slew thee not, but fled away, and hid him hastily
Deep in the press, back plucking his ashen spear from the place,
Nor dared to meet Patroclus, though naked, face to face.
Then smitten of God, and wounded, backward Patroclus reeled
To reach the ranks of Achaea, avoiding that doom revealed;
But Hector, seeing his foeman, for all his valiant heart,
Struck by the biting bronze, back to the rearward start,
Closed with him through the serried ranks, and drove his spear
In at the base of his belly, till the point of bronze stood clear.
Earthward he crashed; and loudly the Argives wailed for woe.
As when high up the mountains a lion has laid low
Some boar of quenchless valour, as they grapple in their pride,
Thirsting alike for water, by some thin runnel's side,
And at last the lion leaves him, gasping his dying breath;
So Menoetius' son undaunted, when he had given death
To many and many a Trojan, by Hector stricken lay.

Then loud the vaunt of the victor rose winging on its way:
'Indeed thou didst deem, Patroclus, that Troy was thine to sack,
And thine the wives of the Trojans, for thee to carry back
As slaves aboard thy galleys, to the land thou lovest dear.
O fool!   The steeds of Hector charge forth in full career
Before these, to defend them; and foremost here I stand,
Among our valiant Trojans, to ward from this our land
Its day of doom.   But thee the vultures here shall eat.
Poor wretch, not Achilles' valour could save thee from defeat!
There in the camp abiding, doubtless he charged thee strait—
"Come not, knightly Patroclus, back where our galleys wait,
Until thy hand in battle has torn the bloody vest
Of man-destroying Hector from his own dying breast."
So doubtless did he charge thee—and, fool, thou didst heed his lie!'
   Then, breathing hard, Patroclus, did thy brave lips reply:
'Boast, Hector, loudly as thou wilt.   For Crŏnus' son
Gives thee the triumph, and Apollo—'twas *these* left me undone,
Easily—from my shoulders *these* stripped my arms away.
Had twenty such as thou art met me amid the fray,
They had fallen—all!—before me and died beneath my spear.
But Lēto's son, and deadly Fate, have slain me here,
And, among men, Euphorbus; and thou art but the third.
And yet I have still to utter—heed thou me well—one word:
Not long shalt *thou* live, either.   Already near at hand
The day of *thy* death also, and a doom of violence, stand—
To fall by the peerless valour of Achilles Aeácides.'
   Thus as he spoke, on Patroclus did death and darkness seize,
And his soul fled forth from his body upon the path to Hell,
Leaving its youth and its manhood, wailing the doom that fell.
And then the glorious Hector to the dead man made reply:
'Sheer doom for me, Patroclus, why wilt thou prophesy?
Who knows if even Achilles, whom fair-tressed Thĕtis bore,
May not go down, hereafter, before my spear in war?'
   With that, upon the fallen he set his foot and thrust,
To free his spear, and the body fell backward in the dust.
Then, with his lance uplifted Hector turned to run
On the swift Achilles' godlike squire, Autómedon,
Eager to strike; but *him* his lightfoot steeds did save,
Those steeds of deathless beauty the Gods to Pēleus gave.

(XVI, 698–867.)

Above the body of Patroclus the combat now became more furious than ever.

So on both sides they battled and an iron clangour there
Rose up to the brazen heaven through the barren fields of air.
But now aloof from the conflict the steeds of Achilles stayed,
Sorrowing, since they knew their charioteer was laid
Dead in the dust by Hector's hand.   In vain Autómedon
With swift lash urged them onward, Diōres' stalwart son—
In vain with words of kindness, with menaces in vain.
They would not stir—not homeward to the Greek ships again
Beside broad Hellespont, nor yet back to the fight
In the wake of the Achaeans.   As a grave-slab stands upright,
Immovable, on the barrow of a man or a woman dead,
So by their fair-built chariot, with earthward drooping head,
Both stood.   And from their eyelids, mourning their driver slain,
To the ground the warm tears trickled, and all their splendid mane
Was soiled, as from the yoke-strap, over the yoke, the hair
Trailed in the dust.   But, seeing, Zeus pitied that grieving pair,
And shook His head, and murmured to His own heart, pondering:
'Why did we ever give you, poor beasts, to a mortal king,
To Pēleus?—ye who are ageless, whom death will never find,
Why should ye share the sorrows of hapless humankind?
For surely unhappier creature, than man, comes not to birth,
Of all that breathe and move on all the ways of earth.'

(XVII, 424–47.)

*At last the Achaeans gained possession of the body of Patroclus, though not
till Hector had stripped from it the arms of Achilles.*

The Struggle for Patroclus

So Ajax spake and the others lifted the dead on high
With arms that strained their utmost.   But there rose a mighty cry
Far back through the ranks of Troy, as they saw Patroclus slain
Upborne by the Achaeans; and on they charged amain,
As hounds, ahead of the hunters, leap on a wounded boar—
Thirsting to tear their quarry they rush far on before,
But when he wheels about in the courage of his might,
They flinch again and scatter, this way and that, in flight.
So the serried ranks of Trojans again and again pressed near
With many a thrust of swordblade and double-pointed spear;
But whenever the two Aiantes whirled round to front them there,
Standing at bay, their colour paled—not one would dare
To head the charge against them and seize the dead they bore.
Thus towards the hollow ships forth from the press of war

They struggled with Patroclus—fierce raged the battle's height
About them, like a devouring flame that sets alight,
With swift and sudden onset, some city's teeming ways,
While houses shrink in that furnace and wind-swept roars its blaze;
So now, as ever onward they strove their way to win,
The roar of steeds and spearmen crashed with unslackening din.
And still, as when a mule-team, straining their stubborn strength,
Heave down some rugged mountain-track the nodding length
Of a beam, or a great ship's timber, and ever as they go
Their hearts are spent with effort and fast the sweatdrops flow;
So the bearers toiled with the body.   But the two Aiantes stood,
Holding the foe behind them, as some ridge clad with wood,
That juts o'er the plain from the uplands, holds back the ruinous force
Of even mighty rivers and turns them from their course
Sharply across the levels, and the great floods chafe in vain;
So did the two Aiantes hold back across the plain
The spears of Troy—yet they followed, and two in the front of these,
Hector in his glory, and Aeneas Anchīsiades.
But as a cloud of starlings, or daws, wild-chattering fly
When they see the small birds' slayer, the falcon, swooping nigh;
So broke the sons of Achaea, wild crying, at the sight
Of Hector and Aeneas, and forgot their joy in fight;
And all about the trench, as the Danaans fled away,
Thick fell the fair-wrought armour, and the battle found no stay.
      So there they raged in conflict like some consuming flame,
But now with the news to Achilles the swift Antílochus came
And found him before the high-horned poops of his galleys, gloomily
Foreboding at heart, already, what things had come to be,
While to his own great spirit he murmured in dismay:
'Ah!—why do the long-haired Achaeans fall back now from the fray
Across the plain to the ships once more, harried and hard bestead?
Let not the Gods accomplish that evil thing I dread,
That prophecy of my mother, that she foretold me once—
How, while I yet was living, the best of the Myrmidons
Should be stricken from the sunlight beneath the Trojan spears!
Dead is Menoetius' gallant son!—too true my fears.
Ah, reckless heart!   Yet I charged him to turn back from the fight,
Once he had saved the ships from fire, nor challenge Hector's might.'
      While thus his spirit brooded, the noble Nestor's heir,
Weeping hot tears, drew nigh him, with bitter news to bear.
'Son of wise-hearted Pēleus, I bring thee now—' said he,
'Would God the truth were other!—news of calamity.
Patroclus—he is fallen.   They battle where he lies,
Naked—for all his armour is bright-helmed Hector's prize.'

Then closed around Achilles grief like a black cloud's pall.
He gathered dust and ashes, with both hands, and let fall
Over his head, till the beauty of his face was turned to shame—
And his nectar-fragrant tunic—with dark dust from the flame;
And the mighty one, mightily fallen, lay in the ashes there,
Outstretched in all his stature, with hands that tore his hair.

(XVII, 722–XVIII, 27.)

*In an agony of grief the hero wept on the sea-shore, till his mother Thĕtis
heard him from the deep and rose with her Nereids to comfort him.*

Achilles' Remorse

So saying she came from her cavern; and with her, tearfully,
The Nereïds went—and about them the surges of the sea
Sundered in twain.   But when they reached Troy's fruitful land,
One behind another they mounted up its strand,
Where round the swift Achilles, close-clustered, stood the ships
Of the Myrmidons.   Beside him, while groans burst from his lips,
Stood his noble mother and, crying, clasped his head,
While the words came winging from her, and all in tears she said:
'My son, what is thy sorrow?   Why dost thou cry "Alas!"?
Tell me now, do not hide it.   For Zeus has brought to pass
That thing thou once didst ask for, with hands upraised in prayer—
That all the sons of Achaea might be driven in despair
Back to their ships, for lack of thee, and their glory turned to shame.'
Then from the swift Achilles, with a groan, the answer came:
'Ah, mother, Zeus of Olympus hath indeed performed to the end
My prayer—but what joy has it brought me?   For fallen lies my friend,
Patroclus, the very comrade I loved and honoured most—
Yea, as myself I loved him—and now for ever lost!
My arms, too, Hector has taken—my arms that shone so brave,
The huge and wondrous weapons that once the Immortals gave
To Pēleus, when they brought thee to be a mortal's bride.
Ah would they had left thee, mother, with the Nymphs of the salt sea-tide,
And only a mortal woman had lain in Peleus' bed!
Thine too will be grief past telling, for a son that shall soon be dead,
Whom never thou shalt welcome returning home again.
For truly the heart within me no longer now is fain
To live, or mix with the living—unless beneath my spear
Hector shall first fall smitten and in his turn pay dear
With his life for the blood of Patroclus, son of Menoetius.'
Then, with tears fast falling, Thĕtis answered thus:

'Alas, how thy days are numbered, if such thy words must be,
My son.   For, after Hector, death waits at hand for thee.'
   Then the swift Achilles answered, stirred deeply, 'Would the grave
Held me already, seeing I was fated not to save
My friend as he lay dying!—far from his native land
He fell, and found in battle no help from this right hand!
What is there left?—to me, homecoming is denied,
And neither to Patroclus, nor my many friends beside,
Could I bring life—nay, death at Hector's hand they found,
While here I sit, an idle encumbrance of the ground—
I that had never an equal in the brazen battle-line
Of Achaea; though in speech there are cleverer tongues than mine!
Ah would that from earth and Heaven all strife were for ever flung,
And wrath, that makes even a wise man mad!   Upon the tongue
Its taste is sweeter than honey, that drips from the comb—but *then*
Like a smother of blinding smoke it mounts in the hearts of men.
So was I stung to anger by Agamemnon the King.
Yet now be the past forgotten, however sharp its sting!
Perforce, we both must master the passion in our breast.
Now will I seek that slayer of him I loved the best,
Hector—if I must perish, I will face it, nor complain,
When Zeus and the other deathless Gods shall so ordain.
Not even the mighty Hēracles could shun his doom—he died.
Though the Son of Crŏnus loved him, better than all beside,
Yet Destiny overcame him, and Hēra's deadly hate.
So I—if now for me also a like end lies in wait,
Well, in death I shall rest.   Let fame tell what I dĭd;
Let many a Trojan woman and deep-bosomed Dardanid,
As from her delicate cheeks her two hands wipe away
The streaming tears, and thick she sobs for him I slay,
Learn that, though long I tarried, I come again to war.
Let thy love not hold me from battle.   Thou canst bend my will no more.'

                                                    (XVIII, 65–126.)

*The Achaeans bearing back Patroclus were still hard pressed by Hector, who
would indeed have recaptured the body, had not Hēra sent Iris to warn Achilles.
He complained that he was weaponless; but Iris bade him simply cross the Achaean
ditch and shout to the battling armies.*

Achilles over the Trench

   Up leapt Achilles dear to Zeus, and Pallas flung
Round his great shoulders her aegis, where many a tassel swung;
But his head the noble Goddess crowned with a cloud of gold
And kindled there a glory blinding to behold.

As when above some city the smoke towers heaven-high,
Far off upon an island, where leaguering foemen lie—
All the day long the townsmen, fighting from their walls,
Grapple in bitter battle; but soon as darkness falls,
Then beacon after beacon flames, and high the glow
Leaps heavenward, to let their neighbour-cities know,
In hope they may sail to succour those townsmen hard bestead;
So flamed that radiant splendour, high from Achilles' head.
Down from the wall to the trench he came; yet still he stayed
Apart from the Achaeans, as his wise mother bade;
But standing there he shouted, and far away as well
Athene called—on the Trojans measureless tumult fell.
As shattering as the clangour of a clarion's call,
When enemies without pity beset a city wall,
So shattering resounded the shout of Aeácides;
And when they heard that voice of bronze, his enemies
Felt their hearts fail within them, and their long-maned horses reared
Back, with their cars behind them, dreading the doom that neared,
And white grew the chariot-drivers to see that splendour spring
From the head of the dauntless Achilles, and burn unwearying,
Enkindled by the Goddess, Athene the flashing-eyed.
Thrice there over the trench the noble Achilles cried,
Thrice on Trojans and famed allies fell wild dismay—
By their own spears slain, by their chariots crushed, twelve of their noblest
    lay.

(XVIII, 203–231.)

So, as the day ended, Patroclus was borne to Achilles' hut at last. The Trojans now held a council and Polýdamas warned Hector to withdraw behind the walls of Troy, since Achilles would now surely return to war. But Hector scorned him and the Trojans applauded in their folly.

Then in the field the Trojans supped; but the Argives kept
Mourning all night for Patroclus; sorely they wailed and wept,
While in their lamentation Pēlīdes led the rest.
Laying his hands of slaughter upon his comrade's breast,
Loudly he groaned, and deeply, as a lion with mighty mane
Whose cubs, far in the forest, some deer-hunter has ta'en
By stealth; too late returning, the lion in his grief
Ranges the glens of the mountains upon the trail of the thief,
In hope at last to find him—so hot his anger runs.
Thus, groaning deep, Achilles cried amid the Myrmidons.

(XVIII, 314–23.)

Meanwhile Thĕtis came to the dwelling of Hephaestus and he consented to make new arms for her son.

So saying he passed from Thĕtis to where his bellows lay,
And towards the fire he turned them all; then bade them play.
Twenty in all, on his crucibles they breathed the flame
And ever their blast fierce-kindling at his pleasure went and came;
Now furious, when he laboured; now sinking back to rest,
Just as Hephaestus willed it, as served his skill the best.
Then tin within the furnace and tireless bronze he cast,
And precious gold, and silver; and next he planted fast
The weight of his massy anvil upon the anvil-stand,
And grasped his mighty hammer and his tongs in either hand.

First a shield he fashioned, stout and heavy to hold,
All bright-inlaid; and round it he set a rim threefold
Of fiercely flashing metal, and a silver belt he made.
Of layers five that shield was; and on it he inlaid
Many a cunning figure, in the wisdom of his heart.

Therein he wrought the Heavens, the Earth, and the Sea apart,
And the sun that wearies never, and the moon with her orb's full round;
There too the constellations wherewith high Heaven is crowned,
The Pleiads, and the Hyads, and Orion in his might,
And the Bear—or 'The Wain' men call her—that through the hours of
night
Turns ever in her station and watch on Orion keeps
And alone of the constellations bathes not in Ocean's deeps.

Next, two cities of men he made, upon two sides—
Lovely they were.   In one were weddings, and feasts, and brides
Borne from their homes through the city amid the merry throngs
Of torches brightly blazing and lilting marriage-songs.
In the dance young men were whirling, and amidst them many a lyre,
Many a flute made music; and, gathered to admire,
In the porches of their houses the women stood and gazed.
But the folk thronged thick in the market.   For there a suit was raised
Betwixt two men that wrangled touching the right to pay
Gold for a death—to the people one urged 'twas his to lay
A full price down for the slaying; but the other still denied,
Refusing aught—to a doomsman they brought it to decide.
Loudly in either's favour the folk stood clamouring,
But heralds stayed the tumult, while in a sacred ring
On polished stones the elders sat—each took in hand
A staff from the thunderous heralds, and up in turn would stand
To speak his doom; and amidst them two golden talents shone
For his reward whose judgment should seem the wisest one.

But round that other city two hosts in war-array

He wrought, with armour flashing.   Two plans before them lay—
Should they sack the town to the utmost, or with the townsmen share,
Taking half of the treasure within that city fair?
But not yet yielded the townsmen.   Secretly they set
An ambush, leaving behind them to man their parapet
Their wives beloved, with their children, and the old men bowed with
    years.
So out they marched; and Ares and Athene led their spears,
Fashioned as golden figures, in garments all of gold,
Fair and of godlike stature, and peerless to behold
In their panoplies; but the mortals he made of meaner size.
But when they came to the place they planned for that surprise,
By a river where the cattle were driven down to drink,
There, in arms of burning bronze, upon the brink
They sat them down; and, before them, two scouts they set to warn
Of the coming of the sheep and the kine with curling horn,
That were hard at hand already—amid them two herdsmen played
Gaily upon their pipes, nor guessed that a trap was laid.
But now the men in ambush burst suddenly in sight
And rounded up the flocks, with fleeces snowy-white,
And that great herd of oxen, while others the herdsmen slew.
But soon as the besiegers, sitting in conclave, knew,
By the clamour among their cattle, each on his chariot leapt
And with lofty-stepping chargers swift in pursuit they swept,
Till now beside the river-bank the full-set battle clashed.
There, as men smote each other, the brazen spearheads flashed;
There Strife was; there was Carnage; and there strode Doom the grim,
Gripping a man unwounded, and a wounded next to him,
And dragged by the feet another across the tumult—dead,
While the mantle over her shoulders with blood was spotted red.
There warriors rushed together, like life, in battle's toil,
Haling, on either side, slain bodies to despoil.

    But next—wide, soft, and fertile—he made a thrice-ploughed field,
And in it many ploughmen hither and thither wheeled
Their oxen; and whenever to the end of his furrow's line
A ploughman came returning, one brought a cup of wine,
Sweet as honey, to cheer him.   So all ploughed stoutly, fain
Quickly to reach the border of that deep loam again.
But behind their ploughs the earth turned black, just like ploughed land,
Although 'twas of gold—a marvel of the craftsman's cunning hand.

    And then he made a king's domain, where reapers reaped,
Wielding their whetted sickles.   Behind, the swathes fell heaped
Along the furrows; next, came binders binding fast
Their sheaves—three were the binders, followed by lads that passed

Armfuls of corn ungathered into their hands to bind.
And there amid the furrows the king stood, glad in mind,
Holding in hand his sceptre, and watched, yet never spoke.
But his heralds were preparing a meal beneath an oak
With a great ox slain in sacrifice; and women there
Cooked a great mess of barley for the reapers' noonday fare.
   Then he made a golden vineyard, beautiful, where clung
Many a mighty cluster.   Black the clusters hung,
But everywhere of silver the poles whereon they grew,
With a wall of bright tin about them, and a ditch of azure hue.
A single path led thither, whereby the pickers came
At vintage.   Lads and lasses, young hearts that knew no blame,
Were bearing in plaited baskets the honey-sweet fruit away
And in their midst on a sweet-toned lyre a boy did play
Enchantingly, and sang to it a fair lament
For Līnus, carolling clearly; and ever as they went,
Their feet kept time together with song and music's fall.
   Next, a herd of cattle, with horns uppointed tall,
He fashioned, bright inlaying the beasts in gold and tin.
Forth from the farmstead, lowing, they galloped out to win
Their pasture, where roared a river and reeds waved on its banks.
Four golden herdsmen followed the cattle's rushing ranks
And nine dogs—swift feet twinkling—trotted behind them there.
But amid the foremost heifers two grisly lions tare
A deep-voiced bull, and dragged him—fearfully he cried,
Bellowing.   Youths and dogs pursued—but now the hide
Of that great steer was ripped apart, and bowels and gore
The two great lions were lapping with their tongues.   Yet all the more
The herdsmen ran, hallooing to each fleet-footed hound;
In vain, for the dogs dared not to bite, but still gave ground,
Leaping aside; or barked, as round they stood afraid.
   Next a wide sheep-pasture the glorious Haltfoot made,
In a fair glen, where flocks with snowy fleeces browsed,
With its steadings, and its pinfolds, and the huts where its shepherds
    housed.
   And there besides was figured by the glorious Haltfoot's hand
A dancing-place, bright-gleaming; such as Daedalus planned
Long since in spacious Cnossus for Ariadne the fair.
Many a much-wooed maiden, many a youth was there,
Dancing, and each in his hand the wrist of another had.
Delicate linen the maidens wore—the youths were clad
In tunics dainty-woven, where smooth the bright oil shone;
Fair wreaths were round the maidens' brows—the youths, each one,
Carried a golden dagger, by a silver baldric bound.

Sometimes with cunning feet lightly they danced around,
Easily as a potter, whenever he would feel
How smooth it runs, with his fingers will twirl his potter's wheel;
Or again, in lines opposing, back and forth they danced
And about their lovely motion a great throng stood entranced,
Watching; amid them a minstrel his lyre divinely swept,
While, to the music's measure, in the midst two tumblers leapt.
    Last, the mighty waters of the Ocean-stream he wheeled
In circle round the margin of that fair-fashioned shield.

(XVIII, 468–608.)

*Next morning Thĕtis brought the arms to Achilles; and he was reconciled
with Agamemnon, who handed over Brīsēïs and the promised gifts of atonement.
Then Achilles armed.*

The Horse Xanthus Warns Achilles

But Alcĭmus and Autómedon toiled busily
Yoking his steeds, and buckled the breast-straps fair to see,
And set the bits in the horses' jaws, and drew back tight
The reins to his stout-built chariot's rail.   Then in his right
Autómedon gripped the glittering lash, and leapt upon his car;
And, donning his helm, Achilles, in arms that gleamed afar
Like the blaze of Hyperīon, sprang after in his turn
And cried to his father's horses, in a fearful voice and stern:
'Now then, my steeds of glory, ye whom Podarge bare,
Bálius and Xanthus, bring back with better care
Your master, after battle, safe to the Danaï,
Nor leave him, like Patroclus, upon the field to die.'
Then Xanthus of the glancing feet bent suddenly
His head and answered Achilles, with long mane falling free
Over the yoke from the yokestrap, till to the dust it bowed,
(For the white-armed Goddess Hēra his tongue with speech endowed):
'For thy safety, great Achilles, this day we *will* take heed;
And yet thy deathday now is near.   Not ours the deed—
A mighty God shall do it, and a resistless Fate.
Not because *we* were heedless, or laggards, did the hate
Of the Trojans strip Patroclus.   He fell in the front of war
By the noblest of Immortals, whom fair-tressed Lēto bore,
That Hector might have the glory.   We are fleet as the western blast—
Of winds, men say, the swiftest—and yet thy doom is cast.
By a God and a man together in the dust shalt thou be flung.'
When Xanthus so had spoken, the Erīnyes stayed his tongue.
But the swift-footed Achilles made answer, gloomily:

'Why warn me, Xanthus, of my doom?   No need for thee!
Well enough I too know it, that here in the Trojan land,
Far from my own loved parents, I shall perish.   Yet this hand
Shall stay not till Troy has swallowed its surfeit of my spear.'
    Then he lashed his swift steeds, shouting, forward in full career.

(XIX, 392–424.)

*So Achilles plunged into the fight.   Aeneas was saved from his fury by
Poseidon, Hector by Apollo; but among the rest of the Trojans there followed a
fearful slaughter and they fled to the river Xanthus.*

But as o'er some parched mountain sweeps a portentous blaze,
Deep through its glens, devouring, deep through its woodland ways—
On every side the whirling wind drives on the flame;
So, like a God, on every side Achilles rushing came
With murderous spear pursuing, till the dark earth ran red.
And as, when a man has yoked his broad-browed steers to tread,
On some fair threshing-floor, white barley in the ear,
Under the hoofs of his lowing beasts swiftly the grain falls clear;
So, while the dauntless Achilles flung to his steeds the rein,
Their hoofs trod down the bodies and the bucklers of the slain.
The rails of his chariot reddened, red ran his axletree,
As from his wheels and his chargers' hoofs the blood-drops scattered free.
On, in pursuit of glory, the son of Pēleus drave,
Dyeing deep in crimson those hands no man might brave.
But when they came to the ford, where eddied swift and fair
Xanthus, begot of Zeus most high, Achilles there
Sundered the fleeing Trojans; and half towards where Troy lay,
Across the plain he hunted (where only yesterday
Before the fury of Hector, headlong the Achaeans fled).
In the path of these, to check them, the hand of Hēra spread
A wall of mist; but the others ran huddling in their haste
Where down the deeps of Xanthus the silver whirlpools raced.
Loud the steep channel echoed, as splashing in they sprang;
Loudly the banks resounded; loudly the shouting rang,
As men swam hither and thither, round in the eddies whirled.
And as when swarming locusts by the fire's hot blast are hurled,
Flying, into a river—for rising suddenly
That blaze flares up resistless, and into the waves they flee;
So were the roaring depths of eddying Xanthus then
Filled by Achilles' fury with jostling steeds and men.
And now the Zeus-sprung hero, dread as a God to behold,
Planted his spear by the tamarisks, and plunged where the river rolled.

(XX, 490–XXI, 18.)

Here Achilles caught, fleeing out of the river, Priam's son Lycāon, whom he had captured once before and sold as a slave. Again the youth pleaded for quarter.

So spoke Priam's noble son, with many and many a word
Of prayer for life; but bitter was the answer that he heard—
'Fool, tell me not of ransom!   Talk not of a price to pay!
Indeed, until Patroclus had met his fatal day,
Dearer my own heart held it to spare an enemy;
Many I took of the Trojans, and sold them oversea.
But now not one shall escape his fate, of those that fall
By God's will into my hand, here before Ilios' wall—
Nay, not a single Trojan; and Priam's sons least of all.
Therefore, my friend, die also.   What help lamenting now?
Even Patroclus died, that was better far than thou.
Look upon me—me also, that am made so strong and fair,
Son of a noble father, whom a Goddess Mother bare;
Yet for *me* too a death of blood, or late or soon,
Stands waiting; for *me* there cometh some morn, or eve, or noon,
When in the clash of Ares shall fall that fatal blow,
Whether it be by a spearpoint or arrow from the bow.'

(XXI, 97–113.)

The River-god Xanthus, finding his channel choked with slain, rose in anger against Achilles, who was soon in danger of being swept away. But Hēra called her son Hephaestus to help, and he subdued the River with his flame. Then battle became general among the Gods themselves. Athene felled Ares and Aphrodite; Apollo refused the challenge of Poseidon; and Hēra chastised Artemis.

Meanwhile Achilles pursued the fleeing enemy to the wall of Troy and nearly took the city. But Apollo encouraged the Trojan Agēnor to resist, then himself took Agēnor's likeness and lured Achilles in pursuit, away from the routed army, back into the Trojan Plain.

The Slaying of Hector

So the fugitives of the Trojans, that had fled as fawns in the brake,
Wiped off their sweat in the city, and drank great draughts to slake
Their thirst, as they leaned on her noble walls; but nearer yet
The Achaeans drew to the rampart, with shields on their shoulders set.
But doom chained the feet of Hector to stand his ground and wait
In front of Ilios still, there by the Scaean Gate.
Meanwhile to the son of Pēleus Phoebus Apollo cried:
'Why dog me still, Achilles, with swift-pursuing stride,
A mortal chasing a deathless God!   Still blind to me,
That I am an Immortal, in thy mad persistency

Thou forgettest the stricken Trojans that fled before thy way.
Safe now they crowd in the city—and thou art run astray.
Yet thou canst not kill me, Achilles.   I am one that cannot die.'
　　Then answered the swift Achilles with a loud and angry cry:
'Thou hast fooled me, far-shooting Apollo, of all the Gods most ill,
Luring me from the city!   Else many another still
Had bit the dust, or ever they came to Ilios' wall.
Thou hast robbed me of mighty glory!   Ay, thou hast saved them all
Full cheaply!—for thou fearest from *me* no punishment.
Ah, had I but the power, sorely thou shouldst repent.'
　　Then back in his proud anger he turned to the town again,
Swift as some steed triumphant races across the plain,
With chariot behind him, galloping easily;
So lightly the son of Pēleus plied nimble foot and knee.
It was the old king Priam that saw him first afar,
Charging across the levels, glittering like the star
That rises up at harvest-tide, and with his light
Outgleams the hosts of Heaven in the blackness of the night—
By men named 'The Hound of Orion.'   Far brightest of them all
His splendour glares, portending evil to befall,
And many a burning fever he brings to hapless man.
So on the breast of Achilles the bronze flashed, as he ran.
But the old king groaned aloud and lifted his hands on high
And beat his head, lamenting, and cried with a mighty cry
To his dear son—for before the gate he saw him stand,
Burning to offer battle to Achilles, hand to hand!
Then piteously old Priam called, with arms outthrown:
'Hector, my own loved son, meet not this man alone
With none of thy comrades by thee—for fear thou perish now
By the hand of this son of Pēleus—he is mightier far than thou,
And merciless!   Ah, that Heaven but held his life as dear
As I—then hound and vulture would soon devour him here,
Dead!—ay, *that* would lighten my heart of bitter pain!
So many fair sons he has robbed me of—some he hath slain,
And some to far-off islands in bondage he hath sold.
Two of them at this moment my eyes cannot behold
Mid all that are fled to the city—my sons by Laóthoë,
Polydōrus and Lycāon—ah, queen among women she!
If yet they live, in the Argive host, why then we will
Pay bronze and gold for their ransom—for treasure we have still
(Such wealth with his daughter Altes gave, grown old in his renown);
But if they are dead, and already to Hades' house gone down,
Bitter indeed for me and the mother that gave them birth,
But still that loss to the Trojans shall seem of lesser worth

If only thou find not also at Achilles' hand thy grave.
Back then, my son, within the wall!—come back to save
The men of Troy and her women—lest now to Pēleus' son
Thou give this crowning glory, and thy own sweet days be done.
Pity thy wretched father—this heart so full of tears,
Still quick to feel.   Old as I am, in the gate of years,
I know that Zeus hath doomed me to look on misery—
My sons hewn down, my daughters haled to captivity,
My palace given to plunder, babes in their helplessness
Smitten against the ground in the bitter battle's stress,
And the wives of my sons dragged headlong by murderous hands to their
     fate;
Ay, and me too at the end, before my palace-gate,
The hounds shall rend and raven, soon as the final blow
Of sword-edge or of spearpoint has laid this body low;
Yea, the dogs I reared at my table, the dogs that watched my door,
Shall couch them at my gateway, when they have lapped my gore,
With frenzy still upon them.   Ah, comely are the young,
Even when slain in battle; even when they are flung
Unburied—even in death, still graceful lies each limb;
But when an old man is fallen, with the dogs befouling him—
Grey head, grey beard dishonoured, and his parts of shame—ah, then
No sight is so full of pity in this world of hapless men.'
   So the old king lamented, with hands that grasped and tare
His locks of grey; yet Hector was moved not by his prayer.
But after him Hector's mother upon the other side
Wept, and unbared her bosom, and lifted her breast and cried,
Wailing with wingéd words: 'My son, revere this breast—
Pity me, Hector!—if ever it lulled thy tears to rest,
Dear one, bear *that* in remembrance, and face thine enemy
Behind our rampart—stand not forth, so recklessly,
To brave him.   For if he slay thee, child of my womb, dear son,
Then never shall I, nor the wife whom thou hast wooed and won
With many a gift, bewail thee, laid on thy deathbed—nay,
The Argive hounds shall tear thee, by their galleys, far away.'
   So the old pair, loud wailing, cried to the son they loved,
With prayer on prayer; but Hector, with courage still unmoved,
While ever the towering Achilles drew nearer, faced him there.
And as some snake of the mountains, coiling before its lair,
Battened on poisonous herbage, with fury in its soul,
Waits for a man, grim glaring from the issue of its hole;
So now with quenchless courage still Hector kept the field.
Against the jut of a tower he leant his shining shield;
And yet, filled with misgiving, to his brave heart murmured low:

'Ah me, if behind our ramparts—within our gates—I go,
Polýdamas will be foremost to blame me in all men's sight.
For he warned me to lead the Trojans within our walls, this night
Of ruin, when the noble Achilles first roused him back to war;
But I—I would not heed him.   It had been better far!
Yet having destroyed my people, by my folly that would not hear,
I cannot face the Trojans and their long-robed wives; for fear
Some meaner man than I am may cry my shame aloud—
"Hector has ruined the people, of his own strength overproud."
So they will say.   Nay, better it would be now for me
Either to face Achilles and return with victory,
Or at least with honour before Troy-wall to die.
And yet—how if on earth, now, I let my bossed shield lie,
And my great helm, and leaning against the wall my spear
Met noble Achilles face to face, and standing near
Promised to give back Helen, with all her wealth, once more,
All that within his hollow ships once Paris bore
Troyward, from whence this quarrel betwixt our peoples fell?—
To yield them to the Atrīdae, and give the Greeks as well
Half of the gathered treasures that in our walls abide,
Taking from all the Trojans a solemn oath to hide
Nothing, but fairly apportion all things 'twixt them and us?
Ah no, what can it profit in my heart to reason thus?
I well might go to meet him, and he—he would not care
For mercy nor for honour, but slay me standing there,
Disarmed, like some weak woman, and helpless.   What avails
To think of bandying with him such bygone dreamer's tales?—
Such love-talk as youth and maiden, whispering apart,
Youth and maiden utter to one another's heart?
Better to clash in battle, with all the speed may be;
We will find whom Zeus of Olympus shall crown with victory.'
    So, waiting there, he pondered; but Achilles now drew near,
Like to the high-plumed God of War.   His dreadful spear,
Of Pēlian ash, he brandished from his shoulder as he came,
With his brazen arms about him aglitter like the flame
Of some great conflagration, or like the rising sun.
But seeing him Hector trembled—from the gate he turned to run,
In flight before that menace too fearful to endure:
And after him leapt Achilles with nimble feet and sure.
Then as a mountain falcon, swiftest of birds that be,
Swoops light in the wake of a trembling dove that turns to flee—
Closely behind he follows, and screaming loud and shrill
Again and again darts after, with heart athirst to kill;
So, furious, swooped Pēlīdes; but Hector edged in flight

Along by the Trojan rampart with hurrying knees and light—
Past the place of the watchmen, past the wild fig wind-swept,
Slanting away from the wall, by the waggon-track they kept,
Till they came to the springs fair-flowing, where from a double source
Out of the earth arises Scamander's eddying course.
Hot from the one the water flows—above, a spire
Of smoke goes up to Heaven, as if from a burning fire;
But the waters of the other, even in summer, flow
As chill as ice, or frozen hail, or wintry snow;
There two wide washing-places, of fair stone, lie at hand.
Ere came the sons of Achaea, while peace lay on the land,
Hither the wives of the Trojans and their lovely daughters drew,
To scour their shining raiment white; and here the two,
Fugitive and pursuer, passed now in headlong race.
Noble was he that fled, but behind him in the chase
A mightier came, and swiftly.   It was no runner's prize,
Oxhide or beast for slaughter, they had before their eyes;
It was for the life of Hector, tamer of steeds, they ran.
Lightly as chariots racing, at the games for some dead man,
Wheel round the course, contending for a guerdon of great price—
A cauldron or a woman; so round Priam's city thrice
Those swift feet fetched their circuit.   And the high Gods watched them
      pass.
Then spoke in their midst the Father of Gods and men—'Alas,
This was a man I loved.   And now I must watch him flee
Around the Trojan rampart.   Sore is the heart in me
For Hector's sake, that hath burnt me so many a bullock's thigh,
Sometimes on Ilios' citadel, and sometimes high
On the peak of deep-glennèd Ida.   And lo, round Priam's town
Now the noble Achilles with swift feet hunts him down.
Therefore, ye Gods, take counsel and ponder well on this—
From death now shall we save him?   Or, noble as he is,
By the hand of Achilles, Pēleus' son, shall we leave him to be slain?'
      Then the flashing-eyed Athene answered him again:
'Lord of the blackening stormcloud and the white lightning's flame,
What words are these, my Father?   Death hath an evil name;
Yet to spare this man that is mortal—long destined for the tomb!
So do!   But not *all* we other Gods can praise Thee for Thy doom.'
      Then Zeus, that gathers the storm-wrack, made answer: 'Have no dread,
Dear daughter, Trītogeneia.   For this that I have said,
I spoke it not in earnest.   Fain would I please thee still.
Hold back no more—thy purpose, just as it was, fulfil.'
So he urged on Athene, that needed no spurring—light
She leapt on her way to earthward, down from Olympus' height.

But ever the swift Achilles pressed hard on Hector's trail,
As when a hound in the mountains pursues through glen and dale
Some fawn it has roused from its resting—and even if its prey,
Baffling it for a moment, in the thicket cowers away,
Still the dog trails it tireless, until it finds the place;
So Hector could not baffle the swift Achilles' chase.
Again and again he spurted towards those strong towers built high
O'er the Dardan gates, still hoping their warders might let fly
Spears from above to defend him; but out into the plain,
Achilles, that kept on the city-side, still edged him back again.
As when in sleep a dreamer would follow one that flies—
In vain he strains to follow, to flee the other tries;
So Hector could not win safety, nor Achilles overtake.
But how indeed should Hector have had the power to break
Still from his doom, if Apollo, for a last time in that hour,
Had not drawn near to speed him and lend his limbs new power?
Yet the noble Achilles warned his men with shaken head
Not to let fly at Hector their sharp spears as he fled,
Lest his own praise have but second place, if another struck him dead.
But when they came for the fourth time where the springs of Scamander
  lie,
Then the All-father lifted up His golden scales on high;
Twin dooms of Death the Destroyer he laid therein—the one
For Hector, the tamer of horses, the other for Pēleus' son—
And held them poised by the middle. Then Hector's doom at last
Sank, towards the pit of Hades—from his side Apollo passed.
Instead, to the son of Pēleus came Athene flashing-eyed
And, standing close beside him, with wingéd words she cried:
'Now, glorious Achilles, beloved of Zeus, shall we,
I trust, bring deathless glory to the Greek camp by the sea,
When we have slain this Hector, insatiate of war.
For *this* day he is destined to flee our hands no more;
However much Apollo, the Archer-king, entreat
His father the Aegis-wielder, writhing before his feet.
But stay awhile and breathe thee. *I* will go and persuade
This fellow to stand at last, and face thee unafraid.'
    Then to the word of Athene he hearkened with good cheer
And stood a moment leaning on his bronze-headed spear.
But to the noble Hector Athene passed from him,
Taking the shape of Deïphobus, mighty in voice and limb,
And the words flew winging from her—'Good brother, hard indeed
Achilles presses on thee, with all his lightfoot speed,
Round Priam's wall; but come now, let us face him here and fight.'
Then answered the mighty Hector, with helmet glittering bright:

'Deïphobus, even aforetime I held thee dearest far
Of all my brothers born to Priam and Hecuba;
But now, with all my heart, I honour thee yet more
Since for my sake, beholding how Achilles pressed me sore,
While the rest remain within our walls, thou comest to my side.'
Then in her turn there answered Athene the flashing-eyed:
'Indeed my honoured mother and my father clasped my knees,
Begging me not to leave them—and my comrades too with these—
For one and all, my brother, they fear him dismally.
Yet with too bitter anguish my heart was wrung for thee.
But come—let us turn our fury to battle, and not spare
Our spears, till we see if Achilles shall slay us both, and bear
To his hollow ships our armour, with our lifeblood dripping red,
Or *thy* hand strike Achilles into the dust instead.'

So with her words of cunning Athene snared his heart;
But when, advancing face to face, the two were close apart,
First spoke the bright-helmed Hector—'Achilles, now no more
I will avoid thy coming, although I fled before
Thrice about Priam's great city, because I feared to face
Thy onset.   My heart has rallied to meet thee in this place,
Hand against hand.   I am ready to perish or to slay.
But let us pledge us by the Gods—for best are They
To witness and watch over our plighted covenant;
No outrage will I do thee dead, if Zeus shall grant
Me strength to stand against thee, and *my* hand leaves thee slain;
Thy glorious arms, Achilles, I will strip, but give again
Thy body to the Achaeans.   The like to me do thou.'

Then the swift Achilles answered, with darkly scowling brow:
'Wretch hated past forgetting, talk not of pacts to me!
'Twixt men and lions, Hector, no covenants can be,
No thought can come of concord betwixt the wolves and sheep,
When only undying hatred in the hearts of both lies deep.
So there can stand no friendship 'twixt thee and me at all,
No covenants—nay, sooner shall one or the other fall
And with his blood glut Ares, Lord of the Bull's-hide Shield.
So summon thy best valour.   For here upon this field
Thou shalt need to show thee a spearman, a warrior stout of will.
No more thou shalt escape me.   Nay, thee shall Pallas kill,
Now, by this hand.   Ay, *now* thou shalt repay my pain,
At last, for all the comrades thy murderous spear hath slain.'

With that he poised and hurled his mighty-shadowed spear;
But glorious Hector saw it, beforehand, and leapt clear,
Crouching low down, while above him the brazen spearpoint flew
And stuck in earth.   But Athene seized it and gave anew

To Pēleus' son; yet Hector, the shepherd of his folk,
Saw not—to great Achilles once again he spoke:
'Thou hast missed me, godlike Achilles! 'Twas not yet thine to know
So surely from Zeus my day of doom! Thou wouldst persuade me so,
But indeed thy tongue in its glibness was playing a cunning part
To make me afraid, forgetting my strength of hand and heart.
Not through the back shalt thou pierce me, flying in the chase;
Nay, drive thy spear athwart my breast, as I charge thee face to face,
If so God hath ordained it. Now look to it!—guard thee too
Against *my* spear. Would to Heaven it ran thee through and through!
Far lighter for the Trojans the weight of war would be,
Once *thou* wert dead. For, truly, no curse they know like thee.'
  With that his mighty-shadowed spear he poised and flung,
Nor missed the son of Pēleus. On his central shield it rung
And far away rebounded. But Hector's wrath grew hot,
That he had hurled his weapon and yet it helped him not.
Dismayed he stood there, lacking a second spear beside;
To his white-shielded brother, Deíphobus, he cried
Loudly, to bring another—no brother now stood near.
Then to his heart said Hector, for now his eyes saw clear:
'Ah now, indeed, the Immortals have summoned me to die.
I deemed Deíphobus, brave heart, was standing nigh;
But Athene has deceived me. He is within our wall,
And my evil end approaches—not far it has to fall,
Now, and nought may avoid it. Such doubtless, was the will
Long since, of Zeus and His Archer-son, that saved me still,
In other days, so surely. Now comes my doom on me.
Yet not, at least, with dishonour, nor tamely let it be,
But with some deed to remember among posterity!'
  So saying he snatched the warsword, trenchant and huge, from his thigh
And gathered himself and sprang—as an eagle towering high
Down to the plain swoops headlong, through vapours black with storm,
On some soft lamb, to seize it, or hare crouched in its form;
So Hector charged before him, whirling his whetted sword.
And Achilles dashed to meet him, his soul within him stored
With rage, his shield's bright splendour gripped close to guard his breast,
While high on his flashing helmet he shook his fourfold crest.
Marvellous in their beauty waved all the plumes of gold
Hephaestus had richly set there. And as, ere night grows old,
Amid the stars in their courses moves on the evening star,
That of all lights in Heaven abides the fairest far;
So in the hand of Achilles his glittering spearpoint shook,
With death prepared for Hector, as he scanned with searching look
The fair form of his foeman, to see where his blow would tell.

Now the rest of Hector's body those bright arms guarded well
That he stripped from the mighty limbs of Patroclus overthrown;
But Achilles' eye discovered that spot where the collar-bone
Links the neck to the shoulder—where life finds through the throat
To death its swiftest passage.   There great Achilles smote,
As Hector charged; and the spearhead pierced his soft neck through.
Yet the ashen shaft with its weight of bronze sheared not his windpipe too,
That Hector, ere he perished, might make a last reply.
But he crashed in the dust and, exultant, out rang Achilles' cry:
'Ah Hector, once, despoiling Patroclus where he lay,
Thou didst hope thyself in safety, and scorn me far away!
Oh fool!   I still was waiting, by our ships upon that shore,
To rise up his avenger—I, mightier in war,
That have loosed thy knees beneath thee!   In shame now, limb from limb,
Vulture and hound shall tear thee, while the Argives bury him.'
Then answered bright-helmed Hector, with breath drawn faintingly:
'By thy life, by thy knees, by the parents that once gave life to thee,
Leave me not by your galleys for Achaean dogs to rend,
But take the gifts my father and honoured mother send—
Bronze and gold in plenty!   And dead let me return
For the Trojans and Trojan women to honour and to burn.'
   But the swift Achilles answered, scowling gloomily:
'Entreat me no entreaties!   Beg not, thou hound, of me
By my father or my mother.   I would my passion's heat,
For what thou hast done, could bring me to carve thee raw and eat;
Sure as there is none living shall keep our dogs away
From gnawing thy skull!—no matter, though thy kindred come to pay
Ten—twentyfold—in ransom, and promise more as well!
Though Priam, the son of Dardanus, should bid them tell
Thy weight in gold—not even so upon thy bier
Shall thy royal mother lay thee, her son, with many a tear!
Nay, but now dog and vulture thy carcass shall divide.'
   Then the bright-helmed Hector made answer, as he died:
'Ah no, too well I know thee and see thee as thou art.
No power had I to persuade thee.   Of iron is thy heart.
Yet beware lest I bring the anger of Heaven on thy head—
That day when Phoebus Apollo and Paris strike thee dead
There in all thy glory, beside the Scaean Gate.'
   With that there darkened o'er him the final hour of fate,
And his soul fled forth from his body, down to Hades' gloom,
Leaving its youth and its manhood, wailing for its doom.
But noble Achilles answered the dead man where he lay:
'Lie there!—and the fate that waits me, I will face it, on the day
That Zeus shall so ordain it, and the Gods that live for aye.'

So saying, he dragged his brazen spear from out the dead
And, laying it down, he wrenched the armour reeking red
From the body, while the Achaeans ran crowding in their haste
To see with what mighty stature, how marvellously graced,
There Hector lay.   Not a man but stabbed him with his spear;
And one would say, as he glanced at his fellow standing near:
'Far softer now, by Heaven, is Hector in his ways
To deal with, than when his wartorch kindled our ships to blaze.'
So did they jest together, and stab him, lying there.
But when the swift Achilles, the noble, had stripped him bare,
He stood amid the Achaeans and swiftly his winged words flew:
'Leaders and lords of the Argives, my own tried friends and true,
Since now the Gods have given into our hands to destroy
This man that wrought more evil than all the rest of Troy,
Come, make we an armed assault all round their city-wall,
To see how the Trojans' spirits stand, since Hector's fall—
Will they turn now and abandon their towering citadel,
Or have they yet heart to fight us, although their champion fell?
Yet no!—within my spirit why should such thoughts arise,
While dead, unwailed, unburied, still by our ships there lies
Patroclus?   How forget him!   Never, while I draw breath
Here in the land of the living and my knees are light beneath!
Though the dead forget in Hades the dead they used to know,
There too I will remember my friend of long ago.
Come then, sons of Achaea, back to the hollow ships
Drag we this body with us, a paean upon our lips:
"We have gained us mighty glory.   Low is great Hector laid,
To whom, like a God from Heaven, the men of Ilios prayed."'

(XXII, 1–394).

*Achilles now trailed the body of the fallen Hector behind his chariot back to
the Achaean ships, while Priam, Hecuba, and Andrómache wailed for the dead.
No less Achilles and his Myrmidons mourned Patroclus.*

The Wraith of Patroclus

But Achilles, by the breakers of the loud-thundering sea
Amid the bands of the Myrmidons, lay groaning heavily.
Where the surges washed the shingle, in a clear space apart
He lay, till slumber took him, easing his heavy heart
And lapping softly round him—for now his bright limbs all
Were weary with chasing Hector towards Ilios' windy wall.
But lo! the unhappy phantom of Patroclus came.
His comely eyes, his stature, his voice were still the same,

Unchanged seemed, still, his raiment; and over Achilles' head
The spectre stood, and called him. 'Thou sleepest now,' it said,
'And in thy thoughts, Achilles, my memory lies forgot.
Living, thou didst love me: the dead thou lovest not.
Ah, bury me soon as may be—let me pass through Hades' gate!
For far the phantom souls of the perished make me wait,
Nor let me cross the River to mingle with their host—
Through the House of Death, with its mighty gates, I drift a wandering
    ghost.
Give me thy hand, ah, give it!—for never shall I return
Back from the House of Hades, once ye have let me burn;
Never again, forsaking our dearest friends, shall we
Sit and plan together. For grim mortality
Hath gaped for me—so 'twas fated, when first I left the womb.
For thee too, godlike Achilles, there waits the selfsame doom—
Under the wall of golden Troy, like me, thou must be slain.
But one thing more I ask thee—make me not ask in vain!
Let not my bones, Achilles, from thine lie far aloof,
But close—as close together we grew beneath your roof,
Since the day when, out of Ŏpus, Menoetius came to bring
Me, but a lad, to your fireside, for a bitter manslaying—
That day when in boyish anger, not knowing what I had done,
Over a game of dice I slew Amphídamas' son.
'Twas then the knightly Pēleus in his own home welcomed me—
Lovingly he fostered and made me squire to thee.
So let our bones lie hidden together in the grave,
Within that urn of gold thy noble mother gave.'
    But the swift Achilles answered: 'Dear heart, what brings thee here?
What need to tell thy wishes? For all this, never fear,
In full I shall perform it; whatever be thy will.
But ah, come closer, closer. Embraced for a moment still,
To sorrow's desperate solace let us give our hearts at last.'
    So saying, hands of yearning towards his friend he cast,
Yet touched him not. For the spectre beneath the earth, like smoke,
Fled, crying shrill. And, astonished, once more Achilles woke
And smote his hands together and with voice of sorrow said:
'Ah God, so there *is* something, e'en in the House of the Dead,
There *is* some soul, some phantom, though life breathes there no more!
For the hapless wraith of Patroclus, weeping and wailing sore,
With word of his last wishes above me hovering came,
All the night long. Ah strange, how still he seemed the same!'
    Then, at his words, with sorrow their hearts grew passionate;
Rose-fingered Morning found them as they wept disconsolate
Around ill-starred Patroclus. But through the camp the King,

Atrīdes, roused his Achaeans to yoke their mules and bring
Wood for the dead man's burning; and sent, to order these,
The kindly Idómeneus' comrade, the brave Meríones.
With axe in hand, and twisted ropes, and the mules ahead,
Uphill and down, this way and that, as the winding trackway led,
They came to the flanks of Ida, mount of the many rills.
There bit their keen-edged axes, as they hewed with eager wills
Many an oak high-crested, till thundering far around
It crashed, and they split the timber, and the mighty logs they bound
Behind the mules; then the stamping hoofs deep in the trackway tore,
Hurrying through the thickets to reach the plain once more.

(XXIII, 59–122.)

Next day Patroclus was burned and funeral games held in his honour. Daily
thereafter Achilles dragged the dead Hector round his comrade's tomb, until on
the twelfth morning Apollo reproached the other Gods with their cruel indifference.
Then Zeus sent Iris to summon Thĕtis.

Then up sprang storm-foot Iris to bear the word He gave.
'Twixt Samos and craggy Imbros in the black gulf of the wave
She plunged; and a mighty roar across the surges sped.
Down she dived to the sea's abyss, swift as the lead
An angler casts in the waters, bearing, with its weight
Set on the horn of a pastured ox, the greedy fishes' fate.

(XXIV, 77–82.)

When Thĕtis had come before him, Zeus warned her that her son must give
back Hector's body: then he sent Iris to Troy to bid Priam ransom his son.

Zeus spake; and storm-foot Iris leapt forth to bear His word:
She came to Priam's palace, and wails and cries she heard.
For there sat his sons in the courtyard, about their sire, and shed
Tears streaming down their raiment; and the old king, with his head
Hid in his cloak, lay amid them.   Upon his neck there clung,
And over his silver locks, thick filth that he had flung
With his own hands upon him, as he rolled there on the ground;
And the wives of his sons, and his daughters, wailed in the rooms around,
Remembering their fallen, so many of the best,
That by the spears of Achaea had died, and lay at rest.

(XXIV, 159–168.)

At Iris' word the old King, despite his wife's despair, loaded a waggon with
ransom and drove off to the Achaean camp.   Zeus sent Hermes to guide him.
Disguised as one of Achilles' Myrmidons, the Herald of Heaven brought Priam
within the Achaean lines, then revealed his godhead and disappeared.

73

So saying, to Olympus with its long ridge stretched afar
Hermes was gone; but Priam leapt earthwards from his car;
The mules he left, and the horses, under Idaeus' care,
But the old man hastened onward, straight to the dwelling where
Was wont to sit Achilles, beloved of God's own heart.
Alone King Priam found him, for his comrades sat apart,
All except two that were serving him—that son of War,
Alcĭmus, and Autómedon.   For just before
He had ceased from meat and drinking, and the table still stood by.
Past all, unseen, great Priam came; and drawing nigh
He clasped the knees of Achilles and kissed those hands of dread,
Those murderous hands, that had smitten his sons—so many—dead.
As when some blinding madness has driven a man to slay,
And he comes from the land that bore him to a country far away,
To some rich house, an outlaw, watched of men's wondering eyes;
So on the godlike Priam Achilles in surprise
Stared, and at one another the rest glanced wondering.
Then to the son of Pēleus in prayer spoke Priam the king:
'Remember, godlike Achilles, thy father—remember how,
Like *me*, at the dismal door of age he too is standing now.
Him too his neighbours harass, it may be, in their greed,
And none he has to defend him, alone in his friendless need;
Yet *he* has at least the comfort of news of thee from Troy,
Living; he can sit dreaming, each day still, of the joy
Of thy safe coming home again.   But all unblest
Am I—who once had sons, the noblest and the best
In all the breadth of Troyland—yet all were doomed to die.
When came the hosts of Achaea, fifty sons had I.
Nineteen my queen had borne me, and the rest of these
The women of my palace.   But loosened lie the knees
Of most by cruel Ares; and one that alone did stand
To save my city, my people, now for his fatherland
By thee has fallen—Hector.   For *him* to the ships of Greece
I come with a priceless ransom, to pray for his release.
But fear the Gods, Achilles, take pity upon me,
Remembering thy father.   Truly my agony
Is worse than his—I have dared what no man born has done—
Pressed to my lips the hand of the slayer of my son!'
    So he spoke, and awakened, deep in Achilles' heart,
Yearning to weep for his father.   Gently he thrust apart
The old king kneeling before him, and then both wept aloud,
Remembering; Priam for Hector, with his old head bowed

Before the feet of Achilles—and Achilles wept as well
At the thought of his own dear father, and how Patroclus fell;
So the roof rang with their sorrow.   But when in passionate grief
Achilles—soul and body—had found at last relief,
Up from his throne he started and pitying that white head,
That white beard of old Priam, he raised him too, and said:
   'Unhappy man, what sorrows, indeed, thy heart has known!
How couldst thou *dare* to visit Achaea's ships alone?
How couldst thou *dare* to face me, who low in the dust have laid
Thy many sons and noble?   Of iron must thy heart be made!
But come, sit here beside me.   And let us lay to rest
The grief in our hearts for a little, however sore oppressed.
No help in bitter mourning, no cure man's heart can find.
This doom the Gods appointed for hapless humankind—
To live in pain; while *They* dwell carefree evermore.
For in the house of Zeus there stand, on Heaven's floor,
Two jars, that hold His gifts to men—one full of ills,
One of good things.   So he for whom the Thunderer fills
A mingled portion, passes, now dark, now happy days;
But to some He gives evil only—a curse lies on their ways,
And frenzied longings hound them across the goodly earth,
By God and man dishonoured.   Most glorious gifts from birth
To Pēleus the Immortals gave—rich, prospering
Beyond all men, he ruled the Myrmidons as king;
Ay, and to him, though mortal, they gave a Goddess-bride.
Yet grief they gave him also; seeing that they denied
The birth of a race of princes to fill his kingly hall,
Granting him but a single son, untimeliest-doomed of all.
He is old now, I cannot help him—far off across the sea
Here before Troy I sit, to grieve thy sons and thee.
Thou too, old man—most happy, men say that thou hast been,
Blest in thy sons and riches, the greatest king between
Lesbos, the isle of Măcar, and, northward, Phrygia's land,
And the great water of Hellespont; and yet, on the other hand,
The will of the Lords of Heaven hath sent thee grief and pain,
That thy city stands encompassed with battles and men slain.
Take courage, then—lament not, comfortless evermore;
For all thy passionate weeping shall never now restore
Thy gallant son—nay, sooner new sorrows shall draw nigh.'
   Then that godlike ancient, King Priam, made reply:
'Ask me not, noble Achilles, to sit upon a throne
While under thy roof my Hector lies, uncared-for and alone.
Ah, give him back, let me see him!   Take the rich gifts I bring.
God grant thee to enjoy them—safe be thy homecoming,

Since thy mercy so has spared me, to look on the sunlight still.'
  Then answered the swift Achilles with a scowl of evil will:
'Old man, rouse not my anger. Freely my mind is bent
Already, to ransom Hector. From Zeus to that intent
My mother came, the daughter of the Ancient of the Sea.
And clearly, too, I can see it, it is not hid from me,
That here to the ships of Achaea some God hath been thy guide.
For truly no man living, though young and strong, had tried,
Else, to enter our leaguer. None pass where our guard waits,
No hand could heave back lightly the bolt that bars my gates.
But rouse me not now to anger, in my grief for my friend that died,
Lest, suppliant as thou art, here at my own fireside,
I spare thee not, but outrage the law that Zeus hath made.'
  So he cried, and in terror the white-haired king obeyed.
Then out through the door Pēlĭdes, like a lion, paced
And, behind, his two companions followed him in haste,
Alcĭmus and Autómedon, best-loved of all
The comrades of Achilles, since Patroclus' fall.
Swiftly they loosed the mules, the horses, from the yoke
And led to their hut the herald that for the old king spoke.
There in a seat they set him; then from the polished wain
Lifted the priceless ransom sent for Hector slain.
But from it they left two mantles, and a tunic fair beside,
To be the dead man's wrapping on his last homeward ride.
Then Achilles called to his handmaids and ordered them to bear
The body apart, and wash it, and anoint it there,
For fear King Priam should see it and his sorrow for his child
Burst out in sudden frenzy, and Achilles too grown wild
Might slay the old man in his fury, and God's law be transgressed.
  So the maidens washed the body, and anointed it, and dressed
In a tunic and fair mantle. Himself Achilles laid
On a bier the lifeless Hector, then with the others' aid
On the polished waggon set him. But groaning bitterly
He cried to his dead comrade: 'Ah, be not wroth with me,
For this that I do, Patroclus, if ever thou shouldst know,
E'en in the house of Hades, that I let brave Hector go.
It was for no mean ransom, it was at his father's prayer;
And on thy grave shall be offered, dear heart, thy rightful share.'
  So spoke the noble Achilles, then turned to his hut once more
And on his settle, bright-inlaid, he sat down as before,
Hard by the other wall, and to King Priam said:
'Old sir, thy son is ransomed, and laid out on his bed,
As was thy wish. Thyself, as soon as day shall break,
Canst bear him home and behold him. But now is time to take

Some thought of food.   For even the bright-haired Níobe

At last took food; although it was her fate to see
Six daughters in her palace, six fair young sons laid low.
For her sons the angry Apollo slew with his silver bow,
By Artemis, the Archer-queen, her daughters died,
Because with the fair-cheeked Lēto Níobe had vied,
Vaunting her many children, while Lēto's were but twain—
Yet by that pair alone those many perished slain.
Nine days they lay in their blood and weltered, left alone,
Unburied (for the people were turned by Zeus to stone):
It was the Gods entombed them, when the tenth day broke at last.
Then, weary with ceaseless weeping, Níobe broke her fast;
But now on the crags of Sípylus, high in that mountain-land
Of desolation—haunted (men say) by the sacred band
Of Nymphs, whose beauty dances by Acheloïus' stream—
In stone she stands; still brooding her god-sent griefs in dream.
Then, noble sire, take comfort.   'Tis time we too sat down
To eat; for *then* thou canst mourn him, when back to the Trojan town,
Thou hast borne thy dear son homeward.   Long, long hast thou to
　　weep.'
　　Then rose the swift Achilles and slew a snow-white sheep
And his companions flayed it—well and in order due
They cut all into morsels and with spits they ran them through,
And carefully they roasted, and removed them one by one.
Then was the flesh divided by the hand of Pēleus' son;
Bread on the board, in baskets fair, by Autómedon was set;
And so to the fare before them they stretched their hands and eat.
But when with food and drinking their hearts were satisfied,
Then Priam, the son of Dardanus, with awe and wonder eyed
The stature of Achilles, his form and face divine;
No less Achilles wondered, gazing at Priam, how fine
The old man was in speaking, how noble to the sight!
Long each looked on the other with wonder and delight,
Then spoke the godlike Priam: 'I pray, let me go to rest,
Fair sir; with peaceful slumber may both our hearts be blest.
For not to these eyes for an instant, till now, has sleep come near,
Since first my son was stricken to death beneath thy spear.
I have but brooded grief untold—yea, I have lain
On the heaped-up filth of my courtyard, writhing there in vain.
But here thy bread I have eaten, and thy bright red wine has passed
These lips of mine that never, till now, had broke their fast.'
　　Then Achilles bade his comrades and his handmaids lay a bed
In the cloister of his courtyard, with purple coverings spread.

(XXIV, 468–644.)

While Priam slept, Hermes reappeared to warn him of the danger of remaining in the camp of his Achaean enemies. The God himself drove the old King's waggon out to the Trojan Plain, then returned to Olympus; so, as morning broke, Hector's body once more entered Troy; and there they lamented him.

The Wail for Hector

First by Andrómache the women's wail was led,
Within her white arms clasping the valiant Hector's head:
'In the flower of thy days, my husband, thou hast died and left me thus,
A widow by thy fireside, with the one child born of us,
Ah misery!—a speechless babe!—what hope have I
To see him grow to boyhood? Ere that, all Troy shall lie
Razed to the dust, since thou, its stay, art overthrown—
Thou that didst save its little ones, its loyal wives, alone.
Soon, now, the hollow ships shall bear hence them and me,
And thou, my child, must follow, to shame and slavery,
Thrall to some king that pities not. Or else some Greek
From a tower's top shall hurl thee—oh grisly death!—to wreak
Revenge for father, or brother, or son by Hector slain.
For many an Achaean full low ere this has lain
Beneath the hand of Hector, to bite the far-flung plain.
Never mild was thy father to meet in the bitter fray;
Therefore it is men mourn him through Ilios to-day.
Ah, Hector, to thy parents sorrow and broken heart
Thou leavest—yet, of all, mine is the bitterest part.
Thou couldst not give me, dying, from thy bed a last embrace,
No last word of thy wisdom, to leave its lifelong trace
Deep on my heart while, night and day, for thee I cried.'
So she spake in her weeping and the women's wail replied.
Then Hecuba uplifted the strain of grief in turn:
'Hector, of all my children my heart did deepest yearn
To thee. Well-loved, in living, wast thou by the Gods on high,
And thee they remembered, even, when came thy doom to die.
For my other sons Achilles, the fleet of foot, would sell
Whenever he took them captive, across the barren swell,
To Samos, or to Imbros, or to Lemnos capped with smoke;
But when *thy* life passed from thee before his sharp spearstroke,
About the grave of Patroclus whom erst thy hand had slain,
He dragged thy mangled body (yet raised not *him* again!);
None the less, pure as the dew is, here before my gaze
Thou liest, and unblemished, as one Apollo slays
Beneath the gentle arrows of his silver bow.'
So she wept, and wakened the endless cry of woe.

Then third among them Helen took up the wailing call:
'To me thou wast ever, Hector, best-loved by far of all
The brothers of that husband who brought me here as bride—
Paris, fair as Heaven—would God I first had died!
Now twenty years together have passed above my head
Since, from the land of my fathers, hither to Troy I fled;
Yet never from *thy* mouth, Hector, harsh word, or wounding, came.
Ay, and if ever another stung me with taunt or blame—
Thy sisters, or thy brothers, or their wives clad gloriously,
Or thy mother—for thy father was ever mild to me,
As if I had been his daughter—*thou* didst restrain them still
With thy gentle speaking, thy gentleness of will.
Therefore for *thee* I sorrow—and for myself undone;
For all the breadth of Troyland holds never another one
So dear as thou, so kindly!   But *me* all men abhor.'

   So Helen cried; and the countless throng caught up her wail once more.
(XXIV, 723–776.)

*During a nine days' truce the Trojans felled timber for Hector's pyre; on the
tenth they burned him and held his funeral feast.*

Similes

Clouds upon Windless Peaks

   Steadfast they stood, as mists that upon windless days
High on the mountain-ridges the Son of Crŏnus stays,
Motionless, while the might of Boreas lies asleep
And all the other blustering winds, whose wild blasts sweep
The shadowy clouds this way and that across the sky;
So the Danaans faced the Trojans, unmoved, and would not fly.
(V, 522–7.)

The Steeds of Heaven

   Then the white-armed Goddess Hēra heeded the words he said
And lashed her steeds; right gladly upon their course they sped,
The pair of them, 'twixt earth and the Heavens' starry ways.
Far as a man can see, till the distance dims with haze,
As he sits on some mountain-vantage to scan the wine-dark deep,
So far spring the horses of Heaven, loud-neighing, at one leap.
(V, 767–72.)

79

The Sere and Yellow Leaf

'Like the leaves in their generations, such is the race of men.
For the wind casts the leaves from their branches to earthward, and again
Others the budding greenwood each springtide brings to birth.
So do man's generations spring up and fade from earth.'

(VI, 146–9.)

The Death of Gorgúthion

But as in a garden a poppy bows its head away,
Weighed down by its seeded ripeness and wet with showers of May;
So, under the weight of his helmet, his head, too, bowed and lay.

(VIII, 306–8.)

Stag and Jackals

They found Odysseus dear to Zeus, where hemmed him still
The Trojans, like tawny jackals that gather from the hill
About some antlered hart, when a shaft hath stricken him
From the hunter's bow.   While warm his wound, and light each limb,
The beast escaped the huntsman; but when the arrow's smart
Has quelled his strength, then the jackals in some dark glen apart
Flock ravening to rend him.   But thither some God leads
A savage lion—then the jackals flee, and alone the lion feeds.
So there about Odysseus, hero of war and guile,
Thick pressed the champions of Troy, though all the while
He warded the doom that threatened, with swift thrusts of his spear:
But now, with his shield like a mighty tower, Ajax drew near
To Odysseus' side; and the Trojans fled scattering in fear.

(XI, 473–86.)

Wasps

'But as bees or supple-waisted wasps, that love to make
Their nests by some rocky pathway, refuse still to forsake
Their hollow homes—unflinching, they meet the spoiler's hand
To guard their brood; so *these* men stout in the doorway stand,
But two against an army; and resolute their will
To yield no step before us, but to perish or to kill.'

(XII, 167–72.)

Nestor's Doubt

As when the deep lies heaving with a great swell, silently,
Sensing a shrill gale's coming, far out across the sea;

Doubtful, the mighty waters now this, now that way flow,
Waiting till from God's Heaven one sure sharp wind shall blow;
So swayed the old man's counsels, divided, to and fro.

(XIV, 16–20.)

Homer
Iliad

The Old Traveller

Swiftly as dart the thoughts of a man long used to fare
Wide in the world, while he muses 'Would I were there!—or there!'
And memories keen with longing from his wealth of wisdom rise;
So eagerly sped Queen Hēra, so swiftly, through the skies.

(XV, 80–3.)

The Fallen Olive-Tree

Sheer through his neck's soft skin the point of the weapon sprang—
Crashing he fell, and above him loudly his armour rang;
Blood stained that hair as lovely as the Graces' locks to behold
And all its plaited tresses, with silver clasped and gold.
As when a man has reared some fair young olive-tree
In a lonely spot where water from a wellhead bubbles free,
And all the winds of Heaven send swaying to and fro
The lovely green of its branches, where white the blossoms blow—
Yet comes the blast on a sudden of a great wind shrieking loud,
And from its trench uproots it, and earthward its head is bowed;
Euphorbus of the ashwood spear so fell, so lay,
Struck down by Menelaus, that stripped his arms away.

(XVII, 49–60.)

The Barren Battlefield

Soon of the shock of battle men surfeit and grow sick.
There are no swathes so heavy as the sword reaps, nor so thick;
But never a thinner harvest than men receive therefor,
Weighed in the scales of God, that casts the account of war.

(XIX, 221–4.)

Achilles' Arms

Then on his arm he settled the massy weight of his shield
That flashed afar its splendour, like the moon's round orb revealed;
Or as when sailors out at sea behold the light
Of some great watchfire blazing, that burns on a mountain-height
Beside some lonely steading; but o'er the heaving foam
The wild winds sweep them helpless, far off from friends and home.

(XIX, 373–8.)

NOTES

The Iliad

'In Troy—there lyes the scene.'   Its splendour is worth picturing.   Behind the city on the steep hill of Hissarlik, mountains fill the background E. and S., culminating 40 miles S.E. in the snowy top of Ida (nearly 6,000 feet), where Hector sacrificed to Zeus and Zeus watched the swaying battle on the Trojan Plain.   To N., just across the Hellespont, stand the bare crags of Gallipoli; 25 miles N.W., beyond the blue Aegean rise the mountains of Imbros, overpeered by the granite peak of Samothrace (5,200 feet), whence Poseidon saw the Achaeans reeling backward, till he hastened to their aid; and 50 miles W. lies the volcanic Lemnos of Hephaestus, where Philoctetes brooded for ten years, marooned with his snake-bite, till the last days of Troy brought him too, at last, his hour.

It is worth visualizing, also, how the epics were presented to their original public.   The early poets seem to have chanted or intoned, accompanying themselves, no doubt very simply, on the lyre.   At an hour and a half, say, a night, *Iliad* and *Odyssey* together might take a month.   But why not?   Ionian princes were not bustling moderns.   And even modern audiences listen to novels on a not wholly dissimilar system from the B.B.C.   Later, the poet was replaced by the rhapsode, the lyre by a long staff, chant by recitation.[1]   The vividest picture of a rhapsode is Plato's Ion (535 B-E), who both lectures on Homer and recites him, 'in all the glory of embroidered clothes and golden diadems' and with all the emotion of the South.   'When I come to a pathetic passage, my eyes fill with tears; when it is grim or terrible, my heart races and my hair stands on end.'   Nor were his hearers behindhand—'I can always see them from my platform weeping or looking aghast in wonder at my words.   For indeed I have to keep a close eye on them—if I can make them cry, it will be for me to laugh over the receipts; whereas if I make them laugh, it is I that will weep, unpaid.'

[Page 8] *Pēleus.*   Son of Aeacus of Aegīna, though his name seems derived from Mount Pēlion in Thessaly.   Zeus loved Thĕtis the Nereid, but was warned that her son would be mightier than his father; he therefore wedded her instead to the mortal Pēleus, to whom she bore the mightier Achilles (a story full of interest for modern psychology).

Note how Homer counts from the outset on his hearers' knowledge of the legendary background—clearly from poems more ancient still.

[Page 8] *Goddess.*   The Muse.   This is the oldest of all references to these mythological persons who have been made responsible for so much (good, bad, and indifferent) in the last three thousand years.   *Mousa* seems to come from an older form *Montia*, related to *mania* (madness), *mantis* (prophet).   In fact, the Muse is the personification of the poet's creative inspiration.   Later three Muses appear; then, in Hēsiod, the familiar nine.   From Piéria, their traditional birthplace north and east of Olympus, their worship spread south; particularly to Mount Helicon (there had been a River Helicon in their first home) and to Hēsiod's village of Ascra at its foot; also to Delphi, where arose their partnership with Apollo.

---

[1] Compare the design (from a Greek vase) on the title-page.

This opening invocation of the Muse was faithfully copied by later epics like *Aeneid* and *Paradise Lost*; but where Homer, swift-footed as Achilles, takes only eight lines to get going with his story, Milton takes thirty-three.

[Page 8] *Atrīdes.* Son of Atreus; here Agamemnon.

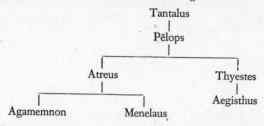

Tantalus
|
Pĕlops
|
Atreus   Thyestes
|
Agamemnon   Menelaus   Aegisthus

[Page 8] Pope's version of this proem, once one accepts his convention, is splendidly spirited, as it mounts up to its sonorous closing Alexandrine:

> *Achilles'* wrath, to Greece the direful spring
> Of woes unnumber'd, heav'nly Goddess, sing!
> That wrath which hurl'd to *Pluto's* gloomy reign
> The Souls of mighty Chiefs untimely slain;
> Whose limbs unbury'd on the naked shore
> Devouring dogs and hungry vultures tore:
> Since great *Achilles* and *Atrides* strove,
> Such was the sov'reign doom, and such the will of Jove! [1]

On the other hand, Pope has here added out of his own head 'spring,' 'heav'nly,' 'gloomy reign,' 'untimely,' 'unbury'd on the naked shore,' 'devouring,' and 'sov'reign doom'; has substituted 'hungry vultures' for 'all *kinds* of birds'; and, to get his climax, has moved the words about the will of Zeus to the end, from their original place two lines earlier. This, in turn, involves a mistranslation. For Homer does not say that the will of Zeus was due to, or dated from, the two kings' quarrel: he merely asks the Muse to begin from that point in the traditional story *where* the two kings quarrelled.

The degree of freedom in translation is a matter of taste; but this seems to me too free.

[Page 8] *Son of Zeus and Lēto.* Apollo. For his birth on Dēlos see the Homeric Hymn, p. 208.

[Page 8] *Chrÿses.* From Chrÿse, a little town on the coast 20 miles S. of Troy. His daughter Chrÿseïs, here a shadowy girl, little knew the disgrace that awaited her twenty-five centuries after her death, as the ill-famed and ill-fated Cressida of Boccaccio, Chaucer, Henryson, and Shakespeare. Benoît de Sainte-Maure in his very medieval *Roman de Troie* (c. A.D. 1160) included a love-story of Troilus and Briseïda (who answers to the almost equally shadowy Brīseïs,

---

[1] Clearly Pope had read, but has, I think, bettered Dryden:

> The wrath of Peleus' son, O Muse, resound;
> Whose dire effects the Grecian army found,
> And many a hero, king, and hardy knight,
> Were sent, in early youth, to shades of night:
> Their limbs a prey to dogs and vultures made:
> So was the sovereign will of Jove obey'd;
> From that ill-omen'd hour when strife begun,
> Betwixt Atrides great, and Thetis' god-like son.

here in Homer the captive of Achilles).   It was Boccaccio who saw fit to change Briseïda into Criseïda.

[Page 9] *Wreath of the Archer Apollo.*   The wreath or band of wool worn on the head of the god's image or of his priest.

[Page 9] *Smintheus.*   Apollo Smintheus, the 'averter of mice' (*sminthoi*), was specially worshipped at Chrȳse, where in the 4th century B.C. the sculptor Scŏpas made a statue of him with a mouse under his foot.   Conceivably a relic of totemism.   The mice were primarily the fieldmice dreaded by the farmer; but even ancient peoples seem already to have suspected the connection of mice or rats with plague.   (Cf. I *Samuel*, vi, 4—golden mice offered by the Philistines.) That connection may be relevant here.

[Page 9] *Tenedos.*   A white-cliffed island off the Troad, famed for its women's beauty.   In Virgil the Greeks hide their fleet behind it, when they feign to have sailed home after building the Wooden Horse.

[Page 9] *Killa.*   Town S. of Mount Ida.

[Page 9] *Bitterly let Thine arrows.* . . .   A famous line, quoted by the ageing Nerva when he wrote to Trajan in Upper Germany, calling on him to share the purple and do justice on Nerva's enemies (A.D. 97).

[Page 9] *Olympus* seems a pre-Greek name for 'mountain' in general (as 'Ida' for 'wooded mountain'), though it came also to be used simply for 'Heaven, sky.'   Of several peaks with this name the most famous, the home of the Gods, rises between Thessaly and Macedonia to 9,754 feet, and its long snow-capped ridge makes a magnificent sight alike from Larissa and from Salonīka.   A. B. Cook's *Zeus* (II, opposite p. 905) gives a fine photograph of its volcano-like summit.   It has kept its hold even on the modern Greek imagination; the monks of St. Dionysios say mass once a year in the chapel of St. Elias on its top; and a folksong quoted by Cook (*Zeus*, I, 104) makes the mountain itself proclaim:

> I seventy mountain-summits have, and two-and-sixty fountains;
> To every bush an Armatole, to every branch a Klephtë.
> And perched upon my highest peak there sits a mighty eagle; [1]
> A mirror, in his talon grasped, he holds on high exalted,
> And in it he his charms admires, and on his beauty gazes.

Local legends in the last century told that a shepherd had once seen there a mysterious palace, columned with white marble; or that the stars came down at night on the mountain—for, once, Heaven and earth met on its summit; but, with the growing wickedness of men, God had withdrawn Himself higher (compare Hēsiod, p. 200).

[Page 9] *And shot.*   In the Greek the line begins with the monosyllable βαλλ' followed by a pause.   Compare Tennyson, *The Last Tournament*:

> But let the drunkard . . .
> Down from the causeway heavily to the swamp
> *Fall*, as the crest of some slow-arching wave,
> Heard in dead night along that table-shore
> *Drops flat*, and after the great waters break
> Whitening for half a league. . . .

[Page 9] *Then spoke the swift Achilles.*   This and the Embassy to Achilles in *Iliad* IX are the first and, with Milton's council in Pandemonium, perhaps the finest of many epic debates.   The *Odyssey* opens with two, one in Heaven, one in Ithaca; but neither Ithaca nor Heaven possessed such a figure as Achilles.

[1] The bird of Zeus, in ancient story.

In general, it should be remembered that to the Greeks epic probably seemed nearer to drama than it seems to us. Some papyri of Homer actually put the speakers' names in the margin, as in a play. Plato's *Ion*, too, makes it clear how dramatic Homeric recitations were.

[Page 10] *Calchas*. The famous seer who had foretold the ten years of the siege. Later legend made him also predict that the fleet could not leave Aulis without the sacrifice of Iphigeneia, nor Troy be taken without Achilles, Neoptólemus, and Philoctētes. A further, typically Greek story told how, after Troy fell, he planted a vineyard in land sacred to Apollo near Myrīna in Aeŏlis. A rival soothsayer warned him he would never drink its wine. Yet the grapes grew, the wine was made, and Calchas scornfully invited the evil prophet to his vintage-feast. But, as he lifted the cup to his lips, he burst into such exultant laughter that he choked and died. 'There's many a slip . . . .'

[Page 10] *Though Atrīdes' self it be*. Already the passionate Achilles grows dangerously tactless.

[Page 10] *Prophet of evil*. Anger makes Agamemnon unfair. Calchas had foretold the fall of Troy after ten years of siege.

[Page 11] *Than my own queen Clytemnestra*. The sister of Helen, and as false. Homer's hearers may well have known that within a twelvemonth Agamemnon was himself to perish by the hand of that jealous queen, when he sailed home with another Trojan mistress, Cassandra daughter of Priam (p. 150).

[Page 11] *Most glorious . . . greediest*. Even at the fiftieth reading this trenchant contrast keeps some of its effective surprise (like Othello's sudden stabbing of himself in the last scene of his tragedy).

[Page 12] *Phthīa*. The kingdom of Peleus, in S. Thessaly.

[Page 12] *Stretch mountains mighty-shadowed*. For all who know Greece, a whole landscape rises up in this magnificently surging line:

Ourea | te skio|enta || tha|lassa te | ēchē|essa.

This may originally have sounded something like: 'Oorăya tay skeoaynta thahlāhsha tay ayk-hayesha.' One can fully share FitzGerald's feeling that the sea must prefer to be called *thalassa*, rather than 'the miserable word "sea."' For the surf-like onrush of the line's second half, compare Tennyson's 'by the long wash of Australasian seas.' Pope is here not very adequate:

> Far hence remov'd, the hoarse-resounding main,
> And walls of rocks, secure my native reign;

whereas Homer's '*shadowy* mountains' call up to the vision both the shadows cast by the clouds *on* the mountainsides and the shadows cast *by* the mountains on gorge and glen.

[Page 12] *And the wise Zeus most of all*. Unconscious irony. Soon Zeus is deliberately to dishonour Agamemnon; and for Achilles' sake.

[Page 12] *Myrmidons*. The people of Phthīa. Achilles brought to Troy fifty ships, each with fifty men. The legend is post-Homeric which tells that they were a race of ants (*myrmēkes*) turned by Zeus into men, to console Aeăcus of Aegīna, Achilles' grandfather, who had lost his people by plague.

[Page 13] *Aegis-bearing Zeus*. The Aegis was a magical goatskin (with a hundred gold tassels, each worth a hundred oxen) wielded by Zeus or his favourite daughter and deputy, Athene; not even the thunder of Zeus could prevail against it. Perhaps its far-off origin lay in a totemistic identification of god and goat.

[Page 13] *So on his silver swordhilt. . . .* Tennyson used this couplet to contrast Pope with Dryden's greater 'real poetic force':

POPE: He said, observant of the blue-ey'd maid;
    Then in the sheath return'd the shining blade.

DRYDEN: He said; with surly faith believed her word,
    And in the sheath, reluctant, plunged the sword.

But perhaps this particular parallel is a little too kind to Dryden.

[Page 13] *Never hadst thou the courage.* Achilles in *his* turn grows fantastically unfair.

[Page 13] *This staff whose leaves of green and boughs shall never spring again.* Similarly in the Tannhäuser legend the Pope avers that sooner his staff shall sprout than Tannhäuser's soul be saved. Miraculously the staff budded, but too late—Tannhäuser had gone back in despair to the Venusberg. Compare M. Arnold, *The Neckan.* Also Aaron's rod, Hēracles' club, Romulus' spear, Joseph of Arimathea's staff, and various saints' legends. Pope burlesques the passage in *The Rape of the Lock*, IV, where the Baron vows—

But by this Lock, this sacred Lock, I swear,
(Which never more shall join its parted Hair;
Which never more its Honours shall renew,
Clipt from the lovely Head where late it grew)
That while my Nostrils draw the vital air,
This Hand, which won it, shall for ever wear.

[Page 14] *Pylos.* Probably the Messenian Pylos, near Navarino, in W. Peloponnesus. A palace of the thirteenth century B.C., with over 600 clay tablets in a script descended from the Minoan, has actually been unearthed on a hill N. of Navarino Bay. Nestor's kingdom seems to have stretched N. to the Alpheius. Others identify Nestor's home with another Pylos, 30 miles further N., in Triphylia.

[Page 14] *He had seen two generations.* With three generations to a century, this makes Nestor perhaps seventy or eighty. He is still lively ten years later in the *Odyssey.*

[Page 14] *Dryas, Exádius, Caeneus, Peiríthoüs.* Heroes of the Lápithae, an ancient Thessalian tribe, whose famous battle with the Centaurs was depicted on the Parthenon metopes at Athens and on the W. pediment at Olympia—one of the finest sculptures in the world. The conflict arose because at the wedding-feast of Peiríthoüs, son of Ixīon and chief of the Lápithae, the drunken Centaur Eurýtion tried to carry off the bride Hippodameia. Finally the Lápithae were victorious, though the Centaurs hammered the invulnerable Caeneus into the ground. This battle was followed by the war which Nestor tells of here.

[Page 14] *Centaurs.* A Thessalian race, half man, half horse; begotten, some said, by Ixīon on the cloud with which Zeus deluded him when he tried to seduce Hēra, Queen of Heaven. They may partly embody the impression made on surrounding Greek tribes by a more primitive horse-breeding race in Thessaly, which of all Greek lands is best suited to cavalry.

[Page 14] *As men are now.* With Nestor there enters European literature that immortal type, the elderly gentleman convinced of the superiority of the good old days when he was young. But Nestor, though loquacious in reminiscence, is a wise and gracious figure. Homer smiles at him, but does not caricature. Nestor is not Polonius.

[Page 15] *Battle for the sake of a girl.* Note Homer's irony. The whole war is actually for a woman—Helen. Pope thinks Achilles himself aware of the paradox; but he does not seem so here—though he puts the point bitterly enough in Book IX (p. 32).

[Page 15] *Blameless Ethiopians.* Conceivably this idea of the Gods feasting with them may be based on some distant knowledge of Ethiopian priest-kings.

[Page 16] *Hēra and her bitter tongue.* Homer's Gods provide not only the majestic background to his human tragedy, but also, curiously enough, its comic relief—the sharp-tongued Hēra, the graceless grace of Aphrodite, the blustering Ares, the halt-footed, shrewd-witted Hephaestus. Thus, by a further irony, the comic relief abominated by neo-Classicist critics really originates with the first and greatest of classic writers.

[Page 16] *Zeus with his dark brows nodded.* These three lines are said to have been quoted by Pheidias as the conception that inspired his own colossal gold-and-ivory statue of Zeus at Olympia (25–40 feet high, as it sat enthroned) a work so majestic, says Quintilian, that it seemed to add something to received religion itself.

[Page 16] *Caÿster.* Lydian river, reaching the sea at Ephesus.

[Page 16] *Asian meadow.* Perhaps from Asias, an ancient king of Lydia; in any case, far as yet from its wide later meaning.

[Page 16] *Scamander* (by the Gods called Xanthus) rose in Ida and flowed down to the Trojan Plain.

[Page 17] *Cranes.* These cross Greece northward in spring, to breed in Macedonia and on the Danube; then return S. in October to winter in Africa. Compare pp. 202, 249.

[Page 17] *Stream of Ocean.* Homer's earth is flat, circular, and moated by the Ocean-stream.

[Page 17] *Pygmies* (Gk. *pygme*—13½ inches). Possibly Homer had dimly heard of this dwarf African race, which was certainly known to the Egyptians; its battling with cranes might be based on ostrich-hunts. Cf. Milton, *Par. Lost*, I, 574, 'that small infantry Warred on by cranes'; Sir Thomas Browne includes among his *Vulgar Errors* (IV, xi) the notion that 'they fight with Cranes upon the backs of Rams or Partridges.'

[Page 17] *Resolute and dumb.* This stern, disciplined silence is one of the few contrasts made by Homer between his Greeks and his Trojans (who even speak the same tongue). Another difference is Priam's oriental harem.

[Page 17] *More dear to the thief than night.* The truth of this description of day-mist will strike anyone who has patrolled in war.

[Page 18] *Iris*, Goddess of the Rainbow, which links earth and heaven; and so Messenger of the Gods.

[Page 18] *Embroidering the tale of all that pain.* Compare the Bayeux Tapestry.

[Page 18] *Her parents.* Leda and Tyndáreüs; though her real father was Zeus, who came to Leda in the shape of a swan.

[Page 18] *Aethra, daughter of Pittheus.* Later legend told that Theseus of Athens carried off Helen from Sparta while yet a girl: her brothers Castor and Polydeuces invaded Attica in his absence, rescued her, and carried off in reprisal Theseus' mother Aethra, making her Helen's handmaid. But the line may be interpolated.

[Page 18] *Thymoetes, Lampus, Hiketāon.* Sons of Laómedon and brothers of Priam.

[Page 18] *Cicadas.* The male insects have a kind of drum on each side of their abdomen with which they make a shrill noise, much loved by the ancients (as by the Chinese), but less poetically compared by modern observers to a scissors-grinder or a railway-whistle. A number of them can be heard a quarter of a mile away. It may be recalled that Tithōnus, another brother of Priam, was actually turned in old age into one of these garrulous creatures (p. 221).

[Page 18] *But when they saw how Helen. . . .* Lessing (*Laocoon* XXI) praises

Homer's skill in describing, not the physical details of Helen's beauty, but its effect even on the old. So Gordon Bottomley in his picture of that beauty's decay, *The Last of Helen*:

> Till, as she made one half-unheeded passage
> Down Lacedaemon street, she heard a moan
> 'Is that the lass of Troy?' and turned and saw
> A lean brown shipman weeping to distortion.
> Then Helen knew she must have grown quite old.

Whereas Constantinus Manasses in twelfth-century Byzantium, cataloguing Helen's charms with more than twenty epithets in eight hexameters, becomes an insufferable bore.

Ronsard, in a sonnet to his own Hélène, recalls this famous scene:

> Il ne faut s'esbahir, disoient ces bons vieillars,
> Dessus le mur Troyen voyans passer Helene,
> Si pour telle beauté nous souffrons tant de peine:
> Nostre mal ne vaut pas un seul de ses regars.

But, with a romantic hyperbole that contrasts with Homer's realist good-sense, Ronsard maintains, like Shakespeare's Troilus, that they should have kept Helen at all costs.

[Page 19] *Would God some death abhorred*. . . . Compare Tennyson's Helen in *A Dream of Fair Women*:

> Whereto that other with a downward brow:
> 'I would the white cold heavy-plunging foam,
> Whirl'd by the wind, had roll'd me deep below,
> Then when I left my home.'

It is not easy to make a Helen seem real; Homer does it by contrasting her divine beauty with an all too human weakness and self-reproach.

[Page 19] *My little daughter.* Hermíone, future wife of Achilles' son, Neoptólemus. Later legend told that her cousin and lover Orestes, son of Agamemnon, had her husband murdered at Delphi and carried her off (see Racine's *Andromaque*).

[Page 19] *Great is he on the throne, and valiant under helm.* Alexander the Great's favourite line of Homer.

[Page 19] *Otreus*, King of Phrygia and brother of Priam's queen, Hecuba (cf. p. 219).

[Page 19] *Mygdon.* Virgil tells how his son Coroebus came to help Troy for love of Cassandra and died trying to save her when the city fell.

[Page 19] *Sangárius* flows into the Black Sea, 100 miles E. of Constantinople.

[Page 19] *Amazons.* Later tradition told that (after the close of the *Iliad*) their queen, Penthesileia, came to succour Troy and was slain by Achilles. The belief in a race of warlike women in Asia Minor, so prominent in Greek art and legend, may possibly derive from contact with Hittite elements where matriarchal customs still survived.

[Page 19] *Antēnor.* Pope ingeniously suggests that it would have been embarrassing for Helen to point out her own deserted husband Menelaus among the Greek chiefs; so that Homer puts his description, instead, in the mouth of Antēnor.

[Page 20] *In the arms of life-giving Earth.* Arnold (*On Translating Homer*) condemns, as 'false' and 'modern sentiment,' Ruskin's comment on this phrase:

'The poet has to speak of the earth in sadness; but he will not let that sadness affect or change his thought of it. No; though Castor and Pollux be dead, yet the earth is our mother still—fruitful, life-giving.' But Arnold seems too severe. Homer was surely capable (like so many later poets) of seeing Mother Earth as both womb and tomb, and of stressing that contrast by the epithet 'life-giving' (φυσίζοος). Cf. the famous simile of the leaves (p. 80); and p. 332.

The whole of this lovely human scene of Helen on the Wall (later imitated by Statius and Tasso) would of course be more appropriate to the first year of the siege than the tenth. But its beauty silences the carpings of probability.

[Page 22] *Shame and blame.* Because Menelaus' victory renews his right to Helen.

[Page 22] *Stung him with mockeries.* There is a strangely modern psychology in this loveless scene between two guilty lovers who cannot admire, but only desire each other, their passion poisoned by contempt.

> If I the death of Love had deeply planned,
> I never could have made it half so sure,
> As by the unblest kisses which upbraid
> The full-waked sense; or, failing that, degrade!
> (Meredith, *Modern Love.*)

[Page 23] *Cránaë.* Island in the Laconian Gulf.

[Page 23] *They loathed him, as the black pit of the grave.* Homer's wise reticence seldom makes moral judgments: yet what a judgment on Paris is here implied!

[Page 23] *The Aiantes.* Ajax the Greater, son of Télamon, and Ajax the Less, son of Oïleus.

[Page 24] *The shepherd hears their thunder.* For this sudden escape from war's horror to the peace of the quiet countryside, compare pp. 28 and 40; and Shakespeare, *Henry VI*, Part III, II, v, 1–54.

It is seldom realized that this great parting-scene between Hector and Andrómache seems to be in fact their last meeting on earth.

[Page 24] *Thēbe.* A town near the Gulf of Adramyttium, S. of Ida and N.E. of Lesbos. Its Cilicians are far removed from their kindred in the historic Cilicia in S.E. Asia Minor.

[Page 25] *Astýanax.* 'Lord of the City.' When Troy fell, the child was flung from its rampart, while Andrómache became the slave of Achilles' son, Neoptólemus.

[Page 25] *Elm-trees*, like willows and poplars, were thought funereal, because fruitless.

[Page 26] *For well in my heart I know it. . . .* These three lines of heroic despair were murmured by the victorious Scipio as he watched the smoke-clouds billow from burning Carthage (146 B.C.) and foreboding struck him for the fate of Rome. They probably haunted more than one English memory in 1940.

[Page 26] *Messēïs.* Near Pharsālus in S. Thessaly, or in the Peloponnese.

[Page 26] *Hypereia.* Near Pharsālus, or in N. Thessaly.

[Page 26] *That my son may win . . . such fame as I have won.* Inconsistent with Hector's forecast of Troy's fall; but a most human inconsistency.

[Page 27] *Gargărus.* The summit of Ida. Cf. Tennyson, *Oenone*:

> Behind the valley, topmost Gargarus
> Stands up and takes the morning.

[Page 27] *The Scales of War.* Compare the symbolic weighing of Hector against Achilles (p. 67) and Milton's imitation (*P. L.*, IV, 996–1004):

Th' Eternal to prevent such horrid fray
Hung forth in Heav'n his golden Scales, yet seen
Betwixt Astrea and the Scorpion sign
Wherein all Things created first he weigh'd,
The pendulous round Earth with ballanc't Air
In counterpoise, now ponders all events,
Battles and Realms: in these he put two weights
The sequel each of parting and of fight;
The latter quick up flew and kickt the beam.

Milton's Deity grandly takes for His balance the actual Sign of the Zodiac, the constellation Libra; yet Milton's weighing loses force because it only shows what *would* happen if Satan fought with Gabriel. And, less dramatically it does not weigh Satan against Gabriel, but one policy for Satan against another. Further, the pair do not fight; no tragedy follows; and who cares about Gabriel, anyway?

The Homeric passages may be influenced by the Egyptian weighing of the soul before Osiris. Cf. too *Daniel*, v, 27 (Belshazzar's feast): 'Thou art weighed in the balances and art found wanting.' Zeus with the scales perhaps appears in art as early as a Mycenaean vase from Enkomi in Cyprus (M. P. Nilsson, *Homer and Mycenae*, p. 268); and Aeschylus wrote a tragedy *The Weighing of Souls* on the combat between Achilles and Memnon, son of the Morning.

[Page 28] *The Trojans Encamp.* 'The most beautiful night-piece that can be found in poetry' (Pope). Most of this passage is translated by Tennyson, in blank verse that suits its quietness admirably:

As when in heaven the stars about the moon
Look beautiful, when all the winds are laid,
And every height comes out, and jutting peak
And valley, and the immeasurable heavens
Break open to their highest, and all the stars
Shine, and the Shepherd gladdens in his heart.

Pope, on the other hand, whose strength lies in Homer's oratorical passages, badly botches this marvellous description.

As when the Moon, refulgent *lamp of night*!
O'er heav'n's *clear azure* spreads her *sacred* light,
When not a breath disturbs *the deep serene*,
And not a cloud o'ercasts the solemn scene;
Around her *throne the vivid planets roll*,
And stars unnumber'd *gild the glowing pole*,
O'er the *dark* trees *a yellower verdure shed*,
And *tip with silver* ev'ry mountain's head;
Then shine the vales, the rocks in prospect rise,
A flood of glory bursts from all the skies:
The *conscious* swains, rejoicing in the sight,
Eye the blue vault, and bless the useful light.

The words in italics are Pope's additions. As pointed out in Mr. Norman Ault's *New Light on Pope*, the poet had studied painting under Jervas and introduces colour-terms into his verse on a scale unknown in English poetry before him. But it remains here a curious method of improving Homer. The emphasis transferred from stars to moon spoils the parallel with camp-fires. The colouring

seems exaggerated for a night-scene.   And the solitary shepherd of the *Iliad* is
ill exchanged for a company of 'conscious swains.'   For part of the point lies
in the contrast between the quiet happiness of this solitary Wordsworthian figure
on the hills and the embattled hosts upon the Trojan Plain.

It may be objected that the stars do not show their full multitudinousness
with a moon; better, at all events, to picture here a crescent moon than a full.

[Page 28] *The bridges of the battle.*   A curious phrase, apparently meaning the
No Man's Land that links two confronted armies.

[Page 29] *Achilles Rejects the Embassy.*   This debate in Achilles' hut is to
me the most burning display of eloquence in all poetry—so splendid in its style,
so subtle in its adaptation to the differing characters, so vivid in its rendering
of Achilles' moods, now courteous, now smouldering with anger, now flaring
to a white heat of hatred.

[Page 31] *Gift-free.*   The Homeric wooer buys his bride with gifts to her
parents; though the opposite custom of dowries is beginning sometimes to
appear.

[Page 31] *Cardámyle*, etc.   Cities of Messenia in S.W. Peloponnese.   Phĕrae
is now Kalamáta.

[Page 32] *So the third day may find me. . . .*   It is with an adaptation of this
line that, in Plato's *Crito*, the white-clad woman seen in a dream by the imprisoned
Socrates foretells his coming death.

[Page 33] *Orchómenus.*   A Boeotian city W. of the Copaic Lake (the draining
of which, as well as trade, may have brought its legendary wealth).   The site
has a Bronze-Age palace and a beehive tomb like those at Mycenae.

[Page 33] *Thebes.*   This seems a relic of very ancient tradition.   For the great
age of Egyptian Thebes was about 1400 B.C.   Its importance began to shift
north to the Delta under Ramses II (1292–25); and by the next century it was
in full decline, though not finally destroyed by Assyria till 663.

[Page 33] *Hellas.*   A district in S. Thessaly, whence the name later spread to
cover all Greece.

[Page 33] *Pytho.*   Delphi, on the craggy flank of Parnassus, above the
Corinthian Gulf.

[Page 34] *If here I stay to battle. . . .*   It is not hard to imagine how much
less sympathetic Achilles would become, with all his wilful egotism, but for
this brooding shadow of an untimely doom.

[Page 35] *The Zeus that reigns in Hades.*   Pluto, brother to Zeus and Poseidon.

[Page 35] *Dólopes.*   In S.W. Thessaly, in the wild valleys round the snow-
capped Tymphrestus.

[Page 35] *Oft hast thou drenched my tunic. . . .*   Pope could not face the
homely realism of these two lines.   He omits them, adding: 'I wish I had any
authority to say these verses were foisted into the text; for though the idea be
indeed natural, it must be granted to be utterly unworthy of Homer.'   (A
niceness somewhat strange in a friend of Swift; to say nothing of some passages
in Pope himself.   But of course the dignity of epic, in eighteenth-century eyes,
required different standards.)

[Page 36] *For Prayers, indeed. . . .*   One of the loveliest, and gentlest,
allegories in literature.

[Page 36] *The Cūrētes.*   Homer, assuming his hearers' knowledge of the tragic
tale of Meleăger, retells it so allusively as to become obscure for the modern
reader.   Oeneus King of Cálydon (near Missolonghi, N. of the mouth of the
Corinthian Gulf) forgot to sacrifice to Artemis.   She plagued him with a boar.
Heroes gathered from all Greece and killed it; but over its hide Meleăger, son
of Oeneus and Althaea, quarrelled with his mother's brother (or brothers); for
he wished to give this trophy to his new love, the huntress Atalanta.   When

he slew his uncle (or uncles), his mother cursed him; and war followed between Cálydon and his mother's kin, the Cūrētes, dwelling in Pleuron, 8 miles W. Meleäger was killed either by Apollo in battle or by his mother when she burnt the fatal brand linked with his life. Homer says nothing of Atalanta or his death; but see Bacchýlides (p. 272) and Swinburne's brilliant *Atalanta in Calydon*.

[Page 37] *Marpessa . . . Idas.* Idas carried off Marpessa from her father and defended her from the passion of Apollo himself. Finally Zeus ordained that she should herself decide between her lovers; and she chose the mortal Idas, fearing with good reason that the deathless Apollo would desert her when she aged.

[Page 37] *Fury.* The Erīnyes, or Furies, were personifications of the curses that pursue the sinner, especially the sinner against kindred. Some of their traits suggest an ancient matriarchal origin.

Compare the incantation they sing over the matricide Orestes in Aeschylus (*Eumenides*, 307–20, 334–46):

> Now link the dance, O sisterhood,
> For lo! the hour
> To tell in grisly chorus,
> How among men we wield the power
> That Fate hath set before us.
> Just we deem our ways, and good.
> For he whose hands are clean and clear
> Hath never wrath of ours to fear,
> His days pass by unshaken;
> But if such a slayer as hideth here
> Our anger shall awaken,
> In righteous witness to the dead
> We rise, for the blood his hands have shed;
> Till a life for a life is taken. . . .
>
> Such the office that eternal Fate
> Spun for *us*, with thread inviolate—
> Evermore to hound implacably
> Him whose wantonness shall dare
> Slay his kindred—everywhere,
> Till the grave!   And even there
> Scant shall be his liberty!
> Over the victim that they bring
> This is the chant the Erīnyes sing,
> Heart-wildering, brain-shattering—
> No such tune as harpstrings play.
> Fettered soul, and senses fey,
> Whoso hears it, wastes away.

See also p. 98.

[Page 38] *If homeward 'tis best to sail.* Achilles' first concession. He will, after all, *perhaps* remain.

[Page 38] *Ajax spake.* The blunt soldier Ajax is by no means 'beef-witted' here. While affecting to accept Achilles' 'No,' he cleverly insinuates a new appeal; and thereby wins Achilles' second concession—if Hector reaches his own ships, he *will* fight. No less characteristic is this burly warrior's contempt for women—why all this stir about a girl, when seven others as good are on offer?

[Page 39] *Star of bale.* The Dog-star, Sirius.

[Page 40] *Their noble mansions in the folds of Olympus' crest.* Cf. the Epicurean Gods of Tennyson's *Lotos-eaters*:

> For they lie beside their nectar, and the bolts are hurl'd
> Far below them in the valleys, and the clouds are lightly curl'd
> Round their golden houses, girdled with the gleaming world.

[Page 41] *Dullard ass.* Pope, while justly admiring the simile's vividness, blenches at calling an ass an 'ass'; so it becomes 'As the slow beast with heavy strength indued.'

[Page 41] *Sarpēdon, Glaucus.*

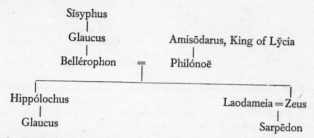

In Lўcia, succession was through the female; and so Bellérophon inherits the kingdom from his wife's father and transmits it to his daughter's son, Sarpēdon, not to his son's son, Glaucus.

[Page 41] *Xanthus.* Not here the Trojan river (=Scamander), but a Lўcian stream reaching the sea 60 miles E. of Rhodes.

[Page 42] *Dear heart, if once escaping. . . . Now let us on.* One of Homer's most famous passages and subject of a well-known quotation in R. Wood's *Essay on Homer* (1769), describing how he called on John Carteret, Earl Granville, to show him the preliminary articles of the Treaty of Paris, a few days before Carteret's death at Bath on January 2, 1763. Finding him very weak, Wood suggested a postponement; 'but he insisted that I should stay, saying, it could not prolong his life, to neglect his duty.' After which he repeated in Greek these words of Sarpēdon.

Pope's burlesque in *The Rape of the Lock*, v, has equal brilliance and good sense:

> Oh! if to dance all Night, and dress all Day,
> Charm'd the Small-pox, or chas'd old Age away;
> Who would not scorn what Huswife's Cares produce,
> Or who would learn one earthly Thing of Use? . . .
> But since, alas! frail Beauty must decay,
> Curl'd or uncurl'd, since Locks will turn to grey,
> Since painted, or not painted, all shall fade,
> And she who scorns a Man, must die a Maid;
> What then remains, but well our Pow'r to use,
> And keep good Humour still, whate'er we lose?

Compare too the words of his sorceress mother to Earl Sigurd of Orkney (the same that fell in 1014 before the Irish at Clontarf), when he consulted her before battle with Finnleik of Scotland: 'I would have reared thee long in my wool-bag, had I known that thou wouldst like to live for ever; but know that it is fate, not the way a man goes, that rules his life. Better die with honour than live with shame.'

[Page 42] *Some boulder. . . .* 'One of the noblest similes in all Homer' (Pope); imitated by Virgil and Tasso.

[Page 42] *Samothrace.* A small, mountainous island (5,250 feet), 40 miles N.W. of the mouth of the Dardanelles.

[Page 42] *Mountain flowers.* Cf. Leaf, *Troy*, p. 11 (of Ida): 'All round the fields of melting snow there springs up in May a glory of colour which those who have seen it are not likely to forget—crocus and hyacinth carpeting the slopes with brilliant orange and blue, mingled in thick beds worthy for the couch of the gods.'

[Page 43] *A castle in the sand.* Nothing in Homer seems more modern than this childish sand-castle that has withstood the tides of 3,000 years.

[Page 43] *Two and twenty cubits* = 33 feet.

[Page 44] *As a little maid will cry.* Imagine such a simile in Milton!

[Page 44] *Agamemnon.* Eustathius, Archbishop of Thessalonica (12th century A.D.), points out the tact with which Patroclus puts this hated name neither first nor last, but obscurely in the middle of the other wounded chiefs, lest it rekindle Achilles' rage.

[Page 46] *No arms left but ours.* Curiously illogical since, if Achilles had his will, there would be no Trojans left for them to fight. But passion scorns logic; and Achilles' utterance gives the measure of his frenzied resentment and of that overweening pride now near its fall.

[Page 47] *Pelasgian.* A pre-Greek race inhabiting Aegean lands (mainly in the north) and apparently related to Lydians and Etruscans.

[Page 47] *Dōdōna.* In N.W. Greece, S. of the lake of Yánina, under the fir-forested slopes of the 6,500-foot Tómaros; probably on the ancient route by which the Achaeans penetrated Greece. The valley itself, 1,600 feet above the sea, with snow lying much of the year on its surrounding peaks, well deserves its name of 'bleak.' Here Zeus had an oracle, where priests or priestesses interpreted the rustling leaves of his oak or oaks (a tree sacred to the Sky-god, as specially liable to be struck by lightning); or the murmur of a sacred spring; or the clash of brazen cauldrons; or the casting of lots. Even in 1929 the Mohammedan monks of a monastery at the foot of Mt. Tomori, in neighbouring Albania, were still sacrificing annually on that summit a white bull to Zeus (Cook, *Zeus*, II, 1171). Cf. Housman, *Last Poems*:

> 'Tis mute the word they went to hear on high Dodona mountain,
>   When winds were in the oakenshaws and all the cauldrons tolled.

[Page 47] *Unwashen feet.* It has been suggested that the priests couched on earth, and left their feet dusty, to strengthen their contact with Mother Earth, consort of the Sky-god Zeus.

[Page 47] *Selloi.* A local tribe; perhaps connected with 'Hellene.'

[Page 48] *From the lips of Apollo.* Cf. Arnold, *Switzerland*, 'Meeting':

> Again I spring to make my choice:
>   Again in tones of ire
> I hear a God's tremendous voice:
>   'Be counsell'd, and retire.'

(Though there seems a touch of grotesque incongruity in transferring this divine warning beneath the Trojan wall to the question whether a young Englishman should love a young Frenchwoman at Thun.)

[Page 48] *Kebríones.* Son of Priam and charioteer of his half-brother Hector.

[Page 49] *Loud didst thou mock.* Patroclus seems better at war than wit. (Pope compares 'those very low jests' which Milton gives his fallen angels in

P. L., vi; though Patroclus at least does not sink to puns). But the main purpose here is to wake our misgivings. Patroclus in his triumph is yielding to that boastfulness which always filled a Greek mind with dismay.

[Page 49] *But quiet in the whirling dust-cloud.* . . . A magnificent line and a half in the Greek. Pope's three seem hardly adequate:

> But where the rising whirlwind clouds the plains,
> Sunk in soft dust the mighty chief remains,
> And stretch'd in death, forgets the guiding reins.

'Soft' seems a particularly unhappy addition.

[Page 49] *When oxen quit the yoke.* Cf. Milton, *Comus*: 'What time the labour'd Oxe In his loose traces from the furrow came.'

[Page 50] *Death at last, Patroclus.* . . . It is curious how repeatedly Homer addresses Patroclus, unlike most other heroes, in the second person—as if he felt for him some of Achilles' tenderness.

[Page 50] *Terrible.* So in the Greek the line begins with δεινός followed by a stop.

[Page 50] *Panthöüs' son, Euphorbus.* This otherwise obscure Trojan has become famous because Pythagoras had the whimsy to pretend that he had himself been Euphorbus in a previous incarnation; and that, during one of his later transmigrations, he had recognized as his own the dead warrior's shield, hung in a temple at Branchĭdae or Mycenae, where it had been dedicated by Menelaus (who kills Euphorbus at the beginning of *Iliad* xvii).

[Page 50] *Boar of quenchless valour.* For this fierceness, Leaf quotes a Mahratta proverb: 'A boar will drink between two tigers.'

[Page 51] *Doubtless did he charge thee.* Hector's complete misconception of Achilles' real attitude seems symbolic of that blindness to his own coming fate which now seizes him in the intoxication of triumph.

[Page 51] *Not long shalt thou live, either.* For this idea that 'truth lives upon the lips of dying men,' compare the warning of Socrates to his judges (*Apology*, 30): 'Next, I am moved to prophesy to you that have condemned me. For now I stand where men grow most prophetic—face to face with death.' It will be noted that detail after detail in the slaying of Patroclus by Hector is repeated in the retributory slaying of Hector himself by Achilles.

[Page 51] *And his soul fled forth from his body.* . . . Two magnificent lines adapted by Virgil for the closing verse of his whole *Aeneid*, when Turnus dies:

> Vitaque cum gemitu fugit indignata sub umbras.

(A verse prophetically appropriate to the poet himself, who was to die uttering the despondent wish that his unperfected life-work should be burned.)

[Page 52] *The warm tears trickled.* As Shakespeare with his stag in Arden, the ancients believed that horses wept (*e.g.* after Caesar crossed the Rubicon), and even elephants.

[Page 52] *The two Aiantes.* See p. 89.

[Page 53] *Antĭlochus.* Nestor's eldest son, himself doomed, after the close of the *Iliad*, to fall before Hector or Memnon and (in later tradition) to have his ashes laid in one urn and one gravemound with those of Achilles and Patroclus, on the shore of Hellespont.

[Page 53] *Patroclus—he is fallen.* 'This speech of Antilochus ought to serve as a model for the brevity with which so dreadful a piece of news ought to be delivered; for in two verses it comprehends the whole affair of the death of Patroclus, the person that killed him, the contest for his body, and his arms in

E   95

the possession of his enemy. . . . The Greek tragick Poets have not always imitated this discretion.' (Pope, following Eustathius.)

[Page 54] *Gathered dust and ashes.* This picture of Achilles' anguish is prominent among the poetic passages carped at, as lacking restraint, by Plato in one of his most intolerant and intolerable moods (*Republic*, 388).

[Page 54] *Zeus hath brought to pass.* The central tragic irony of the whole poem. Achilles' prayer has been granted; and the end is this! Compare Juvenal's great line on the blindness of human desires (x, 111):

> Magnaque numinibus vota exaudita malignis.
> (Vast prayers that Heaven, in its cruelty, hears.)

It is a perfect *peripeteia* (attainment of a result exactly the opposite of that intended), such as Aristotle in his *Poetics* saw to be the very soul of Tragedy; as when Adam and Eve 'knew not eating death,' or Othello 'threw a pearl away Richer than all his tribe,' or Lear disinherited his one true daughter, or Byron was cunning in his own overthrow. 'We are betrayed by what is false within.'

[Page 55] *Then the swift Achilles answered.* . . . The hero becomes more sympathetic than ever before, as his swift and splendid eloquence finds for its theme, no longer the wounds of pride, but the death of comrades loved.

[Page 55] *Wrath that makes even a wise man mad.* These four lines give the essential theme of the whole *Iliad*—an astonishingly human theme (were Homer not so familiar to us) for the *war*-poem of a primitive age.

[Page 55] *Long I tarried:* 15 days.

[Page 55] *Achilles over the Trench.* Translated by Tennyson in another fine fragment.

[Page 55] *Aegis.* See p. 85.

[Page 56] *Clarion.* Homer carefully excludes trumpets from his narrative, but (quite justifiably) is less strict about anachronism in a simile; just as Milton brings Galileo and his telescope into *Paradise Lost.*

[Page 56] *Polýdamas.* Son of Panthöüs and brother of Euphorbus.

[Page 57] *The Shield of Achilles.* An incomparable picture of the Homeric world, given new actuality by modern discoveries of Mycenaean art, such as daggers inlaid with vivid hunting-scenes or the marvellous bulls of the gold cups from Vaphió (see Sir A. Evans, *The Palace of Minos*, III, 131–2; IV, 958–9).

It will be recalled how Lessing in his *Laocoon* contrasts Homer's dynamic description of Achilles' shield, step by step as it is made, with Virgil's too static description (*Aeneid* VIII, 625 ff.) of Aeneas' shield in its finished state, which becomes dull as an art-catalogue. For, while visual art works in space, literature must work in time; so that long static descriptions may fail. But Homer's superiority is due still more, I feel, to its vivid, natural detail. Virgil crams into Aeneas' shield a compendium of eight centuries of Roman history, meaningless to Aeneas himself: Homer, avoiding all pedantry of allusion, simply fills this weapon of war and death with visions of the joy and vividness of living. Perhaps one's only objection is that such a masterpiece seems fitter for museum than battlefield.

Milton has followed (but far from equalled) Homer in the spectacles of human life revealed by Michael to Adam in *P. L.* XI (esp. 638 ff.).

[Page 57] *Pleiads.* Probably 'Doves.' (The constellation is still known in Sicily as 'The Seven Little Doves.') Legend made them daughters of Atlas, changed into stars (according to one version) when pursued by Orion.

[Page 57] *Hyads.* Probably 'Rainy Ones,' from their rising at the commencement of the rainy season. They too were daughters of Atlas, made stars (in one version) after dying of grief for their brother Hyas, slain hunting.

[Page 57] *Orion.* The giant hunter, a Greek Nimrod, loved by Eos and slain by Artemis (p. 229).

[Page 57] *The Bear.* In later legend, the nymph Callisto, loved by Zeus but changed into a bear and set among the stars. Probably Callisto was originally one with Artemis; and the bear may be a relic of totemism. The statement that *only* The (Great) Bear never sets suggests that other constellations round the Pole were not yet named. (See p. 184).

[Page 57] *Doomsman.* Compare the 'lawman' prominent in Icelandic saga.

[Page 58] *Their wives.* Aeneas Tacticus (4th cent. B.C.) tells how the defenders of Sinōpe, being short of men, manned their walls with women and marched them round in full view. But they wisely did not let them throw anything; for 'even a long way off you can tell a woman's throwing' (XL, 4–5).

[Page 58] *Mortals . . . of meaner size.* As in Egyptian art, where giant Pharaohs tower above pygmy subjects.

[Page 58] *Thrice-ploughed field.* The Roman Varro similarly recommends three ploughings—in spring, as the soil dries; in early summer, as it hardens; and in autumn, after the first rains. The value seems to lie partly in preventing pores from forming in the soil, through which the moisture rises by capillary attraction and is lost (M. Cary, *Geographical Background of Greek and Roman History*, p. 16).

[Page 58] *Just like ploughed land, Although 'twas of gold.* Homer already realizes the artistic principle of likeness in difference, which brings out one aesthetic quality (here a change of light and shade) by concentrating on it, while ignoring others; as a bronze statue, concentrating on form and ignoring colour, is more satisfying than the all-round realism of a coloured waxwork.

[Page 59] *Amid the furrows the king stood.* There seems a peculiar charm in this picture of the early world where even a king supervises his own harvest-home (just as the Princess Nausícaä washes the household linen or young princes watch their sheep). 'Such grace had kings when the world begun.'

[Page 59] *Līnus.* Perhaps derived from the Semitic wail 'Ai lanu'—'Woe to us!' Frazer (*Golden Bough*, VII, ch. vii) suggests that the Līnus-song was originally one of the laments for corn-spirit or vine-spirit sung in many lands at harvest or vintage, and sometimes in early days accompanied by human sacrifice. 'To a Greek traveller in Asia or Egypt the foreign words would commonly convey no meaning, and he might take them, not unnaturally, for the name of someone (Maneros, Linus, Lityerses, Bormus) upon whom the reapers were calling.' Frazer also quotes an account of Devonshire harvest-ritual which survived till recent years—'on a fine still evening the "crying of the neck" has a wonderful effect at a distance, far finer than that of the Turkish muezzin, which Lord Byron eulogizes so much, and which he says is preferable to all the bells in Christendom.'

[Page 59] *Daedalus.* The mythic inventor who fled from Athens to serve Minos in Crete, built the Labyrinth to cage the bull-headed Minotaur borne by Queen Pasíphaë, and finally escaped thence on wings of wax and feathers.

[Page 59] *Ariadne.* Daughter of Minos, who loved Theseus, gave him the guiding thread by which he emerged from the Labyrinth, and was forsaken by him on Naxos. Frazer (*Golden Bough*, IV, 75–7) suggests that the Minotaur represented the Sun-god and Ariadne's dance may have imitated the Sun's annual path—perhaps with the magic purpose of keeping him upon his course. 'It is some confirmation that on coins of Cnossus the sun or a star appears in the middle of the labyrinth, the place which on other coins is occupied by the Minotaur.' Sir A. Evans (*Palace of Minos*, III, 66 ff.) found at Cnossus a fresco with a sinuous dance of maidens among olive-trees; and perhaps also the actual site of their dances. He records, too, similar dances by modern Cretans, sometimes with two acrobatic leaders who behaved exactly like the tumblers here in Homer.

[Page 59] *Bright oil.* Apparently to give a gloss to the fabric.

[Page 60] *Hyperīon* ('he that passes on high') was, strictly, the son of Urănus (Heaven) and the father of Hēlios (the Sun), Selēne (the Moon), and Eos (the Dawn). But his name is often, as here, transferred to the Sun himself. The common English pronunciation 'Hypērion' is one of our strangest distortions of classical names.

[Page 60] *Podarge.* One of the Harpies (personified storm-winds). Earlier (XVI, 150) Homer had told how Podarge bore two horses to the W. Wind beside the Ocean-stream. The idea that ordinary mares, too, could be impregnated by the wind is found in Virgil and even in the scientific Aristotle.

[Page 60] *The Erīnyes* (see p. 92). Here they represent, more widely, the laws of Nature; as when Heraclītus says that, if the Sun strayed from his course, the Erīnyes would find him out.

'It is remarked, in excuse of this extravagant fiction of a horse speaking, that *Homer* was authorised herein by fable, tradition, and history. Livy makes mention of two oxen that spoke on different occasions, and recites the speech of one, which was, *Roma, cave tibi. . . .* Spondanus and Dacier fail not to bring up *Balaam's* ass on this occasion' (Pope).

[Page 62] *Even Patroclus died, that was better far than thou.* One of the most famous lines in literature. By repeating it, Callisthenes used to annoy Alexander in his glory. Lucretius puts an adaptation in the mouth of Nature, as she reproaches man for fearing death (III, 1025):

> Lumina sis oculis etiam bonus Ancu' reliquit,
> Qui melior multis quam tu fuit, improbe, rebus.

In turn, this grim consolation stirred Arnold in *Obermann*:

> Yes, as the son of Thetis said,
> I hear thee saying now:
> *Greater by far than thou are dead;*
> *Strive not! die also thou!*

[Page 62] *The Slaying of Hector.* 'This is the book, which of the whole *Iliad* appears to me the most charming. It assembles all that can be imagined of great and important on the one hand, and of tender and melancholy on the other' (Pope). 'Charming' seems a somewhat curious description; but with the rest many readers will agree.

[Page 62] *Phoebus Apollo* had diverted Achilles from pursuit of the vanquished by fleeing before him the shape of the Trojan Agēnor.

[Page 63] *In the blackness of the night.* Actually, in summer Sirius rises close to the sun, and only shines at night in spring and winter.

[Page 63] *Altes.* King of the Léleges, ruling at Pēdasus under Ida. It becomes clear that Laóthoë was more than a concubine and that Priam had, in oriental fashion, more than one full wife.

[Page 64] *Babes . . . smitten against the ground.* Cf. Ps. cxxxvii, 9: 'Happy shall he be that taketh and dasheth thy little ones against the stones.' Homer, however, is less 'happy' about it than the Psalmist.

[Page 64] *When they have lapped my gore.* 'In the place where the dogs licked the blood of Naboth shall dogs lick thy blood, even thine. . . . The dogs shall eat Jezebel by the wall of Jezreel.' (I *Kings*, xxi.)

[Page 64] *Comely are the young.* The Greek passion for beauty, even in death.

[Page 65] *Bandying . . . bygone dreamers' tales.* Lit. 'talking with him of stock

and stone'; apparently with reference to old fairy-tales of human descent from
stones and trees.   Cf. Hēsiod's Bronze-Age men sprung from ash-trees (p. 199);
and similar stories from India, Persia, and Scandinavia.

[Page 65] *Such love-talk as youth and maiden*. . . .   Again Homer's device of
suddenly transporting us from the midst of death to the peaceful happiness
of life.   The lovely repetition of 'youth and maiden' from one line to the next
has been imitated by later poets from Virgil to Hardy.

[Page 66] *The springs fair-flowing*.   These have been sought in vain near Troy;
but where Scamander rises, miles away, on Ida, there actually are two springs
with temperatures of about 45° and 65° Fahrenheit.   Homer seems to have
transferred them, deliberately or in error, from Ida to Troy; perhaps, as Leaf
suggests, confusion arose between 'the springs of Scamander' and 'the springs
on the Scamander side' (of Troy).

[Page 66] *Ere came the sons of Achaea*.   There is something strangely moving
in this glimpse of the happy unheeded years before Troy became a tragic history,
and its contrast with this moment when Troy's hero falls.

[Page 66] *The games for some dead man*, as, in a sense, we feel that Hector
himself is now already dead.

[Page 66] *Round Priam's city thrice*.   Not incredible, for the circuit is under
half a mile (Schliemann, *Ilios*, 142; Leaf, *Troy*, 162 ff.).

[Page 66] *The high Gods watched them pass*.   Like the superhuman spectators
in Hardy's *Dynasts*.

[Page 66] *Tritogeneia*.   'Trĭton-born,' an appellation obscure even to the
Ancients.   Athene was associated with a River Trĭton in Boeotia and a River
Trĭton in Libya.   See L. R. Farnell, *Cults of the Greek States*, I, 266 ff.

[Page 67] *Achilles still edged him back*.   Leaf suggests that Hector kept to
a waggon-track, Achilles to the rougher ground nearer the walls.

[Page 67] *Golden scales*.   See p. 89.

[Page 67] *To the son of Pēleus came Athene*.   Her treacherous intervention
is one of the least pleasant things in Homer.   Why did he do it?   Was it to
deepen the tragedy of Hector, abandoned by God and man, by the Goddess of
his city and by the countrymen he died to save?   Certainly this terrible loneliness
becomes more tragic than if he had simply fallen by Achilles' human power.
And when we read of the doom of great figures in history, does it not often
seem as if Heaven and earth conspired against them?   I can see no other motive.
Achilles loses stature by Athene's help—but for the moment Achilles matters
less.   Athene loses dignity—but Homer cares more about the characters of
his men and women than of his Gods.

[Page 67] *Deïphobus*.   In later legend, wed to Helen after Paris died by the
arrow of Philoctētes; and slain by Menelaus and Odysseus in the sack of Troy
(p. 127).

[Page 70] *Ten—twentyfold—in ransom*.   The same passionate language as
Achilles had used in rejecting the Greek embassy (p. 33).   And now too he is
to prove more generous than his threats.

[Page 70] *And his soul fled forth*.   The resemblances in detail between the
slaying of Patroclus and that of Hector are here clinched by an exact verbal
repetition (4 lines in the Greek).   An eye has been paid for an eye, a tooth
for a tooth.

[Page 71] *The Wraith of Patroclus*.   Hector has died (and it seems crudely
self-complacent to suggest that Homer did not, like ourselves, feel with the
vanquished).   But now Achilles regains the centre of the stage and of our
sympathies.   As Pope says: 'We are now past the war and violence of the
Ilias . . . we may look back with a pleasing kind of horror upon the Anger of
Achilles, and see what dire effects it has wrought in the compass of nineteen

days.' (It is curious how often Pope is more interesting than later Homeric commentators. But Pope was very intelligent; and he regarded the Greek epic as literature, where most of the learned have treated it as learning.)

[Page 71] *Ilios' windy wall.* Cf. Leaf, *Troy*, 180—'"Windy" it undoubtedly is: many a visitor can testify to the tearing wind which sweeps down from the north, and in fact constitutes during most of the summer a serious climatic drawback to the country.'

[Page 72] *Fled, crying shrill.* Cf. *Hamlet*, I, i, 115—'The sheeted dead Did squeak and gibber in the Roman streets.'

[Page 72] *Ah God, so there is something . . . some soul, some phantom.* This detail (with others) is echoed by Propertius in the most moving of his pieces (IV, 7), where he is visited by his dead mistress's ghost and the poet in him for a moment forgets the pedant—'Sunt aliquid Manes: letum non omnia finit':

The dead—the dead are something. With death all is not over.
   Some glimmering shade escapes, when the last ash crumbles grey.
This night my eyes have seen her. She bent above her lover,
   Though now she sleeps for ever by the roar of the harsh highway.

[Page 73] *Uphill and down, this way and that. . . .* The Greek line is a famous instance of the sometimes overrated device of suiting sound to sense (here the bumping of mules along a mountain-track)—'Polla d'ananta katanta paranta te dochmia t' ēlthon.'

[Page 73] *Samos.* Samothrace.

[Page 73] *Horn of a pastured ox.* Sometimes supposed a protection for the line against being bitten through, but probably a shiny lure itself (just as bass can be caught with silver paper).

[Page 74] *Remembering thy father.* Priam had begun with an appeal to Achilles' love for his father; with an appeal to that love he ends.

[Page 75] *Two jars.* A famous passage, condemned by Plato's puritanism (cf. the beautiful epitaph of Philētas, p. 297). The jars can be imagined like those great oil-vessels, big enough for the Forty Thieves, found on sites like Cnossus. Even the *Roman de la Rose* (6812 ff.) imitates Homer's description, with the two jars changed to 'tuns' (*toneaus*), presided over by Fortune.

[Page 75] *Achilles with a scowl of evil will.* Even at this climax of his pathos (far more moving, to me, than the histrionic cries of Lear) Homer will not sacrifice truth to sentiment. Achilles pities; but the tigerishness is still there. Such is the tragedy of war.

Twice is almighty Homer far above
Troy and her towers, Olympus and his Jove.
First, when the God-led Priam bends before
Him sprung from Thetis, dark with Hector's gore;
A second time when both alike have bled
And Agamemnon speaks among the dead.[1]

(Landor.)

[Page 77] *Níobe.* Usually described as daughter of Tantalus, sister of Pĕlops, and wife of Amphīon, who built Thebes with the music of his lyre. Pausanias says that on Mt. Sípylus (5,000 feet), near Smyrna, there was a rock shaped like a mourning woman, whence in summer dropped water like tears (see Frazer, *Pausanias*, III, 552 ff.).

[Page 78] *The Wail for Hector.* Leaf (*Iliad*) quotes a modern account of

[1] See p. 150.

Albanian women's dirges, sung solo in couplets, then repeated by a chorus of neighbours and kin. Cf. the Irish keening in J. M. Synge's *Riders to the Sea*; and also the lament of Sir Ector over the dead Lancelot at the end of Malory. Arnold closely follows Homer in the wailing of the Gods for Balder slain.

[Page 78] *From a tower's top shall hurl thee.* The traditional fate of Astýanax.

[Page 78] *Samos.* Samothrace.

[Page 78] *Capped with smoke.* The meaning of the Greek word is uncertain. But Lemnos, though no longer volcanic, seems once to have been so and was associated, like Etna, with Hephaestus.

[Page 78] *Unblemished.* It seems a characteristic trait of the old Hecuba to lay special stress on the physical side of funerals; cf. her appeal to Hector, p. 64.

[Page 79] *Thou didst restrain them still.* Readers of *Tom Brown's Schooldays* may recall that at this point Arthur was moved to tears, to the disgust of a tougher schoolmate. It is almost needless to say that the next line ('With thy gentle speaking, thy gentleness of will') has been expunged by some editors as 'tautological.' For it is an unfortunate fact that Homer has often engaged the minute attentions of men better fitted by temper for a life-study of grits or snails.

[Page 80] *Gorgúthion.* A son of Priam, shot by Teucer.

[Page 80] *As in a garden a poppy.* Imitated by Virgil (*Aen.* IX, 436) and by Arnold in *Sohrab and Rustum*:

> Like some rich hyacinth which by the scythe
> Of an unskilful gardener has been cut,
> Mowing the garden grass-plots near its bed,
> And lies a fragrant tower of purple bloom,
> On the mown, dying grass—so Sohrab lay,
> Lovely in death, upon the common sand.

Homer seems, however, here to have nodded a little himself; poppy-*buds* hang down, but hardly poppy-*heads*.

[Page 80] *Nestor's Doubt.* Cf. Tennyson, *Merlin and Vivien*:

> So dark a forethought roll'd about his brain,
> As on a dull day in an Ocean cave
> The blind wave feeling round his long sea-hall
> In silence.

[Page 81] *Euphorbus.* See p. 95.

HOMER

ODYSSEY

Aye on the shores of darkness there is light,
  And precipices show untrodden green,
There is a budding morrow in midnight,
  There is a triple sight in blindness keen;
Such seeing hadst thou, as it once befel
To Dian, Queen of Earth, and Heaven, and Hell.

Keats, To Homer.

THE *Odyssey*, for most readers, does not quite equal the supreme moments of the *Iliad*; but it remains an even more perfect whole. The first four Books deal with events in Heaven, where Athene wins Zeus to grant Odysseus' return, and in Ithaca, where his nineteen years' absence has left his wife and son a prey to the island-chiefs that seek her hand; and with that son's search for news of his lost father at Pylos and at Sparta. The next four (V–VIII) tell the release of Odysseus from his seven years' captivity with the Nymph Calypso and his welcome by Princess Nausícaä and the Phaeacians. The next four (IX–XII), justly the most famous, contain the hero's narrative to the Phaeacians of his adventures in the year after Troy fell. The second twelve Books, perhaps at times overlong, relate his return home, his slaughter of the Suitors with the help of his son, and his reunion with wife and father.

The two epics show both striking parallels and striking contrasts. The *Iliad* deals with the love of comrades and of honour; the *Odyssey* above all with the love of wife and home. Achilles is more brilliant than Odysseus; yet he is at times 'passion's slave,' as Odysseus is not. And so the honour Achilles sets his heart upon proves dust, his vengeance vain; but Odysseus, enduring to the end, is saved alike from the fury of ogres and the lure of fair enchantresses. Achilles never sees again his old father nor his son; but Odysseus, by his courage and patience, comes back at last to both. So too with the women-characters. In the *Iliad* loyal wives like Andrómache are dragged to destruction by the fatal beauty of Helen; in the *Odyssey* there is another fatal woman—Clytemnestra, Helen's own sister; but, this time, the true wife, Penelope wins through to final happiness. Like Shakespeare, Homer seems to pass, as he ages, from Tragedy to Romance, from passionate catastrophe to forbearance and endurance and acceptance. I must add, however, that the *Odyssey* seems to me far greater, far less marked by declining power, than *The Tempest* or *Cymbeline*.

For some ancient critics, indeed, the domestic scenes in Ithaca were too realistic, the adventures of Odysseus in faery seas too unreal. Zoïlus (4th century B.C.) jeered at mariners turned pigs; even the sensitive 'Longīnus' (1st century A.D.?) likened the poet of the *Odyssey* to a sinking sun, not less great, but less intense; or to an ebbing Ocean, uncovering strange monsters as its tide turns home. But the modern reader, who has seen realism, and unrealism, and surrealism carried to lengths undreamed of by the more balanced temper of Antiquity, is not so easily disturbed. We are more likely to feel that the *Odyssey* is at times too long and too repetitive—that we could do with less of the Phaeacians and of the Suitors, with fewer interventions by the busy Athene, with fewer mystifications by the wily Odysseus.

Yet if the *Odyssey* is the work of an ageing genius, it has all the same aged less in some ways than the *Iliad*. It may be based in part on folklore and fairy-tale far older than any siege of Troy; yet these keep some of the eternal youth of our own nurseries. And, on the other hand, the indomitable love of a sea-tossed man for wife and home, the struggles of a leader amid hardship and danger to hearten and save his feebler followers—these remain themes closer to modern sympathy than the lust of battle and the pride of slaughter. Further, the story holds our remembrance with a more rounded completeness. In consequence, modern translators have turned far more often to the *Odyssey*. And even the *Iliad* contains nothing finer than the simple words with which Odysseus rejects Calypso's proffered immortality for the sake of an ageing wife and a barren island home; or the picture of Eumaeus in his swineherd's hut, still loyal and humorous and unembittered after a life of ill-luck and servitude; or the death of the dog Argus on his dunghill when he had recognized, after so many years, the master whose disguise no human eyes could pierce. Above all, I think, there lives in my memory the visit of the hero to the legions of the dead on that desolate poplared shore of Queen Persephone. There in this great eleventh book, at the poem's centre, there meet both past and future, the comrades lost long since on the battlefields round Ilios and the prophecy of Odysseus' far-off homecoming, till death shall rise at last for him also, like a quiet mist from the sea. When the wraith of Elpēnor begs only that above his grave be set the oar that he rowed with among his comrades, in dangers and hardships gladdened still by comradeship; when the dead Achilles utters his passionate protest against the empty glories of the tomb—those glories for which he had sacrificed others and himself—as compared with the life of even some poor drudge on earth; when Anticleia tells how she died, not by the painless arrows of Artemis, but of inconsolable longing for the wisdom and gentleness of her lost son—at moments like these life so poignant seems to transcend the artifice of art, art so perfect to redeem the

* E

bitter imperfectness of life. For Homer, as for Shakespeare, perhaps the supreme human quality is loyalty. The *Odyssey* is not merely a tale of changes and chances in perilous seas; it is a tale of loyalties that all those changes and chances failed in the end to break.

ODYSSEY

The poet calls his Muse to sing the tale of that wise-hearted hero who once wandered through the world, after Ilios fell, learning the ways of many lands. Yet all his wisdom could not win a safe return for his comrades, who slew in their folly the cattle of the Sun.

Long after all the other chiefs of Achaea had come back, Odysseus was kept from home by the Nymph Calypso, who loved him, and by Poseidon, who hated him for the blinding of his son Polyphemus. But while Poseidon was away feasting with the Ethiopians, the Gods gathered in Heaven and Zeus spoke among them of the folly of Aegisthus, who stole the wife of King Agamemnon and slew her lord, but was himself slain in vengeance by Agamemnon's son Orestes. Then Athene exclaimed that the guilty Aegisthus had indeed suffered; yet the wise and godfearing Odysseus was still left forgotten by the Gods, a prisoner in Calypso's isle. And so Zeus promised that his homecoming should no longer be delayed.

Then Athene departed to Ithaca to encourage the young Telémachus, Odysseus' son, whose house was beset by the insolent wooers of his mother Penelope. The Goddess took the form of Mentes, a Taphian chief; and Telémachus made her welcome. Marking the Suitors' arrogance, the disguised Athene urged him to assemble the men of Ithaca and appeal to them for justice—let the Suitors quit the palace and Penelope return home to her father, so that he could wed her to another. But Telémachus himself should make a journey to old Nestor at Pylos, and to Menelaus at Sparta, for tidings of his father's fate. After giving this counsel, the Goddess vanished in the shape of a bird; and Telémachus knew now that it was an Immortal he had welcomed unawares. Filled with new courage, he warned the Suitors that he would appeal to an assembly of the Ithacans to make him master in his own house. Hot words passed between him and Antínoüs, the chief of the intruders. Till evening the Suitors revelled; and all that night Telémachus lay awake, planning how to follow the counsel of Athene.

The Debate in Ithaca

But when came early Morning, with fingers rosy-red,
Then the dear son of Odysseus started from his bed;
Dressing, over his shoulder his keen-edged sword he cast,
And bound beneath his glistening feet his shapely sandals fast;

Then hastened forth from his chamber, fair as a God in face,
And bade the clear-voiced heralds call to the meeting-place
The long-haired sons of Achaea.   So at the heralds' call
Quickly the people gathered; and into the midst of all
Telémachus came.   His right hand grasped a bronze-tipped spear
And with twinkling feet behind him two hounds came trotting near.
But Athene shed upon him grace like a God's—thereat
The people gazed in wonder, as forth he strode and sat
Down in the seat of his father, while the elders all made way.
Then first the hero Aegyptius rose—bowed down and grey
With years, yet wise with the knowledge of countless things was he.
His own dear son, in the noble Odysseus' company,
Had sailed with the hollow ships, long since, to the Trojan plain—
Antïphus the spearman, by the savage Cyclops slain
For that last meal he ravened, deep in his mountain-den.
But three more sons were living; one was consorting then—
Eurýnomus—with the Suitors, and two yet stayed to till
The fields of their old father, that grieved and fretted still
For his lost heir.   So now, speaking, he wept the while:
'Hear me, ye men of Ithaca.   Within our isle
There hath not been assembly nor gathering, till to-day,
Since first the noble Odysseus with his galleys sailed away.
Who calls us now together?   Who now has come to stand
So sore in need, among our youth, or the elders of our land?
Has he some news to give us, that first has reached his ear?—
Word of some host embattled marching against us here?
Or has he some other matter, for the common weal, to tell?
An honest man, I doubt it not, that means us well—
God bless him with whatever his heart's desire may be!'
    Then the dear son of Odysseus welcomed joyfully
Those words of happy omen—he waited now no more,
But rose in the midst with eager lips—and the herald Peisēnor
Set in his hand the sceptre, a prudent man and wise.
Then first on the old Aegyptius Telémachus turned his eyes—
'Old sir, the man thou seekest, is here—do thou but heed—
It was I that summoned the people.   For mine is a bitter need.
It is no secret tidings that first have reached mine ear,
No word of a hostile army marching against us here,
Nor any other matter touching our common weal.
On my own home it has fallen, this grief that now I feel—
Nay, double grief!—for lost is my noble sire that once
Was your true king, and loved ye, as a father loves his sons;
And now a greater trouble grows, that utterly,
Ere long, shall ruin our house and disinherit me.

For suitors have beset us, to seek my mother's hand
Against her will—the sons of the lordliest in our land.
To Icárius her father's house they are afraid
To go that *he* might settle the bride-price to be paid
And choose her out a husband that were pleasing in her eyes;
To us instead, day after day, they crowd and sacrifice
Oxen, and sheep, and fatted goats, and feast their fill
And drink our fire-red wine at their own wanton will.
So all our substance runs to ruin.   For now our hall
Has no lord like Odysseus, to save it from its fall.
Too weak for such a task are we—should we but try,
It could but show how feeble, how powerless we lie.
Nay, had I strength, I *would* resist.   Not to be borne
These things are that we suffer—my home laid waste in scorn!
But *ye*—will not *ye* resent it, the evil these men do?
Not feel some shame in the face of all our neighbours, too,
That dwell in the lands about us?   Nay, of the Gods beware,
For fear They wreak upon ye this wickedness men dare!
Ah, by Zeus of Olympus, by Thĕmis I implore,
That gathers the folk to council and speeds them home once more,
Have done, my friends, and leave me to mourn alone at last!—
Or hath my noble father, Odysseus, in the past
So wronged the well-greaved Achaeans with deeds of evil will,
That now with deeds as evil ye persecute me still,
Setting these fellows on me!   In truth, it were better far
If ye yourselves were devouring, men of Ithaca,
My chattels and my cattle—I might have justice *then*!
For here in our city-street, again and yet again,
I would challenge each I met with, till ye paid me back in full.
But now ye heap upon me anguish insufferable.'

   So he spoke in his anger—then flung upon the ground
The sceptre, and burst out weeping.   But the people gathered round
Pitied him, and were silent—harshly no man could bear
To answer the son of Odysseus.   Only Antínoüs there
Cried out: 'What art thou saying, to put us all to shame,
Proud tongue, mad heart of passion!   Why lay on *us* the blame?
We wooers of Achaea have never done thee ill,
Telémachus—'tis thy mother, and her too cunning will.
For now three years are over—and the fourth will soon be gone—
That she cozens the Achaeans, with false hopes leading on
Each in his turn—with promises—with words in secret sent;
And all the while on other ends her heart is bent.
Ay, and in her cunning this other trick she planned.
There in her hall she set a mighty warp to stand

And started to weave upon it a web both fine and vast—
"Since the noble Odysseus," she said, "is dead at last,
Wait yet a while, young wooers, for this hand ye seek to gain,
Until my web is woven—make not my work in vain.
'Tis a shroud for the hero Laertes, when on his head shall fall
Death the grim destroyer, that low at length lays all;
Lest, through the lands of Achaea, women should blame me loud,
That so great a lord, and wealthy, must lie without a shroud."
Such were her words; and our haughty hearts must needs obey.
So there she laboured weaving at that great web each day,
And yet each night, by torchlight, unravelled every thread.
Thus for three years, unnoticed, she fooled us and misled;
But, with the fourth year's coming, as round the seasons ran,
One of her women, knowing all, betrayed her plan
And we caught the queen unthreading that web wrought gloriously.
She finished it, then, with a heavy heart, since so it needs must be.
But we, her suitors, answer thus, that thou mayst know,
Both thou and the folk of Achaea—make now thy mother go
And wed whomever her father bids, whomever her own heart will.
But beware, if the sons of Achaea must vex their patience still
Because of her!—wise though she be, by Pallas taught
Mastery of craftsmanship and subtlety of thought,
Beyond all other women; with such a cunning wit,
That even from ancient days none knows the like of it!
Ay, of the fair-tressed daughters of Achaea none was found—
Not Tyro, not Alcmēne, not Mycēne glittering-crowned—
In cleverness could rival the wise Penelope;
And yet it was past all reason, her latest trickery.
But as long as in her heart this purpose shall hold good
That now the Gods have set there, so long thy livelihood,
Thy substance, shall be wasted.   Win a fair name she may,
By baulking us; but bitter is the price that *thou* must pay.
We will not go to our lands, we will not turn elsewhere,
Till she has wed an Achaean—whomever she may care.'
   Then the prudent Telémachus answered: 'Can I drive from my own door,
Antínoüs, unwilling, the mother that once bore,
Once nursed me?—while my father is lost and far away,
Be he alive or perished!   And how, then, should I pay
Icárius due atonement, if thus of my own will
I hunt away my mother?   Needs must I suffer ill
From the anger of her father; ay, and at Heaven's hand—
For she will call upon me, if I cast her from the land,
The curse of the grim Erīnyes.   Men, too, will speak with wrath
My name—no, I *cannot* utter the word that drives her forth!

But if ye too are angry, still get ye gone at least
Out of my house, and find you some other way to feast,
Off your own wealth—go visit each other's board in turn.
Or, if ye deem it simpler, and it gives ye less concern,
To ruin, unatoning, one household—have your way!
Rob on!   But I will call to the Gods that live for aye,
That haply Zeus hereafter may make ye rue it all.
Then *ye* too, unatoned for, might perish in my hall.'
   So Telémachus spoke.   But Zeus far-thundering
Sent forth from the mountain-summit two eagles on the wing.
Awhile, with the wind behind them, swift on their way they sped,
Side by side together, with straining wings outspread;
But when they were over the meeting-place, with its buzz of eager speech,
Wheeling they clashed, and feathers each rent in clouds from each,
While down they glared on the crowd beneath (and doom was in that
    glare).
Fiercely each other's face and neck their talons tare,
Then over the roofs of the city they vanished, towards the right,
While all the people watched them, in wonder at the sight,
With hearts that deeply questioned what end these signs foretold;
But the hero Halitherses, the son of Mastor, old
And wise beyond all his fellows to divine the flight of birds
And tell what Fate portended, with a prophet's words,
Lifted his voice amidst them in loyal intent and true:
'Men of Ithaca, hearken what now I say to you;
And, above all, the Suitors.   By *them* let my words be weighed;
For a grim fate surges towards them.   Not now for long delayed
Shall be the return of Odysseus to those he loves—maybe
He is near us *now*, preparing doom and butchery
For the Suitors—and many among us shall find their evil day,
Who dwell in far-seen Ithaca.   While yet we may,
Let us plan to check these wooers.   Nay now, let them restrain
Themselves!   Ay, it were wiser for their own sakes to refrain.
I am no unproved prophet.   I speak what well I know.
I tell ye, for Odysseus all things have fallen so
As long since I foretold him, when the Argives went on board
For Troy, and with them Odysseus, our subtle-hearted lord;
I warned him that, full of sorrows, with all his comrades dead,
Home he should come at last, when the nineteenth year was sped,
Unknown to all.   Fulfilment of all these things is nigh.'
   Then shouted the son of Pólybus, Eurýmachus, in reply:
'Away, old man!   Get homeward—to thy children play the seer—
Lest rather for them, it may be, some evil end is near.
I am a better prophet, myself, how things shall go.

There are plenty of birds that flutter in the sunlight to and fro,
And many of them betoken nought.   Odysseus died
Far hence—and it were better, hadst thou perished at his side
Thyself—then thou wouldst not babble so loud of prophecy,
Whetting the wrath of Telémachus, in hope that he
Perhaps may give thee a present to carry home again!
I tell thee—and these my words shall not be said in vain—
If thou that art grown old in years, and counted wise,
Wilt egg this lad to anger, with thy gulleries and lies,
Little cause for rejoicing shall *he* have, first of all,
And on thyself, old sir, we will see such a fine shall fall
As wrings thy heart to pay it—yea, loudly shalt thou cry.
But to Telémachus, now, I give this counsel—ay,
Here before all: thy mother to her sire's house send away,
And her kin shall settle the marriage and the gifts that are to pay,
Such rich gifts as are fitting for a dear-loved daughter's hand.
Till then we sons of Achaea—and I deem that my word shall stand—
Will never cease our wooing, however harsh.   For we
Fear none!—not Telémachus, even!—glib talker though he be!
Nor yet, old man, are we troubled by all thy idle store
Of prophecies—they only shall make thee hated more.
We will waste the goods of Odysseus—ay, without recompense—
So long as the Queen is minded to hold us in suspense,
While here we sit contending who shall possess this prize
Of womanhood, day after day, and have no eyes
For all the other women whose hearts we well might gain.'
    Then Telémachus the prudent answered them again:
'Eurýmachus, and ye others, for what ye have now denied,
No word more will I utter to pray you in your pride.
The Gods, and the folk of Achaea, know well now what is true.
But give me, at least, a galley, with twenty men for crew,
To take me beyond the sea, and back again once more.
For I will sail to Sparta and to Pylos' sandy shore,
To seek news of my father, lost now this many a year.
Maybe some man will tell me—some rumour I may hear
Sent forth by Zeus, who scatters most tidings among men.
If I learn my father is living, and sailing homeward, then
I will endure my troubles another twelvemonth yet;
But if I hear he has perished and his last day is set,
Then back to my own dear country I will return and make
A barrow, and accomplish the last rites for his sake,
Richly as is befitting, and let my mother wed.'
    With that Telémachus sat him down.   But in his stead
Rose Mentor, by great Odysseus beloved in days of old;

Him, when he sailed to Troyward, Odysseus chose to hold
Rule over all his household and keep all safely still,
Obeying old Laertes.   Now with a loyal will,
'Ye men of Ithaca,' he said, 'hearken to me.
Never again let a sceptred king deal righteously!
Never let king be gentle and loving and kind of heart—
Nay, rather a savage tyrant, that makes his people smart!
For all this folk, o'er whom the godlike Odysseus bore
Rule gentle as a father's, remembers him no more.
Little I envy the Suitors—proud men and pitiless—
Their deeds of evil outrage, woven in wickedness:
It is their own heads they hazard, while they riot away
The wealth in the house of Odysseus, whom *they* deem perished—nay,
It is with *ye*, the people, I am angered; that unstirred
And mum ye sit, so many, and utter never a word,
Though few they are against ye, to check the Suitors' pride.'
 Then started up Leiócritus, Euēnor's son, and cried:
'Mentor, thou mischief-maker, thou littlewit, how now!
Wilt thou set this people on us?   But we are more than thou—
Not lightly shalt thou challenge our feasting with the sword.
Nay, though Odysseus' self should come, our island's lord,
And try to hurl us Suitors in our pride from where we sit
Within his hall at banquet, but little joy of it
His wife should have, though sorely she longs to see him there—
An ill death he would die himself, should he but dare
Do battle with so many.   Thy tongue too idly ran.
Back to your fields, good people!   Scatter ye home, each man.
Let Mentor and Halitherses, his father's friends of old,
Speed Telémachus' journey.   Nay, if the truth were told,
For many a long day yet he shall sit here helplessly
For news at home—for I doubt, this voyage will never be.'
So Leiócritus spoke; and swiftly far and wide
At his word the people scattered, each man to his own fireside.

(II, 1–258.)

*Telémachus went down alone to the grey sea and prayed to Athene, who again
appeared to him, now in the shape of his father's faithful friend Mentor, and
promised to find him ship and crew.   Telémachus returned to the palace to gather
provision for the voyage; and there Antinoüs mocked him with words of feigned
friendship.   But he plucked back his hand from Antinoüs' grasp and went his
way, while the Suitors discussed whether he were planning to bring armed help
against them from Pylos or Sparta, or to kill them with poison from Éphyra.
Then Telémachus made the old housekeeper Eurycleia, once his father's nurse,
give him food and wine and swear not to tell his mother Penelope of his voyage,*

till eleven or twelve days were past. *Meanwhile Athene, disguising herself as Telémachus, had borrowed a galley and raised a crew.* *That evening they sailed with a west wind sent by the Goddess herself.* *Next day they reached Pylos, where Nestor welcomed his old comrade's son, but knew nothing of his father's fate; he could only send him on to Menelaus and Helen at Sparta, lending him a chariot and his own son Peisístratus for companion.* *They found Menelaus celebrating the weddings of his son and daughter; but of Odysseus he could only repeat what he had learnt, when driven to Egypt on his homeward voyage, from Prōteus, the Old Man of the Sea.*

The Old Man of the Sea

'The Gods held me in Egypt, longing to sail for home,
For I failed to seek their blessing with an offered hecatomb.
Now off the coasts of Egypt, amid the breakers' spray,
An island lies, called Pharos (as far as in a day
A ship can sail, when behind her the piping gale blows fair).
Good shelter is its haven—men draw their water there,
Dark from the spring, ere seaward they launch their keels once more.
Here the Immortals stayed me full twenty days ashore;
For the winds that bear men's galleys o'er the broad backs of the tide
Blew not, and food would have failed us, and all my men had died,
If the pity of a Goddess had not delivered me—
Eidóthea, the daughter of the Old Man of the Sea,
Prōteus the wise. Compassion had touched her to the heart,
As there she met me wandering, lonely and apart,
While all about the islet my comrades ranged abroad,
Fishing with hooks; for hunger hard at our bellies gnawed.
Near me she stood, and asked me—"Stranger, canst be so blind
Of wit, or in love with sorrow, that here thou sitst resigned,
Prisoned within this island, powerless to seek a way
To get thee hence—while thy comrades lose heart from day to day?"
And then I made her answer—"Whatever Goddess thou,
Not of free will, believe me, do I thus sit here now,
But it seems I must have angered the Gods of the boundless sky.
Yet thou—for nought is hidden from Immortals—tell me why;
Tell me what God thus stays me, nor lets me sail again?
How shall I find my homeward way across the teeming main?"
But the glorious Goddess answered: "I will tell the truth to thee.
This isle is ever haunted by the Old Man of the Sea,
Prōteus the Egyptian, the deathless and the wise,
Who serves the Lord Poseidon, and knows whatever lies

Deep in the sea's abysses.   They say I am his child.
Now couldst thou snare my father and hold him, thus beguiled,
Then *he* indeed can tell thee of the road that must be passed
And how, o'er the deep of the fishes, home thou shalt come at last.
O king of Zeus belovéd, he can tell thee, if thou will,
Whate'er in thy halls has happened, whether of good or ill,
While, far away and weary, o'er earth thou wanderest still."
And then I answered: "Lady, thyself devise the snare,
Lest seeing me, or foreseeing, he may elude me there.
Hard it is for a mortal to give a God a fall."
Then said the glorious Goddess—"So be it.   I tell thee all.
When the sun has mounted, stranger, to Heaven's highest steep,
Then that wise Ancient of the Sea comes from the deep,
While the West Wind, to hide him, breathes dark on the ruffled wave;
There on the shore he lays him, within a hollow cave,
And round him his seals are gathered from the grey heave of the tide,
The brood of the Sea's fair daughter, to slumber at his side;
And foul is the reek of their breathing, with the tang of ocean-brine.
Thither, then, I will lead thee at earliest morning-shine
And find thee a place to lie in—but bring thou comrades three,
Of all in thy well-benched galleys the bravest that there be.
Now these are the old man's magic arts—first he will go
Among his seals and count them, if all be there or no;
But when he has seen and numbered all, then down to sleep
Amidst them he will lay him, like a shepherd mid his sheep.
But soon as ye see him resting, then summon all your might
And all the manhood in you, and mind ye hold him tight,
However he strain and struggle to slip from out your hand.
For he will take, to escape ye, all shapes that move on land,
And into water turn him, and into raging fire.
But still ye shall grip and press him hard, nor ever tire,
Till he takes his ancient likeness—as when among his herds
He first lay down—and asks you your will in human words.
Then do him no more violence, but set the old man free
And ask him, noble hero, what God is wroth with thee,
And how o'er the deep of the fishes ye shall come home at last."
With that beneath the weltering wave the Goddess plunged and passed.
   'So back I turned to my galleys, where beached on the sand they stood,
And deep, as I went, I pondered, and heavy was my mood.
But when I was come to my galley, at the haven, there we made
Supper; and night ambrosial fell; and down we laid
Our bodies by the breakers.   But when the Dawn of day
Shone forth with rosy fingers, again I took my way
Beside the boundless waters, praying in my bitter need,

With comrades three, the surest for any desperate deed.
Then from the sea's abysses the Goddess rose again,
Bringing four sealskins with her, from seals but newly slain,
Wherewith to trap her father; for each of us a lair
In the sea-sand she had hollowed, and now sat waiting there.
So, as we came, in our places she hid each one and laid
The skin of a seal above him.   But never ambuscade
So horrible.   For we sickened, till our very hearts did blench,
With the reek of the sea-bred seals, the intolerable stench.
And indeed what man could endure it, to lie with a beast of the sea?
But again the Goddess saved us, and brought a remedy,
For she laid beneath our nostrils ambrosia, to quell
The stink of the sea-born monsters with its sweet celestial smell.
So there with hard endurance, while morning passed away
We waited; and out of the waters the seals flocked forth and lay
Down in their wonted order beside the breakers' roar;
But with high noon the Old Man came, and on the shore
Found his fat seals and counted, going about and about;
Us too with the first he reckoned, untouched by any doubt,
And then to sleep he laid him—but mightily we cried
And up we leapt and grappled; yet the Old Man on his side
Forgot not his ancient cunning—to a lion with mighty mane
He turned, to a snake, to a panther, to a huge boar; then, again
He shaped him as slippery water, and then as a towering tree;
Yet all the while we gripped him, inescapably.
But when the old magician felt that his strength was done,
At length his tongue was loosened, and he spoke—"O Atreus' son,
What God was it that taught thee to trap me against my will?
What wouldst thou?"   But I answered—"Why seek to deceive me still,
Old sir?   For *all* thou knowest—that here within this isle
Prisoned I find no issue, and my heart grows faint the while.
But thou—for the Gods know all things—I pray thee tell me plain,
What Immortal holds me, nor lets me sail again?
How o'er the deep of the fishes can I come home once more?"
Then he said in answer—"There on the Trojan shore
Thou shouldst have made, ere sailing, a noble offering
To Zeus and the other Immortals, and prayed to them to bring
Thy galleys safely homeward across the wine-dark sea.
For now to behold thy dearest it is not fated thee,
Nor the fair walls of thy palace, nor the land where thou wast bred,
Till first to the stream of Aegyptus, with its waters heaven-fed,
Thou hast sailed again, and offered a holy hecatomb
To all the Gods that hold wide Heaven for their home.
So shall they grant, at last, the return thou yearnest for."

Then my spirit broke within me, that I must sail once more
O'er the gloomy deep to Egypt, a weary voyage and dread;
Nevertheless I answered—"Whatever thou hast said,
Old sir, I will perform it.   But tell me one thing true—
Have all the lords of Achaea come home, with nought to rue,
Whom Nestor and I left behind us, sailing from Troy?   Of these
Did any find death on a sudden amid the stormy seas,
Or in dear arms that loved them, when the toils of war were done?"
But quickly came his answer—"Why ask me, Atreus' son?
No need hast thou to learn it, or search my thoughts.   I know—
It will not be long, when I tell thee, before thy tears shall flow.
For many indeed have perished, though many were saved beside,
Of the bronze-clad chiefs of Achaea.   Yet only two have died
Returning—and in Troyland thou sawest thyself who fell;
And a third is held imprisoned by the wastes of the wide sea-swell.
Know, then, that the Locrian Ajax with his long-oared galleys drowned;
For first of all Poseidon had hurled his ship aground
On the great crags of Gȳrae, yet saved him from the sea;
And he might have lived, though Athene hated him bitterly,
Had not his infatuate blindness madly made him cry
He had scaped the gulfs of the surges despite the Gods on high;
But Poseidon heard him boasting, and his great hands smote amain
On Gȳrae's rock with his trident and split that crag in twain.
Then part stood fast, but the fragment where Ajax sat and cried
Those words of infatuate folly, crashed into the tumbling tide,
And he fell in that waste of waters and perished, drinking brine.
But thy brother's hollow galleys, by Hēra's aid divine,
Escaped from doom; yet nearing the steep of Málea
The storm-blast broke upon them, and bore him out afar
O'er the teeming main, lamenting, to the limits of the land,
Where once the house of Thyestes, in old days, used to stand
And now dwelt his son Aegisthus; but soon the Gods anew
Sent a fair wind to thy brother and home at length he drew.
Then indeed most happy to reach his land at last,
He kissed the earth that had borne him, and his tears flowed hot and fast
With joy to see his country.   But his coming caught the eye
Of the guard that the guileful Aegisthus had set in a tower on high,
With a promise of two talents of gold to be his pay.
There had he watched for a twelvemonth, lest thy brother on his way
Should come unseen to Mycenae, with heart alert for war.
So now that watcher hastened with his warning fast before
To tell his lord Aegisthus.   Quickly the traitor then
Laid his trap, with an ambush of twenty chosen men,
The stoutest of his township, upon the hall's one side,

And on the other a banquet; and hastened forth to ride
With his chariots to summon the shepherd of the land,
Agamemnon, to his table.   (Yet death in his heart lay planned.)
Home then he led his lord, blind to that doom to fall,
And feasted him and slew him, as they slay an ox at stall.
Not one of Atrīdes' comrades came living back again,
Not one of the men of Aegisthus.   There all alike were slain."
   'With that my spirit was broken and there aloud I cried,
Sitting upon the sand; for in my heart had died
All wish to go on living and see the sunlight still.
But when I had rolled upon the ground and wept my fill,
Then spoke again that truthful Ancient of the Sea:
"Cease, son of Atreus, weeping so long, so bitterly.
For never a whit will it profit.   Bethink thee rather how
Thou mayst return most quickly to thine own country now.
Thou shalt find Aegisthus living, or Orestes shall forestall
Thy coming, maybe, and slay him—thou shalt come for his funeral."
So he spoke; and within me the proud and passionate heart
Was gladdened again a little, despite its sorrow's smart,
And the words came winging from me—"Yet tell me one thing more.
Who was that third, held living on the boundless waters' shore?"
And then at once he answered—"The lord of Ithaca,
Laertes' son.   I saw him, held in an isle afar,
And fast he wept as he sat there, in the nymph Calypso's bower.
For there she keeps him bound perforce—he has no power
To sail for home—no comrades, no well-oared ship has he,
To bear him where he would be, o'er the broad backs of the sea.
But as for thee, Menelaus, of Zeus beloved, thy doom
Is not in horse-rearing Argos to die and find thy tomb.
For thee at last to Elysium's plain the Gods shall send,
Where reigns fair-haired Rhădamanthys at the wide earth's utmost end,
And full of ease men dwell there.   There falls no flake of snow,
Nor rain, nor ever loudly the great storms rise to blow;
And there to cool men's faces there breathes from Ocean's breast
The music, shrilly piping, of winds from out the West.
For son-in-law to Zeus thou art, since Helen is thy bride."
So he spoke, then vanished beneath the tumbling tide.'

(IV, 351–570.)

*Such was the story of Menelaus; but meanwhile the Suitors were furious to
find that Telémachus had sailed, for they thought he had only gone into the
country.   At once Antínoüs took ship, with twenty armed companions, to waylay
his return between Samos and Ithaca.   Penelope, hearing of her son's voyage
and danger, was in despair; but Athene comforted her in a dream.   And now*

the Gods again met in council and again Athene complained to Zeus that Odysseus still lay prisoned in Calypso's isle, while an ambush was laid to murder his son. Then Zeus sent Hermes to bid Calypso set the hero free.

The Message of Hermes to Calypso

Then hearkened the Argus-slayer, Hermes the Heavenly Guide,
And swiftly his shapely sandals upon his feet he tied—
His sandals of gold, eternal, that over the salt sea-flow
Bear him, and over the boundless earth, as fleet as the winds that blow.
And he took his wand, wherewith he charms the eyes of men—
Whomever he will—and from slumber awakens them again.
So, wand in hand, did the mighty slayer of Argus fly
And, passing across Piéria, to sea from the upper sky
He swooped; then over the rollers like a gull pursued his way,
That wets, as it chases the fishes, its pinions in the spray
Above the dread abysses of the waters none may reap:
So sped Hermes onward, o'er the myriad-rolling deep.
But when at last he reached that isle at earth's far end,
Up from the purple ocean he turned him to ascend
Landward, until he came to that mighty cavern where
The lovely-tressed Calypso dwelt—and found her there.
High on the hearth a great fire blazed; and sweet the scent
Of burning juniper, with cloven cedar blent,
Breathed through the isle; and lovely her voice from the cavern rang,
While with a golden shuttle she wove her web and sang.
But thickly about her cave grew many a fair green tree—
The alder, and the aspen, and the cypress' fragrancy—
Wherein there nested many a bird of spreading wing,
Many an owl and falcon, and sea-crows chattering
That go about their business in the waters of the deep.
Round that hollow cavern's mouth a vine did creep
In the fulness of its glory, where many a cluster clung:
And close by one another out of the ground there sprung
Four runnels of white water, each flowing a different way
Where meadows soft with parsley, soft with violets lay.
So lovely a spot it was, that even a God whose gaze
Fell there, might stand to behold it in gladness and amaze.
Long looked the Argus-slayer on the beauty of the place;
But when he had gazed his fill, and wondered at its grace,
Into the spacious cave he passed—nor strange his guise
To the noble Goddess Calypso, soon as she met his eyes.
For always the Immortals easily can tell
The faces of one another, though sundered far they dwell.

But Hermes found not beside her Odysseus the great of heart;
For now he sat, as ever, and grieved on the shore apart,
Wringing his soul in anguish with many a tear and groan.
But the noble Goddess Calypso set a bright-glittering throne
For Hermes, then she asked him—'What, Hermes, brings thee here,
God of the Golden Wand—an honoured guest, and dear?
Rarely thou comest.   Speak thy mind.   I would do thy will,
If 'tis a thing that *can* be done, a wish that I *can* fulfil.'
So saying, there before him she set a table spread
With ambrosia, and mixed him a draught of nectar red.
Then the Herald, the Argus-slayer, feasted as she bade;
But when with eating and drinking at length his heart was stayed,
Thus he answered Calypso—'What it is brings me here?
As a God to a God, my answer—as thou bidst me—shall be clear.
It was Zeus that sent me hither—and by no will of mine;
For who would choose to travel such boundless leagues of brine,
By his own wish?   No city is here, of human homes,
Where men bring offerings to the Gods, and goodly hecatombs.
But what the Aegis-wielder's will shall once ordain—
No other God may avoid it, no God may make it vain.
He says that here thou keepest the unhappiest of all
The heroes that once battled about King Priam's wall
Nine years and, in the tenth, sacked it with sword and fire;
Yet, as they turned them homeward, they roused Athene's ire,
So that she sent upon them a storm and a raging sea.
This man—so Zeus hath ordered—send hence with all speed may be,
For he was not born to perish far off from home and kin;
It is doomed he should see again those that he loves, and win
Back to his high-built hall, to his native land, at last.'
    Then through the noble Goddess, as she heard, a shudder passed,
And from her lips in answer the swift words winging sped:
'Ye are harsh, ye are passing jealous, ye Gods!—if to her bed
A Goddess takes a mortal man, and hides it not,
But makes him her own dear husband, ye grudge her happy lot.
When Dawn the rosy-fingered to Orion gave her love,
Ye grudged that too, ye Gods, at your ease in Heaven above—
Him Artemis the maiden, Queen of the Golden Throne,
Slew in Ortygia's island, by her painless shafts o'erthrown.
And when fair-tressed Demeter obeyed her passionate heart
And lay in love with Iásion, in a thrice-ploughed field apart,
Like fate was hers—ere long the tidings of it came
To Zeus, and He smote her lover with the lightning's white-hot flame.
Now me in my turn ye envy, ye Gods, that I should keep
A mortal man, though I saved him, alone, from out the deep

117

Astride the keel of his galley, that Zeus had split in twain
With the white glare of His lightning amid the wine-dark main.
All of his noble comrades had died, with none to save,
And alone he drifted hither, the sport of wind and wave.
I loved him, and I cherished—I dreamed that it might be
I should make him ageless and deathless for evermore with me.
But since what Aegis-wielding Zeus shall once ordain,
No other God may avoid it, no other God make vain,
Hence with him—if Zeus sends him, and hath commanded so—
Across the barren breakers!   I cannot make him go—
I have no well-oared galleys, no mariners are mine
To bear him on his journey o'er the long backs of the brine;
Yet I will counsel him kindly, and hide the truth no more,
That so he may come, at last, safe to his native shore.'
Then the Herald, the Argus-slayer, replied—'Send him away,
And tempt not Zeus to anger, lest He turn on *thee* one day.'

So the mighty Argus-slayer departed, with that word;
But the queenly Nymph, Calypso, now that she had heard
The will of Zeus, went forth and found beside the sea
The noble Odysseus, sitting with eyes that ceaselessly
O'erflowed with tears—such longing to see his native shore
Wasted for him life's sweetness; for the Nymph pleased him no more.
Each night, indeed, beside her in her hollow cave he slept
Perforce—by *her* will, not by his—but daylong wept,
Sitting among the boulders on the borders of the deep.
Staring across the waters that never man may reap,
He wrung his soul with sighing, with tears in anguish shed.
Beside him the noble Goddess came now and stood and said:
'Unhappy man, I pray thee, weep not for ever apart,
Wasting thy life.   For homeward I will send thee with all my heart.
Come now, rise up and hew thee tall timber, and prepare
With the edge of the bronze a broad-beamed raft, and fasten there
A deck above, to take thee across the misty tide.
Water, and bread, and good red wine I will provide,
To cheer thee and stay thy hunger; and bring thee too, with these,
Raiment to wear; and send thee, astern, a favouring breeze.
So shalt thou come, unscathed, back to thy home again,
If so indeed the Immortals in boundless Heaven ordain—
For mightier They than I am, alike to know and do.'
At that the noble Odysseus shuddered through and through
His steadfast heart—with words swift-winging he began:
'Ah Goddess, within thy mind must lurk some deeper plan,
Not my return!—if thou sendst me across the sea's abyss
On a mere raft!—so grisly and grim a sea as this,

Where even swift ships sail not, whose glad sails Zeus doth fill!
To no raft will I trust me, against thy secret will—
Unless thou canst bring thee, Goddess, to swear a great oath to me
Not to contrive against me some new calamity.'
At that the noble Goddess, Calypso, gave a smile
And with her hand caressed him, and said—'Ah, deep in guile
Thou art; not barren-witted! What a thing, now, hast thou said!
But be the Earth my witness, and broad Heaven overhead,
And that down-plunging stream of Styx—the mightiest
And most dread oath there can be, for the lips of all the Blest—
That surely I will not fashion sorrows for thee anew.
I wish thee well; and the counsel that I give thee shall be true
As if for myself I planned it, in straits as sore as thine.
Not evil is my spirit, nor is this heart of mine
Of iron within my bosom, but pitiful indeed.'
Thus spoke the noble Goddess; then home again with speed
She turned, and Odysseus followed. So to her deep cave's door
The Goddess and the mortal together came once more
And, in the seat whence Hermes had lately risen, there
Odysseus sat, and Calypso laid before him fare—
Both meat and drink—such as mortals eat; then face to face
Before the godlike hero the Goddess took her place,
And her handmaids brought ambrosia, and nectar poured;
Then both put forth their hands to the banquet on the board.
But when they two had taken their fill of food and wine,
Then spoke again to Odysseus Calypso the divine:
'Thou subtle Odysseus, seed of Zeus, Laertes' son,
Art thou so eager, truly, at once now to have done
And hasten back to thy own dear home! Yet fare thee well!
What sorrows lie in store for thee, could thy heart tell,
Or ever thou beholdest thy native land again,
Here in my house, beside me, rather thou wouldst remain,
And win a life eternal, however sore thou pray
To see this wife thou longest for, day after day.
For indeed I cannot think it, that any worse I seem
In form than she, or in beauty—for how should a mortal dream
To challenge an Immortal in face or beauty's pride?'
Then to her Odysseus of the many wiles replied:
'Dread Goddess, be not angry. Well it is known to me,
That less in loveliness the wise Penelope
Is than thyself, and meaner in stature to behold—
For human is she; but thou, a Goddess that grows not old.
Yet, even so, day after day, I crave and yearn
For the sight of home again and the day of my return.

And if some God shall break me, far out on the wine-dark wave,
Why, then my heart must bear it, with the patience of the brave.
Many a toil and trouble, by sea, in fields of war,
I have endured.   This also I will bear, as those I bore.'
    But now the sun was setting and darkness closed the day;
Into the inmost cavern together they took their way
And there in each other's arms in the joy of love they lay.
But when the rosy-fingered Dawn once more awoke,
Quickly Odysseus clad him in his tunic and his cloak;
And Calypso too arrayed her, in a long robe of white,
Graceful and finely woven, and round her waist drew tight
Her lovely golden girdle, and set on her head a veil;
Then for the noble Odysseus she planned how he might sail.
First she brought him a mighty axe, with double blade
Of bronze, firm-set on a handle of olive deftly made;
Next she gave him a polished adze; then at her call
To the island's end he followed, where many a tree grew tall,
The alder, and the aspen, and fir-trees heaven-high,
That would swim light—so long they had stood there dead and dry.
Then the noble Goddess Calypso turned home again; but he
Set him to fell the timber and his work went speedily.
Twenty he felled, and trimmed their boughs with the axe away,
And smoothed them all with the adze, till true to the line they lay.
And now the noble Calypso brought augers, and each beam
He bored, and with peg and dowel he made fast every seam.
Broad as the hull of a freighter by a cunning shipwright planned—
No less—the raft of Odysseus grew up beneath his hand.

(V, 43–251.)

*In four days Odysseus had finished his boat.   Calypso brought cloth for his
sail and new raiment for his body; gave him corn, wine, and water; and sent
him on his way with a favouring gale.*

The Sailing of Odysseus from Ogygia

    So then the noble Odysseus with a fair wind off shore
Gladly set sail and, sitting, guided the steering-oar
With all his skill; no slumber could make his eyes forget
Their steadfast watch on the Pleiads, and Boötes slow to set,
And the Bear—or 'the Wain' some call her—that stirs not from her place,
But wheeling round, to the hunter, Orion, keeps her face,
And in the baths of Ocean, alone, can never share.
For the noble Goddess Calypso had bid him keep the Bear

Still, as he sailed, to leftward.   Thus, then, his boat was borne
Seventeen days o'er the surges; but on the eighteenth morn
The nearest shadowy mountains of Phaeacia rose revealed—
Far off o'er the gloomy rollers the land loomed like a shield.

But now at last, returning from Ethiopia,
The Lord Earth-shaker spied him across the waves afar,
From the Solýmian mountains; and seeing him sail the sea,
With shaken head he muttered to his own heart angrily:
'What now!   Past doubt, as I lingered in the Ethiopian land,
The Gods have changed their counsel, from what before they planned
Should be the doom of Odysseus.   He nears the Phaeacian shore,
Where for his chain of sorrows fate holds an end in store.
But still I trust to hound him far on the road of woe.'
So saying, he gathered his stormrack and roused his blasts to blow
From the four winds; trident in hand, he stirred the swell,
Shrouding in mist both earth and sea; and gloom from Heaven fell.
The East wind clashed together with South and stormy West,
And the North wind swooped from Heaven, rolling a vast wave-crest.
Then the knees of Odysseus faltered, and his heart began to quake,
And, with a shudder, thus to his own great soul he spake:
'Ah, bitter!   What end awaits me now?   Indeed I dread
Only too full of truth were the words the Goddess said—
That I must fill my measure of sorrows on the sea,
Or ever I came to my country.   Now all those things shall be:
So terrible a cloudrack throughout the width of sky
Zeus gathers, and heaves the surges, while all His stormwinds cry
From the four ends of Heaven.   Sure stands my utter doom.
Ah thrice and four times happy the Greeks that found a tomb,
Fighting for the Atrīdae, on the great Trojan Plain!
Would that I too had died there!   Would I had found my bane,
When the serried ranks of the Trojans thickly against me sped
Their brazen spears, as we battled above Achilles dead!
Then had the Argives honoured my burial and my fame:
But now has Fate ordained me a wretch's death of shame.'
Scarce had he ceased, when upon him a great wave's plunging swell
Crashed, and his craft spun whirling round—far overboard he fell.
Out of his hand the helm was hurled; then that grim blast
Of winds together battling in sunder snapped the mast,
Flinging sail and yardarm far out across the main.
Long was he whelmed beneath the surf; long, ere he rose again,
Back to the light, from under the rush of the weltering wave,
Dragged down by the weight of the garments divine Calypso gave;
But at last he rose, outspewing the brine that from his head
Poured streaming down.   And yet, battered and buffeted,

Still he did not forget his raft; but through the spray
Plunging he seized and sat thereon, still holding death at bay,
Though ever the racing rollers swept it from side to side.
As when the North wind tosses o'er the plains in autumntide
The thistlestalks whose clusters close-balled together cling,
So the stormwinds whirled it through the surges, shuddering.
Now the East wind tossed it to the West wind to pursue,
Now the South wind flung it to the North to chase anew.

(v, 269–332.)

*In his peril the sea-goddess Leucóthea took pity on Odysseus and gave him
her magic veil. And after Poseidon had departed to Aegae, Athene calmed
the winds. So on the third day Odysseus reached a river-mouth and lay down
in a thicket to sleep. Then Athene appeared in a dream to Nausícaä, princess
of Phaeacia, taking the likeness of a girl she knew, and moved her to go down
to the sea to wash her bridal-linen.*

Nausícaä

So flashing-eyed Athene spoke, and went her way
To Olympus, where stands fast the home of the Gods, men say,
For ever, and no rain falls there, and never wind blows loud,
Nor drifts the snow; but above it, clear and without a cloud,
Stretches the sky, and around it a pure white radiance plays;
There dwell the blest Immortals, rejoicing all their days,
And thither, her counsel given, once more Athene sped:
But now came bright-throned Morning and lightly slumber fled
From Alcínoüs' fair-robed daughter. Yet still her vision seemed
Strange; and she sought her parents to tell them what she dreamed.
Hurrying through the palace she found them still within,
Both her noble sire and her mother—for her mother sat to spin
Sea-purple yarn with her women, by the fireside in the hall;
And she found her father going forth, at the proud Phaeacians' call,
To the council of his chieftains. Then coming very near
Nausícaä said to her father, 'Wilt give me, father dear,
That I may go down to the river, a high and strong-wheeled wain,
To take the fair clothes that lie here soiled, and wash them clean again?
For when with our land's leaders thou sitst at the council-board,
Spotless should be the raiment upon the King their lord;
And five dear sons in this house there are, that call thee sire—
Two wedded, and three lusty lads—all these require
Linen white from the washing, whenever it may be
That they would go a-dancing. And all this falls on me.'

So, lady, at *thee* I wonder; and yet I am sore afraid
To clasp thy knees—with sorrow my spirit still is weighed;
I escaped but yesterday from the wine-dark deep at last,
Where wave and storm have tossed me these twenty long days past,
Since I left Ogygia's island.   God cast me here ashore—
Maybe, here too to suffer.   To hope my sorrows o'er
I dare not—nay, the Immortals, I doubt, ere that will bring
Much else to pass.   But since, after such suffering,
I find thee first, O Queen, have pity!   For save thee
In all thy land or city none else is known to me.
Show me the road to thy township, give me some shred to wear,
If ye have some wrap for the linen that hitherward ye bare.
And whatever thy heart desireth, by the Gods may thy will be done!
Husband and home may they grant thee, and love to make ye one—
Their noblest gift.   For nought better, nought dearer life can give
Than when at home together with hearts united live
Husband and wife—their concord by all their friends is blest;
It is bitter to those that hate them; but their own hearts know it best.'
Then the white-armed princess answered: 'It seems to me thou art
No evil-doer, stranger, nor yet a fool at heart.
But—since Zeus of Olympus to good men and to ill
Sends good or evil fortune, just as His wisdom will—
Bear up beneath thy sorrows; they come, sure, from His hand.
But now that thou art come hither to our city and our land,
Thou shalt not lack for raiment, nor any other thing
That a generous heart should give to a suppliant's suffering.
I will guide thee to our city; we dwellers in this place,
And the countryside about it, are Phaeacians by race;
And as for me, the father that begot me is the great
Alcínoüs, stay and pillar of our Phaeacian state.'
Then she cried to her fair-tressed handmaids—'Stand fast, girls!   Will ye
     flee
At the mere glimpse of a man?   Do ye deem him an enemy?
There is none born, nor shall be, that dares bring threat of spear
Against Phaeacia's marches—the Gods hold us too dear;
Too far mid the washing surges, here at earth's end alone,
We live, to all the traffic of other lands unknown.
'Tis but a hapless wanderer—that needs our care as friends.
All strangers and all beggars 'tis Zeus Himself that sends;
And even a little bounty can be a precious thing.
So quickly, girls, some food now—and drink for the stranger bring,
And bathe him, out of the wind, by the river's sheltering shore.'
Then they halted and called to each other to be afraid no more.

(VI, 41–211.)

125

Then Nausícaä bade her maidens bring clothes and oil in a golden flask for Odysseus. Withdrawing apart, he bathed and clothed himself; and Athene made him so handsome that the princess could not forbear to tell her maidens how gladly she would have such a husband.   Then, after they had given him food and drink, Nausícaä guided him behind her waggon to a poplar-grove outside the city; there she left him to find his way to the palace alone, for fear of the gossiping Phaeacians.   So there he waited and prayed to Athene, who heard him but did not reveal herself, for fear of angering her uncle Poseidon; yet as he went on towards the city, she cast about him a veil of mist; and by the gate she herself met him, disguised as a young girl with a pitcher.   Thence she led him to the palace of Alcínoüs, splendid with doors of gold and walls of bronze, amid orchards bearing fruit from year's end to year's end.   Entering the hall, Odysseus threw himself in supplication, as Nausícaä and Athene had bidden him, at the knees of Queen Arēte and begged her for a passage home. Alcínoüs called the stranger to feast beside him and promised him safe return. Arēte now recognized the clothes Odysseus was wearing; and he told how her daughter Nausícaä had saved him.

Next day Alcínoüs called an assembly and proposed that a ship be chosen to take their guest to his native land.   The ship was launched and then the King invited his lords and Odysseus to a farewell banquet.

Odysseus and Demódocus

But now a herald, leading the bard beloved, drew near;
For indeed the Muse had given to him she held most dear
Both good and ill—his sight she took, but for his own
Gave him sweet poesy.   On a silver-studded throne
The herald Pontónoüs set him, where a column towered high
In the banquet's midst; and hung his clear-toned harp near by,
Guiding the blind man's fingers to find it overhead;
And put a fair table before him, with a basket full of bread
And a cup of wine for drinking, whenever his heart might will.
So the feasters fell to the banquet; but when they had their fill
Of meat and drink, the Muse stirred up the bard to raise
A chant of the glories of heroes, out of that lay whose praise
Rose then as high as Heaven—the strife of Pēleus' son,
And Odysseus, son of Laertes, at the Gods' rich feast begun,
With words whereat men trembled; yet Agamemnon the king
Rejoiced to see the noblest of Achaea quarrelling.
For thus in goodly Pytho Apollo had foretold
Long since, when the son of Atreus had crossed his stone threshold
To question of the future, in the days when first there rolled

Woe's wave on Greek and Trojan, at Zeus the all-mighty's word.
'So sang the glorious minstrel.   But as Odysseus heard,
His great hands plucked his mantle above his noble head,
Burying deep his face in its folds of purple-red,
In shame, lest the Phaeacians should see him as he wept.
Each time that godlike singer ceased, his fingers swept
His tears away, and his mantle back from his brow he drew,
And from his double-handled cup poured wine to the Gods anew;
But each time that the minstrel struck up his song again,
As the lords of Phaeacia bade him, delighting in his strain,
Afresh then wept Odysseus, his head veiled in his cloak.
And yet, of all the Phaeacians, none marked how his sorrow woke—
Only, sitting beside him, Alcínoüs saw him weep,
And noted the grief that shook him, and heard him groaning deep.

(VIII, 62–95.)

*After the feast Alcínoüs called the Phaeacians to let the stranger see their
skill as athletes.   Some of the young men challenged Odysseus to show his own
powers and then, when he refused, grew insolent; until he was stung into hurling
a great stone quoit far further than any man there.   Next Alcínoüs summoned
a band of his young dancers to perform, while Demódocus chanted how Ares
beguiled Aphrodite, but the all-seeing Sun betrayed their love to her husband
Hephaestus, who set a magic net to catch the lovers together.   In it they were
entangled and their shame displayed before the laughter of the Immortal Gods.
Not till Poseidon interceded, would Hephaestus let them go.*

*Odysseus praised warmly the grace of the Phaeacian dancing; and the
flattered king moved his fellow-princes to load their guest with rich gifts in
return.   After sunset Odysseus bade farewell to Nausícaä and was feasted anew
by her father.   Again Demódocus the minstrel was led in; and Odysseus,
sending a portion from his own plate, prayed him to sing the lay of the Wooden
Horse.   So Demódocus sang how the Achaeans built it and hid in it their bravest
heroes, then feigned to sail away; and how the Trojans in their blindness dragged
it into the city and Troy fell, while Odysseus and Menelaus rushed to the house
of Helen's husband Deïphobus.   There, after the fiercest of all his battles, by
the grace of Athene Odysseus prevailed.   Again, as he listened, Odysseus
wept—as a woman weeps above her husband slain; and again Alcínoüs noticed.
Bidding the minstrel cease, he asked the stranger to tell his name and story.
So Odysseus began his tale: 'I am Odysseus, son of Laertes, from Ithaca.
After leaving Troy, the wind bore me to the Ciconian city of Ismărus, which I
sacked.   But my men in their folly would not withdraw in time; so help came
to the Cícones from inland and they drove us to our ships.   For two days Zeus
sent a fearful tempest.   Then it fell and I should have reached my home, but
north wind and current drove me past Cythēra southward across the sea.'*

'For nine days then we were driven by the tempest's ruinous blast
Over the deep of the fishes; and reached on the tenth, at last,
The land of the Lotus-eaters—on the fruit of a flower they feed.
Ashore we went, and water we drew there for our need;
And then by our swift galleys my comrades sat to dine.
But when we all had taken our fill of flesh and wine,
I chose two men, with a herald, and sent them forth to see
What manner of mortal men within that land might be.
Now hardly had they departed on the errand they were sent,
Ere they met with the Lotus-eaters, that (with no ill intent
To seek their ruin) yet gave them of the Lotus-fruit to eat.
But they—when their lips had tasted that fruit as honey sweet,
They lost all will to return, or bring me word again;
There with the Lotus-eaters they craved but to remain,
Gorging upon the Lotus, forgetting their native shore.
So by main force to our galleys I haled them, weeping sore,
And under the rowers' benches, fast bound, I had them laid;
Then the rest of my trusty comrades, fast as they might, I bade
Embark, lest others, likewise, should eat and forget their home;
Swiftly they manned their benches and once more into foam,
With oars in order sweeping, they lashed the rollers gray.
   'So, with hearts still heavy, we sailed upon our way;
And we came to the land of Cyclōpes, lawless and arrogant,
That, leaving all to the deathless Gods, toil not to sow nor plant.
For there without any labour, unploughed, unsown, there spring
Wheat for them, and barley, and great grapes clustering,
Swelled by the rain of Heaven, from whence their wine shall flow.
But never their folk for council meets, nothing of law they know;
High in the tops of the mountains, in hollow caves alone,
They dwell with their wives and children, and each is a law to his own;
But never one to another gives either thought or care.
Now in this land of Cyclōpes a haven lies, and there
Before it a lowly island, not near, nor very far,
Deep-forested.   Therein wild goats past numbering are.
For never a track leads thither, to scare the beasts of the wood;
No hunter comes there, seeking his hardy livelihood
Amid the depths of the forest and the high tops of the hills;
No shepherd feeds his sheep there, his fields no tiller tills.
Unsown, unploughed for ever, bereft of man it lies,
Nourishing nought, save only its goats with their bleating cries.
For the Cyclōpes have no ships, with cheeks vermilion-red,
No craftsmen to make them galleys, wherewith they might have sped

To seek their needs in cities, far off where mortals dwell,
As mariners do, that traffic across the wide sea-swell.
With such they might have made that isle as a garden fair,
For ill it is *not*—all things in their season it might bear.
Meadows it has, low-lying beside the grey sea-flow,
Well-watered, soft with grasses; and in it vines would grow,
Unfailing; and easy its ploughland, and rich the harvest-home
Would be with each new autumn; for fat indeed its loam.
And fair no less is its haven.   A man need not make fast
His galley with stern-cables, or anchor-stones out-cast;
Enough to run her keel ashore, and so remain
Until his heart would be sailing and winds blow fair again.
And there at the head of the harbour, from a cave, there gushes out
A spring of sparkling water, with poplars round about.
Thither some God was, sure, our guide—we came ashore
Through the mirk night, and nothing our eyes could see before;
So thickly the sea-mist hid our ships, and in the height
Of Heaven the moon was lost in cloud, nor gave us light;
So none of us marked that island, none saw upon its strand
The league-long rollers breaking, till our keels had touched the sand.
Then ashore we ran our galleys and furled the sails in each
And ourselves leapt out and landed, there on the foaming beach,
And laid our limbs to slumber, awaiting radiant Dawn.
   'But when appeared the early light of rosy-fingered Morn,
Here and there we wandered, wondering at the isle,
And the Aegis-bearer's daughters, the Nymphs, drove forth the while
The hill-goats from their coverts, to make my men good cheer.
So we all fetched from our galleys curved bow or long-necked spear
And formed three bands of hunters and let our missiles fly;
Then God gave us good hunting.   For there twelve ships had I,
And each had nine goats for its portion; but ten they gave to me.
All the day long, till sunset, we sat there, merrily
Feasting on flesh in plenty and sweet wine at our will.
(For we *had* red wine remaining in the holds of our galleys still,
From the great store of wine-jars we filled and bore away
When we made the sacred city of the Cícones our prey.)
And towards the land of Cyclōpes, quite near across the deep,
We gazed, with its smoking homesteads, its bleat of goats and sheep.
Then, when the sun descended and darkness fell once more,
Again we turned to slumber by the breakers on the shore.
   'But when the Dawn returned, with fingers rosy-red,
I gathered my fellows round me and thus to them I said:
"The rest of you, good comrades, shall wait here my return,
But with my own ship and companions I will sail across to learn

129

What manner of people dwell there, and what their ways may be—
Are they but wild and wanton, dealing unrighteously,
Or kindly unto strangers, with the fear of God in mind?"
With that I climbed my galley and bade my men behind
Follow, and loose her moorings.   Swift were all to obey—
Manning her benches, with their oars they smote the rollers grey.
Soon we had reached the mainland; and where it met the surge,
We caught sight of a cavern, upon its very verge,
Lofty, embowered in bay-trees, with folds for many sheep
And goats; in front was a courtyard, walled round with stones set deep,
With many a lofty pine-tree, and oaks to heaven grown.
And there dwelt a man of monstrous bulk, that all alone
Pastured his flocks in the distance; for dealings none had he
With others, but lived aloof in his iniquity.
Prodigious indeed was the monster—the semblance that he had
Was not like men that live by bread, but some peak forest-clad
That towers mid the lofty mountains, sheer, lonely, and apart.
Then all the rest I ordered, of the comrades dear to my heart,
To stay and guard our galley; but, to share my quest,
I chose out twelve companions—my bravest and my best—
And went; and with me a goatskin of dark, sweet wine I bore,
That Maron, son of Euanthes, had given me long before—
The priest of Apollo, guardian God of Ismărus, was he,
And him we had saved, with wife and child, in piety,
Because he had his dwelling within the holy wood
Sacred to Phoebus Apollo.   He gave me, in gratitude,
Most glorious gifts—seven talents of gold by the craftsman wrought,
And a mixing-bowl, pure silver; and then this wine he brought—
Twelve jars—pure, unmixed vintage—that only his own hand drew,
A drink divine.   About it not even his household knew—
Woman nor man—save himself, and his wife, and one housekeeper;
But when they drank of that sweet red wine, one cupful they would stir
With twenty measures of water; and the bowl wherein it lay
Breathed forth a fragrance of heaven—hard *then* to turn away!
With this I filled a mighty skin, and for the road
With food I stuffed a wallet; for my strong heart seemed to bode
That soon we should be dealing with a man of giant might,
A savage, a contemner of justice and of right.
Quickly then to the cave we came, but found it still
Empty—its lord was feeding his fat flocks on the hill.
So we passed on into the cavern, gazing at all it hid:
There were baskets crammed with cheeses and pens with many a kid,
Many a lamb, close-crowded—yet each in a separate stall,
The first-born, and the later, and the youngest-born of all:

And his milk-vessels were brimming—both bowl and pail—with whey. Homer:
Then eagerly my companions began to urge and pray Odyssey
That first we should take of the cheeses, then drive fast from their pens
Lambs and kids to our galley, and hurry seaward thence.
Yet I would not (well, had I listened!), so much I longed to see
Himself—and what gifts he might give us, in hospitality.
But little joy for my comrades his coming was to bring.
  'So there a fire we kindled and, after offering
To the Gods some of his cheeses, we helped ourselves and sate,
Till he came with his flocks before him, bearing a mighty weight
Of dry faggots to light him at his suppertime within.
He cast them down in the cavern, that it thundered with the din
And all of us fled in terror to the inmost nooks of the rock;
But into the grotto's vastness he drove his fatted flock,
As many as needed milking; leaving the males alone,
Both rams and goats, in the great courtyard.   Then up he heaved a stone
Of boundless bulk, that as door to the cavern's mouth he laid:
Not two and twenty waggons, four-wheeled and stoutly made,
Could have shifted that huge boulder, with its lofty sides and steep.
So down he sat, and milked his bleating goats and sheep
In order, and under each mother he set her young to feed.
Half the white milk he curdled, and gathered it with speed
In baskets of woven wicker; and half in pails he stood,
Leaving it waiting ready to be his evening's food.
But when this toil was finished that he plied so busily,
He lit his fire, and saw us, and called: "Who then are ye,
Strangers?   Whence come ye sailing across the wet sea-ways?
Are ye traders?   Or random rovers, that live to risk your days
Wandering across the surges, to others bringing bale?"
So he spoke; but within us our very hearts did fail
For dread of that deep voice, that body's monstrousness.
Notwithstanding I answered: "We come by weather's stress
Blown off our course, Achaeans, from Ilios bound for home.
For winds from all quarters whirled us across the wastes of foam,
Not by the path we purposed, not by the way we sought—
Doubtless some hidden counsel of Zeus herein was wrought.
Proudly we serve, as sovran, Agamemnon, Atreus' son;
For widest under Heaven is the fame that he hath won,
So mighty a city he plundered, so vast a host he gave
To death.   But, driven hither, we clasp thy knees and crave
Thy welcome—thy gifts, it may be—such gifts as guests may find.
Great sir, we beg thy succour, and pray thee hold in mind
The fear of Zeus.   For, ever, a guest is sanctified—
With guests and suppliants, ever, doth the God of guests abide."

So I said; but he answered, with heart that knew not ruth:
"Stranger, thou art but a fool, or come from far, in truth,
To bid *me* dread the Immortals, or fear lest their wrath should fall.
For we Cyclōpes reck not of the blessed Gods at all,
Nor of Zeus the Aegis-wielder.   For mightier are we.
No heed of Zeus or His anger shall weigh one whit with me
To spare thee or thy comrades, if my heart wills otherwise.
But the stout ship that ye sailed in—tell me, now, where she lies—
Far away have ye left her, at the edge of the land?   Or near?"
So he asked to entrap me.   But I, through many a year,
Had learnt too much to be cozened; I answered with cunning speech:
"Poseidon, the great Earth-shaker, upon the rocky beach
Shattered our ship.   For the sea-wind cast us against a cape
Here upon thy borders.   Myself I found escape
From that sheer pit of destruction, with these men of my crew."
So I spoke; then he answered not, that heart that no pity knew,
But leaping up he snatched at my comrades standing round,
And two he seized, like puppies, and dashed against the ground,
So that the brains flowed from them and stained the earth beneath.
Then joint from joint, for his supper, he hewed them, and with his teeth,
Like to a lion of the mountains, their limbs he turned to tear—
Not flesh, not bones, not marrow, not entrails did he spare.
With a cry at that deed of horror, to Zeus in our distress
We raised our hands; yet our hearts were heavy with helplessness.
But when with the flesh of men the Cyclops now had filled
His mighty maw and, after, with the unmixed milk he swilled,
Down mid his flocks in the cavern he laid him, stretched out straight.
Then with my own stout heart awhile I held debate,
Whether to plunge the trenchant blade beside my thigh
Deep in his chest, where midriff holds liver, creeping nigh
And feeling with my fingers to find the place—and yet
An afterthought withheld me.   For then we had been beset
With a sheer gulf of destruction, unable evermore
To shift the giant boulder that closed his cavern-door.
Therefore, deeply groaning, we waited glorious Dawn.
    'But when there shone forth early the rosy-fingered Morn,
The flame on his hearth he kindled and milked in order due
His goodly flocks, and beneath their dams he set the young anew;
Next, when his busy toil was done, again he cast
His hands on two of my comrades and with them broke his fast;
Then turned his fat flocks to pasture, lifting that ponderous door
Lightly aloft from the cavern's mouth.   And then once more
He laid it back, as closely as a quiver's lid could fall.
So to the hills again, with many a whistling call,

He drove his fatted flocks, while I brooded secretly

Plans for revenge—might Athene but grant that prayer to me.
Then to my heart this counsel, beyond the rest, seemed good.
There lay beside a sheepfold a club of olive-wood,
Still green, by the Cyclops hewn and left, to use when dry.
To us, as we looked upon it, it seemed as thick and high
As is the mast of some black ship with twenty oars,
Some broad-beamed merchant-vessel that plies to far-off shores.
Such, in length and thickness, its trunk was; from its top
I cut, maybe, a fathom, and bade my comrades lop
And smoothe it; and while they smoothed it, I set myself to hew
Its point, and with bright fire charred it, till black and hard it grew.
Carefully then I hid it, heaping it with dung
That everywhere through the cavern in mighty mounds lay flung.
But the rest of my companions I bade draw lots to see
Which of them should venture to lift that beam with me
And twist it round in his eyeball, while fast he lay asleep.
Then the lots fell on the very men I wished to keep—
Four of them; I myself made up the tale to five.
So evening came, and homeward we heard the monster drive
His fleecy flocks; but *now* within the cave he brought
All, leaving none in the courtyard (whether some hidden thought
Moved him, or God so willed it); then up he heaved anew
That rock, and closed the cavern, and each bleating goat and ewe
He milked in order, laying her young beneath each one.
But when at last the toil of his hurrying hands was done,
Seizing two more of my comrades he set himself to sup.
Then in front of the Cyclops I took my stand, a cup
Of dark-red wine in my hands, and with these words began:
"Come now, taste wine, O Cyclops, after the flesh of man.
Now thou canst know what drink divine we carried in our keel.
To offer thee I brought it, in hope thy heart might feel
Some pity, and send us homeward. In truth, too much to bear
Thy fury is—hard heart, what man on earth shall dare
To visit thee hereafter? Thou hast used *us* so ill!"
He took the cup and drained it and felt strange rapture thrill
His soul from that sweet liquor; then begged again for wine—
"Pour me yet more, of thy goodness. And say—what name is thine?
Quickly, that I may give thee a gift thou shalt hold dear.
To us Cyclōpes also the kindly earth each year
Yields wine from mighty clusters that the rain of Zeus makes grow;
But from some fount of nectar and ambrosia *this* might flow!"
So he; and with fire-red wine again I filled his bowl.
Thrice did I fill and bring it, thrice with infatuate soul

133

He drank; but when from the wine-cup the Cyclops' wits grew dim,
Then with words like honey once more I spoke to him:
"My glorious name thou askest, O Cyclops.   Verily
I will tell it; but thou—forget not the gift thou hast promised me.
The name I bear is Noman.   And by that name alone
To my father and my mother and my comrades am I known."
So I said; and he answered, with heart where no pity passed—
"Then, after all his comrades, I will eat Noman the last.
The rest shall die before him.   This is the gift I grant."
Then back he leaned—he fell—he lay, great neck aslant,
Sprawling with face turned upward.   And sleep, that masters all,
Seized him, while from his jaws wine dribbled, and withal,
As he spewed with his load of liquor, gobbets of human meat.
But deep within the embers I thrust our pole to heat
And shouted to my comrades not now to flinch or fear.
Then, as the stake of olive within the fire was near
To burst in flame, and grimly glowed, though green its wood,
Out of the hearth I brought it, while round my comrades stood.
Then truly God inspired us and dauntless grew our mood.
For gripping the bole of the olive, they plunged deep in his eye
Its point; and myself the while, with all my weight, on high
Twisted.   As when a shipwright bores a hole within
The timbers of a galley—beneath, his fellows spin
His drill, as they haul unceasing at the band that makes it twirl;
So did we make our pole with its red-hot point to whirl
Deep in his eye, till a bloodstream came spurting round its glow,
And the fierce heat singed his eyebrow, and either lid below,
While the eyeball burned and, under, its roots a crackling made.
As when, with a mighty hissing, an adze or a great axe-blade
In a bath of icy water by the blacksmith's hand is set,
To temper the steel, and toughen, to greater hardness yet;
So loud about the treetrunk hissed the Cyclops' eye,
And he gave, till the rock re-echoed, a wild and fearful cry.
In terror we darted from him; forth from his eye he tore
The timber, blood-bespattered, and hurled it far before
In frenzy, to all his fellows shrieking and roaring still,
That dwelt in their caverns round him, on many a windy hill.
But they, when they heard his clamour, gathered from every side,
And standing round his cavern, asked him for what he cried:
"What ails thee, Polyphemus, thus with thy shouts to break
The silence of night divine and keep us all awake?
Is some man driving thy flocks away, in spite of thee?
Or murdering thee thyself, by violence or treachery?"
Then the mighty Polyphemus from his cavern cried again—

"Nay, Noman's guile, my comrades, no violence, leaves me slain."
Then swiftly flew their answer—"If alone there in thy cave
None harms thee, from the sickness great Zeus sends, nought can save.
Go pray to our lord father, the Shaker of the Earth."
So saying they departed; and my heart laughed in its mirth,
So well my name had gulled them, my masterpiece of guile.
But in agony and anguish, groaning deep the while,
With groping arms he heaved that boulder from his door,
Then sat him down in the entry, with hands spread wide before,
Hoping to catch any straggler that stole out with his sheep.
So simple he seemed to think me.   But now I pondered deep
What were the wisest counsel, for my men and me to find
Escape from death; long I sat there, weaving in my mind
All my wiles and cunning, as one with life at stake.
For grim the risk.   At last, this plan seemed best to take:
There were rams in his flocks, well-nurtured, with thick fleece on their
       back,
Stalwart beasts and splendid, with wool of deepest black;
Now noiselessly together I lashed them, three by three,
Using the supple withies where slept in his savagery
That monster; so each man beneath three sheep would ride
And while the midmost bore him, another on each side
Defended him from peril.   But I myself took hold
Of one young ram, the finest—face upwards there I rolled
And deep within his noble fleece both hands I pressed
And clung, with all my endurance, beneath his shaggy breast.
Thus then we waited, groaning, the rise of glorious Dawn.
    'But when appeared the early light of rosy-fingered Morn,
Eager to reach their pasture, out rushed his rams again,
While the unmilked ewes stood bleating about their pens in pain,
With udders swelled to bursting.   Their master, though still deep
His anguish, as before him there paused each passing sheep,
Felt their backs with his fingers; yet his folly never found
Underneath their bellies my comrades lying bound.
So last there came to the entrance my own ram, moving slow
With the weight of his wool and me, that slyly lay below;
And I heard great Polyphemus, when he had searched it, say—
"Dear ram, why art thou coming out of the cave to-day
Hindmost of all?   Aforetime, 'twas not like *thee* to pass
After the sheep—nay, foremost, to crop the flowery grass
With great, long strides thou ledst them, and first to the riverside,
First wast thou to remember the fold at eventide;
Yet now thou comest rearmost!   Is sorrow in thy mind
For the lost eye of thy master, whom a scoundrel has left blind—

He and his sorry comrades—when wine had mastered me?
Nevertheless this Noman is not safe yet, maybe.
Ah, if thou couldst but share my thought, couldst thou find speech
To say where the wretch lies lurking, out of my mighty reach,
His skull I soon would splinter upon this floor—his brain
Should spatter round my cavern, and in my heart the pain
Be eased, that I have suffered from this Noman—nothing-worth!"
So saying, through the doorway he let the ram go forth.
But when we were come a little from cave and courtyard, then
I dropped from my ram's belly and turned to free my men.
Then many a fat and long-shanked sheep, with our best speed,
We headed towards our galley; and there with joy indeed
Our comrades saw us living—yet loud they wailed the slain.
But nodding my head, and frowning, I forced them to refrain,
Bidding all rise and hurry to drive our flock aboard
And launch on the salt-sea surges. Into the ship they poured
And, ranged upon her benches, they smote the grey sea-tide.
    'But when we were now as distant as voice could hail, I cried,
To sting the heart of the Cyclops with taunt and mockery—
"He was no such weakling, Cyclops, as he seemed to thee,
Whose men within thy cavern thy violence did devour.
And well was retribution to find thee in its hour,
Thou cruel heart, that by thy hearth wast not afraid
To eat thy guests. But Zeus, and the high Gods, have repaid."
So I spoke; but the Cyclops' wrath blazed fiercer still
And he hurled at us the summit torn from a towering hill.
Just ahead of our dark-blue prow it hit the sea
And under that crashing crag the deep swelled mightily
In one huge wave, that made our ship back shoreward roll
And swept her stern on the beaches. But seizing a mighty pole
I thrust her off and, nodding, to my companions signed
To row amain and snatch us from the doom that lay behind.
So to their oars they bent and heaved. But when, at last,
Twice as far as the first time, seaward our ship had passed,
Anew I hailed the Cyclops—but now on every side
With soft words of beseeching my companions cried:
"Rash heart, why must thou anger this savage man yet more?
But now he hurled a hilltop that swept us back to shore,
Till surely we thought our death was come. Had he but heard
Any among us utter sound, or whisper word,
He would have smashed together our heads and ship and all
With some great jagged fragment—so far his missiles fall!"
And yet not all their beseeching could curb my spirit's pride,
But again to Polyphemus angrily I cried:

"Cyclops, if hereafter any of mankind
Shall ask who was it gave thee that eye so foul and blind,
Say, 'By the sacker of cities, Odysseus, it was done,
Who has his home in Ithaca, Laertes' son.'"
So I said: but groaning the giant answered me:
"Alas, now there finds fulfilment an ancient prophecy.
For here there dwelt among us a mighty man and true,
Tēlemus, son of Eurўmus—of prophecy he knew
More than all men, and among us as prophet he grew old.
All that has now befallen me, his tongue foretold,
And that the hand of Odysseus one day should blind my sight.
But always I had expected some hero clothed with might,
Tall and noble of presence, to come at last—and lo!
A nobody, a puny dwarf, a feeble foe,
Hath mastered me with the winecup, then robbed me of my eye.
And yet come back, Odysseus!   Let me give thee gifts, and cry
Unto the great Earth-shaker to bring thee safe by sea.
For I am son of Poseidon, and my proud sire is he.
His hand—none else among Blessed Gods or mortal men—
Shall have the power, if he pleases, to heal my sight again."
And then in turn I answered: "Would God that thy life and breath
I could destroy, and send thee to haunt the House of Death,
As sure as not even Poseidon shall ever heal thine eye!"
But the Cyclops, with arms uplifted towards the starry sky,
Prayed to the great Earth-shaker—"O Thou that girdlest earth,
O dark-haired Lord Poseidon, if I am Thine by birth,
And Thou art proud of Thy fatherhood, then I implore
That Odysseus, sacker of cities, may see his home no more.
Or, if his fate must bring him to those he loves—to stand
Once more in his high-built palace, there in his native land,
Yet long be his voyage, and evil—perish his comrades all—
Let him find no ship but a stranger's, and sorrow in his hall."
Thus did he pray; and there heard him the God of the Raven Hair.
Then he seized a rock, far vaster yet, and through the air
He whirled and hurled it, straining his immeasurable strength—
Seaward it hurtled, missing our dark-prowed galley's length
Hardly at all—close grazing the oar we steered her by.
Then with that great rock falling the waters swelled on high
In a wave that washed us onward, far as the further shore,
Where waited my other gallant ships and, weeping sore,
My comrades sat in mourning for us that came no more.
So there we beached our galley and ran her up the sand,
And leapt ashore in the rollers that broke along the strand;
Then from our hold we landed the Cyclops' sheep, and fair

We dealt them round, for I wished no man to lack his share.
To me my valiant comrades, for my own portion, gave
That great ram; there on the beaches, beside the breaking wave,
To Zeus that darkens the Heavens, Almighty, Crŏnus' son,
I slew him and burnt his thigh-bones.   And yet that offering done
Zeus heeded not—He was planning how in the days to be
My good ships, my dear comrades, should perish utterly.'

(IX, 82–555.)

*Next Odysseus came to the floating island, walled with bronze, of Aeŏlus,
Warder of the Winds.   For a month he feasted Odysseus; then, for his homeward voyage, gave him all the winds shut in an oxhide bag, except the favouring
west.   But after nine days, in sight of Ithaca itself, Odysseus fell asleep; and
his comrades in their folly opened the bag, seeking treasure.   The winds burst
forth and blew them back to Aeŏlus, who would help no further a man so clearly
hated by the Gods.   In six days more they came to the nightless land of the
Laestrygonian giants.   The three men whom Odysseus sent ashore encountered
the daughter of King Antíphates, and then his Queen, huge as a mountain-crag.
She called to her husband, who devoured one on the spot; then the giant Laestrygonians rushing forth shattered with rocks the eleven ships in the harbour.
Odysseus alone had time to cut his cable and escape to sea.*

Circe

'So thence with heavy hearts we sailed the seas again,
Glad to escape destruction, but sad for our comrades slain,
Until we came at the last unto Aeaea's beach,
The isle of fair-tressed Circe, dread Goddess of human speech,
Sister to grim Aeëtes.   For both they had their birth
From Hēlios, who scatters His light across the earth;
But Perse was their mother, whom Océanus begot.
Landward we brought our galley, in silence, to a spot
That gave her sheltered moorings—some God was, sure, our guide—
And went ashore.   Two days there, two nights, did we abide,
Gnawing our hearts with sorrow and the labours we had borne.
But when once more a third time uprose the fair-tressed Morn,
I girt my keen sword round me and took a spear in hand
And climbed in haste a hilltop that looked across the land,
Hoping to see some tillage, or hear some voice of men.
So to that rugged vantage-point I clambered up—and then
From the far-flung earth before me I saw smoke, as I stood,
Curl up from the hall of Circe, through tangled brake and wood.
Then for a while I pondered and mused within my mind—
Now I had seen that flamelit smoke, should I seek what lay behind?

138

But, after long thought taken, it seemed the wiser way
To turn me back to seaward, where our galley lay,
And dine my men, and send them to seek what they could see.
But, as I neared our vessel, some God must have pitied me,
While there I wandered lonely; for right athwart my way
He made a mighty stag, with towering antlers, stray—
From feeding in the forest down to the riverside,
To drink, the beast was coming, parched with that hot noontide.
In the midst of his back I struck him, as out of the copse he drew,
Full on the spine; beyond it, the point of bronze came through,
And down with a scream he toppled, and breathed his life in the dust.
Hard upon his body I set my foot and thrust,
To free my spear; then laid it beside me upon the ground,
While I gathered withes of willow, and osiers, and wound
A pliant rope—a fathom's length—and tightly bound
The great beast's feet together.   Then towards our galley near
I went my way, supporting my footsteps with my spear
And, with my neck, the carcass.   For, with my one hand free,
He was more than I could shoulder—so huge a beast was he.
At last, where our ship was lying, I let my quarry fall
And standing beside my comrades I cheered them one and all—
"Come, though your hearts be heavy, we cannot pass away,
My friends, to the House of Hades before our destined day.
Up then!—while yet our galley holds store of food and drink,
Let us eat, and not let hunger thus make our spirits sink."
They heard and straight they hearkened; there by the barren sea
From over their heads they drew their cloaks and dazedly
Stared at my stag—so huge he was.   But when at last
They had satisfied their wonder, with washen hands they passed
To dress that noble banquet.   And so, till day was done,
On sweet wine we sat feasting and boundless venison.
    'But when the sun was sunken and darkness come once more,
Down to sleep we laid us by the breakers on the shore.
But soon as shone the Morning, with fingers rosy-red,
I gathered all my comrades round, and thus I said:
"Friends, since we know no longer which way eve's darkness lies,
Nor where the dawn—know neither where the sun doth rise
To light the world, nor where he sets—come, let us make
What plans we may.   Myself, I see no choice to take.
For when to yon rugged summit I climbed, in front of me
I saw but an island circled with a rim of endless sea.
Low lay the land before me.   But I saw there, as I stood,
Smoke in the midst upcurling through tangled brake and wood."
Then, at my words, within them the very hearts did bleed,

Recalling Antíphates the Laestrygonian's deed,
And the rage of the savage Cyclops, that gnawed the flesh of men;
Great tears they shed and loudly their sorrow wailed again.
Yet, since for all their weeping no profit came of it,
My men in their bright armour I counted there and split
Into two bands, with each a captain at its head—
I took the one; the other, godlike Eurýlochus led.
Then lots in a brazen helmet we cast without delay
And brave Eurýlochus' lot leapt forth.   Upon his way
With two and twenty comrades, all in tears, he went,
Leaving us behind them as loud in our lament.
Away in those wooded valleys, built on a far-seen site
They found the house of Circe, of smooth stone gleaming white;
But many a lion about it and wolves of the mountain ranged,
Whom with her evil potions Circe had witched and changed.
And yet on my men they leapt not—but rose up from the ground,
With their long tails fawning, and ramping all around,
As dogs, when their master rises from his table, round him spring
Fawning (for well they know his custom is to bring
Dainties they love); so round them those wolves with great claws played,
And lions, grisly monsters—sore were my men afraid.
But now, as they stood at the gateway of the courtyard, they could hear
The voice of that fair-tressed Goddess, carolling sweet and clear
As she wrought at a mighty web, immortal in its grace,
So fine, so full of glory as hands divine may trace.
And then out spoke Polites—the best of men was he,
The nearest and the dearest of all my company:
"Friends, at her loom, within there, I hear someone that sings
So sweet and clear, that with it all the chamber rings,
Be it woman or Goddess.   But quick now, let us call!"
Then at his word my comrades shouted one and all,
And quick she came, and opened that gleaming portal wide,
And bade them enter—blindly, they followed her inside.
Only Eurýlochus, doubting no good would come of it,
Lingered without.   But couches, and chairs for them to sit,
The Goddess brought, and mixed them a draught of honey pale
And cheese and barley and Pramnian wine—and drugs of bale
Therewith, to kill remembrance of their own fatherland.
But when they had drunk her potion, with the wand in her right hand
She struck them, and drove them forth, and penned them in her sty.
Swine's heads, swine's shape, swine's bristles were theirs now, and the cry
Of swine; yet lived within them, unchanged, the minds of men.
So, piteously screaming, she shut them in their pen,
And acorns, and wild cherries from the cornel-tree, and mast,

The food of swine in their wallow, down at their feet she cast.
But back to our swift black galley Eurýlochus ran to tell
News of his lost companions, whom that swift doom befell.
Not a single word could he speak at first, hard though he fought
For utterance; so deeply his heart was overwrought—
Tears filled his eyes, his longing was but to weep and wail,
Until, as all astonished we questioned him, this tale
Of how his comrades perished, at last his lips could frame:
"As thou badest, noble Odysseus, across the woods we came—
We found within a valley a noble house—and there
Beside a mighty loom a voice was singing fair,
Whether of woman or Goddess. But when my comrades cried,
Quick she came forth, and opened her shining portal wide,
And bade them in. Then I, misdoubting some foul play,
Waited. But my companions—they vanished clean away—
Not one came back; though sitting by the gateway long I stayed."
So he; then over my shoulder I cast my mighty blade
Of bronze, with silver studded, and round me slung my bow,
And bade him come to guide me the way that I should go.
But round my knees he flung his arms, imploringly—
"Drag me not there, thou dear to Zeus!—ah, suffer me
To stay behind. For I know it—thou wilt not come again—
Nor thou, nor our companions. Let us that yet remain,
Fly—if so it may be, we scape our evil day."
Then to his prayer I answered—"Nay then, Eurýlochus, stay.
Here by our black ship's hollow side drink thou and feed;
But go I must—upon me there lies too stern a need."
So from our ship on the beaches I turned away inland,
Across those vales enchanted; but now, when near at hand
Stood that great house of Circe, with all her gramary,
And close I came to its gateway, there Hermes met with me,
The God of the Golden Wand; like a young lad's his face,
With the first down upon it, when youth hath fairest grace.
At once he cried in greeting, with a hand that clasped my own—
"Whither, unhappy man, across these hills alone,
Not knowing this land about thee? In Circe's house thy men
Lie shut in the shapes of swine, each in his darkened den.
And now to their rescue comest thou? I tell thee clear
Thou too shalt not win homeward, but share their prison here.
But enough!—for I will save thee and snatch thee from thy doom.
Now listen—when thou comest into Circe's room,
A magic herb thou shalt carry, to keep thee safe the while.
But, first, hear all the secret of Circe's deadly guile—
She shall mix for thee a potion wherein her drugs lie hid,

And yet it shall not enchant thee—the virtue shall forbid
Of the herb that I will give thee—see now, I tell thee all.
But when on thy body Circe shall let her long wand fall,
Then rush headlong upon her, sword drawn as if to kill—
Then in terror she shall offer her beauty to thy will.
And thou shalt not refuse her, but take her love; that so
She may give thee a kindly welcome and let thy comrades go.
But make her swear a mighty oath, by the Gods on high,
To plot no more against thee, nor yet, when thou shalt lie
All naked there, to rob thee of thy manhood and thy worth."
So spake the Argus-slayer and gathered from the earth
A growing herb, and gave it, and showed what form it wore—
Black was its root, but a blossom as white as milk it bore.
The Immortals call it "Mōly"—to dig it where it springs,
Is hard indeed for a mortal; but the Gods can do all things.
So towards the long Olympus Hermes went his way
Across that wooded island; and I passed on, where lay
The house of Circe before me, with deeply musing breast.
There I stood by the gateway of that Goddess lovely-tressed,
And shouted loud.   Then swiftly she heard me, as I cried,
And out she sped, and opened her gleaming portal wide,
And bade me in—I followed; but my heart was dark with gloom.
On a throne with silver studded, fair-carven, in her room
She bade me sit, with a footstool beneath my feet, and made
A draught for me in a golden cup, and there she laid
Her magic drug, with evil hidden in her thought.
But when I took and drank it, and still no spell was wrought,
Lifting aloft her wand, she struck me, with the cry—
"Out!—get thee gone to thy comrades and wallow in their sty."
But with sharp sword uplifted, even as Circe said
Those words, I rushed upon her, as if to strike her dead;
Then under its point with a shriek she ran—her arms she threw
About my knees and from her, wailing, the winged words flew—
"Who art thou?   Whence come hither?   Thy parents?—say!   Thy
        land?
Thou hast drunk, yet nought enchants thee.   I do not understand;
For never yet could mortal against my drugs stand fast,
Once he had drunk my potion and betwixt his teeth it passed;
But in *thee* there lives a spirit that yields not to my spell.
Thou art surely the subtle Odysseus?—of thee did Hermes tell,
The God of the Golden Wand, that one day thou shouldst come,
In thy swift and sable galley, from Troy returning home.
Nay, sheathe thy sword in the scabbard—and let us turn to rest
Within my bed together, as lovers breast to breast,

That, thus made one, henceforward we may trust each other still."

Then in my turn I answered—"How ask for my good will,
When thou hast witched my comrades, here in this house, to swine;
And now thou wouldst trap me also, with treacherous design
Bidding me to thy chamber to sleep within thy bed,
Meaning, when I am naked, to leave my manhood dead,
A thing of nought.   Nay, Goddess, to love thee I am loth,
Unless thou first canst bring thee to swear a mighty oath,
Never to purpose evil against me evermore."
Then without gainsaying, as I bade her, so she swore;
And when she had sworn that solemn oath, and sealed it fast,
In the beauteous bed of Circe I laid me down at last.
   'But meanwhile Circe's maidens—four of them had she
Within her house—to their labours bent them busily.
(From water-springs, or woodlands, those handmaids had their birth,
Or the sacred streams that seaward go gliding o'er the earth.)
One on the high-seats in the hall began to strow
Fair coverlets of purple, with linen cloths below;
And one before the high-seats tables of silver spread
And laid upon them baskets, all golden, for the bread;
And a third within a mixing-bowl of silver poured
Wine honey-sweet, and ranged gold goblets on the board. . . .
Then a grave dame of the household brought wheaten bread to me
And many a dainty, gracious in her hospitality,
Bidding me eat.   But I—I had no heart for food,
My mind was filled with other things and thoughts of little good.
But Circe, seeing how there I sat, yet never laid
Hands on the fare before me, with sorrow still downweighed,
Stood at my side, and from her the words came winging fleet—
"Why dost thou sit, Odysseus, as a man struck dumb, nor eat
Nor drink what stands before thee?   Why gnaw thine own heart now?
Art still afraid of treachery?   No cause hast thou
To fear—have I not taken a mighty oath and sure?"
So she spoke; and I answered—"But who then could endure,
What man of honour, Circe, to sit him down and feast
On food and wine, while his comrades yet lingered unreleased—
Till he saw them standing before him, safe again and free?
But if thou wouldst have me eat and drink, in verity,
Release them—and let me see the men that I love, at last!"
So I; but already Circe, with wand in hand, had passed
Forth from the hall, and opened the doorways of her pen,
And out, in the shape of boars full-grown, she drove my men.
There they stood before her, and passing through them all
She smeared their skins with another charm, that made to fall

From off their hides the bristles, where a moment since they grew
By the queenly Circe's baleful power.   To men anew
They changed—but men grown younger than they used to be,
And taller in their stature, and goodlier to see.
And now once more they knew me—with tears of joy and love
They crowded round and wrung my hands—the roof above
Rang with their cries, till pity even in Circe woke.
Again then, drawing near me, the noble Goddess spoke:
"Son of Laertes Heaven-sprung, Odysseus subtly-wise,
Get thee down to the beaches, where thy swift ship lies;
Haul her ashore, leave hidden in the sea-caves all your gear
And arms, and bring behind thee thy loved companions here."
So to the Goddess' bidding I bowed my spirit's pride,
And back I turned to the beaches; and there at my ship's side
I found my loved companions, sitting with evil cheer,
Lamenting in their anguish and weeping tear on tear.
But, as the calves in a homestead rush skipping to meet the cows,
When back they come to the farmyard from the pasture where they browse,
Full of sweet grass at eventide—no pens can keep
Those young things back—with lowings that never cease, they leap
All around their mothers; so, seeing me, they streamed,
Weeping, all around me; and to their hearts it seemed
As if they were come, at last, safe homeward from afar,
To the land that bore and bred them, to craggy Ithaca.'

(X, 133–357, 371–417.)

*For a year they stayed feasting with Circe; then the comrades of Odysseus
reminded him of home.   So he called on the Goddess to fulfil her promise and
let him sail for Ithaca.   But to his horror she replied that first he must voyage
to the Land of the Dead beyond the Ocean-stream, to consult the wraith of
Teirésias the Seer.   At this he wept sitting upon her bed, with soul that no
more desired to see the sun.   But at last he asked Circe for guidance; and she
told him how he must sail before the north wind across the Ocean Stream, until
he came to the desolate shore of Persephone, with its groves of poplar and willow;
and must there sacrifice to the powers of Death.   She herself brought a ram and
a black ewe; and Odysseus led his despairing comrades to their ship.*

The Kingdom of Death

'But when we were come to the shore and our black ship again,
First from the beach we hauled her down to the glorious main,
And then once more within her we set her sails and mast,
And stowed the sheep for sacrifice.   But thick and fast
We wept as we went aboard her, and with fear our hearts were wrung.

144

Meanwhile the fair-tressed Circe, dread goddess of human tongue,
Behind our dark-prowed galley wafted a helping breeze
To fill our sail and friend us far off across the seas.
So, when our gear was set in place, then down at last
We sat, and with wind and helmsman swift on our course we passed.
All day with bellying canvas onwards our vessel flew,
Till sank the sun, and o'er earth's ways the shadows of evening drew—
And there lay earth's end before us, where deep-flowing Ocean swells,
There lay the land and the city where the race of Cimmerians dwells,
Wrapped deep in mist and darkness.   For never the glorious rays
Of Hēlios look upon them—neither when up the ways
Of starry Heaven he rises, nor when he sinks again;
But a grisly gloom hides ever that race of hapless men.
Thither we came, and beached our ship, and set on land
The sheep we were to offer; then down the Ocean-strand
We passed, till we found before us the place that Circe told.
There I bade Perimēdes, I bade Eurýlochus hold
The victims fast, and drew my sword, and dug a pit,
In length and breadth a cubit, and round the edge of it
I poured out three libations for all the hosts of dead—
Mead, and sweet wine, and water, and over these I spread
White barley.   Then, with many a prayer, I cried aloud
To the fleeting wraiths of the perished.   To slay for them I vowed
A barren heifer, my finest, and burn upon its pyre,
If ever I came to Ithaca, rich offerings in the fire;
And for Teirésias only, apart from all the rest,
A great ram, black all over, in all my flocks the best.
But when I had called to the nations that Death hath laid asleep,
With prayer and with promise, I slit the throats of the sheep
Over the pit, and the dark blood flowed.   Then round me from the gloom
Of Erebus there gathered the spectres of the tomb—
Young brides, and youths unwedded, ar d old men's weary years,
And maids in their tender girlhood, with young hearts new to tears,
And, from the grapple of Ares, many a mighty man
Slain with the bronze of battle—still red their armour ran.
From every side they gathered, and round my trench they drew
With a terrible cry, in their thousands.   Then pale with fear I grew.
But still I cheered my comrades, and the slaughtered sheep that lay
Struck down by the sword that spares not, I bade them take and flay,
And burn them, and call for succour on the Gods that rule the dead,
On the mighty name of Hades and Persephone the dread.
But I myself, unsheathing the keen blade from my thigh,
Sat by the trench, forbidding the thin wraiths to draw nigh
And drink the blood, ere I questioned Teirésias the seer.

'Then first the soul of Elpēnor, my comrade, flitted near;
For in no grave, as yet, beneath wide earth he slept—
We had left his body behind us, unburied and unwept,
In Circe's hall at departing—pressed with such haste were we.
But now I was filled with pity—his face I wept to see
And the words came winging from me: "Art come to this land of night,
More fleet on thy feet, Elpēnor, than even our black ship's flight?"
Then with a groan he answered: "Some evil spirit's hate
And measureless draughts of the winecup—these brought me to my fate.
For on Circe's roof I had laid me and, waking, heeded not
To descend by the way I mounted—the ladder I forgot.
So from the housetop, headlong down, I plunged and fell
And my neck from my spine was shattered and my spirit sped to Hell.
But now, by those thou hast left behind, so far away,
By thy wife, and by the father that watched thy childhood's day,
By thy own son Telémachus, that waits thee there,
Thy only son, I beg thee, listen to my last prayer.
For well I know that, returning from Hades' house, awhile
Thou wilt stay thy stout-built galley again at Aeaea's isle.
There, O my lord, I charge thee, once more remember me,
Nor leave me unwept, unburied, as thou sailest out to sea;
Lest haply the wrath of Heaven upon thy head I bring.
But burn me there and, with me, the arms of my warfaring,
And heap a mound above me, beside the grey sea-flow,
The grave of a man unhappy, for men unborn to know;
Do this for me, I beg thee; and on my barrow raise
The oar I pulled with my comrades, living, in other days."
So he spoke. And I answered: "All this, as thou hast prayed,
Unhappy friend, I promise." But while, with sorrow weighed,
We sat and talked—on the one side I, with naked sword
Over the blood; on the other, this phantom that implored—
The wraith of Anticleia, my own dead mother's soul,
The great Autólycus' daughter, that I left alive and whole,
Sailing to sacred Troy—before my eyes she came.
Then my heart filled with pity, and I wept. Yet all the same,
Despite my grief, I let not the wraith of her draw near
The blood, till I first had questioned Teirésias the seer.
But now the soul of the Theban, Teirésias, from the dead
Came forth, with a golden sceptre; and it knew me, and it said:
"Son of Laertes Heaven-sprung, Odysseus subtly-wise,
Why art thou come, unhappy, away from the sunlit skies
Hither, to set thy gaze on the dead men's joyless land?
Nay, lift thy whetted warsword —back from the blood-pit stand—
That I may drink and tell thee the truth that shall abide."

Sheathing my silver-studded sword, I stood aside
And let the blameless prophet drink of that blood dark-red;
And then, "Thou seekest ever to reach thy home," he said,
"Most glorious Odysseus—return were honey-sweet:
Yet harsh shall Heaven make it.   Not lightly shalt thou cheat,
I think, the great Earth-shaker, whose hatred thou hast won—
So deeply broods his anger for thy blinding of his son.
Yet even so, it may be, though worn with many an ill,
Safe ye may come, if thou master thy own and thy comrades' will,
When in your stout-built galley, escaped from the purple deep,
Ye make Thrīnacia's island, and find the goodly sheep
And cattle, there at pasture, that the Sun-god calls his own,
To whom, all-seeing, all-hearing, all things on earth are known.
Now if ye leave his herds unhurt, if ye fix fast
Your thoughts on home, sore-troubled ye may win home at last.
But, if ye dare to harm them, surely I prophesy
Doom for thy ship and comrades.   And though thou shouldst not die,
Yet long-delayed and evil shall be thy homecoming.
Thy comrades lost, to thy country a stranger ship shall bring
Thee only; and there also thou shalt find new troubles bred—
Insolent men, that gather with many a gift to wed
Thy noble queen, and raven the wealth within thy hall.
Thou shalt, indeed, avenge thee on their violence, one and all;
But when, there in thy palace, thou shalt have slain this horde
Of suitors, by thy cunning or in open clash of sword,
Forth yet again thou must wander, bearing an oar with thee,
Until thou findest a nation that knows not of the sea;
That eat their food unsalted, and never heard before
Of ships with cheeks of crimson, or the fairly-fashioned oar
That wings swift galleys onward.   The sign that thy quest is done
Shall be this token I tell thee, a clear and certain one—
When by the way there meets thee another wandering man
That, seeing the oar on thy shoulder, calls it 'a winnowing-fan,'
Plant there its polished shaft upright in the earth, and bring
Unto the Lord Poseidon a noble offering—
A ram, and a bull, and a mating boar; then turn thee home
And give to the Gods, wide Heaven's lords—to each—a hecatomb,
In order due.   For thyself, Death from the sea shall rise,
Most peacefully, when a calm old age weighs down thine eyes,
Amidst thy happy people.   And this is verity."
And then I said in answer: "These threads of doom for me,
Doubtless, the Gods themselves have spun.   Yet I implore,
Teirésias, declare me the truth of one thing more.
I see here my own dead mother, yet her spirit sits apart,

Silent, beside the pit of blood, and has no heart
To speak one word to her son, or look me in the face.
How shall I make her know me?   Lord, tell me, of thy grace."
And then he made me answer: "Easily that is said,
Do but as I shall bid thee.   Of all the gathered dead,
Those that thou shalt suffer to come to the blood and drink,
Will speak to thee, and truly; but those that from its brink
Thou holdest off, to the darkness, hushed as they came, shall fade."

'Then back to the House of Hades the lord Teirésias' shade
Vanished, and so ended the soothsay of the seer;
But I kept my place, unmoving, till my mother's wraith drew near
And tasted of that dark-red blood—and lo, she knew
My face; and from her, wailing, the words of sorrow flew—
"My son, how com'st thou hither, to the land that is dark for aye,
Living?   For the living, not easy is the way.
From Troy hast thou come hither, wandering about the main
So long, with ship and comrades?   Hast not yet come again
To Ithaca?   Not seen, yet, thy wife that waits for thee?"
And then I answered, "Mother, by grim necessity
Here in the House of Hades I seek the prophet's lore
Of Teirésias the Theban.   Not yet to Achaea's shore
Have I come near, nor planted my foot on Ithaca.
I wander and I suffer, since first I sailed afar
To Ilios, land of noble steeds, to fight at Atrīdes' call.
But tell me true, my mother, on thee what fate did fall?—
What doom of Death that strikes men down?   Some lingering ill?
Or did Artemis the Archer-queen descend to kill
Thee with her gentle arrows?   What of my father's fate?
Of the son I left behind me?—do they still uphold my state,
Or has some other seized it, because men deem me dead?
And my wife—how stands her purpose?   What thoughts lie in her head?
Does she yet guard my home and son?   Or is her hand
Now given to the noblest of all the Achaean land?"
But my noble mother answered: "Indeed, enduring all,
Thy wife abides in her sorrow at home within thy hall,
And her days and nights are wasted with tears that never cease.
None hath usurped thy honours; still in untroubled peace
Telémachus holds thy acres and sits at the banquet-board
In each man's hall, as befits a justice-dealing lord,
For all men give him welcome.   But ever thy father keeps
Away from the city, upon his lands; no more he sleeps,
Now, in a bed with rugs and bright-hued blankets strown.
In winter, like the bondsmen, where the ash of the hearth is thrown,
Close to the fire he slumbers, in ragged raiment clad;

And when the summer cometh and the harvest groweth glad,
At random, in some corner of his fruitful vineyard's shade,
Low on a heap of withered leaves the old man's limbs are laid.
Loading his heart with sorrow, lamenting he lies there
For the fate that has come upon him; and his years grow hard to bear.
So I too came to perish—'twas not the unerring bow,
The painless shafts, of the Archer-queen that laid me low;
No sickness came upon me, such as wastes away
The life from the limbs of man in hideous decay;
It was, my noble Odysseus, my long yearning for thee,
Thy gentleness, thy wisdom, that took sweet life from me."
So she spoke; and longing awoke within my heart
To clasp my mother's spirit—three times there did I start
Forward, to press her to me—three times I saw her shape
Like to a dream, a shadow, between my hands escape.
Then deeper yet the anguish that on my spirit lay
And I cried with words swift winging—"Ah, why wilt thou not stay,
My mother, that for a moment—even in Hell—embraced,
The chill comfort of weeping, together, we might taste?
Or art thou only a phantom that the dread Persephone
Hath sent, with yet sorer sorrow to wring the heart in me?"
But my noble mother answered, "Unhappiest in thy lot
Of all men born!—my child!—Persephone cheats thee not.
This is the fate of *all* men, once that their days are done.
Then the sinews knit no longer the flesh to the skeleton;
For those the scorching flames of the funeral-pyre devour,
Once life has left our gleaming bones—and from that hour
The soul must flutter dreamlike.   But haste thee on thy way
Back to the light, and remember, and tell thy wife one day."'
    (*Next there rose up before Odysseus the dead heroines of ancient legend.*)
    'And next I saw Īphimĕdeia, that was Alōeus' bride,
But claimed she had lain in love by Lord Poseidon's side.
And indeed she bore twin-children (though their years had little length),
The glorious Ephialtes, and Ōtus' godlike strength.
Never—save great Orion's self—grew sons so tall
Or half so fair on Earth, that gives her grain to all.
At nine years old, nine cubits was the span from left to right
Across their mighty shoulders, and fathoms nine their height;
And they threatened to bring the onrush of their battle-cry
Against the lords of Olympus, the Gods that never die;
Ossa upon Olympus, and Pēlion's forest-crown
They planned to pile on Ossa, to hurl the Immortals down.
Ay, and they would have done it, had years been theirs to grow.
But the son of Zeus and fair-tressed Lēto laid them low,

Or ever the beard upon their cheeks had time to spring
Or the down had veiled their faces with youth's fair blossoming.
And Phaedra I saw, and Prŏcris, and Ariadne the fair,
Daughter of baleful Minos, her whom once Theseus bare
From Crete towards Athens' sacred soil—and yet did gain
No joy thereof—by Artemis his love was slain,
At the word of Dionysus, in Dia's sea-girt isle;
And Clýmene, and Maera, and Eríphyle the vile,
That sold for the lure of gold her own dear husband's life;
And many another daughter, many another wife
Was there, of the race of heroes—more names than I can say,
For deathless Night, ere I finished, would long have waned away. . . .
    'But when the souls of the women had been dispersed apart,
This way and that, by Persephone, the pure of heart,
The wraith of Agamemnon, the son of Atreus, came,
Grieving, with all his comrades, whose end had been the same—
To die in the hall of Aegisthus.   At once he knew me well,
So soon as he drank of the dark-red blood; then swiftly fell
His tears, and loud was his crying, and wide his arms he spread,
Longing to clasp me to him—in vain—for the strength was fled
And the force that lived aforetime within each supple limb.
Then I too wept, beholding, and sore I pitied him,
And the words came winging from me—"Most glorious king of men,
Agamemnon son of Atreus, what fate befell thee, then,
Of Death the all-destroying?   Did Poseidon master thee,
Raising some blast of bitter winds across the sea?
Or upon land didst thou perish, by spears in the battle-line,
Striving to drive away men's fair-fleeced sheep or kine,
Or fighting to make some city and its womenfolk thy prize?"
And then he said in answer, "Odysseus subtly-wise,
Son of Laertes Heaven-sprung, Poseidon slew not me,
Raising a blast of bitter winds across the sea,
Nor did I die in battle by foemen's spears on land.
Nay, it was by Aegisthus my death and doom were planned—
By him and my wife accurséd.   For he bade me to his hall
To feast, and left me butchered, like an ox within its stall.
So, by a death most pitiful, I perished; there as well,
Slaughtered without ceasing, round me my comrades fell,
As white-tusked swine in the courtyard of some great, wealthy lord,
Slain for bridal or banquet, to fill the festal board.
Oft indeed thou hast seen the slaying of men before,
Whether in single combat, or the headlong clash of war;
But deeper had been thy pity to see us lying dead
Mid the mixing-bowls and tables of that banquet richly spread,

While red ran the floor about us, with our own blood defiled.
But pitifullest of all, to me, the cry of Priam's child—
Cassandra—as Clytemnestra, my false wife, stabbed her there,
Clinging to me, while vainly I raised my hands in prayer
And beat the earth, as I struggled, with the sword deep in my side.
But my queen, like a shameless hound, turned from me where I died,
Too cruel to close my eyelids, my lips left gaping wide,
As my spirit fled to Hades.   There is indeed on earth
No creature more appalling—more shameless—brought to birth,
Than the woman whose heart conceives such things as hers conceived—
Murder for her own husband!—I whose fond heart believed
Glad faces of children and servants should greet me at my door!
But she with her hellish heart hath shamed for evermore
Herself and the race of women—even the innocent ones."
At that I cried in answer, "By God, on Atreus' sons
Terribly the Thunderer hath let His anger smite—
And all through the wiles of women.   For Helen's sake in fight
We have fallen in our thousands; and Clytemnestra planned
This treachery for thee, still far in the Trojan land!"
Then in his turn he answered: "Therefore bear this in mind—
Not to thy own wife, even, suffer thy heart grow kind,
Tell her not all thy counsel—enough that thou tell her part,
Keep thou the rest of thy knowledge well hidden in thy heart.
And yet I know, Odysseus, no wife shall murder thee,
For truly Icárius' daughter, the wise Penelope,
Is perfect in her prudence, in all her ways discreet.
Still a young bride, I remember, we left her when our fleet
Set sail for Troy; at her bosom she was nursing, then,
Her baby, that now, no doubt, takes his full place with men—
Ah happy!—for *him* his father's eyes once more shall see,
And he shall embrace his father, with the love that a son's should be.
But *my* wife would not suffer *me* to gaze my fill
On *my* dear son—she slew me first.   Nay, hearken still,
This counsel too I give thee—bring not thy ship to shore
Openly, but in secret—let none trust woman more.
And tell me this, Odysseus—I charge thee tell me true—
Of my son, that he yet is living, have ye heard tidings new?
In Orchómenus is he?   Or amid Pylos' sand?
Or haply with Menelaus, in the wide Spartan land?
It cannot be that, already, Orestes' days are done."
And then I made him answer: "Why ask me, Atreus' son?
Be he dead or alive, I know not.   Nay, idle words are ill."
   'But as in our grief and anguish we stood there weeping still,
The spirits of Achilles and Patroclus came,

Antílochus, too, and Ajax, of all the Achaean name
Next to the noble Achilles in form and feature's grace.
Then the soul of swift Pēlídes knew, as of old, my face
And quick came his cry of sorrow—"Odysseus subtly-wise,
Son of Laertes Heaven-sprung—what wilt devise,
What madness next, rash spirit!   How couldst thou dare the deep
Of Hell, with its senseless phantoms of weary souls that sleep?"
So he spoke; but I answered, "Achilles, without peer
In all the hosts of Achaea, it was to seek the seer
Teirésias—to ask him for counsel how to come
Safely at last to Ithaca, my rocky home.
For not yet to Achaea have I sailed, not even now,
Nor trod the soil that bore me.   I suffer still.   But thou
Art blest beyond all, Achilles, that lived or yet shall live;
Glory to thee, as to Heaven, we Argives used to give,
In life; and now in Hades thy honour standeth chief.
Therefore let death, Achilles, not give thee *too* much grief."
But then at once he answered—"Talk not smooth words to me
Of death, most noble Odysseus.   Far sooner would I be
A serf, in thrall to a landless man, that scarce had bread,
Than lord it here in Hades o'er all the perished dead.
But come now, tell me tidings of the brave son I begot—
Did *he* too come as a leader to the war by Troy, or not?
And tell me of noble Pēleus—of him what canst thou tell?
Among my folk of the Myrmidons does he still live honoured well?
Or lies he now neglected in Hellas and Phthīa's land,
Because the years have left him feeble in foot and hand?
For now he lacks to defend him, there in the light of day,
These arms that once had vigour the mightiest to slay,
When I fought for the Achaeans on the great Trojan Plain.
Ah, could I but for a moment stride through his doors again,
As once I was, good reason they should have to curse my might—
These men that deal him dishonour and do his age despite!"
So he spoke; and I answered, "Indeed what days befall
Thy noble sire, I know not.   But I can tell thee all
Of thy dear son, Neoptólemus.   It was with me
He sailed, in my hollow galley, from Scyros oversea
To join the well-greaved Achaeans.   And when, at Troy, we sought
For counsel, *he* was the foremost, always, to speak his thought,
And never amiss; excepting Nestor the divine,
And me, none could outspeak him; and when in the battle-line
On the Trojan Plain we grappled, thy son would never stay
Within the ranks of our serried host—deep in the fray
He plunged ahead before us—none could outdo his might

And fast men fell before him in the grisly shock of fight.
Nay, I could never name them, the many he laid low
In battle for the Argives.   And with how fierce a blow
He felled that son of Tēlephus, Eurýpylus the brave!—
Thick his Kēteian comrades around him found a grave—
All for the gold that bought a woman's treachery!
Yet a comelier foe, save Memnon, never these eyes did see.
And when the chiefs of Achaea under my command,
Were entered into that Horse of Wood Epeius planned,
The other lords and captains sat wiping eyes grown dim
With tears, and their strong limbs trembled; but never, watching him,
Did I see in thy son's fair features paleness or trace of tear;
Nay, all the while with his fingers he clutched at his heavy spear
Of bronze, and at his swordhilt, praying me to let him go
Down from the Horse, impatient for the Trojans' overthrow.
But when we had sacked King Priam's tall city utterly,
With a noble share of plunder he put again to sea,
Unscathed of sword or spearhead in all the press of fight;
Though ever it is but blindly that the blows of Ares smite."
I ceased; and the swift Achilles through the mead of asphodel
With giant strides departed, gladdened to hear how well
His son had won the glory of a mighty man of war.
  'Then other wraiths of the perished flocked round me, grieving sore,
Asking the fate of their dearest: there was one soul alone
Stood far and angry—Ajax, the son of Télamōn—
Because by the ships I worsted him, when both we sought
The armour of Achilles, that his goddess-mother brought
For prize, and the sons of the Trojans, and Pallas, made award.
Ah, would I had never won them!—so valiant a lord
Because of it earth covered—of warriors the best,
After the great Achilles, and in beauty comeliest!
So now, with gentle words, I called to him—"Ajax, son
Of Télamon the blameless, even though life be done,
Canst thou not, even yet, forget thy wrath with me
For those arms accurst?—ah, truly, for our calamity
To the Argives Heaven gave them!   For fallen art thou, our tower,
Mourned no less than Achilles by the Argives to this hour.
Let none be blamed—'twas Zeus, implacable in hate
Against the hosts of Achaea, that brought thee to thy fate.
Nay, then, dear lord, come hither—let us speak as friend to friend;
At last lay aside thine anger, thy pride that nought can bend."
So I cried, but he answered not; and silent thus
He passed with the souls of the perished to the gloom of Erebus.'

(XI, 1–224, 305–330, 385–564.)

After Ajax, Odysseus saw Minos sitting in judgment and Orion hunting the
shades of the beasts he had slain on earth; Tityus devoured by vultures, Tantalus
hungering and thirsting, Sisyphus heaving his stone.   But then the Dead
crowded on him in such myriads that he and his comrades fled in terror and
sailed again for Aeaea.   After burying Elpēnor, they put forth again and came
to the Sirens' isle.

The Sirens; Scylla and Charybdis

'Thus I revealed to my comrades the warning Circe gave;
But on her way in the meantime swiftly our good ship drave
Towards the Sirens' isle.   For behind us the breeze blew full and fair.
Yet now on a sudden dropped the wind, still grew the air,
And by God's will on the surges a hush of slumber lay;
Then, rising, my companions lowered and stowed away
Our sail, and with their oarblades of pinewood polished bright,
Sitting upon their benches, they lashed the waters white.
But a great round of wax I took, and hewed it small
With my sword's keen blade, then kneaded the fragments one and all
With strength of hand, till quickly the wax to softness came
Under the blaze resistless of our Lord the Sun-god's flame.
Therewith I stopped the ears of all my comrades fast;
Then, hand and foot, they bound me to the socket of the mast,
With ropes lapped tight round the mast itself; and so once more
Took their place on the benches and smote the surges hoar.
But as we neared the Sirens and stood now within hail,
Racing lightly upon our course, they did not fail
To see our swift keel's onrush; and clear their singing came:
"Hither, renowned Odysseus! Achaea's noblest name!
Bring in thy ship to shoreward and hear our song at last.
For by us never a sailor will steer his black hull past,
Till first he has stayed to hearken to our voices' honeyed call—
Then gladdened in heart he goes his way, and a wiser man withal.
For well we know what sorrows, of old, in Troy's broad land
Trojans and Argives suffered at the Immortals' hand;
Whatever betides, we know it, through all earth's fruitful bounds."
Thus did their lovely voices call; and those sweet sounds
So lured my heart to hear them, that with a frowning brow
I signed to my men to loose me.   But only the harder now
They rowed, and Perimēdes and Eurýlochus hastily,
Rising, with yet more bonds, and tighter, fastened me.
But when we had passed upon our course, and now no more
I heard those voices singing upon the Sirens' shore,

Quickly my dear companions took out the wax again,
That stopped their ears, and loosened the bonds where my limbs had lain.
  'But soon as we left the Sirens' isle, I saw a smoke
And a mighty surf, and heard its thunder as it broke.
Then from the hands of my comrades the oars dropped in dismay—
Splashing they dipped in the surges—and now our ship lost way,
As the long blades ceased to urge her on; but in each ear,
Passing along the gangway, I uttered words of cheer:
"Come now, long since, my comrades, our hearts have learnt to brave
Danger—this is no greater than when in his hollow cave
The violence of the Cyclops robbed us of liberty;
Yet even thence by my counsel, and courage, and wit came we.
I trust we shall live to remember this peril too one day.
But listen now to my counsel—let one and all obey—
You rowers, keep your benches and smite the deep sea-wave,
In hope that from *this* doom also the hand of Zeus may save;
And thou at the helm, mark well my word, and understand,
Since the steering-oar of our galley is given to thy hand!
Away from the smoke and the surf, by the cliff-side make her run—
Take care lest she swing out yonder and leave us all undone."
  'At once they obeyed my orders.   But never a word I said
Of Scylla—that fell destroyer, that overmastering dread;
Lest my comrades in their terror, if of her too I told,
Should drop their oars together and huddle in the hold.
Yet Circe's hard commandment in *that* hour I forgot,
Nor bethought me of her warning that I should arm me not.
Clad in my splendid armour, with two long spears in hand,
High on the platform by the prow I took my stand;
For I hoped from the front of my galley to catch the first glimpse plain
Of yon crag-lurking monster, that meant my comrades' bane.
Yet nowhere could I see her; though weary grew my eyes
As I searched the crag-face looming, all misty, to the skies.
So, groaning in our horror, we sailed that narrow way.
Upon the one hand Scylla, and on the other lay
Divine Charybdis, sucking the salt deeps in her wrath;
As boils on the flame a cauldron, so, when she spewed them forth,
Up in confusion seethed the seas, and spray like rain
On the very crest of the crag-wall on each side fell again;
And whenever she sucked the salt sea down, we saw how deep
The inmost whirlpool weltered, while all the rocky steep
Boomed, and the far sea-bottom stood plain before our sight,
Where dark the sandy eddies swirled—with fear my men grew white.
But, as we stared at Charybdis, fearing that all was o'er,
In that same instant Scylla out of my galley tore

Six of my best and bravest.   Just as I turned my eyes
Back to my ship and comrades, I saw above me rise
The hands and feet of them, haled aloft; and heard them call
Loud on my name in anguish, for the last time of all.
Just as when a fisher, with a long rod in his hand,
To catch small fish, on a jut of rock will take his stand,
Then casting his cunning bait, his line with its ox-horn sheath,
Draws them panting and struggling up from the wave beneath;
So they too, panting and struggling, were lifted to her lair
And at her cavern's entry Scylla devoured them there,
Stretching their arms out towards me in that dread agony.
No sight so full of pity, as this, e'er fell to me,
In all my weary wanderings o'er the pathways of the sea.'

(XII, 165–259.)

*Now they drew near to Thrīnacia and Odysseus urged his men to sail by.
But they were too sea-weary.   Wind-bound there for a month, at last in their
hunger they killed, while Odysseus slept, the forbidden cattle of the Sun.   Then
the Sun-god cried to Zeus for vengeance—else he would go and shine in Hades
among the Dead.   So Zeus struck the ship with lightning and Odysseus alone
was left floating on her mast.   Escaping again from the whirlpool of Charybdis,
after nine days he drifted ashore on Calypso's isle.*

*Such was Odysseus' story, which so delighted the Phaeacians that they loaded
him with further gifts before he sailed.   All night the ship sped on, while
Odysseus slept; at dawn the sailors disembarked him, still sleeping, on Ithaca.
But as they neared Phaeacia on their homeward voyage, the still wrathful
Poseidon turned ship and men to stone.*

Odysseus' Return to Ithaca

So the noble Odysseus wakened, once more on his native ground,
And yet, long exiled, knew it not; for all around
By Pallas Athene, child of Zeus, a mist was thrown
(Till she could tell her purpose) to keep him still unknown;
Lest his wife, or his friends, or his people should see him now returned,
Before he had dealt to the Suitors the doom their deeds had earned.
So now all things before him seemed unfamiliar—
The sure and sheltering havens, the tracks that wound afar,
The trees in their summer glory, the great crags falling sheer.
To his feet he leapt, and looked on the land he held so dear,
Then groaned aloud, and smiting with both hands heavily
His thighs he cried in anguish—'Alas, unhappy me!

Upon what unknown country, this time, have I been thrust?
Are they savage men that dwell here, and wanton, and unjust?
Or hospitable to strangers, fearing the Gods on high?
What shall I do with all this wealth?   Whither shall I
Turn now myself?   Ah better, had the Phaeacians spared
Their gifts—had I discovered some other king that cared
To help me in his greatness, and send me home again!
I have no place where, hidden, these treasures might remain;
Yet here I dare not leave them, for other hands to steal.
Ah shame!—the lords and princes of Phaeacia did not deal
Wisely with me, nor justly (as I deemed), that on the shore
Of this strange land they left me, when indeed they swore
To set me on far-seen Ithaca—yet did it not!
Now may the Zeus of Suppliants not leave their crime forgot—
He that regardeth all men and makes the wicked fall!
But come, let me look to my chattels and tell the tale of all,
For some, maybe, they have pilfered, before they sailed away.'
So he counted those fair cauldrons, and tripods, where they lay,
And the gold and the raiment woven fair; but not one thing
Was wanting—then he turned him, again, to sorrowing
For his own home, and wandered beside the thunderous deep
With slow, sad steps.   But nigh him, like a lad that watches sheep,
Athene came—a delicate lad, like a king's son to behold,
With a fine-wove cloak on his shoulder, hanging in double fold,
And sandals under his shining feet, and in his hand a spear.
Glad at the sight grew Odysseus and swiftly drawing near,
He said: 'Now hail to thee, stranger—for thine is the first face—
Friendly I trust it may be—that I meet within this place.
Give shelter now, I pray thee, to these my goods and me—
As of a God I beg it, a suppliant at thy knee.
And tell me *one* thing truly, to set my heart at rest—
What land is this?   What country?   And by what race possessed?
Is it some isle far-seen at sea?   Or but a strand
Sloping down to seaward from the heart of the rich mainland?'
And then the bright-eyed Goddess, Athene, made reply:
'Nay, thou art simple, stranger, or far thy home must lie,
If *this* land's name thou knowest not!   Not so obscure
A land it is—nay, many know well its name, be sure,
Whether they dwell to eastward and the first morning's light,
Or away, beyond, to westward and the shadows of the night.
Indeed it is but rugged, no land where horsemen ride,
Yet not too poor its soil is, although it lies not wide;
For its harvests are past all telling, and well its vineyards yield.
It lacks not rain, nor dew that gladdeneth the field;

All manner of timber fills its woods; good grass is here
For goats or kine; and water-springs, that fail not through the year.
Therefore even in Troyland men know of Ithaca,
Stranger; although from Achaea they say Troy lies full far.'
Then joyful was noble Odysseus, the enduring, when he heard—
Happy in his dear land, according to the word
Of the Aegis-bearer's daughter, Athene.   Then again
The words came winging from him—and yet he told not plain
All of the truth, but checked himself before he spake,
(For still in his heart the cunning was watchful and awake):
'Indeed far overseas, in the wide Cretan land,
I had heard of Ithaca—and lo, on its shore I stand,
With all my wealth about me!   To my sons as much again
I left and fled to exile, because my hand had slain
Idómeneus' dear son, Orsílochus the fleet,
Who was the swiftest runner among the men of Crete.
For he had tried to rob me of all my rightful part
In the spoils of Troy (that cost me such bitterness of heart
Amid the shock of battle and the wild surges' roar),
Because I would not follow his father to the war
At Troy, nor court his favour, but led my band alone.
So, as he came from the country, with a comrade of my own
I laid wait by the wayside, and struck him going by
With my bronze spear.   Thick darkness had hidden all the sky
And none there was to behold us, as I left him lying dead.
But when with my keen spearpoint I had slain him, then I fled
To a ship of the proud Phoenicians and prayed them aid me there;
From the plunder I had gathered I paid them an ample share,
And begged them to give me passage and land me in Pylos bay
Or the goodly land of Elis, where the Epeians sway;
But off that coast a violent wind blew them to sea,
Hard though they fought—if they failed me, it was not willingly.
So from our course we were driven, here upon this shore,
By night, and made the harbour by hard toil at the oar.
Of supper, though all faint for food, we took no care,
But landed from our galley and lay down as we were.
Then a sweet slumber seized me, so wearied out was I;
But *they* unladed all my goods and let them lie
Beside me, as I slumbered outstretched upon the sand;
Then went aboard and sailed for the fair Sidonian land,
Leaving me here forsaken, in my heart's bitterness.'
Then smiled the bright-eyed Athene and, with a fond caress,
Laid her hand on Odysseus.   A woman now seemed she
Tall, and fair, and skilful in glorious artistry,

And with wingéd words she answered—'Ah, cunning past compare
And crafty were he could catch thee!—ay, though a God it were!
Thou incorrigible trickster, thou subtle-witted one,
Not even here, in thy country, art thou willing to have done
With the crookéd words and stratagems that please thee so?
But come, let us say no more of this—full well we know,
Both of us, to dissemble—there is no man may vie
With thee in guile and policy, and first am I
Of Gods in craft and counsel.   Not even *thou* didst see
That I was Athene, child of Zeus, who ceaselessly
Care for thee, through all perils, and guard thee to the end.
It was I that made the Phaeacians to treat thee as a friend,
And now I am come hither, to counsel thee and hide
These gifts that the lords of Phaeacia gave thee in their pride,
Before they sent thee homeward, by my purpose and design.
But now will I tell thee truly what toils shall yet be thine
Within thy noble palace.   Bear them, since so thou must.
Tell nought to man or woman—to no one shalt thou trust
To know thou art come wandering home.   With no word said,
Suffer thou thy sorrows and the wrongs heaped on thy head. . . .'
And then the mist she scattered, that all the land stood plain;
But the long-enduring Odysseus rejoiced to see again
His home, and kissed its earth, the giver of man's bread;
Then to the Nymphs he lifted his hands in prayer, and said:
'Daughters of Zeus, O Naiad Nymphs, I did not dare
Hope ever again to see you.   Hear now my loving prayer.
Hail!   We will bring ye offerings, as once we used to bear,
If by the grace of Athene, that drives the spoil of spears,
I live, and my own dear son grows ripe to manhood's years.'

(XIII, 187–310, 352–60.)

Then Athene helped Odysseus to store his treasures in the cave and counselled him to seek shelter with the faithful swineherd Eumaeus, while she brought back Telémachus from Sparta.   For disguise she changed Odysseus to an old beggar-man in a bald stag's hide.   After he had nearly been torn to pieces by the swineherd's dogs, Eumaeus gave him food and a bed; and the seeming beggar told such vivid stories of his own past life and encounters with Odysseus, that his delighted host, while still refusing to believe in Odysseus' imminent return, called for the best of the swine to be brought forth and killed.   Then Odysseus asked Eumaeus how he himself had first come to Ithaca.   And Eumaeus told how he had been kidnapped in childhood.

'Beyond Ortygia there lies an isle
Called Syria—if ever thou hast heard its name erewhile—
Where in his courses turns the sun: not very wide,
But fertile—rich its vintage, and rich its harvest-tide,
And fair its sheep and cattle.   No famine that land sees,
Nor there on hapless mortals fall hateful maladies;
But when at last white-haired with age its people grow,
Then Artemis and Apollo, Lord of the Silver Bow,
Come with their gentle arrows and deal death from their hands.
Now in that isle two cities are, that share its lands,
And both of these obeyed my father's sovranty,
Ctēsius, son of Ormĕnus; and like to the Gods was he.
Thither there came Phoenicians, famed mariners and bold,
But greedy—with countless trinkets stored in their black ship's hold.
Now we had a Phoenician woman, there in my father's hall,
Skilled in splendid handiwork, and beautiful, and tall;
Her those cunning Phoenicians beguiled and led astray.
For first, as she washed her linen, close to their ship, one lay
Beside her as a lover (and *that* will quickly blind
A woman, though before it she bore a blameless mind).
And, after, he asked her who she was, whence she had come,
And quick she answered, pointing to my father's high-built home:
"From the city of bronze, from Sidon, I boast to draw my blood—
The daughter of Árybas, whose wealth flowed like a flood.
But once on a time sea-robbers, Taphians, kidnapped me,
As home I came from the country, and bore me oversea,
To the lord of that great house yonder.   And well they made him pay."
Thereto that other answered, with whom by stealth she lay:
"Wouldst thou like to sail back homeward, with *us,* to Phoenicia,
And see that high-built house where thy father and mother are,
Yet living?—for rumour has it they are wealthy people still."
Then replied the woman—"Indeed it were my will—
Most gladly—if *you* are willing, ye mariners, to swear
An oath, in truth to bring me safely and surely there."
So she said: and the sailors, just as she bade them, swore;
And soon as that solemn promise was sealed and pledged, once more
The woman spoke among them: "Now silence!   Let none talk
One word to me, if ever ye meet me as I walk
Either about our market, or yet beside our spring—
Not one of you—lest haply some listener hear and bring
Tidings to my old master, and he suspect our plan
And bind me in bitter fetters, and do ye, every man,

To death. So mark my counsel; gather the freight ye need,
And when your ship has laded her merchandise, with speed
Send home to me, up yonder, a messenger to say,
And I will come, with whatever gold I can take away.
Still more to pay my passage, if it may be, I will bring—
For the son of my good master is my own fosterling—
Such a sharp little lad, that beside me goes trotting where I come.
And if on board I bring him, then for a pretty sum,
Ye can sell the boy, wherever ye sail, to strangers oversea."
With that to the noble house of my father home went she.
So, for the space of a twelvemonth, they stayed there in our isle,
Gathering goods in plenty to their hollow ship the while;
But when they were ready for sailing and their stores were stowed in her,
In secret to the woman they sent a messenger,
To my father's house—a fellow of cunning manifold,
Carrying a necklace of amber beads and gold.
But, as my lady mother and her handmaidens all
Stood busy with eyes and fingers about it in the hall,
Bargaining to buy it, then to my nurse alone
With never a word he nodded—and back to his ship was gone.
So by the hand she took me and out of the door she led,
And there in the porch she found tables and winecups spread,
That had been used by the feasters waiting on the king,
Now gone to their seats in the market, for the people's gathering.
Quickly she snatched three goblets and stuffed them in her dress,
And all the while I followed, in childish heedlessness.
By then the sun was setting, and dark grew every street,
As down to the glorious haven we came on hurrying feet;
At once aboard their vessel, a good ship and a fast,
The strangers climbed, and drew us up, and off we cast
On the wet sea-ways; and behind us Zeus sent a favouring breeze.
Six days on end, both day and night, we sailed the seas;
Until, when Zeus had brought the seventh morn again,
By Artemis the Archer-queen my nurse was slain—
Headlong, as dives a gannet, into the hold she fell.
So, for the seals and fishes, out into the swell
They flung her; and left me lonely, there in my misery.
But to Ithaca their galley was swept by wind and sea,
And here Laertes bought me, with the wealth he had in store;
And that was how for the first time my eyes beheld this shore.'

(XV, 403–84.)

*Meanwhile at Sparta Athene warned Telémachus in a dream not to delay too
long away from home and to avoid the ambush laid for him by the Suitors. So*

next morning he departed, with many gifts from Menelaus and Helen. Even as he left, an eagle swooped down and carried off a great white goose from the courtyard; and Helen interpreted it as an omen of the return of Odysseus to take vengeance on the Suitors. When Telémachus had reached his ship near Pylos and was about to sail, he was besought for passage by one Theoclýmenus, a seer, who was fleeing from a blood-feud; and granted it. Again Athene sent a fair wind; and sailing by night they eluded the Suitors' ambush. They made land near the cot of Eumaeus; and after sending the ship on to the city and entrusting the seer Theoclýmenus to his own comrade Peiraeus, the young prince went on foot to visit Eumaeus, who greeted him like a long-lost son and made ready a meal for him. The disguised Odysseus amused himself by asking Telémachus why he did not slaughter the Suitors. Telémachus explained that he was an only son and could not rely on the people against so many chieftains. Then he sent off Eumaeus to tell his mother of his safe return; and so found himself alone with his unknown father.

Odysseus and his Son

Then close at hand came Athene. A woman now seemed she,
Tall, and fair, and skilful in glorious artistry;
And stood in the sight of Odysseus by the door of the swineherd's cot.
Telémachus' eyes were turned away—he saw her not
(For the Gods show not their presence for every man to mark);
But clear she was to Odysseus, and the dogs—they did not bark,
But far across the steading they fled with a frightened whine.
Then with her brows she beckoned him; and at her sign
The noble Odysseus quit the room. Past the great wall he sped,
That ringed the yard, till he faced her. And then Athene said:
'Son of Laertes Heaven-sprung, Odysseus subtly-wise,
Tell thy son now the secret and cast away disguise;
And when ye have planned for the Suitors the death that they shall die,
Begone to the glorious city. A little while, and I,
With heart athirst for battle, will be beside ye there.'
Then lightly she touched Odysseus with the golden wand she bare;
About his limbs a mantle and a tunic she let fall
Of spotless white, and made him younger and more tall,
And filled again his hollow cheeks, and bronzed his skin,
And turned to its former darkness the beard upon his chin.
Therewith once more she vanished; and again Odysseus passed
Back to the hut—but on him his dear son gazed aghast
And turned away in terror, deeming it must be
Some God; and the words flew from him—'Stranger, thy look to me

From what it was seems altered, all in a moment's space;
Changed are the clothes upon thee, and the colour of thy face!
Sure, thou art one of the Gods that hold the Heaven's height.
Ah, grace!—that we may win us favour in Thy sight,
With golden gifts and offerings.   Have mercy now, I pray!'
Then answered the noble Odysseus, the long-enduring—'Nay,
I am no God—why liken *me* to the Gods above?
But indeed I am the father that thou mournest, for whose love
Thou hast suffered so many sorrows from the violence of men.'
So saying, he kissed his son; and then, and only then,
Burst forth the tears he had checked so long, unflinchingly.
But Telémachus, mistrusting that this indeed could be
His father, cried, 'My father—Odysseus—*thou* art not!
Thou art some God that beguiles me, to make my hapless lot
Bitterer still.   Could a mortal contrive by his own wit
Such wonders!—unless a God were at hand to accomplish it,
Making him seem, at pleasure, now aged and now young.
Old thou wast but a moment since, with foul rags round thee flung,
And now thou art like the Immortals that hold the boundless skies!'
Then answered him again Odysseus the subtly-wise:
'Nay, think it not too wondrous, nor past belief, that thus
Homeward thy own dear father is come, Telémachus.
There is no other Odysseus that shall come after me.
Long have I suffered—wandered long—by land and sea,
But here I stand, in the twentieth year, on my native shore;
And this is the work of Athene, that drives the spoil of war.
'Tis she that shapes me as she will—for hers the power—
Now as an aged beggar, and again, in the selfsame hour,
As a man yet young, and nobly clad.   Not hard it is
For the Gods of boundless Heaven to do such things as this—
To crown a man with glory and again to make him base.'
Down he sat as he said it—then to his sire's embrace
Telémachus ran, and clasped him with tears outflowing fast.
Then both were seized with longing to ease their souls at last
And loud they wept together, loud as wild birds give tongue—
Sea-eagles, or vultures crooked of claw—whose callow young
Countryfolk have stolen, before their wings were grown;
So sorely son and father together wept alone.

(XVI, 157–219.)

Then Odysseus, after concerting with Telémachus how to slay the Suitors,
sent him on to the palace.   He himself, changed back by Athene to beggar's
shape, followed with Eumaeus.   On the way he was insulted and kicked by
the goatherd Melanthius, who was leagued with the Suitors.

But as they talked, laid near them a dog upraised his head,
And pricked his ears to listen—Argus, that once was bred
By Odysseus' self, the stout of heart, yet all for nought.
For ere the hound was grown, far off his master fought
Round sacred Troy.   Then Argus with the young men used to go,
Hunting the goats of the mountain, hunting hare and roe;
But now the old dog, forgotten, with his master far away,
Stretched on a mighty midden before the palace lay,
Where dung of mules and oxen waited the farmhands' wain
To fetch it and to scatter on Odysseus' broad domain.
There outstretched lay Argus and the ticks swarmed in his hide;
And yet, when he saw Odysseus, standing close beside,
He wagged his tail, and backwards he let fall either ear,
Too weak to creep to his master.   But the king wiped off a tear,
Turning away, as he saw him, to shun Eumaeus' eyes
(It was not hard); and, quickly, he asked 'But wherefore lies
This dog on the midden, Eumaeus?   It is strange to see him so,
For noble he is to look on—though indeed I cannot know
If ever he was as fleet as he is fine to see,
Or only for show, as the hounds that haunt men's tables be,
That great men feed of their bounty because they are fair to the eye.'
Then to him Eumaeus, the swineherd, made reply:
'Thus fares the hound of a master that far away lies dead.
But were he the same to-day, in muscle and in head,
As when Odysseus left him, sailing for Troy, indeed
Thou wouldst see a hound most matchless, alike for strength and speed.
There was never a beast could escape, with Argus on his trail,
In the depths of the deepest forest.   He tracked them without fail.
But now he is fallen on evil days.   Dead lies his king,
In some strange land, and the women neglect the helpless thing.
For when, to give them orders, they have no master there,
Servants will never trouble to do what needs their care.
Ay, once the doom of bondage falls on a man, that day
Zeus, that beholdeth all things, takes half of his worth away.'
To the great house then Eumaeus turned, and strode inside
Straight for the hall, where gathered the Suitors in their pride.
But over the eyes of Argus Death's sable shadow passed,
Now he had seen his master, in the twentieth year, at last.

(XVII, 290–327.)

Odysseus too entered the palace and sat down on the threshold of the hall,
where Telémachus sent him meat and bread; then he rose and went begging
among the feasters, until the arrogant Antinoüs, now returned from his un-

successful ambush, struck him with a stool.   News of this inhospitable outrage
reached Penelope in her chamber; indignant, she summoned the old beggar to
come and see her; but he answered that it would be wiser in the evening, after
the Suitors had departed.   Now appeared another, younger beggar, Irus, who
picked a quarrel with Odysseus.   The Suitors amused themselves by setting
the pair to box; Odysseus, after breaking Irus' jaw, hauled him out into the
court.   Then he tried in vain to warn Amphínomus, who had shown him more
kindness than the others there.   Now Penelope herself came forth and showed
herself before the Suitors, more beautiful than ever.   She reproached Telémachus
for letting the old beggar be harmed; and the Suitors for wasting the wealth of
the woman they sought, instead of bringing wooers' gifts.   In shame they heaped
presents upon her.   But the trials of Odysseus were not over.   The maid
Melantho railed at him; and Eurýmachus threw a stool, which hit the cupbearer.
At length the Suitors went; then Odysseus and Telémachus cleared all weapons
from the hall.   Next, Penelope came to question the stranger.   He told a long
tale of his Cretan origin; of how he had once seen Odysseus in Crete; and of how
the hero was now in Thesprōtia, ready to return.   The grateful Penelope
ordered her maids to bathe the stranger's feet; but he refused to be touched except
by an old woman.   So Penelope called his own nurse Eurycleia, who wept to
see how this beggar resembled her lost master.

Odysseus and Eurycleia

So the old nurse took a basin of brass bright-glittering,
Wherein she was wont to wash men's feet—cold water from the spring
She poured there first in plenty, then added warm thereto.
But at once away from the fireside in haste Odysseus drew
And sat with his face to the shadow.   For now he guessed she might
Lay hands on his scar, and know it, and bring the truth to light.
Then drawing near she bathed her lord—and in a flash
She knew that place where the boar's white tusk had left its gash,
When he went where Autólycus dwelt, with his sons, on Parnassus side—
His mother's noble father, with whom none living vied
In theft and subtle swearing.   It was from a god on high
He had that gift—for to Hermes many a savoury thigh
Of lamb and kid he offered, and Hermes stood at hand
To bless him still.   Now it happened, to Ithaca's fair land
Autólycus came, and found there his daughter's new-born son.
Upon the knees of his grandsire, when suppertime was done,
Eurycleia laid her nursling, and spoke these words withal:
'Autólycus, bethink thee, by what name wilt thou call
The dear son of thy daughter, this child of many a prayer?'
And Autólycus made answer—'Why then, the boy shall bear,

Good son-in-law and daughter, this name that I choose for him.
For now I am come hither in anger great and grim
With many a man and woman on this rich earth—and so
Call him "Odysseus"—"the man of wrath." When he shall grow
To youth, and come to that great house of his mother's kin,
That stands beneath Parnassus, with all my wealth therein,
I will choose him a present from it, and send him homeward glad.'
So when to claim that bounty Odysseus came, a lad,
Autólycus made him welcome, and the sons of Autólycus' race,
With many a kindly greeting, many an embrace;
And his mother's mother, Amphíthea, with arms outspread
Clasped him and pressed her kisses on his comely eyes and head.
But Autólycus bade his famous sons let food be brought—
Speedily they obeyed him, and out they went and caught
A bullock of five summers, and flayed him with a will,
And hewed the limbs asunder, and severed them with skill;
Then upon spits they roasted and served the portions round.
So all day long, until the sun sank underground,
They revelled, and no man lacked his fill of the equal feast;
But when the sun was sunken and the dusk of night increased,
To rest they turned, and upon them the boon of sleep was shed.
But when upsprang the early Dawn, with fingers rosy-red,
The sons of Autólycus roused them, with their hunting-hounds, to chase,
And with them noble Odysseus. To the beetling mountain-face
Of forest-clad Parnassus and up its dales wind-swept
They turned and quickly clambered; till, as the first sun leapt
O'er earth from Ocean's deep and softly flowing tide,
Into a glen the beaters came. In front there cried
The hounds on the trail of the quarry, while followed at their back
Autólycus' sons and with them—on the very heels of the pack—
Shaking his mighty spear, Odysseus ran before.
But there in the heart of a thicket lay couched a monstrous boar—
No wet blasts of the tempest could pierce that tangled lair,
Never the glittering shafts of the sun could enter there,
No driving rain beat through it—so dense it grew and deep,
And dead leaves lay within it, piled in a mighty heap.
But now, as he lurked, about him the feet of hounds and men
Grew loud, as they hurried onward—at once from out his den
The beast, with eyes all burning and roughly bristled crest,
Rose face to face before them. In front of all the rest,
Long spear in stalwart hand, all eagerness to kill,
Odysseus sprang. But against him the boar struck swifter still.
Above his knee, and through his flesh, with a sidelong blow,
The tusk went tearing deeply; yet spared the bone below.

But down through the beast's right shoulder Odysseus drove his spear,
And out again beyond it the glittering point stood clear,
And the boar in the dust fell screaming, and breathed his life away.
Then the good sons of Autólycus took up the prey,
And the wound of noble Odysseus, the godlike, close and well
They bound, and the dark blood's flowing they staunched with a chanted
    spell;
Then hastened swiftly homeward, back to their father's door.
There, with his sons, Autólycus healed him once more,
And gave him glorious presents, and so in a little while
Sent him back rejoicing, home to his own dear isle
Of Ithaca.   Returning, a happy sight was he
To his sire and his noble mother: they asked him eagerly
Whence came that scar upon him, and he told them all the truth,
How his thigh was wounded by the boar's white tooth,
Hunting high on Parnassus, beside Autólycus' sons.

  So now the old nurse's fingers, feeling his leg, at once
Came on the scar, and knew it—she dropped his foot to the ground,
That his leg smote hard on the basin, making its brass resound,
And tipped it back, and the water was scattered along the floor.
With joy she was filled, and anguish—fast her eyes brimmed o'er
With tears, and in her throat she felt the utterance choke;
Then, seizing the chin of Odysseus, thus his old nurse spoke:
'Indeed thou art Odysseus, my dear child—yet for such,
Master, I never knew thee, till I felt thy body's touch!'
So saying, Eurycleia turned to her mistress, fain
To tell that her dear husband was come safe home again.
But Penelope saw nothing—she might not understand,
For Athene rapt her thoughts away.   But with one hand
Odysseus groped, and gripped his nurse's throat, and near
He dragged her with the other, and whispered in her ear—
'Old mother, wilt thou slay me!—thou that upon thy breast
Didst nurse me once!   Behold now, long troubled and distressed,
Home I am come to my country, in the twentieth year, at last;
But since some God hath opened thine eyes to me, hold fast
Thy tongue, lest any other should know me in this hall.
For else, I tell thee surely—and so it shall befall—
If over these proud Suitors God gives me victory,
I will not show thee mercy—though thou didst foster me—
When I leave the other handmaids within my palace slain.'
Then the wise Eurycleia answered him again:
'Dear son, what word is this has passed between thy teeth?
Thou knowest how firm my spirit, how sure my heart beneath.
I will be as rock unyielding, as iron; so thou shalt find.

Another thing I tell thee—and take it well to mind:
If God lay low before thee the Suitors in their pride,
I will name thee all the women that here in thy house abide—
Which do thy name dishonour, and which are pure in deed.'
Then answered the subtle Odysseus—'Nay now, old nurse, what need?
Why shouldst thou tell? Myself, I will watch and judge each one.
But keep thine own tongue silent, and let the Gods' will be done.'

(XIX, 386–502.)

Eurycleia fetched more water and bathed Odysseus' feet. Then Penelope asked his counsel—should she stay with her son, or wed again to save his heritage from utter wreck? She had dreamed that a great eagle slew twenty of her geese, then a voice said 'The geese are the Suitors and I, the eagle, thy husband.' Odysseus answered her that the dream interpreted itself. Yet Penelope still doubted—there are indeed dreams that pass through the Gate of Horn and tell the truth, but others come from the Gate of Ivory, only to deceive. She was resolved now to set a trial for the Suitors—whoever should most easily string the bow of Odysseus and shoot an arrow through the openings in twelve axeheads, should win her hand. Odysseus approved; for her husband, he said, would be home again before they could perform it. Then Penelope left him and he lay down in the covered porch. There the women who were the Suitors' paramours passed laughing to their lovers. Odysseus debated whether to rise and slay them; but spared them for one night more. As he tossed sleepless, Athene appeared in woman's form and gave him comfort. Near dawn he heard Penelope weeping; unable to bear it, he rose and prayed Zeus for an omen. Zeus thundered in Heaven; then Odysseus heard a slave-woman pray, as she toiled at her quern, that this might be the last flour she ever ground for the Suitors. Again the goatherd Melanthius reviled him; but the neatherd Philoetius greeted the old beggar who so resembled his lost master. Again the Suitors discussed the murder of Telémachus; but an omen dismayed them. At the feast Ctesippus hurled an ox-hoof at Odysseus; and Telémachus threatened death to any that wronged his guest. Then Agelāus again urged him to make his mother wed. Again Telémachus answered that he could not constrain her.

The Vision of Theoclýmenus

So Telémachus spoke. But Pallas Athene sent
Madness upon the Suitors, and quenchless merriment.
They laughed—but the lips they laughed with, seemed no more their own
And it was as the flesh of their feasting with drops of blood were strown;
Wet grew their eyes, and dark their hearts, with bodings dim descried.
Then amid them the godlike prophet, Theoclýmenus, cried:

'Unhappy men, what ails ye all? For to my sight
Your heads are veiled, and your faces, and your knees, in gloom like night.
There rises a noise of wailing—I see your faces wet
With tears—on wall and rafter red stains of blood are set.
The courtyard is filled with phantoms—the porch with wraiths that fly
Down to the gloom of Erebus. Gone from the sky
The sun!—and an evil darkness thickens over all!'
Then merrily laughed the Suitors in answer through the hall;
And Pólybus' son, Eurýmachus, lifted his voice and said:
'This new-come stranger, comrades, is wandering in his head.
Out with him, men, to the city. Let him shift to the market-place,
Since here in the house he finds such gloom before his face.'
But the godlike prophet answered, 'Nay, Eurýmachus, nay,
Of thee I ask no escort, to bring me on my way.
I have eyes of my own, and ears, and feet to take me hence,
And a heart here in my bosom not wholly reft of sense.
With these I will get me gone, since clearly I see the shape
Of doom that strides upon ye—not one man shall escape
Of you that haunt Odysseus' house and woo his wife for bride,
Doing all men outrage, in the blindness of your pride.'
   So saying he strode from that noble hall, and went his way
To the threshold of Peiraeus, that welcomed him. But they
Interchanging glances, turned to make them sport
Against Telémachus, because of the guests he brought;
And thus, in their youth's vainglory, they cried with mockery:
'When was there ever a man with guests so ill to see,
Telémachus, as *thine* are! We are brought this beggared oaf,
Ignorant, decrepit, greedy of wine and loaf,
Mere useless cumberer of the earth. And by and by
Follows this other fellow, that needs must prophesy.
Wouldst thou but take my counsel, indeed it were far the best
In a many-oared ship to set the pair, and sail them west
Out to the land of the Sicels—good profit we might win.'
So the Suitors jested. But deaf to their idle din,
Telémachus, in silence, gazed towards his father there,
Till he should loose upon them grim hands that would not spare.

(xx, 345–86.)

Now Penelope went to her treasure-chamber to fetch Odysseus' bow. Long
she wept above it, then descended to the Suitors in the hall. Eumaeus and
Philoetius also wept at the sight of their master's bow; and Antínoüs railed
at them savagely. Telémachus dug a trench in the earthen floor of the hall
and set up the twelve axes to shoot through. First Leiōdes tried in vain to
string the bow. Then Antinoüs bade Melanthius light a fire and grease the

weapon. But still none could string it. Meanwhile Odysseus led Eumaeus and Philoetius from the hall and revealed himself, showing the wild boar's scar; then cut short their tears of joy to give them orders for the coming fight. As the three returned to the hall, Eurýmachus was vainly struggling with the bow. Antínoüs proposed that they defer the trial till to-morrow, since to-day was the feast of Apollo. But Odysseus begged to be allowed to try. The Suitors raged and Antínoüs threatened to kill him; but Penelope interposed—did they fear she would wed this beggar? Then Telémachus spoke out, bidding his mother go back to her household, for the disposal of his father's bow was his. She went, and Eumaeus was bringing the bow to Odysseus, when the menaces of the Suitors made him halt. But Telémachus drove him forward again with threats fiercer still.

The Slaying of the Suitors

So Telémachus spoke; then laughter loud and gay
Rose up among the Suitors, and with it died away
Their bitter rage against him; but along the hall there passed
The swineherd, and laid the bow in Odysseus' hand at last;
Then called to Eurycleia and said to her, apart:
'Telémachus commands thee, Eurycleia, thou wise heart—
Bar the strong doors of the women's hall; and though ye hear
Uproar within these walls, or cries of pain and fear,
Ply ye your work in silence, and come not forth to sight.'
Never a word she answered him, but fastened tight
The doors of the fair-built chambers wherein the women slept.
Then from the house, in silence, swiftly Philoetius crept,
And closed the gates of the high-walled court, and left them bound
With a curved ship's cable, of byblus, that lay there on the ground
Under the porch of the gateway. Then back to the hall he went,
To the seat whence he had risen, and sat with eyes intent
Upon the face of Odysseus, as he handled and turned the bow
This way and that, and tried it on every side, to know
If worms at the horn had nibbled, while left by its lord it lay.
But towards each other the Suitors glanced, and one would say:
'Of bows, it seems, this fellow is a judge exceeding wise!
Maybe just such another by his own fireside lies,
Or else he is minded to make him one!—with touch so fond
He turns it over and over, this rascally vagabond!'
And then of those young wantons another would reply:
'And much good may it bring him!—as sure as by and by
He shall have the strength to string it!' So sourly jested they,
But now the subtle Odysseus, so soon as every way

He had turned the great bow and scanned it, at once, as easily
As a man that is skilled with the lyre and a master of minstrelsy
Slips a new string upon its peg, when at each end
He has knotted the twisted sheep-gut—so did Odysseus bend
That mighty bow in a moment; then with his right hand tried
The string—as sweet as a swallow, under his touch, it cried.
But there fell on the Suitors blank dismay, and white to see
Their faces went.   Zeus thundered, loud and bodingly;
And glad the enduring heart of noble Odysseus grew
That the Son of subtle Crŏnus sent that clear sign and true.
He seized a swift-winged arrow, beside his table set
With naked point (for the others lay closed in the quiver yet,
Although those sons of Achaea were soon to feel them bare),
And gripping the bridge of the bow, and sitting still in his chair,
Drew backward string and arrow-notch, then with a steady aim
Let the shaft fly—through the axeheads, from first to last, it came,
That arrowhead with its weight of bronze, and missed not one,
But cleared them all, and sped onward.   Then Odysseus cried to his son:
'Telémachus, the stranger that sits to-day in thy hall
Hath shamed thee not.   I have hit the mark; and it took no toil at all
To string thy bow.   My manhood abides unweakened still
And the Suitors lied, when they mocked me with words of evil will.
But now is the hour to make ready, while the light is clear to see,
Supper for the Achaeans; and then, with melody
And dance to crown the banquet, gaily we will carouse.'
So saying the godlike Odysseus made sign with knitted brows
To his dear son; and swiftly Telémachus girt his brand
About his waist and, gripping his spear in his right hand,
Beside his seat, bright-helmed in bronze, with his father took his stand.
   But now the subtle Odysseus his rags from his shoulders flung
And with bow and well-filled quiver to the great threshold he sprung;
At his feet he spilt the arrows, out on the floor of the hall,
And shouted to the Suitors, 'The trial that settles all
Is ended—now for a target that none hath tried, to see
If I can hit—if Apollo will grant that feat to me.'
Such were the words of Odysseus, and he aimed a deadly shaft
At Antínoüs, as he lifted in his fingers for a draught
A fair, gold, two-eared goblet.   Death troubled not his mind—
For who indeed at a banquet would ever dream to find
Black doom, from a single foeman, howsoever brave,
With feasters thick about him?   But Odysseus' arrow clave,
With deadly aim, his gullet, and pierced his soft neck through,
And Antínoüs slid sideways—from his hand the winecup flew,
As the arrow struck; from his nostrils a blood-jet spurted thick;

And he spurned the table from him, with a last sudden kick,
That its dainties all—roast flesh and bread—across the floor
Were scattered in defilement.   Then with a wild uproar
The Suitors filled the palace, seeing their comrade fall,
And leapt from their seats in fury, scanning the fair-built wall
This way and that, for weapons; but never a shield they spied,
Nor mighty spear to arm them; then angrily they cried
Their rage against Odysseus—'A curse upon thy play,
Stranger, of taking men for mark!   Thou hast shot this day
The last of all thy matches.   Sure stands thy doom in truth,
Seeing that thou hast murdered the very noblest youth
In Ithaca.   Now vultures shall tear the flesh of thee!'
For thus they deemed, not dreaming that he had purposely
Struck down the dead—so little could their childish folly tell
That the ends of doom were fastened upon themselves as well.
Then cried the subtle Odysseus, with lowering brows and black:
'Dogs, indeed ye trusted that never could I come back
From the land of Troy—and therefore ye feared not to lay waste,
My house, and force my women to lie in your arms unchaste,
And woo, while I yet was living, my wife in my despite;
Neither dreading the Gods, that hold the Heaven's height,
Nor recking that good men's anger upon your deeds should fall.
Lo now!   The ends of destruction are fast upon ye all.'
Then terror seized upon them, and white their cheeks were grown,
But no man dared to answer, save Eurýmachus alone—
'If *thou* art Odysseus of Ithaca, after so long
Returned, indeed the Achaeans have done thee wanton wrong,
Alike to lands and household; and justly thou hast said.
And yet the man that was guilty of all this lies there dead—
Antínoüs!   By *his* doing these things were brought to be;
Not so much that he wished or sought to wed Penelope—
Nay, he was plotting, rather, to be lord of this fair land,
Himself, when thy son had fallen in ambush by his hand.
But Zeus forbade.   He has perished.   Therefore have mercy thou
On us that are yet thy people.   And we will gather now
Enough through the land to repay thee for all that is spent of thine,
Both meat and drink; each bringing, in atonement, twenty kine:
Bronze too and gold we will give thee, till thy heart is satisfied.
Till then no man may blame thee, fierce though thy wrath abide.'
Then Odysseus cried in answer, scowling dark with ire—
'Eurýmachus, though each gave me the whole wealth of his sire—
All that ye now possess, all ye can gather more,
Not even so from slaughter would I hold my hands, before
Ye Suitors have paid to the utmost the evil ye have done.

Therefore this choice is left ye—fight with me now, or run,
Hoping that some among you may still escape your fate:
Yet surely I deem there are others for whom death lies in wait.'
At that the hearts within them and the knees of all grew weak,
But again among his fellows thus did Eurýmachus speak—
'My friends, he will not spare us, with his deadly hands, nor show
Mercy; and, now he has armed him with quiver and polished bow,
He will shoot us down, as he stands there on the stone sill of the door,
Till he kills us all.   Come, remember our ancient joy in war—
Against his death-winged arrows take each of you for targe
A table; then out with your swords, and at him!—make a charge,
All as one man!   From the threshold and the doorway let us try
To thrust him—then out through the city, to raise the hue and cry!
And then this man will quickly have shot his last, maybe.'
So saying, against Odysseus, shouting terribly,
He leapt, with his two-edged blade of biting bronze laid bare.
But against him noble Odysseus let fly a shaft, and there
It struck his chest by the nipple—the whizzing arrow tore
Its way athwart his liver—his sword fell to the floor,
And sprawling over a table, with huddled limbs, he crashed,
While the double-handled goblet, and the food, on the ground were
     dashed.
His two feet spurned the settle, his forehead beat the ground
In the anguish of the dying; and in night his eyes were drowned.
Then against the renowned Odysseus in turn Amphínomus leapt—
Face to face he charged him and out his sharp sword swept,
In hope to fight the doorway clear.   But swifter yet
Telémachus hurled, behind him, and the brazen spearpoint met
Amphínomus 'twixt the shoulders and out through his breast it thrust,
And he fell with a crash, and his forehead hurtled into the dust.

(XXI, 376–XXII, 94.)

*Then Telémachus ran to fetch arms for his father to wield, when his arrows
should be spent, and for their two faithful servants.   On the other hand the
false goatherd Melanthius began stealing weapons from the storeroom for the
Suitors; but he was caught and bound by Eumaeus and Philoetius.   Athene
showed herself to encourage Odysseus, first in the shape of Mentor, then as a
swallow perched on the rafters.   A new charge by six of the boldest Suitors
failed; then Athene raised her Aegis and in panic the survivors scattered through
the hall, only to be slain.   The minstrel Phēmius and the herald Mĕdon were
spared; the rest lay in heaps of blood and dust, like a draught of fishes tumbled
gasping on the shore.   The twelve faithless handmaids who had given their
love to the Suitors, were made to wash the floor and bear out the dead; then
hanged together by Telémachus from a single hawser.   The traitor Melanthius*

was mutilated and slain. *Now Eurycleia ran with the glad news to Penelope;
but her mistress would not believe. It must be some God, she said, that had been
provoked to punish the Suitors' insolence. She came and sat opposite Odysseus,
searching him silently with her eyes. At last he turned away, ordered the
minstrel to strike up a dance-tune to deceive the men of Ithaca, and went to bathe.
Returning and finding Penelope still cold, he ordered a bed to be prepared for
him alone. Then, to test him, she ordered that his great bed be made up
outside their marriage-chamber. Odysseus knowing that one post of his bed
had been formed by the immovable trunk of an olive, cried out in anger that it
should have been changed. Then at last Penelope doubted him no more.*

The Reunion of Odysseus and Penelope

But her knees at his words were loosened and the heart within her breast
Melted—so well she knew those tokens manifest;
And straight she ran to Odysseus, weeping, and kissed his head,
Clasping her arms about his neck; and then she said—
'Be angry no more, Odysseus!—for thou wast ever first
Of men, in understanding. Our lives the Gods have curst;
To share the happy years of youth and, side by side,
Pass to the threshold of old age—this They denied.
But ah, do not reproach me, do not feel bitterly,
That I did not, in that first moment, open my arms to thee.
For, always, deep within me I felt my heart to fail
With terror, lest some stranger should come with a cunning tale
To trap me—there *are* so many that speak things false and fair.
And, indeed, the Argive Helen, daughter of Zeus, had ne'er
Given her love and her body unto a foreign face,
Had she but seen beforehand that one day in disgrace
The warlike sons of Achaea would bring her home again.
So she was tempted of Heaven to a deed of shame—in vain,
Too late, she saw her blindness; too late did she discern
That bitter fault, whence sorrow on *our* lives fell in turn.
But now, since the certain tokens of our bride-bed thou hast told,
That the eyes of no one living have looked on from of old,
Save thine and mine and, beside us, one handmaiden's alone,
Actor's child, who was given by my father for my own,
When I wedded thee, and has warded our marriage-chamber door—
My heart thou hast persuaded, that was so hard before.'
Yet deeper, then, the craving for tears within him grew
And clasping the wife he loved, the loyal and the true,
Odysseus wept; and as lovely as land at last in sight
To swimmers whose stout vessel with wave and tempest's might

Poseidon breaks—from the surges hardly a handful swims
At length to land, with the brine close-crusting all their limbs,
And dear seems the earth beneath them, escaped from death abhorred—
So sweet and dear to her was the sight of her own loved lord.
Long, long about his neck her two white arms clung fast.
The rosy-fingered Morning would have found them there at last
Still weeping, if Athene, the bright-eyed, had not made
This too her care—the passing of the long Night she delayed,
Nor suffered Dawn by the Ocean-stream on her golden throne
To yoke her fleet-foot coursers, Lampos and Phaëthōn,
That to the eyes of mortals bring back day's radiancy.
Then said the wise Odysseus unto Penelope:
'Dear wife, let us not linger, for my labours are not o'er,
Not even now; new toils, past telling, lie in store,
Bitter and long to accomplish, that will not be denied.
For so to me the spirit of Teirésias prophesied,
When down I went to the house where Hades sits as king,
In hope to win my own and my comrades' homecoming.
But now, dear wife, to bedward let us turn us—so 'twere best—
That we may take together, at last, the joy of rest.'

(XXIII, 205–55.)

Penelope asked what was the quest that Teirésias had laid upon him; and Odysseus told how he must travel forth again till he found a race that knew nothing of the sea. Then, after he had sacrificed to Poseidon and the other Gods, he should live in peace, till from the sea a quiet death came to him at last. So the old nurse and the housekeeper lighted them to bed and they renewed their love of long ago. Then Penelope told all she had suffered from the Suitors; and Odysseus related all his wanderings from Troy to Ithaca. When morning, long delayed by Athene, came at last, Odysseus set forth with Telémachus, Eumaeus, and Philoetius to find his old father on his farm. Meanwhile the ghosts of the Suitors flitted to the world of the Dead, where Agamemnon recognized one of them, and learned from him the whole tale of the slaying, and blessed Odysseus that he had a wife whose loyalty should be famous for ever.

Odysseus and his Father

Now Hermes of Cyllene called to the world beyond
The wraiths of the fallen Suitors—in hand he bore his wand,
Fair-wrought in gold, wherewith he charms the eyes of men
To sleep, and out of slumber awakens them again.
With it he roused the Suitors, and led them—shrieking shrill
They followed; as squeaking flutter the hosts of bats that fill

The nooks of some great grotto, if one shall chance to fall
From the chain that clusters clinging to the cavern's rocky wall.
So, gibbering, on Hermes the Saviour in his flight
They followed, where he led them on the mouldering paths of night—
Past the great gateway of the Sun, past Ocean's streams,
Past the White Rock they hastened, past the Land of Dreams,
Until at the last they came to the Meadow of Asphodel,
Where the phantoms of the weary, the souls of the perished dwell. . . .

    But Odysseus found his sire alone; the old man plied
His spade by a tree in his vineyard, with gaiters of stitched oxhide
About his calves, and gauntlets against the thorns that tore;
Nought but a cap of goatskin upon his head he wore,
And mean and patched and filthy was all the old man's dress;
For his heart cared but to deepen his own unhappiness.
But when the noble Odysseus, the enduring, saw him there
Wasted with many years, and his heart weighed down with care,
Under a lofty pear-tree he turned away to weep.
And afterwards, for a little, he stood and pondered deep—
Should he embrace his father, and kiss him, and tell him plain
That now in his native country his son was home again?
Or ply him at first with questions, and find how all things lay?
But, as he thus debated, it seemed the better way
First with deluding speech to try the old man's mood.
And so the noble Odysseus strode up to where he stood;
But still at his root Laertes toiled, with downbent head,
Till close there came beside him his glorious son and said—
'Old sir, indeed thou lackest no knowledge how to till
A garden—all about thee bears witness to thy skill.
Each plant, each vine, each fig-tree, each olive here and pear,
Ay, every garden-plot in this orchard shows thy care.
Yet must I say—and I pray thee, be not vexed with me—
Thou art, thyself, cared for but ill. For heavily
Weighs thy old age, and mean and squalid is thy dress;
At least, if thy lord neglects thee, 'tis not for idleness!
But indeed thou hast no semblance of a bondsman in thy face
Or stature—thou seemest, rather, like one of royal race—
One that might live in comfort and pass from bath and food
To a down-bed, to slumber as soft as old men should.
But answer me my question now, and tell me clear—
What man hast thou for master? Whose is this orchard here?
And tell me too, is this isle indeed—I fain would know—
Ithaca?—as one told me a little while ago,
Who met me coming hither—not lively of wit was he,
For he would not answer me fully—nay, hardly heeded me,

When I asked if a friend that once I loved were living now,
Or dead and gone to Hades' hall.   But listen, thou,
I will tell thee all my story, that thou mayest understand.
Once there came a stranger to my dear fatherland,
Whom I gave entertainment—indeed he pleased me more
Than ever wandering stranger that came to my house before.
He claimed that his home was Ithaca—his sire, he said,
Laertes, son of Arceisius.   So him I led
To my own roof, and gave him a hearty welcome there;
For I loved him well, and my household had plenty and to spare.
Then, as for a guest of honour, rich gifts for him I brought:
A mixing-bowl, solid silver, with flowers overwrought,
I gave him, and seven talents of finely fashioned gold;
Twelve coverlets, and as many cloaks of single fold;
Twelve tunics and twelve mantles, fine-woven; and thereto
Four women, of the fairest, with fingers skilled to do
Handiwork to perfection—and let him choose the four.'
Then his old father cried aloud, lamenting sore:
'Stranger this *is*, indeed, the isle of Ithaca—
But mad with pride and outrage the men that hold it are.
Alas, thy generous gifts to *him* are thrown away!
Be sure, hadst thou found him living in Ithaca this day,
Both gifts and warmest welcome from him thou wouldst have won;
For indeed he had been bounden to requite such kindness done.
But come now, give me an answer, tell all the truth to me—
How long ago, then, was it, that thus hospitably
Thou didst receive that hapless guest?   *My son* he was—
If son I had!—but him, far from his home, alas,
Far from his friends, the fishes within the wave did eat,
Or upon land wild beast and bird.   No winding-sheet
His mother wrapped around him; we might not mourn our son;
And the wife whom in days past over his rich gifts wooed and won,
The wise Penelope, stood not beside his bier
To close her husband's eyelids, with many a dirge and tear—
The last sad meed of honour that the dead have for their due.
But tell me now what I long to know, and tell me true—
Who art thou?   Whence come hither?   Thy parentage?   Thy land?
And where is the swift galley—far off or close at hand?—
That brought thee, and thy good comrades?   Or didst thou travel, say,
Aboard some ship of others, that left thee and sailed away?'
Then in his turn there answered Odysseus the subtly-wise:
'The truth indeed I will tell thee, and free from all disguise.
I come from Álybas, from a house well known to fame;
My father is King Apheidas, Polypēmon's son; by name

Epēritus they call me.   And now, far off my course,
Towards Sicánia sailing, God drove me here perforce;
But my ship lies away from the city, out on the open shore.
As for Odysseus, four years now are past, and more,
Since from the coast of my country away to sea he stood—
Unhappy man!   Yet the omens at his going boded good,
With birds on the right hand flying—gladly upon his way
I sped him, glad he departed.   For indeed he hoped one day
That we should meet in friendship, with generous gifts, again.'
Then the old man's eyes were darkened with the gloom of bitter pain—
He seized black dust and ashes in both his hands to shed,
With cries and lamentations, upon his hoary head.
But, at the sight of his sorrow, Odysseus' pity woke
And suddenly from his nostrils anguish past bearing broke.
He ran to embrace his father, and kissed his face, and cried—
'The son thou weepest, father—he stands here at thy side!
Home I am come to my country, after nigh twenty years;
Cease thy lamentations, cease thy bitter tears,
And hark to the very truth—for quickly it must be said.
I have left within my palace the Suitors lying dead—
Avenged are the shame and outrage and ill they loved to do.'
Then cried the old Laertes—'If this indeed be true
And *thou* art my son Odysseus, then show me now some sign,
Some token past all doubting, that I may know thee mine.'
Then again there answered Odysseus the subtly-wise:
'First, here upon this ancient scar turn thou thine eyes,
Where once high on Parnassus the boar's tusk wounded me,
When thou and my noble mother sent me from home to see
Her sire beloved, Autólycus; that I might claim
The gifts the old man promised, when, long before, he came
To Ithaca.   And listen—I will tell thee all the trees
Thou gavest me in this fair garth—for all of these,
As a little boy, I begged thee—through this orchard following
Thy steps, of their names I asked thee, and thou toldst me everything.
Thirteen were the pear-trees, and the apple-trees were ten
Thou gavest, and forty fig-trees—and thou didst promise, then,
I should have fifty vine-stocks, that in succession came
To ripeness—ay, the clusters on no two showed the same,
As the passage of God's seasons swelled them upon the bough.'
But the old man's knees were loosened, melted his heart, as now
He knew for sure the tokens thus by Odysseus told—
Round his dear son he clasped his arms.   And in his hold
Odysseus seized his father, swooning as if to death.
But then, as he recovered his senses and his breath,

Once more spoke old Laertes—'Ah, Zeus, as in the past,
Ye Gods yet hold Olympus' height—if thus at last
The Suitors have been punished for their pride's iniquity.
And yet my heart misgives me, that now right speedily
The Ithacans against us may gather, armed for war,
And call to their aid the cities of Cephallēnia.'
Then noble Odysseus answered—'Take heart, no need for fear!
Let us turn into the house now, beside the orchard here;
I have sent Telémachus thither, before me, to prepare,
With the neatherd and the swineherd, food for our midday fare.'

(XXIV, 1–14, 226–360.)

*While Odysseus, Laertes, and Telémachus sat to eat, Rumour flew through
Ithaca with tidings of the Suitors' death. The mourners gathered their slain
from the palace. Then Eupeithes, father of the fallen Antínoüs, roused the
people with his cries for vengeance, though Mĕdon the herald and Halitherses
spoke against him; and so the most part of the men of Ithaca came marching
towards Laertes' farm. But, with the approval of Zeus, Athene leapt from
Heaven to intervene. Odysseus, his father, his son, and their servants were
now armed and facing the rebels. Athene again took the shape of Mentor
and encouraged old Laertes, who hurled his spear and slew Eupeithes. Then
Odysseus and the rest charged, and the Ithacans fled. But Zeus cast a flaming
bolt from Heaven to stay the strife; and between Odysseus and his people peace
was restored at last.*

NOTES

[Page 106] *Suitors have beset us*. Telémachus lists them in *Od.* XVI—52 from Dulíchium (perhaps part of Cephallēnia), 24 from Same (perhaps the other part of Cephallēnia), 20 from Zacynthus, 12 from Ithaca. Total, 108. It has been suggested that this would overcrowd the hall of Odysseus and that the passage should be deleted; but it seems niggling to check a poet so precisely by the size of actual remains at Tiryns or Mycenae.

[Page 106] *Bride-price*. See p. 91.

[Page 106] *Icárius*. Brother of Tyndáreüs, the father of Helen (though she was actually child of Zeus) and Clytemnestra. The recurrent contrast in the *Odyssey* between the true wife, Penelope, and these two fatal women is heightened by their close kinship—they are first cousins. Tradition told how Icárius so loved his daughter that, when she wedded Odysseus, he tried to keep the young couple with him at Sparta. But the home-loving Odysseus would not give up Ithaca and, setting his wife in his chariot, took the road north from Lacedaemon. Even then Icárius followed, begging at least his daughter to stay. At last Odysseus bade her choose. In silence she drew her veil across her face. So Icárius understood what, gentler than Cordelia, she would not say—that she must follow her husband; and, resigning himself, set up by the wayside a statue of Modesty—the same, Pausanias fondly believed, as he saw by the road north of Sparta fourteen hundred years later, in the second century A.D. (III, 20, 10).

Other accounts linked Icárius with Cephallēnia or Acarnānia—which would be much nearer for the Suitors.

[Page 106] *Thĕmis*. Goddess of law and order. In *Il.* XX Zeus bids her convene the assembly of the Gods.

[Page 106] *Warp*. The vertical threads that were first hung from the top bar of the loom; after which the horizontal threads of the woof were woven through them with the shuttle.

[Page 107] *Tyro*. Daughter of the Thessalian Salmōneus and mother, by Crētheus, of Aeson, father of Jason; by Poseidon, of the evil Pĕlias and of Nēleus, the father of Nestor.

[Page 107] *Alcmēne*. Mother of Hēracles (p. 342).

[Page 107] *Mycēne*. Daughter of the Argive river Inăchus, who gave her name to Mycenae.

[Page 110] *With ye, the people, I am angry*. Homer's attitude to the multitude is curiously like Shakespeare's—sympathy and even admiration for individuals, amused contempt for the gullibility, baseness, and savagery of the many-headed beast when it lacks leadership. These truths, indeed, have changed little in thirty centuries. Mme Dacier well points out that in the *Iliad* common men perish by the folly of their kings—or, as Horace puts it, 'Quicquid delirant reges, plectuntur Achivi'; whereas in the *Odyssey* it is the wisdom of their king that struggles, often in vain, to prevent common men from perishing by follies of their own. (This applies both to the comrades of Odysseus and to his subjects in Ithaca.)

[Page 110] *Pylos*. Probably the Messenian Pylos, near Navarino (p. 86).

[Page 111] *Pharos* is less than a mile from the coast where later rose Alexandria—indeed it has ceased to be an island. But this coast was then Libya,

and Egypt only began some 25 miles eastward, at the Canopic mouth of the
Nile. True, a short day's-sail; but, in any case, what is this inaccuracy
compared with 'sea-coasts of Bohemia'? It may, indeed, be the Bolbinitic
(Rosetta) mouth that Homer has in mind (see Rhys Carpenter, *Folktale, Fiction,
and Saga in the Homeric Epics*, 98–9); that would make 40 miles.

Pharos was important to early navigators on these dangerous coasts with
their shoaling waters and often low-lying land. 'From Paraetonium [near Mersa
Matruh] in Libya to Joppa in Hollow Syria,' says Diodorus, 'a voyage of over
5000 stadia, the only safe harbour is Pharos.' But it was easy to be windbound
there. If the sailing-season be put at 210 days, says Bérard (*Les Phéniciens et
l'Odyssée*, 11, 75), on more than 180 the wind is liable to be between N. and E.

[Page 111] *Prōteus*. Bérard (11, 49) connects Pharos with Pharaoh, and
Prōteus with *prouiti* ('*la Sublime Porte*'), another of Pharaoh's titles. Indeed
Egyptian priests assured Herodotus that Prōteus was a king of Memphis (cf.
Euripides, *Helen*). Egyptian romances from papyri tell of magic transformations
and of Pharaohs skilled in magic; indeed the putting of magical constraint even
on the Gods is typically Egyptian. On the other hand, such resemblances can
be overstressed. Other Greek deities, like Nēreus and Thētis, have powers of
shape-changing (appropriate to their watery nature); or, like Nēreus and Glaucus,
foreknow the future.

[Page 112] *Sea's fair daughter*. Amphitrīte (p. 228).

[Page 112] *Take . . . all shapes*. Similarly Thētis when seized by Pēleus,
Nēreus when grappled by Hēracles. Cf. too *Tam Lin*:

> They 'll turn me in your arms, ladye,
> An aske but and a snake;
> But hauld me fast, let me na gae,
> To be your warldis make.

> They 'll turn me to a bear sae grim,
> And then a lion bold;
> But hauld me fast, let me na gae,
> The father o' your child.

> They 'll shape me in your arms, ladye,
> A hot iron at the fire;
> But hauld me fast, let me na gae,
> To be your heart's desire.

(See F. J. Child, *English and Scottish Popular Ballads*, Pt. II, 336 ff., for parallels;
including a modern Cretan tale amazingly close to the legend of Pēleus and
Thētis, and a Scandinavian ballad which, curiously enough, deals with the family
of a king and queen of *Egypt*.)

[Pages 112–13] *Ambrosial, ambrosia*. Though it is generally the food of the Gods,
which can make even men immortal, ambrosia is also used by Hēra in the *Iliad*
as a cosmetic perfume, and by Thētis to keep the corpse of Patroclus from
corruption. In short, it is a fragrant substance defying death, decay, and the
odours of decay. 'Ambrosial' night has been taken to mean 'fragrant'; but
the vaguer sense 'holy' seems more likely.

[Page 113] *All the while we gripped him*. Some ancient critics asked how they
could grip water; other ancient critics, more intelligent, replied that Prōteus
only produced a visual illusion of water.

[Page 114] *The Locrian Ajax* was the lesser Ajax, son of Oïleus, in contrast
to the greater Ajax, son of Télamon. He appears in the *Iliad* as a smaller,
lighter-armed warrior, good with the spear and swift of foot, but of harsh and

aggressive temper. Tradition told that, when Troy fell, he dragged the even fatal Cassandra from Athene's altar and was nearly stoned by the Greeks for sacrilege. Hence Athene's hatred for him here. To atone his crime, the Locrians (on the mainland opposite N. Euboea) were doomed for a thousand years to send annually two noble maidens, chosen by lot, to serve as priestesses in Athene's temple at Ilios (if they escaped being killed by the Ilians on their way there). Greek conservatism actually continued this custom till nearly A.D. 100.

The Locrians continued also to honour Ajax as a hero and left a vacant place for him in their battle-line (as some Spanish convents left a place at table for St. Theresa). A warrior of Croton who tried to pass through this gap in the ranks of the Italian Locrians, was badly wounded and had to seek healing from the hero's spirit on the White Island, near the mouth of the Danube, where he was supposed to dwell immortally with Achilles, Helen, Patroclus, the greater Ajax, and Antílochus.

[Page 114] *Gȳrae's rock.* Off Mýconos or Tēnos; or (more probably) near Cape Caphēreus in S.E. Euboea.

[Page 114] *The house of Thyestes,* by one tradition, stood on the island of Cythēra, S. of Málea; though at this moment Aegisthus was away, waiting for Agamemnon at Mycenae.

[Page 115] *Elysium.* This description recalls the Egyptian Happy Fields of Yalou, or Aalu, in the far west, where the grain grew seven cubits high and the blessed sat beneath never-dying foliage, cooled by a never-failing north wind. Compare Euripides, *Hippolytus,* 742–51:

> Where, while apples round them redden,
>   Sing the Hesperides,
> And the Sea-god guards, to ships forbidden,
>   His purple western seas.
> For there, in Atlas' keeping,
>   Lies Heaven's sacred bound,
> There springs divine rise leaping,
>   There Zeus for aye hath found
> Peace, and the kindly Earth doth bless
> The Gods' eternal happiness.

Cf. too Tennyson, *Morte d'Arthur* (Avilion):

> Where falls not hail, or rain, or any snow,
> Nor ever wind blows loudly; but it lies
> Deep-meadow'd, happy, fair with orchard-lawns
> And bowery hollows crown'd with summer sea.

[Page 115] *Rhădamanthys,* son of Zeus and Europa, and brother of Minos, ruled on earth so justly that he was made either king of the Blest, or (with Minos and Aeăcus) judge of the Dead in Hades.

[Page 115] *Samos.* Probably Cephallēnia, or part of it.

[Page 116] *Argus-slayer.* The meaning of *Argeiphontes* as title of Hermes was obscure to the later Greeks themselves. It may mean merely 'bringer of brightness.' But it was often associated with the legend that when Io, beloved of Zeus, was turned into a cow, the jealous Hēra set as guard over her the many-eyed Argus (the starry sky?); then Zeus in his turn sent Hermes to lull Argus asleep and kill him.

[Page 116] *Piéria.* The Muses' land, N. and E. of Olympus.

[Page 116] *Calypso* means 'the concealer.'

[Page 117] *By no will of mine.* The Heavenly Herald is not very polite to his hostess. Still he shows some tact in conveying his own reluctance to bring this bad news.

[Page 117] *Athene's ire.* Against the Locrian Ajax for his sacrilege (p. 182) and against the Greeks for leaving him unpunished.

[Page 117] *Hides it not.* Public opinion among the Immortals (as among some human societies) tolerates discreet liaisons of Goddesses with mortals, but not open misalliances.

Note that Calypso, with a mistress's egotism and a Goddess's pride, does not even discuss here the wishes of Odysseus. No doubt she might have replied that, like most mortals, he did not know his own good.

[Page 117] *Ortygia*, 'Isle of Quails' (common in the Aegean in summer), is here probably Dēlos.

[Page 117] *Iásion* was loved by Demeter in Crete, where she bore him Plutus (Wealth)—a clear relic of the Sacred Marriage common in fertility rituals. Frazer (*Golden Bough*, VII, 208-9) mentions a W. Prussian custom whereby the woman representing the Corn-mother enacted the mock-birth of a Corn-baby on the harvest-field.

[Page 117] *Thrice-ploughed* should perhaps here be 'triple-furrowed,' with reference to the three ritual furrows traced at the opening of the ploughing-season, as was done in China by the Emperor (E. A. Armstrong, *Class. Rev.*, 1943, p. 3).

[Page 118] *Pleased him no more.* Realist amid all his romance, Homer implies, in two brief syllables (*eti*, 'still'), that *at first* Odysseus had not found unpleasing the divine beauty of Calypso.

[Page 118] *Raft.* For details of this construction, apparently not unlike flat-bottomed rafts used in the Red Sea, cf. Bérard, *Les Phéniciens et l'Odyssée*, I, 295 ff.

[Page 118] *If so indeed the Immortals . . . ordain.* Calypso's feminine resistance to the Almighty will is delicately drawn. She tells Hermes she cannot transport Odysseus; she does *not* tell Odysseus that Zeus has ordered his release; and a few lines later she still tries a last persuasion to keep him.

[Page 119] *Styx* ('Abhorred'), one of the rivers of Hell, but also identified with a gloomy stream in N. Arcadia, whose source (now the 'Black Water' or 'Dragon Water') plunges from the snows of Mount Chelmos over 600 feet of precipice on the mountain's northern face; so that in winter, when clouds are low, it seems to drop from Heaven itself (see the admirable description in Frazer, *Pausanias*, IV, 250). Any God who swore falsely by it, had to spend a year in trance, nine years in banishment; and Psyche, in the tale of Apuleius, was forced by the cruel Venus to fetch water from its dragon-warded fount. See also my *From Olympus to the Styx* (2nd ed.), p. 322 ff.

[Page 119] *Whence Hermes had lately risen.* So close has Odysseus come to immortality. And yet he refuses it for wife and home—a strange and pleasing contrast to those edifying hagiologies of the Dark and Middle Ages where, on the contrary, men are admired for trampling, in the hope of eternal bliss, on every tie of human tenderness.

[Page 119] *Dread Goddess . . . those I bore.* One of the noblest passages, I think, in Greek—or any—poetry. It is a pity that Pindar and the Attic dramatists, smaller men than Homer, persisted in degrading Homer's hero to a sort of human fox.

For the stoical last line, cf. Odysseus' later saying—'Bear up, my heart within me. Thou hast borne a yet bitterer thing'; and the resolute refrain of the Anglo-Saxon *Lament of Deor*—'That is passed over; so this may also.'

[Page 120] *True to the line.* A string covered with chalk or ochre was held tight near the wood's surface, plucked back, and then allowed to fly forward to mark it with the straight line required.

[Page 120] *Pleiads, etc.* Since there was then no Pole Star, Greek sailors steered by the Great Bear. But the Bear was not above the Pole, and it moved —hence the need to check it by other constellations. Thus shortly before dawn in October (cf. Calypso's grapes and fire) about 1000 B.C. Arcturus would be E., the Pleiads W., Orion S. W., and the Bear's two eyes (our Pointers) aligned nearly N. and S., with her body stretching away N.E. (See Prof. D'Arcy W. Thompson in *Proc. Class. Ass.* 1929, pp. 28–9.) Odysseus is bearing E. from Calypso's far-western isle.

Professor Thompson adds that the Great Bear does set now in the Mediterranean, though she did *not* 'about 800 or 900 B.C., and for some centuries before.' This seemed to me admirable evidence for Homer's date (it *is* so used in a recent history of Greek Literature) and I consulted astronomers. But by the kindness of H.M. Nautical Almanac Office I am informed that even the star of the Bear furthest from the Pole (η U. Maj.) only began to set in the Mediterranean about A.D. 800, not B.C.

[Page 121] *Phaeacia* (Schéria), was later identified with Corcȳra, the modern Corfu. But Homer's geography, whatever its substratum of fact, remains a thing of faery.

[Page 121] *Like a shield*, laid flat on earth, convex side up.

[Page 121] *Solýmian mountains.* There were Sólymi in Lўcia and a Mount Sólyma above the Lўcian Phasēlis. But here too it seems vain to chase poets too closely with atlases. Though Lўcia might be on Poseidon's way back from Ethiopia, it is ill-suited for observing Odysseus W. of Greece.

[Page 121] *Ah thrice and four times happy....* On this line hangs a story well illustrating what Homer meant to Greece and Rome. According to Plutarch (*Quaest. Conviv.*, 737A), the Roman Mummius after taking Corinth in 146 B.C. ordered a boy among the captives to show his qualifications by writing something in the sand; bitterly the young Corinthian traced this verse; and the conqueror, despite his famous Philistinism, was so moved that he released the lad with his whole family. (It was in this same year 146 that Scipio made his Homeric quotation in view of burning Carthage, p. 89.)

[Page 122] *Thistlestalks.* The dead branches dry into balls that blow across country or whirl high in air; so that in the Russian steppes they are called 'wind-witches.'

[Page 122] *Leucóthea.* Ino, wife of Áthamas, when her husband ran mad and killed their son Learchus, leapt with her other boy Melicertes from the crag of Mŏlouris (p. 262) into the sea and became the sea-goddess Leucóthea.

[Page 122] *No rain falls there.* This vision of Heaven is imitated by Lucretius (III, 18 ff.) and by Tennyson in his *Lucretius*:

> The Gods, who haunt
> The lucid interspace of world and world,
> Where never creeps a cloud, or moves a wind,
> Nor ever falls the least white star of snow,
> Nor ever lowest roll of thunder moans,
> Nor sound of human sorrow mounts to mar
> Their sacred everlasting calm.

[Page 122] *To tell them.* Nausicaä does *not* tell them her dream. It would have been rather tedious. We can suppose, if we will, that she changed her mind on the way.

[Page 122] *A high ... wain.* Two-wheeled chariots had small wheels to keep their centre of gravity low; four-wheeled waggons could have larger wheels and so be 'high.'

[Page 123] *Washing-places.* Plutarch (*Quaest. Conviv.*, 627) conducts a learned discussion between several speakers on the problem why the Princess did not wash her clothes in the sea! Any washerwoman could have told him.

[Page 123] *As the Archer-queen....* Adapted by Virgil (*Aen.* 1, 498 ff.) to describe Dido. Not very happily; for it is far less suited to a queen in her city than to Homer's Princess playing by the wild sea-shore (though it has been pleaded that both Artemis and Dido have masculine qualities).

[Page 123] *Erymanthus.* Arcadian mountain, home of the monstrous boar slain by Hēracles as one of his Labours.

[Page 123] *Taÿgetus.* The snowy mountain-wall above the smiling vale of Sparta.

[Page 123] *The Princess cast the ball.* Sophocles wrote a lost play *Nausícaä*, in which he himself acted the Princess, being (we are told) specially skilful at ball-play. Eustathius suggests that the game here was that in which the thrower makes as if to cast the ball at one player, then suddenly sends it to another.

[Page 124] *Odysseus ... crept forth.* This scene was painted by Polygnōtus in the Propylaea at Athens.

[Page 124] *Dēlos.* Presumably the Greek fleet is supposed sailing to Troy from Aulis, by way of Dēlos, Chios, and Lesbos. For sacred palms cf. p. 211.

[Page 125] *For nought better.... Husband and wife.* One of the central themes of the whole *Odyssey*; whereas the *Iliad* turns rather on love, anger, and forgiveness between man and man. When Coventry Patmore imagined that in married happiness, as treated in *The Angel in the House*, he had found the greatest subject in the world, unaccountably neglected by poets before him, he himself unaccountably forgot Homer.

[Page 126] *His sight she took.* Perhaps one source of the tradition of Homer's blindness (cf. p. 4). But there is no reason why the creator of Demódocus may not, in these two moving lines, really have been thinking of his own loss of sight—like Milton in *Paradise Lost*.

[Page 126] *Pytho*, Delphi.

[Page 127] *Cícones.* On the Thracian mainland, N. of Samothrace. Odysseus could excuse his attack (if he thought excuse needed) by their having helped Troy.

[Page 128] *Lotus-eaters.* Odysseus, caught off Málea by one of the N.E. gales common in the Levant, would be driven on to the coasts of Tripolitania or Cyrenaica. Strabo and Ptolemy located Lotus-land more precisely in Djerba Island in the Gulf of Gabes—one of the few refuges for the seaman between Pharos and Tunis-Carthage. Bérard (*Les Phéniciens et l'Odyssée*, II, 100 ff.) points out that its inhabitants, still noted for their hospitality, live largely on fruit owing to the difficulty of growing anything else; and that the absence here of any scenic description, so unlike the rest of Odysseus' voyage (or Tennyson's *Lotos-eaters*), would suit the dull monotony of the N. African coast. Such details are easily overstressed; but there is no reason why Homer should not have used seamen's tales of the Mediterranean, as Shakespeare in *The Tempest* used seamen's tales of Bermuda.

[Page 128] *Lotus-fruit.* Sometimes identified as a sort of date, or the fruit of the jujube-tree (see Herodotus, IV, 177; Theophrastus, *Hist. Plant.*, IV, 3). One can hardly imagine forgetting home for the sake of either; but the 'lotus' was also used to make wine, which might be more effective. Still, it is futile to botanize in Elfland.

[Page 128] *Land of Cyclōpes.* This next episode would specially interest the Phaeacians, who (says *Od.* VI) had once themselves lived next the Cyclōpes, but migrated to Schéria to escape neighbours so unpleasant.

Three kinds of Cyclōpes appear in ancient legend: (1) workmen of Hephaestus, smithying the bolts of Zeus in volcanic Etna or the Lipari Islands; (2) builders of giant 'Cyclopean' walls like those at Mycenae and, still more, Tiryns (the smallest of whose blocks, says Pausanias, not two mules could shift—and indeed they remind the modern traveller of the vast crags used for door or missile by Polyphemus); (3) this Homeric race of pastoral savages, located by later tradition round Etna. Bérard's idea of them as personified volcanoes may suit (1), but hardly (2). Grimm's solar myth seems *not* convincing. The curious thing is that folktales about the blinding of a giant ogre (often one-eyed), frequently followed by an escape under cover of a sheep or sheepskin, have been found in Jugoslavia, Roumania, Esthonia, Lithuania, Finland, Lapland, Russia, Germany, Gascony, Ireland, the Basque country, Syria, Turkey, Persia, and *The Arabian Nights* (Sindbad). (See Frazer, *Pausanias*, v, 343–4.) Some psychologists would say that, like other giant-stories, they give a child's-eye view of the adult; and that the putting out of the eye is a variation on the castration of Urănus by his son Crŏnus and other Oedipus-fantasies. I should be slow to contradict them.

[Page 128] *Vermilion-red.* Coloured with cinnabar (sulphide of mercury), one of the oldest of pigments.

[Page 129] *They might have made that isle as a garden fair.* Here appears already that colonizing eye which was to spread Greek settlements from S. Russia to Marseilles.

[Page 130] *Prodigious indeed was the monster.* Note that Homer's hearers seem expected to know already that Cyclōpes are one-eyed. There is no mention here of that vital peculiarity, though the whole story turns on it.

[Page 131] *After offering To the Gods some of his cheeses.* The piety of Odysseus is contrasted from the start with the Cyclops' godlessness.

[Page 133] *Olive-wood.* It is hard to imagine making a mast, or even a straight pole, from an *olive*-tree. But the emendation 'pinewood' is hard to fit into the text. (The objection that pinewood burns even when green—even if that is *always* true—seems less cogent.)

[Page 133] *Mast of some black ship.* Imitated by Milton (*P. L.*, 1, 292–4):

> His Spear, to equal which the tallest Pine
> Hewn on Norwegian hills, to be the Mast
> Of some great Ammiral, were but a wand.

[Page 133] *After the flesh of man.* '"Cyclops, here, have a drink after that jolly meal of man's mutton"—so Rouse aptly renders.' This is the comment of Professor Stanford's recent (and excellent) edition of the *Odyssey*. So far have we travelled from the excessive dignity of Pope, to a state of mind that does not even comprehend what dignity is. There is nothing in the Greek about 'jolly,' nothing about 'mutton'; in fact, nothing whatever to suggest this tone of humorous vulgarity. It sheds no light on Homer; but only too much on one side of the twentieth century.

[Page 134] *Plunged deep in his eye Its point.* Here Pope (and it is *not* one of the books of the *Odyssey* that he farmed out to Broome or Fenton) exemplifies the opposite extreme of ridiculous mock-sublimity:

> Urg'd by some present God, they swift let fall
> The pointed torment on his visual ball.

[Page 135] *Noman's guile.* This punning device may seem excessively childish; but no more childish than actual happenings of the Middle Ages. About

1290 a certain Radulfus discovered that in the Scriptures 'nemo' (Noman) signified Christ; he even preached before the future Boniface VIII a sermon on 'the precious treasure of this most glorious Noman.' For example, 'Noman hath seen God,' 'Noman hath ascended into Heaven.' He was finally refuted by an opponent of more sense and wider reading, with such devastating counter-quotations as 'To Noman did God give easy occasion of sin,' 'God . . . would therefore have Noman damned everlastingly.'

[Page 135] *Dear ram.* Homer's sympathies, like Shakespeare's, are wide; for a moment here they embrace even Polyphemus.

[Page 137] *As sure as not even Poseidon. . . .* In his triumph even the prudent Odysseus falls for a moment into *hubris.* He is to pay bitterly.

[Page 138] *Aeólus* was later associated with the Lipari Islands; especially with Stromboli, whose volcano is apparently very sensitive to atmospheric changes. But as Eratósthenes wisely said, we can map the voyage of Odysseus when we have found the cobbler who sewed the bag of the winds.

From Lapland and Shetland to New Guinea and Tierra del Fuego, sorcerers have made a business of supplying favourable winds on reasonable terms. Scott visited an old lady of ninety in the Orkneys, who produced them for sixpence by simply boiling her kettle. Kaffir wizards would catch the winds in a pot; Finns sold them in knots. (See Frazer, *Golden Bough,* I, 319 ff.)

[Page 138] *Nightless land of the Laestrygonian giants.* This almost continuous day seems based on dim rumours of the far north. Later localizers put the Laestrygonians (rather unconvincingly) near Leontini in Sicily or Formiae in Italy.

[Page 138] *Circe.* Similarly located, in later days, at the rocky promontory of Circeii, near Terracina. Already Hēsiod gives her two sons by Odysseus—Agrios and *Latinos.* On the other hand she has confusing eastern associations, probably older. Thus Circe, daughter of the Sun, dwelling in Aeaea, has for brother Aeētes, son of the Sun, ruling at Aea (at E. end of the Black Sea); and in *Od.* XII, 3 her home is by the rising-places of the Sun. Circe (*Kirke*) may mean 'she-falcon' (*kirkos,* 'hawk,' connected with *kuklos,* 'circle,' from its wheeling flight).

[Page 138] *Aeētes,* king of Aea or Colchis, from whom Jason carried off his daughter Mēdēa and the Golden Fleece.

[Page 138] *Perse,* daughter of Ocean.

[Page 138] *I saw smoke . . . brake and wood.* Two of the most romantic lines in Greek literature. Rhys Carpenter (*Folktale, Fiction, and Saga in the Homeric Epics,* 18–9) points out how typically like a *Märchen* is this whole episode of the witch's house in the lonely wood.

[Page 139] *Which way eve's darkness lies. . . .* These lines have caused difficulty. The stag was suffering from the sun's heat: therefore the sun was visible to take bearings by. But Circe is not far from the Laestrygonians. Early voyagers in the far north may well have been amazed not only by the long days, but by the sun's rising and setting almost in the north. Compare the astonishment of the Phoenicians who circumnavigated Africa for the Pharaoh Necho at finding, S. of the equator, the sun passing north of them. Herodotus himself cannot believe it (IV, 42). In short, Odysseus *can* see sunrise and sunset, but no longer knows in what direction they are.

[Page 140] *Eurýlochus,* a kinsman of Odysseus (brother-in-law, says a scholiast), is one of those weak and foolish characters who try to compensate their sense of inferiority by habitual opposition; until finally he destroys himself and his shipmates by instigating them to eat the cattle of the Sun.

[Page 140] *Pramnian.* From Mt. Pramnon in the Aegean island of Icária.

[Page 140] *To kill remembrance of their own fatherland.* Like the lotus. His repetition of this idea suggests that such forgetfulness seemed particularly dreadful to the poet.

[Page 140] *Yet lived within them, unchanged, the minds of men.* Cf. Austin Dobson, *The Prayer of the Swine to Circe*:

> For us not now—for us, alas! no more
> The old green glamour of the glancing sea;
> For us not now the laughter of the oar—
> The strong-ribbed keel wherein our comrades be;
> Not now, at even, any more shall we,
> By low-browed banks and reedy river places,
> Watch the beast hurry and the wild fowl flee;
> Or steering shoreward, in the upland spaces
> Have sight of curling smoke and fair-skinned foreign faces.

[Page 141] *But go I must.* A totally different character, in its unflinching loyalty, from the Machiavellian Odysseus drawn by Attic dramatists and Roman poets.

[Page 142] *Mōly*, has been identified with garlic (sometimes used against magic) or hellebore (an old remedy for madness). But is garlic 'hard for a mortal' to gather? In S. Europe one sometimes wishes it were harder. Hellebore, however, *was* believed dangerous to pick; compare the mandrake (see Theophrastus, *Hist. Plant.*, IX, 8, 7–8; and my *Works of J. Webster*, I, 226–7). Yet such identifications seem rather idle.

[Page 144] *Homeward . . . to craggy Ithaca.* A pathetic touch—none of them were ever to see Ithaca again.

[Page 144] *Teirésias*, one of the most famous of ancient seers, is prominent in the *Oedipus Tyrannus* and *Antigone* of Sophocles, the *Bacchae* of Euripides, the *Bathing of Pallas* of Callímachus (p. 300). In life, said one legend, he had been both a man and (seven years) a woman; in Hades, by the special grace of Persephone, 'He alone has the breath of wisdom—the rest are fleeting shades' (*Od.* X, 495—a line applied by the aged Cato to the younger Scipio, as the only Roman capable of taking Carthage).

[Page 144] *The Kingdom of Death.* This 11th book of the *Odyssey* is outstanding. It is closely followed by Virgil in *Aeneid* VI, by Arnold in *Balder Dead*. It recalls, too, the vision of Engidu in the Epic of Gilgamesh; though with all the superiority of Greek art to Sumerian. Some, indeed, will prefer its passionate, yet compassionate humanity even to the *Inferno*. Parts of it may be later additions; but few things even in Homer equal these scenes with Elpēnor and Anticleia, with Agamemnon, Achilles, and the grimly silent Ajax.

Localizers like Virgil and Bérard have fixed on Lake Avernus, in the volcanic landscape of Naples; but this seems to narrow and degrade an episode that belongs, more mysteriously, to the desolate Ocean-shore at the world's end. The perpetual darkness of the Cimmerians, like the perpetual day of the Laestrygonians, may be a reminiscence of the far N. or N.W. (Both peoples live not far from Circe, and therefore not far from one another.)

[Page 145] *The Cimmerians.* Not the historic Cimmerians of S. Russia, who invaded Asia Minor in the eighth-seventh centuries B.C. Possibly the name here may be connected with the Cimbri, who had their early historic home in Jutland, but might once have been found further S.W. Though Procópius is a far later writer (6th century A.D.), it is curious that he both describes how in 'Thule' (perhaps Scandinavia?—it is 'ten times greater than Britain') the sun does not set for forty days in summer nor rise for forty in winter (VI, 15), and also tells how certain villagers on the Ocean-coast, subject to the Franks, had

nightly to ferry over to the Land of the Dead (a mysterious island called 'Brettia')
the souls of the departed; who were invisible, yet weighed the boats down to
the gunwale. (See Pauly-Wissowa, *Real-Encyclopädie*, 'Kimmerier,' and J. B.
Bury in *Klio*, VI (1906), 79–88; and compare some Irish legends.)

[Page 145] *Ocean-strand.* On the *farther* side of the Ocean-stream.

[Page 145] *Cubit.* Here, to be precise, a cubit of 15 inches.

[Page 145] *Young brides and youths unwedded....* These six marvellous
lines some Alexandrian critics wished to excise, for reasons more suitable to
attorneys than poets. Foolish objections were also raised to ghosts being in
armour or wounded; the spectres of Hamlet's father and Banquo would have
worried them badly.

[Page 145] *Then pale with fear I grew.* 'There seems no reason why
Odysseus should be seized with panic' (Merry and Riddell). So courageous
are commentators.

[Page 146] *Elpēnor.* This poignant episode has also been condemned by
some modern critics, on grounds as comic as its poetry is tragic.

[Page 146] *Autólycus.* For this famous trickster, whose name was used by
Shakespeare for his roguish pedlar in *The Winter's Tale*, see pp. 165, 284. Later
tradition made him actually the son of his patron, the mischievous God
Hermes.

[Page 146] *It knew me.* Teirésias, specially privileged, can know and address
Odysseus without drinking the blood (which he takes, presumably, to *strengthen*
his powers); Elpēnor, like Patroclus (p. 72), can also recognize and speak to
the living, because he is still unburned; but to the other souls the blood is
indispensable. For primitive associations of blood with life and soul, and blood-
offerings to the dead, see Frazer, *Pausanias*, V, 227–9.

[Page 147] *Thrīnacia.* Later identified with Trīnacria, that is, Sicily.

[Page 147] *Death from the sea shall rise.* Later generations degraded this
into a stupid tale of Telégonus, son of Odysseus and Circe, coming to Ithaca in
search of his father and killing him in ignorance, with a fishbone-spear; after
which he suitably wedded Penelope, and Telémachus Circe—a foolish farrago,
merely of psychological interest for its double Oedipus-motif. But in Homer
the future remains as quietly mysterious as in *Crossing the Bar*. Not for *his*
prudent hero any fantastic last voyage such as imagined by Dante and
Tennyson.

[Page 148] *My mother's wraith drew near.* I may be fanciful, but it is perhaps
not quite without significance that, whereas the other shades forbidden to drink
merely drifted back into the darkness, the shade of Anticleia has waited all this
while near her son, as if, even without the blood, she dimly knew him.

[Page 148] *None hath usurped thy honours.* Telémachus is as yet a boy of
only thirteen or fourteen; not for some time will the Suitors arrive, to plague
Penelope for the four years before Odysseus' return.

[Page 149] *It was, my noble Odysseus....* I know no scene between mother
and son in all literature that seems to me to equal this—so tender, yet so bleak
in its brave despair. Swinburne, in those later years when he had himself
become a ghost, regains for a moment some of his old life as the desolate Dunwich
beaches recall to him this strand of Persephone:

> Here the wise, wave-wandering, steadfast-hearted
>   Guest of many a lord of many a land
> Saw the shape or shade of years departed,
>   Saw the semblance risen and hard at hand,
> Saw the mother long from love's reach parted,
>   Anticleia, like a statue stand. . . .

Here, where never came alive another,
   Came her son across the sundering tide
Crossed before by many a warrior brother
   Once that warred on Ilion at his side;
Here spread forth vain hands to clasp the mother
   Dead, that sorrowing for his love's sake died.

(By the North Sea.)

[Page 149] *Like to a dream, a shadow.* So, for Virgil's Aeneas, the wraith of wife or father slips away—'par levibus ventis volucrique simillima somno.'

[Page 149] *Dead heroines.* This Dream of Fair Women may be a later addition. Similarly with the tormented souls on p. 154.

[Page 149] *Ephialtes and Ōtus.* These young giants, 54 feet high, 13½ broad, imprisoned Ares thirteen months in a bronze vessel, whence he was only rescued by Hermes.

[Page 149] *Son of Zeus and . . . Lēto.* Apollo.

[Page 150] *Phaedra*, daughter of Minos and queen of Theseus, played Potiphar's wife to her stepson Hippolytus; then hanged herself.

[Page 150] *Prŏcris*, daughter of Erechtheus king of Athens, wedded Céphalus, who was loved by Eos, the Dawn. Jealously spying on her husband as he hunted, she was killed by him in mistake for a wild beast among the bushes. By one account she was Odysseus' own great-grandmother; but this was hardly in Homer's mind.

[Page 150] *Ariadne*, originally a nature-goddess akin to Aphrodite, has here already become a human heroine, daughter of Minos, who gave Theseus the clue of thread to lead him from the Labyrinth and fled with him, only to be abandoned in Dia (either the small island N. of Cnossus or, in later tradition, Naxos). Later writers told that she became bride of Dionysus, who crowned her with a golden crown that became a constellation; but Plutarch (*Theseus*, 20) mentions a version that she died in childbirth.

[Page 150] *At the word of Dionysus.* According to one suggestion he told Artemis that Ariadne had lain with Theseus in the Goddess' sacred grove.

[Page 150] *Maera.* A companion of Artemis, but slain by her for having become the mistress of Zeus, to whom she bore Locrus, one of the founders of Thebes.

[Page 150] *Clýmene*, daughter of Minyas and mother, by one account, of Phaëthon, by another, of Atalanta.

[Page 150] *Eriphyle*, wife of the Argive prophet-king Amphiarāüs, was bribed by Polyneices to make her husband join the doomed expedition of the Seven against Thebes; for this she was slain by her son Alcmaeon.

[Page 150] *The wraith of Agamemnon.* This is presumably the passage praised by Landor (p. 100).

[Page 151] *No creature more appalling.* Here opens that long series of misogynist utterances by European writers, against which the Mēdēa of that supposed misogynist Euripides already protests. It is far from the view of Homer himself; he makes Penelope and Nausícaä shine only more brightly against the dark background of some of their sisters; but the fury he lends Agamemnon shows how well he has noted the way in which angry males generalize from their own experience. Pope, with his eighteenth-century politeness—or rather Broome, who seems to have written the notes to Pope's *Odyssey*—is comically shocked at the tactlessness of Odysseus in repeating Agamemnon's tirade— 'Why does he chuse to relate such a story before a Queen and her daughter? In short, I think they ought to have torn him to pieces, as the Ladies of *Thrace* served *Orpheus*.'

[Page 151] *All through the wiles of women.*   Odysseus might have added that Agamemnon's own mother Aerope had previously helped to bring a curse upon her race by taking Thyestes for lover.   But Agamemnon might not have relished the reminder; and the legend may be later.

[Page 151] *Icárius*, brother of Clytemnestra's father Tyndáreüs; so that, as already pointed out, the loyal Penelope is first cousin to the frail Helen and the cruel Clytemnestra.

[Page 151] *Orchómenus.*   Either the Arcadian Orchómenus, or the Boeotian (p. 91).

[Page 152] *Talk not smooth words to me.*   One of the gloomiest passages in literature—all the bitterer, in its irony, when we recall that it is precisely for this same empty glory that Achilles while he lived flung away both his own life and thousands more.   Cf. Arnold, *Balder Dead*:

> Better to live a serf, a captured man,
> Who scatters rushes in a master's hall,
> Than be a crown'd king here, and rule the dead.

[Page 153] *Eurýpylus*, son of Télephus, King of Mysia.   His mother Astýoche, as covetous as Eríphyle (note the recurrence here of the theme of evil women), was bribed by her brother Priam with a golden vine to send her own son to fight and die at Troy.

[Page 153] *Kēteian.*   Possibly the same as 'Hittite.'

[Page 153] *Memnon*, son of Eos and Tithōnus, coming to Troy after the close of the *Iliad*, slew Antílochus but was slain by Achilles.   The morning dews, it was said, were the tears of the Dawn-goddess inconsolable for her lost son.

[Page 153] *Epeius*, son of Pánopeus, devised with Athene's help the Wooden Horse.   Odysseus then contrived its entry into Troy.

[Page 153] *Asphodel.*   A pallid plant, common in Greece on waste places and so in graveyards.

[Page 153] *Sons of the Trojans.*   The Trojan prisoners in the Greek camp were asked which of the competitors, Ajax and Odysseus, had done their country more harm.   Defeated, Ajax slew himself.

[Page 153] *He answered not.*   'Quite independently of its wording, sometimes a writer's bare conception can impress us by its magnificence; as, for example, the silence of Ajax in Odysseus' Visit to the Dead is finer than any words could be' ('Longīnus'; 1st century A.D.?).   So too Virgil's Dido turns away in silence, when Aeneas meets her among the shades.

[Page 154] *Orion.*   Page 97.

[Page 154] *Títyus*, giant son of Earth, assaulted Lēto and was slain by Apollo, Artemis, or Zeus.

[Page 154] *Sísyphus.*   The cunning king of Corinth (p. 284).   Anyone who has toiled on a hot morning up the 2000 feet of his Acropolis and pictures the human bondage needed to fortify such a site, will see the appropriateness of his punishment—the eternal rolling of a stone up a mountainside.

[Page 154] *Sirens.*   Two in Homer; later, often three.   Half birds, half women, they are associated with death, and common on early Greek tombs (cf. the Egyptian soul-bird).   Circe had warned Odysseus that their meadow was full of mouldering bones—presumably the victims had simply starved, unable to tear themselves away.   Later tradition located them in the Sorrento area.   (For other parallels see Frazer, *Pausanias*, v, 171.)

Note that the temptation offered by the Sirens to the *wise* Odysseus (as, in the end, by Satan to Christ in *Paradise Regained*) is *knowledge*—their own possession of it they display by at once knowing who he is.

H

[Page 154] *Scylla and Charybdis*. Later (and not very convincingly) located in the Straits of Messina. Scylla with her twelve dangling legs and six heads, fishing for dolphins and sea-monsters, might be partly based on a giant squid; though of course squids do not live halfway up cliffs or yelp like puppies.

[Page 156] *Ox-horn sheath*. Cf. p. 100. The horn may be protection for the line, or a bait.

[Page 156] *Ship . . . to stone*. A tree-covered islet (Pondikonisi) is still pointed out at Corfu as 'The Ship of Odysseus' (it also, curiously enough, suggested to the painter Boecklin his 'Island of the Dead').

[Page 157] *Then he turned him, again, to sorrowing*. The practical Odysseus always takes action, if action is possible, before indulging emotion—strong though his emotions are. Anguished by his mother's wraith, he yet remembers that he must speak first to Teirésias; so here he decides to make sure of his chattels before giving way to his grief.

[Page 158] *Idómeneus*, son of Deucálion and grandson of Minos.

[Page 158] *Phoenicians*. Some have tried to turn Homer's Phoenicians into Minoans. But Homer definitely mentions Sidon—once the chief Phoenician city, though later eclipsed by Tyre which, like Venice, enjoyed the greater safety of an island. The Phoenician opportunity came with the fall of Minoan sea-power; and they resolutely took it, if it is true that Utica was founded by 1100 B.C. and Gades (Cadiz) in the century that followed.

[Page 158] *Epeians*. The name almost always used by Homer for the inhabitants of Elis.

[Page 160] *Ortygia, Syria*. Probably Délos and Sÿros (now Sÿra), which is 'beyond' Délos for a poet in Asia Minor, though not, of course, for Eumaeus himself in Ithaca.

[Page 160] *Where in his courses turns the sun*. Commonly rendered 'where the sun sets,' 'towards the sunset.' But this does not really translate *tropai*, which means 'solstice.' Solstices may not much interest the average modern; but to the primitive farmer, as Hésiod shows, they are highly important to watch. P. Waltz (*Revue des Études Homériques*, 1931, pp. 3–15) takes Homer to mean that from Ortygia (Délos) at summer-solstice the sun is seen to set over the N. tip of Sÿros. But Pherecÿdes of Sÿros (c. 550 B.C.) had on that island a *helio-tropion* or instrument for observing solstices. Given that neighbouring Délos was sacred to the Sun-god, Pherecÿdes may have been carrying on an older, religious practice. The meaning here, then, might be, rather, that from the N. tip of Sÿros men watched the Sun-god *rise* over his own Délos at the *winter*-solstice (cf. Stonehenge); and one might render '(Sÿros) where are (observed) the turnings of the sun.'

[Page 160] *Nor . . . hateful maladies*. Bent's muleteer on Sÿra assured him of the recent death of an old lady aged 130; and added that in past days people used to live so long on this healthy island that they had to be pushed over a special precipice, thence called Geronsi—'For the old.'

[Page 160] *Taphians*. Pirates, probably inhabiting a group of islands between Leucas and the mainland.

[Page 162] *Dogs*. Cf. Theócritus (p. 308) where the dogs sense the approach of Hecate; and medieval superstitions about their foreboding of deaths.

[Page 164] *The Death of Argus*. It has been rashly said that *all* poems about dogs are bad. Here is at least one exception; though it might be hard to find many others. 'I do not know anything more beautiful or more affecting in the whole poem.' (Footnote in Pope's *Odyssey*.)

[Page 164] *Too weak to creep*. As Eustathius points out, this is ingenious as well as moving. Had Argus still had strength for demonstrations, Odysseus' disguise would have been penetrated.

[Page 165] *Autólycus.* See pp. 146, 284.

[Page 165] *Subtle swearing.* I.e. subtle equivocations (like those of the Delphic oracle), which would avoid downright perjury.

[Page 166] *Man of wrath.* The Greek pun (Odysseus—*odyssamenos*, 'having grown angry') could be vaguely reproduced, were it worth it, by saying 'Since many, both man and woman, are grown odious to me, call him "Odysseus."'

[Page 168] *Through the openings in twelve axeheads.* Either through the holes in twelve axeblades (some ancient blades being shaped like a D, with one aperture in them, or like a B, with two apertures); or through the sockets of twelve axeheads laid horizontally on wooden supports, without their handles, to make a discontinuous tube. But it would be a very narrow tube; and the description of their being set up by Telémachus suggests that the handles of the axes *are* present, and are fixed upright in the earthen floor; this favours the first view. In either case it is a test both of skill (to aim straight) and of strength (to give the arrow an extremely flat trajectory).

[Page 168] *The Vision of Theoclýmenus.* Perhaps the most eery passage in all Homer.

[Page 168] *The lips they laughed with, seemed no more their own.* They are hysterically losing control and no longer seem themselves. Cf. Tennyson, *The Princess*:

> and all the ladies, each at each,
> Like the Ithacensian suitors in old time,
> Stared with great eyes, and laugh'd with alien lips.

[Page 168] *As the flesh of their feasting with drops of blood were strown.* Cf. p. 409 and the boding vision before the burning in *Njal's Saga*—'the whole board and the meat on it are one gore of blood.' Others have compared Cassandra's second-sight in the *Agamemnon*, Belshazzar's feast, and Banquo's ghost.

[Page 169] *Veiled . . . in gloom.* Celtic superstition likewise believed that the doomed might appear shrouded in a mist of death. Cf. the spae-wife's vision of James I of Scotland in Rossetti's *King's Tragedy*.

[Page 169] *Sicels.* Probably early inhabitants of Sicily.

[Page 170] *Women's hall.* Apparently opening not on the main, men's hall, but on the courtyard outside this main hall.

[Page 170] *Byblus.* Papyrus, whose fibres could be used for ropes as well as for writing material.

[Page 170] *Horn.* The bow seems made of two horns coupled by a bridge.

[Page 171] *The great threshold.* The hall has apparently only one, large door leading into the court. This single escape for the Suitors is now barred by Odysseus and his son.

[Page 175] *Now Hermes of Cyllene. . . .* This whole passage about the passing of the Suitors to Hades is suspected of being a later addition. But, whether or no, its opening is fine.

[Page 176] *The White Rock.* Unknown. (One fanciful mind has suggested Dover Cliff!)

[Page 176] *Odysseus found his sire alone.* This episode also has been thought a later addition. But I find it hard to believe that this poem on the love of home could have failed to show us the meeting of Odysseus with that father of whom we have heard so much, as well as with mother, wife, and son. The scene bears a distant likeness to the meeting of Achilles with the aged Priam which closes the *Iliad*.

[Page 176] *Tell him plain.* Why does not Odysseus do this, instead of tormenting his unfortunate old father? Eustathius charitably suggested that he feared a too sudden shock of joy for Laertes. But it seems rather that Odysseus finds it too hard to tell anyone anything plainly till he has made sure of his ground—like Pope, who 'could not take tea without a stratagem.' How long, he seems to ask himself, can he mystify the old man without being recognized? But humanity breaks in again, very movingly, at the moment when Odysseus is swept out of all his tortuousness by a sudden wave of pity and affection.

[Page 178] *Sicánia.* Apparently Sicily, whose oldest population, the Sicans, was driven west by an invasion of Sicels from Italy.

HESIOD OF ASCRA

(*c.* 800 B.C. ?)

By such examples taught, I paint the lot,
As Truth will paint it, and as Bards will not.   Crabbe.

LESS impersonal and self-effacing than Homer, Hēsiod tells how his father
had migrated from the Aeŏlic Cyme in Western Asia Minor to the village
of Ascra at the foot of Mount Helicon in Central Greece—'evil in winter,
in summer intolerable.'   His *Works and Days*, a mixture of moral treatise
and farmer's manual, is addressed to his idle brother Perses, who by bribing
the 'gift-devouring princes' had gained an unfair share of their common
heritage.   Hēsiod is also credited with a theological poem, the *Theogony*
('Generations of the Gods').   As so often, this traditional authorship has
been questioned; as so often, with little reason.

Hēsiod is a poet of superstitious, but laborious peasants ('of Helots,' said
the contemptuous Spartan king, Cleómenes), while Homer is the poet of
proud Viking princes.   From Homer's glorious fictions Hēsiod turns to
harsh and homely truths; he values the virtues, not of war, but of peace;
not of the rich, but of the poor—hard work, prudence, honesty, thrift.
There is, indeed, country-life in Homer also—in the lovely similes, in the
Shield of Achilles, in the cot of the swineherd Eumaeus; but it remains
country-life as seen by a spectator rather than a toiler—as Chaucer sees it,
not Langland.   Even Eumaeus turns out to be a kidnapped prince; just
as in Malory even the hermits of the good old days are gentle-born.   Homer
too loved the rich damp blackness of new-ploughed earth; but on Hēsiod's
hands we seem to feel the very blisters made by the handle of the plough.
This poet has himself reaped, sweating, where the sun cracked the hillsides
of Ascra, or shivered behind his team as the winds of winter whistled from
the bleak forests of the North.   Hēsiod is Europe's first realist.

On his *Works and Days* Virgil modelled the *Georgics*; but Virgil, like
Homer, remains a court-poet.   He has an artistry, a refinement, a sensitive
pity for the world, that are far removed from the sardonic old Boeotian.
Yet each is admirable in his different way; if he has less imagination, Hēsiod
has the blessed reality of writers—they are none too common—who really
know the things of which they write; a reality more solid than Wordsworth's
mystical rusticities, or the somewhat idyllic Berrichons among whom George
Sand regained her sanity.

And with all his realism Hēsiod remains a Greek—he feels the loveliness, as well as the harshness, of Nature.   As we wander among his rock-strewn valleys, suddenly there comes the quiet benison of spring-rain, or the cuckoo's call along the hills, or the peace of summer afternoons as he sits, for once at ease, in a great rock's shadow, gazing out across the blue distance of that sea he so distrusts.   He has a sympathy of his own with the creatures of the wild, like another ploughman thousands of years later in the fields of Scottish Ayr.   And he is not only a realist, like Tennyson's Lincolnshire farmers: in his dour way, he is an idealist also.   Two things he preaches tirelessly—Work and Justice.   At times he recalls the strivings after righteousness of Amos, the herdsman of Tekoa, of our own Langland on his grey-misted Malvern Hills, of Crabbe among the muddy streams and harsh shingles of Aldeburgh.   Shrewd, hard, close-fisted, this peasant who reveals at moments the wry humour of Hardy's countryfolk, has also, like some of them, thoughts that scan wonderingly the eternal Heavens and this Earth that seems only to worsen with the years.   So that, while in one direction he is an ancestor of the artificial poets of pastoral, in another he foreshadows the philosophic poets of later Greece with their more reasoned cosmologies.

True, his *Theogony* seems a far more shadowy work than the *Works and Days*.   Its war in Heaven has not the marble dignity of Milton, who trod the purple heights of Helicon, not its foothills; nor the elaboration of Keats, whose *Hyperion* is a far-off descendant of Hēsiod as well as of Milton.   For us, it is Hēsiod's picture of the Farmer's Year that remains vividly alive; recalling, to all who have known them, the barren limestone-ridges that are still Greece, the hum of bees among their prickly scrub and pallid asphodel, the oxen ploughing far below, the rhythmic rise and fall of the peasants' mattocks among the young-leaved vines—that blending of grey mountainside and blue-shimmering sea that still makes Hellas one of the poorest, yet loveliest, of European lands.

WORKS AND DAYS

Summary

1. *There are two kinds of emulation—one evil, that breeds war and strife; one good, that toils for excellence.* (1–27.)

2. *Do you, Perses, follow the good emulation, and exert yourself; instead of pursuing the evil and cheating me, your brother, in law-suits.* (28–41.)

3. *The evil of all unrighteousness, the universal necessity of toil, are witnessed by the tale of Pandora and the past Ages of the World.   Now in our Age of Iron, alas, might is become right, as the hawk said to the nightingale.* (42–212.)

4. None the less it is better for kings and commoners alike to keep justice;
as for you, foolish Perses, work and honesty are the only way. Then there
follow precepts for agriculture; precepts for navigation; precepts for living; and
precepts about lucky and unlucky days. (213–828.)

The Fall of Man and The Early Ages of The Earth

We have shared already our father's goods; and besides thy share,
Thou hast robbed me richly, brother, by speaking false and fair
To gift-devouring princes.   Such suits delight their soul,
The fools!—that have never learnt how 'Half is more than whole,'
Nor know that life can be happy on mallow and asphodel.
For, alas, the Gods keep hidden the way to wealth too well;
Else, one day of labour easily could have brought
Food to last thee a twelvemonth, lying and doing nought;
Idle above the chimney might hang thy steering-oar,
And neither ox nor patient mule need toil for evermore.
But God hath taken such ease away, and hidden it,
Angry that He was cheated by Prometheus' cunning wit.
So Zeus ordained us sorrow, and fire He hid from men.
Yet the hero-son of Iápetus stole it again
For mortals' sake, in a fennel-stalk, from Zeus the wise;
Then spake the Lord of Thunder, whose wrack benights the skies,
In wrath: 'O soul most subtle, Iápetiónides,
Thou hast stolen fire, and tricked me—thy heart it well may please.
Yet sorely shalt thou repent it!   And men unborn!   In vain!
Such a curse will I send to requite them—a curse they shall rush to gain,
Embracing in their blindness the thing that is their bane.'
So spoke the Sire of Gods and men.   Loudly His laughter rolled;
And the glorious Hephaestus He bade with speed to mould
Clay and water together—to shape them, and mingle there
The voice and might of a mortal, and a face divinely fair,
To form a sweet maid's loveliness.   'But all the art
Of the loom, and the weaver's cunning, Pallas shall teach her heart;
And golden Aphrodite about her brow shall set
Grace, and the pangs of passion, that pines men with regret;
And last the Argus-slayer, God's herald, shall compound
The soul of a thief therewith, and the heart of a shameless hound.'
Such was the word of Crönus' son.   The Gods obeyed;
And straight the glorious Haltfoot in the form of mortal maid
Fashioned an earthen image, as the Lord of Heaven planned.
Bright-eyed Athene decked her with robe and girdleband;
And then the heavenly Graces and sovran Peitho dressed

Her beauty with chains all golden; and the Seasons lovely-tressed
Wreathed around her forehead all the flowers of spring:
But in her heart, by the counsel of Zeus loud-thundering,
The Argus-slayer planted the faith that still must fail,
The stealthy soul of the thief, and the crooked and cunning tale;
The power of speech he gave her, and called the woman's name
'Pandora,' because to her making all the Olympians came
With gifts—for the undoing of all the sons of earth.

But when this snare escapeless, this pit, was come to birth,
Her the glorious herald, the Argus-slayer bore,
By the will of Zeus, as a gift, to Epimetheus' door,
In whose heart *then* the warning of Prometheus lay forgot—
To turn from his door all gifts of Zeus, and take them not,
For fear some doom of evil befall the sons of men.
He took her; and once the curse was his, too late he saw it *then*.

For hitherto all mortals on earth were living still
Unvexed by bitter labour, untouched of any ill,
Free from the pains of sickness that lays life in the dust;
But *now* from the jar that held these plagues, the hands of the woman thrust
The lid, and let them scatter, for the ruin of humankind.
Only Hope was left there, a captive still confined,
Caught in the mouth of the vessel.   For ere she escaped—the last,
Once more the hands of Pandora had shut the jar's lid fast
(Thus the Aegis-wielder, the Lord of Tempests, willed).
But those other, infinite curses roam loose in the world; and filled
Is all the earth with evils, with evils filled the sea.
Maladies stalk at noonday, bringing men misery,
And maladies steal through the darkness, unlooked-for and unheard
(Zeus made them, in His wisdom, to wander without word).
And so no man may avoid it, whatever He ordain.

But here is another story, if thou wilt listen again,
And well my tongue can tell it—of the years when first began
The race of Gods (heed thou my words) and the race of Man.

First of all, the Immortals, who high Olympus hold,
Created that earthly race which bears the name of Gold.
Those were the years when, still, in Heaven Crönus reigned
And men lived happy as Gods, with hearts that no cares constrained,
Free from all toil and travail.   Never upon them hung
The burden of age—with hands and feet for ever young
They revelled and made merry, till Death, like a gentle rest,
Ended those lives untouched of pain, in all ways blest.
Ever the kindly cornlands, that no man toiled to till,
Brought forth their harvests' bounty; and all men lived at will,
Crowned with every blessing, on their own fields quietly.

Long since the dust has hid them; but still, by God's decree,
They haunt the world as spirits, that guard men and befriend,
Bringing us wealth and plenty.   This glory crowns their end.

  Next, the Lords of Olympus fashioned in their place
A second breed, of Silver—but theirs was a meaner race,
Neither in flesh nor spirit like to the men of Gold.
The infants in their houses were a hundred winters old
Ere they could leave their mothers, or cease their childish play;
Yet once they had reached the years of youth, then brief their day
And evil, by their folly.   For, with infatuate pride,
They outraged one another, and to the Gods denied
Worship, and sacrifices, such as all men have laid
On Heaven's holy altars.   Therefore, because they paid
No honour to the Immortals who hold Olympus' height,
Zeus in His anger smote them—and earth hid them from sight.
And yet 'Blest souls' men call them still, in the world below;
Lesser are these in honour—yet honoured even so.

  Then from the hand of Zeus, in turn, a third race came,
Far changed from the breed of Silver; from Bronze it took its name.
Grim, strong men, sprung from ash-trees—*they* had no other care
But War with its pain and outrage.   Bread for their daily fare
These would not eat; their hearts of adamant were made,
Ruthless—and vast their vigour, and from their shoulders played
Great brawny arms, with hands resistless and untamed.
Bronze were their weapons; bronze their tools; of bronze they framed
Their dwellings (for unknown yet was black iron in the world).
Yet, to extermination by their own violence hurled,
They passed to the house of Hades, its chill and mouldering gloom,
Nameless—their fury faded in the blackness of the tomb,
And they left behind for ever the glorious light of day.

  But when the dust had hidden this race in its turn away,
Then Zeus, the son of Crŏnus, created in their stead
A fourth upon the kindly earth—more nobly bred,
More just—the godlike Heroes, as demigods revered,
The last that dwelt in the boundless world, before our race appeared.
But evil strife destroyed them, and the grim battle's roar—
Some before Thebes of the Seven Gates, as they made war
For the flocks of Oedipus, in the Cadmeian land;
And some in the host that sailed, far off, to the Trojan strand
Across the sea's abysses, for fair-haired Helen's sake:
There they found the slumber that nothing more shall wake.
But on some the Almighty Father another home bestowed,
Another life, at the world's far end, where no men find the road;
There dwell the happy Heroes, with hearts for aye at rest,

Beside deep-eddying Ocean, in the Islands of the Blest,
Where thrice in the passing seasons from bounteous earth is born
The harvest in its splendour—and honey-sweet its corn.

But ah, that I were not living in this fifth age of the earth!
Would I had died aforetime, or later come to birth!
For now is the Race of Iron.   Never shall these by day
Find rest from toil and trouble; and the night-time shall not stay
Their ruin; but the Gods shall give them sorrows without cease
(Though *some* good with their evils be mixed for even these).
And yet for this race also hath the will of Zeus prepared
Doom—in the days when their children shall come to birth grey-haired.
For then indeed all concord of son with sire shall end,
And the host shall hate his guest, the friend shall hate his friend;
The ancient love of brothers in those days shall not hold,
And children shall dishonour their parents growing old.
Yea, they shall revile them with bitter words and rude,
And hardened hearts, that fear not God—small gratitude
Shall aged sire and mother receive for all their care.
Might shall be right, and city shall plunder city bare.
But they that are keepers of faith, and just, and of good intent—
To these shall none give honour; nay, to the insolent
And doers of all outrage.   For men shall lose their shame,
And in force of hand shall their justice be—they shall defame
The nobler with crooked speeches, and seal them with perjury;
And to all such as suffer shall cling implacably,
The hateful joy of malice—ill tongue and evil face.
Then to rejoin the Immortals, quitting the human race,
Quitting the wide-wayed earth, once more, for Heaven's height,
With snowy mantles veiling their beauty from men's sight,
Honour at last, and Righteousness, shall flee away,
Leaving but pain and anguish and griefs that nought can stay.

But now will I tell our princes (they have wit enough) a tale—
The words the hawk once uttered to the dapple-necked nightingale,
As in his claws he gripped her, and towered through the cloudy skies.
Pierced by those curving talons, his prey with piteous cries
Lamented; but her captor rated her rudely—'Now
Why squeaking, wretch?   There holds thee one stronger far than thou.
Where I take thee, thou must follow, for all thy minstrelsy.
For my dinner I can eat thee, if I will, or set thee free.
Fools struggle with the stronger.   Defeat is all they gain
And to humiliation they add but bitterer pain.'
Such were the words of the falcon, with swift wings quivering wide.
But thou—heed justice, Perses, and puff not up thy pride.

(*Works and Days*, 37–213.)

Evil to choose is easy, of her thou canst find thy fill;
For close she dwells beside thee, and smooth the road to ill.
But the way that leads to Goodness the Gods made full of sweat,
Long is the path, and steep, for those whose face is set
Towards *her*; and the start is stony.   Yet once thou hast gained the height,
Although before so painful, at length it groweth light.

(287–92.)

Bid him to dine that loves thee, leave him that hates alone,
But him be sure to summon, whose house stands near thine own.
When trouble comes in the village, the neighbours run at sight;
But thy kin at a distance linger to pull their girdles tight.

(342–5.)

Drink deep when the winejar's opened, or when 'tis running low;
In the middle, spare.   Too late, when the dregs begin to show.
What to thy friend thou owest, pay it him full and fair.
When thy own brother borrows, smile—but have witness there.
By trust alike and *dis*trust has many a man sped ill.
Let no hip-wagging woman cajole thee to her will
(When 'tis thy barn she covets) with her flattering fond deceit;
Who puts his trust in woman, trusts himself to a cheat!
Thou art wise if thou begettest but one son to sustain
Thy father's house—then the plenty within its walls shall gain.
And a second son thou mayest leave, if thou die old;
Nay, for still more, if He will, can God find wealth untold.

(368–79.)

Wed, above all, a woman that dwells not far away;
And look well ere thou leapest, lest thou make thy neighbours gay.
For a good wife is the fairest prize that life can bring;
But as for a wife that is evil—there is no grislier thing—
Some greedy slut that, goodly although her husband be,
Roasts him without a fire to raw senility.

(700–5.)

Take care to keep thy name untouched of ill report.
For evil reputation—easily it is caught,
But heavy it is to carry, and hard to cast away.
Nothing perishes wholly that many have come to say.
Ay, Reputation also is a Goddess, in her way.

(760–4.)

One carpenter hates another, potter hates potter still,
The beggar envies the beggar, the singer the singer's skill.

(25–6.)

A small ship—thou mayst praise her; but set thy goods in a great.

(643.)

Rustic Wisdom

Autumn Ploughing

Take heed, what time thou hearest, high in the clouds, the crane
Calling her yearly call, for plough-time come again,
Crying that the rains of winter once more are nearing now—
Bitter her voice to his hearing, that hath no team to plough.

(448–451.)

Spring Ploughing

But if thou art late with ploughing, remedy thou hast still;
When, from the leaves of the oak, the cuckoo calleth shrill
For the first time, and gladdens all men to the wide earth's end,
Then on the third day after, if Zeus vouchsafe to send
Good rain that fills the hoofprint of an ox—just fills, no more—
Late ploughers then shall prosper as they that ploughed before.
But note these things with a mindful heart—mark in their hour
The signs of the grey spring's coming, and the seasonable shower.

(485–92.)

Summer

But when up stalks from the ground House-carrier turns to climb,
Fleeing from the heat that the Pleiads bring, past is the time
For digging vines—with sickles keen, call out thy men to the corn,
And shun the seat in the shade, and lie not late till morn.
Now, in the days of harvest, when the hot sun tans the skin,
Now is the time to be stirring forth, thy sheaves to win;
Rise with the very daybreak, that thy life pass free from need;
A third part of thy labour those hours of Dawn shall speed.
Dawn is the toiler's, the traveller's friend—she that each day
Sets forth so many a wanderer, world over, on his way,
And on so many an ox's neck once more the yoke doth lay.
But when the artichoke flowers—when with quick-quivering wings
Through the heavy heat of summer the shrill cicada sings
And, perched in a tree's green leafage, pours out his piercing notes,
Then wine is at its finest and fattest then are goats;
Women, most wanton; and weakest, men.   For the Dog-star's heat
Scorches the skin on their bodies and parches head and feet.
Then in a great rock's shadow, with milk-bread, let me lie,
And Biblian wine, and milk from goats just going dry,

202

And flesh of an uncalved heifer, fed in a forest-glade,
Or kids first-born of their mother.   So let me sit in the shade,
With a bellyful within me, sipping at my ease
The fire-red wine, and turning to face the western breeze.
(571–94.)

Autumn

After the sun has turned him, for the space of fifty days,
While summer draws to its ending and men sweat in his blaze,
Then is the time for sailing.   For never a tempest then
Shall shatter the timbers of thy ship, nor drown her men,
(Unless the heart of Poseidon, the Shaker of the Land,
Or Zeus, the Lord of Heaven, their certain doom hath planned;
For all good hap, and evil, lies lastly in God's hand).
Then steady blow the breezes, and the sea's wrath lies asleep;
So fear not—trust thy vessel to the winds, and on the deep
Launch her, and see her cargo tightly stowed aboard.
Yet turn with thy best speed homeward, linger not abroad
Till the new wine, and the tempests that break the summer's drouth,
With winter hard behind them—when grim gales from the south
Lash the deep to fury, and earthward heavily
Zeus hurls his rains autumnal, and savage grows the sea.
There is another season, for sailing, in the spring,
When on the fig-tree's summit the first leaves opening
Stretch as wide as the footprints a crow sets on the earth;
'Tis then the springtime sailing comes.   But little worth
I hold it—for such ventures full little love I bear.
They are but snatched occasions.   Perilous.   Yet men dare
These also, in the folly of their infatuate mind.
For money is very life to hapless humankind.
Yet death at sea is a bitter thing.   So heed me well,
Store in thine inmost heart these counsels that I tell;
And trust to no hollow ship all that thou callst thine own—
Keep most ashore, and venture the lesser part alone.
'Tis ill to find in the wave the grave of thy happiness,
Ill to o'erload thy waggon with weight so merciless
That the axle splits, and thy lading is spilt and spoilt with the fall.
Keep to the mean.   Due measure is ever best of all.
(663–94.)

Winter

But beware the month of Lēnaion, ill days of bitter frost,
Days that would flay an ox, when the wide seas are tossed
203

By Boreas, blowing hard from the horse-pastures of Thrace,
And land and woodland bellow, as he wrenches from their place
Amid the glens of the mountains many an oak high-crowned,
Many a stalwart fir, and flings them to the ground,
Till the multitudinous forest shouts with a single cry.
Shivering under their bellies the tails of the wild beasts lie,
For all the fur that warms them—through the shaggiest breast it goes,
Through the hide of the ox himself that icy tempest blows,
And through the goat's lank hair—the fleece of the sheep alone
With its thick wool can baffle that blast from the northward blown.
It sets an old man running; and yet it cannot come
To the tender maiden sitting by her mother's side at home,
Of the golden Aphrodite as yet all unaware.
Ay, warm in an inner chamber—soft limbs new-bathed, and fair
With olive-oil—she lays her down and slumbers sweet
Through the winter days, when No-bones must sit and gnaw his feet
Alone in his fireless house and the depths of his dismal den;
For never forth to pasture the low sun lights him then.

(504–26.)

But pass thou by the smithy and the warm seat in the sun,
In winter, when for the cold no work in the fields is done,
(E'en then a stirring fellow can still increase his store);
For fear the bleak December bring misery to thy door
And thou press, with a vagrant's hand grown thin, a foot grown fat and
        sore.

(493–7.)

Theogony

Religion

First, of the Heliconian Muses be my song,
To whom the great and holy heights of Helicon belong;
Whose soft feet sway for ever by the violet-shadowed spring
And round about the altar of Crónion the King.
With lovely bodies newly bathed in Hippocrēne's fount,
Or Olmeius the holy, or Permessus, on the mount
Of Helicon at its highest they gather for the dance—
Ay, beautiful past telling their rushing footsteps glance.
Thence 'tis their way to wander, wrapt in a mantling cloud,
Across the night, with voices choiring sweet and loud,

In praise of the Aegis-wielder and in Queen Hēra's praise
Who passes, Lady of Argos, gold-sandalled on her ways;
In praise of bright-eyed Athene, daughter of Zeus most high,
In praise of Phoebus Apollo, and Her whose arrows fly
Swift in the chase; of Poseidon, that girds and shakes the earth—
Grave Thĕmis—Aphrodite with her dancing eyes of mirth;
Of fair Diōne, and Hēbe, with forehead golden-crowned,
Of Dawn, and the Sun's great circle, and the Moon's fair-shining round;
Of Lēto, of Iápetus, of Crŏnus subtly wise,
Of Earth, and boundless Ocean, and Night in her sable guise,
And the rest of the race of Heaven, the race that never dies.
  Fair too was the song they taught, one day, to Hēsiod,
Feeding his flock on Helicon, the Mount of God.
Thus on the mountain-silence the Olympian Muses broke,
The Aegis-wielder's daughters, and thus to me they spoke;
'Shepherds of wild and wasteland, ill-famed, ye bellies blind,
Many a falsehood like to truth our tongues can find,
Yet many a true word also, when truth is to our mind.'
  So spake the Daughters of Zeus, whose words are verity,
And a wondrous staff, of deathless bay, they plucked and gave to me.
                                        (*Theogony*, 1–31.)

Daemones

  To spirits thrice ten thousand by God's will 'tis assigned
Through all the fruitful earth to watch o'er humankind.
Deathless, hidden in darkness, wandering everywhere,
They watch all judgments given, all evil that men dare.
                                        (*Works and Days*, 252–5.)

Poetry

  For it is the Archer Apollo, and the Muses, that inspire
All minstrels upon earth, all players of the lyre,
Just as of Zeus come princes. Blessed is he among men
Whom the Muses love—like honey the words flow from him then;
And if with heart new-burdened by sorrow overstrong
Some man sits bowed, and a servant of the Muses lifts his song
To tell of the ancient heroes, or hymn with praise the blest
Immortals, that have their dwelling on high Olympus' crest,
Swiftly even the mourner casts off the load that lay
Upon his heart—by the Muses' gift his cares are smoothed away.
                                        (*Theogony*, 94–103.)

Mountains

Earth bare the long-ridged mountains, within whose fair depths dwell
The Nymphs divine, in the valleys that run 'neath peak and fell.

(Theogony, 129–30.)

The Coming of Aphrodite

And by her side went Eros, and Passion followed fast,
As the new-born Aphrodite to the host of Heaven passed;
For her kingdom and her glory she holds for aye assigned
Both among Gods in Heaven and among humankind—
The maiden-whispers of love, its smiles, and its deceit,
And all its loving-kindness, its fulfilment honey-sweet.

(Theogony, 201–6.)

THE HOMERIC HYMNS

ALTHOUGH other poets of the early period also wrote epics
> Presenting Thebes, or Pelops' line,
> Or the tale of Troy divine,

not one of them seems to have shown the greatness of *Iliad* and *Odyssey*,
and only a few fragments remain.   Like the civilization of its birthplace
Ionia, on the western edge of Asia Minor where life was softer than in the
Greek motherland, the Homeric epic was a spring-flower; first to bloom
and first to fade.   Yet in its decline this Homeric tradition could still produce
most of the so-called 'Homeric Hymns.'   They are not comparable with
Iliad or *Odyssey*.   Mortals are usually better subjects for poetry than gods.
But the six best of these poems deserve far more readers than they have
found.

In all, our collection of 'Homeric Hymns' contains thirty-four pieces.
Four of them—those to Apollo, Aphrodite, Demeter, and Hermes—are of
some length (290–580 lines); two—those to Pan and Dionysus—are briefer
(49 and 59 lines); the rest are very short (3–22 lines) and presumably mere
preludes to longer recitals.

The four longest seem the oldest.   Indeed the Hymn to Apollo is
assigned to Homer himself by Thucydides, who quotes its old poet's final
farewell to the daughters of Dēlos.   All, however, must be later than
Iliad and *Odyssey*.   *Aphrodite* and the Dēlian section of *Apollo* seem perhaps
as old as the eighth century; *Demeter* and *Hermes* probably seventh-century;
and the rest younger.

HYMN TO APOLLO

The first half of the *Hymn to Apollo*, here translated, seems composed
for the God's festival on Dēlos.[1]   We have to imagine ourselves on a little
islet of yellow sand and granite, three miles long, with, in its midst, the low
granite hill (370 feet) of sacred Cynthus.   It is crowded with pilgrims for
the festival; as they still crowd to the neighbouring isle of Tēnos for the
festival of the Virgin, during which the Italians treacherously torpedoed
the Greek cruiser *Helle* in 1940.   Round the horizon of Mediterranean blue

---

[1] The rest of the hymn (177–546) deals with the Delphic Apollo and seems a later,
inferior addition.

stretches one of the most marvellous seascapes in the world—mountain-island after mountain-island, east and west and south and north—Sȳra, Gýaros, Tēnos, Mýconos; Paros, with its veins of marble; Naxos, where Theseus left Ariadne; Serīphos, where Dánaë drifted ashore in her floating chest with the baby Perseus, who was one day to sever the Gorgon's head. And now among the white-robed pilgrims from Attica and Ionia an old blind poet takes his stand to sing of the nativity of the Sun-god, whom his mother Lēto, despite the jealous persecution of Hēra, the Queen of Heaven, bore at last to Zeus, here on the isle of Dēlos.

This Nativity of Apollo presents a vivid contrast to the Bible story of the Nativity of Christ. In both, indeed, there is the jealous persecutor—Hēra or Herod; in both there is the mother's hard search for shelter before the divine child is born. But where the Hebrew thinks of ethics—of the blessing of the humble, of the peace for men of good will—the Hellene turns to aesthetic beauty, to the dazzling splendour of the youthful God of Song. Here is no poor inn, no hay-filled manger, no shepherds with their flocks in the cold midnight; instead, the sunlight beats on golden Dēlos and blue-dancing Aegean, on the radiant grace of Olympian Goddesses, on the proud, wilful splendour of eternal youth. None here invites the weary and heavy-laden with the promise of rest; the Gods of Greece are like Nature, as modern man sees her—often divinely beautiful, but often amoral, often indifferent, or ruthless, to the ephemeral sufferings of mortality. 'How comfortless!' some may cry; but I suppose a Greek might have answered—'Comfortless, yes; but profoundly true. It is not just because of their beauty that our Gods of Olympus still haunt your European mind; it is because of their strange symbolic truth to the ways of the Universe. We loved life, but without illusions; as a man may love a woman who is beautiful, splendid even, but—in the end—cruel.'

Hymn to the Delian Apollo

(8th Century B.C. ?)

Now shall my song remember Apollo, Lord of the Bow,
At whom the Immortals tremble, what time they see him go
Through the house of Zeus. To their feet they spring, each from his
    throne,
As Phoebus comes with his bright bow bent; and Lēto is left alone
By the Son of Crŏnus sitting, the Lord of the thunder-rack.
Then she closes her dear son's quiver, and makes his bowstring slack,
And off his stalwart shoulders she lifts his bow in her hands
To a peg of gold, on the pillar that by his father stands.
Last, to his place she leads him. Now Zeus upon the board,
To welcome his son, the nectar in a golden cup hath poured;

Then the Immortals take their thrones; and the heart of Lēto stirs,
To think that such an archer, so mighty a son, is hers.
Hail to thee, blest among mothers!   For children of glory are thine,
O Lēto—our lord Apollo and the Maid of the bow divine.
In Ortygia thy daughter, on Dēlos' rocks thy son
Thou barest, by the palm-tree, where Inōpus' waters run,
On the ridge of Cynthus resting, till thy travail-time was done.

But how shall I praise thee, Apollo, whom songs so many praise?
For all the ways of songcraft—O Lord, they are thy ways,
Through all the meadowed mainland and the islands of the sea;
All high hills, too, thou lovest, all peaks are dear to thee,
That tower amid the mountains, all streams that seaward sweep,
And beaches that slope to the breaker, and havens of the deep.
Shall I tell how Lēto, resting on Mount Cynthus, gave thee birth,
There in the rocky islet, to thee, the joy of earth,
Alone in sea-girt Dēlos, while round on beach and cove
Before the piping sea-wind the dark-blue billow drove?
There she bore thee, master of all men near or far.
For lord thou art of the Cretan land, of Attica,
Of Aegīna's isle, and Euboea, with her ships far-famed at sea,
Of wave-washed Peparēthus, Aegae, Eirésiae;
Lord of the Thracian Athos, of Pēlion's looming crest,
Of Sámothrace and Ida, with her ridges woodland-dressed,
Of Scyros and Phocaea, of Autócane capped with cloud,
Lord of the smoke-topped Lemnos, and Imbros deeply ploughed,
Of Lesbos the fair, where Măcar dwelt, of Aeŏlus' race;
Of Chios, that most fruitful of isles that the seas embrace;
Lord of the craggy Mĭmas, and Claros glittering bright,
Of Córycus' beetling headland, and of Aeságea's height;
Lord of well-watered Samos and Mýcale towering bold,
Milētus, and that city of the Méropes of old,
Cos, and the lofty Cnīdus, and Cárpathus tempest-blown,
Of Naxos, and of Paros, and Rhēneia's isle of stone.

So far, ere travail seized her, world over, Lēto passed—
Where should her son find refuge, find him a home at last?
For all these feared and trembled—there was not one to dare
Shelter the babe Apollo, however rich they were;
Until at last to Dēlos the Lady Lēto came,
And words from her lips flew winging, and she called the islet's name:
'Dēlos, wilt *thou* give welcome to my son?   Upon thy ground
Wilt *thou* let Phoebus Apollo his golden temple found?
For no man else (thou knowest) will build amid thy rocks
And small hope thine to be rich in kine, or white with flocks;
From *thy* soil shall no harvest, no orchard come to be.

But, if the Archer Apollo once sets his shrine on thee,
Hither shall all the nations gather with sacrifice
And from thine earth for ever the smoke of incense rise,
Measureless.   Thou shalt nourish with fruits of *other* lands
All those that dwell within thee, though barren lie thy sands.'
    She spoke, and Dēlos gladdened, and swift came her reply:
'Lēto, great Coeus' daughter, most glorious!—glad were I
To be in truth the cradle of thy son, the Archer-king—
For ill indeed is my name on earth; and *he* would bring
Glory to me, past telling.   And yet my fears are stirred—
I will not hide it, Lēto—by a rumour I have heard.
'Tis told me that Apollo shall be one proud of heart,
That he shall bear hereafter a proud and princely part,
Alike among Gods and mortals, through all the fruitful earth.
For *that* my mind misgives me.   I fear when he comes to birth
And looks upon the sunlight, I shall but wake his scorn,
Who am but a rocky islet, barren and forlorn.
I fear he may spurn me beneath him and tread me under the foam,
And the depths of the weltering surges be mine eternal home;
That he may seek some fairer land, more worth his love,
Wherein to build his temple and plant his hallowed grove,
While polyps breed within me and black seals make their den
Upon me at their pleasure, left desolate of men.
But if, of thy grace, great Goddess, thou swear an oath to me,
That here his first fair temple, his oracle, shall be,
Throughout the earth thereafter let him turn on other ways,
For I know that his names are many, and wide shall be his praise.'
    Then Lēto swore that mighty oath the Immortals swear—
'Witness the Earth beneath me, and the Heaven's upper air,
And the down-dropping stream of Styx—the deadliest,
The holiest thing that ever Immortal lips attest—
Here shall the grove of Phoebus and his fragrant altar stand
And he shall honour Dēlos like no other land.'
    When Lēto thus had sworn it and her oath had found its close,
Dēlos rejoiced for her new lord's birth.   But bitter throes,
And passing expectation, on Lēto fell; in pain
Nine days, nine nights she travailed.   Beside her sat, in vain,
Rhea and Diōne, the mightiest powers to save,
Thĕmis and Amphitrīte from the deep-moaning wave,
And others still.   (Yet Hēra, the white-armed, came not nigh,
Throned in the hall of Zeus whose rack benights the sky.)
One only—Eileithyia, who soothes the agony
Of mothers, still knew nothing; 'neath the golden clouds sat she
On Olympus' height, by Hēra in her jealousy beguiled,

Who knew that the fair-tressed Lēto should bear a peerless child.
   But to seek for Eileithyia the Immortals in their need
From that fair isle sent Iris, and promised for her speed
A necklace of nine cubits, all strung on threads of gold;
Bidding her go in secret, lest Hēra's word withhold
The coming of Eileithyia.   Then on her wind-swift feet
Iris arose and hastened, far off, to that high seat
Of the Gods on the sheer Olympus.   And straightway from its hall
She summoned Eileithyia and with winged words told her all,
As the Immortals bade her—quickly she gained her prayer
And like frightened doves, together, they darted through the air.
But soon as Eileithyia touched Dēlos, suddenly
The birth-pangs fell on Lēto, and the longing to be free.
On the soft grasses kneeling, tightly her arms she cast
About the palm of Dēlos.   And all at once there passed
A smile across the face of earth—and forth he sprang
To the light of day, Apollo!   Loud through the island rang
The cry of the Immortals; and then, O Archer-lord,
Over thy limbs the water, stainless-clear, they poured,
And wrapped a robe of the fine-spun wool, snow-white, around,
And about thee for a girdle a band of gold they bound.
But the golden-sworded Apollo knew not his mother's breast;
Ambrosia sweet, and nectar, unto his lips were pressed
By the deathless hands of Thĕmis.   And Lēto's heart grew glad
To think what a mighty archer, and stalwart son, she had.
   But, at the taste of that food divine, no girdling gold,
No swaddling bands, O Phoebus, thy quivering limbs could hold.
And as thy limbs were loosened, in the Immortals' ear
The voice of Phoebus Apollo on a sudden rang out clear;
'Let me love the cry of the lyre, let me love the bended bow,
And the will of Zeus, that fails not, through *me* mankind shall know.'
Then up he leapt, far-striding o'er earth's immensity,
The Archer-god Apollo, with his tresses tossing free;
And the Goddesses marvelled at him, and in Dēlos' heart was bliss
That the son of Zeus and Lēto had chosen her for his,
Before all lands, all islands.   Yea, Dēlos flowered with gold,
As on some mountain-summit the woodland flowers unfold.
   But thou, far-shooting Apollo, Lord of the Silver Bow,
Now upon craggy Cynthus up and down didst go,
Now through the isles and nations didst wander to and fro.
For many thy sacred groves, many thy temples be,
And all high hills and headlands were ever dear to thee,
All peaks amid the mountains, all seaward swirling streams;
Yet Dēlos, O Apollo, to thy heart the dearest seems.

There gather to thy glory the long-robed Ionians,
They and their honoured wives, their daughters and their sons:
There, when the lists stand ready, faithfully they throng
To gladden thee with boxing, and with dancing, and with song.
A man might dream them ageless and deathless evermore,
Who sees the Ionians gather upon the Dēlian shore,
And marks with what grace they bear them, and rejoices there
In the glory of their manhood and their women girdled fair,
Their swift ships, and the riches of the proud Ionian race.
And there, too, is a wonder that the years shall not efface—
The mustered maids of Dēlos, who serve the Archer-king.
For first the praise of Apollo their lips in chorus sing,
The praise of Lēto his mother, and his sister's deadly bow;
Then, of men and women that lived long years ago
They chant, till all who listen their life's own cares forget;
And last their quick tongues mimic the dancer's castanet,
And the speech of many a country, till each man seems to hear
His own tongue calling to him—so subtle-sweet their ear.

Now the grace of Apollo upon us, and the grace of Artemis;
And so farewell to you, maidens; and in days after this
Remember, whenever a stranger and wanderer over earth
Hither shall come and ask you—'What minstrel is most of worth,
Of all that sail to Dēlos? Whose songs have sweetest fall?'
Then shall ye make this answer to his question, one and all—
'A blind man; craggy Chios is his homeland—and 'tis he
Whose songs of all are noblest for all the years to be.'
And I will spread your glory, wherever I shall go
Among earth's teeming cities, as I wander to and fro;
And verily they shall believe me, for indeed the truth is so.

(1–176.)

HYMN TO APHRODITE

Just as the *Hymn to Apollo* is full of the wind of Greek seas, so is the *Hymn to Aphrodite* of the wind of the Greek mountainside, that keen wind of Ida which still blows two centuries later through the pages of Bacchýlides, when Hēracles beholds the wraiths of the dead in Hades—'many as the dry leaves the wind tosses up the sunlit ridges of Ida, among the grazing sheep.' [1] Of its kind, I think, Greek poetry has produced nothing finer.

[1] P. 271.

The poem begins with a vision of Aphrodite, symbolizing the reproductive force of Life; as in Lucretius, and in Tennyson's *Lucretius*—

> The all-generating powers and genial heat
> Of Nature, when she strikes thro' the thick blood
> Of cattle, and light is large, and lambs are glad
> Nosing the mother's udder, and the bird
> Makes his heart voice amid the blaze of flowers.

For ultimately the legend of Anchises and Aphrodite seems to belong to the familiar type of ancient tale that symbolizes, under the brief loves of Goddess and mortal (Cýbele and Attis, Aphrodite and Adonis, Demeter and Iásion, Seléne and Endymion), the beauty of spring's awakening, the brevity of summer's pride, the sadness of the swiftly declining year.

So here the poem tells how Aphrodite's power dominates alike Gods and men, birds and beasts and creatures of the sea. Only three of the Immortals are proof against her—Artemis, who embodies that other virginal side of Nature which the hunter or the shepherd meets, in the silence of the forest or on the lonely ridges of the hills; Athene, who incarnates the mind of man in wisdom and in war, in art and craft; and Hestia, the Goddess of hearth and home, where the wildness of passion is tamed and sanctified. All others the Goddess of Love can bow to her will. And so, to humble her pride in her omnipotence, Zeus ordained that she should herself fall in love—in love with a shepherd-lad on Ida, Anchises the cousin of Priam, King of Troy.

Then the tone grows gay, ironic, mischievous, to tell how 'the Laughter-lover' was thus snared in her own net, and how by woman's wit she gained her end. But suddenly upon this smiling sensuousness there breaks the cry of human passion—as if a child at play had loosed a wild thing from its cage. And now, as love finds fulfilment, there sounds the deeper note of human tragedy:

> Mortal beside the Undying he lay—and knew it not.

For a moment the tension relaxes, while through the hush of evening the herds up on Ida turn their heads towards home. Then a new climax, as the Goddess who had seemed but a girl resumes her godhead, and her fair imperious figure towers to the very roof, and she wakens her sleeping lover to the anguish of her pride and shame at the infatuation by which Zeus made her fall. This mood in its turn yields to a quieter sadness, as she calls up before Anchises the vision of Age and Death—the decrepitude that palsies the bright limbs of Tithōnus, the doom that awaits, after many a generation, even the half-immortal Dryads whose green arms wave in the winds of Ida. And so to the close, with its mingled hope and warning—the promise of the child unborn that shall uphold the House of Troy, the menace that awaits him who betrays in his folly the secrets of the Gods (as one day Anchises was to do).

It is hard to guess a writer's intentions across so many centuries; but hard also to believe that these swallow-swift turns and wheelings of the poet's mind are merely fortuitous caprice. In half an hour's space he has passed from Heaven to earth and from earth back to Heaven, from Olympus to Cyprus, from Cyprus to Mount Ida, from youth to age, from Love to Death. So the builders of the tiny Ionic temple of the Wingless Victory on the Acropolis of Athens did not find even a frieze less than eighteen inches high too small to hold, on three sides the swaying tides of battle, on the fourth the conclave of the Olympian Gods. [1]

Europe has other poems like this in theme; but the difference of treatment remains more striking than the likeness. 'The machinery of the Pagans,' says Johnson, 'is uninteresting to us: when a Goddess appears in Homer or Virgil, we grow weary.' But not here. And, again, Paul Valéry: 'Vénus est bien difficile à peindre. Puisqu'elle porte toutes les perfections, il est à peu près impossible de la rendre vraiment séduisante. Ce qui nous captive dans un être, ce n'est pas ce degré suprême de la beauté, ni des grâces si générales: c'est toujours quelque trait particulier.' Yet here that individuality comes to life. The frivolous lay of the loves of Ares and Aphrodite sung by Demódocus in the *Odyssey* at the court of Phaeacia shows no such feeling for the beauty of Nature or the tragedy of Man; it is a mere occasion for cynical court-jests. Ovid's tale, where Venus openly flings herself at Adonis, is neat, light-hearted, and heartless as a *Conte* by La Fontaine. Shakespeare's *Venus and Adonis*, fleshy as a Rubens painting, and spotted all over with foolish cleverness, is only saved by its occasional lovely lines, and by its dumb creatures—hare and horse, boar and snail, dive-dapper and lark:

> My sighs are blown away, my salt tears gone,
> Mine eyes are turn'd to fire, my heart to lead.
> Heavy heart's lead, melt at mine eyes' red fire!
> So shall I die by drops of hot desire.

Not even the molten lead can warm the frozen reader. Fortunately Shakespeare found other styles than this.

Yet these three far cruder poems have been much more read than the Homeric Hymn: ignored by the ancients, it has been hardly more noticed by the moderns. The only worthy trace of it known to me in English literature is Tennyson's *Tithonus*. Already in the pages of *Oenone* Tennyson had visited the glens of 'many-fountain'd Ida,' with their fawning panthers. His *Tithonus*, though it owes little in style to Aphrodite's telling of that

[1] For a discussion of the technical subtleties of the Greek original see H. N. Porter, 'Repetitions in the Homeric Hymn to Aphrodite' in *Amer. Journal of Philol.*, lxx, 249 ff.

legend in her Hymn, yet echoes—with a difference—the world-sadness of
the Greek; that 'immeasurable sadness' nearer to the real heart of Tennyson
himself than any 'larger hope':

> The woods decay, the woods decay and fall,
> The vapours weep their burthen to the ground,
> Man comes and tills the field and lies beneath,
> And after many a summer dies the swan. . . .
>
> Yet hold me not for ever in thine East:
> How can my nature longer mix with thine?
> Coldly thy rosy shadows bathe me, cold
> Are all thy lights, and cold my wrinkled feet
> Upon thy glimmering thresholds, when the steam
> Floats up from those dim fields about the homes
> Of happy men that have the power to die,
> And grassy barrows of the happier dead.

It remains one of Tennyson's finest poems.   And yet its grey gloom lacks
that dancing changefulness of light and shade which make the Homeric Hymn
so radiantly alive.   The English poem closes with a prayer for death: but
the Greek with a promise of birth.   The English seems autumnal as its
dank, mist-bound woods: the Greek as springlike, despite its sense of human
sorrow, as the wind of an April morning.   Each time I read these Hymns
to Aphrodite or Apollo, which even for Thucydides were already ancient,
they bring back this sense of flushed and unspoilt youth.   The page grows
dim; the walls turn air; the wind and sun of other years in Greece return.
Once more, at the tale of Lēto's travail upon Dēlos, round the horizon
loom the blue mountain-shapes of the Cyclades above the glitter of the
Aegean, as once from a surf-tossed boat I watched them dancing round the
little yellow islet where the God of Light was born:

> Alone in sea-girt Dēlos, while round on beach and cove
> Before the piping sea-wind the dark-blue billow drove.

Is it merely the graceful fancy of a bygone race, this vision of the
mysterious power of Love that can bow the loftiest and noblest in supplication to the young and unknown; that masters alike the Lord of Olympus
and the lad who keeps his cattle on the hills; that brings ecstasy, and falls
asleep, and passes on the winds like a morning-dream—yet leaving behind
it the seed of the eternal future, as well as the sorrow for the irrevocable
past; that reigns in resistless domination not over mankind alone, but over
the wild things also of earth and sky and sea?   Call her 'Aphrodite,' or
'Nature,' or 'the Life-force,' or 'the Will to Live'—names may alter, the
reality endures—tender yet wanton, beautiful yet pitiless, immortal yet
amoral.   And no less living here is that other side of Nature—the virginal,

the aloof, the lonely—the Nature that watches us across the unsullied snow of the high peaks or amid the bracken of the whispering forest—her whose stern splendour our poet calls "Ἀρτέμιδα κελαδεινήν"—'Artemis of the hunting-cry'—as she halloos her hounds upon their endless chase. The same two powers, Aphrodite and Artemis, the Nature that is love and the Nature that is loneliness, meet again face to face in the *Hippolytus* of Euripides, in the *Pervigilium Veneris* of the declining Empire. Both are here: both are eternal. Only yesterday an English poet uttered anew, in some of the most perfect lines in English poetry, the same bitter cry of the mortal lover of Nature forsaken by his cold immortal mistress—as Artemis forsook the dying Hippolytus, as Aphrodite left Anchises on the sunset slopes of Ida:

> Tell me not here, it needs not saying,
> What tune the enchantress plays
> In aftermaths of soft September
> Or under blanching mays,
> For she and I were long acquainted
> And I knew all her ways. . . .
>
> Possess, as I possessed a season,
> The countries I resign,
> Where over elmy plains the highway
> Would mount the hills and shine,
> And full of shade the pillared forest
> Would murmur and be mine.
>
> For nature, heartless, witless nature,
> Will neither care nor know
> What stranger's feet may find the meadow
> And trespass there and go,
> Nor ask amid the dews of morning
> If they are mine or no.[1]

To all mankind she comes, whether on Ida or Cithaeron, Brocken or Bredon, or under the Eildon Tree; from all, at last, she goes.

Hymn to Aphrodite

Of the Golden Aphrodite tell to me, Muse, the ways,
Who sends on the Gods in Heaven love's sweet desire, and sways
All races of men that perish, and the fleeting fowls of air,
And the myriad beasts the lands bring forth, and all that the oceans bear.

[1] A. E. Housman, *Last Poems.*

The fair-crowned Cytherēan, they heed her one and all,
But three there are she snares not, three that contemn her call.

   First, the bright-eyed Athene, the Aegis-bearer's child—
On the golden Aphrodite *her* heart has never smiled.
For *her* delight is the clash of fight, where Ares stands,
Battle, and war, and the splendour that springs from the master's hands;
Hers is the craftsman's cunning, whom first her wisdom taught
To fashion the waggon's timbers and the chariot bronze-inwrought;
And the skill that quickens maidens' wit, to broider fair,
As soft they sew by the fireside's glow—'twas she that set it there.

   Next, Artemis of the hunting-cry, Queen of the shafts of gold—
Her too no Aphrodite, with all her smiles, can hold.
She loves but the bow of the hunter and the beasts she smites on the hills,
And the harping, and the dancing, and the cry of the Nymphs that thrills,
And the shadows of the forest, and the cities of righteous folk.

   And a third there is whose maiden heart Love never woke,
Nor the deeds of Aphrodite—Hestia, eldest daughter
Of Crŏnus the crooked in counsel.   Although for bride there sought her
Poseidon and Apollo, queenly she said them nay,
And with a vow she sealed her word, that never shall pass away,
Laying her hand in witness on the Aegis-bearer's head,
To abide through the years for ever inviolate and unwed.
To her, instead of wedlock, Zeus gave another grace—
Hers is the hearth in the heart of home, for her abiding place,
And of sacrifice the fairest, and honour in every shrine,
And in human hearts the dearest praise of all the host divine.

   These three, then, Aphrodite has never the power to move,
These three the sweet cheat snares not.   Else from the might of Love
Nothing escapes—not mortal men, not Gods above.
Yea, Zeus, the Lord of Thunder, Allmightiest, Prince of Praise,
She has beguiled his wisdom and led him wandering ways,
Oft as she would, and laid him by many a mortal's side,
Forgetting the love of Hēra, his sister and his bride,
The noblest child of Rhea and the subtle Crŏnus bred,
The true wife and the queenly, whom Zeus the all-wise hath wed,
Of all Immortal faces herself the loveliest.
So, in return, Zeus wounded the Cyprian's own white breast
With sweet desire for a mortal's love.   Once she had lain,
She too, at last in a mortal's arms, then never again
Should she vaunt in the halls of Heaven with sweet, disdainful smile,
The laughter-loving Cypris, how oft she could beguile
High Gods to seek the kisses of the daughters of the earth,
And from their seed immortal bring mortal sons to birth,
Or daze the daughters of Heaven with love for mortal men.

Therefore in Aphrodite Zeus awakened then
Sweet longing for Anchises, fair as the Heaven's kings,
As he kept his kine on Ida, mount of the many springs.
The laughter-loving Cypris, she saw him, and her heart
Maddened with measureless longing.   Swiftly she fled apart
To her fragrant shrine in Paphos, far on the Cypriot shores,
Tree-girt, asmoke with incense, and shut its shining doors.
Round her the Graces gathered, and bathed her beauty there
With water, and oil ambrosial, that makes more fair
Even the Gods undying.   New-clad and golden-bright,
Once more the Laughter-lover soared through the cloudy height—
From the sweet airs of Cyprus to Troy and Ida's head,
Mount of the many waters, mother of beasts, she sped.
Over the hill, to the neatherds' byre, she passed; and as she came,
The grey wolves followed, fawning, and lions with eyes on flame,
And bears, and lightfoot leopards, devourers of the deer.
The Goddess smiled to see them; and on all, both far and near,
She cast her lure of longing—back to their forest-dens,
Pair by pair, they vanished, down the darkness of the glens.
But herself to the herdsmen's huts she came, built well and fair,
And alone she found Anchises, left by his comrades there
In his god-given beauty.   For all the rest were gone
With their herds to the mountain-meadows; and he was left alone,
Striding forth and backward, while the cry of his harp rang clear.
Then Zeus-born Aphrodite stepped forward and drew near,
Changed to the form and stature of a young unwedded maid,
Lest his eyes discern her godhead and the hero grow afraid.
Then Anchises saw and wondered—so beautiful she seemed,
So tall she towered before him, so gay her garments gleamed.
For the robe that rippled round her, shone like a fire ablaze,
Richly her twisted armlets, her earrings flashed their rays,
Round her soft throat fair chains of gold glanced fitfully,
Light from her soft breasts shimmered, like moonlight, strange to see.
Then passion gripped Anchises.   Swift was his greeting given—
'Hail to Thee, Queen, whoe'er Thou art among the Blessed in Heaven!
Whether the bright-eyed Pallas, or Thĕmis high of heart,
Or Lēto, or Aphrodite, or Artemis Thou art,
Or one of the deathless Graces come earthward, it may be,
Who walk, men say, in Heaven in the high Gods' company;
Or one of the Nymphs that harbour in springs whence rivers rill,
Or deep in the lovely woodland, or up the grassy hill.
Now on some far-seen summit that looks across the lands
For Thee will I build an altar, and bring Thee with my hands
Fair gifts through the circling seasons.   But Thou—in the Trojan town,

O Goddess, of Thy goodness grant me to win renown.
Let me leave good sons behind me.   Long let my own days run,
Happy among my people, seeing the light of the sun.
Let me come, at last, to the door of eld, before I die.'
    Then the Aegis-bearer's daughter, Aphrodite, made reply:
'Nay, Anchises, noblest of men that are born of earth,
Why liken *me* to a Goddess?   Mine is no Heavenly birth.
I am but a mortal woman, that of earthly mother came,
Daughter of famous Otreus—if ever you heard his name—
Lord of the well-walled cities of all the Phrygian land.
Yet the tongue of the Trojans also, like mine, I understand;
For my nurse at home was a Trojan born.   My mother dear
Gave me, a little child, into her hands to rear.
But now the Argus-slayer has caught me away unseen,
The God of the Golden Sceptre from the Golden-shafted Queen,
From Artemis of the hunting-cry, round whom we danced and played,
Many a Nymph, past number, many a long-wooed maid.
The Argus-slayer seized me, God of the Golden Wand—
O'er many a tilth and ploughland he bore me, and beyond
Many a waste and wilderness, untilled of men,
Where beasts devouring wander, deep in the shadowy glen—
I thought that never again should I feel the kindly ground.
For the bride-bed of Anchises, the God said I was bound,
To be the wife you wedded and bear strong sons to you;
He said it, and pointed towards you, then swiftly away he flew,
The mighty Argus-slayer, back to the Heavenly Gate—
And to you I came—for upon me hard lay the hand of Fate.
But now, by Zeus and the noble hearts that gave you birth,
I beg you (for, sure, no dastards bred such a son of worth),
Take me a maid as I am, that nothing know of love,
Home to your noble mother, home to your sire, to prove;
And to your brothers show me, bred of the selfsame race—
Let them judge if this bride before you will bring your blood disgrace.
Then to my land of glossy steeds, to Phrygia,
Send word at once to my father, to my mother that mourns afar—
Much gold, and woven dresses, they will send you back again.
The noble gifts they offer, let not your hand disdain;
But make the banquet ready for the lovely bridal-day,
The feast that all men honour, and Gods that live for aye.'
So in his heart she made the sweet love-longing stir,
And passion gripped Anchises, and swift he answered her:
'If you are a mortal maid indeed, of woman bred,
And the great Otreus is your sire, as you have said;
If Hermes, the Herald of Heaven, truly has brought you here,

To be my wife for always, unto my latest year,
Then there is no man living, there lives no hand divine,
Shall have the power to hold me before I have made you mine,
Now!—no, not even Apollo, though from his silver bow
The Archer-king should slay me with the arrows of his woe.
Face fair as the Immortals, once let me share your bed,
And then the House of Hades may close above my head!'

Hard by the hand he gripped her. With eyes cast down for shame
Upon the earth, and bending her face away, she came,
The laughter-loving Cypris, to the bed of the prince spread fair
With many a fleecy mantle, and furs of the forest bear
Above them, and hides of deep-mouthed lions, that his own hand
Had stricken to death aforetime, high in that mountain-land.
But when they two together in that fair bed were laid,
He drew the gems aglitter from the body of the maid,
Brooches and twisted armlets, earrings and chains of gold;
And loosed the girdle round her, and drew off fold by fold
Her garments in their glory, and laid them, soft and still,
On a seat with silver studded. Then, by the high Gods' will,
Mortal beside the Undying he lay—and knew it not.

But at the hour's returning when the herdsman seeks his cot
With his fat sheep and his cattle, home from the flowery field,
Then the eyes of Anchises deep in sweet sleep she sealed.
Once more she clad her body, a Goddess glorified,
In the beauty of her raiment, and stood at his bedside.
But now to the rooftree rose her head, and from her face
Shone in its deathless splendour the Cytherean's grace.
Out of his sleep she roused him and called him clear by name—
'Up!—wilt thou never waken? *Now* do I seem the same,
Dardanides, to thy vision as in the morning light
When this face for the first time dawned upon thy sight?'
With that cry in his ears on a sudden he started in surprise;
Then, at the sight of that proud neck, those flashing eyes,
He shrank away, in his mantle hiding his comely face,
And the words came winging from him, and he begged the Goddess' grace:
'I knew it in that first moment, when I saw Thee—well I knew
That Thou wert indeed a Goddess. 'Twas *Thy* tongue spoke not
    true.
But, by the Aegis-bearing Zeus, have mercy Thou—
Leave me not, I beseech Thee, on earth to linger now
A feeble, strengthless shadow! For that man wastes away,
Who once in the arms immortal of a daughter of Heaven lay.'
Then the Aegis-bearer's daughter, Aphrodite, made reply:
'Courage, Anchises, noblest of men that are born to die.

Fear not too much—from me thou hast no ill to fear,
Nor from the other Immortals.   For Heaven holds thee dear.
And now a loved son shall be born thee.   He shall reign as the Trojans'
     king,
And children of thy children, years without end, shall spring.
His name shall be called "Aeneas," for deep and bitterly,
When I sank to the bed of a mortal, the heart was shamed in me.
But indeed, of all earth's peoples, the children of thy race
Have ever stood next the Immortals in comeliness and grace.
So Zeus the all-devising for his beauty skyward bore
The fair-haired Ganymēdes, to dwell there evermore,
Honoured among the Blessed, glorious to behold,
As he draws the deep-red nectar from the mixing-bowl of gold.
Fathomless was the sorrow that on Trōs his father lay,
Mourning the loss of his vanished son, long day by day,
Not knowing whither had whirled him the storm-blast from on high.
But the heart of Zeus was softened, hearing that father's cry,
And he bade to King Trōs in requital a team of steeds be given—
Such steeds as draw, high-prancing, the chariots of Heaven—
And sent the Argus-slayer, his messenger, before
To tell how Ganymēdes god-like evermore
Should live—unaged, undying.   That word came not in vain;
The Trojan ceased from weeping, glad grew his heart again,
As his steeds with the feet of the tempest swept down the Trojan Plain.
Of your race too came Tithōnus, fair as the high Gods are,
Whom Eos gold-enthronéd bore from your land afar,
Then came to Zeus, whose storm-rack benights the skies with gloom,
To beg that her love for ever might live, nor see the tomb.
So the Son of Crŏnus nodded to her prayer, and grudged it not.
Ah fool, the Queen of Morning, there as she prayed, forgot
To ask for Youth eternal and shear grim Age away!
So, while his lovely youth endured, rejoicing, gay,
With Eos gold-enthronéd, the Daughter of the Morn,
He dwelt by the Stream of Ocean, at the round earth's utmost bourn.
But, when on that fair countenance, that noble head,
To grey the first hair faded, the Goddess left his bed,
Yet lovingly still she cherished him, within her hall,
With glory of fair raiment and food ambrosial.
Then, when the hateful course of age had run its length
And even to lift his limbs her lover lost the strength,
Best in her heart the Goddess deemed to set at last
The old man in a chamber with shining doors shut fast.
There still his voice chirps ceaseless on, but dead and cold
The manhood lies that quickened in those lithe limbs of old.

Not like to him would I wish for *thee* to live for aye,
Immortal among the Immortals.   If, as thou art this day
In comeliness and beauty, thou couldst for ever be,
To have thee for lord and husband were then no grief to me.
But now—without any pity, swift on thine head shall draw
The doom that waits on all men, that the very Gods abhor,
Old age, the grim, the weary.   And, as for me, my name
Always henceforth in Heaven must bear its bitter shame
Because of thee.   Aforetime, my power held all in dread,
For all the Gods in Heaven to women of earth I led
With my love-wiles and love-whispers.   But now, the name of love—
Never my lips dare speak it, henceforth, in Heaven above,
Since this folly came upon me, past utterance, terrible,
That to the bed of a mortal, infatuate, I fell.
And now beneath my girdle I bear, I too, a child.
But him, when he sees the sunlight, the Nymphs of the mountain-wild
Shall take to their deep bosoms.   This high and holy peak
Is theirs, and no haunts of mortals, no haunts of the Gods they seek.
Long are their days of living, ambrosia is their bread,
And in the Gods' fair dances their whirling footsteps tread.
By the keen-eyed Argus-slayer, alone, their love is won,
Or by the wild Silēni, where under the mountains run
Fair caverns deep in the darkness.   But with them, at one birth,
For each an oak, or a pine-tree, springs from the nurturing earth,
Towering green and lonely, high on the mountainside,
In groves no woodman touches, by the high Gods sanctified.
But when at last for the Dryad draws near the doom of death,
First, where it grows on the hillside, each fair tree withereth.
Down from the trunk the branches fall, the bark grows dry,
And the life of the Nymphs, too, passes from the sunlight, and they die.
These, then, shall be the nurses to watch and tend my son.
And when to lovely childhood he grows, as the seasons run,
The Nymphs shall lead him hither, for thine own eyes to see:
And again in his fifth summer will I bring him back to thee,
And thou shalt learn my purpose.   At sight of that young face
In the first flower of its springtide, fair as the Gods in grace,
Thy heart shall leap rejoicing.   Then shalt thou take the boy
And bring him down beside thee to the windy walls of Troy.
But as for thy dear son's mother, if thou art asked of men,
"Who bore him under her girdle?"—beware, Anchises, then!
This be thine answer (remember!)—"They say he was the child
Of a flower-faced Nymph of Ida, where wave the woodlands wild."
But if, with the mind of a madman, thou boast vaingloriously
That the fair-crowned Cytherēa once gave herself to thee,

Then Zeus shall loose in his anger his reeking bolt on thy head.
Therefore take heed what I tell thee.   My latest word is said.
Mind well thy mouth, nor name me.   Of the wrath of the Gods beware.'
She ceased, and vanished, soaring, through the windy wastes of air.

   Lady of fair-tilled Cyprus, O Goddess, fare thee well.
My tale of thee is told now, of another will I tell.

NOTES

[Page 197] *Gift-devouring princes*. Homer's heroes have dwindled to petty local oppressors—more like the Suitors in Ithaca.

[Page 197] *Half is more than whole*. Cf. *Ps*. xxxvii, 16: 'A little that a righteous man hath is better than the riches of many wicked'; *Prov*. xv, 16–7: 'Better is little with the fear of the Lord than great treasure and trouble therewith. Better is a dinner of herbs where love is, than a stalled ox and hatred therewith.' But Hēsiod's adage is of wider scope and allied to the fundamental Greek moderation of 'Nothing too much.'

[Page 197] *Mallow and asphodel*. The poor ate mallow-shoots and asphodel-bulbs. Asphodel, for all its poetic name, is a pallid, scraggy plant, common on barren patches throughout Greece.

[Page 197] *Prometheus* ('Forethought'), the Titan, son of Iápetus and brother of Epimetheus ('Afterthought'), was originally a trickster like the Norse Loki, but later idealized as a champion of man against Heaven's harshness. The *Theogony* tells how he tried to dupe Zeus by dividing the sacrificial ox into two portions—the flesh covered with the paunch and the bones within a rich roll of fat. Though seeing the trap, Zeus chose, as Prometheus had hoped, the fat and bones (the part that Greek ritual in practice gave the Gods); but he punished the deceiver by depriving him and mankind of fire.

[Page 197] *Iápetus*. Father of Prometheus, Epimetheus, and Atlas the up-holder of the sky. Perhaps an ancient figure of Asiatic mythology, as his name seems to recur in the Biblical Japhet.

[Page 197] *Fennel-stalk*. Giant fennel-stalks, some 5 feet long and 3 inches thick, with hard rind, and pith that burns slowly like a wick, were still used for carrying fire in Greek lands as late as the 19th century.

[Page 197] *His laughter*. 'He that sitteth in the heavens shall laugh' (*Ps*. ii, 4). Homer smiles sometimes even at Zeus; but in Hēsiod it is Zeus that grimly laughs. This grave Boeotian is less at home on Olympus.

[Page 197] *Argus-slayer*. See p. 182.

[Page 197] *Soul of a thief*. . . . It is curious how this strain of misogyny recurs in world literature—in Semōnides (p. 239), for instance, Euripides, the Old Testament, the Early Fathers, the *Roman de la Rose*, Chaucer, Milton, Pope, Strindberg, Tolstoy. Whereas the corresponding term *misandry* does not even exist. Nor, on the other hand, do women or women-writers seem to idealize Man as men have often idealized Woman. Probably no poet has ever expressed *both* attitudes towards the feminine with more vehemence than Euripides. For example:

> Fearful the violence of the raging sea;
> Fearful the force of torrent and of flame;
> Fearful is penury, and a thousand ills
> There are beside; but none so fell as woman—
> No written word has power to say how evil,
> No tongue has power to tell it. If any God
> Created them, *He* was an evil genius—
> That let Him know—and hated all mankind.

(Fr. 1059.)

And yet, in a famous women's chorus of the *Mēdēa* (410–30), it is as if he were answering such passages as this in Hēsiod—

> Backward the Streams of Righteousness are driven—
> All things lie confounded, Justice overborne.
> Men are turned to traitors and their solemn pledges given
> In Heaven's sight forsworn.
> 'Tis time earth's songs were altered, to sing of Woman's fame—
> Ay, honour shall be rendered, at last, to Woman's name;
> No more the ancient slanders shall hold us up to scorn.
>
> And *they* shall be silenced, the bards of old that chide us,
> Harping still their stories of false wives that fell.
> Well for men that Phoebus, the Lord of Song, denied us
> The poet's godlike spell!
> Else *we* had sung our answer, and loud our lips had rolled
> To men a chant of challenge. For Time, from years of old,
> Many a tale of the dealings 'twixt us and men could tell.

[Page 197] *Peitho.* Persuasion, Allurement, Temptation.

[Page 198] *The Seasons lovely-tressed . . . all the flowers of spring.* Misogynist though he is, Hēsiod makes the creature very fascinating.

[Page 198] *Pandora.* Originally an epithet of Earth—'all-giver'; though here she becomes the primeval *femme fatale*.

[Page 198] *The jar,* which Pandora had brought with her (cf. Homer's twin jars of good and evil in the house of Zeus). Like Homer with his tale of Meleāger (p. 36), Hēsiod here seems to assume his hearers' knowledge and tells his story in allusive and abbreviated form. Frazer (*Pausanias*, 1, 24, 7 and note) compares an ancient Peruvian legend that the Creator sent to the Inca Huayna-Capac a box containing all maladies in the shapes of butterflies which, when the box was opened, infected the whole world.

[Page 198] *Only Hope.* Commentators have debated whether Hope is one more plague (cf. p. 402) or a consolation-prize. But allegories, though seldom delicious as peaches, like them should not be pressed. Hēsiod seems simply to mean that, in a world filled with evils, Hope yet abides persistently with man. In Pope's words:

> Hope springs eternal in the human breast;
> Man never is, but always to be blest.

[Page 198] *Race . . . of Gold.* Like other dreams of Golden Ages, this seems psychologically a reflection of man's nostalgia for the happy days of childhood. But it would, perhaps, be over-fanciful to see in the hundred-years childhood of the Silver Age that follows, a reflection of the not uncommon psychological resistance to growing up.

[Page 199] *Sprung from ash-trees.* The wood used for spear-shafts. See too p. 99.

[Page 199] *Of bronze . . . their dwellings.* Cf. beehive tombs like the Treasury of Atreus at Mycenae, with its bronze doors and roof-rosettes; and the legends of Dánaë shut in her brazen tower, of Eurystheus hiding from Hēracles in his brazen pot.

[Page 199] *The godlike Heroes.* Hēsiod has not done badly in dating the heroic era of the sieges of Thebes and Troy at the close of the Bronze Age and on the eve of the Iron.

[Page 200] *All concord of son with sire shall end.* Cf. *Mark* xiii, 12: 'Now the brother shall betray the brother to death, and the father the son; and children shall rise up against their parents and shall cause them to be put to death' (after all, we have ourselves seen such things in our own century): and the still grimmer Sibyl's Prophecy from the *Edda* (Vigfusson and York Powell, *Corpus Poeticum Boreale*, II, 625):

> Brother with brother shall grapple in battle,
> Kin that are closest, shall couple and care not,
> Harsh shall the world wax, and heedless of whoredoms—
> An axe-age, a sword-age, when shields shall be shattered
> A storm-age, a wolf-age, ere the world's ending.

[Page 200] *Honour and Righteousness.* Aidōs and Nemesis—roughly, the self-condemnation pronounced by the individual conscience and the general condemnation pronounced by the public conscience.

[Page 200] *Hawk . . . nightingale.* The first European fable. The hawk, though Hēsiod leaves it unsaid, corresponds to the 'gift-devouring princes.' Cf. the fable of cat and ratons in *Piers Plowman*, equally veiled and equally directed against insolent barons. (Those interested will find a parallel between Hēsiod and Langland in my *Studies French and English.*) Here the point is: 'The great are ruthless as the hawk. But let us follow justice. God pays in the end.' Cf. the Latin distich quoted by Salimbene (1221–*c.* 1288):

> Milvus ait pullo, dum portaretur ab illo,
>   'Cum *pi pi* faris, non te tenet ungula talis.'

> 'In vain "Peep-peep!" you squawk,' to the chicken quoth the hawk,
> As through the air he bore it; 'these claws of mine ignore it.'

[Page 200] *Dapple-necked.* Ordinary nightingales apparently are not 'dappled.' But Ovid likewise (*Met.* VI, 669) speaks of the nightingale's neck as still bearing traces of her murder of her child Itylus.

[Page 201] *Worldly Wisdom.* Sainte-Beuve justly compares some of this shrewd but prosaic prudence to the homely precepts of Benjamin Franklin (*Poor Richard's Almanac*).

[Page 201] *Evil to choose is easy.* Cf. the Delphic oracle p. 407.

[Page 201] *Long is the path and steep.* A famous passage, imitated by Simōnides, referred to by Plato and Xenophon. Cf. *Matthew*, vii, 13–4:, Wide is the gate, and broad is the way, that leadeth to destruction . . . strait is the gate, and narrow is the way, which leadeth unto life'; and Donne, *Satyres*, III. 'On a huge hill Cragged, and steep, Truth stands.'

[Page 202] *Crane.* See p. 249 and compare Aristophanes, *Birds*, 709–12:

> For first we show how the seasons go, autumn and winter and spring,
> And *then* ye know it is time to sow, when the crane flies chattering
> Towards Libya's shore; then the skipper can snore, by the chimney his rudder
>   leaving,
> And Orestes takes note to get him a coat for his winter nights a-thieving.

[Page 202] *The heat that the Pleiads bring.* They rise with the sun in May.

[Page 202] *House-carrier.* The snail.

[Page 202] *Biblian wine.* Not known. Possibly 'Biblian' does not mean 'brought from Biblis,' but indicates a *type* of wine, made locally in Boeotia.

[Page 203] *Wave . . . grave.* Corresponding to a jingle in the Greek— 'meta kūmasi pēmati kursai.'

[Page 203] *Lēnaion.* Late Jan.–early Feb.

[Page 204] *No-bones.* The cuttlefish. Aristotle (*Hist. of Animals*, VIII, 2) says this vulgar error that they eat themselves arose from the finding of tentacles that had really been bitten off by congers. Cf. the old idea of the bear sucking his paws in winter:

> And when these fail'd, he 'd suck his Claws,
> And quarter himself upon his Paws.
>
> (Butler, *Hudibras*.)

[Page 204] *Helicon.* The Muses' mountain (5800 feet), N. of the Corinthian Gulf and S.E. of the far more imposing Parnassus (8200 feet). Hēsiod's Ascra topped a high conical hill E.N.E. of Helicon.

[Page 204] *Violet-shadowed spring.* Aganippe, supposed to give inspiration to the drinker. Perhaps a source near the monastery of St. Nicholas in the Valley of the Muses, at the N. foot of Helicon, close to the River Archontitza, which seems the ancient Permessus.

[Page 204] *Crónion.* Zeus.

[Page 204] *Hippocrēne.* 'The Horse's Fount' (because produced by a blow of Pegasus' hoof) lies in a firwood-glade near one summit (Zagara) of Helicon. On the summit itself, 100 paces E., stands a chapel of St. Elias, probably on the site of the altar of Zeus mentioned here (Frazer, *Pausanias*, V, p. 158).

[Page 204] *Olmeius.* River flowing from Helicon to the Copaic Lake.

[Page 205] *Diōne.* Daughter of Heaven and Earth, and at Dōdōna the consort of Zeus; sometimes given as the mother of Aphrodite.

[Page 205] *Hēbe.* Youth, daughter of Zeus and Hēra; cupbearer, like Ganymede, of the Gods; and wife of Hēracles in Heaven.

[Page 205] *Hēsiod.* Some have argued that 'Hēsiod' here is not the same person as 'me' below; *i.e.* the *Theogony* is not Hēsiod's. But it seems much more like a Greek poet to sign his own work by putting his name at its beginning than to name a predecessor while himself remaining modestly anonymous.

[Page 205] *Many a falsehood . . . many a true word also. . . .* Here in two lines is the scope of all poetry. Herrick made them the motto of his *Noble Numbers*.

[Page 205] *The mourner casts off the load. . . .*

> Qui chante
> Son mal enchante.

Compare Montesquieu's astounding statement that he had never had a grief which an hour's reading could not cure.

HYMN TO THE DELIAN APOLLO

[Page 209] *Ortygia*: 'Quail-island.' Probably here Rhēneia, severed from Dēlos by a narrow channel.

[Page 209] *The Cretan land etc.* Roughly the poet circles the Aegean— S., W., N., and E. Peparēthus is an island E. of Mt. Pēlion; Aegae, perhaps an island off Euboea; Eirésiae, perhaps an island in the Thermaic Gulf near Thessalonica; Autócane, opposite Lesbos; Mĭmas, the mountain facing Chios, with Córycus at its S. end; Claros, on the Asiatic coast, N.E. of Samos. (Aeságea is unidentified.)

[Page 209] *All these feared.* Because of Hēra's jealousy.

[Page 210] *Coeus.* A Titan, son of Heaven and Earth.

[Page 210] *Rhea*, daughter of Heaven and Earth, wife of Crŏnus, mother of Zeus, Poseidon, Hades, Hēra, Hestia, and Demeter; in origin, one of the many Mother-goddesses of the ancient Levant.

[Page 210] *Diōne.* Likewise daughter of Heaven and Earth (see p. 227).

[Page 210] *Thĕmis.* Justice. Another daughter of Heaven and Earth; in fact, the Goddesses of the old order here gather to the birth of the radiant deity of the new.

[Page 210] *Amphitrīte.* Goddess of the Sea, wedded to Poseidon.

[Page 210] *Eileithyia.* Goddess of Childbirth.

HYMN TO APHRODITE

[Page 218] *Anchises*, cousin of Priam.

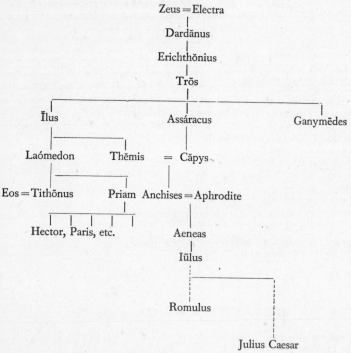

[Page 217] *From the might of Love Nothing escapes.* Cf. Sophocles, Fr. 855:

> My children, Love is more than Love alone,
> For Love hath also many another name.
> Ay, Love is Death; Love is a power eternal;
> 'Tis passion's heady wine, 'tis wailing anguish,
> 'Tis frenzy at its starkest. Love hath all—
> Strong purpose, utter peace, wild violence.

It melts its way into the hearts of all
That breathe on earth—what does not yield to Love?
It moves the plunging fishes of the deep,
Seizes the four-foot creatures of the land,
Flutters its wings among the birds of air:
Nor beasts nor men escape, nor Gods in Heaven.
With Love what God that wrestled hath not found
A triple overthrow?   If I dare say it—
And why may I *not* say what is the truth?—
Love masters Zeus Himself.
Love needs no spear, no swordblade, to confound
The wisest plans alike of God and man.

[Page 218] *Ida*.   Source of the Scamander, Granīcus, and Æsēpus, and still
a 'mount of many springs,' lies south of Troy, along the north shore of the Gulf
of Adramyttium, and rises in its highest point, Mount Gargărus, to nearly 6,000
feet.   Still each summer, like a Swiss alp, its uplands are grazed by herdsmen
from the country round.   In late May, when the lower lands are already beginning to parch, they begin driving up their beasts to the new grass that springs,
starred with crocus and hyacinth, in the wake of the receding snows.   Indeed
Leaf found a stone cattlefold on the very summit.   The mountain, he says, was
still held holy by the local Mohammedans and still covered with forests of pine
and oak.

It is also of interest that, while the Troad, north of Ida, has severe winters
with deep snow and fifteen to twenty degrees of frost, the coast south of Ida is a
sort of Riviera, free from lasting snow, rich in olives, and famous in antiquity
for its fertility (Leaf, *Troy*, pp. 11, 202, 218)—as if the two sides of the mountain
still symbolized the meeting of the lovely Aphrodite and the hardy Anchises.

[Page 219] *Argus-slayer*.   See p. 182.

[Page 219] *Otreus*.   See p. 88.

[Page 220] *That man wastes away*.   Probably because of the jealousy of the
Gods.   Thus Orion was slain by Artemis for having loved Eos, or by Apollo
for having loved Artemis.   Zeus slew Demeter's lover Iásion; and in his own
arms perished Sémele by the guile of the jealous Hēra.

[Page 221] *He shall reign as the Trojans' king*.   The Homeric idea (*Iliad* xx,
307–8) was that the House of Aeneas was to rule in the Troad.   Strabo locates
them at Scepsis, north of Ida.   The legend of Aeneas' voyage to Italy seems to
begin with Stesíchorus (6th century B.C.).   Later still came the tradition that
Aeneas founded Lavinium and his son Iūlus (Ascánius) Alba Longa, whence in
its turn sprang Rome.   The belief that the Julian Gens in particular descended
from Iūlus was sufficiently living in Cæsar's day for him to give 'Venus Genetrix'
as the password at Pharsālus and Munda.

[Page 221] *Aeneas*.   An imaginary derivation of 'Aineias' from *ainos*
('terrible').   The true etymology is unknown.

[Page 221] *Ganymēdes*.   This story of his being carried off by a whirlwind is
earlier than the familiar version in which he is borne away by Zeus in the shape
of an eagle, or by the eagle of Zeus.

Or else flush'd Ganymede, his rosy thigh
    Half-buried in the eagle's down,
Sole as a flying star shot thro' the sky
    Above the pillar'd town.
                                Tennyson.

[Page 221] *His voice chirps ceaseless on*.   Later versions definitely state that he was turned into a grasshopper or cicada, emblem of garrulous age.   When we recall that Memnon, son of Tithōnus and Eos, was identified by the Greeks with the colossal statue of Amenhotep III, near the Egyptian Thebes, which uttered a musical cry each dawn, it seems conceivable that the withered immortality of Tithōnus himself may have been suggested to the Greek imagination by the wizened eternity of the Egyptian mummy in its shining sarcophagus.

[Page 222] *Silēni*.   Wild men depicted in early art with *horse*-ears and, often, *horse*-legs and tail.   They are much confused with Satyrs; who, however, by association with Pan, tend to become *goat*-like.

[Page 222] *Forthe Dryad draws near the doom of death*.   Hēsiod (Fr. 171) gives the following table of expectation of life for nymphs—

> 1 crow = 9 generations of men
> 1 deer = 4 crows
> 1 raven = 3 deer
> 1 phoenix = 9 ravens
> 1 nymph = 10 phoenixes.

Clearly, however, this version bears no relation to the comparatively brief life of a tree.

[Page 223] *Zeus shall loose in his anger his reeking bolt*.   Legend told that, despite this warning, Anchises (by one account, when flushed with wine) could not keep his secret and was accordingly paralysed, blinded, or even killed by the lightning of Zeus.   Many sites are assigned to his grave, from Ida to Arcadia and Italy.   Virgil makes him share the wanderings of Aeneas as far as Trápani in Sicily: there he died and was buried, with a hero's shrine, on Mount Eryx.

PART TWO

FROM ARCHILOCHUS TO ALEXANDER
7th–4th centuries B.C.

ARCHÍLOCHUS OF PAROS

(earlier 7th century B.C.)

HOMER had been as impersonal as Shakespeare in his plays: Archílochus becomes as personal as Shakespeare in his sonnets. But personalities easily grow bitter—Archílochus is the father of European satire. He was, too, the illegitimate son of a noble father and a slave mother; that may have helped to make him feel at war with the world, like Shakespeare's illegitimate Edmund, and to scoff at it, like Shakespeare's Bastard Falconbridge.

His questionable birth (says tradition) caused another Parian noble, Lycambes, to break off the betrothal of his daughter to the poet, who retaliated with lampoons so savage that Lycambes and both his daughters hanged themselves. He took part in the colonization of the North-Aegean island of Thăsos, which he hated; fought the Thracian natives of the mainland—his flight from whom on one occasion he celebrated in a poem of famous irony, which caused him to be banned from Sparta; and finally fell in battle against the men of Naxos. (It is not the worst soldiers that own laughingly to being afraid.) Tradition adds that the Delphic oracle cursed the man who had slain 'the servant of the Muses.'

Time has left us only fragments that do not make it easy to understand why some ancient critics should have ranked Archílochus next to Homer himself; though they justify Quintilian's praise of his style as 'vigorous, terse, vibrating—full of blood and sinew.' He remains the type of poet who has more strength than sweetness, hate than love, passion than wisdom —like Juvenal, Villon, Skelton. Theirs is not the highest type of poetry: yet literature would be poorer without them. And so Archílochus too finds his place in that garland into which Meleăger, in the first of European 'Anthologies,' gathered the infinitely diverse flowers of Greek poetry:

> Sweet as the honeysuckle that springs from its own sowing,
>   Here is Anácreon's singing, his nectared elegies,
> And Archílochus' thorny blossoms, in their tangled thicket growing,
>   Bitter as the spindrift that drives across the seas.

Life and Art

A henchman sworn of Ares, Lord God of war, I live,
And a master of that beauty the Muses' hands can give.

(E. Diehl, *Anthologia Lyrica Graeca* i, p. 211.)

233

The Freelance

For me my spear is kneaded bread; wine from the Thracian land
My spear is; and, to drink it, I lie with spear in hand.

(p. 211.)

The Better Part of Valour

Some Thracian now goes strutting with the shield I left behind me,
    Under a bush—a peerless shield—regretfully.
However—I came home living.   Plague take it! I will find me
    Another one hereafter—and just as good to me!

(p. 213.)

Girlhood

    A branch of myrtle in her happiness
    She held, and a rose's beauty; and her hair
    Fell shadowing deep her shoulders and her back.

(p. 218.)

Too Versatile

    Many a trick the wise fox knows;
    But the hedgehog has *one*, worth a lot of those.

(p. 241.)

Sursum Corda

Heart, my heart, with cares past curing thou that liest sore opprest,
Lift thee up now and defend thee.   Grapple closely, breast to breast,
Foes that lie in ambush for thee—undismayed and undistrest!
When thou winnest, let not all men see thee too triumphant stand,
When thou losest, hie not homeward there to lie and mourn unmanned.
Grieve in sadness, joy in gladness, not past measure—thine to know
How the tides of human fortunes must for ever ebb and flow.

(p. 230.)

TYRTAEUS OF SPARTA

(later 7th century B.C.)

Legend described Tyrtaeus as a lame Athenian schoolmaster sent at the
request of the Spartans to raise their morale in the Second Messenian War
(*c.* 630 B.C.?). It may indeed be true that, like Alcman of Lydia, he was
no Spartan born. Patriotic war-poetry, however, like hymns and other
too purposeful art, seldom reaches the heights. Few would name Campbell

234

as a favourite poet, or wish to multiply the *Marseillaise*. Tyrtaeus' work shows, too, some of the monotonous grimness of Sparta, with her iron laws and her iron money, her black broth and her barrack communism. When he copies Homer, he shows his own inferiority. Homer's Priam laments the unsightliness of an old man butchered in contrast to the grace, even in death, of the young; as an appeal to Hector to pity him and not defy Achilles single-handed, this becomes moving poetry. But Tyrtaeus twists it round into propaganda for the young to fight—even dead they will be handsome; and what was pathetic becomes slightly morbid and disgusting.

Still Tyrtaeus remains a characteristic figure; and his picture here of the miseries of the refugee has an only too modern bleakness.

'Dulce et Decorum'

It is a fair death, fighting in the front of battle
    For the cause of country like the brave to fall;
But to flee his city, his fields of corn and cattle,
    And beg!—among man's sorrows *this* is worst of all.
A banished wretch, with aged sire and her that bore him,
    With his little children and the wife he wed,
To all men he is hateful, wherever he comes, and o'er him
    Beggary is master, and the cry for bread.
A brand he brings upon his fathers; ay, disgraces
    His body's grace; and with him all blame and shame must live.
Therefore, since dishonour and scorn in all men's faces,
    Both for him and his children, wait on the fugitive,
For our sons, for Lacedaemon, for this land that gave us birth,
Fight and die, accounting mere life of little worth.

            (E. Diehl, *Anthologia Lyrica Graeca* I, p. 9.)

ALCMAN OF SPARTA

(later 7th century B.C.)

Alcman, perhaps a Greek of Sardis in Lydia who migrated to Sparta, wrote choral songs, especially for maidens—the earliest Greek lyrics, apart from a few lines of Terpander, that survive.

The Old Poet to his Maiden Choir

Ah voices sweet as honey, ah maiden songs divine,
Faint grow my limbs and fail me! Would the halcyon's lot were mine!—
Wherever the white foam flowers, with my fellow-birds to fly,
Sea-purple bird of the springtime, blithe heart where no cares lie.

            (Diehl, II, p. 34.)

Vesper

Now sleep the mountain-summits, sleep the glens,
The peaks, the torrent-beds; all things that creep
On the dark earth lie resting in their dens;
Quiet are the mountain-creatures, quiet the bees,
The monsters hidden in the purple seas;
And birds, the swift of wing,
Sit slumbering.

(p. 27.)

MIMNERMUS OF COLOPHON

(later 7th century B.C.)

You promise heavens free from strife,
*   Pure truth, and perfect change of will;*
But sweet, sweet is this human life,
*   So sweet, I fain would breathe it still.*

W. Cory, *Mimnermus in Church*.

In temperament, Mimnermus is an even completer contrast to Tyrtaeus than Rossetti to Meredith, or Pater to Carlyle. The softer Greek cities on the Asiatic riviera had been the first part of Hellas to flower: they were to be the first to fade. Mimnermus turns like Ovid, or Omar Khayyám, or Herrick, to gathering rosebuds, and the sadness that it brings. A flute-player himself, he loved a flute-girl, Nanno, who inspired much of his poetry. Despite a fine fragment on courage, he may perhaps be called the first European decadent. But, like many decadents, he remains a brilliant minor artist.

'Gather ye rosebuds'

Ah, what is life?—what is joy?—but Aphrodite the golden?
    Let me die, when I am gladdened no more by things like these—
Her gifts honey-sweet, and the bed of love, by none beholden,
    And all the flowers of youth, that are so sweet to seize,
For the hands of man and woman. But he who is once o'ertaken
    By grim old age, that makes him ugly at once and base,
With misery and anguish his heart without cease is shaken,
    No more to the sun rejoicing, thenceforth, he turns his face.
Hateful he grows to boyhood, a scorn to women's gaze—
Such is the bitter burden God made life's latter days.

(Diehl, 1, p. 39.)

'The Sated Guest'

I would that free from sickness, untouched by cares and tears,
The doom of death might take me at the end of sixty years.

(p. 41.)

The Labours of the Sun

No day released from labour to the Sun-god's self is given;
   No hour of rest for his horses, no hour of rest for him,
From the moment when there rises, across the height of Heaven,
   Dawn the rosy-fingered, leaving Ocean's rim,
Till he sinks to the bed all golden, fair-fashioned for his sleeping,
   That bears him back to eastward, round the circling seas,
Wrought by the hand of Hephaestus with wings that, swiftly sweeping,
   Waft him over the wavetops, from the Hesperides
To the Ethiop shore, where his horses, his headlong chariot wait
Once more, till mounts the Morning again through her eastern gate.

(p. 42.)

HYMN TO DIONYSUS
(7th–6th century B.C.?)

Despite a certain vividness, this piece seems markedly inferior to the best 'Homeric Hymns,' such as *Apollo* or *Aphrodite.* At moments the hand of the poet shakes; and in general Dionysus himself is less attractive than many of the Olympians. There clings about him too much of that decadent romanticism and fanaticism of which his worship remains the eternal symbol. It is characteristic that Homer hardly mentions him; yet Greek wisdom realized that it is perilous too much to repress the instinctive and impulsive forces of human nature. The Puritan Pentheus is torn in pieces by the Bacchanals; the wiser Apollo grants his tumultuous younger brother a share in the Delphic sanctuary. All the same Dionysus remains to this day one of the supreme dangers to the civilization so laboriously and precariously built by man.

Hymn to Dionysus

Of him that had for mother the glorious Sémele
I will sing, of Dionysus—how by the barren sea
Upon a jutting headland he stood revealed once, fair
As a stripling in his flower of youth, with raven hair
Tossing about his shoulders, and a mantle purple-wove
Round his broad chest. But, swiftly, in sight a tall ship hove,

237

Manned by Tyrsēnian pirates, cleaving beneath her stem
The waste of wine-dark waters—ill hour it was for *them*!
Seeing him they nodded each to each, and speedily
They sprang ashore, and seized him, and dragged with savage glee
Aboard their ship.   For they deemed him a prince that they had caught,
Son of some king by Heaven blest; and bitter gyves they brought.
But lo! nothing could hold him—the bonds all slid away
From his hands and feet and, before them, he sat there, smiling gay
With eyes of blue.   Then the steersman, seeing such things befall,
Cried aloud in warning to his comrades one and all:
'Madmen, what God is this that ye seize and bind in vain!—
A mightier one is here than *our* ship can contain.
Zeus it must be, or Poseidon, or the Lord of the Silver Bow,
Apollo!   For only Immortals were ever fashioned so,
That dwell on high Olympus—and none of mortal birth.
Come, let him go in freedom across the dark-loamed earth,
Delay no more, unhand him!—for fear that in wrath he cast
Some great gale loose against us, some tempest's raging blast.'
     But angrily the captain made answer: 'Keep an eye,
Fool, on the wind behind us, and hoist full sail on high.
This lad is for *men* to handle.   If it go as I have planned,
To Cyprus, or to Egypt, or the Hyperborean land—
Or further yet—I will ship him.   He shall tell us in the end
The names—ay, and the riches—of family and friend,
Seeing that fate was minded to throw him in our way.'
     With that he hauled at mast and sail; and every stay,
As the breeze swelled out the canvas, they stretched taut to the blast.
But suddenly before their eyes strange wonders passed—
First of all, through their swift black ship gushed streams of wine,
Sweet to the taste and nostril, while a fragrance all divine
Floated around—the seamen stood gaping at the sight.
All up the sail went climbing a vine to left and right,
Loaded with hanging clusters; and high aloft the mast
Dark coils of winding ivy, bright with its flowers, clung fast,
All beautiful with berries; and the thole-pin of each oar
Stood wreathed with green.   To the helmsman, they cried to steer for
     shore;
But, from the prow of the galley, the God's self met them there,
Like a grisly lion, with thunderous roar; and a shaggy bear,
Rising erect in her fury, by his wonder-working power,
Amidships stood, while forward they saw the lion lour,
Terrible.   Then to sternward they huddled, shuddering,
Around the righteous steersman.   But, with a sudden spring,
The lion seized the captain; and the crew, all mad to flee

That evil end, plunged headlong into the sacred sea
And changed at once to dolphins.   But, unlike all the rest,
The God pitied the helmsman, and held him back, and blessed:
'Courage, thou noble heart!   I am well pleased with thee.
But *I* am Dionysus, the Lord of Revel—he
Whom Zeus begot on Cadmus' child, His own loved Sémele.'

Son of fair Sémele, farewell!   No man shall raise
Sweet song, save he remember to yield thee too thy praise.

SEMONIDES OF AMORGOS

(*c.* 600 B.C.)

Semōnides 'of Amorgos' (in the Cýclades), so called to distinguish him
from his greater namesake, Simōnides of Ceos, was by birth a Samian and
took part in colonizing Amorgos about 600 B.C.   His iambics provide an
early example of satire that attacks, not individuals like the lampoons of
Archílochus, but a class or type.   Characteristically, he here takes for his
subject (like Juvenal, Chaucer, Dunbar, Skelton, Pope, and so many others)
that eternal topic—woman.   It is, indeed, curious that satire—not wholly
to our credit—seems a verse-form almost exclusively cultivated by men;
though perhaps men might retort that women make up for it in conversation
—not to mention novels like Jane Austen's.

Women

God from the first created diversely
The minds of women.   One from a bristly sow
He made, within whose house the goods and chattels
Lie filthy, tumbling higgledy-piggledy,
While she, the slattern, dressed in dirty clothes
Sits in her muck and fattens.
    Another kind, God made from a vicious vixen—
Omniscient.   There's nothing, good or bad,
Escapes *her* comprehension.
Evil she'll twist to good, and good to evil,
Just as, from day to day, the whimsy takes her.
    Another has a dog's soul—nimble mongrel,
That needs must know all, hear all, everywhere
Nosing, and scurrying, and giving tongue,
Though none be there to bark at.   Nothing stops her,
Not threats, not gentleness—not though in rage
One lifted up a stone and dashed her teeth out.

239

Even as guest, sitting at others' tables,
Still, unabashed, she plies her futile yapping.

  Then there's another sort the Olympians made
From simple clay—a half-wit, knowing nothing—
Nor good, nor bad—all that *she* understands
Is eating—*that* apart, she has not sense,
In the depth of the worst winter God can send,
Although she's shivering, to pull near the fire.

  Another was created from the sea,
Two persons in one body—one day laughing,
So gay that any stranger seeing her
At home, will sing her praises—'Never woman
So sweet in all the world, so lovable!'
Let a day pass—and she's insufferable,
To come near or to look at; in a frenzy,
Like a bitch with puppies, snapping at everyone,
To friend and foe a universal shrew.
Just as the sea will often lie so calm
And gentle—sheer delight to all that sail it—
Through summer days; and no less often rages
In a convulsion of deep-thundering breakers.
Nothing in all the world's so like such women.

  Another's made from a dusty, stubborn ass
That only blows and endless objurgation
Can make consent to labour.
And all the while, day-long, night-long, she eats—
Eats at the table, eats in a private corner.
In love, no less, she is omnivorous,
Greedy to grasp whatever lover comes. . . .

  Another's born of a dainty, long-maned filly,
Shying away from trouble and drudgery—
Never ask *her* to grind flour, or to finger
Dishes, or empty slops.
As for an oven—lest a smut fall on her,
She'll not go near it.   *Her* love's tyranny.
Never a day but twice or thrice she washes,
And daubs herself with perfume; and her hair,
Flows deep, smooth-combed, all shaded o'er with flowers.
A lovely thing to look at, such a woman,
For other men; but a curse to him that has her—
Unless he be a king or a dictator,
To glorify his fancy with such toys.

  Then there's the ape.   *She* is, beyond compare,
The deadliest pest of all that Zeus has sent us—

A sort of woman that 's so foul to look at,
She 's the laughter of the town, as she goes by—
Short-necked, and wooden-jointed; limbs like sticks,
And skimpy-hipped—poor miserable man,
That has this monster for a bed-fellow!
But every trick she knows, and every cunning,
Just like an ape—she cares not who may laugh.
She does no kindnesses, her only thought,
Her study, all day long, is simply this—
To vent her utmost malice.

    Last there 's the bee—and lucky he that finds her!
For she alone is a woman without reproach
And in her hands life blossoms and bears fruit.
Beloved and loving, she grows old beside
Her husband, mother of children fair and honoured;
Her name shines out among all womankind,
And on her ways a grace lies, like the Gods'. . . .

A man can gain no prize on earth that 's better
Than a good woman, nor grislier than a bad.

(Diehl, 1, p. 248.)

CLEOBULUS OF LINDUS?

(6th century B.C.)

Cleobūlus of Lindus in Rhodes, perhaps a Carian by birth, was counted among the 'Seven Sages.' A fragment of Simōnides reproaches him for impiously comparing in this poem the duration of a mere mortal monument with that of the eternal forces of Nature.

Midas' Tomb

Here, a maiden of bronze, I stand on Midas' grave,
And as long as runs the water, as long as tall trees wave,
As long as the sun, to light us, and the bright moon mount the sky,
As rivers flow, and the breakers along their beaches cry,
Beside this tomb of sorrow my shape its vigil keeps,
To tell the traveller passing that here King Midas sleeps.

(Homeri Opera, ed. T. W. Allen, v, p. 157.)

ALCAEUS OF MYTILENE

(born c. 620 B.C.)

Alcaeus was a Lesbian aristocrat, driven into fifteen years of exile by his political opponents, whose extreme democracy, as so often in history, tended to throw up dictators. Finally his enemy Pittăcus, before laying down his power in 580 B.C., forgave the poet and allowed him to return home. A great fighter (though, like Archílochus, he once threw away his shield and wrote a poem about it) and a great hater, he took as his main themes love, wine, and war. But most of his work is lost and his chief memorial remains that Alcaic stanza which Horace was to adopt in many of his finest odes. With Alcaeus the lyric becomes as passionately personal as elegy and iambus had been in the hands of Archílochus; but here, for us, he is overshadowed by his contemporary and countrywoman, Sappho.

The Footsteps of Spring

The flowery spring—I heard her, coming upon her way.
A bowl of honey-sweet wine! And mix it fast as ye may.

(Diehl, I, p. 431.)

To his Brother in the Service of Nebuchadnezzar

Homeward from earth's far ends thou art returned
With gold-and-ivory swordhilt—ay, and well
By service to thy comrades *that* was earned,
The men of Babylon; who saw thee quell
So stout a champion, in single fight.
Of five royal cubits, in his giant height,
   But one span short he fell.

(p. 412.)

A Country's Greatness

It is not streets where proud-roofed mansions stand,
Nor masonry of ramparts deftly planned,
   It is not dockyard, quay, or jetty,
   That, in themselves, can make a city—
But *men*, with hearts to use what comes to hand.

(J. M. Edmonds, *Lyra Graeca*, I, p. 339.)

SAPPHO OF MYTILENE

(born c. 610 B.C.)

Yea, they shall say, earth's womb has borne in vain
New things, and never this best thing again;
Borne days and men, borne fruit and wars and wine,
Seasons and songs, but no song more like mine.

Swinburne, *Anactoria*.

Like Alcaeus, Sappho—or Psapho—belonged to the aristocratic party in Lesbos; and like him suffered exile, perhaps in Sicily. One of her poems reproaches her brother Chǎraxus because in Egypt he fell into the toils of the courtesan Rhŏdōpis or Dōricha, whom he ransomed and married (see the epigram on p. 318); though she afterwards forgave him. On the other hand later stories of her own vain passion for Phǎon, which drove her to hurl herself from the Leucadian headland, seem pure myth. She appears on the contrary to have married and had a daughter Kleïs, 'fair as the golden flowers, dearer to me than all the Lydian land.' Tradition makes Sappho herself small, dark, and not beautiful.

That towards other women she felt passions perhaps in her eyes 'passing the love of men,' has given rise, like the similar background of Shakespeare's *Sonnets*, to much learned cant and hysteria. In some Greek communities feelings of this kind were accepted and honoured; if modern psychology knows better the danger of such departures from the normal, that is no reason for trying, like many modern scholars, to garble the plain language of the past.

Sappho remains a supreme example of the Greek gift, so lamentably rare to-day, of combining subtlety and simplicity, plainness and dignity, in a style so tense, yet terse, as to defy the translator. It rings as naturally as the spoken word—yet here are words such as few lips ever spoke. Perhaps its nearest modern counterparts are to be found in some lyrics of Musset, Heine, Christina Rossetti, and A. E. Housman. It may recall, too, that natural grace of language which has enabled some women (like Dorothy Osborne, for instance, or Julie de Lespinasse) to write better letters, even when they could not spell, than far greater male masters of literature. True, Sappho's poetry is as narrow as it is intense; her one subject is love; none the less her poems remain, in the phrase of Meleāger, 'few—but roses.'

Like the 'Alcaic,' the 'Sapphic' stanza has become familiar through the odes of Horace; it has even been one of the few Greek metrical forms to bear, in some degree, transplantation into English, in the hands, not indeed of Isaac Watts or Canning, but of Swinburne.

To Aphrodite

Aphrodite, daughter of Zeus, undying
Goddess, throned in glory, of love's beguilements,
Do not now with frenzy and desperation
      Utterly crush me.

Hear and come!—if ever before Thou heardest
Cry of mine, that called from afar Thy succour;
Then, in haste, with chariot swiftly harnessed,
      Forth from the golden

Hall of Zeus Thy father, to me Thou camest—
Then Thy lovely sparrows from Heaven swept Thee
O'er the dark-loamed earth, through the ether beating
      Swift wings together.

Fast they brought Thee hither; and Thou, most blessed,
With a smile of heavenly lips didst ask me,
What it was I suffered; and why I called Thee
      Hither to aid me.

'Tell me what it is, then, that most thou cravest,
Heart so full of madness?—who *is* it, Sappho,
Passion must awake to desire and love thee?
      Who is it wrongs thee?

'For, although she shun thee, she soon shall seek thee;
Though she scorn thy presents, herself shall bring them;
Though she love thee not, yet she soon shall love thee!—
      Yea, though she would not.'

Come again to-day, then, as once Thou camest.
Save my soul from sorrow, that grows too bitter—
Grant my heart's desiring—be Thou my helper,
      Thou, Aphrodite!

                  (Diehl, 1, p. 325.)

The Beloved

Him I hold as happy as God in Heaven,
Who can sit and gaze on your face before him,
Who can sit and hear from your lips that sweetest
      Music they utter—

Hear your lovely laughter, that sets a-tremble
All my heart with flutterings wild as terror.
For, when I behold you an instant, straightway
    All my words fail me;

Helpless halts my tongue; a devouring fever
Runs in flame through every vein within me;
Darkness veils my vision; my ears are deafened,
    Beating like hammers;

Cold the sweat runs down me; a sudden trembling
Sets my limbs a-quiver; my face grows paler
Than the grass in summer; I see before me
    Death stand, and madness.

(p. 327.)

The Lost Friend

Atthis, our own loved Anactória
In Sardis dwells afar,
And yet, there too, of us her memories are;

Recalling other days—how once you were,
To her, divinely fair,
And with your song no singing could compare.

Now among Lydia's daughters that dear head
Shines, as when day is fled
The risen moon, with fingers rosy-red,

Outshines the stars, and flings her glory wide
Across the salt sea-tide,
Across the many-flowered countryside,

While fair her dew falls on the flowering rose,
And where soft anthrysc grows,
And where in bloom the melilōtus blows.

Yet, Atthis, still, of *you* her memories wake,
Where'er she goes, and make
That gentle heart grow heavy for your sake.

'Come back!' she cries.   We know.   For many be
The ears of Night; and She
Brings us that cry across the sundering sea.

(p. 371.)

To a Rich Uncultured Woman

Dead you shall lie, for ever, a name that none recall;
  For never you gathered roses upon the Muses' tree.
Dim as you were in living, there too in Hades' hall
  You shall drift where only phantoms faint and forgotten flee.

(p. 354.)

Forsaken

Moon's set, and Pleiads;
  Midnight goes by;
The hours pass onward;
  Lonely I lie.

(p. 368.)

Lost Heart

I cannot, sweetest mother,
  My loom I cannot mind;
Delicate Aphrodite
  With longing leaves me blind.

(p. 376.)

The Maid Unwed

As the sweet apple reddens, high up against the sky,
High on the highest branch, where the pickers passed it by,
Forgetting—ah, no, not forgetting—they never could reach so high.

(p. 376.)

Lost Maidenhead

As the hyacinth high on the mountains under the shepherds' tread
Lies trampled, and to earthward bows down its purple head. . . .

(p. 377.)

Evensong

All things thou bringest, Hesper, that the bright Dawn did part—
Sheep and goat to the fold, and the child to the mother's heart.

(p. 378.)

SOLON OF ATHENS
(c. 640–c. 560 B.C.)

Apart from drama (and prose-poetry like some of Plato's) the Athenians
seem to have been less gifted poetically—though we are so dazzled by the
other brilliance of Athens that no one apparently dares to say so—than many

smaller and obscurer Greek cities. Attica produced few non-dramatic poets besides Solon; and even Solon is a rather prosaic poet. His poetry is nearly all politics; as the poetry of that other supposed Athenian, Tyrtaeus, is nearly all military. But it is fair to add that few politicians have written poems even as good as Solon's.

His birth was noble. He is said to have nerved his discouraged country-men to renew their efforts to drive the Megarians from Salamis, the island at the very gates of Peiraeus, by a poem of which part is given below. He certainly in his archonship of 594 B.C. brought back some political and economic justice to his troubled city. But, like most moderates, he displeased extremists on either wing; and, after vainly warning Athens of the growing threat of despotism, the old statesman who had disdained to make himself dictator died under the dictatorship of Pisistratus.

In temper Solon of Athens remains closer to Hēsiod in the neighbouring Boeotia than to most other poets before him; he shows the same practical morality, the same passion for justice. But the finest of his works was his life.

The Shame of Losing Salamis

Why, then, let Phōlegandros or Síkinos be my city,
  Not Athens! Be my country some other land than this!
For now through all the world our shame shall make men witty—
  'This is an Attic fellow, beaten from Salamis.'

(Diehl, 1, p. 21.)

The Rise of Dictatorship

As on the fiery lightning followeth the thunder,
  As from the cloudrack comes the driving hail and snow,
From men of power comes a city's ruin; so it falls under
  A despot—by their folly its folk to bondage go.
Once a man is exalted, hard he grows to restrain.
Already the time is on ye to see that issue plain.

(p. 28.)

THEOGNIS OF MEGARA

(c. 540 B.C.)

A complete contrast to the enlightened liberal Solon is the embittered conservative Theognis, from the adjacent city of Mégara on the Isthmus of Corinth. But if Theognis was a smaller man, he was a better poet. Like

Alcaeus and Sappho, he too was driven out by democrats to taste the bitter bread of exile. He typifies indeed the recurrent tragedy of the aristocratic landowner fighting a lost battle against the new money-makers in trade and industry; of the gentleman outdated by the parvenu. In Tchekhov or Galsworthy, after twenty-four centuries, the same conflict is still there; but the political hatred of Theognis has a passion of bitterness such as England, happily, has seldom even conceived.[1]

Nor were his private passions happier. His poems to his loved squire, Cyrnus, show as agonized an alternation of affection and resentment, admiration and scorn, as the Sonnets of Shakespeare.

It is not surprising to find the philosophy of such a man darkening into pessimism—anguish at youth's passing, loathing for the relentless inroads of old age, fury at the lack of loyalty or justice in the world. At moments, he might be Byron (without the humour); or Baudelaire (without the decadence). It is easy to understand why this sombre, yet indomitable aristocrat should have deeply appealed to Nietzsche.

But, after all, whatever such violence of passion may do to a man's happiness, it can be the lifeblood of poetry, when it goes with a sense of beauty—such as Theognis shows in passages like his description of the nativity of Apollo, where he even, for once, forgets himself. Theognis remains a minor poet; but no other Greek poetry, before or after him, (except perhaps Palladas) achieves quite the same power of bitterness.[2] Perhaps his nearest counterpart is, at moments, a poet of our own century, A. E. Housman—

> Ay, look: high heaven and earth ail from the prime foundation;
>> All thoughts to rive the heart are here, and all in vain:
> Horror and scorn and hate and fear and indignation—
>> Oh why did I awake? when shall I sleep again?

The Soldier

> See from yon looming summit the beacon, Cyrnus, beckon,
>> Like to a tongueless herald, that tells of tearful war.
> Get our swift steeds bridled—little the time, I reckon,
>> Until the ranks of foemen are barring the path before.
> Soon they will be upon us—they lie not far behind,
>> Unless the Gods in Heaven have left my judgment blind.

(ll. 549–54.)

[1] Cf. the comment of a Greek officer on hearing of the 1945 election-results—'I suppose Churchill has taken to the hills?'

[2] Criticism is complicated by the intrusion of other poets' work in the collection that bears his name.

The Wanderer

I have travelled to Euboea and her plains with vineyards growing,
   I have travelled, in times past over, to the shores of Sicily,
And to glorious Lacedaemon, and seen Eurōtas flowing
   Amid his reeds; most noble was their hospitality.
And yet, for all their kindness, no gladness filled my breast:
So true it was that all men must love their own land best.

(783–8.)

The Refugee

I heard, O Polypāïdes, I heard the bird's shrill crying,
   That comes to tell the tiller that time has come to plough,
And it stabbed the dark heart in me, to think my lands are lying,
   My flowered fields, in keeping of other masters now;
That no team of mine goes straining against the yoke this day,
Since by its cursed pilots our city's cast away.

(1197–1202.)

Against the Demos

Now to my prayer in season, O Zeus of Olympus, hearken!
   After so many evils, give me some good again.
Let me die, if I find no respite, amid my days that darken,
   If I cannot avenge me and pay back pain for pain.
This were but just. Yet of justice upon these evil-doers,
   What sign, though they keep the riches that from my hands they tore?
The robbers! Poor as a hound I have fled from my pursuers—
   All, in the torrent's fury, I lost ere I came to shore.
Ah, could I drink their dark-red blood! Could some just power
Govern it so, and grant me, at last, to have my hour!

(341–50.)

An Eye for an Eye

Now fall the height of Heaven in headlong ruin above me,
   Where it hangs its brazen menace above the heads of men,
If I give not love and helping to all the hearts that love me,
   And to all that hate I give not havoc and hate again!

(869–72.)

Vendetta

Speak fair to him that hates thee, till he falls in thy hand at last,
Then linger not for reasons, but pay him for the past.

(363–4.)

Poverty

Whatever the worth of a man, yet poverty can bring him
    Lower than burning ague, or grey senility.
Sooner than bear it, Cyrnus, better a man should fling him
    From crags that no foot can clamber, or down the gulfs of sea.
He dare not do a deed, he cannot utter sound,
Once penury has chained him.   His very tongue lies bound.

(173–8.)

Friendlessness

The exile has never a friend of loyal and steadfast will;
Bitter enough is exile; but *this* is bitterer still.

(209–10.)

Plutocracy

In most men's eyes one virtue, alone, is worth endeavour—
    Riches.   It seems that nothing, save this, shall profit us!
Vain to be self-controlled as Rhădamanthys, clever
    As Sīsyphus aforetime, that son of Aeŏlus
Who came back even from Hades by his wisdom, and persuaded
    By the cunning of his speeches even Persephone,
That dims men's minds with Lethe, till their memory hath faded—
    Never another mortal devised such subtlety,
Once the dark cloud of Death around his head had risen
    And he reached the land of shadows, that the souls of the perished fill,
Beyond those dark-blue portals which evermore imprison
    The wraiths of the departed, so sore against their will.
Yet Sīsyphus the hero even from thence ascended
    Back to the light of the sun, so much his wise heart knew.
But vain is it now to be gifted with skill in speech as splendid
    As was the godlike Nestor's, that made false things seem true;
Vain, though thy speed in the race leave the Harpies overtaken
    And outrun Boreas' sons, winged feet through the heavens hurled.
This truth let all mankind henceforward trust unshaken—
    Gold it is that holds now dominion through the world.

(699–718.)

Eugenics

A ram or a stallion, Cyrnus, of good stock each man chooses,
    Or an ass for siring—we seek the purest race
For cattle! But, in marriage, not our noblest now refuses,
    If gold enough goes with her, the base child of the base.

Now an ignoble lover by never a girl is dreaded,
  So he be rich—the wealthy, and not the good, must speed.
Money it is, men worship.   The honourable have wedded
  The mean, and the mean the noble.   Wealth has confounded breed.
Wonder no more, my Cyrnus, if the blood of our city still
Degenerates, when good things are thus confused with ill.

(183–92.)

Race

Ne'er yet from the root of a squill did rose or hyacinth wave;
Nor came a son of freedom from out the womb of a slave.

(537–8.)

Critics

Pass with all men's approval through life to Hades' portals
  None can—none ever could, of all that have come to birth.
Not even He that reigns o'er mortals and Immortals,
  Zeus, the son of Crŏnus, can please all men on earth.

(801–4.)

'Hurler avec les Loups'

Among the mad, none madder; and in the company
Of the virtuous, for virtue there is no man like me.

(313–4.)

Protective Colouring

Be like the twisted polyp that coiling round a boulder
  Takes the rock's own colour, whatever hue it be;
So change thine own complexion to humour each beholder.
  Better by far is cunning than steadfast constancy.

(215-8.)

Loyalty

'I loathe a man that 's evil.   My face in my veil I 'll cover
  And pass him by as lightly as a bird flies from the snare.'
'I hate a gadding woman, I hate a wanton lover
  That in another's acre would thrust his own ploughshare.'

(579–82.)

The Beloved

To thee, my love, for ever I have given wings to raise thee
  To fly the wide world over, to cross the infinite sea,
Swift as a thought: laid lightly on the lips of men that praise thee
  At every feast and revel in the midst thou too shalt be.

251

And youths in the flower of their beauty, to the flute's clear voice replying
  With voices as clear and lovely, in order due shall sing
Of thee; and when thou goest to that place of bitter crying,
  Deep in earth's abysses, where Hades sits as king,
Not even in death shall thy glory fade, thy memory wither,
  Thou shalt not lie forgotten, not even in the grave;
Through Greece, through the Isles, my Cyrnus, thou shalt wander, hither,
  Journeying for ever o'er the tireless, teeming wave;   [thither,
Riding, but not upon horses.   Not steeds, but the glorious guerdon
  Of the Muses shall bear thee onward, the Violet-garlanded;
All that love *them* hereafter, shall make *thy* name the burden
  Of a song that sounds for ever, till earth and sun be dead.
And yet for all this, my Cyrnus, I am nothing in thine eyes!
Shameless, thou hast deceived me, like a little child, with lies.

(237–54.)

The False One

Now at his hour Love rises, while all the earth is springing,
  Springing into blossom with all the flowers of May.
Out of lovely Cyprus, Love comes and wanders flinging
  His seed in hearts of menfolk through all the world away.
Alas!   Love came and whispered to thee of me, and bade
That thou shouldst turn elsewhither and leave my love betrayed.

(1275–78B.)

The Adder

Thou hast stolen again—I know it—on the path thy feet did follow
  Before this, in thy falsehood, our old love to forsake.
Begone!—by all Gods hated, by all men known for hollow—
  Thou whom I clasped to my bosom, a cold and spotted snake.

(599–602.)

Love's Blindness

When two men hate, my Cyrnus, they find traps hard to lay:
But a lover finds a lover a trifle to betray.

(1219–20.)

The Broken Chain

I love the lad no longer; I have spurned my bitter sadness;
  I am escaped rejoicing from the toils of misery.
The fair-crowned Cytherēa has delivered me from madness;
  Boy, thou art fair no longer, no longer fair to me.

(1337–40.)

'Cherchez Fortune Ailleurs'

I drank at a spring, time was, where dark the water bubbled;
　　Sweet it seemed to my lips, and fair to my eye its gleam.
But now some foot has befouled it, with mud it lies all troubled;
　　Another fount I must find me, drink from another stream.

(959–62.)

'Vive hodie'

Now is the time to surrender our hearts to merry-making,
　　While life's fair things can give us a joy that is not vain.
For the glory of youth goes by us, swift as a thought, o'ertaking
　　Even the speed of steeds whose charging hoofs amain
Whirl some king in his car to the press of the spear-fought fray,
Over the young green furrows, exulting on their way.

(983–8.)

Dust to Dust

Make merry, heart within me.　Others shall come to birth
So soon, and I be lying but blackened earth in earth.

(877–8.)

The Years

'Alas for grim old age!　Alas for youth!' I cry—
The one so swift departing, the other drawing nigh.

(527–8.)

The Problem

Dear Zeus, at Thy ways I wonder.　For all that live adore Thee,
　　The power to Thee, and the glory, all mankind accord:
There is not a heart, not a thought, but stands revealed before Thee;
　　There standeth no dominion to match with Thine, O Lord.
How then can Thy wisdom look in so indifferent fashion
　　On those whose deeds are evil, and who deal righteously?—
Whether a man refrain his heart; or sate his passion
　　In works of overweening and iniquity?

(373–80.)

Despair

Not to be born at all is the happiest lot for mortal,
　　Never to open eyelids on the bright shafts of the sun:
Or, born, as soon as may be to pass beyond Death's portal,
　　To pull earth's heavy mantle above him and have done.

(425–8.)

The Stoic

What is my fate to suffer, my Cyrnus, knows no cure:
What is my fate to suffer, I fear not to endure.

(817–18.)

Nativity

Lord Phoebus, when our Lady, the gracious Lēto, bore Thee
  Beside the round mere's margin, when Thou camest from her womb,
While her slim hands clasped the palm-tree, all Dēlos to adore Thee,
  Fairest of the Immortals, grew fragrant with perfume,
Ambrosial, passing measure—then laughed the endless earth
And the deep seas' hoary surges made answer in their mirth.

(5–10.)

IBYCUS OF RHEGIUM

(mid 6th century B.C.)

Íbycus of Rhēgium in southern Italy later removed to the court of Polýcrates in Samos. Only fragments of his work survive; but his ancient reputation was based on the grace and fire of his love-lyrics. A legend, retold in Schiller's poem, related that he was murdered by robbers and called, as he died, for vengeance to a flight of cranes winging overhead; the robbers repaired to the theatre at Corinth and one of them, seeing cranes pass over, whispered to his fellow: 'The cranes of Íbycus!'—an indiscretion which brought them to summary justice.

Passion without Respite

Only in spring do the quince-flowers quiver
Blossoming deep in the garden-close
Sacred to maidenhood, where from the river
Many a quickening channel flows;
Only in spring do the vine-flowers throng
Under the leaves; but all year long
No rest my passion knows.
Sent by the Cyprian (as from the north
Headlong the Thracian tempest breaks,
While from its gloom the lightnings shoot),
Raving it smites me in its wrath,
Shrivelling all—to the very root
My heart it shakes.

(Diehl, II, p. 53.)

HIPPŌNAX OF EPHESUS

(*c.* 540 B.C.)

Little remains of one who seems to have been a sort of Villon, consorting with outcasts and criminals, and adapting their slang to his verse. One authority credits him with the invention of parody. He certainly did invent what was called 'the lame iambic' (*scaʒon*) with a dragging close of three long syllables. Clearly, like Donne, he wished to fit harsh sound to harsh sense.

Misogynist

Two days a woman's best—the day she's wed,
The day she's carried from your doorway—dead.
(Diehl, I, p. 302.)

Economy

Out of the jug we drank; there was no cup
(The boy fell down on that and smashed it up).
(p. 272.)

Pugilist

Take my overcoat and hold it—I'll hit Būpalus in the eye.
Ambidexterous I am; and so I never aim awry.
(p. 283.)

PHOCYLIDES OF MILETUS

(*c.* 540 B.C.)

A writer of verse aphorisms, who may perhaps claim to be one of the founders of the epigram in its modern sense—a short poem with a point.

'In Huts where Poor Men Lie'

This said Phocýlides, also; where men live lawfully,
Better a crag-built township, than follies of Nineveh.
(Diehl, I, p. 49.)

The Exception that proves the Rule

The Lěrians are evil; all!—and not just a few—
All except only Prŏcles. And Prŏcles is Lěrian too!
(p. 48.)

(*c. 570–c. 485* B.C.)

Anácreon, though most famous for poems he never wrote—imitations ranging from the Alexandrian to the Byzantine period (see p. 333), has become the prototype of Epicurean poets such as La Fontaine and Herrick.   In him the decadence of Ionia, already visible in Mimnermus, has gone further still.   Liberty has given place to foreign invader and domestic tyrant; the old energy and daring have died away; rosebuds remain.   In the words of Landor:

> But where the land is dim from tyranny,
> There tiny pleasures occupy the place
> Of glories and of duties; as the feet
> Of fabled fairies, when the sun goes down
> Trip o'er the grass where wrestlers strove by day.

At courts like those of Polýcrates in Samos, or Hipparchus in Athens, Anácreon surrendered himself to a graceful frivolity that gaily defied the years.   He had fought in youth and, like Archílochus and Alcaeus, had written a poem on losing his shield; but now he turned from Ares to Aphrodite and Dionysus, to become the poet of love, wine, and humorous old age—a character well symbolized in the legend that he died at eight-five by choking with a grape-pip.

The Coy Mistress

Thracian filly, why so heartless?   Why, so shyly sidelong glancing,
    Hold me ever at a distance, like a fool with wit untried?
I could clap a bridle on ye, very well, for all your prancing;
    Down the course I well could rein ye, make ye wheel the way I guide.
Yet a while, across the pastures, go your ways with light feet dancing—
    You have still to find the master that shall curb ye and shall ride.

(Diehl, I, p. 470.)

War's Folly

Timócritus fought well.   This is his grave.
For Ares spares the coward; and not the brave.

(*Anthologia Palatina*, VII, 160.)

XENOPHANES OF COLOPHON
(*c. 565–470* B.C.)

With Xenóphanes, though himself a poet as well as a philosopher, begins the long war of philosophy against poetry.   Here he is a forerunner of

Plato and Tolstoy.   Born at Cólophon in Asia Minor, then driven by the Persian invader to migrate to South Italy and Sicily, the old sage speaks of having tossed his thoughts up and down Hellas for seventy years.   A monotheist and doubter of the senses, he was counted the founder of the Eleatic School continued by Parménides, a profounder thinker but worse poet.

Wickedness of Poets

Homer and Hēsiod fathered on the Gods' divinity
All deeds most blameful and shameful that here on earth there be—
Yea, thieving and deceiving and adultery.

(Diehl, I, p. 58.)

Anthropomorphism

If oxen, or lions, or horses had hands like men, they too,
If they could fashion pictures, or statues they could hew,
They would shape in their own image each face and form divine—
Horses' gods like horses, like kine the gods of kine.
'Snub-nosed are the Immortals, and black,' the Ethiops say;
But 'No,' the Thracians answer, 'red-haired, with eyes of grey.'

(p. 58.)

The Agnostic

Of the Gods and these other matters none knows the verity—
No man that lived before us, no man that yet shall be.
However full-perfected the system he hath made,
Its maker knoweth nothing.   With fancy all 's o'erlaid.

(p. 62.)

Rainbow

She, too, whom men call 'Iris' is but a mist in the skies,
That shimmers green, and scarlet, and purple in men's eyes.

(p. 62.)

Athleticism

Now if a man shall show him in speed of foot the faster
    On that ground to Zeus made holy, where the fount of Pisa flows
Through Olympia, or at wrestling shall prove himself the master,
    Or at the pentathlon, or the boxer's bitter blows,
Or from the grim pancration shall rise a winner,
    He seems in the eyes of his city more splendid than before;
His to eat henceforward at the public cost his dinner
    And a gift from the public treasure shall go to increase his store;

His the seat of honour at every celebration—
    And as richly is *he* rewarded whose coursers take the prize,
Though less in worth than *I* am!   For of nobler estimation
    Than the strength of men or horses is the wisdom of the wise. . . .
Nay, though a man shall conquer beside the banks of Pisa,
    Small cause to be glad his city shall gain from such as he;
From the curses of disorder no such triumph frees her,
    That cannot fill the coffers of her treasury.

(p. 55.)

HYBRIAS THE CRETAN

(6th or early 5th century B.C.?)

The Freelance

My golden hoard is spear and sword
And the bull's-hide shield I bear before me;
With these I plough and reap my bread,
And sweet wine from the grape I tread;
These make my slaves as lord adore me.

But they that fear good sword and spear
And bear no bull's-hide shield before them—
Louting low on bended knee,
These must salute my majesty—
As King of Kings I lord it o'er them.

(Diehl, II, p. 128.)

HYMN TO PAN

(5th century B.C.?)

Though included among the 'Homeric Hymns,' this piece is generally believed not earlier than the fifth century B.C., when the worship of Pan, originally a local Arcadian God, became more widely spread—witness the legend that during the Persian invasion of 490 the famous runner Pheidippides, sent by Athens to hasten Spartan aid, was met returning across Mount Parthénius, near Tégea, by Pan himself, who asked why the Athenians did not worship him and promised his help in the coming fight.   This promise Pan kept at Marathon by casting on the Persians that 'panic' terror with which he can fill the lonely wanderer in the silence of the hills; as Wordsworth knew—

    I heard among the solitary hills
    Low breathings coming after me and sounds
    Of indistinguishable motions, steps
    Almost as silent as the turf they trod.

258

Hymn to Pan

Of the dear son of Hermes, O Muse, sing now to me,
That goat-foot, hornéd lover of ringing revelry,
Who wanders the woodland valleys, while his lightfoot Nymphs dance round;
Where never a goat can clamber, along the crags they bound,
Calling to Pan, the shepherd-god, with shout and song—
Pan of the glorious locks unkempt, to whom belong
All peaks, all snowy summits, all stony mountain-ways.
Through the tangled brakes of the forest, now here, now there, he strays—
Sometimes the rivers lure him down to their gentle flow,
Sometimes he turns to scramble, by rocks where none may go,
Up to a towering hilltop, to see where his sheep may lie;
Often the long white ridges behold him hurrying by,
Often with keen, wild glances he scours the upland glen,
Tracking his prey; and returning from his chase in the twilight then
On the reeden pipe of a shepherd he plays his music lone—
No nightingale can utter a strain of lovelier tone,
When in the flowery springtime, perched amid many a leaf,
With notes as sweet as honey she trills her song of grief.
Then round him the lilting voices of the Nymphs of the mountain ring,
As by the dark-black water, bubbling from a spring,
Their light feet trip, and the echoes, high from the hilltop, call.
But the God, with his twinkling steps, through their dances leads them all,
Now through the midst of them whirling, now this, now the other side,
Rapt by the music, and wearing a reddish lynx's hide;
Soft round them lies the forest-lawn and, perfumed sweet,
The hyacinth blends, and the crocus, with the grass beneath their feet.
But the song of the Oreads tells of the blessed Gods on high
And of the long-ridged Olympus; and, above the rest, they cry
The praise of the Gods' fleet herald, of Hermes swift to aid,
And how of old to Cyllēne, to his sacred woodland's shade,
In Arcadia, mother of flocks, land of fair springs, he sped
And there that son of Heaven the sheep of a mortal fed;
For now a tender longing in his heart had come to flower
For Drÿops' fair-tressed daughter. The lover found his hour;
And so in her home for Hermes she brought a dear son to birth,
Twy-hornéd and goat-footed, a lover of noisy mirth—
So monstrous, that his mother, dropping him, fled afeared
From the sight of those grim features, that bristled with a beard.
But quickly Hermes the Helper lifted him where he lay
And owned his son; and within him the heart of the God grew gay.
Then Heavenward in haste he turned, wrapping the child
Warm in the furry skin of a hare of the mountain-wild,

And took his seat in Olympus and showed his little lad
To Zeus and the other Immortals—and all of them grew glad,
But most of all Dionysus delighted in the boy.
So 'Pan' was the name they gave him, since he filled 'ALL' Heaven with joy.

Farewell, O Lord, I have brought Thee prayer alike and praise;
And I will sing thy glories, anew, in coming days.

SIMONIDES OF CEOS

(c. 556–467 B.C.)

During his long career Simōnides of Ceos (in the Cýclades, off Attica)
wrote both elegiac and lyric poetry. He was patronized by various ruling
personages—Hipparchus at Athens, the Scópadae in Thessaly (until their
banquet-hall fell on their impious heads), and Híero at Syracuse; but he was
also a friend of the democrat Themistŏcles. Ancient tradition accused him
of avarice—which probably means merely that, like Shakespeare, he was a
business-like poet. On the other hand he was especially famous for his
power of pathos, so that for Catullus the extremity of sorrow is something
'sadder than the tears of Simōnides.' That quality is illustrated by his
song of Dánaë; but even here, and still more in his epigrams, the restraint
is not less intense than the sorrow. With Aeschylus (whom he is said to
have defeated in a contest for the best epigram on the dead of Marathon),
Simōnides remains the most representative Greek poet of the great period
of the Persian Wars.

• *Dánaë Adrift*

*Acrisius, king of Argos, was warned by the Delphic oracle that if his
daughter Dánaë had a son, that son would kill him. He therefore shut her
up in a tower of brass; but Zeus loved her, and descended into her room in
a shower of gold. Acrisius then set his daughter and the infant Perseus adrift
in a coffer: but they were cast ashore on the isle of Serīphos. Perseus grew
up, killed the Gorgon Medusa, saved Andrómeda from the sea-monster, and
at the funeral-games for Polydectes, king of Serīphos, accidentally killed his
grandfather with a discus that he threw.*

When she was set in her carven chest,
Whirled by the wind from crest to crest
            Of heaving sea,
On Dánaë's heart fell horror—her tears began to run
And babe to breast the mother pressed, crying 'O little son,
        For me is misery,

But thou, my innocent one—
Calmly thou sleepest; and nought to thee
      This brass-nailed chest of woe;
Nought is the starless midnight, nought is the dark-blue gloom
Of the wave that welters by us and flings its driving spume
      Upon thy curls below;
Nought is the sea-wind's wailing—so soft thy face is laid
On mine, within the purple of my mantle fast asleep.
Nay, terror has no terror, for *thee*—else how dismayed
Thy little ears would listen, to hear thy mother weep!
Sleep on, my babe; sleep, restless sea; sleep, boundless ill
That breaks my heart!   O Father, O Zeus, be it thy will
      To save us and to spare.
      Yet, if too bold my prayer,
If I transgress Thy justice, forgive, forgive me still!'

                         (Diehl, ii, p. 69.)

Life's Best

    Health is the best that Heaven sends;
    Next, to be comely to look upon;
    Third is riches, justly won;
    Fourth, to be young among one's friends.

                         (p. 183.)

The Backbiter

Much I guzzled, much I tippled, and of slander many loads
I vented—now I rest here, Timócreon of Rhodes.

                         (p. 97.)

The Unlooked-for Bargain

Here Brótachus of Gortȳna, a Cretan born, is laid;
Who came on no such errand, with thought of nought but trade.

                         (p. 112.)

Lost at Sea

Thou hast but foreign earth, O Cleisthenes, to hide thee,
    For Death found thee, a rover, far in the Euxine foam.
The sweetness of returning to thy country was denied thee;
    Never again thou camest to sea-girt Ceos home.

                         (p. 111.)

Lost at Sea

Ah, misty Géraneia, ill crag, thou shouldst stand facing
    Where Ister, where endless Tánaïs far off through Scythia flow!—
Not here where the Sea of Scīron is white with rollers racing
    And where along the gorges of Mŏlouris swirls the snow.
Cold, cold upon thy waters he drifts; and emptily
His tomb cries here of the sorrow he found upon the sea.

(p. 89.)

The Hound's Grave

Although beneath this grave-mound thy white bones now are lying,
    Methinks, my huntress Lўcas, the wild things dread thee still.
The memory of thy deeds tall Pēlion keeps undying,
    And the looming peak of Ossa, and Cĭthaeron's lonely hill.

(p. 113.)

The Dead of Athens at Chalcis (506 B.C.)

We died in the glen of Dirphys; here by our country's giving
    This tomb was heaped above us, high on Eurīpus' shore.
'Twas earned.   For young we lost the loveliness of living,
    We took instead upon us the bursting storm of war.

(p. 92.)

The Dead of Sparta at Thermópylae (480 B.C.)

Take word to Lacedaemon, passer-by,
That here obedient to their laws we lie.

(p. 94.)

The Dead of Sparta at Plataea (479 B.C.)

These men, to set a crown of ever quenchless glory
    On their dear land, cast round them Death's cloak of cloudy gloom.
Yet even in death they die not.   For still their valiant story
    Lifts them again to honour, from out the House of Doom.

(p. 107.)

PINDAR OF THEBES
(c. 518–c. 438 B.C.)

Pindar was born just outside Thebes, and a charming legend tells how
one day bees dropped their honey on the infant's lips (compare p. 331). Little
is known of his life; but his fame covered the Greek world, from northern
Macedon to southern Cyrēne. He was welcomed at the courts of Syracuse

and Ácragas in the west: in the east the Rhodians are said to have inscribed one of his odes on the wall of Athena's temple in letters of gold.   Even after his death, each night at Delphi, as the shrine of Apollo was closed, the spirit of the poet was summoned to dine with the god.   Even a century later, in Alexander's sack of Thebes,

> The great Emathian conqueror bid spare
> The house of Pindarus, when temple and tower
> Went to the ground.

And even to-day he can intoxicate staid scholars into hyperboles of praise that do not always observe his own doctrine of moderation.

Of his seventeen volumes of lyrics, apart from fragments, about a quarter survives—his poems on athletic victors.   This is not the section of his poetry most of us might have chosen; but, actually, it seems to have contained his best work.   After all, it was the side of life that he seems most passionately to have loved.

For the translator Pindar remains one of the most impossible poets in the world.   To render him literally, as Cowley says, can only give the impression that one madman has translated another.   It is not merely that his music is lost; even these surviving libretti are in metres complicated beyond the resources of an accentual prosody like ours.   Similarly with the style; it is enough to look at a literal prose version to see how remote from English is this strange blend of gorgeous phrases with shattering banalities, of excessive artifice with extreme simplicity of mind, of naïve personal comments with elaborate mythical allusions; which meant as much to him, no doubt, as Scripture to Milton, but mean little to us—especially as what he finds edifying often strikes us as the reverse.   He tumbles intertwisted metaphors over one another like a Metaphysical poet; yet he would have loathed our Metaphysical poets, as he loathed all 'clever devils' with less in them of lion than fox.   Indeed Pindar, like Spenser, shows how moderately intelligent even distinguished poets can be.   At times, like Lully, 'il n'a pas le sens commun; il n'a que le génie.'

Pindar's power does not lie in the pedigrees of totally unimportant athletes, or the victories of mules that lived twenty-four centuries ago, or the misbehaviour of minor deities who never lived at all.   It lies in a splendour of phrase and imagery that suggests the gold and purple of a sunset sky.   I can do little more than try to convey by a few brief extracts some faint reflections of that splendour.[1]   The physical prowess that so inspired Pindar was a good deal more shrewdly appraised by Xenóphanes and by Euripides (compare pp. 257, 287); but in beauty of form (as in lack of profundity) he recalls, at his best, the radiant Hermes of Praxíteles, found in the ruins of that Olympia which the poet loved so well.   This praiser of athletes

---

[1] There are complete translations by, amongst others, E. Myers (1874), C. J. Billson (1928–30), L. R. Farnell (1930–32), J. E. Sandys (1937), R. Lattimore (1947).

was, curiously enough, one of the most purely aesthetic artists there have ever been. We cannot hear his music; we cannot see his dancers; but his pure poetry still lives.

The Coming of Jason to Iolcus

Pélias, after usurping the throne from his brother Aeson, was warned by the Delphic oracle to beware of a one-sandalled man. One day Aeson's son Jason, reared to manhood by the centaur Chīron in his cave on Mount Pēlion above Iolcus, came down to the city to claim his father's birthright; crossing the torrent Anaurus he lost one of his sandals; and Pélias recognized in him the man of fate. That fate he delayed by persuading Jason first to seek the Golden Fleece from Colchis in the Black Sea. So from all Greece gathered the Argonauts to help him in his quest.

What was it first began their voyaging?
What adamantine nails of peril held them fast?
It was foretold to Pélias the king
He should find death at last
By the hands, or the plans unfailing, of the proud Aeólidae.
For from the navel of Earth, fair mother of many a tree,
Chill on his subtle spirit there struck the word of God—
'To far-seen, famed Iolcus shall come—then heed thy danger,
Whatever it may cost thee—from the huts of the hills a stranger
With a single sandal shod.

'Native or foreign, of him shalt thou beware!'
Years passed. And a wondrous stranger *came*, two spears in hand;
On his bright limbs he wore the garb men wear
In the Magnesian land;
But over it—strange mingling—a leopard's hide was flung,
To ward the hurtling rainstorms, and on his shoulders hung,
Unshorn, his rippling tresses in their young and glorious grace.
Then he put to proof his manhood, as he strode forth, swift, untrembling,
Into the midst of the people, as there they thronged assembling
Within the market-place.

Known to no man he stood there. Yet they whispered in their awe:
'Who *is* he? Not, surely, Apollo? Nor the brazen-charioted
Lover of Aphrodite? And now, 'tis said, no more
Are the sons of Īphimĕdeia—in gleaming Naxos dead
They lie, the lordly Ōtus and Ephialtes the brave;
And Títyus, too, the resistless shafts of Artemis have slain,
Those shafts whence nought can save,
To warn all men from longing for loves too high to gain.'

(Pyth., IV, 70–92.)

264

The Mercenary Muse

Freely, with glorious harp in hand, of old men rode away
In the car of the gold-crowned Muses, Thrasybūlus, and let play
Their singing shafts in praise of some young face,
Upon whose comeliness the witching grace
Of fair-throned Aphrodite lay.

For then no miser was the Muse, no hireling yet was she;
Not yet were the honeyed songs of sweet Terpsíchorē
Sold in the mart, their cheeks with silver spread;
But *now* she cites that word the Argive said,
That word too full of verity—
When wealth and friends, together, from him ran,
"'Tis money,' quoth he, 'money maketh man.'

(Isthm., II, I–12.)

The Magic of Melody

O golden lyre, by Apollo and the Muses violet-crowned
Alike beloved; so soon as thy quivering prelude rings,
The feet of dancers bound
In the glory of their motion, and their voices heed thy strings.
Even the warrior lightning, with his spears of quenchless flame,
Thou stillest—even the eagle of Zeus thou makest tame;
There on God's sceptre he sleeps with folded wings.

The king of birds sits drooping his crook-beaked head, his eyes
Locked in enchanted darkness, and soft the feathers o'er
His shoulders fall and rise,
To the throbbing of thy music.   The very God of War
Forgets his savage spearthrusts and dreams in peace an hour—
In the Muses deep of bosom, and Apollo, lies such power
Even o'er hearts that live for evermore.

But all things that Zeus loves not, they tremble as they hearken—
On land, on the raging surges—when sing the Piérides;
Yea, Typhōs the hundred-headed, o'er whom Hell's shadows darken,
That foe of Gods, yet fears the voice of these.
Bred in the famed Cilician cave, his shaggy chest
'Neath Cyme's sea-beat headlands, now, and Sicily lies low,
And o'er him columned Etna lifts heavenward her snow,
That biting snow she nurses, year-long, on her breast.

But from her inmost caves rise vomited
Pure streams of fire approachless; like a river, all the day
Their flame-lit smoke goes swirling, all night they glare blood-red,
While on their seaward way
They roll great stones in thunder.   And ever—things of dread
To see—to hear of, even—flame-fountains skyward soar
From that fell monster, fettered there outspread
Betwixt earth's floor and Etna with her dark-leaved forest-head,
While rock-jags goad his great back evermore.

(Pyth., I, 1–28.)

Dēlos

Child of the sea, marvel of earth, made firm for aye,
That art to men
'Dēlos'—but to Olympus' Gods a star,
In earth's blue distance glittering afar.

(Prosodion; J. E. Sandys, Pindar, p. 560.)

Athens

O city of light and song, town of the violet crown,
Bulwark of Hellas, glorious Athens, walls of divine renown.

(Dithyramb, p. 556.)

Spring

When the Seasons clothed with purple have flung their chamber wide,
And fragrant Spring leads back her flowers, as nectar sweet,
Then on the earth divine beneath men's feet
Are violets strewn; then rose-wreathed locks blow free,
And flute and song resound on every side,
And dancers praise the diademed Sémele.

(Dithyramb, p. 554.)

The Poet's Praise

No sculptor I of forms whose feet stand clinging
Idly for ever to a pedestal;
From every ship and boat, my song, go winging
With thy sweet call,
Forth from Aegīna's harbour—everywhere
Name the stout Pytheas, Lampon's son,
Crowned now in Némea's pancration,
Though not yet blooms on his young cheek the down
Life's summer shall mother there.

(Nem. ,v, 1–5.)

The Poet's Power

Yet Homer has told of Ajax' worth, and sent his glory ringing
Wide through the world, as he chanted to the beat of his staff of bay,
With godlike words for after-poets' singing.
For noble verse to all eternity
Goes forth clear-voiced; and, with it, upon its endless way
O'er fruitful earth and sea,
The light of splendid deeds shines out unquenched for aye.

(Isthm., IV, 37–42.)

Mortality

Yet, though a man have riches, and none so fair as he,
And his in the games a victor's strength, let him bear in mind alway,
Those limbs he garbs are fashioned of mortality—
He too, when all is over, must don a cloak of clay.

(Nem., XI, 13–6.)

Moderation

Not in *every* generation do virtues long-descended
Breed men of might.   Not *always* do the black fields bounteously
Give harvest; not with *every* summer ended
Like wealth will load the fragrant-blossomed tree;
But with changeful alternation.   So too for humanity

Fate stands.   What God's disposal shall ordain us,
No token tells.   And yet we launch out evermore
On perilous quests—our wanton hopes enchain us—
The tides of foresight lie beyond our lore.
Keep measure in ambition.   Sharp the pain
Of mad hearts craving what no hand shall gain.

(Nem., XI, 38–48.)

Content at Home

'Shall I, then, covet riches?   The lot that the Blest have made
Mine, here in Ceos, shall I then cast away
For foreign greatness?   Nay!
I should be, always, afraid.
Crave not, my heart, the land of the cypress-tree,
Crave not the pastures under Ida.
My little land of oaks—I seek nought wider;
Here strife nor sorrow vexeth me.'

(Paean IV, 46–53; J. E. Sandys, Pindar, p. 530.)

Courage in Exile

'When some great oak-tree, glorious in men's gaze,
Falls humbled by the trenchant axe, and its boughs in the dust lie broken,
Though now but a barren stock, it still gives token
Of its true worth, as it ends in the wintry blaze;
Or when, above towering columns, it holds aloft the weight
Of the palace of some alien lord—hard though its burden weighs,
And its old home lies desolate.'

(Pyth., IV, 263–9.)

God and Man

One is the race of Gods and men; and yet, though Earth,
One common Mother, brought them both to birth,
Man is a thing of nothing, and Theirs the eternal sky,
In brazen strength for ever.   But in us too can lie
Some godlike touch of heart or soul,
Though day and night we wander, powerless to descry
Where Fate hath drawn our goal.

(Nem., VI, 1–7.)

Elysium

While we in night lie hidden, there in the world below
Bright shines the sun; in the meadows about their city's wall
The fruits of gold hang heavy, crimson the roses blow,
From fragrance-breathing boughs the shadows fall. . . .
With steeds, and games of strength, and games of skill,
And music they make merry; perfect peace
Wreathes all their days with flowers;
While perfumes fill
That lovely land, where without cease
From the Gods' far-flaming altars the mingled incense towers.
But, opposite, the livid streams of night
Belch blackness infinite. . . .

(Dirge; J. E. Sandys, Pindar, p. 586.)

BACCHYLIDES OF CEOS
(c. 510–c. 430 B.C.)

Bacchýlides was the son of Simōnides' sister and, like his uncle, a lyric
poet who found favour at the court of Syracuse.   Till 1896 he remained
little more than a name; but in that year the British Museum acquired a

papyrus in some two hundred fragments, containing about a thousand lines of his poetry. It had been written, probably, in the first century B.C.; was found by natives in Egypt; and was published in 1897.

Beside the passionate inspiration of Pindar, Bacchýlides is a much quieter and more even poet—like Marvell beside Milton. Indeed the Greek treatise *On the Grand Style* falsely attributed to 'Longīnus,' which probably dates from the first century A.D., when it argues (very reasonably) that faulty genius stands above faultless talent, takes Pindar as an example of genius, Bacchýlides of faultlessness. All the same Bacchýlides will seem to many a far better poet than is implied by Pindar's contemptuous comparison of him and his uncle Simōnides to 'jackdaws chattering against the eagle.' Certainly he is far less impossible to translate.

The Eagle (*to Híero of Syracuse*)

As towering through the height
Of Heaven with swift brown wing
The eagle cleaves his flight,
That messenger of Zeus the Lord of Thunder,
King of All—
Proud in his strength whereunder
All lesser birds shrill-twittering
Cower and fall
(For through the boundless earth no peaks can stay him,
No foam that flies
From the steep surge of sleepless seas dismay him,
As through the wild waste skies
Before the western gale
Those great soft pinions sail,
A marvel in all men's eyes)—

So, free as he, I have infinite flights before me
Whereon my song may soar
To praise ye, whom dark-haired Nīke crowns with glory,
And the bronze-breasted God of War.

(Odes, V, 16–34.)

Croesus

In 546 B.C. Croesus, the rich king of Lydia—encouraged (says the story) by an ambiguous Delphic oracle that if he crossed the River Hălys he would destroy a mighty empire—attacked Cyrus king of Persia. After an indecisive battle he retired; and his capital, Sardis, was stormed by the Persians. Cyrus, however, spared his fallen enemy.[1] The version given here, which makes Apollo

[1] See the enchanting narrative of Herodotus, I, 76 ff.

save the pious Lydian king by a miracle, in return for his many offerings to Delphi, may well have been of Delphic origin.

Thronged now the shrines with revel and sacrifice,
    The streets, with festival and dances;
    Before the fane of Phoebus glances
The gold of tall, rich tripods, past all price;

And there beside the banks of Castaly,
    Through the wide precinct of Apollo,
    To prayer the files of Delphians follow—
Praise Him, with gifts!—the best of Saviours He!

Witness that day when Sardis
    Was sacked of the Persian horde,
As the doom of Zeus appointed;
    Yet the Lydian horsemen's lord,
King Croesus, was delivered by Apollo,
    God of the Golden Sword.

For when on Lydia's Lord so sudden fell
    That day of weeping and disaster,
    Scorning to bow before a master
He built outside his bronze-walled citadel

A mighty pyre, and mounting there on high
    With his true Queen, his young Princesses,
    That sobbed and tore their radiant tresses,
He lifted hands to Heaven with the cry—

'Is this, O haughty God,
    Thy gratitude divine?
Where lingers Lēto's son,
    While falls Alyattes' line?
Thus are my gifts and offerings, past all telling,
    Repaid by Pytho's shrine?

'My city falls to Persian sword and flame;
    With blood Pactōlus' golden waters
    Run crimson; and our wives and daughters
Are dragged from their rich palaces in shame.

'Then welcome horror!—Death is kindliest.'
    He called—and a soft-paced Lydian lighted
    That tower of timber.   But crying, affrighted,
The maidens clung about their mother's breast.

For ever man's heart finds grimmest
    Death when it rises nigh.
Yet, as a glittering tongue
    Of fierce flame quivered high,
To quench its yellow glare, a cloud black-looming
    Zeus drew athwart the sky.

Nought is too hard to Heaven's ordering hand;
    So then did the God of Dēlos bring
    Slim-ankled maidens and ancient king
Far, far away to the Hyperborean land:

Because, of all men, honouring things divine,
He gave the most to Pytho's hallowed shrine.

(III, 15–62.)

Hēracles and the Wraith of Meleāger

Hēracles, descending to Hades to fetch the three-headed hound Cerberus, there saw the phantom of Meleāger, whose sister Dējanīra he was destined to wed on his return to earth—but to his own undoing. (For she sent her husband a tunic smeared with the poisoned blood of the centaur Nessus, believing it a love-philtre; and in his agony Hēracles had himself burnt on Mount Oeta.)

Once the sacker of towns, men say,
Matchless son of the lightning's Lord,
Down from the sunlight took his way,
To where lightfoot Persephone
Dwells in Hell's obscurity,
To catch that hound with jaggéd teeth
Whelped by Echidna the abhorred.
And there in Hades' House beneath
He saw, beside Cōcȳtus' flow,
The hapless shades drift dense and deep,
As wind-tossed leaves amid the sheep
Up Ida's sunlit headlands blow;
And glorious in the midst of these
He marked one mighty spearman go,
The wraith of Porthaónides.

Soon as Alcmēna's hero-son
Saw that armed ghost glittering,
Swift on his bow he stretched the string,
Twanging shrilly, and thereon
From his opened quiver slipped,
In haste, an arrow brazen-tipped.

271

But Meleāger's shade descried
That face well-known and, standing forth,
'Son of mighty Zeus,' he cried,
'Stay!—and lay aside thy wrath.

'Shoot not bitter shafts in vain
At the spectres of the slain.
Nay, fear not *me*!'   Then wondering said
The royal son of Amphítryon,
'What God—or who of mortal birth
Begot the like of thee on earth?
Say, in what country wast thou bred?
Who slew thee?   *Such* a champion
The Queen of Heaven girdled fair
Would gladly use, to lay me low;
Yet Pallas of the golden hair
Shall be my succour, well I know.'
But Meleāger answered him
(While with tears his eyes grew dim),
'What Heaven's will has ordered so,

'For men to alter, hard it is.
Else my own horse-taming sire,
Oeneus, had appeased the ire
Of mighty, white-armed Artemis.
But vain his prayers.   In vain to slay
Before the flower-crowned Virgin's shrine
Herds of goats and red-backed kine—
Nought could turn her wrath away.
A boar of boundless strength she sent,
A brute most pitiless, to vent
The full tide of his fury, where
Danced once the maids of Cálydon.
Our vineyards with his tusks he rent,
Our sheep, and every mother's son
That crossed his rage, he slaughtered there.

'Against him gathered all the flower
Of Hellas.   Six days savagely
We fought the beast, till came the hour
God gave the Aetōlians mastery.
Then we laid our dead to rest,
Whom his wild-shrieking onset tore—
Ancaeus—Agelāus, best

Of my brave brothers; ay, of all
Whom once in Oeneus' glorious hall
My mother, Queen Althaea, bore.

'And others, too, doom's bitter lot
Destroyed.   For She that loves the chase,
Lēto's fierce daughter, quieted not
Her anger; no less savagely
Against the stout Cūrētes we
Clashed in battle, face to face,
For the sake of that monster's tawny hide.
By me, with many more beside,
Íphiclus and brave Áphares,
My mother's gallant brothers, died.
For nought of kin stark Ares knows;
And nought the hurtling javelin sees,
Thirsty for the blood of foes,
To this or that breast bringing death,
Just as God's will ordereth.

'But no such thought could make less hard
My mother's anger—Thestius' child;
Fierce, fearless woman, evil-starred,
She turned to compass death for me.
From its chest carved curiously,
Forth with lamentations wild
She brought and lit the magic brand
Of sudden death, that destiny
As limit of my life had planned.
It chanced I stood in act to slay
Brave Clýmenus, Daípylus' son,
Whose fair form I had overrun
Before their city's towers (for they
Were fleeing routed, one and all,
Back to Pleuron's ancient wall).

'Then did my sweet life fail from me—
I felt my strength go ebbing fast,
And wept—alas, how bitterly!—
To leave behind youth's radiant years!'
Then, for the first time and the last,
Amphítryon's fearless son, they say,
Felt his own eyes fill with tears,

Pitying him that passed away
So haplessly.   He answered then:
'Not to be born is best for men,

'Nor ever to behold the sun;
Yet, since it profits not at all,
To weep for sorrows that are done,
Best speak of what may still be won.
Say then if still in Oeneus' hall
Any maiden daughter be,
In breed and beauty like to thee?
For gladly, if I had my will,
Her beauty would I take for bride.'
Then gallant Meleāger's shade
Answered: 'On the day I died,
A single lovely-throated maid,
Dējanīra, dwelt there still,
A girl as yet—nought knoweth she
Of golden Love's sweet witchery.'

                                        '(v, 56–175.)

The Coming of Theseus towards Athens

Aegeus, king of Athens, had a child by Aethra, princess of Troezēn.   Growing up, the young Theseus set out to find his lost father in Athens; slaying on his way many robbers and evil-doers—Periphētes, Sĭnis, Scīron, Kerkyon, and Procrustes.

CHORUS

Lord of Athene's holy hill,
    The grace-loving Ionians' king,
Why is the bronze-mouthed trumpet loud
    With calls to war and mustering?
Are hostile armies near?
    Do enemies invade
Our realm's frontier?
    Or evil robbers raid
From out our shepherds' hands
The flocks that graze our lands?
    What makes thy soul dismayed?
Speak, lord.   For, sure, if ėver king there were
    Could call to arms a host
    Of valiant youth, that boast
Is thine, Pandīon and Creūsa's heir!

A messenger is come with speed
  By the long road from the Isthmus here,
With word of many a marvellous deed
  Wrought by a mighty stranger's spear.
He hath slain Sïnis in fight,
  The great Earth-shaker's son,
Unmatched in might.
  Foul Scïron he hath done
To death and, in Crommyon's glen,
The swine that ravened men;
  And outwrestled Kerkyon;
And faced at last by a mightier than he,
  Procoptes cast from him
  Polypēmon's hammer grim.
I dread what the end of all these things may be.

CHORUS

Who is this stranger?   Do they say
  From whence he hails?   What garb he bore?
Comes he marching on his way
  With a mighty host of war?
Or leading but a few
  Followers of his own,
As travellers do
  That visit lands unknown?
What valour and strength were his
To quell such men as this!
  Surely by God alone
To scourge all evil-doers he is sent?
  How else should he prevail
  O'er foe on foe, nor fail?
But Time shall bring these things accomplishment.

AEGEUS

Of but two servants he is lord,
  'Tis said; and, slung from his shoulder white,
He bears an ivory-hilted sword;
  A spear in each hand, burnished bright;
A thick Thessalian wrap,
  A tunic of purple fair,
And a Spartan cap
  To crown his golden hair;

But deep within his eyes
A flame—such flames as rise
Where the fires of Lemnos glare.
In years a lad; yet his heart is set on fight
And the clash of swords at play;
And his journey's goal, they say,
Is Athens—land that glories in the light!

(XVII, 1–60.)

PRAXILLA OF SICYON
(*c.* 455 B.C.)

A lyric poetess, of whom little is known.

'*Neither Maid nor Wife*'

O fair face at the window, looking down alone—
Face of a maid, and yet—loosed now thy maiden zone.

(Diehl, II, p. 130.)

EMPEDOCLES OF ACRAGAS
(*c.* 494–*c.* 434 B.C.)

Empédocles seems to have been a Greek Paracelsus—part scientist, part quack. In his poem *Of Nature* the scientist describes how the universe is built of air, earth, fire, and water, now mingled by love, now severed by strife or repulsion; in his *Purifications*, the miracle-worker claims to be himself divine, and preaches reincarnation, purification, and vegetarianism. The real Empédocles appears to have died in the Peloponnesus, not (as in the legend followed by Matthew Arnold) to have leapt down the crater of Etna.

Karma

There stands a decree of Destiny, from the immemorial past,
A law of the Gods, that fails not, with weighty oaths sealed fast:
That if ever a blessed spirit, born to eternal life,
Shall stain his guilty hands with blood, or swayed by strife
Shall falsely swear, and burden his soul with perjury,
For thrice ten thousand years his banishment shall be.
From the seat of the Blest he shall wander in ceaseless shapes of change,
Through the bitter paths of Being, doomed without rest to range.
For the might of the aether flings him to seaward, and the main
Spews him upon earth's threshold, and earth to the sun again,
And again to the eddying aether by the bright sun he is hurled,
From one to another driven, abhorred through all the world.

(H. Diels, *Fragmenta der Vorsokratiker* (1922), I, p. 267.)

Pre-Existence

A lad, and a lass, aforetime it was my lot to be,
And a bush I was, and a bird, and a dumb fish in the sea.

(p. 268.)

PLATO
(c. 428–c. 348 B.C.)

This is no place for a detailed account of the most famous of philosophers, who in his too austere maturity banned poets from his ideal state, except under the bleakest of censorships. In his more gracious youth, however, he had himself been a poet; and some of the epigrams attributed to him may be genuine, though the last two selected here are generally thought spurious.

Love Lies Sleeping

We came to a wood and within it, where dark its shadows run,
Fair as a rosy apple, lay Cytherēa's son.
He had not his quivered arrows, he had not his curving bow,
Under the leafy branches we spied them hanging low;
But there lay Love himself among the roses red,
Smiling, locked in the toils of sleep, and overhead
On those sweet lips, from a honeycomb, brown bees their honey shed.

(Anthologia Palatina, XVI, 210.)

Love's Apple

I throw my apple towards you. If you will love me, take it
    And give me in repayment your own maidenhead:
If your will is what I would not, yet keep it still; and make it
    Your lesson of how swiftly all loveliness is fled.

(V, 79.)

Ecstasy

As I kissed Ágathon, my soul
    All but passed away:
To my very lips, poor wretch, she stole—
    So close her Heaven lay.

(V, 78.)

The Young Astronomer

At the stars thou gazest, Aster. Ah, would that I could be
That sky with its myriad eyes, to fix them all on thee!

(VII, 669.)

The Young Astronomer Dead

Awhile, O Dawn-star of the living,
    On life thy light was shed.
Now death hath made thee Hesper, giving
    New radiance to the dead.

(VII, 670.)

'Passing the Love of Women'

For Hecuba, for Troy's daughters, a doom of tears and sorrow
    The Destinies appointed, from the hour that they were born.
Your triumph was won, my Dīon; but lo, upon the morrow,
    Your spacious visions likewise the high gods flung to scorn.
Yet in your wide-wayed city, honoured at last, you rest,
O Dīon, whose love once maddened the heart within this breast.

(VII, 99.)

'Quand Vous serez bien Vieille'

I Laïs, whose proud laughter mocked Hellas; whose alluring
    Thronged thick my gates with lovers, to the Paphian give my glass:
Since now to see my likeness, as it is, grows past enduring;
    Since I no more may see it, as in old days it was.

(VI, 1.)

Pan's Piping

Hush now, O wooded hill of the Dryads! Hush your leaping
    Down from the rocks, ye fountains! Hush, myriad-bleating ewes!
For along his reeden pipe now Pan Himself is sweeping
    His supple lip to waken the sweet cry of the Muse;
And with feet untired for dancing about him gathered gleam
The Dryads from the forest, the Naiads from the stream.

(IX, 823.)

TIMOTHEÜS OF MILETUS
(c. 450–360 B.C.)

Timótheüs may have been better as a musician—we have no evidence (his vast popularity at the time is none). But as a poet, since the discovery of part of his *Persians* in 1905, he is remarkable among Greek writers as being, for once, really detestable—crude, vulgar, blatant, and ridiculous. It is this which adds a very modern irony to the boast that follows.

'Contemporaneity'

I sing no out-of-date matter,
For our new songs are better.
Crŏnus was master aforetime,
But Zeus is the monarch of *our* time.
The old Muse—hence let her get her.

(Diehl, II, p. 150.)

PARRHASIUS OF EPHESUS
(*c.* 400 B.C.)

Parrhasius, one of the most famous painters of antiquity, was no less famous for his pride and dandyism. 'No one,' says Pliny, 'ever enjoyed reputation more insolently.' He claimed divine descent from Apollo and pretended, with Blake-like assurance, to have painted his Hēracles from visions of the hero in person.

The Artist's Last Word

I say it, though none believe me. I say that clear for ever
  Henceforth the furthest limits of the painter's art stand set
By this my hand. Beyond it shall pass no man's endeavour;
  Though the beauty that men blamed not, was never fashioned yet.

(Athenaeus, XII, 543E.)

ERINNA
(mid 4th century B.C. or later?)

A poetess said to have died at nineteen, but ranked with Sappho by some ancient judgments, though little of her work survives. Her chief poem was a lament, *The Distaff*, for her dead girl-friend Baucis.

The Eternal Silence

Nought to the far-off Hades but an empty echo cries.
There, mid the dead, is silence. My voice in the darkness dies.

(Diehl, I, p. 486.)

CLEANTHES OF ASSOS (IN MYSIA)
(*c.* 331–232 B.C.)

Cleanthes, disciple of Zēno and second of the great Stoic philosophers, is said to have begun life as a boxer. He composed philosophical works in prose and a *Hymn to Zeus*. The Stoic creed, not very intelligent, but with a bleak nobility of its own, pictured the world as governed by 'unalterable law,' '$\dot{\eta}$ $\epsilon\dot{\iota}\mu\alpha\rho\mu\epsilon\nu\eta$'; and happiness was to be found by the sage only in complete and passive acceptance of this law—all other seeming goods and ills are illusory.

The Stoic's Resignation

Lead ye me on, O God and Destiny,
To the end ye have appointed.   Without flinching,
Still I will follow.   For, though I turned craven
And cried ye nay, yet I must follow still.
(J. U. Powell, *Collectanea Alexandrina*, p. 229.)

PERSES
(late 4th century B.C.)

The God of the Lowly

Little am I among lesser gods; but call in season
    Even on me, and I hearken.   Yet ask me for nothing grand.
Things that a god of the people may look to give in reason,
    When a poor labourer prays him—these lie in Tӳchon's hand.
(*Anthologia Palatina*, IX, 334.)

ADDAEUS OF MACEDONIA
(late 4th century B.C. ?)

Probably a contemporary of Alexander the Great, for whom he wrote an epitaph.

The Pensioned Ox

His yoke-ox, growing feeble with age and years of ploughing,
    Alcon its master pitied, and saved from the blood-stained knife,
Honouring its true service; mid the meadow-grasses' soughing
    Knee-deep it lows, contented and furrow-free for life.
(VI, 228.)

NOTES

ARCHILOCHUS

[Page 234] *The Freelance.* Cf. Hybrias, p. 258.

[Page 234] *Wine from the Thracian land.* Wine of Ismărus, the same as Odysseus used to fuddle Polyphemus.

[Page 234] *Some Thracian.* More precisely 'Saïan,' a tribe near Abdēra. Evidently the incident occurred in some clash between the Greek colonists of Thăsos and the natives on the mainland. Archílochus' laughter at his own discomfiture was imitated by Alcaeus, Anacreon, and Horace (who fled at Philippi in 42 B.C.).

[Page 234] *When thou winnest . . . When thou losest. . . .* Cf. that noble praise of the Elizabethan soldier Sir Francis Vere—that none seeing him return from a victory could have known that he had not lost, none seeing him ride back from defeat have guessed that he had not won.

ALCMAN

[Page 235] *The halcyon's lot.* It was believed that the male halcyon, growing old, was borne through the air by the female birds. Here the old poet, too frail to dance, wishes half sadly, half laughingly, that he were a sea-bird and his chorus of Spartan girls could bear him soaring on his way.

[Page 236] *Vesper.* Bowra (*Greek Lyric Poetry*, p. 73) suggests that the scene of this is the Vale of Sparta (which lies in such smiling, un-Spartan fruitfulness under the snowy mountain-wall of Taÿgetus). But I feel that the poem's landscape needs the sea: at Sparta this lies 20 miles away, hidden beyond the southward hills.

In Sept. 1780, on the wall of a forest-hut on the Gickelhahn near Ilmenau Goethe wrote his *Wandrers Nachtlied*:

> Über allen Gipfeln
> Ist Ruh,
> In allen Wipfeln
> Spürest du
> Kaum einen Hauch;
> Die Vögelein schweigen im Walde.
> Warte nur, balde
> Ruhest du auch.

(He is said to have come on the poem again in August 1831, at 82, and to have sadly repeated its last two lines.)

MIMNERMUS

[Page 236] *Ugly at once and base.* Or, with a different reading, 'that brings to one level ugly and comely alike.'

[Page 237] *At the end of sixty years.* Solon wrote a poem in reply, suggesting *eighty* years as better.

281

HYMN TO DIONYSUS

Dionysus' adventure with the pirates is depicted in relief on the choragic monument of Lysícrates at Athens (334 B.C.).

[Page 238] *Tyrsēnian.* Here probably 'Pelasgian' (pre-Greek race in Aegean area), though later applied to the Etruscans (who may have been of the same stock).

[Page 238] *Hyperborean land.* A legendary country 'beyond the North Wind' (though it is doubtful if this ancient etymology is right). Cf. p. 291.

CLEOBULUS?

[Page 241] *Midas.* The name of several Phrygian kings, the most famous being that legendary monarch who got into trouble (like some modern governments) by turning everything to gold; and was credited (like many critics of all ages) with ass's ears, bestowed on him by the angry Apollo for tastelessly preferring the flutings of the Satyr Marsyas (p. 392) to the God's own lyre.

ALCAEUS

[Page 242] *To his Brother.* Antiménidas, driven from Lesbos like Alcaeus by the popular party, took service with Nebuchadnezzar (605–562 B.C.) and must have fought this duel against some Syrian, Jewish, or Egyptian champion.

[Page 242] *Five royal cubits.* $5 \times 20\frac{1}{2}$ ins. $= 8$ ft. $6\frac{1}{2}$ ins. A span $= 3$ ins. or a little over. The giant therefore stood 8 ft. $3\frac{1}{2}$ ins.

[Page 242] *A Country's Greatness.* Cf. Whitman:

A great city is that which has the greatest men and women,
If it be a few ragged huts, it is still the greatest city in the whole world.

And Cobbett: 'It is *men*, and not *machines*, that constitute a nation.'

SAPPHO

[Page 244] *The Beloved.* Sappho's love seems to be sitting next her bridegroom at the wedding-feast in her father's house. Catullus addressed a rendering of the poem to his mistress Clodia, whom he called 'Lesbia.'

[Page 245] *And madness.* Adopting Bergk's conjecture ἄλλα—'distraught.'

[Page 245] *Atthis.* One of Sappho's pupils. At first sight, Sappho had thought her a child lacking in grace; but the feeling deepened, until Atthis forsook the poetess for a rival—Andrómeda. A fragmentary line still recalls Sappho's grief—

'I loved thee, Atthis, once, in days long past.'

[Page 245] *Anactória.* Another of the girls in Sappho's circle (the restoration of her name here is conjectural). Whoever it was, she has here left Lesbos, presumably as a wife, for the Lydian capital, Sardis, 100 miles away.

[Page 245] *Outshines the stars.* Cf. Sir Henry Wotton on Elizabeth of Bohemia:

You meaner beauties of the night
That poorly satisfy our eyes
More by your number than your light,
You common people of the skies;
What are you when the moon shall rise?

282

[Page 245] *Anthrysc.*   An umbellifer.

[Page 245] *Melilōtus.*   Melilot, a clover specially rich in honey.

[Page 246] *To a Rich, Uncultured Woman.*   The first clear statement in European poetry of literary immortality (cf. Sappho's fragmentary line—'I say that some shall remember us, even in years to come').   It becomes much more emphatic in Theognis (p. 251).

[Page 246] *Forsaken.*   Possibly folksong, not Sappho's.   Adapted by A. E. Housman in the poem beginning:

> The weeping Pleiads wester,
>   And the moon is under seas;
> From bourn to bourn of midnight
>   Far sighs the rainy breeze.

Cf. also Ronsard (ed. Vaganay) IV, 164:

> Ja la lune s'est couchée,
> La poussiniere est cachée,
> Et ja la my-nuit brunette,
> Vers l'Aurore s'est panchée,
> Et je dors au lict seulette.

[Page 246] *The Maid Unwed.*   This and the next two fragments come from a marriage-song.   Cf. Catullus, 62.

[Page 246] *Evensong.*   Cf. Byron, *Don Juan*, III, cvii:

> Oh, Hesperus! thou bringest all good things—
>   Home to the weary, to the hungry cheer,
> To the young bird the parent's brooding wings,
>   The welcome stall to the o'erlabour'd steer;
> Whate'er of peace about our hearthstone clings,
>   Whate'er our household gods protect of dear,
> Are gather'd round us by thy look of rest;
> Thou bring'st the child, too, to the mother's breast.

Also Housman, *Epithalamium*:

> Happy bridegroom, Hesper brings
> All desired and timely things.
> All whom morning sends to roam,
> Hesper loves to lead them home.
> Home return who him behold,
> Child to mother, sheep to fold,
> Bird to nest from wandering wide:
> Happy bridegroom, seek your bride.

But neither, I think, equals the simple brevity of Sappho's fragment.

Certain other fragmentary verses attributed to Alcaeus and Sappho have been sometimes taken as a gallant address from poet to poetess followed by a crushing retort from her to him (Diehl, I, pp. 386, 416):

> 'Pure and violet-crowned, honey-smiling Sappho,
> Somewhat would I say—but my tongue is shamefast.'
> 'Were good the aim that makes you so passionate,
> Did not your tongue stir something dishonourable,
>   No shame would bow your eyes to earthward;
>   Frank would your speech be of things more honest.'

283

But (1) it is not certain that the first line belongs to this context at all; (2) the other five lines *may* be part of a dialogue-poem of Sappho's (like Horace's quarrel with Lydia, *Odes*, III, 9); but Sappho's poem may only present fictitious persons in a fictitious situation.

SOLON

[Page 247] *The Shame of Losing Salamis*. The story is that, weary of war with Mégara for the island of Salamis, the Athenians made it a capital offence even to propose renewing the struggle; Solon evaded this by feigning madness and reciting in the market-place a patriotic poem (from which these lines are taken), with such success that the law was rescinded and he led his countrymen to a new and victorious campaign. He is said, when he died, to have had his ashes scattered over the island he had won for Athens.

[Page 247] *Phŏlegandros, Sĭkinos*. Obscure islands S.W. of Naxos, N.W. of Thera (Santorin).

THEOGNIS

[Page 249] *Polypäïdes*. The young Cyrnus, son of Polypas.

[Page 249] *The bird's shrill crying*. The migrant crane (p. 202).

[Page 249] *An Eye for an Eye*. Not very Christian, but very forcible.

[Page 250] *Rhădamanthys*. A Cretan king, son of Zeus and Europa, and brother of Minos. So just was his reign on earth, that he was made ruler of the blessed in Elysium, or one of the judges of the dead in Hades.

[Page 250] *Sĭsyphus*, King of Corinth, was a byword for cunning. He outwitted even Autólycus (p. 146), who used to steal his cattle, by fastening under their hoofs lead plates with the legend 'Stolen by Autólycus,' so that he could track them down. He enchained even Death, till Ares rescued him; then, coming himself to die, Sĭsyphus bade his wife not bury his body. Thereby he was enabled to get leave of absence from Hades, that he might punish this impious woman; and, once returned to earth, gaily overstayed his leave. Finally Hermes dragged him back to the Netherworld, where he was punished by having to push a rock up a mountain through eternity.

[Page 250] *Harpies*. Personified storm-winds.

[Page 250] *Boreas' sons*. Zētes and Cálaïs, the wing-footed sons of the North Wind by the Athenian princess Oreithyia, whom he carried off. They sailed in Argo and fought the Harpies.

[Page 250] *Eugenics*. Plato (*Republic*, 459A) elaborates the same view into his genial scheme for nationalizing love and the family.

[Page 250] *A ram*. Theognis' own city, Mégara, was noted for its sheep and its boors (also, curiously enough, for its philosophers); so that Diogenes could jest that it was better to be a Megarian's ram than his son. (Cf. Shaw's proposal that children be periodically shot like partridges, in the hope that they might then be as carefully preserved.)

[Page 251] *Critics*. Cf. the Bulgarian proverb—'Not even God can please everybody.'

[Page 251] *Loyalty*. Apparently a lovers' quarrel, the woman speaking first.

[Page 251] *The Beloved*. Perhaps the most eloquent of all Theognis' poems. Cf. Shakespeare, *Sonnets*, 55:

> Not marble, nor the gilded monuments
> Of princes, shall outlive this powerful rhyme. . . .

For the sudden sting in the tail of the poem (which has needlessly bothered some commentators) cf. the next piece and the endings of *Sonnets* 84 and 92:

You to your beauteous blessings add a curse,
Being fond on praise, which makes your praises worse.

But what's so blessed-fair that fears no blot?
Thou mayst be false, and yet I know it not.

[Page 252] *The Broken Chain.* Cf. Sir Thomas Wyat, *He Rejoiceth that he had broken the Snares of Love*:

Was never birde tangled in lyme
That brake awaye yn better tyme,
Then I that rotten bowes ded clyme,
And had no hurte, but scaped fre.
Now ha! ha! ha! full well is me,
For I am nowe at libertye.

[Page 253] *I drank at a spring.* Cf. Shakespeare, *Sonnets*, 35:

No more be griev'd at that which thou hast done:
Roses have thorns, and silver fountains mud.

And *Othello*, IV, ii, 60 (of Desdemona): 'The fountain from the which my current runs.'

[Page 253] *The Problem.* Cf. G. M. Hopkins, in his bewildered *Justus quidem tu es, Domine*:

Thou art indeed just, Lord, if I contend
With thee; but, Sir, so what I plead is just.
Why do sinners' ways prosper? and why must
Disappointment all I endeavour end?

[Page 253] *Despair.* This clear-eyed melancholy, which yet, for centuries, did not sap Greek vitality, already appears in Homer (p. 52) and in legends like that which tells how King Midas, having captured a Silēnus, hoped to learn precious wisdom from its lips: but was only told that the best thing for man was not to be born; the next best, to die as soon as possible. Or again there is the tale of Cléobis and Biton (Herodotus, I, 31), whose mother, priestess of Argive Hēra, prayed the Gods to reward her sons' piety with the best gift Heaven could give—that same night they died in their sleep. (Their sixth-century statues have been found at Delphi.) The same theme is the burden of the most famous chorus of the *Oedipus at Colonus*, written by the fortunate and popular Sophocles at the close of his long life:

He that craves in life a span
Past the common lot of man
Sets his heart, past questioning,
On a vain and empty thing;
Whoso lives beyond his share,
Slowly sees the creeping years
Leave no trace of gladness there,
Turning all his joys that were
Into things more close to tears;
Till One alone is left to heed his call—
One no bridesong gladdeneth,
Nor yet dance, nor music—Death,
That brings an end of all.

Never to be born is best;
Next to that, far happiest

285

He that hastens from his birth,
Fast as may be, back to earth.
Soon as, with its follies light,
On its way our Youth is past,
Then, of sorrows infinite,
What is spared us?—tongues that bite,
Faction, battle, slaughter—last,
There comes Old Age, the strengthless, the accurst,
Age that knows no love, no friend,
On whose solitude attend
Griefs of *all* griefs the worst.

Similarly in a fragment of Euripides, *Cresphontes* (Fr. 449):

Wiser it were to gather and lament
For every babe that enters this sad world;
But when man dies and all his trouble's over,
Bear him with joy and blessings from his home.

Cf. Tennyson, *Tithonus:*

the homes
Of happy men that have the power to die,
And grassy barrows of the happier dead.

Note, however, that this later Greek pessimism goes beyond Homer's. Zeus may call man the unhappiest of created things; but he does *not* say it is better never to be born or else to die as soon as possible. The difference suggests a certain decline in Greek vitality.

[Page 254] *The Stoic.* No ill motto for the twentieth century.

[Page 254] *Nativity.* Cf. the *Hymn to Apollo* (p. 209).

[Page 254] *The round mere.* A round pool near the shore of Dēlos, where in historic times swam the sacred swans of Apollo. The *Hymn* had located the birth at the foot of Cynthus, a quarter of a mile away from the pool.

IBYCUS

[Page 254] *Quince-flowers.* Our word 'quince' is really the plural of 'quine,' 'coyn,' from Latin (*malum*) *Cydonium*, 'apple of Cydonia' (now Canea), in Crete. Like apples, quinces were love-symbols (cf. pp. 246, 277).

HIPPŌNAX

[Page 255] *Misogynist.* The authorship is not certain. Cf. Prior:

Women 'twixt sheets are best, 'tis said,
Be they of holland or of lead.

[Page 255] *Būpalus.* A Chian sculptor detested by Hippōnax.

PHOCYLIDES

[Page 255] *The Exception.* Adapted by Porson in his satire on Gottfried Hermann:

The Germans in Greek
Are sadly to seek;
Not five in five score,
But ninety-five more:
All; save only Herman—
And Herman's a German.

ANACREON

[Page 256] *The Coy Mistress*. Anácreon may have met his Thracian girl when he fled in 545 B.C. with his fellow-citizens of Teos (S.W. of Smyrna) before the invading Persians to Abdēra on the coast of Thrace. The poem is imitated by Ronsard (ed. Vaganay), III, 270: 'Pourquoy comme une jeune poutre De travers guignes tu vers moy?'

XENOPHANES

[Page 257] *Wickedness of Poets*. Similar criticisms of the morality of traditional theology recur in Pindar and, above all, Euripides. Cf. *Heracles Mad*, 1341–6:

> I cannot think Gods do adultery,
> Nay, I have ever scorned, and ever shall,
> To dream a God can bind a God with chains,
> Or one be born by Fate another's master.
> For God, if God indeed, has need of nothing.
> These are but poets' old unhappy tales.

[Page 257] *Anthropomorphism*. Still more neatly in Montesquieu: 'Si les triangles avaient un dieu, il aurait trois côtés.'

[Page 257] *Rainbow*.

> There was an awful rainbow once in Heaven:
> We know her woof, her texture; she is given
> In the dull catalogue of common things.
> Philosophy will clip an Angel's wings.   Keats, *Lamia*.

[Page 257] *Athleticism*. In the Greek world, as in ours, professionalism in sport and the consequent idolatry of athletes became a curse. Euripides is said himself to have trained in youth as one; but in a fragment of his *Autolycus* he attacks them more bitterly even than Xenóphanes.

> Now of ten thousand curses that plague Hellas
> None is more pestilent than this breed of athletes,
> Who never yet discovered how to live,
> And could not, though they would. . . .
> Oh, they go brave in youth, the strutting ornament
> Each of his city.   But once grim age has clutched them,
> *Then* see them slinking threadbare, out at elbows.
> It gets no praise of me, our Grecian way
> Of gathering in multitudes for *their* sakes,
> Making a festival for such idle toys.
> For what stout wrestler, or what nimble runner,
> Or discus-thrower, or brave jawbone-breaker,
> Profits his country with the crown he wins?
> Will they go grappling in the grip of war,
> Quoits in their hands?   Or in the clash of shields
> Will wrestlers' trips o'erthrow the enemy?
> None meddles with such fooleries, when he faces
> Steel!   Keep your wreaths to honour wiser heads—
> For good men, temperate leaders of their land,
> Whose words can put a curb on reckless doings,
> And calm strife and sedition.   *These* are gifts
> To bless alike our country and all Hellas.

See also Norman Gardiner, *Olympia*; and, for stories of typical Greek athletes, the chapter on Olympia in my *From Olympus to the Styx*.

[Page 257] *Pentathlon.* 'Five contests'—running, long jump, discus-throwing, javelin-throwing, and wrestling.

[Page 257] *Grim pancration.* The epithet was deserved. The pancration was a kind of all-in wrestling and boxing where everything was allowed—arm-twisting, kicking in the stomach, and so forth—except only biting and gouging. It went on till the vanquished held up his hand—or, sometimes, died.

[Page 258] *Less in worth than* I *am.* An almost Shavian freedom from false modesty!

HYBRIAS THE CRETAN

A drinking-song (cf. Archílochus, p. 234) or perhaps a song for a war-dance (see Bowra, *Gk. Lyric Poetry*, pp. 437–43). It was translated by T. Campbell and may recall Peacock's equally spirited *War-Song of Dinas Vawr*:

> The mountain sheep are sweeter,
> But the valley sheep are fatter;
> We therefore thought it meeter
> To carry off the latter.

[Page 258] *Bull's-hide shield.* It is disputed whether the Greek *laiseion* means shield of hide, or hide used in place of a shield (which seems rather poor for such a fire-eater as Hybrias), or some kind of body-armour.

[Page 258] *My slaves.* Greek *mnoïai*, the name given to public serfs in Crete (cf. Sparta's Helots). Possibly connected with 'Minos,' Greek invaders having enslaved a pre-Greek Minoan race.

[Page 258] *King of Kings.* The Greek *megan basilea*, 'Great King,' suggests an allusion to the Great King of Persia.

HYMN TO PAN

[Page 259] *Long white ridges, i.e.* of the whitish limestone common in Greek lands.

[Page 259] *On the reeden pipe of a shepherd.* Cf. p. 278.

[Page 259] *Cyllēne.* A mountain in N.E. Arcadia (7,800 feet), where Hermes was born.

[Page 259] *Drÿops.* Son of Apollo by Dia, daughter of Lycāon, King of Arcadia. She hid her babe in an oak (*drys*), whence his name Drÿops—appropriate enough to the grandfather of a woodland god.

[Page 260] *Pan.* The Greeks derived the name from *pan*, 'all' (it is more probably connected with a root *pa*, found also in 'pasture,' 'pastoral'; so that Pan would mean 'the Feeder,' 'the Shepherd').

SIMONIDES

[Page 261] *Life's Best.* Authorship doubtful.

[Page 261] *Timócreon* of Iálysus in Rhodes, a famous athlete and eater, became after the Persian conquest of his country a buffoon of the Great King at Susa. When the Persians were defeated in 480, he hoped Themistŏcles might secure him an amnesty to return home. Disappointed, he lampooned the Athenian as having taken his money, then broken the bargain. The flight of Themistŏcles himself to Persia naturally delighted Timócreon, who sang: 'I am not the only fox to lose his tail.' Here Simōnides, who had been a friend of

Themistŏcles, retaliates. (In the Palatine MS. some scribe has made on this epigram the engaging comment: 'Just like my uncle.')

[Page 261] *Gortўna*.   In S. Crete, S.S.W. of Cnossus.

[Page 262] *Géraneia*.   A mountain-mass (4,500 feet) barring the Isthmus W. of Mégara.

[Page 262] *Ister . . . Tánaïs*.   Danube . . . Don.

[Page 262] *Scīron*.   This famous robber used to make travellers wash his feet on the Scironian Cliffs (at the S.E. end of Géraneia), then kicked them over into the sea for a tortoise to eat; until Theseus served him to his own tortoise.

[Page 262] *Mŏlouris*.   A neighbouring crag over which Ino leapt with her child Melicertes into the sea, after her husband, King Áthamas, had run mad and killed her other son.

[Page 262] *The Dead of Athens at Chalcis*.   After her expulsion of the despot Hippias in 510, Athens was attacked by Sparta, the Boeotians, and the Chalcidians.   In 506 the Athenians defeated the Boeotians near the Eurīpus, then crossing into Euboea won a second victory over the Chalcidians on the same day.

[Page 262] *Dirphys*.   A peak in mid Euboea (5,725 feet), whose lovely pyramid of snow haunts everywhere the walker in N.E. Attica.

[Page 262] *Eurīpus*.   The narrow strait at Chalcis (now bridged) between Euboea and the mainland.

[Page 262] *Thermópylae*.   The famous pass between Mt. Oeta and the sea, opposite the N.W. tip of Euboea, where Leŏnidas fell with 300 Spartans and 700 Thespians.   Since translating this, I see that W. L. Bowles (1762–1850) anticipated my second line:

> Go tell the Spartans, thou that passest by,
> That here obedient to their laws we lie.

In 1833 'Christopher North' gave preference to Bowles's version, out of five by other writers and forty-eight by himself.   (See *Oxford Book of Greek Verse in Translation*, p. lxv.)

[Page 262] *Plataea*.   Under Mt. Cĭthaeron in Boeotia, where in 479 the Greeks finally defeated Mardonius and the Persian army left by Xerxes.

PINDAR

[Page 264] *The Coming of Jason*.   From an ode written for the victory of King Arcésilas of Cyrēne in the four-horse chariot-race at the Pythian Games of 462.

[Page 264] *Aeólidae*.   Jason was son of Aeson, son of Crētheus, son of Aeŏlus.

[Page 264] *Navel of Earth*.   Delphi, at earth's centre; as Zeus found by releasing from the earth's opposite extremities two eagles which met there.

[Page 264] *Far-seen*.   Or perhaps 'sunlit.'

[Page 264] *Single sandal*.   Jason lost the other while fording the Anaurus.

[Page 264] *Magnesian land*.   Coastal Thessaly from Ossa to Pēlion.   Perhaps Pindar means here a close-fitting dress suited to its wooded mountains.

[Page 264] *Lover of Aphrodite*.   Ares.

[Page 264] *Sons of Īphimĕdeia*.   For these young giants see p. 149.

[Page 264] *Tĭtyus*.   Another giant, slain for trying to ravish Lēto or Artemis. Near Pánopeus was shown his gigantic grave; and the *Odyssey* describes him in Hades, sprawling over nine acres, while two vultures tore his liver.   It seems doubtful, however, if the brilliant picture of Jason's beauty is really enhanced by adding these vast figures.

[Page 265] *The Mercenary Muse*. Written for Thrasybūlus, nephew of Thēron despot of Ácragas; probably after the despot's death, perhaps after the fall of the dynasty. Pindar himself, like Simōnides, took rewards for his odes; but here he seems regretting that general necessity, in this poem freely offered to a friend whose family has now fallen. There may be also a hit at the supposed avarice of Simōnides.

[Page 265] *Terpsíchore*. Muse of choral lyric.

[Page 265] *Cheeks with silver spread*. Perhaps with allusion to dancers sticking silver coins on their cheeks. But it may be only one of Pindar's audacious metaphors.

[Page 265] *The Argive*. A certain Aristodāmus.

[Page 265] *The Magic of Melody*. For a chariot-victory of Híero, despot of Syracuse, at the Pythian Games of 470. The poem opens with this famous passage on the civilizing power of music.

[Page 265] *The eagle of Zeus*. Cf. Gray, *Progress of Poesy*:

> On Thracia's hills the Lord of War
> Has curb'd the fury of his car,
> And dropt his thirsty lance at thy command.
> Perching on the sceptred hand
> Of Jove, thy magic lulls the feather'd king
> With ruffled plumes and flagging wing:
> Quench'd in dark clouds of slumber lie
> The terror of his beak, and lightnings of his eye.

[Page 265] *Typhōs*. A monster who battled against the Gods and was whelmed by Zeus beneath Etna.

[Page 265] *Cyme*. Cumae, 10 miles W. of Naples, in another volcanic area. Here in 474 Híero's navy had defeated the Etruscans.

[Page 265] *Etna*. At the mountain's foot, about 474, Híero founded the city of Aitna. Possibly this ode was sung at the installation of his son Deinómenes as its king. There had been a a violent eruption of Etna in 479, lasting perhaps till 476.

[Page 266] *Dēlos* means 'clear' (though the derivation of the island's name is uncertain). Pindar here alludes also to its other ancient name, Astérie (from *aster*, 'star').

[Page 266] *Made firm*. Previously a floating island, Dēlos was made fast for Apollo's birth.

[Page 266] *Athens*. From a dithyramb in praise of Athens (474 B.C.). The gratified Athenians repaid the poet with 10,000 drachmas; and Aristophanes mocks his countrymen for their persistent vanity about this description of their city. 'Violet-crowned' has been explained (too fancifully) as referring to the purple of sunset on Hymettus, or of the neighbouring sea. But violet wreaths were presented to the Gods or worn by men at the vernal Dionysia; and perhaps Athens herself is here conceived as a festal deity, crowned with violets like Aphrodite, the Muses, or the Graces (see A. B. Cook in *Journal of Hellenic Studies*, 1900).

[Page 266] *The Poet's Praise*. For an Aeginetan lad, victor at Némea in the pancration (see p. 288).

[Page 266] *From every ship and boat*. Pindar's verse seems rather difficult for sailors and fishermen. But cf. W. Whitman: 'In vessels that sail my words sail, I go with fishermen and seamen and love them'; and the singing of Tasso by Venetian fishermen.

[Page 266] *Though not yet blooms*. . . . Lit. 'though he does not yet show

on his cheek the summer-ripeness which is the tender mother of vine-like down.'
No poet ever recked less of mixing metaphors; whether always with success,
remains a matter of taste.

[Page 267] *Content at Home.* From a papyrus giving part of a Paean to the
Delian Apollo, composed to be sung in Ceos. Pindar, praising content at
home, quotes King Euxantius of Ceos, son of Minos by a Cean mother (perhaps
a far-off memory of Minoan supremacy in S. Greece). For, though offered a
seventh share, beside the sons of Minos and Pasíphaë, in the hundred cities of
Crete, he preferred his own quiet isle.

[Page 267] *Cypress-tree . . . oaks.* Crete was famous for its cypresses; Ceos
for its oaks (*Quercus aegilops*). Bent describes it as still covered by a million
and a half of them, their acorn-cups producing the valonia used in tanning.

[Page 268] *Courage in Exile.* Towards the close of *Pythian* IV Pindar tact-
fully appeals to Arcésilas King of Cyrēne to amnesty the exiled noble Damóphilus,
quoting this utterance which he ascribes to the exiled Oedipus.

[Page 268] *From the Gods' far-flaming altars. . . .* Adapted by Tennyson
for the close of his *Tiresias*:

> And every way the vales
> Wind, clouded with the grateful incense-fume
> Of those who mix all odours to the Gods
> On one far height in one far-shining fire.

BACCHYLIDES

[Page 269] *The Eagle.* A fine companion-piece to the sleeping eagle of
Pindar (p. 265). The ode celebrates the victory of Híero of Syracuse in the
horse-race at Olympia (476).

[Page 269] *Ye.* Híero and his brothers.

[Page 269] *God of War.* Probably refers to the Syracusan defeat of Carthage
at Himera (480).

[Page 270] *Thronged now the shrines. . . .* These two lines are usually referred
to rejoicings at Syracuse for Híero's victory at the Olympiad of 468 B.C. in the
four-horse chariot-race (the previous stanza had described the acclamations at
Olympia itself). But it seems simpler to pass direct from Olympia to Delphi
(where the 'rich tripods' are offerings from the rulers of Syracuse).

[Page 270] *Castaly.* The spring of Apollo, gushing into a square rock-hewn
basin from the Phaedriad crags which tower sheer above Delphi.

[Page 270] *Bronze-walled.* Adorned with bronze plates.

[Page 270] *Alyattes.* The founder of Lydian power (*c.* 617–560). Croesus
was son of Alyattes, son of Sadyattes, son of Ardys, son of Gyges.

[Page 270] *Pactōlus.* A small stream flowing W. of Sardis to join the
Hermus. Gold was anciently found in its reddish mud.

[Page 271] *Hyperborean land.* Here in the far north Apollo was sometimes
imagined to pass the winter. Its inhabitants, pious vegetarians, lived without
war or sickness for a thousand years; till, wearying of this tranquil existence,
they leapt garland-crowned from a rock into the sea.

[Page 271] *Hēracles and the Wraith of Meleāger.* Earlier in this poem
Bacchýlides has warned his patron Híero to remember in his good fortune that
none can prosper always—witness the fates of Hēracles and Meleāger.

[Page 271] *Sacker of towns.* Hēracles, son of Zeus by Alcmēna (wife of
Amphítryon King of Thebes) sacked Troy, Pylos, and Oechalia. As one of
his Twelve Labours, he was sent by his cousin Eurystheus to fetch Cerberus,
the three-headed Hound of Hell.

[Page 271] *Echidna,* a primitive monster, half woman, half snake, some-times located in Scythia, was credited with a large, miscellaneous, and unpleasant progeny—Cerberus, the Hydra, the Chimera slain by Bellerophon, the Dragon of the Hesperides, the Dragon of the Golden Fleece, the Sphinx, Scylla (p. 155), the Gorgons, the Nemean lion, and the eagle that ate Prometheus' liver.

[Page 271] *Cōcȳtus,* 'Wailing,' one of the streams of Hell.

[Page 271] *As wind-tossed leaves. . . .* A sudden flash of sunlight across the gloom of Hell.

[Page 271] *Porthaónides.* Meleāger, son of Oeneus, son of Porthāon.

[Page 272] *Queen of Heaven.* Hēra, who persecuted Hēracles in her jealousy of his mother Alcmēna.

[Page 272] *Meleāger answered. . . .* Contrast Homer's version (p. 37). Here too no word of Atalanta; though Euripides in a lost play made Meleāger's passion for her the root of the tragedy.

[Page 273] *Magic brand.* For similar folklore in which a man's life is bound up with fire or other external objects, see Frazer, *Golden Bough,* II, 265, XI, 103.

[Page 274] *Not to be born is best.* See p. 253.

[Page 274] *Ionians.* Here Athenians. Athens regarded herself as mother-city of Ionia.

[Page 275] *Sĭnis,* son of Poseidon, waylaying travellers at the Isthmus, tied them to two pine-trees bent earthward, so as to be torn in half when the stems were released; till Theseus did the like to him.

[Page 275] *Scīron.* See p. 289.

[Page 275] *Crommyon,* 12 miles E. of Corinth.

[Page 275] *Kerkyon,* another son of Poseidon, at Eleusis, wrestled with all comers and killed them.

[Page 275] *Procoptes* (or Procrustes), apparently son of Polypēmon, fitted his victims to his famous bed, stretching them if too short, lopping them if too long.

[Page 276] *Lemnos.* For its volcanic nature see p. 101.

PRAXILLA

[Page 276] *'Neither Maid nor Wife.'* Cf. Sir Henry Taylor, *Elena's Song:*

> Quoth tongue of neither maid nor wife
> To heart of neither wife nor maid—
> Lead we not here a jolly life
> Between the shine and shade?
>
> Quoth heart of neither maid nor wife
> To tongue of neither wife nor maid—
> Thou wagg'st, but I am worn with strife
> And feel like flowers that fade.

PLATO

[Page 277] *Ăgathon* (c. 445–401). A brilliant but decadent tragic dramatist, friend of Euripides and butt of Aristophanes. He appears also as a speaker in Plato's *Symposium,* whose setting is the celebration at Agathon's house of his first victory, in 416.

[Page 277] *Aster.* Supposedly a youth with whom Plato studied astronomy.

[Page 278] *Dīon,* a wealthy Syracusan, son-in-law of the elder Dionysius, despot of Syracuse, became an ardent disciple of Plato. Banished by his brother-in-law, the younger Dionysius, he lived at Athens (366–57); then, returning with troops, mastered Syracuse. But he made himself unpopular and was murdered by a fellow-Platonist, Callippus, in 353. Platonist ventures into practical politics were, indeed, singularly unsuccessful.

[Page 278] *Laïs.* There were at least two famous courtesans of the name. This is perhaps the elder or eldest, who lived at Corinth in the later 5th century and counted among her lovers the hedonist philosopher Aristippus (who philosophically commented: 'She is mine, I am *not* hers'). On her grave there stood a lioness (often associated with Aphrodite), tearing a ram. Prior has adapted this epigram:

> Venus, take my votive glass,
> Since I am not what I was;
> What from this day I shall be,
> Venus, let me never see.

TIMOTHEÜS

[Page 279] '*Contemporaneity.*' It is said that in conservative Sparta, at the music-festival of the Carneia, one of the Ephors snatched from Timótheüs the eleven-stringed lyre he had introduced in place of the old seven-stringed instrument, and hacked four of its strings away.

CLEANTHES

[Page 280] *The Stoic's Resignation.* An adaptation of these lines by J. A. Symonds was put on his tomb.

PERSES

[Page 280] *Tychon.* God of luck, perhaps connected with Priāpus.

PART THREE

ALEXANDRIAN PERIOD

3rd–2nd centuries B.C.

PHILĒTAS OF COS

(c. 300 B.C.)

AN elegiac poet and grammarian, who was tutor to the children of
Ptolemy I of Egypt and one of the poetic masters of Theócritus.

'Nothing is here to wail'

I mourn you not, best friend.   Much good and fair
You knew.   Of evil, too, God sent your share.

(Stobaeus, *Florilegium*, CXXIV, p. 616.).

ARATUS OF SOLI

(c. 315-c. 240 B.C.)

J'ai l'esprit tout ennuyé,
D'avoir trop étudié
Les Phénomènes *d'Arate;*
Il est temps que je m'ébatte
Et que j'aille aux champs jouer.
Bons Dieux! qui voudrait louer
Ceux qui collés sur un livre
N'ont jamais souci de vivre.

Ronsard.

Wordsworth looked forward to a poetry of science.   But it has hardly
arrived, though the idea of it was already known to the ancients.   With his
versified astronomy, the *Phaenomena*, Arātus attained a reputation hard now
to understand; he was imitated by Virgil, quoted by St. Paul, translated by
Cicero, Germanicus Caesar, and the fourth-century Avienus.   In a sense
Arātus revives the didactic epic of Hēsiod, as Apollonius Rhodius the heroic
epic of Homer.   But where Hēsiod's work smells of rain-wet earth, that of
Arātus reeks of the lamp.   He has none of the passion of Lucretius' *De
Rerum Natura*, none of the charm of Fontenelle's prose in his *Sur la Pluralité
des Mondes*.   Alexandria, indeed, produced too much *Professorenpoesie*.
Arātus wrote also a poem on medicines, shorter pieces, an edition of the
Odyssey, and a critical work on Homer; but these are lost.

297

Often the birds of mere or main, with ceaseless dives,
Plunge headlong into the waters; or the swallow drives,
With belly that skims the ripples, about the lake for hours;
Or that race not so happy, whom the watersnake devours,
The fathers of the tadpole, within their shallows croak;
Or the lonely tree-frog murmurs, as soon as dawn hath woke.
Oft, when a storm is coming, along some jutting strand
The chattering crow betakes him towards the shelter of the land;
Or, from his head to where his shoulders first begin,
Splashes himself by a riverside, or dives full in,
Or with loud caws by the water stalks round and round again.
And oxen, too, give warning of the coming of the rain,
Lifting their heads towards Heaven and snuffing at the air;
And from their hollow homes in haste the ants will bear
The eggs that are their treasure; and quickly up the wall
The centipede goes swarming; and widely wandering crawl
Those worms that men have named 'the sable earth's entrails';
While all the race of Chanticleer, through wings and tails,
Peck eagerly for vermin, or loudly gurgling go,
With a sound as when dripping water on water drops below.

(Phaenomena, 942–62.)

CALLIMACHUS OF CYRENE

(c. 310–c. 240 B.C.)

Un petit ruisselet a toujours l'onde nette;
Aussi le papillon et la gentille avette
Y vont puiser de l'eau, et non en ces torrents,
Qui tonnent d'un grand bruit par les roches courants.
Petits sonnets bien faits, belles chansons petites,
Petits discours gentils, sont les fleurs des Charites.

Ronsard.

Callimachus is a typical Alexandrian poet. For the Alexandrians
laboured under the difficulties that beset creative writers in an age when
literature has passed one of its great periods and they grow painfully conscious of living in the lengthening shadow cast by giant predecessors. They
are heirs to great wealth, yet they feel impoverished; they are more cultured
than their fathers, yet more sterile; their shelves teem with books, their
heads with knowledge, yet they lack the old passion, energy, and life. For
when the past becomes more than the present, memories than hopes, then a

man—or a race—is growing old. And so, in this autumnal atmosphere, some of the Alexandrians turned to science; some to scholarship; some to a sort of literary Parnassianism, despising the popular, avoiding the trite, striving by elaboration of technique and depth of learning to find and gather laurels yet uncut. Poets like Callímachus took the view of Théophile Gautier that the artist must work, like a gem-engraver, in a hard medium; the view of Edgar Allan Poe that poems must essentially be brief—or at least that they must *now* be brief. 'A big book,' said Callímachus, 'is a big curse.' Other poets, like Apollonius of Rhodes, still hoped by more curious erudition and subtler psychology to revive the spacious glories of the epic. Others still, like Theócritus—the most successful, turned back from the hot and hustling streets of giant Alexandria to nature and the piping of simple shepherds among the eternal silence of the hills. Unfortunately writers are often not content to leave their theories of art for practice to prove and for time to judge; between Callímachus and Apollonius there broke out a wordy warfare of barbed epigram and bitter allusion —dust of a day now covered in the dust of years.

Callímachus, born in Cyréne, became a schoolmaster at Alexandria, then an official of its library (where he played a chief part in compiling the catalogue), antiquarian, critic, and literary historian, as well as poet. Of the 800 volumes attributed to him, our chief remains are six *Hymns*, parts of his *Aitia* (*Origins*) and of his *Hécale*, and some epigrams, which include his finest work. His *Hymns* cannot challenge their 'Homeric' predecessors; what they gain in erudition, they lose in poetry; the pages that follow include the best part of the best among them, *The Bathing of Pallas*. The *Aitia* seems to have been on similar lines to Ovid's *Fasti*—a form giving scope in its antiquarian framework for anecdotes like the romance of Acontius and Cydippe, retold by Morris in his *Earthly Paradise*. The *Hécale* is about an old woman who entertains Theseus on his way to fight the Marathonian Bull, and rambles on about a miscellany of matters to her guest—a typical attempt to treat an old theme from a novel angle. But, for the artist, novelty proved a will-o'-the-wisp; then as now. His essential aim, I believe, should be not 'progress'—that he can leave to scientists—but perfection; not to be new, but to be true. If he has personality, novelty can take care of itself—it will come unsought. Work that chases the new seldom lives to grow old.

Callímachus' *Lock of Berenice* is likewise lost, though we have a Latin version by Catullus. Its theme—that a newly discovered constellation was really one of the queen's tresses—takes us into the frigid world of court-poetry, as dull under the Ptolemies as under the Bourbons. Yet fate is a grim ironist; no astronomical flatteries were to save Queen Berenice from being murdered by her own son.

Callímachus was a dominant figure in his day. He deeply influenced Roman poets like Catullus, Propertius, and Ovid. But, like many neo-classic poets of the eighteenth century in France and England, he seems often to have let his heart be cramped by his head, his creation be inhibited by his self-criticism. He remains a somewhat cold writer, who can strike out fine flashes, but kindle no enduring fire. Hence the superiority of his epigrams. For himself, he *was* right to prefer short poems; and there was wisdom in the advice he attributed to Apollo—that a poet should offer fat beasts, but slender verses. It is when Callímachus mourns for the dead schoolgirl whose stories will never again delight her playmates, for the dead friend with whom he will never again talk down the sun to setting, that his voice after all these centuries once more becomes alive.

The Bathing of Pallas

Maidens, in Thebes Athene loved once a nymph past measure,
 One nymph of her chosen comrades she cherished best of all—
The mother of Teirésias. She took no pleasure
 Save with her friend; and whenever to Thespiae's ancient wall
Or to Corōnēa, beside Courálius' river,
 Where, fragrant with their incense, her grove and altars are,
The Maiden Goddess drove her team—ay, or whenever
 She sped to Háliartus, through the fields of Boeotia,
Often she took Charīclo in her chariot beside her;
 And unless, when the Nymphs were gathered for talk or dance, her friend
Was foremost there, Athene felt all her joy denied her:
 Yet bitter grief for Charīclo lay waiting in the end.
It helped not that Athene had loved her once so dearly.
 For it chanced that one day, unclasping their raiment on the Hill
Of Helicon, where the Horse's Spring runs sparkling clearly,
 They bathed—as the hush of noon o'er the mountainside lay still.
Ay, 'twas the hour of noontide, as they bathed there, those two only,
 While deep the silence brooded upon the mountain-peak;
But into that holy place with his hound came, wandering lonely,
 Teirésias (there darkened the first beard on his cheek),
And athirst past all endurance, he turned where that stream rose springing:
 Alas! For there he discovered the beauty none may see.
No ill he meant. But, in anger, Athene's voice rose ringing—
 'What evil spirit hath led thee this road of calamity?
Henceforward, Euēreides, no light shall ever quicken
 Thine eyes again.' As she said it, upon him closed the dark.
Speechless he stood—his tongue with sudden horror stricken,
 And fast in the grip of anguish his knees grew stiff and stark.
But loud screamed the Nymph, his mother—'My queen, to the son I cherish
 What hast thou done? Is it *thus*, that ye Gods show loving care?
Thou hast robbed my child of his vision! O son born but to perish,

Thine eyes have beheld Athene with breast and body bare—
But never again the sunlight!   O heart with sorrow shaken!
O peaks I shall shun for ever—hillsides of Helicon!
To exact so much for so little!   For a few deer he had taken,
For a few fawns, ye have stolen the eyesight of my son!'
So cried that weeping mother; then, in her arms enfolding
Her dear son, with such wailings as nightingales awake,
Led him away.   But Athene grew pitiful, beholding
The sorrow of her comrade; and thus in turn she spake:
'Take back, dear heart and honoured, those words of fierce misprision.
Not by *my* doing was it, that thy son hath lost his eyes.
No joy it is to Athene to rob youth of its vision;
But thus the solemn edict of the Son of Crŏnus lies—
Who sees an Immortal's beauty (save the God himself reveal it)
For that moment's revelation a bitter price must pay.
And what is done, honoured lady, no power can repeal it;
Such was the thread Fate spun him, upon his life's first day,
When he came from the womb of his mother.   But thou, take what is given,
And bear, O Euēreides, the doom of destiny.
How many sacrifices shall be burnt one day to Heaven
By Aristaeus, and Cadmus' child, could they but see
Their only son, Actaeon—even with eyes that fail him!
Yet, though he shares the hunting of the mighty Artemis,
The shafts they shot together on the hills shall not avail him,
Nor all their days of hunting, against the doom that's his,
When he shall see, unwilling, bare in the pool before him
The beauty of his Goddess; for then his hounds shall run
To banquet on their master, and everywhere she that bore him
Shall search the woods to gather the bones of her own son.
Yea, *that* day she shall call thee "most blest"—"a happy mother"—
Since safe to thy arms, though blinded, he came from the mountain-brake.
Dear friend, grieve not too sorely; I promise many another
Honour to this thy son, henceforward, for thy sake.
A prophet I will make him, and bards unborn shall utter
His name, as far the greatest of any earthly seer.
He shall know which birds betoken good—and which birds flutter
Idly—and which come winging with signs for men to fear.
Boeotia shall hearken to the words of God he showeth,
And Cadmus and, thereafter, the great Labdácidae.
I will give him a mighty staff, to guide him where he goeth;
A long life I will give him, and many his years shall be.
And even in death his wisdom, alone, shall keep its worth,
Honoured of Him that gathers the peoples of the earth.'

(Hymns, V, 57–130.)

The Parnassian

Once in the ear of Apollo said Envy, privily:
'I honour only a poet with songs wide as the sea.'
But, spurning Envy from Him, Apollo thus replied:
'Full flows Assyria's river; yet thickly down its tide
The sweepings and the scourings of the earth wash weltering:
But her servants bear to Demeter—not draughts from *any* spring—
Nought but the flower of waters, that from some fount divine
Rills in a slender streamlet, unsullied, crystalline.'

(Hymns, II, 105–11.)

The Aesthete

I loathe bards' commonplaces.   No beaten track delights me,
    Where the feet of multitudes go thronging soon and late.
I hate light loves and easy.   No public fount invites me.
    Everything that is common do I abominate.

(Epigrams, XXX, 1–4.)

The Dead Playmate

For Crēthis the teller of stories, for that sweet head so clever
    At common task or playtime, the maids of Samos call
Oft and in vain.   But that gay tongue sleeps here for ever
        The sleep that waits them all.

(XVIII.)

Don Juan

The huntsman, Epicȳdes, across the mountains follows
    The track of every hare, the slot of every hind,
In the teeth of frost and blizzard.   But if a comrade hollows—
    'See, one is down!—before you!'—to that he has no mind.
Such is my love: so eager to follow all that flies,
Onward it sweeps disdaining what at its mercy lies.

(XXXIII.)

The Dead Poet

One told me, Heraclītus, you were dead; and left me weeping,
    As once more I remembered how often down the west
We talked the sun to setting.   And now—dust in earth's keeping—
    Old friend from Halicarnassus, long since, it seems, you rest.
Yet still the songs you sang us, your Nightingales, abide:
Not Death's own hand can seize them, that clutches all beside.

(II.)

'Pulvis et Umbra'

'Sleeps Cháridas beneath you?'   'If you would ask concerning
  The dead son of Arimmas, from Cyrēne, here he lies.'
'What of the grave, friend?' 'Darkness.' 'What of the dead's returning?'
  'False.' 'What of Pluto?' 'A fable.   What dies for ever dies.
This is the truth.   Would you rather some pleasant fairy-tale?
Why then, in Hell for a penny fat oxen stand on sale.'

(xv.)

The Misanthrope

'Now you are buried, Timon, is the darkness worse, or the light?'
'The dark.   For ye swarm yet thicker, here in the House of Night.'

(v.)

THEOCRITUS OF SYRACUSE

(c. 310 B.C.–?)

Ah! leave the smoke, the wealth, the roar
Of London, and the bustling street,
For still, by the Sicilian shore,
The murmur of the Muse is sweet.
Still, still the suns of summer greet
The mountain-grave of Helikê
And shepherds still their songs repeat
Where breaks the blue Sicilian sea.

Andrew Lang.

Theócritus serves as an example of what a real poet *can* do even if he has
the misfortune to be born in an age of decadence, when everything seems
already said.   Probably a Syracusan by birth, he spent part of his life in the
green and pleasant island of Cos, off south-west Asia Minor, and in the vast
new city of Alexandria.   Hence he is a poet of both town and country,
loving the country as only those can who have stifled in great towns.

Like Callímachus, he felt that long poems risked tedium; his *Idylls* (that
is, 'Short Pieces') are sketches of town and country life, of heroic legends,
of happy or unhappy love.   The first of regular pastoral poets, he remains
the finest.   For though his countryside is already somewhat idealized (it is
enough to contrast the harsher realism of Hēsiod), he did at least know his
shepherds, while some of his successors give the impression of never having
talked to a real rustic in their lives.   Hence Theócritus contrives to keep an
admirable balance between realism and romance.   Even with the most vivid
figures of Attic drama one seems to hear and feel the tread of the tragic
buskin: but those of Theócritus still go springing with bare brown feet
across the grass and rock of Cos or Sicily.   More actual than Virgil or

Spenser, he does not on the other hand, like Wordsworth, sometimes give his countrymen too much an air of oaf or boor. Theócritus, indeed, could not have written *Michael*; but then neither could Wordsworth have created the passionate young sorceress of Theócritus. Here is none of the grey brooding mystery of the cloud-raked crags of Westmorland; but no Greek poet since Homer has painted so vividly the sunlit beauty, yet sadness, of Mediterranean hillside and Sicilian sea.

Daphnis

THYRSIS

Sweet is the whisper, goatherd, of yonder pine that sings
There by the running water—and sweet your piping rings.
Next to Pan's self, in music, yours is the mastery—
If He were to win the horned he-goat, yours would the milch-goat be;
Or, if Pan chose the she-goat, then yours the kid to win—
And a kid is delicate eating, till her milking days begin.

GOATHERD

Sweeter your song flows, shepherd, than the murmuring tone
Of the streamlet plashing yonder, down from its lofty stone.
If, matched with you, the Muses for *their* prize chose the sheep,
Then yours the lamb, as second. Or if they chose to keep
The yeanling, then its mother were yours as next in skill.

THYRSIS

By the Nymphs, I beg you, goatherd, I beg you, on this hill
Sit you down for a little, where the tamarisks grow, and play
Your pipe. And I will be watching that none of your goats shall stray.

GOATHERD

Ah, shepherd, pipe we may not. Not in the hushed noontide.
For fear of Pan we may not. For then on the mountainside,
Tired with the chase, He slumbers. And savage of heart is He
And the snarling anger hovers at His nostrils, perilously.
But come—the sorrows of Daphnis, O Thyrsis, you can sing,
So sweetly that never a herdsman can match your carolling.
Then hither beneath the elm-tree—come hither now and sit,
Here, with the carved Priāpus and the Spring-nymphs opposite,
Where the shepherd's seat and the oak-trees are. And if for me
You sing as well as once you sang, in rivalry
With Libyan Chrŏmis, you shall have—to milk her thrice—
My goat that, though twin her kidlings, yet brims the milkpail twice;

304

And my deep dish of ivy-wood, with sweet wax polished well,
Twin-handled, fresh from the chisel, still full of the clean wood-smell.
Round its lip, at the top, there twists an ivy-spray—
Ivy-leaves dotted, between, with berries golden-gay;
And there within—as a God might carve—is a woman in the pride
Of splendid robe and headband; and by her, on each side,
A fair and long-tressed lover.   Passionately that pair
Of rivals bandy insults; but she—she does not care.
At one she glances smiling—and then she turns again,
Inclining more to the other.   But *they*—from love's long pain
Their eyes are ringed with blackness.   Yet all their labour 's nought.
Next these, an aged fisher on a rugged rock is wrought—
There, with the look of one that is labouring hard and fast,
The old man stands and gathers his great net for a cast.
He is straining the strength of his body to the utmost, you can tell,
All round his neck so tensely the corded muscles swell;
For though his hair is grizzled, hale as a youth is he.
Next, a little aside from that ancient of the sea,
Is a vineyard purple-clustered, growing fair and tall;
Close by, there sits to guard it, upon a loose stone-wall,
A little lad; and, near him, two foxes—one that goes
Along the vines, devouring; with all the guile she knows,
The other stalks his wallet, determinedly intent
On a more solid breakfast.   But he—he is wholly bent
On plaiting a lovely locust-trap, with asphodel and reeds,
And lost in that loving labour nor food, nor vines, he heeds.
Lastly, a lithe acanthus goes twining about the bowl.
It is a thing of rapture, a sight to witch your soul.
I bought it from a sailor of a Calydnian ship,
For a goat and a great, white, cream-made cheese.   But never lip
Of mine has touched its virgin wood—'tis yours this day,
And welcome, friend!—if only you 'll sing your lovely lay.
Come, I speak true!   Your song now!   For take it you cannot
Down to the House of Hades, that makes all things forgot.

THYRSIS (*sings*)

Lift up the song, dear Muses, lift up the herdsman's song.
Thyrsis from Etna calls you—Thyrsis the sweet of tongue.
While Daphnis' heart was breaking, ah Nymphs, where were ye then,
Where were ye?   In vales of Pindus?   In Tempe's lovely glen?
For, sure, by broad Anāpus ye were not wandering,
Nor high on the peak of Etna, nor by Ācis' holy spring.
Lift up the song, dear Muses, lift up the herdsman's song.

305

For him the very jackals, the wild wolves howled and cried;
Even the lion from the thicket sorrowed when Daphnis died.
  Lift up the song, dear Muses, lift up the herdsman's song.

Round his feet, as he lay there, mourning with heavy cheer
Stood many a calf and heifer, many a mighty steer.
  Lift up the song, dear Muses, lift up the herdsman's song.

First, Hermes came from the mountain, and said—'Who makes thee weep,
Dear son? Who is it, Daphnis, that stirs thy heart so deep?'
  Lift up the song, dear Muses, lift up the herdsman's song.

The neatherds came—the shepherds—the goatherds—to his side,
And asked what evil ailed him. Priāpus came, and cried,
'Why grieving, wretched Daphnis?—while now by every rill
For thee the girl goes wandering, by every woodland, still?'
  Lift up the song, dear Muses, lift up the herdsman's song.

'Searching for thee!—oh feeble, feckless in love, art thou.
"The neatherd" once men called thee—no better than goatherd now!'
  Lift up the song, dear Muses, lift up the herdsman's song.

'The goatherd, craven creature, watching his he-goat cover
The bleating flock, cries weeping—"Had I but been their lover!"'
  Lift up the song, dear Muses, lift up the herdsman's song.

'So thou, as girls go gaily laughing in thy sight,
Weepest—"Ah, to join them in their dances, what delight!"'
But the herdsman answered nothing; he bore his bitter doom
Of passion, uncomplaining; he bore it to the tomb.
  Lift up again, dear Muses, lift up the herdsman's song.

Last, with her lovely laughter, came Cypris—secretly
Laughing, yet nursing anger still—'Daphnis,' said she,
'Once thou didst boast in wrestling thou couldst o'ermaster Love:
Is Love not a grimmer wrestler?—thou under, he above?'
  Lift up again, dear Muses, lift up the herdsman's song.

Then Daphnis groaned in answer: 'Ah, Love, thou thing of pain,
Love abhorred and accursèd; Love, thou mortal bane,
Now indeed thou deemest that my last sun is set;
But Daphnis, even in Hades, shall make Love suffer yet.'
  Lift up again, dear Muses, lift up the herdsman's song.

'To Ida—go!—to Anchises!   Runs there not a tale,
Of herdsman and Cyprian there, mid oak and galingale?'
   Lift up again, dear Muses, lift up the herdsman's song.

'And ripe, too, is Adonis—one herdsman more for thee!—
Who hunts the cowering hare and all the beasts that flee.'
   Lift up again, dear Muses, lift up the herdsman's song.

 Nay, turn thee back to the battle, face Diomēdes now
And say: "I have conquered Daphnis, the herdsman—meet me *thou*!"'
   Lift up again, dear Muses, lift up the herdsman's song.

'Farewell, ye wolves, and jackals, and bears in your mountain caves,
Ye shall meet the herdsman Daphnis no more where woodland waves,
No more in brake or coppice.   Arethusa, evermore
Farewell!—and ye, fair rivers whose floods down Thymbris pour.'
   Lift up again, dear Muses, lift up the herdsman's song.

'It is Daphnis calls upon ye, whose herds once roamed your hills;
Daphnis, whose steers and heifers were watered at your rills.'
   Lift up again, dear Muses, lift up the herdsman's song.

'O Pan, O Pan, where art thou?   Wherever thou treadst this while—
Tall Maenălus, long Lycaeon—to this Sicilian isle
Come!—from the grave of Hélice, come to me here—
From that high mound of Arcas, that even the Gods revere.'
   Now cease your song, dear Muses, now cease your herdsman's song.

'Come hither, take my panpipe—the honeyed scent is cast
Still, from the wax, O Master, that binds its fair lip fast:
Down to the House of Hades I am dragged by love at last.'
   Now cease your song, dear Muses, now cease your herdsman's song.

'Now let the briar and bramble bear violets, if they will;
On the juniper let blossom the dainty daffodil.
Since Daphnis dies, come chaos!   Let pears on the pine be found;
Let the hind turn now on the hunter and worry the hunting-hound;
Let the music of nightingales by owls from the hills be drowned.'
   Now cease your song, dear Muses, now cease your herdsman's song.

So saying, his voice fell silent.   To lift that fallen head
In vain strove Aphrodite.   The Fates had spun his thread.
The Stream of Death took Daphnis—and down its flood was borne
The singer loved of the Muses, the youth no Nymph could scorn.
   Now cease your song, dear Muses, now cease your herdsman's song.

Now bring your bowl and the goat, for me to milk and do
Libation to the Muses.   Muses, farewell to you!
Farewell!   I will bring ye hereafter a song that is sweeter still.

Ah Thyrsis, I wish you honey, yes, honeycombs, to fill
Your tuneful mouth, and figs from Aegilus to eat,
Sweet figs—for never cicada was heard to sing so sweet.
Here is the bowl.   Now try, friend!—smells not its fragrance good?
You would think the fruitful Seasons in their fount had steeped its wood.
Hither, Kissaitha!   Milk her!   And you, ye goats, take care!
Have done with your wanton gambols, lest the he-goat catch ye there.

(Idylls, 1.)

The Sorceress

Where are my leaves of laurel?   Quick!—lay them in my hand,
Thestўlis.   And my philtres!   And twist a crimson strand
Of finest wool on the vessel's lip.   I mean to cast
A spell on my heartless lover.   Wretch, that for twelve days past
Has left me!—although he knows not, am I living yet or dead?
No more on my door he batters.   Ah, shameless!   Has Love led—
Love and the Queen of Desire—that fickle heart astray?
To Tīmāgĕtus' wrestling-school, at morn, I will take my way—
Find him and curse his unkindness; but spells of fire this night
Shall bind him first.   O Selēne, fair shine thy lovely light!—
While low to Thee, and Hecatē, I sing, who fills with dread
The very dogs as She comes, through the blood, through the graves, of the
        dead.
Hail Hecate, Queen of Terror—be near me Thou to the end!
Such power as once to Circe, or Mēdēa, Thou didst lend,
Or to fair-haired Perimēde—such may my magic be!
   My wheel, draw that man hither, oh draw him home to me!

Now wastes in the flame the barley—come now, more quickly!—throw,
Thestўlis!   Wretched girl, what leaves you dreaming so?
Am I grown so vile in your eyes—a jest to you too at last!
Scatter the barley, saying 'It is Delphis' bones I cast.'
   My wheel, draw that man hither, oh draw him home to me!

Delphis has done me wrong—I burn these leaves of bay
For Delphis.   And as this laurel crackles and burns away,
Bursting to flame in an instant, leaving no ash behind,
Let a fire as fierce, as wasting, round the limbs of Delphis wind.
   My wheel, draw that man hither, oh draw him home to me!

Now will I burn the corn-husks.   O Artemis, Thy spell
Can shatter all that's hardest—ay, the adamant of Hell.
The dogs howl, up through the city!   They hear the Goddess pass,
Thestӯlis, by the crossways!   Beat—quickly!—on the brass!
My wheel, draw that man hither, oh draw him home to me!

Listen!   The winds lie silent, and silent lies the sea,
But nothing can quiet the anguish that fills the heart in me.
For all my soul lies flaming for him that has betrayed
My love to its undoing—left me no more a maid.
My wheel, draw that man hither, oh draw him home to me!

Now as this wax is melted, so by the Goddess' power,
May *he* melt, Myndian Delphis, with passion at this hour.
As my brazen roarer circles, by Aphrodite's will
Let him circle, mad with passion, about my doorway still.
My wheel, draw that man hither, oh draw him home to me!

Thrice now I pour libation—and thrice, O Queen, I cry—
Whether this night beside him woman or lad may lie,
Let them fade from his mind forgotten, as once from Theseus' mind
The fair-tressed Ariadne, in Dīa left behind.
My wheel, draw that man hither, oh draw him home to me!

Arcadia breeds the horsewort, the herb whose longing thrills
Mare and filly to madness, galloping through the hills;
So might these eyes see Delphis race from the wrestling-school
To dash against my doorway, mad as a raving fool.
My wheel, draw that man hither, oh draw him home to me!

I take this stolen tassel, that from Delphis' mantle came,
I tear it and toss its fragments in the fiercest of the flame.
O Love, why wilt thou cling so, bleeding me white, to slake
Thy thirst, O Love devouring, like horseleech from the lake?
My wheel, draw that man hither, oh draw him home to me!

I will pound a poisonous lizard and bear the brew to him
To-morrow.   But take these simples, now while the night hangs dim,
And over his threshold knead them, Thestӯlis, and say,
With muttering mouth, 'I am kneading Delphis' bones away.'
My wheel, draw that man hither, oh draw him home to me!

She is gone.   How shall I mourn, now, my lost love's memory?
Ah, where begin?   Who was it, first brought this curse on me?

Eubūlus' daughter, Anaxo, was chosen out to bear
A basket to Artemis' temple; and in procession there
Many a beast should follow—a lioness as well.
  Listen, O Queen Selēne, how first in love I fell.

Theumáridas' nurse, the Thracian, poor soul that now is dead,
Came from her house close by us, and begged me hard, and said,
We *must* go see that pageant.   And I (oh, unhappiness!),
I let her tongue cajole me—o'er a fair long linen dress
I cast Cleärista's mantle, and then we went our way.
But with half our path behind us, where Lўcon's gardens lay—
  Listen, O Queen Selēne, how first in love I fell—

I noticed Eudamippus, walking together there
With Delphis—but more golden than helichryse the hair
Gleamed on their cheeks, and brighter, O Moon, their breasts than Thou,
(For the athletes had been trying their glorious strength but now).
  Listen, O Queen Selēne, how first in love I fell.

I saw him—and madness seized me—and my poor heart took flame.
Blanched was all my beauty.   I gave no heed what came
In all that day's long pageant.   Home how I found my way,
I know not.   Ague shook me.   Shivering I lay
On my bed ten days together, ten nights—till all my hue
As sallow and as yellow as the dye of Thapsus grew.
  Listen, O Queen Selēne, how first in love I fell.

I pined to a thing of skin and bone; my long hair fell—
Ah, what old beldame's cottage, that dealt in charm or spell,
Did I not haunt?   Yet it helped not.   And ever the days slipped past—
Till to my maid I uttered all of the truth at last.
  Listen, O Queen Selēne, how first in love I fell.

'Thestўlis, for this madness find me a remedy.
I am sick for Delphis, body and soul.   Go now for me
To the school of Tīmāgētus, and watch—there oftenest
He comes; and *there* is the seat that of all he loves the best.'
  Listen, O Queen Selēne, how first in love I fell.

'When you have found him alone there, nod quickly with your head
And whisper "Sīmaetha calls you"—and bring him.'   So I said,
And away she went and, returning, hither home she brought
The youth in his glorious beauty.   At sight of that face long sought—
  Listen, O Queen Selēne, how first in love I fell—

As there he came through my doorway, so lightly, I grew cold
As ice through all my body.   Down from my forehead rolled
Sweat like the pelting raindrops—I could not utter sound
As faint as the moan for its mother, of child in slumber drowned.
I lay with every limb, like a puppet, stiffened fast.
My loveless lover scanned me; and then, with eyes downcast—
   Listen, O Queen Selēne, how first in love I fell—

Taking his seat, 'Sĭmaetha,' he said, 'as narrowly
As *I* outran fair Philīnus once, now *you* have outrun *me*,
In calling me to your bedside, before uncalled I came.
Else, by the joys of Eros, I *had* come, all the same—'
   Listen, O Queen Selēne, how first in love I fell—

'Two or three comrades with me, before this eve was old,
With apples of Dionysus wrapped in my mantle's fold,
My head enwreathed with the poplar beloved of Hēracles,
And twined with purple ribbons.   And then—if you should please—'
   Listen, O Queen Selēne, how first in love I fell—

'To give us ready welcome, then all would have been well;
For gay am I and gallant, as all our youth can tell.
With a kiss from your lovely lips, I could have slept once more.
But, had you barred me out and bolted fast your door,
We had axe and torches ready, at need, to break our way.
So, as it is, to Cypris my thanks in full I pay—
To Cypris first and, next, to you—that from the fire
Have snatched me by your summons, when already my desire
Had left me half in ashes.   In truth Love's hotter far
Than the blaze Hephaestus kindles in his forge of Lípara.
He can hound with his bitter madness the young lass from her room
And the bride but a moment risen from the warm bed of her groom.'
   Listen, O Queen Selēne, how first in love I fell.

Such were the words he uttered—and I, poor fool, gave ear,
And took his hand, and beside me on the soft bed drew him near.
Then flesh against flesh grew melted, and now our faces flushed
With a new warmth and, between us, passed whispers softly hushed.
Alas, O Queen Selēne, not long the tale to tell—
All I could give was given—to love's embrace we fell.
And yet till now there was nothing that he found in me to blame,
Nothing I found in *him*; but now, to-day, there came
Our flute-girl Philista's mother, and Melixo's, just as Morn
Climbed rosy from the Ocean, by her swift steeds upward borne;

And said, among her gossip, that Delphis certainly
Was fallen in love with another—if woman or lad it be,
For sure she could not tell me—only he sat all day
And drank wine, neat, to Eros; then suddenly rushed away
To wreathe, he said, with garlands the door of that love of his.
So the old woman tattled.   But very truth it is.
For thrice a day, or four times, he used to haunt my door
And he left his Dorian oilflask, here in my care, before;
But now, since last I saw him—twelve days!   Ah, doubt it not,
He has turned to another pleasure, and *my* love lies forgot.
So now I will try upon him, if the flame can work its spell;
Then—if he still torments me—against the Gate of Hell
He shall knock—by the Fates I swear it!   Such salves in my chest I save,
Which that Assyrian stranger once taught to me, and gave.
But Thou, farewell, O Mistress.   Turn to the Western Sea
Thy horses—I will bear it, this grief I took on me.
Farewell, O Moon, I bid Thee, throned in Thy lovely light;
Farewell, ye stars that follow on the noiseless wheels of Night.

(*Idylls*, II.)

The Festival

So, as we lay there resting, thick rustled overhead
Many an elm and poplar, while babbling down its bed
Out of the Nymphs' own cavern a sacred water sprang,
And deep in the woodland shadows the dusky crickets sang,
Making a busy music.   And where the brambles lay,
Thick with their thorns, the tree-frog sat crooning far away.
There trilled the lark, and the linnet piped, to the wood-dove's coo,
And over the bubbling wellhead ever the brown bees flew.
There all smelt sweet of summer, all smelt of autumn sweet,
There at our sides the apples, the pears fell at our feet,
Tumbling in headlong bounty; while earthward, overcome
By the riot of fruit upon them, bent the branches of the plum.
    Then from the mouths of the wine-jars was the four-years' seal torn free.
Ah Nymphs of high Parnassus, ye Nymphs of Castaly,
Was it ever such wine as yonder, that in Phŏlus' craggy cave
To Hēracles aforetime the Centaur Chīron gave?
Was it ever such peerless nectar that by Anāpus' stream
Sent reeling round his sheep-fold the giant Polypheme,
Who hurled at ships whole mountains?—as we mingled with your spring,
O Nymphs, by Demeter's altar?   Be it mine, *again*, to bring
A mighty fan for setting in her corn-heap, while She stands
Smiling, with gathered corn-ears and poppies in her hands!

(*Idylls*, VII, 135–57.)

Hylas

Not, Nicias, as we dreamed once, for us alone was Love
Begotten—whoever his parent, among the powers above;
How lovely is life's loveliness, not first are we
To feel, whose mould is mortal, who no to-morrow see.
Long since that iron heart of the son of Amphítryon,
That braved the lion of the mountain, by the love of a lad was won—
By the young beauty of Hylas and the grace of his tossing hair.
He taught the boy those lessons, with a loving father's care,
That had made himself a hero, sung in the mouths of men;
Never an hour could part them—not the high noon, nor when
The white-maned steeds of Morning charged up the Heaven's steep,
Nor when the piping chickens were looking up to sleep
Where aloft on the sooty rafter their mother flapped her wings—
That the boy might grow to a manhood perfect in all things,
A yokefellow true and trusted, after the hero's heart.
    Then fell the days when Jason made ready to depart
In quest of the Golden Fleece; and now on every hand
Each warrior of valour, the flower of every land,
Flocked to the muster—among them, to rich Iolcus' shore,
That man of many labours, whom once Alcmēna bore,
The heroine of Mīdeia; and in his company
Came Hylas, where fair-benched Argo lay beached beside the sea—
Argo, that like an eagle, soaring the watery waste,
Passed untouched through the Clashing Rocks, and onward raced
Towards the deep mouth of Phāsis—while rooted crags grew *they*.
But, at the Pleiads' rising, when Spring has gone her way,
And on the upland borders the young lambs flock to feed,
Then to the quest before them the heroes gave their heed;
The thwarts of hollow Argo they manned, and spreading sail
On the third day reached the Hellespont, before the south-west gale;
And moored her within Propontis, where the Kiānians' kine
Drive broad through the loam their furrow, till bright their ploughshares shine.
Then springing ashore her rowers made ready at evenfall,
Pair by pair, their supper—but a common couch for all;
For many bladed rushes, much galingale grew deep
There in the mead; and they mowed them, to make soft beds to sleep.
    But now for water Hylas, the golden-haired, was gone,
To cook the supper of Hēracles and dauntless Télamon
(For ever they ate as comrades beside the selfsame board).
Brazen pitcher in hand, quickly he came where poured
A spring from a lowly hollow—thick grew the rushes there
Thick the dark celandine and pale-green maidenhair,

And parsley lush, and reed-grass that loves the marsh's cool.
And *there* lay the Nymphs' own dancing-place, within the midmost pool,
Those sleepless Nymphs, from whose dread power the peasant flies—
Euneica; Mālis; Nycheia, with springtime in her eyes.
So, as the boy bent o'er the brink, in haste to dip
The wide mouth of his pitcher, all at once their grip
Closed on his wrist—for passion had thrilled their hearts to see
The Argive lad—and his body went shooting suddenly
Down the dark depths; as when, from Heaven, a star ablaze
Shoots on a sudden seaward, and sailor to sailor says:
'Quick, lads, and lighten sail aloft—'tis coming on to blow!'
The Nymphs on their knees took Hylas, there in the depths below,
With gentle words of comfort to charm away his tears;
But great Amphítryon's son, tormented now with fears,
Strode forth to seek his squire, with trusty club in hand
And curving bow, such as Scythians wield, beside Maeōtis' strand.
Thrice he thundered 'Hylas!' with the strength of his stalwart frame,
And thrice the boy cried answer; but his voice so faintly came
From the pool's depth, that far he seemed, although so near.
Then, as a lion devouring, when falls upon his ear
In his lair high up the mountains the cry of some young fawn,
Rushes to seize his quarry; so through the pathless thorn
Hēracles went searching, in anguish, far and wide.
Stubborn indeed are lovers—far o'er the countryside
He tramped, forgetting Jason, by thicket, hill, and dale,
While Argo, with all aboard her and ready-hoisted sail,
Waited.   At last, near midnight, the heroes lowered once more
Her yard, to bide his coming.   But onward still he tore,
Blindly and madly searching, by raging Love possest.
   So was the lovely Hylas numbered with the Blest;
But bitterly the heroes called curses on the name
Of Hēracles, 'the deserter,' that quitted, to his shame,
The thirty thwarts of Argo; and so afoot came he
Unto the Colchian kingdom's inhospitality.

(*Idylls*, XIII.)

The Hunter Hunted

In the leaf-strewn cavern, Daphnis, thy wearied limbs lie sleeping,
    While for the beasts on the mountain thy hunting-nets are spread;
But see, to hunt the hunter, into thy cave comes creeping
    Pan, and Priāpus with him, that wreathes his lovely head
With the yellow-blooming ivy.   Quick, Daphnis, quickly!   Flee—
Up, and shake off the slumber that softly steals on thee!

(*Epigrams*, III.)

'And Thou beside me Singing in the Wilderness'

Not all the Isle of Pĕlops, nor King's treasures past appraising,
  Nor feet more fleet than wind are anything to me.
I will sing beneath this boulder, with my arms about you, gazing
  At our flocks together grazing and the sea of Sicily.

(Idylls, VIII, 53–6.)

Lovers' Meeting

Have you come then, O my darling!—with the third night's end, at last!
Have you come!   Ah, love-sick lovers grow old ere a day be past.

(Idylls, XII, 1–2.)

Transience

Lovely the rose; and yet—its beauty Time deflowers:
Lovely in spring the violet—but brief its hours:
White is the lily—but fast it falls, and fades away:
White is the snow—but it melts from earth's face where it lay:
Lovely the loveliness of youth—yet lives but for a day.

(Idylls, XXIII, 28–32.)

AUTÓMEDON OF AETOLIA or THEOCRITUS

(3rd century B.C. ?)

Ill Merchandise

O man, on thyself have mercy.   What madness bids ye follow
  The sea, when the year grows stormy.   Too fast, at best, life flies.
In haste for shining Thăsos, from Syria the Hollow,
  Unhappy Cleonīcus, you sailed with merchandise.
Ill merchandise, Cleonīcus!   You that sailed recklessly
As the Pleiad set, with the Pleiad yourself sank under sea.

(Anth. Pal., VII, 534.)

NĬCIAS OF MILĒTUS

(early 3rd century B.C.)

This poet-physician was a friend of Theócritus, who addressed two of his *Idylls* to him, and another to his wife, with the gift of an ivory distaff.

The Wayside Fount

Traveller the long way wearies, under my poplars seat thee;
   Draw near and to my waters bow down thy thirsty head.
And far away, hereafter, still may my memory greet thee.
   Me Sīmus made for Gillus, his son, that here lies dead.

(Anth. Pal., IX. 315.)

DIOTĪMUS or LEONIDAS OF TARENTUM

(4th–3rd century B.C.)

Lightning

Unherded came the cattle from the hills with falling even,
   Home to the byre, and about them the snow-drifts gathered deep.
But under an oak their herdsman lay.   For fire from Heaven,
   In the night that knows no waking, had stretched him there asleep.

(Anth. Pal., VII, 173.)

LEONIDAS OF TARENTUM

(early 3rd centnry B.C.)

Leōnidas celebrates in one of his epigrams a victory won in 274 B.C. by
that Pyrrhus of Epīrus who had vainly tried to save the poet's native
Tarentum from Rome.   He seems also to have wandered to the Eastern
Mediterranean and may possibly be portrayed in the 'Lycidas' of Theócritus' seventh *Idyll*.   Poor himself, he wrote many of his poems on the
poor.   'Love had he found in huts where poor men lie.'

The Cricket's Grave

Though little be the tombstone, O passer-by, above me,
   Though it lies thus lowly in the dust before your feet,
Give honour to Phīlaenis, good friend, that she did love me,
   Her once wild thistle-climber, her clamberer in the wheat,
Her cricket, her sweet songster, whom for two years she cherished,
   Loving the sleepy music of my whirring wing.
She has not forgot me: she gave me, when I perished,
   This tiny tomb in honour of so versatile a thing.

(Anth. Pal., VII, 198.)

The Goatherds' Thank-offering

Athwart the whirling hailstones, through the darkness of December,
  Fleeing from the headlong blizzard and the bitter cold that kills,
A lonely lion and ancient, and gaunt in every member,
  Came down on a fold of the goatherds that haunt high up the hills.
They cowered, their goats forgotten, with the fear of death before them,
  And unto Zeus the Saviour wildly they turned to pray;
But that great beast of the darkness sat out the storm, nor tore them,
  Nor fell upon their cattle, but stalked from the fold away.
And so for Zeus of the Hilltops, they raised in memory
That marvel fairly painted upon this stout oak-tree.

(VI, 221.)

The Shepherd's Last Sleep

Shepherds all, that wander this ridge of the mountains, feeding
  Your flocks of goats and fleecy sheep, grant now to me,
Cleitágoras, a little boon yet kindly, heeding
  My prayer in the name of Earth and Queen Persephone.
Let your sheep bleat still beside me, and sitting on a boulder
  Softly let pipe a shepherd to his flock that feeds beneath;
And let the countryman gather, ere each spring grows older,
  Rathe meadow-flowers and twine them to make my tomb a wreath;
And bring from the flock the mother of some fair lamb, and setting
  Her udder full of milk above my gravestone's base,
Let the white stream spirt upon it.   Deem not the grave forgetting;
  Even the dead can render a grace for a kindly grace.

(VII, 657.)

The Farmer's Rest

Spare to this humble hillock, this stone that stands so lowly,
  Where poor Alcímenes slumbers, one word in passing, friend,
Though beneath briar and bramble it now lies hidden wholly—
  Those same old foes that, living, I fought with to the end.

(VII, 656.)

POSEIDIPPUS

(3rd century B.C. ?)

The Courtesan to Aphrodite

O thou that hauntest Cyprus, and Milētus, and Cythēra,
  And that proud Syrian plain where the hammering horsehoofs roar,
Let Calliston, O Goddess, of Thy grace to Thee be dearer;
  Never she turned a lover, disdainful, from her door.

(Anth. Pal., XII, 131.)

Sappho

Long since your bones have mouldered; long, Dōricha, the binding
  Of your curls, long all the fragrance from your robe has passed away,
That you flung round fair Chăraxus and caught him in its winding
  And breast to breast lay drinking, at the dawning of the day.
But the white page of Sappho lives on and lives for ever,
  Breathing in its sweetness your name thrice-blest the while,
That Naucrătis shall remember while ships shall breast her river,
  Standing in from seaward to the long lagoons of Nile.

(Athenaeus, XIII, 596C.)

ASCLEPIADES OF SAMOS

(early 3rd century B.C.)

Asclēpĭādes is praised by Theócritus as a master-poet, together with
Philētas; and his work compared by Meleāger, in his garland of poets, to
'wind-flowers.'

The Coy Mistress

Your maidenhead—you grudge it?—for what?   Beyond Death's river
  You will find no lover waiting, lass, the day you die,
Love's joys are for the living.   In Hades' house for ever,
  Ashes and bone, proud maiden, we shall slumber, you and I.

(*Anth. Pal.*, V, 85.)

Joy's Crown of Joy

O sweet is snow to June-parched lips; when winter's over,
  Sweet the west wind of springtime to sailors o'er the sea;
Yet sweeter beneath one mantle when lover lies by lover
  And both, O Love, breathe blessings upon the name of Thee.

(V, 169.)

Light Love

With Hermíone the witching as I played once, she was wearing
  A girdle of many colours, O Love, about her waist,
Broidered in golden letters—'Love me!   Yet no despairing,
  If you behold my beauty by a new love's arms enlaced!'

(V, 158.)

318

Bitter-Sweet

Ah me, once Archeädes pressed near and ever nearer;
 To-day, not even in play our glances meet again.
Not even Love the honeyed is always sweet; yet dearer
 Often he grows to lovers, when his joy has turned to pain.

(XII, 153.)

'Fill the Can and Fill the Cup'

Drink, drink, Asclēpïädes.   What use to wail your sorrows?
 Are you the first that Cypris beneath her heel hath thrust?
Your heart the first that felt how grim Love whets his arrows
 And bends his bow for smiting?   You live.   Why gnaw the dust?
Come, pour the wine!—no water!   Look, in the east, Dawn's finger!
 Must we wait for the laggard lantern that bids men bedward creep?
Then here's a health, wan lover.   Brief, brief our time to linger,
 Poor fool, ere we are lying, night without end, asleep.

(XII, 50.)

NOSSIS

(c. 300 B.C.)

A poetess of Locri in South Italy.

The Rose of Love

Than love there's nothing sweeter.   No joys are worth the weighing
 Beside it.   Even honey I spit from off my tongue.
Whom Love's Queen never kissed—I, Nossis, leave this saying—
 She knows not what the rose is the summer's flowers among.

(Anth. Pal., V, 170.)

ÁNYTE OF TEGEA

(early 3rd century B.C.?)

A poetess of whom little remains; but some of it gifted with an effortless
simplicity worthy of her native Arcadia.

The Spring of Hermes

Beside the grey sea-shingle, here at the cross-roads' meeting,
 I, Hermes, stand and wait, where the windswept orchard grows.
I give, to wanderers weary, rest from the road and greeting:
 Cool and unpolluted from my spring the water flows.

(Anth. Pal., IX. 314.)

Never again rejoicing in the surges that I sunder
  Shall I toss my neck aloft, as I leap from gulfs of sea;
Nor, circling round a galley, at its fair prow snort with wonder,
  Proud to find it fashioned in the shape of me.
For the dark-blue rollers hurled me high on the land's dry breast
And in this narrow shingle I am laid to rest.

(VII, 215.)

Death the Leveller

In life, Mānēs the slave; but, since he died,
As great as King Darīus in his pride.

(VII, 538.)

APOLLONIUS RHODIUS

(*c.* 280–*c.* 200 B.C.)

Apollonius, poet, scholar, and finally librarian of Alexandria, was a native of that city, and appears to have withdrawn for a time to Rhodes in consequence of his famous quarrel with Callímachus as to whether poems should be long or short. His attempt to revive the glories of the epic with his *Argonautica* (5,835 lines) hardly proved his case; for that poem lives to-day, not as a whole, but by episodes like Mēdēa's love for Jason. With all his learning, Apollonius lacked the art to give his story a unity like Homer's; it seems too long; yet even so he omits some of the most moving incidents of the original legend—the coming of the young Jason to Iolcus, so magnificently told by Pindar (p. 264); the final quarrel with Mēdēa, on which Euripides wrote his tragedy; and the death of the hero, struck by the falling sternpost of Argo, which forms the fitting close of Morris's *Jason*. These human touches are ill replaced by deserts of fabulous geography and antiquarianism. The strength of Apollonius lies in his power of romantic description, above all in his picture of Mēdēa's passion, which was one day to help Virgil in creating Dido. When this bookish poet turns to analyse the growth of love in a girl's heart, her hesitations, her conflicts, his own heart strangely quickens and he becomes a forerunner not only of Virgil, but of medieval romance and the modern novel. Only one character of his epic lives; to her it owes what life it still retains.

The Sailing of Argo

Pélias usurped the kingdom of Iolcus from his brother Aeson; but Aeson's infant son, Jason, was brought up by the centaur Chīron on Mount Pēlion. Growing to manhood, the young hero descended to Iolcus to reclaim the throne;

*but his uncle impelled him first to sail to Colchis in the Black Sea and bring back
the Golden Fleece of the winged ram which had once borne their cousin Phrixus
to the Colchian land. For this quest Jason gathered the greatest heroes of all
Greece; and for them was built the ship Argo, whence their name of Argonauts.*

But far astern of Argo her whitening wake was seen,
As when a footpath glimmers amid the meadows' green;
And the Gods gazed down from Heaven on the vessel and her crew
Of race divine, the noblest that then the sea-ways knew;
From highest peaks of Pēlion the Nymphs that lurk
Within his glens, looked wondering on Athene's handiwork
And all the heroes in her, heaving at the oar;
But down from the mountain's summit came Chīron to the shore
And stood there up to the fetlocks, where frothed the grey sea's foam,
To wish them, with great hand waving, a glad returning home;
While the Centaur's wife beside him held high above the swell
In her arms the babe Achilles, for his father's last farewell. . . .
Then over the watery pathways, up from the gulfs of sea,
Little and great, the fishes came gambolling merrily.
As when behind their shepherd, filled with sweet grass, his sheep
Troop in their countless thousands home to the fold to sleep—
Gaily he goes before them, playing a shepherd's song
Sweet and shrill on the pipe of Pan; so dense a throng
Of fishes followed Argo, as the fresh breeze filled her sail.
Soon there sank from sight behind them, misty-pale,
The rich Pelasgian corn-lands; racing down the bay,
They watched the mountain-walls of Pēlion pass away.
Cape Sēpias sank.   Before them Peirésiae rose afar,
And, clear in the summer sunlight, the coasts of Magnesia,
And Scíathus' isle, and the barrow where Dŏlops lies beneath—
That evening, there they landed, for the wind turned in their teeth.

(*Argonautica*, I, 545–58, 572–86.)

*When they reached Colchis its king, Aeētes, would only give up the Fleece if
Jason could first yoke two fire-breathing bulls, plough with them the Field of
Ares, sow it with dragon's teeth, and slay the earth-born warriors who sprang up
from that seed.   That task would have been impossible even for Jason, had not
Mēdēa, the king's daughter, fallen in love with the young stranger.*

The Heart-searchings of Mēdēa

Now night drew darkness over earth; far out at sea
Sailors aboard their ships were watching Hélice
And the stars that shape Orion—the traveller on his way,
And by his gate the porter, felt drowsy—slumber lay

On the eyes of the mother, even, whose little ones had died.
Hushed was the city's echoing roar; no watchdog cried,
Now, through the streets; the gloom, fast thickening, grew dumb.
And yet to the eyes of Mēdēa no such sweet sleep would come.
For still her love of Jason, and sorrow for his sake,
And fear of the bulls in their giant strength, held her awake—
Sure, in that field of Ares, miserably lost,
The youth would die! With torment, the heart in her was tossed,
As round a room the sunlight is flung back from the face
Of water in pail or cauldron poured—in endless chase
Headlong hither and thither its sparkles wheel and whirl;
So leapt her heart, and quivered, in the bosom of the girl.
With pitying tears her eyes grew wet; and all her frame
Shuddered with inward anguish as with a smouldering flame.
Through each fine nerve, through the meeting of head and nape, it pressed
(For there the ache is keenest, when the Loves that know not rest,
Let loose upon men's hearts the arrows of their pain).
Now she resolved to reveal him her magic—now again
Resolved she would not give it; but die herself as well—
Then vowed she would neither perish nor yet bestow the spell,
But still endure to the end, dumb though infatuate.
So down she sat and said, her soul torn with debate:
'Ah, wretch! To what choice of evils must I turn me in my grief?
Whatever I do, my spirit fails, nor finds relief.
Nothing can quench its fever. Ah, would that Artemis
With the swiftness of her arrows had struck me down ere this!—
Or ever I looked on Jason, or the sons of Chalcíope
Set foot on the coasts of Achaea! To bring us misery
Some God, or some Erīnys, has sent them here again.
Nay then, let Jason perish, if destiny ordain
His death in the field of Ares! If I fashion him the spell,
How hide it from my parents? What story can I tell?
What stratagem can save him from being overthrown?
Can I meet him without his comrades?—can I go to him alone?
Ah bitter, although he perish, e'en then what hope have I
Of respite from unhappiness?—though he should die,
His memory will haunt me still. Nay now, have done
With shame, have done with honour! Once that my hand has won
His life, let him sail in safety—wherever he would be!
And then, his quest accomplished, let *that* day bring to me
Death!—no matter whether from a beam of the roof I sway,
Throat in a noose; or swallow some poison swift to slay.
And yet, although I perish so, they will heap my name
With insults—ay, every city shall shout aloud my shame,

Through many a land!   And here, from tongue to taunting tongue
Of all the Colchian women, shall my ill fame be flung—
"A girl that in her passion for a stranger's foreign face
Died covering her parents and her home with black disgrace,
A lewd and blinded wanton!"   What scorn must I not bear!
Ay me for this infatuate heart!   Better it were
This night in my maiden chamber should make an end of me,
Dead none knows how, delivered from all their calumny,
Rather than such dishonour—too foul for lips to say.'
With that she sought, arising, a casket wherein lay
Her many drugs—some healing, and some of deadly bane,
And on her knees she set it down, while in her pain
For the fate now come upon her, her tears streamed on unstayed,
Till wet grew all her bosom.   Now her resolve was made
To choose some deadly venom there—to taste and die;
Unhappy lass, already she was turning to untie
With feverish hands the coffer—yet suddenly there fell
Upon her spirit horror of the hateful gloom of Hell.
Long dazed and speechless there she sat—now rose up clear
Before her eyes, in vision, the joys that make life dear.
She thought again of the pleasures that gladden the living still,
She thought of her gay companions—as a maiden will;
And as she recalled all these, with longing, one by one,
Sweeter it seemed, once more, to look upon the sun,
And she put aside the casket from off her knees again,
Swayed by the will of Hēra.   And now her plan grew plain.

(III, 744–819.)

Accordingly Mēdēa met Jason in the temple of Hecate.

So without voice, without murmur, they stood there face to face,
As oaks or towering pine-trees stand rooted in their place,
Side by side, unmoving, high up among the hills,
When winds are hushed—but, sudden, a gust through their branches
      thrills
And they whisper with infinite voices.   So now before Love's gale
Those two were doomed, in a moment, to tell their whole hearts' tale.

(III, 967–72.)

*Then Jason begged her to help him; as Ariadne, daughter of Minos king of
Crete and Queen Pasíphaë, once helped Theseus in his danger, and reconciled
her father to him and sailed away aboard his ship, to find undying glory and a
place among the stars.*

So he spoke in her honour.   Downward she cast her gaze,
With a smile like the Gods' own nectar; and, kindled by his praise,
Her heart was melted in her.   Once more his eyes she met,
Not knowing, of all she must tell him now, what word to set
First—for all together they crowded to her tongue.
Irresolute no longer, she drew from where it hung
By her fragrant waist, the magic charm; and swift and glad
He grasped it.   She would have taken the very life she had
Within her breast, to give him; happy in his desire—
So dazzling, from Jason's golden head, Love flashed his own sweet fire.
For indeed the youth had stolen her own bright eyes away
And the heart within her wasted, as wastes in morning's ray
The dewdrop on a roseleaf.   Now on the ground they cast
Their eyes, ashamed—now, between them, looks swift and sudden passed,
With lovelight in their glances and radiance in their smile;
Then, faltering, spoke the maiden, that dumb had stood this while:
'Listen now, while I tell thee the succour I have planned.
When thou hast gone to my father and taken at his hand
Those deadly teeth from the Dragon's jaw, that thou must sow,
Wait, until half the night is gone, and half is still to go;
Then wash thee in the waters of the river's tireless speed
And alone, far from thy comrades, clad in a sable weed,
Thou shalt dig a hole in a circle's shape, and in the pit
A new-grown ewe thou shalt slaughter—hew not the flesh of it,
But burn it whole on a pyre, by the pit's edge mounded high.
On Hecate, only-begotten of Perses, thou shalt cry
And pour from a cup the sweetness wrought by the hiving bee;
But when thou hast duly prayed her to look with grace on thee,
Then from the blazing pyre draw back—and let no sound
Of footsteps, no dogs' baying, tempt thee to turn around,
Or look behind, lest the rites that thou hast wrought be vain
And in evil case to thy comrades thou go thy ways again.
But steep this charm in water, as breaks the morning light,
And smear it, like oil, on thy naked limbs—then infinite
Thy strength shall wax, till thou feelest in battle thou art peer
Not merely of men, but of deathless Gods.   And on thy spear
Spread it, on sword and buckler—no lance of earth-born men
Shall pierce thee, no flame resistless have power upon thee, then,
Breathed from those grim bulls' nostrils.   Only a little while
Thou shalt be thus—for a single day; but from thy trial
Flinch not!   And this I tell thee, to help thee in thy need:
When thou hast yoked yon raging bulls, and ploughed with speed,

By thy valour and thy manhood, the length of that stubborn field,
And sown are the teeth of the Dragon, and thou seest rise revealed
The Giants from the dusky furrows, thick as the corn in spring,
Then cast a great stone among them, by stealth!—and, as ravening
Hounds for their meat do battle, they too shall turn to smite
Each other.   Then plunge, thyself, headlong into the fight.
So, far away from Aea, thou shalt bear the Fleece with thee
To Hellas home—wherever thou wilt—wherever thy heart would be.'

So she spoke, and in silence her eyes on the earth she cast,
And down her perfect cheeks the hot tears hurried fast,
In grief to think in a little he must launch across the main,
Far from her side.   Then, anguished, she spoke to him again,
Searching his face, and seizing his hand in her distress—
For now no more her glances were bowed in bashfulness:
'And yet, if thou comest, ever, safe to thy home one day,
Remember the name of Mēdēa.   And when thou art far away,
I will remember also.   But I beg thee, tell me where
Thy home is?   Across the waters whither wilt thou fare?
To Orchómenus the wealthy shall thy journey bring thee near?
Or the island of Aeaea?   And who then—tell me clear—
Who was this famous maiden—the child of Pasíphaë?
For unto the king, my father, sister by blood was *she.*'

Such were her words; but, in Jason, the maiden's tears awoke
The pitiless power of passion; and thus in turn he spoke:
'Surely I cannot think it, that either by night or day
I ever shall forget thee, if home I find my way,
From death escaped unscathed, back to Achaea's shore,
And Aeētes does not set us some worse trial than before.
But if, indeed, thou askest where my own country is,
Listen—for no less happy am I to tell thee this.
There lies a land—and, around it, rise up the mountains wild—
Rich in fair flocks and pastures, where once Iápetus' child,
Prometheus, had for offspring the noble Deucálion,
Who was the first of menfolk to sit on a kingly throne.
Shrines to the Gods, and cities, he too was first to found.
"Haemónia," that land is called, by all the dwellers round.
There my own home, Iolcus, stands; and there as well
Many another township.   Their peoples ne'er heard tell
Of the name of Aeaea's island; but Mínyas, 'tis told,
Mínyas, sprung of Aeŏlus' line, went thence of old
And built Orchómenus once, nigh the Cadmēan wall.
And yet why talk of things that matter not at all?—
Of my home?—of Ariadne, King Minos' child far-famed?
(For so indeed that maiden of high renown was named,

Of whom thou bad'st me tell thee.)   As Minos, for his child,
Loved Theseus, I would thy father with *us* were reconciled.'
    So Jason spoke to soothe her, with words of gentleness;
But bitterly she answered, angry and comfortless,
While within her spirit all pain and passion stirred:
'In Greece, maybe, it is honour to keep a plighted word.
But not such is Aeëtes, as the lord of Pasíphaë,
King Minos, by thy telling was.   Nor liken me
To Theseus' love.   Nay, talk not of hospitality!
I say but this—when thou comest at last to Iolcus, still
Remember me!   And I—despite my parents' will—
I shall remember, always.   May there come from far away
Some word, some bird of message, to tell me, on the day
Thou shalt forget!—or a tempest upon its stormwings sweep
My body hence to Iolcus, far out across the deep—
There to reproach thee, face to face, that from this land
'Twas I alone that saved thee once!   Ay, let me stand,
A sudden guest, undreamed-of, that day by thy fireside!'
    With that the tears burst from her and miserably she cried;
But quickly Jason answered: 'Ah, lady, let thy birds,
Thy storm-winds wander where they will.   All idle words!
If ever thou comest thither, to Hellas, thou shalt then
Be honoured among women, reverenced of men.
Like to a God they shall worship thee; because for some,
Thanks to thy wit, safe homeward once more their sons are come;
Loved husbands some shall owe thee, or their brothers, or their kin,
Delivered from destruction.   Then shalt thou make within
My bedchamber thy bridal-bed; the love we plight,
Nothing shall break, till round us Death draws the last long night.'

                                                            (III, 1008–1130.)

THEODŌRIDAS OF SYRACUSE

(later 3rd century B.C.)

On a Shipwrecked Sailor

Here lies one that made shipwreck.   But thou, sail on.   The day
We foundered, other vessels still kept their onward way.

                                                            (*Anth. Pal.*, VII, 282.)

DĀMĀGĒTUS
(3rd–2nd century B.C.)

The Last Word

O famed Phocaean city, with this last cry despairing
   Theāno passed to the darkness wherein no man may reap:
'Apellichus my husband—ah bitterness past bearing!—
   Where *are* you, in your galley far off across the deep?
So close stands Death beside me—would but to God that I
Could feel your hand, to hold it, dear heart, before I die.'
                                 (*Anth. Pal.*, VII, 735.)

THỲMOCLES
(3rd–2nd century B.C. ?)

'*And Left the Thorn*'

Maybe now you remember my solemn warning given:
   'Sweet is the hour of blooming, the hour of bloom is fleet—
So fleet it can outsoar the swiftest bird in Heaven.'
   Lo, on the earth, already, your flower lies at your feet.
                                   (*Anth. Pal.*, XII, 32.)

PHAEDIMUS OF BISANTHE
(3rd–2nd century B.C. ?)

Lost at Sea

I mourn for Polyanthus, who died new-wed, O stranger;
   Here his young wife laid him, Aristágore;
The Aegean surges sank him by Scíathus in their anger,
   And nought but bone and dust came home to her from sea.
For that ill-fated body, as dawn was breaking through,
Into Torōne's haven, O friend, the fishers drew.
                                   (*Anth. Pal.*, VII, 739.)

ANON
(late 3rd century B.C. ?)

The Humbling of Sparta

Lacedaemon, land unconquered, that no foeman's foot molested,
   Lo now the destroyers' campfires by Eurōtas smoking high!
Felled lie thy trees; on shadeless fields thy birds have nested,
   Crying; but the wolves that listen hear now no sheepfolds cry.
                                   (*Anth. Pal.*, VII, 723.)

DIONYSIUS THE SOPHIST
(2nd century B.C.?)

The Rose-girl

Rose-girl, fair as a rose is, what do you come to sell?
Is it yourself, or your roses? Or them and yourself as well?

(Anth. Pal., v, 81.)

ANTÍPATER OF SIDON
(later 2nd century B.C.)

A Greek poet who moved in Roman society and is mentioned by Cicero.

The Vengeance of the Nymphs

The hunting-hound of Midas, Lampon, perished thirsting,
    Though in the face of death fiercely and hard he fought.
With his paws he dug where the earth lay damp; but no stream came bursting,
    So deep, in its sluggard darkness, slept that blind spring he sought.
Too late, as he sank down lifeless, it flowed. Ah, surely you
Were angered, O Nymphs, with Lampon for all the deer he slew.

(Anth. Pal., IX, 417.)

Himself He could not Save

Dāmis the Nysaean of a little bark was master,
    Bound from Ionian waters south to Pĕlops' shore.
Out of her course and reckoning wild seas and storm-winds cast her,
    But safe with all aboard her he brought her in once more.
Yet, as their anchor gripped the rocks, escaped from danger,
    The old man's head sank forward, chilled by that snow-swept gloom:
To the haven where they would be, he brought those others, stranger,
    But himself made fast for ever within the Port of Doom.

(Anth. Pal., VII, 498.)

The Poetess Erinna

Terse-tongued and sparely worded was the singing of Erinna,
    And yet on those brief pages the Muses' blessing came;
Therefore the memory fails not, that her words had power to win her,
    No shadowy wing of darkness casts night upon her name;
While we, earth's latter singers, O stranger, are left lying
    To moulder unremembered, in heaps past numbering.
Better the muted music of the swan than all the crying
    Of jackdaws chattering shrilly across the clouds of spring.

(VII, 713.)

The Sea-birds crying above the Ruins of Corinth

Where are the towers that crowned thee, the wealth that filled thy portals,
  Thy beauty, Dorian Corinth, whereon men stood to gaze?
Thy proud dames sprung from Sisyphus, thy shrined Immortals,
  Thy palaces, the myriads that swarmed along thy ways?
Not a trace, not a trace, unhappy, hast thou left behind in falling—
  All has been seized and ravened by the wild throat of war.
We only, Ocean's children, are still left calling, calling,
  The sea-birds of thy sorrows, along thy lonely shore.

(IX, 151.)

Orpheus

No more shall stones nor oakwoods on thy sweet music follow,
  Nor the beasts that know no shepherd—O Orpheus, never again.
Never again shalt thou lull asleep the stormwind's hollo,
  Nor the hail, nor the driving blizzard, nor the booming of the main.
Now thou art dead.   All the daughters of Memory went wailing
  Loud for thy loss; and loudest, thy mother, Calliope.
Why groan for our children perished, when we see how unavailing
  Even the Gods to hinder their sons' mortality?

(VII, 8.)

BION OF SMYRNA
(later 2nd century B.C.)

Bion, who seems to have moved from Smyrna to Sicily, is one of the last Greek bucolic poets, writing Idylls (not merely pastorals) in the tradition of Theócritus.   The *Lament for Bion*, translated below, states that he was poisoned by jealous rivals.   His best-known poem (if really his) is the passionate but florid *Lament for Adonis*; the amusing trifle printed first here is much closer to the *Anacreontea*, or to the Cupids in the Pompeian House of the Vettii.

Love Hunted

A lad that was a fowler, deep in a leafy grove
Was stalking birds, when lo, he spied the wingéd Love,
Sitting high up on a box-tree bough.   Then at the sight,
Thinking how fine a bird was here, in wild delight
One within another he fixed each jointed rod
And hither stalked, and thither, the flutterings of the God—
Till at last the lad in anger that he could not catch his prey,
Threw down his reeds, and ran to a ploughman old and grey,

Who first had taught him fowling; and when his tale was said,
Pointed where Love was sitting.   But the ancient shook his head,
And smiled at the boyish hunter, and answered him—'Beware
Of that same bird—and seek not to hunt him, nor to snare.
It is a savage creature.   Shun him; and well for thee,
So long as thou failst to catch him—once thou art man, then he
That flees away so nimbly, shall no more flee at all,
But turn unsought of a sudden and on thy head shall fall.'

(J. M. Edmonds, Greek Bucolic Poets, IV.)

Love's Tryst

Hesper, thou golden light of Love's Queen sprung from the sea,
Hesper beloved, thou glory of Night's black mystery,
Brighter the moon than thou art, yet bright art thou above
All other stars—I greet thee.   To the shepherd that I love
As I go serenading, in the moon's stead light the sky;
For her new crescent is set too soon.   No thief am I,
I do not seek through the darkness travellers for my prey;
I love.   And 'tis to thy honour to help love on its way.

(IX.)

ANON

LAMENT FOR BION

(later 2nd century B.C.)

Homere est mort, Anacreon,
Pindare, Hesiode, et Bion,
Et plus n'ont souci de s'enquerre
Du bien et du mal qu'on dit d'eux.

Ronsard.

This *Lament for Bion* used to be attributed to Moschus of Syracuse, who, however, probably lived (*c.* 150 B.C.) before Bion.   Over-long and over-emphatic as it is in places, it remains one of the greatest of elegies, the model for more than one famous poem of after-times.   In the words of Andrew Lang:

And dirge to dirge that answers, and the weeping
    For Adonaïs by the summer sea,
The plaints for Lycidas and Thyrsis (sleeping
    Far from 'the forest ground called Thessaly')
These hold thy memory, Bion, in their keeping
    And are but echoes of the moan for thee.

330

For us, in a sense, these lines seem a dirge not only for a fallen poet, but for a fallen race—for the end of the poetry of a free Hellas.   The second century saw both Sicily and Greece itself prostrate beneath the eagles of Rome.

Lament for Bion

Weep, wooded glens; weep, Dorian wave; ye rivers, weep,
Lamenting Bion the lovely, that now is laid asleep.
Grieve, all ye green things growing; mourn now, ye forests all;
Defaced let all your flowers in withered clusters fall.
Grow deeper red with sorrow, rose and anemone;
Wild iris, thou that bearest 'Alas' inscribed on thee,
Grave it yet deeper—cry it!—the lord of song lies low.
   Lift loud, Sicilian Muses, lift loud your chant of woe.

Ye nightingales sad-singing, deep in each leafy tree,
Tell to Arethusa, where she flows through Sicily,
That dead is the herdsman Bion—that, now his race is run,
Poesy's self hath perished and Dorian song is done.
   Lift loud, Sicilian Muses, lift loud your chant of woe.

Wail out, ye swans of Strȳmon, by the waters where ye lie,
Raise the dirge above him with your own mournful cry—
Such notes as your own throats utter, when your years are waxen old.
By you be the Nymphs Bistónian and Oeagrus' daughters told
This bitter news—'the Orpheus of Dorian song lies cold.'
   Lift loud, Sicilian Muses, lift loud your chant of woe.

No more the cattle listen to hear his sweet voice ring;
No more by the lonely oak-trees he sits him down to sing;
His now is Lethe's music, in realms where Death is king.
In silence lie the mountains; the kine that roamed their ways
So happy, now stand lowing and lose the heart to graze.
   Lift loud, Sicilian Muses, lift loud your chant of woe.

For thy death untimely, Bion, Apollo's self bereaved
Wept; and black-clad Priāpi, and Satyrs for thee grieved;
The Pans of the wood lamented the ending of thy years;
The forest Naiads wailed thee, and their waters turned to tears.
Amid her rocks mourns Echo, sad that she sings no more,
Lacking thy songs to answer.   The day thy life was o'er,
The fruit fell from the orchards, no flowers were left alive,
No fair milk flowed from the udder, no honey from the hive.

There was death and dearth in the honeycomb.   Nay, what was left
Of sweet for men to gather, of *thy* honey bereft?
  Lift loud, Sicilian Muses, lift loud your chant of woe. . . .

Thy pipe who shall inherit, O poet past compare?
Who shall lay lip to *thy* sweet reed?   Ah who shall dare?
For there thine own lips' sweetness, thy fragrant breath abides,
And still within its hollows thy long-lost music hides.
To Pan shall I leave it hallowed?   Yet even His lips divine
May fear to wake its pipings, lest He fail to match with thine.
  Lift loud, Sicilian Muses, lift loud your chant of woe. . . .

With thee have perished, herdsman, all of the Muses' joys,
The lovely lips of maidens, the mouths of winsome boys.
The Loves with clouded faces about thy body cry;
Thy memory makes Cypris with a bitterer yearning sigh
Than her last kiss to Adonis, the day he came to die.
  Lift loud, Sicilian Muses, lift loud your chant of woe. . . .

Alas and alas, when the mallow dead in the garden lies,
Or the pale-green parsley withers, or the lush-curled anise dies,
Yet they rise anew and quicken when spring returns again.
But we the strong, the mighty, the wise, we sons of men,
When we die and the earth is o'er us, ah then how long, how deep,
Unhearing, unawaking, night without end we sleep!
Thou too, in silence huddled, now liest slumbering,
And yet the Nymphs still suffer the ceaseless frog to sing!
They are welcome!   Scant the beauty that *it* has power to bring.
  Lift loud, Sicilian Muses, lift loud your chant of woe.

Poison they gave thee, Bion, yea, poison at the last;
How turned it not to honey, as thy sweet lips it passed?
What heart could be so savage, for the songful lips of thee
To brew and bring his venom—hater of melody!
  Lift loud, Sicilian Muses, lift loud your chant of woe.

On *them*, at least, fell justice.   But still for thy darkened day
My tears flow on—ah if only my feet could find the way,
Like Orpheus I would have trodden the track to Hell below—
Like Hēracles, like Odysseus, in years of long ago—
In Hades again to see thee, again thy song to hear,
If yet for Death thou singest.   Ah, in Perséphone's ear
Pipe, sweet and shrill, some cowherd's tune from Sicily.

She too was once Sicilian—in Aetna's glens played she
And knows the Dorian music—thou canst not pipe in vain!
As to Orpheus, for his harping, of old she gave again
Eurydice, so thy pipings, O Bion, yet shall make
The Queen of Death restore thee to thy mountains.   Could I wake
Such music, I would go piping to Death's self for thy sake.

(*Lament for Bion.*)

ANACREONTEA

Love and my selfe (beleeve me) on a day
At childish Push-pin (for our sport) did play.
                                        Herrick.

This collection of Anacreontic imitations was long supposed to be the
genuine work of Anacreon, who thus paradoxically gained his immortality
largely by poems written after he was dead.   Internal evidence however
makes it clear that the pieces there assembled range in date from the second
or first century B.C. to Byzantine times.   Those given here may be roughly
placed between about 150 B.C. and 350 A.D.

Decadent of course they are; like the Amoretti on the walls of Pompeii,
they illustrate how beauty degenerates to prettiness.   But there is no need
to break butterflies because they are not eagles.   Grace is not contemptible
in a world that has none too much of it.   If the Renaissance overvalued
these gay trifles, modern critics have surely been too hard on work that could
inspire some of the most charming verse of poets like Ronsard or Herrick.

The Old Reveller

All the women tell me:
'Anacreon, you're old now.
Just look in your own mirror—
You'll see your hair has fallen
And bald is all your forehead.'
Of my hair I can say nothing,
Whether it's there or vanished;
But this at least I *do* know—
All the better reason
For the old man to be merry,
The closer Fate approaches.

(*Anacreontea,* 7.)

333

Vive Hodie

I ask not Gyges' riches,
The mighty Lord of Sardis;
Gold doth not bewitch me;
I have no praise for tyrants.
I only care for perfumes
To drench my beard with fragrance;
I only care for roses
To wreathe around my temples;
To-day is all I care for—
Who knows aught of to-morrow? ...

(8.)

Catalogue

If you can tell the number
Of leaves in all the forests,
Or count how many billows
Through all the seas go surging,
I 'll appoint you, and no other,
To be my loves' Recorder.
First, then, write in your reckoning
'Twenty loves from Athens—
With fifteen supplementary.'
And next, put down, 'From Corinth—'
Oh, simply strings of others.
For Corinth 's in Achaea,
That swarms with lovely women.
Then my affairs in Lesbos,
And downward to Ionia,
And Caria, and Rhŏdos—
They total some two thousand.
What!—lost your count already!
There 's Syria to come yet,
And my passions at Canōpus,
And Crete (in Crete there 's nothing
You cannot find—for Love there
Runs riot in every city).
And what of my statistics
Beyond the Straits of Gades,
And the times my heart forsook me
In Bactria and the Indies!

(14.)

334

'Come, fill the cup'

The black earth's always drinking,
There drink from earth the forests;
The sea drinks up the rivers,
The sun drinks from the ocean,
And the moon, she drinks the sunlight.
Then, why my friends, reproach me
If I share their taste for drinking?

(21.)

Beauty's Power

Nature gave horns to cattle,
And hoofs she gave to horses,
And nimble heels to rabbits;
To lions, mighty grinders,
And fins she gave to fishes;
To birds, their wings for flying,
To men, wise understanding.
Had she forgotten women?
Ah, no!—she gave them beauty,
Instead of shield and buckler,
In place of pikes and lances.
Ay, fire and sword are weaker
Than a pretty woman.

(24.)

Love's Nestlings

You, my dearest swallow,
Spring by spring returning,
Build your house for summer;
Winter comes—you vanish
Back to Nile or Memphis.
But Love in me sits making
His nest through *all* the seasons.
One Passion will be sprouting
His feathers; one, half-hatching;
One, in the egg-shell merely.
And from these greedy nestlings
Goes up a ceaseless babel.
In turn each little Passion
Is reared up by a bigger;
And, soon as grown, they set them,
To lay a clutch of new ones.
What *shall* I do about it?—
For such a buzz of Passions
Begins to leave me speechless!

(25.)

335

Love's Stratagem

Once in the hours of midnight,
When the Bear was wheeling
Alongside of Boötes,
And all the earthly nations
Lay locked in weary slumber,
To my bolted doorway
Eros came a-knocking.
'Who bangs so loud?' I shouted;
'Who breaks upon my dreaming?'
But Eros answered: 'Open!
I'm only—don't be frightened—
A little boy.   I'm lost, though,
And wet through in the darkness,
There's not a glint of moonlight.'
And so, just feeling sorry,
I rose at once, and lighted
A lamp, and went to open.
A little boy I saw there,
With bow, and wings, and quiver;
So by the fire I set him,
With my hands I warmed his fingers,
And from his hair all dripping
I wrung out streams of water.
But when he'd ceased to shiver,
'My bow!' he cried, 'let's try it,
To see if all that wetting
Has harmed at all my bowstring.'
He bent his bow—his arrow,
To the very heart it stung me.
Then up he jumped, loud laughing:
'My host, congratulate me!
My bow's all right—it's only
Your heart will give you trouble!'

(33.)

Cicada

Oh lucky you, cicada,
Singing in the tree-tops,
Happy as a monarch,
And tipsy with a dewdrop!
You are lord of all you look on,
Of all that ploughlands furnish,
Of all that woodlands foster.

336

His friend the farmer thinks you—
You never did him damage;
And all men pay you honour,
Sweet harbinger of summer!
Dearly the Muses love you,
And dearly, too, Apollo—
He gave your piercing music.
The years press not upon you,
O clever, earth-born songster;
No blood is yours, no sorrow—
You are all but an Immortal!

(34.)

Love and the Bee

Once Love among the roses
Touched a bee asleep there,
All unawares—it stung him.
Then loud and high he shouted
For that smarting in his finger;
Half running and half flying,
He fled to fair Cythēra,
And cried: 'I'm dying, mother!—
It's killed me and I'm dying.
A little serpent stung me,
All winged—"a bee" they call it,
The people in the country.'
But she answered: 'If a bee-sting
Can hurt you so, my Eros,
What do you think they suffer
Whom *you* sting with your arrows?'

(35.)

NOTES

III. ALEXANDRIAN PERIOD

ARATUS

[Page 298] *Fathers of the tadpole.* It is curious to see Greek poetry here for a moment attacked in its decline by the pompous periphrases characteristic of French and English neo-classic verse (e.g. 'the whisker'd vermin race').

[Page 298] *Along some jutting strand The chattering crow. . . .* Imitated by Virgil with magnificent alliteration (*Georgics*, I, 388–9):

> Tum cornix plena pluviam vocat improba voce
> Et sola in sicca secum spatiatur harena.

With ringing voice then calls for rain the unconscionable crow
And lonely stalks the sandbanks, with solemn steps and slow.

CALLIMACHUS

[Page 300] *The Bathing of Pallas.* Cf. Tennyson, *Tiresias.*

[Page 300] *Thespiae, Corōnēa, Háliartus.* Cities of Boeotia.

[Page 300] *Charīclo.* Wife of Euēres and mother of Teirésias (p. 188).

[Page 300] *Horse's Spring.* Hippocrēne (p. 227).

[Page 301] *Aristaeus and Cadmus' child.* The hunter Actaeon, son of Aristaeus by Cadmus' daughter Autónoë, catching sight of Artemis as she bathed on Cĭthaeron, was changed by the angry Goddess to a stag and rent by his own hounds.

[Page 301] *Labdácidae.* The royal house of Thebes. Labdăcus, grandson of its founder Cadmus, was father of Laĭus, the father of Oedipus.

[Page 301] *Him that gathers. . . .* Hades, who calls to him the nations of the dead.

[Page 302] *Envy.* A hit at Callímachus' rival Apollonius, upholder of long poems.

[Page 302] *Assyria's river.* Euphrates.

[Page 302] *The Dead Poet.* W. Cory's beautiful rendering of this ('They told me, Heraclitus, they told me you were dead') is probably the best-known version of any Greek epigram. Certainly it is not easy to equal. It is, however somewhat free; in the Greek, news of his friend's death is not directly *brought* to Callimachus—it merely transpires in the course of some conversation, as an event already distant—'*long since,* it seems, you rest.'

A poem by this Heraclītus, apparently, is *Anth. Pal.*, VII, 465.

[Page 303] *Cháridas.* Seemingly a philosopher. With epitaphs like this, and many others in the *Greek Anthology*, one may contrast the stupendous dictum of Wordsworth: 'Without the belief in immortality . . . neither monuments nor epitaphs . . . could have existed in the world.'

[Page 303] *Timon.* This half-legendary misanthrope, supposedly of the late fifth century B.C., is mentioned by Aristophanes and figures, nearly six centuries later, in the dialogues of Lucian.

[Page 304] *Pan*. See p. 258.

[Page 304] *Daphnis*, the legendary founder of Sicilian pastoral, was son of Hermes by a nymph who bore, or exposed, him in a grove of laurel (*daphne*), whence his name. He grew up a handsome neatherd, piping on the hills of Sicily and beloved by Apollo, Pan, and Priāpus, by nymphs and womankind. But he died young, either because he loved a nymph and was punished by her for infidelity with blindness; or (as here) because, like Hippolytus, he defied love and incurred the wrath of Aphrodite. She kindled in him a passion for a girl; but he resisted, until, against Aphrodite's wish, his heart broke.

[Page 304] *Sing*. Presumably in a low tone that will not disturb Pan as piping would; unless we suppose Pan's ear specially liable to be irritated by panpipes. For superstitious dread of the hush of noon among the hills cf. p. 258.

[Page 304] *Priāpus*. Rustic God of fertility.

[Page 305] *My deep dish*. Admirably discussed by A. S. F. Gow in *Journ. of Hell. Studies*, 1913, p. 207 ff. and in a note on this passage in his *Theocritus*. The Greek word here is *kissybion*, a type of vessel wide and rather shallow; 'deep,' therefore, must only mean 'deep of its kind.' (Odysseus offers wine to Polyphemus in one, p. 133.) Hence I have used 'dish'—cf. Shakespeare, *Rich. II*, iii, iii, 150: 'My figured goblets for a dish of wood.' The *interior* of the bowl seems to have the fisherman occupying a circle at its centre; the concentric ring between this inner circle and the bowl's rim would then be filled on one side by the woman and her two lovers, on the other by the boy and his two foxes. On the *outside*, we may picture the acanthus leaves rising all round from the bowl's base, while the ivy encircles its exterior above. Greek pottery provides instances of a very graceful ivy-pattern with alternating leaves and clusters of berries. The work here seems to be in coloured relief; possibly when waxed this would withstand moisture; but Gow suggests that Theócritus has transferred to wood the kind of work he had seen in metal. The general description recalls the more elaborate Shield of Achilles in Homer (also the Hēsiodic Shield of Hēracles).

[Page 305] *Calydnian*. Calydna or Calymnos is an Aegean island N. of Cos. Another reading gives 'Calydonian' (from Cálydon in Aetōlia).

[Page 305] *Where were ye?* Cf. Milton, *Lycidas*:

> Where were ye, Nymphs, when the remorseless deep
> Closed o'er the head of your loved Lycidas?

Similarly Shelley, *Adonais*:

> Where wert thou, mighty Mother, when he lay,
> When thy son lay, pierced by the shaft which flies
> In darkness?

To which Dr. Johnson might have replied by asking what had 'nymphs' to do with Edward King, or 'mighty Mothers' with John Keats. Here in Theócritus such an invocation seems less artificial; for, after all, Daphnis is the son of a nymph and Hermes, and himself beloved of nymph and Pan.

[Page 305] *Anāpus*. River flowing into Syracuse harbour.

[Page 305] *Ācis*. Now Fiume di Jaci; a river of Etna fabled to have sprung from the blood of the fair young Ācis, crushed by Polyphemus, his rival for the love of the sea-nymph Galatēa. The ancient name survives also in the neighbouring town of Aci Reale.

[Page 306] *Lion*. As exotic in Theócritus' Sicily as in Shakespeare's Arden;

though Herodotus mentions them even in fifth-century Macedonia as attacking Xerxes' baggage-camels.

[Page 306] *Hermes.* Daphnis' father.

[Page 306] *Priāpus*, as god of fertility, is here the cynic advocate of purely physical passion.

[Page 306] *The girl.* Whom Daphnis, in revolt against Aphrodite, refused to let himself love.

[Page 306] *He bore his bitter doom.* Cf. the stoicism of Sĭmaetha, p. 312.

[Page 307] *Diomēdes.* From whom Aphrodite fled at Troy (*Iliad*, v.).

[Page 307] *Arethusa.* A Nymph beloved by the hunter Alpheius in the Peloponnese. Fleeing to the isle of Ortygia, off Syracuse, she was turned into a spring. Alpheius himself then became the river that flows through Olympia, and plunged to reach her under the western sea. Her head, surrounded by dolphins, appears on some lovely coins of ancient Syracuse.

[Page 307] *Thymbris* (or Thybris). Perhaps a mountain N.W. of Syracuse.

[Page 307] *Maenălus* (5,115 feet). In Arcadia, sacred to Pan.

[Page 307] *Lycaeon* (4,660 feet). In Arcadia, with a temple of Pan and also an altar of Zeus, where human sacrifices were offered, perhaps as late as the Christian era.

[Page 307] *Hélice.* The nymph Callisto, mother by Zeus of Arcas, was changed into the Great Bear (Hélice), while her son became Arcturus or Boötes. Gow suggests that Theócritus is here recalling the tradition that Pan himself was son of Hélice and twin-brother of Arcas.

[Page 307] *Down its flood was borne.* Perhaps a reminiscence of the other legend that Daphnis, after being blinded, plunged from a cliff into the sea.

[Page 308] *Aegĭlus.* On the W. coast of S. Attica, and famous for its figs.

[Page 308] *Cicada.* See p. 87.

[Page 308] *The Sorceress.* Sĭmaetha, helped by her maid Thestӯlis, tries witchcraft to win back her lover Delphis.

[Page 308] *Hecate*, Artemis, and Selēne (the Moon), are three aspects—infernal, terrestrial, celestial—of the same divinity.

[Page 308] *Perimēde.* Perhaps the same as Agamēde, a famous sorceress, daughter of that Augeas whose notorious stable was cleansed by Heracles.

[Page 308] *My wheel.* For the whole magic technique see Gow, *Theocritus*, and his article in *Journ. of Hell. Studies*, 1934, p. 1 ff. The wheel has a string threaded through two holes near its centre, and the ends tied; by holding the end of a loop in each hand, with the wheel in the middle, and alternately pulling and slackening, the wheel is rotated back and forth. This little engine the Greeks called *iynx*, lit. 'wryneck.' The bird of that name, belonging to the woodpecker family, at mating-time curiously writhes its neck, as if to attract its mate; and it was obvious sympathetic-magic to spreadeagle one of these unfortunate fowl on a magic wheel, as a love-charm (Pindar says Aphrodite first invented it to make Mēdēa love Jason); later, the wheel alone was used, without the bird, but still with the bird's name. A. R. Burn (*World of Hesiod*, p. 83) quotes a charm used by N. African Arabs to recover a runaway slave—a beetle tethered by a string to a nail. As the beetle walks round and round, continually shortening his tether, so the fugitive will be drawn home.

The incantation that follows here has the magic number of nine quatrains.

[Page 309] *Beat—quickly!—on the brass.* The conjuror has to be on his guard against the dangerous spirits he conjures up. The howl of dogs betrays Hecate's coming: the brass is to keep her from coming too perilously near.

[Page 309] *Wax.* Cf. D. G. Rossetti, *Sister Helen*: 'Why did you melt your waxen man?' The magic use of puppets is old as Ancient Egypt and a case was reported in the Highlands as recently as 1909 (see also Frazer, *Golden Bough*,

1, 66 ff.).   But here, of course, the wax is not necessarily shaped into a figure; it may be used simply as a substance, like the barley, laurel, and bran.

[Page 309]   *Myndian.*   From Myndus on the coast of Caria.

[Page 309]   *Roarer.*   *Rhombos,* 'bull-roarer,' as used by Australian natives; a long rectangle of wood whirled round on a string (it can also be made diamond-shaped, or of metal).   See Index to Frazer, *Golden Bough,* under 'bull-roarer.'

[Page 309]   *Dīa.*   Naxos, where Theseus forsook Minos' daughter Ariadne, who had saved him from the Labyrinth.

[Page 309]   *Horsewort.*   Greek *hippomanes,* 'horse-maddener.'

[Page 310]   *Helichryse.*   Our Goldflower or Goldilocks, a plant with yellow flower-clusters, used for garlands.

[Page 310]   *Dye of Thapsus.*   From a shrub producing a yellow dye, said to be found at Thapsus, near Syracuse.

[Page 311]   *I grew cold, etc.*   Cf. Sappho, p. 245.

[Page 311]   *With eyes downcast.*   Like the very different Odysseus, p. 20.

[Page 311]   *Philīnus.*   Probably an allusion to a real athlete, Philīnus of Cos, who won the stadium at Olympia in 264 and 260, as well as many other events.

[Page 311]   *Apples of Dionysus.*   Presumably love-symbols, cf. p. 277. Dionysus was a god of fruitful trees, not only of the vine.

[Page 311]   *Poplar beloved of Hēracles.*   He was supposed to have brought the white poplar to Greece from the banks of Ácheron in the N.W.

[Page 311]   *Torches.*   Perhaps not only for light, but also to burn the lintel at the point where the door turned in it.

[Page 311]   *Lípara.*   The Aeolian (now Lipari) islands are volcanic; two, Híera and Strongўle (now Vulcano and Stromboli), being active.

[Page 312]   *The Festival.*   In this poem one Simíchidas (apparently Theócritus himself) describes his walk with a friend to a winnowing festival (July or August) in Cos.   On the way he meets the goatherd Lycidas (possibly a disguise for a fellow-poet) and the pair have a friendly singing-match.   The close, given here, pictures the actual festival at the farm.   The piece has been thought a memory of the days when Theócritus, Leōnidas of Tarentum, Asclēpīădes, Nīcias, and others formed a school of young poets round Philētas (p. 297).   But this is guessing (see Gow, *Theocritus* and his article in *Classical Quarterly,* 1940, p. 47 ff.).

Like Homer's similes, this passage proves that, when they chose, the Greeks could be second to none in appreciating, and describing, natural beauty.

[Page 312]   *Phōlus.*   A centaur, son of Silēnus by a nymph.   Dionysus, when Phōlus adjudged him the isle of Naxos, which was claimed also by Hephaestus, rewarded him with a jar of wine—to be opened only when Hēracles should come. Four generations later Hēracles duly came.   But when the jar was broached, the other centaurs crowded to the scent and a battle followed in which Hēracles slew many of the intruders and among them, by accident, the wise Chīron, who could only escape from his agony and die, by surrendering his immortality to Prometheus.   Phōlus too perished by picking up in curiosity one of Hēracles' arrows, poisoned with the Hydra's venom, and dropping it on his own foot.

[Page 312]   *Anāpus.*   See p. 339.

[Page 312]   *With your spring.*   The Greeks were sensitive to the qualities of water from different sources and its suitability for mixing with wine.   I have heard of modern villagers on Pēlion debating the merits of their rival springs.

[Page 312]   *Fan.*   Winnowing-fan, like a broad-bladed oar (cf. p. 147).

[Page 312]   *While She stands.*   Probably some festival-effigy of the Corn-mother (see Frazer, *Golden Bough,* VII, 208, 135, 151 etc.).

[Page 312]   *Poppies.*   Though it makes the picture less beautiful, truth must add that these were probably poppy-*heads,* which it was customary to give to

Demeter; not poppy-*flowers*. In Cos the poppy blooms as early as April and would be over in August.

[Page 313] *Nīcias*. Physician, poet, and friend of Theócritus (see p. 315).

[Page 313] *Son of Amphītryon*. Hēracles.

[Page 313] *Mīdeia*. The city of Electryon, Alcmēna's father, on a hill of some 800 feet on the E. edge of the Argive plain. In this neighbourhood in 1926 was found an unplundered Mycenaean beehive-tomb, with a buried king, queen, and princess. See A. W. Persson, *The Royal Tombs at Dendra*.

[Page 313] *Clashing Rocks*. The Symplēgades, two moving rocks near the Bosphorus, which crushed ships between them, till Argo slipped through with damage only to her sternpost; after which they became fixed. Similar tales occur in folk-lore. See J. R. Bacon, *Voyage of the Argonauts*, 79–80.

[Page 313] *Phāsis*. The river of Colchis or Aea, the kingdom of Aeētes, at the E. end of the Black Sea, S. of Caucasus (one day to produce the no less ruthless Stalin).

[Page 313] *Pleiads' rising*. In May (p. 226).

[Page 313] *Kianians*. The city of Kios stood on the S. shore of the Sea of Marmora, 40 miles S. of Constantinople.

[Page 314] *Nymphs . . . midmost pool*. Even in twentieth-century Greece this fear of water-nymphs, now called 'Nereids of the river' or 'of the spring,' had not died. (For a modern Hylas, see J. C. Lawson, *Modern Greek Folklore and Ancient Greek Religion*, p. 161.) The belief that one's image in water is one's soul, is world-wide and lies also behind the tale of Narcissus (who pined away because his soul had been seized; cf. Frazer, *Golden Bough*, III, 94).

[Page 314] *Maeōtis*. Sea of Azov.

[Page 314] *Thrice he thundered 'Hylas!'* At the local Mysian festival of Hylas sacrifice was offered by the pool and the priest thrice called 'Hylas!', though only echo answered. To cry 'Hylas!' became a proverbial phrase for waste of breath.

After reading these three lines of Theócritus to F. T. Palgrave, about 1857, Tennyson added: 'I should be content to die if I had written anything equal to this.' Apollonius also told the story of Hylas (probably before Theócritus) in his *Argonautica*: but far less brilliantly.

[Page 314] *Daphnis*. Page 339.

[Page 315] *Transience*. The idyll from which this comes is generally thought spurious.

AUTOMEDON

[Page 315] *Syria the Hollow*. 'Hollow Syria' was the depression between the ranges of Lebanon and Anti-lebanon; but sometimes included the coast.

[Page 315] *The Pleiad set*. At dawn, *i.e.* in early November.

LEONIDAS

[Page 317] *The Shepherd's Last Sleep*. Cf. André Chénier, *Mnaïs*:

> Que vos agneaux du moins viennent près de ma cendre
> Me bêler les accents de leur voix douce et tendre,
> Et paître au pied d'un roc, où d'un son enchanteur
> La flûte parlera sous les doigts du pasteur.

POSEIDIPPUS

[Page 318] *Chăraxus.* Sappho's brother (p. 243).

[Page 318] *Sappho.* The point is: 'Though Sappho wrote against you, she made you immortal.'

[Page 318] *Naucrătis.* Assigned to the Greeks by King Amāsis as a free port, on the Canōpic branch of the Nile, some 50 miles E. of Alexandria; after whose foundation by Alexander Naucrătis decayed.

ASCLEPIADES

[Page 318] *The Coy Mistress.* Rendered by Ronsard (ed. Vaganay), IV, 299, but without his usual grace:

> Dame au gros cœur, pourquoy t'espargne-tu
> Faisant d'un rien l'apuy d'une vertu?

[Page 318] *West wind.* Or with another reading, 'the Crown'—a constellation rising in spring.

APOLLONIUS RHODIUS

[Page 321] *Cape Sēpias, etc.* Magnesia is the coastland from Ossa to Pēlion; Sēpias, its S.E. cape (where Pēleus caught his bride, the sea-nymph Thĕtis, and many of Xerxes' ships were wrecked in 480); and Scíathus an adjacent island. Peirésiae is unknown; apparently a site in Magnesia.

[Page 321] *Dŏlops,* son of Hermes, died and was buried in Magnesia. Argo has here reached the S. outlet of the Gulf of Págasae. As I once neared the same point in a small Greek steamer, the dolphins still danced about us as in this tale of two thousand years ago.

[Page 322] *Chalctope.* Sister of Mēdēa. Her sons had joined the Argonauts and now shared their peril.

[Page 324] *Perses.* A Titan.

[Page 325] *Aea.* Colchis, the kingdom of Aeētes.

[Page 325] *Aeaea.* The isle of Circe, Aeētes' sister, in the far west (p. 187).

[Page 325] *Pasĭphaë.* Another sister of Aeētes; wife of Minos, mother of Ariadne and (by a bull) of the Minotaur.

[Page 325] *Deucálion.* The Greek Noah. Escaping the deluge with his wife Pyrrha, he became the father of Hellen, the Hellenes' ancestor.

[Page 325] *Haemónia.* Ancient name of Thessaly. The antiquarian in Apollonius now begins, as so often, to run away with the poet.

[Page 325] *Mĭnyas.* Great-grandson of Sīsyphus (p. 284) the son of Aeŏlus.

[Page 325] *Orchómenus.* Page 91.

[Page 325] *Cadmēan.* Theban.

[Page 326] *But bitterly she answered. . . .* When this passionate Oriental girl begins to speak, Apollonius regains his poetry.

DAMAGETUS

[Page 327] *Phocaean city.* Phocaea (30 miles N.W. of Smyrna), mother-city of Massilia, the modern Marseilles. Theāno seems buried outside its city-gate.

PHAEDIMUS

[Page 327] *I mourn.* Perhaps the lament is thought of as uttered by the figure of a weeping woman on the tomb.

[Page 327] *Torōne*, 65 miles N.N.E. of Scíathus, on the middle prong of Chalcídice.

THE HUMBLING OF SPARTA

[Page 327] *Campfires.* It had long been the Spartan boast that their women had never seen the smoke from an enemy's campfires; but in the fourth century this boast ceased to be true—370–69, Theban invasion under Epaminondas; 222–1, surrender to Antígonus of Macedòn after Sellasia; 219–8, invasion by Philip V of Macedon; 207, devastation by Philopoemen, general of the Achaean League, after his victory at Mantinēa; 195, surrender of Nabis, tyrant of Sparta, to Flamínīnus; 188, capture by Philopoemen. In *Oxyrhyncus Papyri* No. 662 there is a very similar epigram, by Amyntas, which definitely names 'the unconquered Philopoemen' and suggests that the reference here also is to his invasion of 207 or, less probably, that of 188. The obscure word in the second line rendered 'destroyers' should possibly be a proper name 'Olénian,' from Ōlenus, a city in Achaea. But this was a very obscure township, a few years later not even inhabited.

[Page 327] *On shadeless fields thy birds have nested.* All fruit-trees being felled by the invader. Mackail compares Stesíchorus' warning to the Locrians not to grow too proud 'lest their cicadas chirp on the ground.'

ANTIPATER OF SIDON

[Page 328] *The Vengeance of the Nymphs.* This may be by Antípater of *Thessalonica.*

[Page 328] *Ionian waters . . . Pělops' shore. I.e.* sailing down the Greek W. coast to Peloponnesus. (The Īōnian Sea, supposed to be called after the nymph Io, is to be distinguished from Īōnia in Asia Minor.)

[Page 328] *Erinna.* See p. 279.

[Page 329] *Ruins of Corinth.* Destroyed by Rome in the same year as Carthage, 146 B.C.

[Page 329] *Sīsyphus.* Legendary founder of Corinth (p. 284).

[Page 329] *Sea-birds.* Lit. 'halcyons,' whose plaintive cry particularly struck the Greeks. Cf. A. Chénier, *La Jeune Tarentine*:

> Pleurez, doux alcyons! ô vous, oiseaux sacrés,
> Oiseaux chers à Thétis, doux alcyons, pleurez!
> Elle a vécu, Myrto, la jeune Tarentine!
> Un vaisseau la portait aux bords de Camarine.

[Page 329] *Orpheus*, after Eurydice's death from a serpent's bite, was torn in pieces by Bacchanals. Cf. Milton, *Lycidas*:

> What could the Muse herself that *Orpheus* bore,
> The Muse herself, for her inchanting son
> Whom Universal nature did lament,
> When by the rout that made the hideous roar,
> His goary visage down the stream was sent,
> Down the swift *Hebrus* to the *Lesbian* shore?

[Page 329] *Booming of the main.* Cf. Gray, *Bard*:

> Cold is Cadwallo's tongue
> That hush'd the stormy main.

[Page 329] *Love Hunted*.   Imitated by Ronsard (ed. Vaganay), II, 420, *L'Amour Oyseau*.

[Page 329] *Each jointed rod*.   Fowlers used a set of jointed sticks, like some fishing-rods, the end one made sticky with birdlime.

LAMENT FOR BION

[Page 331] *Dorian*.   Greek pastoral used a Doricized epic diction.   Theócritus was born in Dorian Syracuse and had lived in Dorian Cos.

[Page 331] *'Alas' inscribed on thee*.   The Greek term 'hyacinthos' includes the iris; and the wild iris familiar to walkers on Greek hills is delicately pencilled with lines that can be read as AIAIAI (AI = alas) or, the other way up, as a series of Υs (initial of Hyacinthus).   Hence the legends that this 'sanguine flower inscrib'd with woe' first sprang from the blood of Hyacinthus, a beautiful youth accidently killed by Apollo with a discus; or from the blood of Ajax (Aias) when he slew himself in rage at being worsted by Odysseus in the contest for Achilles' arms (p. 191).   (See my *From Olympus to the Styx*, 2nd ed., p. 80.)

[Page 331] *Arethusa*.   Page 340.

[Page 331] *Strȳmon*, now Struma, flows through Orpheus' native Thrace.

[Page 331] *Waxen old*.   Swans being supposed to sing before death.

[Page 331] *Bistónian*.   The Bistónes were a Thracian tribe.

[Page 331] *Oeagrus*.   Father of Orpheus, by the Muse Callíope.

[Page 331] *Priāpi*.   Rustic deities of fertility.

[Page 332] *Alas and alas. . . .*   Adapted in youth by Wordsworth (*Works*, ed. de Selincourt, I, 286):

> Ah me, the lowliest children of the spring,
> Violets and meekest snowdrops, when they lie
> Nipped in the faded garden, soon again
> Put forth fresh leaves and breathe another year,
> But we, the great, the mighty and the wise,
> Soon as we perish, in the hollow earth,
> Unwakeable, unheard of,[1] undisturbed,
> Slumber a dull interminable sleep.

Later, part of these lines was embodied in the last Duddon sonnet, 'Afterthought':

> Still glides the Stream, and shall for ever glide;
> The Form remains, the Function never dies;
> While we, the brave, the mighty, and the wise,
> We Men, who in our morn of youth defied
> The elements, must vanish.

Cf. too Arnold, *Thyrsis*:

> For there thine earth-forgetting eyelids keep
> The morningless and unawakening sleep.

[Page 332] *The frog* looks like a personal allusion to some detested bard.

[Page 333] *She too was once Sicilian*.   It was in the fields of Enna (Castrogiovanni), forty miles W.S.W. of Etna, that

> *Proserpin* gathring flours,
> Herself a fairer Floure by gloomie Dis
> Was gatherd, which cost *Ceres* all that pain
> To seek her through the world.

---

[1] Wordsworth has mistaken the meaning; it should be 'unhearing.'

Cf. Arnold, *Thyrsis*:

> But when Sicilian shepherds lost a mate,
>   Some good survivor with his flute would go,
> Piping a ditty sad for Bion's fate;
>   And cross the unpermitted ferry's flow,
>   And relax Pluto's brow,
> And make leap up with joy the beauteous head
>   Of Proserpine, among whose crowned hair
>   Are flowers first open'd on Sicilian air,
> And flute his friend, like Orpheus, from the dead.
>
> O easy access to the hearer's grace
>   When Dorian shepherds sang to Proserpine!
>   For she herself had trod Sicilian fields,
> She knew the Dorian water's gush divine,
>   She knew each lily white which Enna yields,
>   Each rose with blushing face;
> She loved the Dorian pipe, the Dorian strain.
>   But ah, of our poor Thames she never heard!
>   Her foot the Cumner cowslips never stirr'd;
> And we should tease her with our plaint in vain!

This singing to Persephone recalls the story of her appearance in a dream to Pindar, complaining that he had left her, alone of the Immortals, without a song—but when he came to her kingdom, he should sing her praises too. Within ten days he died. But afterwards an aged kinswoman of his dreamed that the poet recited to her a poem on Persephone; which, on waking, she wrote down. (Cf. the curious tale of Mozart's *Requiem*.)

[Page 333] *I would go piping to Death's self for thy sake.* So in a fragment of the comic poet Philēmon (*c.* 361–262 B.C.) a character exclaims:

> If, as some say, my friend,
> In very deed the dead had consciousness,
> I had hanged myself to see Euripides.

ANACREONTEA

The Greek metre of these little pieces ($3\frac{1}{2}$ iambic feet), here reproduced, is similar to that of Longfellow's *Hiawatha* less the first (stressed) syllable.

[Page 334] *Vive Hodie*. Imitated by Baïf and by Ronsard (ed. Vaganay), III, 256:

> Du grand Turc je n'ay souci,
> Ni du grand Souldan aussi:
> L'or ne maistrise ma vie,
> Aux Rois je ne porte envie.

[Page 334] *Gyges*, bodyguard of Candaules King of Lydia, conspired with the Queen and killed his master (*c.* 685). He made Lydia powerful and attacked Ionia, but was slain in battle by the Cimmerians about 652.

[Page 334] *Catalogue*. For this 'Leporello-list' cf. Ronsard, III, 268 ('Si tu me peux conter les fleurs'):

> Conte, apres, six cens à la fois
> Dont à Paris je me vy prendre,
> Conte cent millions, qu'à Blois
> Je pris dans les yeux de Cassandre.

[Page 334] *Gades.*   Cadiz.

[Page 334] *Bactria.*   Between Hindu Kush and Oxus.   Its city of Bactra is now Balkh.

[Page 335] '*Come, fill the cup.*'   Cf. Ronsard, III, 268 ('La terre les eaux va boyvant').

[Page 335] *Beauty's Power.*   Cf. Ronsard, III, 136 ('La Nature a donné des cornes aux toreaux').

[Page 335] *Love's Nestlings.*   Cf. Ronsard, III, 339 ('Si tost que tu sens arriver'):

> L'un a des ailerons au flanc,
> L'autre de duvet est tout blanc,
> Et l'autre dans le nic s'essore:
> L'un de sa coque à demy sort,
> Et l'autre en a rompu le bort,
> Et l'autre est dedans l'œuf encore.

And contrast the serious passion of Íbycus on the same theme, p. 254.

[Page 336] *Love's Stratagem.*   Cf. Ronsard, III, 121 ('Du malheur de recevoir'):

> Il estoit minuict, et l'Ourse
> De son char tournoit la course
> Entre les mains du Bouvier. . . .

and La Fontaine's *L'Amour Mouillé*; also Herrick, *The Cheat of Cupid*:

> One silent night of late,
>   When every creature rested,
> Came one unto my gate,
>   And knocking, me molested.

Cherubini set the episode to music in his opera *Anacreon* (performed at Paris in 1803).

[Page 336] *A little boy.*   The Greek idea of Eros grows younger with the centuries—first a youth, then a boy, then the mischievous urchin of the Hellenistic age.

[Page 336] *Cicada.*   Cf. Ronsard, III, 263 ('T'oseroit bien quelque Poëte Nier des vers, douce Alouëte?')—where cicada is replaced by lark.

[Page 337] *Love and the Bee.*   Cf. Ronsard, III, 249, beginning:

> Le petit enfant Amour
> Cueilloit des fleurs à l'entour
> D'une ruche, où les avettes
> Font leurs petites logettes.

Also Herrick, *The wounded Cupid*:

> *Cupid* as he lay among
> *Roses*, by a Bee was stung.

Spenser breaks the bee upon a wheel of lumbering prolixity in his Madrigal IV.

[Page 337] *Cythēra.*   The island of Aphrodite, S. of Peloponnese.

PART FOUR

ROMAN AND EARLY BYZANTINE PERIOD

1st *century* B.C.–6th *century* A.D.

MELEAGER OF GADARA

(c. 135–c. 65 B.C.)

MELEAGER of Gadara in Palestine—'the Syrian Athens,' he calls it—
migrated to Tyre and, in later life, to Cos, where lived (perhaps his last love)
the girl Phānion.   A Cynic philosopher and writer of humorous essays, he
also composed short poems and gathered in his 'Garland'—a selection of
such poems by himself and others—the first of those anthologies from which
our *Palatine Anthology* was to grow.

The Baby Hare

A little hare new-littered, from my mother's breast they tore me
    (Long my ears and taper, swift my baby feet),
But in her bosom fair-skinned Phānion took and bore me—
    Lovingly she gave me flowers of spring to eat.
No more I missed my mother.   But of surfeit unbeseeming
    And banquets overgenerous I fattened and I died.
Next her cottage then she laid me, that in dreaming
    She might see my grave for ever by her own bedside.

                                    (*Anth. Pal.*, VII, 207.)

Love for Sale

Sell him!—just as he lies there in his mother's arms a-sleeping!
    Sell him!—why should I trouble to rear this saucy thing?
With his nails that scratch so sharply, and all amid his weeping
    These sudden shouts of laughter; snub nose and wanton wing!
A brazen, lynx-eyed creature, as babbling as a crier,
    A savage that is brutal to his own mother dear,
An utter monster!   Come, we'll sell him.   Any buyer,
    Outward bound, that wants an infant?   Here now, here!
But look, what tears, what pleading!   Ah, never fear I will—
It shan't be sold!   Live happy, here with my Zēnophil.

                                      (V, 178.)

Hue and Cry after Love

O yes!   O yes!   O yes!   I have lost him, Love the gipsy.
    A moment since he fluttered from my bed, at break of day.
Weeps sweetly; laughter roguish; and the child's tongue runs as tipsy;
    Saucy, and swift, and his shoulders with quiver and wings are gay.

N   351

His father's name? God knows it. For Heaven and Earth disown him,
    And Ocean swears this urchin was never child of his;
Through all the world he's hated, by all who've ever known him—
    Take care lest he be setting new traps for hearts ere this.
But ah!—there he is!—do you see him? In his lurking-place he lies.
I have caught you, archer, ambushed in Zēnophil's bright eyes.

(V, 177.)

'Lenten ys come with Love to Toune'

Now the white violet's blooming, and that lover of the showers,
    Narcissus, and the lilies that go climbing up the hill,
And now, delight of lovers, spring-flower among the flowers,
    Sweet rose of Persuasion, blossoms my Zēnophil.
Ah meadows, vain your laughter, in vain your shining hair:
Than all your fragrant garlands the lass I love's more fair.

(V, 144.)

The Siren

Asclēpias, child of passion, bright eyes like the calm sea's blue,
You lure to sail for Cythēra whoever looks on you.

(V, 156.)

'O lente, lente'

Grey daylight, loathed of lovers, how listless-slow your crawling
    Round the earth, now another in the arms of Dēmo lies!
When mine was that slim body, malignantly forestalling
    My happiness how swiftly, each morn, you used to rise!

(V, 173.)

Love's Last Sacrament

If aught, my Cleobūlus, befall (for what shall save me,
    Whom Love's fires have left wasted, as a brand that smouldereth?),
Make drunk with wine, I pray you, my urn before you grave me,
    And write these words upon it: 'The gift of Love to Death.'

(XII, 74.)

The Bride of Death

No bridal, but Death for bridegroom Cleärista found her,
    The night she first unfastened her knot of maidenhood.
That eve by her bridal-chamber the flutes blew shrilling round her,
    And beating on its doorway the merry-makers stood—

352

But lo, they cried in the dawning with a voice of lamentation,
  And Hymen, stricken silent, changed to a funeral strain,
And the selfsame pinewood torches that glittered in their station
  Round her bride-bed, lit her the road none comes again.

(VII, 182.)

MELEAGER or PHILODEMUS
The Coquette

Well my heart warns me, saying: 'Flee, flee from Heliodora!'
  Too bitterly it remembers past jealousy and pain.
So says my heart.   Yet what strength have I to flee before her?
  She warns me too, the wanton—then kisses me again.

(V, 24.)

PHILODEMUS OF GADARA
(*c.* 110–*c.* 40 B.C.)

Philodēmus was an Epicurean philosopher patronized by L. Calpurnius Piso (consul 58 B.C.), the father of Caesar's wife Calpurnia.   Cicero, though detesting Piso, praises Philodēmus; Horace quotes him, and perhaps owed a good deal to his influence.   In a villa at Herculaneum, probably belonging to Piso, was found a room with busts of philosophers and papyrus-rolls of philosophy, largely by Philodēmus himself, which may have been the poet's library.

Moonlit Love

Lady of Night, twy-hornéd, lover of nightlong dances,
  Look through the latticed windows, O Moon with thy quivering ray,
On my golden lass, Callistion.   Immortal glances
  May linger unforbidden on mortal lovers' play.
Sure on us both, O Moon, there rests thy benison—
Once was thine own heart kindled to love Endymion.

(*Anth. Pal.*, V, 123.)

Years of Discretion

I have loved—but then who has not?   Frolicked—who has not tasted
  Such frolics once?   Done follies—'tis a god that makes us fools.
Enough!   Fast round my temples the dark hair dwindles, wasted
  By silver threads, foretelling the years when folly cools.
We played while it was playtime.   Now that the season brings
Farewell to that, we 'll turn us to think of wiser things.

(V, 112.)

353

Diodōrus Zōnas was an orator of repute at the time of Mithridates' invasion of Rome's eastern provinces (88–7 B.C.).

'The Lip of this Poor Earthen Urn'

Hand me the sweet cup fashioned from that clay,
Whence I was born, where I shall lie one day.

(*Anth. Pal.*, XI, 43.)

Harvest-Home

To the Winnowing Demeter, from his ploughland's scanty measure,
  To the Seasons, whose fair footsteps glide down the furrowed fields,
These motley seeds of pulse, these few ears from the thresher,
  Upon this three-legged table the poor Hērōnax yields,
The tiny tithe of a little.   No broad lands his to till,
Heir of a narrow portion here on the barren hill.

(VI, 98.)

The Little Ghost

Ferryman that rowest the barge the buried fare on,
  With all its freight of anguish, across Death's reedy mere,
Give to the child of Cínyras, O gloomy Charon,
  A kindly hand for climbing to thy boat, as he draws near.
For the little one trips in his sandals; yet he will fear to tread,
Barefoot, the sandy beaches of the River of the Dead.

(VII, 365.)

The End of a Venture

I pile the chill sea-shingle with my hands above thee sleeping,
  A cold and breathless body, here upon the shore.
For the last rites to rest thee no mother renders weeping,
  These limbs that the waves have wasted she shall behold no more.
Only the lonely beaches in their friendless desolation,
  They were thy only welcome beside the Aegean Sea.
This little sand I give thee, and many a lamentation,
  Stranger.   So bitter a bargain thy trading brought to thee.

(VII, 404.)

THYILLUS
(mid 1st century B.C. ?)

The Dead Dancer

Aristion, so swift once to toss her tresses curling
    And her castanets that rattled in praise of Cýbele,
Lightly beneath the pine-boughs to the horned flute's music whirling,
    She that would mix no water, as she quaffed her winecups three,
Rests here beneath the elmtree-shade; now no more lovers
    Gladden her heart, no vigils of maddened midnight hours.
A long farewell, all revels, all follies!   Now earth covers
    The sacred head that, once, went bright with wreathéd flowers.
(Anth. Pal., VII, 223.)

ERŶCIUS OF CYZICUS
(mid 1st century B.C.)

The Trophy

This horn of full two cubits from his bull that turned a rover
    And scorned the herd, its herdsman, the Ambraciot Saon, tore.
Long he tracked the truant the bushy gorges over,
    Up the glens, and found him on a torrent-shore,
Cooling hoof and flank there.   Sideways from the river
    The beast charged at its master.   But with a single blow
Of his club he dashed its horn off, and hung it here for ever,
    On the wild-pear by his steading, where sweet his heifers low.
(Anth. Pal., VI, 255.)

CRINAGORAS OF MYTILENE
(c. 70 B.C.–c. A.D. 18)

Crinágoras took part in an embassy from Lesbos to Julius Caesar at
Rome in 45 B.C.; and in another to Augustus at Tarraco in Spain in 26–5 B.C.
He became a sort of court-poet to the imperial family, writing poems for
Octavia, Marcellus, Tiberius, and others.

Hunter's Thanksgiving

O caves of the Nymphs fresh-flowing, that scatter from your fountains
    Down this craggy hillside your brimming streams headlong;
O little shrine set at the feet of Bassae's mountains,
    That Pan with his crown of pine makes echo to his song;

Ye junipers honoured of hunters, of many a long year's growing,
　Ye cairns heaped high by the wayside for our Lord Hermes' grace,
Be kindly and receive these gifts of my bestowing,
　These spoils of the stag from Sōsander, since ye have blessed his chase.

(Anth. Pal., VI, 253.)*

ANTIPATER OF THESSALONICA

(time of Augustus)

This poet and rhetorician was patronized by L. Calpurnius Piso (Consul 15 B.C.), for whose sons Horace composed his *Ars Poetica*, and wrote an epigram on Octavian's foundation of Nicópolis after the victory of Actium (31 B.C.).

The Wife's Prayer

Cýthere the Bithynian in prayer sets me before Thee,
　Cypris—Thy marble image, wrought by the sculptor's art.
For this small gift grant a greater—Thou art kind when we implore Thee—
　She only prays that her husband be one with her in heart.

(Anth. Pal., VI, 209.)*

The Desolation of the Cyclades

Ah lonely isles, fragments of earth, that with his thunder
　The wild Aegean girdles, like a belt about you thrown,
How have ye lost, unhappy, your splendour and your wonder,
　As desolate as Siphnos or Phŏlegandros grown!
It is Dēlos, once the dazzling, that has made you share her mood—
She that was first to suffer this doom of solitude.

(IX, 421.)

Hero's Tower

Here it was once Leander crossed; here beats the swelling
　Strait that brought a lover—and her he loved—to dust,
Here stands the ruined tower, that once was Hero's dwelling,
　Where of old she kindled the lamp that failed their trust.
Here, in one grave together, they lie—still crying in vain
Against the wind that grudged them to each other's arms again.

(VII, 666.)

POMPEIUS THE YOUNGER OF MYTILENE

(time of Augustus)

This is probably Marcus Pompeius Theóphanes, son of Theóphanes of Mytilene, historian and politician, who became an influential friend of Pompeius, Caesar's rival, persuaded him to restore the freedom of Mytilene, and wrote a history of his eastern campaigns. He was made a Roman citizen by Pompeius, taking the name Gnaeus Pompeius Theóphanes, and after his death received divine honours from his grateful country. His son, our poet, became in his turn procurator of Asia under Augustus and a friend of the future emperor Tiberius, who however drove the poet's son and grandson to commit suicide in A.D. 33.

'In Fields where Roses Fade'

The peerless lass who gathered the lilies of the Graces,
   Herself, to all beholders, of flowers the loveliest,
Now Laïs sees no longer where high in Heaven races
   The Sun's team golden-bridled. She rests as all must rest.
Farewell, wan, jealous lovers; farewell now, feast and wine;
Farewell the lamp of midnight that watched Love's secret shrine!

(Anth. Pal., VII, 219.)

Mycenae Fallen

If I, Mycenae, moulder in dust and desolation,
   Humbler, to eyes that behold me, than a bare and barren stone,
Go, look on the towers of Troy that beneath my domination
   I trampled in their glory, and left Priam's palace lone.
Learn there my ancient greatness. If Time has worked his will,
Sufficient unto mine honour is Homer's witness still.

(IX, 28.)

ALPHĒUS OF MYTILENE

(1st century A.D.—perhaps time of Augustus)

Homer

Still we behold Troy city from her foundations shaken,
   Still in our ears there echoes the wail of Andrómache,
And we watch the moiling Ajax, and Hector stripped, forsaken,
   Haled by the car of Achilles beneath Troy towers we see.
So mighty the Muse of Homer, not one land's pride alone,
To whom all Europe and Asia yield honour as their own.

(Anth. Pal., IX, 97.)

Lost now are the homes of the heroes.   Scarce here and there a city
  From the dust lifts its head a little, where the sons of the gods were born.
And such wert thou, Mycenae, as I passed, a thing of pity—
  Even the goats of the mountain have pastures less forlorn.
The goatherds pointed towards thee.   And I heard an old man say,
'The Giant-built City, the Golden, here it lay.'

(IX, 101.)

DIODORUS OF SARDIS
(time of Augustus)

This Diodōrus, orator and historian, was a kinsman of Diōdorus Zōnas
(p. 354), and a friend of the geographer Strabo.

The Gods Forget

The poet Diodōrus has left these lines that cover
  A mother, dead untimely, who here for ever sleeps.
She died to bear her baby.   And this stone mourns above her,
  Athenaïs, daughter of Mēlo, whom Jason her father weeps
And all the women of Lesbos.   But Thou upon that day,
O Artemis, didst hearken but to Thy bloodhounds' bay.

(*Anth. Pal.*, VI, 348.)

SATYRUS
(1st century B.C.–1st century A.D. ?)

The Voice of the Hills
(On a statue of Echo)

High up the mountain-meadow, Echo with never a tongue
Sings back to each bird in answer the song each bird hath sung.

(*Anth. Pal.*, XVI, 153.)

MARCUS ARGENTARIUS
(early 1st century A.D.)

Serenade

Wake, Īsias, lips of fragrance, lips ten times sweeter, tasted,
  Than spikenard—see, this garland in your dear hands I lay,
Blooming to-night; but withered, to-morrow morn, and wasted—
  Only too true a token of your fair flower's decay.

(*Anth. Pal.*, V, 118.)

'For All the Saints and Sages . . .'

A fathom of earth shall be yours in death; no more thereafter
   To look on the sun in Heaven and the pleasant things of life.
Then crown the cup with wine unmixed, and drink with laughter,
   Clasping your arm, my Cincius, about your lovely wife.
If you deem that the sage's soul lives on, I bid you know
Both Zēno and Cleanthes passed to that deep night below.

(XI, 28.)

BIĀNOR
(early 1st century A.D.?)

'In Huts where Poor Men lie'

This man that is mean, that is nothing, this drudge—he too is known
To Love; he too can call another's heart his own.

(Anth. Pal., XI, 364.)

MYRĪNUS
(1st century A.D.)

Love the Shepherd

Thyrsis the village-shepherd, with the flocks of the Nymphs in his keeping,
   Thyrsis that pipes as sweetly as Pan on the reedy stem,
Flushed with wine in the noontide, under the pine lies sleeping—
   But Love Himself has taken the crook, and shepherds them.

(Anth. Pal., VII, 703.)

ĪSIDŌRUS AEGEATES
(1st century A.D?).

The Farmer Lost at Sea

To far-off shores as merchant the false sea's promise drew me,
   Éteocles, forsaking the fields I used to reap.
I rode the Tyrrhene surges.   But they rose and overthrew me.
   My ship and I were swallowed, head foremost, in the deep
Under the thrust of the tempest—ah, different far the gale
That fans the floor of the thresher, and swells the seaman's sail!

(Anth. Pal., VII. 532.)

ANTÍPHILUS OF BYZANTIUM

(mid 1st century A.D.)

Simple Pleasures

Give me a mattress aft and a good tarpaulin's shelter,
    A-thunder with the drumming of the inblown spray;
A roaring fire on the hearth-stones and, boiling helter-skelter,
    A pot with its rumble of bubbles that merrily dance away;
Let me watch the cook-boy cooking, and for my table clear me
    A rough ship's plank, and on it let a strip of canvas lie;
A game of pitch-and-toss, and the bo'sun's pipe to cheer me—
    Such luck I had just lately; hail-fellow-well-met am I!

                                      (Anth. Pal., IX, 546.)

The Elms of Prōtesilāus

Long, O Prōtesilāus, long shall thy fame be chanted,
    Thou foremost in the onset that brought Troy's doomed wall down.
Deep-foliaged elms above thee long since the Nymphs have planted,
    Where thy grave lies facing, far off, the hated town.
Yet still thy trees are angered. For when they tower descrying
    With their tops the Trojan rampart, then fade and fall their leaves.
How deep that hate of the heroes, if passion so undying
    Even in senseless timber still lingers and still grieves!

                                        (VII, 141.)

LUCÍLIUS

(mid 1st century A.D.)

A grammarian and satirist patronized by Nero. His numerous short
pieces, mostly of a rather thin humour, influenced the Roman poet Martial
and conform to our later idea of the 'epigram' as a brief, pointed poem.

The Champion's Statue

Apis his fellow-boxers here have set,
Because he never injured mortal yet.

                              (Anth. Pal., XI, 80.)

The Portraitist

Eutўchus paints: and twenty sons he's got—
And not a single likeness in the lot.

                                    (XI, 215.)

The Miser's Entertainment

Asclēpīădes the miser, about his chamber peering,
  Spied a mouse and asked it—'Dear mouse, what wilt with me?'
Sweetly the mouse smiled answer—'Good friend, no cause for fearing!
  We only look for lodging; not hospitality.'

(XI, 391.)

JULIUS POLYAENUS
(1st century A.D.)

Possibly C. Julius Polyaenus, duumvir of Corinth under Nero.

The Wanderer

Though Thine ears be filled with voices—voices that pray Thee fearing,
  Voices that praise Thee, thankful because their prayers were heard,
Lord of the sacred Schérian Plain, O Zeus, give hearing
  Unto me too, and grant me, with Thine unfailing word,
An end at last of exile—grant, in my native soil,
A home from all my wandering, a rest from all my toil.

(Anth. Pal., IX, 7.)

ARCHIAS
(1st–2nd century A.D. ?)

Labour Lost

'Flee from Love,' you warn me? Lost labour! How should I
Escape on foot, pursued by a creature that can fly?

(Anth. Pal., V. 59.)

ARCHIAS OF BYZANTIUM
(The same? 1st–2nd century A.D. ?)

A Seaside Grave

Here lies the shipwrecked Thēris. Landward the rollers threw me,
  But my very dust cannot forget the sleepless sea.
Under the crags that the salt surf splits, by the deep that slew me,
  Here the hands of strangers have dug a grave for me.
Yet even among the perished, now and for evermore,
My sad soul listens loathing to the breakers' boom and roar.

(VII, 278.)

ARCHIAS OF MYTILENE

(The same? 1st–2nd century A.D.?)

'*Ah, Poor Faun, Poor Faun!*'

Alas, thy poor beast's body hangs for the winds to batter,
    Swinging aloft from the branch of the shaggy mountain-pine,
High, high aloft.   Ah to challenge Phoebus Himself, O Satyr,
    Child of the peak of Cĕlaenae—what fatal folly thine!
Never again shall we listen, we Nymphs, as thy fluting thrills,
With its wood-notes sweeter than honey, across the Phrygian hills.

(VII, 696.)

GLAUCUS OF NICÓPOLIS

(1st–2nd century A.D.)

Pan the Lover

'Now, all ye Nymphs, tell me truly of Daphnis—where shall I find him?
    Here has he been?—and rested his white kids by the way?'
'Yes, yes, O piping Pan.   And letters here behind him,
    Cut in the bark of the poplar, he left for thee, that say:
"Pan, Pan, in Málea seek me—come, Pan, to Psōphis' hill;
Come, for I shall be there."'   'Farewell to you, Nymphs, I will.'

(*Anth. Pal.*, IX, 341.)

On the Cenotaph of One Lost at Sea

Not a sod hath Erăsippus to entomb him, not a boulder;
    His grave is all this ocean outspread before thine eyes.
For ship and master perished.   Far off his white bones moulder,
    Lost, and only the sea-mews can utter where he lies.

(VII, 285.)

RUFĪNUS

(2nd century A.D.?)

The Happy Mean

I do not love a wanton, I do not love a prude.
One is too easy winning, and one too long pursued.

(*Anth. Pal.*, V, 42.)

'*This Same Flower that Smiles to-day*'

I send thee, Rhŏdocleia, this garland's flowery splendour,
    That my own hands have gathered to twine a crown for thee.

362

Here are violets purple-glancing, and rosebuds, and the slender
    Narcissus—here are lilies and the dewed anemone.
Wreathe them around thy temples and cease from scorn, proud maid:
Like my wreath thou flowerest, and like my wreath shalt fade.

(v, 74.)

LUCIAN OF SAMÓSATA
(c. A.D. 115–c. 185)

This Voltaire of antiquity was first apprenticed to a sculptor, then became
an advocate at Antioch, a disciple of the philosopher Dēmōnax at Athens,
an itinerant lecturer in Italy and Gaul. In his old age he was made procurator of a district in Egypt. His fame rests on his satirical prose.

On a Child

Little Callímachus harsh Death bore hence
In his fifth summer's heedless innocence.
Yet do not weep for me. Of life I knew
Little; but little of life's sorrows too.

(Anth. Pal., VII, 308.)

PTOLEMAEUS OF ALEXANDRIA
(c. A.D. 100–178)

Claudius Ptolemaeus, who gave his name to the 'Ptolemaic system,'
wrote not only on astronomy, but also on astrology, chronology, geography,
and music.

The Scientist

I know well I am mortal, a feeble thing and fleeting;
    Yet when I watch the wheelings of myriad star on star,
My feet touch earth no longer. It is as I were eating,
    At the high God's own table, of Heaven's ambrosia.

(Anth. Pal., IX, 577.)

STRĂTO
(mid 2nd century A.D.)

'Gather ye Rosebuds'

Drink on, love on, not always lover by love reposes;
    Not for everlasting shall we drink, Dāmócrates.
Let us pour *ourselves* the perfume, let us wreathe *ourselves* with roses,
    Ere others come to carry to our graves such gifts as these.
Let my bones yet quick within me drink down the wine that 's red—
And all Deucálion's deluge may drown them lying dead!

(Anth. Pal., XI, 19.)

(2nd–3rd century A.D.)

Oppian of Cilícia wrote a poem on fishes and appears to be a different person from Oppian of Apǎmeia (in Syria) who about the same period wrote a poem, less good, on hunting. Fishes may seem a chilly theme for poetry (though Leigh Hunt and Rupert Brooke did brilliantly with them); but in fact much of the 3,500 lines of the *Halieutica* is interesting and amusing. These are not negligible qualities, even in poetry (though too many poets have seemed to regard themselves, in virtue of their lofty vocation, as licensed bores). Oppian knows something of his subject; and there is much to be said for writing verse even about fishes, which at least are real, rather the type of lyric so superabundant during the last century and a half which assumes it important to acquaint mankind with all the minor private emotions of the writer's ego—'I and a thrush,' 'I and the moon,' 'I and she,' 'I and God.' The best of Oppian, late and obscure as he is, shows both imagination and feeling—there are moments when this Greek Izaak Walton seems touched with all the tenderness of the Ancient Mariner towards the creatures of the deep.

Dolphin and Seal

Ah with what heart of wonder, on calm and windless days
Or when the breeze blows gently, thou mayest stand to gaze
Upon that gay and lovely sight, from thy ship's side,
Where gracefully flock the dolphins, the beauty of the tide!
Together in front the young ones come, like youths unwed,
As if in mazy circles of the whirling dance they sped;
Next, close behind their offspring, there swim, a guardian band,
The big ones and the leaders. As through spring meadowland
After the lambs the shepherds go following, as they graze;
Or as, when homeward children troop, from learning the Muses' ways,
After them come their tutors, watching from behind
Over the little ones' modesty, and guiding heart and mind
(For years bring man discretion); so the dolphin-parents all
Swim in the wake of their young, lest aught untoward befall.

And no less love for her children the mother-seal shows.
For breasts she has, like the dolphin, whence milk for her infants flows,
And when the hour comes on her to bear her travail-pain,
Landward she comes to be lightened—and not amid the main.
Twelve days in all on the beaches she hides with her young new-born;
Then, taking her whelps in her arms, upon the thirteenth morn
Seaward she goes, delighting in her children; as it were,
To show them the home of their fathers. So, if a woman bear
A babe in the land of strangers, then back to her own country

Returns, and the place where she was born, happy all day is she,
Nursing the child in her arms, bringing before its sight
The home that bred its mother—ever she hugs it tight
With a joy that nothing wearies; but the child—it stares at all,
With eyes uncomprehending, in its parents' house and hall.
So that wild creature of the deep, she too displays
Before her young the waters and all their wondrous ways.

Ah Gods above, we see, then, not only humankind
Loves, before all, its children, with a fondness that can bind
More dearly than life or the sunlight: even the savagery
Of beast, or bird, or the ravening fishes of the sea
Feels—wild, untaught, resistless—this passion too; and still
For their little ones—not grudging, but with an eager will—
They face death and the anguish of each extremest ill.

(Halieutica, 1, 670–708.)

The Dolphin's Death

Now, of the ways of dolphins, this wonder too I hear,
For which I do them honour.   When there at last draws near
The sickness that shall end them, unpitying, well they know
Their life is done; then coastward from the great deeps they go
And running themselves ashore on the beach's yielding sand,
There breathe their last; preferring to meet their doom on land,
In hope some man may find them and (still remembering
Their loving gentleness of heart) may stay to fling
A mound of shingle o'er them, feeling he honours so
The Earth-shaker's holy messenger; or else the flow
Of the wild-weltering surges may heap their sandy bed;
Lest the creatures of the waters should see their lord lie dead,
Or from some beast that hates them their bodies suffer shame.
So their virtue and their courage abide to the end the same,
Even in death; and they sully not the dolphin's ancient fame.

(II, 628–41.)

The Mullet and the Hook

But up soon swims our mullet, lured by the scent; the hook
He eyes at first from a distance, and with a sidelong look,
Searching the snare that waits him; as a stranger in the land,
Where three well-trodden trackways meet, comes to a stand
For all his haste, and sometimes to the leftward way his mind
Leans more—and yet anon to the right he grows inclined.
Down each in turn he gazes, with thoughts like eddying tides,
Veering hither and thither—'tis long ere he decides.

So mix in the mind of our mullet endless perplexities,
Dreading a trap, yet drawn to the harmless food he sees.
At last temptation gains him, and near he swims to his fate—
Yet then starts frightened backward.   Many a time the bait
He touches—then terror takes him, and off he darts in dismay.
As when some little girl, while her mother is away,
Seeing some thing she would touch or taste, yet does not dare,
For fear of her mother's anger.   And yet she cannot bear,
Hard as she tries, to turn away.   But now she creeps
Towards it, and now draws backward; now through her heart there leaps
A sudden resolution—then panic!   And evermore
She keeps her sharp-eyed glances turning towards the door.

(III, 499–519.)

QUINTUS SMYRNAEUS

(late 4th century A.D.?)

Even while the Roman Empire was falling before the barbarians, it did
not seem to its poets too late to retell the fall of Troy sixteen centuries before.
Quintus Smyrnaeus (also called Quintus Calaber because the MS. was found
in Calabria) in his *Sequel to Homer* somewhat laboriously narrates the course
of the struggle from Hector's death to the shipwreck of the Greek conquerors
on their homeward voyage; thus bridging the gap between *Iliad* and *Odyssey*.
The episode of Oenone's death on her false lover's funeral-pyre is perhaps
the best part of his work and not unworthy of comparison with the poems
of Tennyson and Morris.

The Death of Oenone

*Oenone, daughter of the River-god Cĕbrēn, was deserted by her husband
Paris for the sake of Helen.   Wounded by Philoctētes with one of the arrows
of Hēracles, which were poisoned with the Hydra's blood, Paris came back to
Oenone begging to be cured; but she drove him away in scorn and he died, little
regretted by the city he had doomed.*

One noble heart, one only, grieved in sincerity—
Oenone's.   Not with the women that mourned in Troy was she;
But far away at home, in the bed where used to sleep,
In other days, her husband, she lay to moan and weep.
As when, high up the mountains, the woods stand mantled white
With snows that the western tempest has scattered in its flight
Across the glens—and now the east wind and the sun
Melt them once more—with torrents the long hill-ridges run
And in those swirling waters, chill though they be, the vast

366

Drifts that had choked the valleys, soften and thaw at last;
So now the heart of Oenone with intolerable pain
Melted, as she sorrowed for that husband loved in vain.
Then, as the sobs burst from her, to her own heart she said:
'Ah God, for my fatal folly! Ah God, that I were dead!
I loved my luckless husband—with him I dreamed to spend,
Even when years grew heavy, life to its honoured end,
In concord still unbroken. But the high Gods willed not so.
Ah, would the dark Fates had whirled me hence, long years ago,
The day that he was destined to leave me and forget!
But, though he lived to forsake me, I will dare one high deed yet—
To die with him, since the daylight is grown a hateful thing.'
    So saying, piteously she wept; remembering
Her husband, that had accomplished his bitter destiny.
Like wax before a flame, she wasted secretly,
Shunning the eyes of her father, her fair-robed handmaids' sight;
But when from the breadth of Ocean uprose the flooding Night
O'er this fair earth, to mortals bringing rest at last,
While sleeping lay her father and the servants, like the blast
Of some wild storm through the doors she broke, and away she raced
On hurrying feet; as a heifer, high in the mountains, chased
By passion rushes headlong on her way to find her mate—
Losing all fear of the herdsman, she dashes desperate,
Searching the glades of the woodland for the lord she longs to meet.
So down the long track Oenone hurried on flying feet,
In frenzy to fling herself on the raging funeral-flame.
Weariness she felt not. Fast and more fast she came,
Hounded by Love and unpitying Fate. In the night-hung ways
She feared not the shagged wood-creatures—so feared in other days.
On, over rock and crag of the hill-thickets, she sped
Unfaltering; she battled through every torrent-bed;
While, looking down upon her, the fair Moon from above
Pitied her haste, still mindful of her own ancient love
For Endymion the noble; and from the firmament,
Glittering in glory, lit the long road she went.
    And so at last, through that mountain-land, she came to where
The other nymphs round Paris stood wailing in despair.
There he lay wrapped in fervent flame; for, gathering
From every side, the shepherds for their comrade and their king
Had piled, as a last sad service of their sorrow, one vast heap
Of faggots from the mountain; and round they stood to weep.
But she—when she saw him lying there, no more she cried,
That broken heart; but, wrapping her mantle close to hide
Her lovely face, leapt headlong upon the blazing pyre.

Loud rose the wails of the watchers, as she clasped him in the fire;
Aghast the nymphs beheld her, flung on her husband's breast,
And low to her heart one whispered, as round the flame they pressed:
'Ah, mad indeed the folly of Paris that forsook
His own true wife and faithful, and a wanton mistress took—
Ruining himself, and his city, and all the Trojan folk.
Fool, that could care so little for the loyal heart he broke!
Yet she, though no more he loved her—nay, hated her to death,
Still loved him more than the sunlight!'   So beneath her breath
Murmured a nymph.   But there, amidst that blaze, to burn
They lay, henceforth for ever forgetting morn's return.
But the herdsmen stood in wonder, as wondered long ago
The Argive host, that day they saw Evadne throw
Her arms about her husband, Cápaneus, by the fire
Of Zeus consumed.   But when, within that raging pyre,
Both Paris and Oenone were both together made
One dust, they quenched the embers with wine at last, and laid
The bones within an urn of gold; and o'er the pair
They heaped a mighty burial-mound; and planted there
Two standing stones, with faces for ever turned apart—
Recalling still that ancient bitterness of heart.

(x, 411–489.)

NONNUS OF PANOPOLIS

(early 5th century A.D.)

With Nonnus of Panópolis in Egypt, who seems to have lived at Alexandria, Antiquity can be seen merging into the Middle Ages.   He wrote both a poem on Christ, paraphrasing the Gospel of St. John, and a poem on Dionysus in no fewer than forty-eight books, for which his name is at least remembered and by some has been admired.   But his poetry seems more remarkable for quantity than quality; this gigantic epic recalls those prehistoric monsters that developed to colossal size on the eve of extinction. The old sonority of the hexameter still echoes here; indeed Nonnus himself introduced new refinements into its structure; but his taste remains lamentable.   Like Ovid, he is too clever; but he is not so clever as Ovid.   Writing a dozen centuries after Homer, he has not yet learnt what Homer already knew—that an epic needs unity and is unlikely to obtain it merely by having a single dominant hero; especially if it begins long before that hero's birth. Nonnus however starts with his hero's grandfather—Cadmus.   Eventually Dionysus is born, conquers India, and ascends to Heaven.   But he hardly takes the reader with him.   The extract which follows, describing Dionysus' view of Tyre, is an example of that fanciful ingenuity which Nonnus did possess.

Tyre

With joy he saw that city which the Shaker of the Earth
Has girt with sea—though not wholly its waters ring her girth.
For such her shape as the Heavenly Moon's, what time she weaves
Almost her perfect round, yet one side still she leaves
Not wholly full.   But his wonder redoubled as he gazed—
So linked in one were earth and sea.   For wave-embraced
Lies Tyre; to the land united, yet by the waters bound
Upon three sides, as a girdle she gathers them around.
There in her poise unshaken, like a swimming girl lies she,
Her head and neck and bosom surrendered to the sea,
With arms submerged beneath the deep to left and right,
And body whereon the surges about her break in white.
Thrust against Earth, her mother, her two feet still remain;
But the great Earth-shaker holds her in his resistless chain,
A watery lover floating round—as if he grasped
His bride, with her neck beloved in his surging arms enclasped.
   So still at Tyre Bacchus marvelled.   For nowhere save in her
The neatherd followed his calling beside the mariner,
Piping along the beaches; there by the goatherd's side
The fisherman hauled in his net; with oars the tide
Was sundered and, close beside it, the tilth by the ploughman's share;
Where the woodlands met the waters, woodmen and sailors there
Stood talking—boatmen and shepherds.   Together he heard combine
The roar of waves, the lisp of leaves, the lowing of the kine.

(Dionysiaca, XL, 311–34.)

GLȲCON

(4th–5th century A.D. ?)

Life's a Jest

All's dust, all's laughter, all's nonentity;
From blind unreason rise all things that be.

(Anth. Pal., X, 124.)

PALLADAS OF ALEXANDRIA

(*c.* 400 A.D.)

Fango è il mondo.
Leopardi.

Pallădas is perhaps the most embittered writer of all antiquity.   He hated
his marriage; his profession of schoolmaster; the monks now swarming
over Egypt; the Christian mob of Alexandria that hurled down its pagan

statues and later murdered Hypatia (A.D. 415); he hated life itself. Yet his intensity has a certain ferocious power, recalling that greater figure of Dean Swift who could find only in the tomb peace at last from 'the savage indignation that lacerates the heart.' With him, night has almost fallen on the ancient world.

Ballet

Memphis, the snub-nosed dancer, danced Daphne and Níobe:
Níobe, just like a stone; Daphne, just like a tree.

(Anth. Pal., XI, 255.)

'To-morrow is a New Day'

Still, as each night dwindles, new-born each dawn we find us;
 All of our former lifetime is irrevocably past.
What we did yesterday, lies *now*, estranged, behind us;
 The life that still is left us, to-day begins at last.
Count not, you that are old, your long years passed away:
For all your years departed are yours no more to-day.

(x, 79.)

The World's Stage

Life's but a puppet-play. Play out your own,
Have done with earnest! Or—plod on and groan.

(x, 72.)

Vanity of Vanities

Naked I came on earth; naked to earth return:
Why toil in vain, when naked is the end mine eyes discern?

(x, 58.)

The Slaughter-house

For Death we all are nurtured, the greatest and the least,
Like fatted swine for the slaughter, to die as dies the beast.

(x, 85.)

Yahoo

O man, keep in remembrance how thy father first begot thee,
 And let *that* memory put thy vanity to scorn.
Too much thou hast let the vapours of Plato's dreams besot thee,
 Calling thee 'immortal,' calling thee 'Heaven-born.'
Of clay thou art. Why so proud, then? And even this too vainly
 Glozes the truth, and garbs it in a too presumptuous dress.
For thou indeed wast begotten, to put the matter plainly,
 Merely of wanton lust and a drop of filthiness.

(x, 45.)

Life is a voyage of peril. Before its tempests driven,
  Often we make worse shipwreck than ever ship at sea.
No pilot except Fortune to guide our helm is given,
  And none knows to what ending the course she sets shall be.
To some shall fall fair weather; for some shall ill winds blow;
Yet one for all is the harbour, deep in the night below.

(x. 65.)

The End

We men of Hellas live now turned to dust,
Feeding on naught but dead men's buried hopes;
For all the world to-day 's tossed upside down.

(x, 90, 5–8.)

MUSAEUS

(later 5th century A.D.)

By Sestos town, in Hero's tower,
  On Hero's heart Leander lies;
The signal torch has burned its hour
  And splutters as it dies.
Beneath him in the nighted firth,
  Between two continents complain
The seas he swam from earth to earth
  And he must swim again.

Housman.

I

None knows whence sprang the tale of Hero and Leander. Possibly it was a local legend, growing up round a tower at Sestos which may once have served as beacon for this crossing of the Dardanelles. It might, even, be partly founded on fact; it is well known that in May 1810 Byron swam from Sestos to Abydos. He took just over an hour. For though the distance for a crow is only a mile and a quarter, the two-knot current caused by the constant overflow of the Black Sea into the Mediterranean forced him to swim four. But Leander had to make the trip both ways. According to Leaf (*Troy*, p. 382) this is normally impossible, unless by landing *ten* miles below Hero's Tower. In any case the feat could not become a habit, at all seasons, in water noted for its coldness and an area noted for its high winds. Besides, any young man in his senses would have found a boat.

In any case the theme of this ancient love-story is more ancient still; it occurs already in an Egyptian love-lyric:

> The love of my darling lies on the farther side,
> And between us the river rolls,
> And on a sandbank waits a crocodile.
> I go down to the water, I face the stream,
> My heart fails not amid its current,
> And under my feet the waves are like firm land.
> Her love it is that makes me strong,
> For me she is magic against the waters.

But it is in Latin literature that the legend of Leander first appears; Virgil cites him in the *Georgics* (III, 258–63) as an instance of the universal power of passion over man and beast:

> And what too of that youth whose soul was set alight
> By Love that knows not pity, to swim at blind midnight
> Seas tossing with the tempest? Above, great Heaven's door
> Thundered, and loud the breakers along that rocky shore
> Howled answer; yet nought could hold him—neither his parents' cry,
> Nor that unhappy girl his death would doom to die.

A little later comes the first known allusion in Greek poetry—an epigram by Virgil's younger contemporary Antípater of Thessalonica, purporting to be written beside the lovers' grave (see p. 356).

On the other hand the tale seems unlikely to have been known to writers before (at earliest) the Alexandrian period. Its romantic tone is typically Hellenistic; and if the tradition were older, we should expect to find some reference to it before Virgil, seeing that we find so many after him—in Ovid, Strabo, Pomponius Mela, Lucan, Statius, Silius Italicus, Martial, under the early Empire; in Fronto in the second century, Ausonius in the fourth, Musaeus in the fifth, Agathias and Paulus Silentiarius in the sixth. The wide popularity of the story is also proved by frescoes at Pompeii; by a mosaic and a relief found at Zaghouan in North Africa; and by coins of Sestos and Abydos under the Roman Empire, which show the lover swimming and the maiden high on her tower.

Not even the Dark Ages could extinguish the memory of Hero's lamp. The legend reappears in the twelfth-century Byzantine romance of Nicētas Eugenianus, *Drosilla and Charicles*; and in the thirteenth-century Provençal tale of *Flamenca*, where it forms part of the repertory of troubadours. Dante himself recalls it in Purgatory (XXVIII, 71–5):

> Ma Ellesponto, là 've passò Serse,
> Ancora freno a tutti orgogli umani,
> Più odio da Leandro non sofferse,
> Per mareggiare intra Sesto ed Abido,
> Che quel da me, perch' allor non s'aperse.

Chaucer, too, planned to include in his *Legend of Good Women* the fate of 'Erro.'

With the Renaissance the old love-story renewed its youth. Aldus printed the poem of Musaeus at Venice in 1495. Scaliger thought it finer than Homer. Bernardo Tasso retold it in Italy; Boscán in Spain. In 1541 appeared Marot's French version; in 1598, Marlowe and Chapman's English adaptation. There are four allusions to the tale in Shakespeare, more in Burton. Nash burlesqued it in his *Lenten Stuffe*, turning Leander into a ling, Hero into a herring. In the seventeenth century Scarron wrote another burlesque, slightly wittier; in the eighteenth, Voltaire's butt, Le Franc de Pompignan, turned the subject into a tragedy and a curious German, Hermann von der Hardt, discovered in it a political allegory—Leander was Byzantium, Hero Rome, her lamp the minister Stilicho! Then the Romantics in their turn took up this ancient romance—Byron in the opening of *The Bride of Abydos*, Schiller in his ballad, Grillparzer in a play, *Des Meeres und der Liebe Wellen,* whose five laborious acts have perhaps less life in them now than the six simple lines of Leigh Hunt (who himself retold the story in not outstanding verse):

> I never think of poor Leander's fate
> And how he swam and how his bride sat late,
> And watched the dreadful dawning of the light,
> But as I would of two that died last night.
> So might they now have lived and so have died:
> The story's heart, to me, still beats against its side.

But it was not only to the hearts of the literary that the legend found its way. In the ballads of simple folk this memory of sorrow has spread through Piedmont, France, Catalonia, the Netherlands, Germany, Scandinavia, Carniola, Hungary, even the far-off Ukraine. Here the lovers' names are forgotten, their race, their time—all except that love strong as death which the waters could not drown:

> Jadis, auprès d'Arles,
> Vivaient deux amants.
> Ce qu'est bien rare en France,
> Ils étaient constants. . . .   (Metz district.)

> 'Bel amant, si vous y venez,
> J'y mettrai flambeau pour enseigne.
> Tant que le flambeau durera,
> Jamais l'amour finira. . . .'   (Pays de Dôle.)

> Es wirbt ein schöner Knabe
> Da überm breiten See
> Um eines Königs Tochter.
> Nach Leid geschah ihm Weh. . . .

Hero becomes the nameless daughter of a castle in Bavaria—Leander turns knight and swims for her the Staffelsee. Hero takes the veil at a convent in the Chiemsee—Leander turns monk in the neighbouring monastery; but a jealous nun puts out the light. Hero is transformed to a princess of Hungary; Leander as a prince tries to swim to her across the Danube; and on their graves occurs a miracle familiar to readers of our own ballads of the Borderside:

> Sur l'un on planta
> Une tulipe blanche rayée;
> Sur l'autre on planta
> Une tulipe toute rouge.
> Les âmes des amoureux
> Devinrent des tulipes vivantes,
> Et elles croissaient, croissaient toujours,
> Jusqu'à ce qu'elles purent s'embrasser.

Even the Punjab, it is said, can show the grave of two lovers who perished like Hero and Leander. This simple tale which (unless it too springs from some older *Märchen*) began on the narrow strait between Europe and Asia, was to travel eastward to the Indus and westward to the Atlantic.[1]

II

Of Musaeus 'the Grammarian,' as he is called, nothing is known; except that he seems to have lived in the later fifth century A.D., after Nonnus of Panópolis in Egypt, who was his main model, and in the days of Procópius of Gaza, who addresses two fulsome letters to a Musaeus that may be our poet. In other words, Musaeus was separated from Homer by a distance almost as great as separates Musaeus from us. Classical Greek poetry had already lived some thirteen or fourteen centuries; apart from a few epigrams, this poem is for us its dying utterance. But though Musaeus is one of the last of Greek poets, he is not the least. He should not be underrated just because he is late, and simple, and not ashamed to borrow from the past. Those who think his subject easy may be advised to read the other poets who have tried it. The cure is not likely to need repeating.

Some five hundred years before Musaeus wrote, Ovid (unless it was a clever imitator) had already composed two imaginary letters between the lovers (*Heroïdes*, 18 and 19), which were to provide posterity with their other main source of the story. These verse-epistles are typical Ovid; neat, smooth, bright—and heartless. Not a tear stains his Muse's paint; not a sob cracks the enamel on her cheek. Leander's passion is so hot that he does not feel the coldness of the water; he has swum so often that

[1] For further details on the diffusion of the Leander-legend see the edition of Musaeus by E. H. Blakeney (Oxford, 1935) and that by T. Sandre (Amiens, 1924), which very conveniently reprints many of the relevant texts.

there is almost a beaten track across the Hellespont. Hero, practical maiden, suggests that if he cannot swim so far as Sestos, they should at least meet and kiss on a wave-top. And both lovers keep mythological dictionaries under their pillows. Aeŏlus, Daedalus, Endymion, Ceyx, Tithōnus, Phrixus, Andrómeda—the whole stage-army of gradus-figures dances dutiful attendance. And yet if it is epigrams one wants, perhaps there is more point—and truth—in four lines of Martial (*De Spectaculis*, 25), which Voltaire thought worth translating:

> They say the bold Leander, towards sweet Hero cleaving
> The waves that dragged already his tired body down,
> Cried, poor lad, to the surges high around him heaving:
> 'Spare me—I go to meet her: *returning*, let me drown.'

But paradox seldom makes poetry. The trouble with Ovid is that he really wants his reader, not to pity his lovers, but to admire the poet himself. That folly, throughout his career, was to stultify his gifts. A writer can sell himself to cleverness, as Faust sold himself to Mephistopheles; but a bout of tawdry brilliance in the world is a poor exchange for a soul.

Marlowe (though he wrote a tragedy on Dr. Faustus) made this very mistake in his *Hero and Leander*. The poem has indeed been glorified by Swinburne in one of his critical ecstasies as standing out 'alone amid all the wide and wild poetic wealth of its teeming and turbulent age as might a small shrine of Parian sculpture amid the rank splendour of a tropic jungle.' But Marlowe's poem seems more like the jungle than the shrine. He remains far closer to Ovid than to anything Greek. His poem, with Chapman's continuation, is seven times as long as Musaeus; but quantity is not quality. Every paragraph is bedizened with quips, quirks, and conceits. Pages go on Hero's costume, which includes—

> Her kirtle blue, whereon was many a stain,
> Made with the blood of wretched lovers slain.

For Marlowe's Leander, the love of this fair murderess is not enough; Neptune too must be enamoured of him (for Marlowe could not resist exhibiting his own homosexuality); and even the waves of Hellespont—

> mounted up intending to have kiss'd him,
> And fell in drops like tears because they miss'd him.

Chapman, when he took up the theme, was not to be outdone; he makes the drops of brine that trickle from Leander as he comes ashore, die for love before the earth entombs them, leaving their souls behind them as froth upon the sea. Then descends the Goddess Ceremony—

> Her flaming hair to her bright feet extended,
> By which hung all the bench of deities;
> And in a chain, compact of ears and eyes,
> She led Religion. . . .

But let us leave Ceremony to comb the deities out of her hair. This curious poem has pleased; power of some sort it must therefore possess. Marlowe's part of it does offer moments of beauty, moments of genuine feeling; it is at least much superior, I think, to Chapman's continuation, which combines shuffling obscurity with snuffling morality; but it may be wondered whether the gift of sincerity is really so common in life that critics need to lavish eulogies on work so void of it.

Unfortunately even sincere work is no guarantee against boredom. That seems the trouble with Schiller's ballad and Grillparzer's play. The gaudy harlotries of Marlowe have at least a sort of life; but these later works, though noble, strike cold and dead as funeral monuments with the stiff, polished whiteness of Carrara marble. Similarly Leigh Hunt's poem on the subject, while it has feeling, lacks force—it is too much like Keats and water. Decidedly Hero and Leander do not make an easy subject. One returns with increased respect to the Greek of Musaeus, or even the simple, honest French into which Marot rendered him.

It is true that Musaeus himself has some discoloured patches of decadence. His brief narrative may invite comparison with the best of the Homeric Hymns or of Theócritus; but the comparison is often damaging. He too slips at times into Ovidian conceits. Leander stripping by the surf of Hellespont talks frigidly of the flames of love as being yet more terrible than the watery sea. And the poet's worldly-wise cynicism about a woman's 'No' being really 'Yes' is paraded till it grows a little tiresome. His style shows a curious carelessness about repetitions of phrase. He loves prettiness too much and restraint too little. Yet on the whole he remains wise enough not to spoil a good story with coxcombries. And after all how few poets of any race or time have known how to tell a story! Musaeus does keep his eye on the object. He retains some of the brevity and rapidity of Homer. Above all, as he nears the fatal ending, his pace smoothly quickens, like a river as it nears a cataract. His characters may be simple outlines, like figures on a Greek vase; but the lines remain firm and clear. He is really moved by the passion of his lovers, by the loneliness of Hero's tower, by the beauty and terror of the sea. Romantic though Musaeus may be, he gives a saner answer to life than the charnel cynicism of Pallădas. After more than a thousand years of use, the Homeric hexameter still resounds and races in his hands, like the breakers on those beaches close to Troy where the long roll of its music first began.

ἀεὶ δ᾽ἀνὰ νύκτα καὶ ἠῶ
ἐξ ἁλὸς ἠνεμόεντος ἐπιβρέμει οὔασιν ἠχή.

But in my ears alway
Only the windy surges that thunder night and day.

And the climax of his eloquence comes, where it should, at the moment when Hero takes her wave-tossed lover to her arms and that brief union is sealed at last. Perhaps even the old Ionian master who sang of the happiness of Odysseus and Penelope joined again after their long years parted by the sea, would not have found his far-off descendant unworthy of him here. This night that curtains the doomed lovers recalls, no longer the garish glare of Marlowe, but that nobler mind which drew the last darkness round Romeo and Juliet.

Hero and Leander

Tell of the lamp that witnessed Love's secret, Goddess, tell
Of the youth that fared to his nightly tryst across the black sea-swell;
Of Sestos and Abydos, of Hero the midnight bride,
And that dark troth that never the deathless Dawn espied.
For I sing of Leander's swimming, of the lamp that faithfully
Served the Cytherēan and bore across the sea,
For Hero, bride of darkness, the message of her love—
That lamp which was Love's glory once; which Zeus above,
When its long task was over, should have hung in Heaven afar,
High in the constellations, and named 'Love's Pilot-star.'
For it shared the pain and passion of two lovers to the last,
A sure, unfailing herald of their sweet vigils passed
Together—till broke upon them the tempest's bitter blast.
O Goddess, sing Thou with me that final night that found
The lamp at last extinguished, Leander lost and drowned.
    There stand two cities facing across the salt sea-flow—
Sestos and Abydos. Now Love once bent His bow
And shot against them both a shaft that set aflame
A young man and a maiden. 'Maid Hero' was her name,
And the name of the youth, Leander—by all men called 'the fair.'
The youth dwelt in Abydos, in Sestos she—a pair
In feature like each other, and each the brightest star
Of the cities that had bred them. If thou shouldst come so far
As Hellespont, look for that tower where, lamp in hand,
Hero of Sestos stood, to light her love to land;
Look for the ancient Abydos, whose sea-resounding strait
Mourns, methinks, still the passion of Leander and his fate.
    How was it, then, that Leander, there in Abydos, fell
Deep in love with Hero, and won her love as well?
Hero the fair and lovely, of the race of Heaven bred,
Was Aphrodite's priestess and dwelt, as yet unwed,
Far away from her parents, in a tower beside the sea—
Herself a second Cypris. But with maiden modesty

She took no part when gathered the women of the land,
Nor when the lasses of her age danced, graceful, hand in hand;
She dreaded women's gossip and their jealous-tongued surmise
(For women look on beauty, always, with jealous eyes)
And ever to Aphrodite she prayed with many a prayer,
Many an offering made to Love, that He might spare—
He and His Heavenly Mother—His quiver's dreaded fire.
In vain!—she could not shun those shafts where burns desire.

For now the holy feast of the Cytherēan came,
That Sestos holds in Adonis and Aphrodite's name;
And so in all their thousands the pilgrims flocked to keep
That festival—they gathered from the isles that fringe the deep,
From Thessaly, from Cyprus amid her seas embayed;
Through all Cythēra's cities there was no woman stayed,
Not a dancer left in the forest-glens of fragrant Lebanon.
All those, too, that dwelt nearer to that gathering were gone—
The Phrygians, the townsmen of Abydos o'er the strait,
And every youth that loved fair maids.   For soon and late,
Whenever comes word of a festival, such youths it brings,
Not so eager to honour the Gods with offerings
As to eye the beauty of the young girls gathered there.

Now Hero went her ways about the temple, fair
As is the bright-cheeked Moon, scaling the eastern skies—
So dazzling was her beauty, as it flashed on all men's eyes.
Like budding rose of double hue, those cheeks aglow
Against the whiteness of her skin; there seemed to blow
A meadow full of roses through all the loveliness
Of her young limbs; and under the pure white of her dress
Rosy shone her ankles, as she glided on her way,
Grace in her every motion.   False are old tales that say
Three were the Heavenly Graces born—in Hero's eye,
In that sweet smile, men saw a hundred Graces lie.
Ay, here was a priestess worthy of Aphrodite found!
So, as she stood outshining every woman round,
And gave the Cyprian worship, the Cyprian's self she seemed.
Smitten was every young man's heart—not one but dreamed
How happy, could he hold her within his arms at last.
Wherever through that fair-built shrine her footsteps passed,
All eyes, all thoughts, all hearts pursued her as she went.
And one young man amidst them cried out in wonderment—
'I have been in Lacedaemon, I have seen the Spartan town,
Famed for its maids contending, that strive for beauty's crown;
But never I looked on lass like this, so fair, so fine—
Has Cypris found for servant some younger Grace divine?

378

I have strained my eyes with gazing, yet never gazed my fill--
Glad would I die, if only Hero would grant my will!
No God on high Olympus I envy for His bliss,
Were I but wed to Hero, were she but mine to kiss.
Yet, if I may not love a maid that serves Thy sanctity,
Ah, grant me, Cytherēan, a bride as fair as she!'
    So cried one youth among them.   But in silence and apart
Many another hid his pain, with frenzy in his heart.
Yet thou, ill-starred Leander, by her young glory stirred—
Thou couldst not hide, like them, thy wound without a word.
Once that fire-breathing arrow had struck thee unaware,
Without the beauty of Hero life seemed too poor to bear.
Higher the fire of Eros blazed, as her bright glances came,
Till his heart was grown one seething sea of quenchless flame.
For the perfect beauty of women, that gains their glory, stings
Man's heart with a keener anguish than wingéd arrow brings.
'Tis through the eye that shaft is shot—yea, eyes can dart
A pang that fast spreads downward, until it strikes the heart.
Fear seized on him and wonder, shamelessness and shame—
Hard beat his heart; he blushed, to find a girl could tame
His soul; yet her beauty dazed him—then passion conquered fear,
Joyful he felt his courage rise, and pressing near
With swift and noiseless footsteps, he stood before the maid;
Yet sidelong still his glances hither and thither played
And still his eyes, in silence, pleaded his cause.   But she—
Soon as she had divined his passion's subtlety,
Her heart leapt at his beauty; and yet with tongue as tied,
Though secret signs betrayed her love, she turned to hide
Her lovely face from Leander—then she would turn again
To catch his look.   Now clearly he saw her longing's pain—
And happy he to find that she did not scorn his heart!
But, while he sought occasion to speak with her apart,
Folding up all its splendour, to westward sank the day
And bright in the east rose Hesper, upon his twilit way.
Then, as he saw the mantling dark stride up the sky,
Leander followed Hero and drew more boldly nigh;
Gently his hand had taken her fingers rosy-red,
With a sigh drawn deep from his inmost heart.   No word she said,
But from him, as in anger, she plucked her rosy wrist.
Yet well divined Leander her heart could now resist
No more—he grasped undaunted her bright-embroidered dress
And drew her onward with him to that rich shrine's recess;
Then, with steps that faltered, after him Hero came,
As one still all unwilling; and with a woman's blame

Loud she cried to Leander—'Stranger, what violence!
To drag me!—a girl unmarried!—what, hast thou lost all sense!
Find someone else to bring here, and take thy hand from me!
I come of wealthy parents—how angry they would be!
I am the Cyprian's priestess—not for thy touch am I,
But maiden still.   Nay, dream not within my bed to lie.'
So, as girls will, she threatened.   But when Leander heard
This storm of woman's bluster, passionate word on word,
Well he knew that token of the yielding of the maid.
For when the tongue of woman grows loudest to upbraid
Some youth, it gives good warning that sweet love-talk is near.
So on her white and fragrant neck he kissed his dear
And cried, from a heart aflame with passion through and through—
'O Love, O second Cypris, O second Pallas too!
For how should I liken *thee* to the daughters of the earth?—
Nay, to the daughters of Heaven, that from Zeus took their birth.
Happy the sire that begot thee, the mother that once bare—
Ay, blest the womb that carried thee!   But hear my prayer,
Take pity on this passion that overmasters me.
Since thou art Love's own priestess—seek Love's reality!
Come to me and fulfil her law, perform her mystic rite—
What use has Aphrodite for a maiden acolyte?
It is not virgins Cypris loves.   If thou wilt please
To learn her fair commandments, her faithful mysteries,
A bed of bridal waits for thee.   Dost thou adore
The Cyprian?—then welcome Love's sweet, bewitching law.
Save me, thy suppliant now—thy lover, if I may—
Whom Love with His shafts has stricken, and made, for *thee*, His prey.
As Hermes, God of the Golden Wand, once brought and gave
Hēracles the dauntless to Omphăle for slave,
So me, not the subtle Hermes, but Love's own Queen has brought
To thee.   By Atalanta, the Arcadian, be taught,
That loved her maidenhood too dear, and scorned the bed
Of Milánion her lover—yet, when upon her head
Fell Aphrodite's anger, to him she had loved not,
She gave herself.   Then listen, love; lest Cypris' wrath grow hot.'
    So with love's soft beguilements he won her to his way,
So to his will he wrought her, loud as she said him nay.
Low on the ground she bent her eyes, no word she said,
But hid away her face, with shame flushed rosy-red,
And while with her foot she scraped the floor, in bashfulness
Often about her shoulders closer she drew her dress.
(For all such signs betoken that a maiden means to yield
And by her very silence a girl's 'Yes' is revealed.)

Already maiden Hero was stung with the desire
Of Love the bitter-sweet, and felt His gentle fire
Burn her, as she trembled before Leander's grace.
But while, in her confusion, earthward she bowed her face,
Leander's passion-drunken eyes were fastened still
Upon her delicate neck, yet could not gaze their fill;
And so at last, with cheeks aflush for lovely shame,
She gave Leander answer, and sweet her accents came—
'They would melt a stone, O stranger, the words that thou canst say.
Who was it taught thy tongue its sweet, seductive way?
Alas, who was it brought thee first to Sestos here?
Yet vain are all thy pleadings.   For how should I hold dear
A dubious, wandering stranger?   How yield my maidenhead?
With holy bonds before the world we may not wed—
That were against my parents' will.   And shouldst thou make—
Thou but a strolling stranger—thy home here for my sake,
How couldst thou keep the secret of our passion hid?
Tongues are so full of slander; the thing a man once did
Most secretly, in the market he hears loud throats proclaim.
But tell me now, in frankness, thy country and thy name.
For thou hast mine already—to many is Hero known.
My home is a skiey tower, sea-beaten, where alone
I dwell with a single handmaid, there on the beach before
The wall of Sestos city, beside the breakers' roar,
With nought but the sea for neighbour—'twas my harsh parents' choice.
There are no young men's dances; *there* to me comes no voice
Of any girl-companion—but in my ears alway
Only the windy surges that thunder night and day.'
And again she hid her blushes deep within her cloak,
With shame renewed, and self-rebuke, for what she spoke.
    But, pierced to the quick, Leander set him to devise
How he should meet this challenge and gain his passion's prize.
For cunning Love makes keener the hearts He takes in thrall,
Healing the hurt His own hand gave.   He conquers all,
And yet to His own true servants wise counsellor is He.
So now He helped Leander with His own subtlety;
Hot with passion and quick of wit, the young man cried:
'For love of thee, dear girl, I will cross that angry tide—
Yes, though the deep be seething and never a ship dare sail,
I will not fear the weltering wave—I will not fail,
For all the surges' thunder, upon my way to thee.
Each night to thy arms thy lover shall come wet from the sea—
Ay, swim the racing Hellespont.   Not far at all
My home is, but before thee—behind Abydos' wall.

381

Let but a single lamp, as darkness falls, be lit
Far off upon thy dizzy tower; that, watching it,
I may steer as Love's own vessel, thy lamp before my eyes
For pilot-star—not Boötes, late-lingering in the skies,
Nor bold Orion, nor yet the never-setting Wain.
So shall I come to harbour on Sestos shore again.
Only beware, belovéd, of the bitter winds of night,
Lest they blow out thy lantern, that is the beacon-light
Of all my life—and thus I cast my youth away.
But if indeed thou askest that I in turn should say
My name—it is Leander—to fair-crowned Hero wed.'

  So when between the two these words of troth were said,
That they should love in secret, and that her lamp should be
The herald of their meeting, each night, across the sea,
That when she kindled it, then he should swim the deep,
They vowed themselves each other's, in a night that knew not sleep;
And yet at last must sever, reluctant—to her tower
Climbed Hero; but Leander, lest in the midnight hour
He lose his course, well noted the tower's landmarks, then
To the broad lands of Abydos and its great walls sailed again.

  All day they sighed for Darkness, as their bridesmaid to bring
The sweet, hid strife of lovers, the nightlong whispering;
At last She rose, black-mantled, to all men bearing rest,
Save to passionate Leander. Then, while each breaker's crest
Broke thundering up the beaches, with straining eyes he sought
That far-seen sign of secret tryst, that lamp with sorrow fraught.
But Hero, as daylight faded and night's blue darkness came,
Set forth her lamp. And swiftly as Hero's lamp took flame,
Love kindled too Leander's impetuosity.
As blazed her lantern, blazed his love. He heard the sea
Boom with its maddened breakers along that echoing shore,
And for a moment trembled—then summoning once more
His courage, to his heart he cried with words of cheer—
'Ay, dread is Love, and fierce the sea. Yet shall I fear
The sea, that is but water, when Love flames wild in me?
Flinch from that flame, my heart, not from the watery sea.
On now, where Love is calling! What though the surges rave?
Hast thou forgot that Cypris Herself sprang from the wave,
And is mistress of the waters, as of thy own heart's need?'

  Then bare he stripped his lovely limbs, and bound with speed
His tunic hard about his head, and with a leap
Plunged from the shore, committing his body to the deep;
Then towards the lamp's far twinkle struck out with all his force,
With arms for oars, like vessel self-steered upon her course.

But Hero, lamp in hand upon her dizzy height,
Against the deadly veering gusts kept safe her light,
Shielding it with her mantle; till on the haven-strand
Of Sestos, spent with labour, her lover came to land.
On towards the tower her lantern led—there by its door,
Silent, she clasped him in her arms, still panting sore,
While fast from all his body the water dripped—then led
Into her maiden-chamber, where stood their bridal-bed.
His skin she bathed, and anointed his body fragrantly
With oil of roses, to take away the harsh tang of the sea;
Then in her bed, piled deep with rugs, laid him to rest,
Still breathing hard, and drew him with fond words to her breast—
'Ah love, so sorely tried as never lover yet,
O dear and sore-tried love, the bitter waves forget!
Forget the booming breakers, the harsh, fish-reeking brine,
And rest thy weary body within these arms of mine.'
He hearkened; then her girdle he loosened, and the will
Of glorious-hearted Cypris they turned them to fulfil.
A bridal it was where no man danced; no voice of minstrel praised
Hēra, Queen of Wedlock; no marriage-hymn was raised.
Round *that* bride-bed no torches filled the night with flame,
No revellers light-footed whirling about them came,
Their bridal-song no father and well-loved mother led—
Nay, in Love's crowning hour 'twas Silence strewed their bed
And shut their marriage-chamber; 'twas Darkness decked the bride,
And Night that gave them blessing.   Nor by his true love's side
Did Dawn behold the bridegroom, in the happy sleep of home—
Back, by then, to Abydos he was plunging through the foam,
With passion all unsated still aching in his breast.
    Thus lived the long-robed Hero, though never her parents guessed,
A maid by day, by night a bride—how oft the twain
Sighed for the sun, impatient, to sink to the west again!
So, by Love's compelling, they tasted secretly
The joys of the Cytherēan, in trysts no man might see;
Yet but a little while they lived—soon passed away
The bliss they found together in their passion's stormy day.
For when the wintertide was come, and frosts lay white,
And the wild winds went shrieking across the heaven's height,
And ocean's depths were troubled, and gales with never a break
Lashed to fury the furthest seas, and made to quake
Their bottommost abysses; when, upon either strand
Of Hellespont, the sailors had hauled high up on land
Their black ships, out of reach of the treacherous winter sea—
Not even the seas of winter had power to frighten thee,

O gallant-souled Leander. Still from Hero's tower
Beamed the lamp to light thee, back to thy bridal-bower,
Urging thee on to defiance of the raging gulfs between.
Ah pitiless light and faithless! Far better had it been
If the unhappy Hero had borne those winter days
Apart from her Leander, and left unlit the rays
Of that brief star of bridal. But *too* strong was desire,
Too strong was fate. So tempted, once more she lit her fire—
A bridal-torch no longer—ah now the torch of doom!

The night had come, when winds deep-breathing through the gloom,
Winds with their blasts like whistling spears, most furiously
Fall—and with fiercest onset—upon the surf-torn sea;
And now Leander, straining to reach his true love's breast,
Weltered amid those bellowing waves, from crest to crest,
Now mid the hurtling waters roller on roller dashed,
And sea and cloud were confounded, while all around him crashed
Blast against blast in battle—for now the east wind whirled
Against the west, the north wind on the south its fury hurled,
And infinite rose the tumult of that loud-thundering tide.
But from the pitiless surges ill-starred Leander cried
To sea-born Aphrodite, again and yet again,
And to the lord Poseidon, the master of the main,
And begged the North Wind's pity, for Oreithyia's sake.
In vain—what Doom had destined, not Love Himself could break.
This way and that, resistless, the raging breakers beat
Over his drifting body; faint grew his thrusting feet;
His tireless hands no longer could breast the surges—fast
Between his lips, despite him, the swirling waters passed
And a bitter draught he drank of the overmastering sea.
One ruthless gust extinguished that lamp of treachery,
And with it the doomed Leander's life, with it his passion died.

Against the storm's blind fury bitterly Hero cried,
Already half foreboding her lost Leander's fate,
As hours passed, yet he came not. Still, as the night grew late,
Sleepless she stood there, weeping, in agony of thought.
Dawn lightened; yet no lover to Hero's eyes it brought.
She strained her sight, far scanning the league-long rollers' spray,
In case, when her lamp had failed him, he might have missed his way
And still she might see him drifting. But when, on the rocks below,
She saw the surges batter his body to and fro,
Rending the broidered robe upon her bosom's white,
Down she leapt, whirling headlong, sheer from her tower's height.
There on her true love's body, maid Hero's life was done:
Not Death Himself denied them the joy that made them one.

384

DAMASCIUS OF DAMASCUS

(earlier 6th century A.D.)

Damascius, last head of the Neo-Platonic school of Athens closed by Justinian in 529, took refuge with six fellow-philosophers at the court of Chosroës of Persia; but they found Persia, too, no Paradise; finally they were granted leave to return with an amnesty, by a clause in a treaty between Chosroës and Justinian (see Gibbon, XL).

'The Vasty Halls of Death'

In body alone was Zōsime
A slave.   And now her body's free.

(*Anth. Pal.*, VII, 553.)

JULIANUS PREFECT OF EGYPT

(mid 6th century A.D.)

On Anácreon

Oft and often I sang it, I will cry it yet from the tomb:
'Drink, ere ye wrap around you the mantling dust of doom!'

(*Anth. Pal.*, VII, 32.)

The Bride of Sixteen

Anastasia, fair blossom of the Garden of the Graces,
    Betimes you came to the bride-bed, untimely to the tomb.
Sadly your sire, your husband, go now with tear-stained faces;
    For you weeps even, it may be, the Ferryman of Doom.
For here by his side that loved you, not twelve months you had seen,
And now the earth is o'er you, a bride of but sixteen.

(VII, 600.)

Her Picture

Just as she was, the painter has caught Theódote.
Would he had failed, and let us forget our misery.

(VII, 565.)

Laughter to the Last

Queen of the phantom faces that no smiles ever brighten,
    Yet give Demócritus welcome, as he comes, Persephone,
Though dead, still gaily laughing.   Laughter alone could lighten
    Even thy mother's burden, what time she mourned for thee.

(VII. 58.)

MACEDONIUS THE CONSUL

(mid 6th century A.D.)

'The consular' would be more exact—it was a Byzantine rank or dignity, which could be conferred on those who had not actually held the office of consul.

Farewell to the Sea

Amyntĭchus the aged, when his fisher's days were ended,
    Swathing about his trident his leaden-weighted net,
Prayed to the Lord Poseidon, with his old arms extended
    Towards the salt-surging ocean, and eyes that glistened wet:
'Thou knowest, Lord, I am weary. Bitter the years that bow me,
    But young, and strong to break me, is my mate Poverty.
Now, for the old man's failing breath, bid earth allow me
    Bread, if Thou wilt, O Master alike of land and sea.'

(Anth. Pal., VI, 30.)

'Betwixt a Sleep and a Sleep'

Thou gavest me birth, Eileithyia; Earth, thou wilt hide me sleeping.
    Farewell to you both. I have finished the race you measured me.
I go, not knowing whither. For whence I came to your keeping,
    I know not, neither who made me, nor yet who I may be.

(VII, 566.)

PAULUS SILENTIARIUS

(died A.D. 575)

Paulus, called 'Silentiarius,' as chief of the thirty Silentiarii or Gentlemen of the Bedchamber at the Byzantine court, wrote also two poems on Santa Sophia, one of which was recited at the reopening of the church after an earthquake, in 563. It appears, however, from his verses (and those of his contemporaries) that both Christianity and marriage could still sit lightly on high officials in sixth-century Byzantium. Nor, contrary to the popular idea, do they seem a whit less pessimistic than their pagan forefathers.

Broken Tryst

Late lingers Cleophantis. And now begins to flicker
    The third lamp; now in silence falters and fails its fire.
Ah that the fever in my heart were quenched yet quicker,
    That my passion ceased its burning, sleepless with desire!
How oft by the Cytherēan she swore to come to me
To-night!—but nothing, nothing for God nor man cares she.

(Anth. Pal., V, 279.)

Love-Madness

They say that men whose veins with a mad dog's venom sicken,
    Everywhere see in the water the phantom beast they hate;
And mad was Love, it may be, when his fierce fangs left me stricken,
    Left me, soul and senses, maddened and desolate;
For in the whirling river, in the ocean wave I see,
Ay, in the brimming winecup, the lovely wraith of thee.

(v, 266.)

Stronger than Death

How long in stealthy silence must we watch with glances hidden?
    How long must our eyes encounter with looks of secret fire?
Enough, let us speak our anguish! And if we are still forbidden
    To find in each other's arms the sweet end of desire,
Then the sword shall cure our sorrows. Far better, side by side
To live one life together, or together to have died!

(v, 221.)

The Dead Ballet-dancer

Lips sealed in iron stillness, no more henceforth for ever
    Will you mime us, Chrȳseomallus, the men of olden days
With gestures of golden silence. Ah happy heart and clever,
    How bitter now your dumbness, that once we loved to praise!

(vii, 563.)

'The Rest is Silence'

'My name was—' 'Does it matter?' 'My country—' 'Can it profit?'
    'My lineage was splendid—' 'Though squalid, who cares now?'
'My days were full of honour—' 'Though base they were, what of it?'
    'Here rests at last my body—' 'Who heeds thee? What art *thou*?'

(vii, 307.)

AGATHIAS SCHOLASTICUS OF MYRINA
(A.D. 536–582)

Agathias, born at Myrĭna in Aeŏlis, studied at Alexandria before taking up a legal and official career at Constantinople, where he became a Scholasticus (high legal functionary of the imperial court). He married the daughter of his friend Paulus Silentiarius; wrote a history, continuing Procópius, of the years 552–58; and made a collection of contemporary epigrams which is one of the sources of our *Palatine Anthology*.

The Maid's Complaint

Ah, young men have less sorrow—a harder lot, and cheerless,
    Life has laid upon us, tender-hearted maids.
For *they* have young companions; and free of tongue and fearless
    Into his comrade's ear each lad his heart unlades.
They have sports to kill their troubles, they roam abroad unchidden,
    They can distract their longing with the hues of the painter's art.
But we are begrudged the very sun: alone and hidden,
    At home must we sit brooding in the darkness of our heart.

                           (*Anth. Pal.*, v, 297.)

The Swallows

With sighing and with sorrow all my nights are bitter,
    And when at last comes dawning, to grant my grief some grace,
Then, breaking that sweet slumber, outside the swallows twitter
    And bring anew the teardrops hurrying down my face.
Once more my swollen eyes must watch; once more pursues me
    The memory of Rhŏdanthe; once more my heart is wrung.
Ah, envious chatterers, be still! Can ye accuse me
    That it was I who severed your Philomēla's tongue?
Go—cry among the mountains. There ye may settle, grieving
    For Ítylus, above the hoopoe's craggy nest.
Spare me a little slumber—maybe, some dream deceiving
    May lay me for a moment upon Rhŏdanthe's breast.

                           (v, 237.)

'A Kiss within the Cup'

I have no love for the winecup. If thou wouldst have me taste it
    And lose my wits, then pledge me—I take it from thy hand.
Hard indeed to be sober, when once thy lips have graced it.
    A cupbearer so lovely, how should my heart withstand?
For then the cup will carry a kiss to me from thee,
And low its lip shall whisper a tale of ecstasy.

                           (v, 261.)

'Here Lies a most Beautiful Lady'

I saw a tomb by the wayside, as I went towards Corinth city,
    The tomb of the ancient Laïs, for so its letters tell,
And wept. 'Though I never saw you, yet still,' I said, 'I pity,
    Still for your story's sake, Lady, I greet you well.
Ah the young hearts that ached for you!—and lo, to-day
You dwell by Lethe, all your beauty turned to clay.'

                           (VII, 220.)

To Pan

These fields unsown the ploughman Stratonīcus hallows
   To Thee for all Thy goodness, O Pan that loves the hill.
Here feed thy flocks in gladness, rejoicing in these fallows,
   That from henceforth the ploughshare shall leave uncloven still—
Haunt for a happy lover. For joy in it thy bride
Shall Echo be and lay her, at last, her love beside.

(VI, 79.)

Spring Sailing

With calm the seas grow purple now. No storm-winds sunder
   Roller from furrowed roller, or toss their whitened mane;
No more around the headlands the surges crash in thunder,
   Then backward flung go swirling out to the deep again.
Now the west winds are blowing, and the swallow chirps preparing
   Once more her bridal-chamber, her wattled house of straw.
Grey mariner, take heart then, whether you go faring
   Past Syrtis, or the shingle of the far Sicilian shore.
Burn but a wrasse on my altar, or a gurnard red, and pray
To Priāpus, God of the Harbour, before you sail away.

(X, 14.)

ARABIUS SCHOLASTICUS
(mid 6th century A.D.)

A Byzantine lawyer under Justinian.

A Villa by the Bosphorus

With vineyards and with woodlands, with gardens and with rivers
   Filled am I, and gladdened by the neighbour sea;
And the fisher and the farmer from each side come as givers
   Of all the happy bounties of field and foam to me;
And for them that rest within me falls lulling on the ear
The fair cry of the ferry, or bird that carols clear.

(Anth. Pal., IX, 667.)

JOANNES BARBUCALLUS
(mid 6th century. A.D.)

The Desolation of Bērytus

Stay not for *me*, O sailor, your vessel's swift careering;
   Shorten not sail for *me*. My haven's turned to sand;
Here lies a tomb. Some happier port shall hail you nearing,
   As, with her beat of oarblades, your galley makes to land.
Thus the Gods of the traveller, and Poseidon, bade it be:
Farewell, O men that wander alike by earth and sea.

(Anth. Pal., IX, 427.)

NOTES

IV. ROMAN AND EARLY BYZANTINE PERIOD

MELEAGER

[Page 351] *Love for Sale.*   Turned by Ronsard into a sonnet for Hélène (ed. Vaganay, II, 272):

> Qu'il me soit arraché des tetins de sa mere,
> Ce jeune enfant Amour, et qu'il me soit vendu.

But the epigram hardly gains by being stretched to fourteen lines.

[Page 351] *Brutal to his own mother.*   Wounding her with his arrows; as when he made her fall in love with Adonis.

[Page 352] *His father's name.*   Eros was credited with most various parentage —no parents at all; Chaos; Heaven and Earth; Heaven, or Zeus, or Ares, or Hermes, or Hephaestus, and Aphrodite; Hermes and Artemis; Aether and Night; Zephyr and Iris; Poros (Wealth) and Penia (Poverty), etc.

[Page 352] *The Bride of Death.*   Imitated by Herrick, *Upon a maid that dyed the day she was marryed*:

> That Morne which saw me made a Bride,
> The Ev'ning witnest that I dy'd.
> Those holy lights, wherewith they guide
> Unto the bed the bashfull Bride,
> Serv'd but as Tapers, for to burne,
> And light my Reliques to their Urne.
> This *Epitaph*, which here you see,
> Supply'd the *Epithalamie*.

Pretty; but the tragedy is gone.

PHILODEMUS

[Page 353] *Endymion.*   A young king, shepherd, or hunter, of Elis or Caria, loved by Selēne, the Moon; who, by one account, bore him a liberal progeny of fifty children.   He was granted eternal sleep and eternal youth, either at his own desire or from Selēne's wish to have him always hers.

ZONAS

[Page 354] *The End of a Venture.*   With poems on drowned mariners such as this and those on pp. 261, 262, etc., compare what is perhaps the finest of Heredia's imitations of the Greek Anthology—*Le Naufragé*:

> Avec la brise en poupe et par un ciel serein,
> Voyant le Phare fuir à travers la mâture,
> Il est parti d'Égypte au lever de l'Arcture,
> Fier de sa nef rapide aux flancs doublés d'airain.

Il ne reverra plus le môle Alexandrin.
Dans le sable où pas même un chevreau ne pâture
La tempête a creusé sa triste sépulture;
Le vent du large y tord quelque arbuste marin.

Au pli le plus profond de la mouvante dune,
En la nuit sans aurore et sans astre et sans lune,
Que le navigateur trouve enfin le repos.

O Terre, ô Mer, pitié pour son Ombre anxieuse!
Et sur la rive hellène où sont venus ses os,
Soyez-lui, toi, légère, et toi, silencieuse.

From Egypt, with clear sky, breeze following free,
While in his wake the Pharos' fires grew pale,
At the rising of Arcturus he set sail
In his swift bronze-beaked ship, triumphantly.

Alexandria's Mole no more his eyes shall see.
In sands ungrazed of even a kid, the gale
Dug his sad sepulchre; there, as they wail,
Winds of the deep twist some sea-withered tree.

In the darkest hollow of the shifting dune,
In the night where gleams nor morn, nor star, nor moon,
Let the tired mariner sleep now at will.

O Earth, O Sea, pity his troubled shade,
And on that Greek shore where his bones are laid,
Be light above him, thou; and thou, be still.

THYILLUS

[Page 355] *Cýbele.* The Asiatic Mother-goddess. For her orgiastic worship, see Catullus, *Attis*; Frazer, *Golden Bough*, V, 278.
[Page 355] *Horned flute.* Made of boxwood, but curved like a horn.

CRINAGORAS

[Page 355] *Bassae.* In Arcadia, with one of the loveliest of all ruined temples.
[Page 356] *Cairns.* 'Hermes' may be connected with *herma*, 'a heap of stones' and was perhaps originally a daemon inhabiting a sacred stone or cairn.

ANTIPATER OF THESSALONICA

[Page 356] *Thy marble image.* As it is a 'small gift,' doubtless a statuette.
[Page 356] *Siphnos, Phôlegandros.* Small islands in the Cýclades. Cf. p. 247.
[Page 356] *Dēlos.* In the second century B.C. the sacred island became a prosperous port. Rome made it a free harbour (166), so ruining Rhodes; twenty years later the destruction of Corinth removed another rival. In Dēlos market 10,000 slaves are said to have changed hands in a single day. But about 87 B.C. the island was plundered by a general of Mithridates, and 20,000 massacred. It suffered further from pirates, then from Caesar's refounding of Corinth (46 B.C.). Pausanias (2nd century A.D.) speaks of it as deserted, but for its temple-attendants. It is even told that Athens, trying to sell it, could find no buyer.

[Page 357] *Laïs.* See pp. 278, 293, 388.

[Page 357] *Mycenae.* Destroyed by Argos in 468. Diodorus Sículus, under Augustus, says it had lain desolate ever since. But there must be some exaggeration here; for it had some inhabitants in the Macedonian period, and its youth were carried off by Nabis tyrant of Sparta (early 2nd century B.C.). See Frazer, *Pausanias*, III, p. 97.

DIODORUS

[Page 358] *Artemis.* Goddess both of hunting and of childbirth.

MARCUS ARGENTARIUS

[Page 359] *Zēno, Cleanthes.* The first and second heads of the Stoic School.

ANTÍPHILUS

[Page 360] *Prōtesilāus.* A Thessalian hero, killed in the first landing at Troy; according to one version, because he knew the first ashore was doomed, he deliberately sacrificed himself. The Gods allowed him to revisit for three hours his young wife Laodameia; after which she pined away, or killed herself (cf. Wordsworth's priggish poem on her). The story of the withering of the branches of the trees on his grave in the Thracian Chersonese (Gallipoli), whenever they grew tall enough to see Troy, recurs in Pliny (*Nat. Hist.*, XVI, 88).

JULIUS POLYAENUS

[Page 361] *Schérian.* The Schéria where reigned Alcínoüs in the *Odyssey*, was identified with Corcȳra (Corfu).

ARCHIAS OF MYTILENE

[Page 362] *Poor beast's body.* Athene invented the flute but, disgusted by her own grotesque appearance when playing, flung it away. It was picked up and mastered by the Phrygian Satyr Marsȳas, who in his vainglory challenged the harper Apollo himself. The victor was to do what he would with the vanquished. Apollo, who sang while he played, was judged victor (except by Midas, who thus earned his ass's ears); and Marsȳas was hung on a pine and flayed. Even in historic times his skin was on view at Cĕlaenae in South Phrygia (70 miles E. of Laodicea); if you played a Phrygian tune, it would quiver with emotion; but a strain in praise of Apollo left it sullenly unmoved.

The River Marsȳas, said to have sprung from the satyr's blood, rises in a reedy lake on the mountain above Cĕlaenae, the supposed scene of the contest. The story is sung by Callicles in Arnold's *Empedocles*.

GLAUCUS OF NICOPOLIS

[Page 362] *Daphnis.* Page 339.

[Page 362] *Málea.* Here an Arcadian city, not the cape in Peloponnese.

[Page 362] *Psōphis.* Also in Arcadia, now the village of Tripótamo.

RUFINUS

[Page 363] *Violets purple-glancing, etc.* It was a clever lover that found all these flowers in bloom at the same time. But, after all, the botany of *Lycidas* itself is equally poetic. For, as pointed out by A. Sidgwick, Milton strews the hearse with three kinds of berries, none of which would have appeared when King was drowned on August 10, and with eleven kinds of flowers, nine of which would then be over.

PTOLEMAEUS

There is a not untypical contrast between this scientific modesty and the artist's arrogance of Parrhasius, p. 279.

STRATO

[Page 363] *Deucálion.* Page 343.

OPPIAN

[Page 364] *The mother-seal.* Cf. Buffon and Daubenton, *Histoire Naturelle*, XIII: 'Les femelles mettent bas en hiver; elles font leurs petits à terre sur un banc de sable, sur un rocher, ou dans une petite île et à quelque distance du continent; elles se tiennent assises pour les allaiter, et les nourissent ainsi pendant douze ou quinze jours dans l'endroit où ils sont nés, après quoi la mère emmène ses petits avec elle à la mer, où elle les apprend à nager et à chercher à vivre; elle les prend sur son dos lorsqu'ils sont fatigués.' For the seal's human ways cf. a Welsh poem of Gwilym Dyved (E. Rhys, *South Wales Coast*, 296):

> Bald-head, bald-tail—see him rise!
> Ware him: he hath woman's eyes;
> Ware him, where he lies asleep.
> Years before he knew the deep,
> Three salt tears his change began,
> When he changed from mortal man.

See too the ballad of *The Great Silkie o' Sule Skerrie.*

QUINTUS SMYRNAEUS

[Page 366] *Quintus Calaber.* Cf. Tennyson, *To the Master of Balliol* (dedication of *The Death of Oenone*):

> a Grecian tale re-told
> Which, cast in later Grecian mould,
> Quintus Calaber
> Somewhat lazily handled of old.

[Page 367] *Endymion.* Page 390.

[Page 368] *Cápaneus,* one of the seven heroes who marched against Thebes, had boasted that not even the fire of Zeus should keep him from scaling its wall; as he scaled it, the lightning blasted him. His wife Evadne burnt herself with his body on the pyre.

NONNUS

[Page 369] *Neatherd ... mariner.* Cf. p. 389.

393

PALLADAS

[Page 370] *Niobe*.   Turned by grief to a stone (p. 100).

[Page 370] *Daphne*.   Turned into a laurel-tree when pursued by Apollo.

[Page 370] *The World's Stage*.   Cf. the dying Augustus: 'Do you think I have played well?'   After which he quoted a Greek comic epilogue:

> If any worth you found in this poor play,
> Clap now!—and send us gaily on our way.
>
> (Suetonius, Augustus, 99.)

Similarly Beethoven in his last illness: 'Plaudite, amici, finita est comoedia'; while Berlioz put at the beginning of his Memoirs, in French, and at the end of them in English, the words of Macbeth (v, v, 24):

> Life's but a walking shadow, a poor player
> That struts and frets his hour upon the stage,
> And then is heard no more.

[Page 370] *Vanity of Vanities*.   Cf. *Job*, i, 21: 'Naked came I out of my mother's womb and naked shall I return thither' (on which the dying Friedrich Wilhelm I, father of Frederick the Great, made the perfect Prussian comment: 'No, not quite naked, I shall have my uniform on').

[Page 371] *Life is a voyage of peril*.   Cf. Swinburne, *Erechtheus*:

> Death at last for all men is a harbour; yet they flee from it,
>   Set sails to the storm-wind and again to sea;
> Yet for all their labour no whit further shall they be from it,
>   Nor longer but wearier shall their life's work be.

And contrast Tennyson's *Crossing the Bar*.

MUSAEUS

[Page 377] *Sestos*.   On the coast of Gallipoli, opposite Abydos, on the Asiatic shore.   Here crossed Darĭus, to invade Scythia; here Xerxes built his two bridges, to invade Greece; here Alexander in his turn invaded Asia.

[Page 380] *Omphălè*.   Daughter of Iardănus King of Lydia.   When Hēracles was stricken with sickness for his murder of Ĭphĭtus, an oracle revealed that to be cured he must serve three years as a slave.   Hermes then led him away and sold him to Omphălè.

[Page 380] *Atalanta*.   Daughter of Iăsus or Schoenus.   Her jealous father made all her suitors run a race against her; the defeated were put to death.   But Aphrodite gave Milánion three golden apples so beautiful that Atalanta stopped to pick them up and her lover won.

[Page 382] *Boötes*.   The constellation containing Arcturus.   It has been suggested that the description 'late-lingering,' which is taken from *Odyssey*, v, 272, is due to the brilliance of Arcturus, which keeps it visible for some time after dawn.

[Page 384] *Oreithyia*.   Daughter of Erechtheus, King of Athens, carried off by Boreas the North Wind.

DAMASCIUS

[Page 385] *In body alone. . . .*   This epigram, with slight variations, recurs in an inscription found at Homs in Syria and dated A.D. 537.

JULIANUS

[Page 385] *Demócritus (c. 460–370).* One of the founders of atomism, made the basis of his ethics *euthymia*, 'cheerfulness'; later tradition contrasted him and Heraclītus as the Laughing and Weeping Philosophers.

[Page 385] *Laughter alone could lighten Even thy mother's burden.* The Homeric Hymn to Demeter tells how the Goddess, in search of her daughter Persephone carried off by Pluto, came to Eleusis and was at last brought to laugh and take food again by the jests of the serving-maid Iambe. Allen, Halliday, and Sikes in their edition of the Hymns compare a Sardinian story that the Virgin, inconsolable after the Crucifixion, was at last moved to smile by a frog who told how seven of her children had been killed at one fell swoop by a cartwheel.

MACEDONIUS

[Page 386] *Master alike of land and sea.* As giver of springs, Poseidon the Earth-shaker was also its fertilizer.

[Page 386] *Eileithyia.* Page 210

PAULUS SILENTIARIUS

[Page 387] *Mad dog's venom.* Actually human beings suffering from rabies feel thirst and long to drink; but the attempt (sometimes even the sound, or the thought, of water) may bring on choking spasms of the throat-muscles.

Ronsard has adopted the idea in one of his sonnets to Hélène (ed. Vaganay, II, 257):

> Je voyois, me couchant, s'esteindre une chandelle,
> Et je disois au lict bassement à-par-moy,
> Pleust à Dieu que le soin, que la peine et l'esmoy,
> Qu'Amour m'engrave au cœur, s'esteignissent comme elle.
>   Un mastin enragé, qui de sa dent cruelle
> Mord un homme, il luy laisse une image de soy
> Qu'il voit tousjours en l'eau: Ainsi tousjours je voy,
> Soit veillant ou dormant, le portrait de ma belle.

But the Greek seems more intense in its brevity. Indeed few Greek poems are so passionately romantic as this, and the next.

AGATHIAS

[Page 388] *Philoměla's tongue.* The Thracian king, Tēreus, wedded to Procne, daughter of Pandīon King of Athens, ravished her sister Philoměla and, for secrecy, cut out her tongue. In revenge the two sisters fed Tēreus on the flesh of his own son, Procne's child Ítylus. When Tēreus pursued the murderesses, he was changed into a hoopoe, Procne into a nightingale, Philoměla into a swallow. The hoopoe with his golden crown of feathers is still one of the most spectacular of Greek birds, wintering in Africa and returning in spring. It nests in holes in walls or trees.

[Page 388] *'A Kiss within the Cup.'* Cf. Ben Jonson, *The Forrest*, 'To Celia' (based on Philóstratus, *Love-letters*, 355, *c.* A.D. 200):

Drinke to me, onely, with thine eyes,
    And I will pledge with mine;
Or leave a kisse but in the cup,
    And Ile not looke for wine.
The thirst, that from the soule doth rise,
    Doth aske a drinke divine;
But might I of Jove's *Nectar* sup,
    I would not change for thine.

[Page 388] *Laïs*. See p. 293.

[Page 389] *Syrtis*. The Syrtes were the dangerously shoaling waters off Tripolitania and Cyrenaica—the Greater Syrtis being the Gulf of Sidra, S.W. of Benghazi; the Lesser, the Gulf of Gabes, N.W. of Tripoli.

[Page 389] *Priāpus*. Page 340.

ARABIUS

[Page 389] *Villa by the Bosphorus*. Cf. Nonnus on Tyre, p. 369; also the Delphic oracle to the Megarians, that they should colonize the mouth of the Euxine 'where the red deer and the fishes go feeding side by side.' (They then founded Byzantium.)

BARBUCALLUS

[Page 389] *Bērytus* (Beirut) in Phoenicia, on St. George's Bay (where he slew the dragon), was destroyed by earthquake in A.D. 551. Gibbon (ch. xliii) speaks of the city as 'illustrated by the study of civil law, which opened the surest road to wealth and dignity; the schools of Berytus were filled with the rising spirits of the age; and many a youth was lost in the earthquake, who might have lived to be the scourge or the guardian of his country.' ('Scourge' is, perhaps, a little hard on the legal profession.)

[Page 389] *Poseidon*. The Earth-shaker, from whom earthquakes come.

APPENDIX I

PIECES OF UNKNOWN DATE OR AUTHORSHIP

Hymn to Ares

THIS is included among the Homeric Hymns; but is thought to belong to the imperial period, perhaps to the fourth or fifth century A.D.

Ares, in might surpassing, gold-helmeted charioteer,
Shielded warder of cities, bronze-armoured lord of the spear,
Whose strong hand wearies never, nor the great heart in thee;
Stay of Olympus, fighter for Right, father of Victory,
Terror of all that withstand thee, champion of the leal,
Sovereign lord of valour, thy red orb thou dost wheel
Through the sevenfold paths of Heaven, above whose third great sphere
Thy fiery-breathing horses still whirl thee, year on year.
Saviour of men, and giver of gallant youth, O shine
Upon our life from above with thy own calm light divine,
Thy fortitude in battle.   Oh might I shake from me
The bitterness of evil, and bend obediently
My heart's deceiving passions, its violence control,
That drives me to hideous conflict.   Give courage to my soul,
Thou Blessed One, and the kindly reign of Peace for evermore,
Away from the clash of battle and the brutal dooms of war.

PHILĪTAS OF SAMOS

'Man is Born to Sorrow'

Says this gravestone sorrow-laden: 'Death has taken to his keeping,
   In the first flower of her springtime, little Theódotē.'
But the little one makes answer to her father: 'Cease from weeping,
   Theódotus.   Unhappy all men must often be.'

(Anth. Pal., VII, 481.)

DIOSCÓRIDES OF NICÓPOLIS

The Old Slave

A Lydian I, a Lydian slave; and yet, O master,
   To Timanthes, your old fosterer, a freeman's tomb you gave.
Long be your life, dear lord, fair days without disaster;
   And if, grey-haired, you follow, I am yours yet in the grave.

(Anth. Pal., VII, 178.)

ANON

The Young Bride

Timárete, ere she wedded, gave the coif that tamed her tresses,
  To Thee, O Lady of Limnae, and her drums and her lovely ball;
To Thee her dolls, as is Thy due, and her dolls' dresses,
  O Artemis the Maiden, maiden she gave them all.
Stretch out, dear daughter of Lēto, above Timárete
Thine hand, and the pure in heart guard with Thy purity.

(Anth. Pal., VI, 280.)

The Secret

I loved, I kissed, I was happy, I conquered, her love is mine;
But *her* name, and mine, and our story shall Love alone divine.

(V, 51.)

My Lady Wine-pot

You with the smooth round belly, and lofty neck ascendant,
  One-eared, lank-throated creature, with bubbling mouth and small,
Handmaid of Love and the Muses, Lord Bacchus' gay attendant,
  Lightly laughing hostess, when revel 's in the hall,
Why are you full of liquor, when no drop 's passed my lip;
Then dry, when I am drunken? You wrong good-fellowship.

(V, 135.)

On an old Tippleress

By the vats of Dionysus, where the sacred vine-juice splashes,
  Many a cup I emptied, with no water mixed at all.
No dusty grave for Myrtas! This wine-jar crowns my ashes,
  Symbol of merrymaking, and my gay memorial.

(VII, 329.)

Siesta
(On a statue of Pan)

Fling yourself here, O traveller, in the lush meadow-grasses
  And rest your limbs, aweary from the road that seemed so long;
Here Zephyr's breath shall soothe you, as soughing low it passes
  Through the pines, and round you cicadas chirp their song;
Here the shepherd of the uplands shall pipe beside the fountain
  His noontide song, where shady the plane-tree coppice grows.
Shun for to-day the Dog-star's glare; and cross the mountain
  To-morrow. Trust the counsel that Pan himself bestows.

(XVI, 227.)

Hermes the Hermit

(On a statue of Hermes)

Desolate is my station here on the height, O stranger.
  No choice of mine.   Archélochus has set me here.
No mountain-lover is Hermes, nor ever a hilltop-ranger—
  To me, my friend, the trodden thoroughfare is dear.
Yet since he loves not neighbours, but only solitude,
Hither Archélochus brought me, me too, to share his mood.

(XVI, 256.)

The Dead Child

So young, the little Callaeschrus—ah, Death, why must thou take him,
  Thou heart that no pity softens, ear that no prayers placate?
Now in the House of Hades the Queen of Death shall make him
  Her little page to play with.

But his home lies desolate.

(VII, 483.)

Death in Boyhood

It is not death that is bitter—*that* for all men stands fated—
  But when, before his parents, a boy's young life has fled.
No bride I had, no bridal-song.   I died unmated,
  In life beloved of many, dear now to the myriad dead.

(Kaibel, *Epigr. Graec.*, 373.)

'The Hunter Home from the Hill'

Here I stand, the gravestone that tells where you are lying,
  Pericles, son of Archias, and how you loved the chase;
And all about your tomb horses and hounds a-crying
  And hunting-spears stand ready, and stakes with nets in place—
But, ah, in stone!   And around you lightly the wild things leap,
While you lie here, but twenty, lost in the last long sleep.

(*Anth. Pal.*, VII, 338.)

'The Whole World Kin'

Hades laid hand upon me while yet my years were blooming,
  Aethérius' son, Rūfīnus; and here within this earth
That held my sires before me, they laid me for entombing,
  Son of a noble mother, yet brought in vain to birth.

To the flower of youth I ripened; of lore I learnt the rarest:
  Ah, for the grave my youth was; my learning, for the pyre.
Weep o'er these lines, O stranger, ere on thy road thou farest;
  Surely among the living thou too hast son or sire.

(VII, 558.)

On a Stone at Corinth

O noble heart, Sabīnus, of the great love we cherished
  Only this little stone keeps now the memory.
But always I shall miss you.   I beg you, among the perished
  Drink never a drop of Lethe to dim your thought of me.

(VII, 346.)

Harvest Home

Dear Earth, within Thy bosom grant rest and long forgetting
  To old Amyntĭchus, for all his toil for Thee;
So many a wreath of vine-leaves Thou wearest of his setting,
  So many a grove of olives, green eternally.
With garden and with orchard, with Demeter's golden glory
  He gladdened Thee, with channels of water murmuring.
Therefore, O Earth, lie gently upon those temples hoary,
  And make the grass above him grow fair with flowers of spring.

(VII, 321.)

The Old Bee-Master

Ye Naiads, ye high pastures, where the cold gusts go sweeping,
  Tell to the bees returning upon their springtide way,
That on a night of winter, while for the hares light-leaping
  The old Leucippus waited with his snares, he passed away.
No more shall he tend his bee-hives, so lovingly; yet still
The glens of the shepherds mourn him, who dwelt high up the hill.

(VII, 717.)

The Dead Fowler

Once with his sling Ariston, poor weapon of the lowly,
  To gain himself a living would hunt the flying geese,
Nearer and ever nearer he stalked them, softly, slowly,
  As they fed, their sharp eyes glancing sideways without cease.
Now he is dead.   And idle his whizzing sling must lie,
While, over the grave of their hunter, onward the wild geese fly.

(VII, 546.)

The Blessing of the Dead

Mariner, ask not whose these ashes be,
But chance thyself upon a kindlier sea.

(VII, 350.)

'He Fell Among Thieves'

If ever you come to Phthīa, with her vineyards greenly growing,
    And to Thaumácia, stranger, that ancient city, tell
How upward through the woodlands of desolate Málea going
    You found this stone that marks where the son of Lampon fell—
Derxias, slain by robbers upon his lonely way
To glorious Lacedaemon; by stealth, not open fray.

(VII, 544.)

Heraclītus to his Popular Critics

The voice of Heraclitus—'Why fret me with disputations,
    Fools?   Not for you I laboured, but for those that understand.
One man to me is a million, to me unnumbered nations
    Nothing.   This is my answer, still, from the dead man's land.'

(VII, 128.)

The Sage

I, Epictētus, was a slave; a cripple, I;
And poor as Irus the beggar; and dear to the Gods on high.

(VII, 676.)

Fortune's Freehold

Achaeménides once, Menippus now they call him
    That holds my acres; soon, another's I shall be.
My old lord thought he owned me; the new, whatever befall him,
    Dreams I am *his*.   I am only—Fortune's property.

(IX, 74.)

The Common End

I am dead, but I wait your coming.   For another you shall wait.
Alike for all men living, wide stands the Dead Man's Gate.

(VII, 342.)

401

All Roads Lead to Death

To Hades' gate the road runs straight, with never a turning,
  Whether you go from Athens, or from Méroë.
Though far from home you perished, nothing is here for yearning:
  Fair sets the wind for Hades from all the lands there be.

(X, 3.)

Better Unborn

Dionysius, of Tarsus, here doth rot,
Sixty, ne'er wed.   Would God my sire had not!

(VII, 309.)

'And in the Grave we're Safe, surely'

Farewell now, Hope and Fortune.   You get no more of me.
I am come home to harbour.   Go, fool posterity!

(IX, 49.)

'Après Moi le Déluge'

Once I am dead, let earth go up in flame.
My cares are done.   To me 'tis all the same.

(VII, 704.)

NOTES

APPENDIX I

Hymn to Ares

[Page 397] *Red orb.*   This allusion to Mars as a planet is one sign of the poem's lateness.

[Page 397] *Third great sphere.*   Sun, moon, and planets were thought to revolve round the earth in the following order of nearness—moon, sun, Venus, Mercury, Mars, Jupiter, Saturn.   Thus Mars is 'third' from outside.

DIOSCORIDES

[Page 397] *Your old fosterer.*   The dead man had been a *paidagōgos* (whence our 'pedagogue'), that is, a trusty slave looking after his young master from six or seven till puberty and attending him to school and gymnasium.   Cf. p. 364.

[Page 398] *Limnae* ('the Lakes'), on the border of Sparta and Messēnia, in a glen 6 miles north of Kalamáta, had a famous temple of Artemis (Frazer, *Pausanias*, III, p. 427). In its girlish simplicity this seems to me one of the most moving of ancient (or modern) short poems.

[Page 399] *Death in Boyhood*. From a tomb near Aezani in Phrygia.

[Page 399] *Aethérius*. Perhaps the so-named brother of the Neo-Platonist Simplicius (time of Justinian).

[Page 399] *Son of a noble mother*. Or possibly 'son of Agathe.'

[Page 400] *Lethe*. The infernal river of forgetfulness.

[Page 400] *Tell to the bees*. Brand, *Popular Antiquities* (1913), p. 480, mentions various similar superstitions about bees—that, if master or mistress dies, they will die too, unless moved away; or that their hives must be turned round, as the body is borne from the house. *The Oxford Book of Greek Verse in Translation* (p. 760) gives a still closer parallel from Mark Twain's *Huckleberry Finn*, where the bees must be told of a death before next sunrise, or die themselves.

[Page 401] *Thaumácia* ('Wonderful'). Now Dhomokó, a township north of Lāmia, where the mountain wall suddenly opens before the traveller from the south and reveals the great peak-encircled amphitheatre of the Thessalian Plain. The view is 'wonderful' indeed; though not more so than the number of biting creatures when I once passed a sleepless night in a house there.

[Page 401] *Málea*. Easternmost of the three southward prongs of Peloponnese.

[Page 401] *Heraclītus* of Ephesus (*c.* 500 B.C.). Famous alike for his view of the universe as ceaseless flux, for his pride, and for his obscurity of language.

[Page 401] *Epictētus* (*c.* A.D. 55–135), a Phrygian slave of one of Nero's freedmen, was converted at Rome to Stoicism and, when Domitian expelled philosophers, retired to Nicópolis in Greece, where his teachings were taken down by his disciple Arrian.

[Page 401] *Irus*. The sturdy beggar who quarrels with the disguised Odysseus at the palace in Ithaca (p. 165).

[Page 401] *Fortune's Freehold*. Cf. the Chinese poem quoted by Lin Yutang (*The Importance of Living*, 1938, p. 41):

> What pretty, golden fields against a hill!
> Newcomers harvest crops that others till.
> Rejoice not, O newcomers, at your harvest;
> One waits behind—a new newcomer still!

[Page 402] *Méroë*. On the E. bank of the Nile, between Atbara and Khartoum.

[Page 402] *Better Unborn*. Cf. Hardy, *Human Shows, Far Phantasies*, 'Epitaph on a Pessimist (From the French)':

> I'm Smith of Stoke, aged sixty-odd,
>> I've lived without a dame
> From youth-time on; and would to God
>> My dad had done the same.

[Page 402] *Farewell now, Hope and Fortune*. Famous especially in its Latin form, which may, indeed, be the original and was put on Petrarch's tomb at Arqua. Gil Blas inscribed it on his cottage near Valencia (Book IX, ch. x.), Lord Brougham on the portal of his château at Cannes. Dumouriez adopted it as his motto from *Gil Blas*; and Goldsmith has it in Greek at the end of the preface to his *Citizen of the World*.   Benserade set an adaptation on a tree in his garden at Gentilly:

> Adieu, Fortune, Espoir! adieu, vous et les vôtres!
> Je viens ici vous oublier.
> Adieu toi-même, Amour, bien plus que tous les autres
> Difficile à congédier!

(See J. Hutton, *The Greek Anthology in France*, p. 514.)

[Page 402] *Après moi le Déluge*.   Apparently a tragic fragment.   The first line was a favourite quotation of Tiberius.   Nero, says Suetonius, went one better and, when the line was quoted to him, replied: 'No; while I am still *alive*.'

APPENDIX II

THE ORACLE OF DELPHI[1]

'The Oracles are dumm,
No voice or hideous humm
  Runs through the arched roof in words deceiving.
Apollo from his shrine
Can no more divine
  With hollow shreik the steep of *Delphos* leaving.'

DELPHI lies at the heart of Greece. Indeed ancient legend put it at the navel of the earth itself—so Zeus had found, by releasing simultaneously from the eastern and western verges of the world two eagles which met at Delphi. Even to-day its landscape remains typically Greek in beauty of colour and splendour of form. In the words of the 'Homeric Hymn' to Apollo:

  Towards the West wind its face is turned; above it lean
  The mountain-crags; and beneath it there runs a rough ravine.

Northward rises the 8,000-foot wall of Parnassus; southward, Mount Kirphis; west and south-west the valley opens to reveal the snow-crowned peaks of Aetōlia and the Peloponnese. Delphi itself clings perched on a mountain-ledge; overhead tower the red-brown and slate-green of the Phaedriad crags; beneath, the grey-green olives of the Pleistus gorge tumble steeply towards the vaster olive-groves of the Vale of Sálona, flanked on their left by the blue Bay of Itéa, 2,000 feet below. As Flaubert says, it was a stroke of genius to choose such a site for Apollo's oracle. That choice seems to have been already made in Minoan days (*c*. 1500 B.C.).

Naturally (like most religious centres) Delphi became the seat of imposture as well as faith; but though its priests were often cunning, often corrupt, in the earlier centuries of Greek history they did their part to civilize their world. Less idealistic than the prophets of Israel, they were also less ferocious. The maxims they carved upon their shrine—'Nothing too much,' 'Know thyself'—may not seem highly inspired or inspiring: but they expressed a fundamental sanity that can outlast much inspiration. And so it has seemed worth giving here, as epilogue, a brief selection from the hexameters into which the Delphic prophets were wont to turn the incoherent utterances of their priestesses, intoxicated by the vapours of the sacred chasm—a typical example of the Greek way of imposing conscious

[1] See H. W. Parke, *History of the Delphic Oracle*, 1939; and, for further details, the chapter on Delphi in my *From Olympus to the Styx*.

control even on raptures from the Unconscious.   For some of these oracles
are linked with the finest or most typical memories of the Greek race.   That
some of them were fabricated after the event, may be likely enough; but
even if fabricated they remain *ben trovati* and psychologically interesting.
And some are memorable poetry.   Indeed legend told that the magnificent
roll of the hexameter was first heard in the summons for bird and bee to
come and build the God, with wax and feathers, the earliest of his Delphic
shrines:

Ye birds, bring hither your feathers: bring hither your wax, O bees.

First, then, some instances of the moral teaching of Delphi.   Here, for
example, is an utterance recalling more than one passage of the Bible that
sets righteousness above the fat of rams:

Draw near with heart unsullied to the pure house of Apollo,
 O stranger; sprinkled only with water from the spring.
For the good, one drop suffices; but he whom ill deeds follow,
 Though all great Ocean cleanse him, shall find his guilt still cling.
(Anth. Pal., XIV, 71.)

It was long remembered, too, at Sparta how one Glaucus, being summoned
by certain Milesians to repay a sum left with him by their father, asked the
God if he should dare deny the trust on oath.   The reply was grim:

Son of Epicȳdes, well indeed—for a while—
Thus to win thee a windfall by perjury and guile.
Swear then!   Since even for honest men Death waiting stands.
Yet Oath has a child, that bears no name, and wears no hands,
No feet—yet fleet to pursue the trail of treachery,
To reach and ruin the guilty, and all his race to be.
Better the lot that the loyal leaves to *his* posterity.

The frightened Glaucus begged the God's forgiveness, and duly paid his
debt.   But his race died out of the land (Herodotus, VI, 86).   Aelian, again,
(*Var. Hist.*, III, 44) tells how three youths bound for Delphi were attacked
by robbers.   One was hard-pressed; the second fled; the third, running
to help his comrade, by mischance killed him.   To the coward, as he entered
the shrine, the Pythia cried:

Thou hast left the friend forsaken they were slaying before thy face:
I will tell thee naught.   Begone now, from my fair and holy place!

To the other:

Thou didst slay thy friend in helping.   His blood lies not on thee.
For this, only the whiter thine innocence shall be.

Again, Apollo is said to have snubbed Gyges, the rich lord of Lydia, by
answering that an obscure peasant of Psōphis in Arcadia was a happier man

than he; and to have told a wealthy Magnesian from Asia that all his lavish sacrifice was less welcome than the cake and incense offered by a poor pilgrim from Arcadian Methydrium. But one of the noblest of these utterances, however apocryphal, is the counsel supposed to have been given by Apollo to Lycurgus, the law-giver of Sparta (which might well be remembered by some modern politicians):

> Two roads there lie before thee, that issue diversely.
> One leads to the home of Honour, the house of Liberty,
> And one to the gate of Bondage—*that* is the path to flee.
> The first way, it is trodden by brave men hand in hand,
> That fear not and that hate not. By *this* lead on your land.
> The second, it is followed by the fool who cannot dare,
> And the frenzied heart of faction. Of *that*, before all, beware.
>
> (Diodōrus Sículus, VII, 12.)

For a time, indeed, Delphi was able to render practical service also, as the eighth, seventh, and sixth centuries B.C. saw white sail after white sail vanish over the blue horizons of Greek seas, bearing colonists to Africa and the Euxine, to Thrace, Italy, and Sicily. For, as a centre of pilgrimage, Delphi became also a centre of information and initiative. Battus of Thera, for example, coming to Delphi about his stammer, was told to his astonishment to colonize Libya. Reluctantly sailing with two ships, he settled in an island off its coast; after two years of hardship he and his men returned and complained to Apollo—only to be met with the withering retort:

> If thou, that hast never been to Libya rich in sheep,
> Knowest it better than I that *have*, indeed thy wit is deep.
>
> (Herodotus, IV, 157.)

So the weary Battus sailed back, settled in Libya proper, and there flourished; even to having his stammer duly cured by the shock of meeting a lion.

But it was naturally in the politics between state and state that the interventions of Delphi became most memorable and called for the greatest astuteness. Thus the Spartans coveted Arcadia; and with one of his famous ambiguities the God replied:

> For Arcadia ye ask me. 'Tis much—ye ask in vain.
> In Arcadia too many stout acorn-eaters live
> Who shall beat back your onset. And yet this gift I give—
> For your stamping feet to dance in, I grant ye Tégea's plain,
> I grant, for your rods to measure, all Tégea's fair domain.

But the Spartans were worsted even by the men of Tégea; it was as prisoners-of-war that they measured its fields and hopped among its clods (Herodotus, I, 66). Yet in the Greek mind, with its admiration for subtlety and wit, this divine Machiavellianism seems to have roused no resentment.   Those who read the riddle wrong, felt they had been fairly caught.

But as the world widened for Hellas, this game grew more complex, even with the adroitest ambiguities.   The story is familiar how Croesus king of Lydia set a scientific test for the various Greek oracles by sending envoys to ask what he was doing on the hundredth day from their departure. Proudly Apollo replied:

> I know the deep sea's measures, I know the count of its sand,
> And him I hear that speaks not and the dumb I understand;
> And now to me, in spirit, of lamb's flesh comes the smell,
> Broiled in a brazen vessel with a tortoise hard of shell;
> Yea, brass is laid beneath it and brass above as well.

(Herodotus, I, 47.)

This convinced Croesus, who had in fact been boiling a lamb and a tortoise together in a brazen cauldron, that at least Delphi could be relied on; so he now asked his real question—should he attack the rising power of Cyrus the Persian?   And there came the famous equivocating answer:

> If Croesus crosses the Hălys, he shall ruin a mighty realm.

(Aristotle, Rhetoric, III, 5.)

When Croesus had thereby ruined his own country and become a Persian captive, tradition told that the fallen king sent his own chains as an ironic offering to the God who had so ill repaid his past munificence; but Apollo replied that, though even he could not alter what had been doomed for Lydia, he had at least saved the king's life.   But even if this answer satisfied Croesus, Delphi was soon to make a far more serious blunder, as the Persian turned on Greece itself.   Perhaps the priests had been taught respect for Persia by the fate of Lydia; perhaps with their wide knowledge they were too well informed about the terrible resources of this new empire; in any case, as Xerxes mustered his armies, Delphi spread only alarm and despondency.   It frightened the Cretans into an ignoble neutrality; it gave the same advice to Argos:

> Deep though thy neighbours hate thee, the high Gods hold thee dear.
> Abide behind thy rampart and ready grip thy spear
> And guard thy head—the headpiece shall bring the body clear.[1]

(Herodotus, VII, 148.)

The Spartans on the other hand were menaced by the oracle with ruin:

> Dwellers in wide-walled Sparta, before the Persian horde
> Your great and glorious city is doomed to sack and sword;
> Or the land of Lacedaemon, if this be spared, instead
> From the house of the Heraclïdae must mourn a monarch dead.

---

[1] Perhaps the head is the ruling class, the body the masses.

Not the strength of bulls nor lions shall force your foe away;
For in his arm is the might of Zeus.   He shall not stay,
Till either your king or country is fallen for his prey.

(Herodotus, VII, 220.)

With those words ringing in his ears King Leōnidas marched out to die at
Thermópylae.   But it was above all in his answer to Athens that Apollo
piled horror upon horror, with the eloquence of another Isaiah:

Ah wretches, for what do ye linger?   From your homes to the ends of
    earth
Flee!—from your craggy hilltop, from the circling walls of your birth.
For the head and the body of Athens are tottering to their fall,
Her hands and her feet wax feeble, her reins grow faint, and all
Darkens with doom; upon her, to ruin and to break,
Come fire and the edge of Ares, in the Syrian chariot's wake.
Many another towered town—not only thine—
He shall sack; to the flame devouring he shall give many a shrine,
Where the images of the Immortals now stand and drip with sweat,
Quaking for dread, and the walls with dark blood glisten wet,
As it runs from the roof, presaging the doom that cometh sure.
Hence from my holy place, and steel ye to endure.

(Herodotus, VII, 140.)

In their despair at a denunciation so frightful the Athenian envoys, by
the counsel of a friendly Delphian, returned as suppliants to the temple and
threatened, unless they could be vouchsafed some glimmer of hope, to stay
there till they starved.   Then the God relented a little:

In vain with her prayers, her wisdom, Athene labours still
To move the Lord of Olympus and turn Him from His will.
But one thing more I will tell thee—yea, it shall stand as fast
As adamant—when conquered lie all thy lands at last,
Far as the march of Cĕcrops and divine Cĭthaeron's glen,
The Thunderer shall grant to Trītogĕneia then
A wooden wall, that shall not fall, to save thy race.
Yet when they march against thee, by land do thou not face
The horsemen and the footmen in their thousands—turn away
And give them ground—to meet them shall come another day.
Ay, Salamis divine, full many a mother's son
Thou shalt slay, at Demeter's seedtime, or when her harvest 's done.

(Herodotus, VII, 141.)

The reference to Salamis remains curious.   If the Delphians had falsified
their oracle in retrospect, they would have wished to falsify it much more.
It seems a not inconceivable guess that some mind like Themistŏcles,

shrewdly awake to the importance of sea-power and to the strategic value of Salamis in conjunction with a land-defence of the Isthmus of Corinth, might have deliberately prompted the allusions to 'wooden walls' and to Salamis itself.[1] In any case Greece was saved by men who kept their courage when even Gods, and experts, despaired. And yet, when the victory was won, the Greeks forgave the defeatism of Delphi (which at least claimed the miraculous repulse of a Persian detachment sent against the holy place) and offered there part of their booty. None the less the glory of the shrine never quite recovered. It could still utter in the centuries that followed oracles that became memorable, such as its mysterious praise of Socrates—that no man was wiser than he [2]—and its supposed predictions of the victories of Epaminondas, of the murder of Philip of Macedon, of the fall of Pyrrhus, of the rise of Rome. But it was to be ironically discounted by Thucydides, seized by the Phocians, plundered again by Sulla. Under the Empire, Nero slighted it, Hadrian patronized it. Indeed there is still a sort of faded charm about the reply Delphi is related to have given to Hadrian's enquiry about the birth and descent of Homer:

> Thou askest what the country and what the family
> Of that immortal Siren?   From Ithaca was he;
> Polycaste, daughter of Nestor, was she that gave him birth
> And Telémachus the father of that wisest bard on earth.
>
> (*Anth. Pal.*, XIV, 102.)

There are Homeric scholars who have done far worse.   But by now the oracle was mostly reduced to giving prose answers to trivial domestic inquiries; and Plutarch describes the Pythia of his day as a simple peasant-girl. Yet long verse-utterances still occur also, even when the rise of Christianity was bringing the close of a thousand years of Delphic fame— for example the long piece of verse on Plotīnus finely, though too freely, translated by F. W. H. Myers in his essay on 'Greek Oracles.' And, whatever their authenticity, Apollo was never credited with lines of more poetic sorrow than those with which he is supposed to have replied to Julian the Apostate, before that last champion of dying paganism marched to his own death beyond the Euphrates:

> Say ye to Caesar: 'Fallen our fair-built columns lie.
> Phoebus hath left his temple, his laurel of prophecy,
> His speaking spring—yea, even the spring that spake is dry.'

But even to-day the spirit of Ancient Greece can be felt, perhaps, more intensely at Delphi than anywhere else.   The snows of the long-ridged

---

[1] A similar explanation, I find, has been put forward by Prof. Parke in his history of the oracle.

[2] Later amplified and distorted into the form:

> Wise, Sophocles; wiser, Euripides;
> But Socrates is wiser yet than these.

Olympus still tower, indeed, in snowy splendour or roseate flush above the long Thessalian plain; yet Thessaly, after the legendary glories of Jason and Achilles, soon declined into a backward part of Greece and it does not hold the enchanted associations of the south. The Acropolis of Athens, again, remains incomparable; yet round it stretch the glare and clatter of a modern city.   But at Delphi, as one sits among the white and yellow flowers of one more spring, with the bees humming over them and the wild birds whistling among the rocks, as in the distant days when they built Apollo's shrine of wax and feathers, while the Gulf of Corinth turns a deeper azure and a white cloud-fleece trails along Mount Kirphis and Apollo sinks again westward towards Aetōlia, here still breathes the essential Hellas.   Here are only the ancient crags of Parnassus and the ruins of Apollo's holy place—little modern but the humble village-roofs of Kastrí.   And yet it is not merely a matter of futile brooding over a vanished past.   Apollo is dead; but part of the ideal he symbolized is not.   'Nothing too much'—'Know thyself'— these have not lost their meaning; modern politics, modern psychology have only deepened it.   In this rocky valley the God of reason and control long ago yielded a place beside him to his ecstatic and untamed younger brother, Dionysus; and that myth can still symbolize the eternal need for balance in the human soul—the danger alike of crushing the primitive and unconscious within us, or of surrendering to it.   And here where dwelt the God of so many poets who died 'leaving great verse unto a little clan,' one remembers by contrast our own overcrowded modern world, tormented by the problems which that overcrowding brings to a humanity that risks losing in quality what it gains in quantity.   (How much better if, like Apollo's Daphne, nine-tenths of us were changed to trees!)   And one may be allowed to dream that mankind in centuries to come, learning the lesson of our fate and living in the natural beauty of a less populated earth, as an aristocracy of human beings with machines for slaves, might turn once more towards that ideal of free and sane individuality which Hellas, with all its many faults, has left as its unique bequest to a world that has never wholly forgotten it.

INDEX OF POETS